2017 COSTS FOR REMODELING

Compiled and Edited by

Bill O'Donnell

Publisher

San Francisco & Vicinity

ISBN 978-1-365-67722-9

411 Walnut Street, Suite 6579, Green Cove Springs, FL 32043-3443
1-800-858-5629 - www.RemodelMAX.com

QUICK REFERENCE GUIDE

About the *RemodelMAX* Cost Estimating Manual

The RemodelMAX cost estimating manual is divided into 37 numbered sections, with sub-sections indicated by a black band with white title. Categories in sub-sections are indicated by bold, capitalized titles.

Each page has 7 columns – Description, Unit, Direct Labor, Direct Materials, Direct Total, Selling Price and Man-hours.

Description

This column contains a description of the task to be performed, or in some cases the materials needed. You will find the words 'premium', 'average' and 'economy' often used to indicate a different price category. These descriptions are used on items that tend to have a large price variation between brands, styles and quality. It is important for you to make sure that you understand what your customer is expecting in quality and/or style on their project, and select the corresponding item.

Unit

Unit is simply the way in which the item is quantified. For example LF, or lineal feet, is often used with trim. The LF would be the measurement around the room where the trim is to be installed, or the perimeter of the room. SF, or square feet, is often used with wall coverings like drywall and paneling. The SF would be the square feet of coverage of the wall. For example hanging one sheet of 4' x 8' drywall would be 32 SF.

Direct Labor

Direct Labor is the actual cost of performing the task without overhead & profit. We have added into the Direct Labor the normal amount of non-productive time such as breaks and waiting on materials. Included in this amount is the basic wage paid, unemployment insurance, Workman's Compensation Insurance, Social Security and Medicare tax, and approximately 9.75% for benefits such as vacation, sick leave and medical benefits.

Direct Materials

Direct Materials is the cost to you of materials both used and wasted on the project. A reasonable waste factor has been added to each item. Remember, you pay for the materials in the dumpster.

Direct Total

Direct Total is simply Direct Labor and Direct Materials added together.

Selling Price

Selling price is the recommended price to charge your customer. In all cases the Direct Labor figure has been multiplied by 1.67. This gives you a 40% gross profit on labor. Many Direct Materials have also been multiplied by 1.67. The exception is high cost items, such as bathroom fixtures, kitchen cabinets, heating and cooling units and appliances. These items have been multiplied by 1.20.

Man-hours

Man-hours is simply the amount of time allotted in Direct Labor to complete the task. All Man-hour figures have been determined using only one category of labor. In other words, rough-in for a toilet was determined on the Direct Labor cost of a plumber, not a plumber and helper. Wall framing is determined on the Direct Labor cost of carpenters, not a mix of carpenters and helpers.

Every effort has been made to provide up-to-date cost information. Material and labor costs fluctuate throughout the year. No warranty or guarantee is made as to the accuracy or correctness of the information contained in this manual. The publisher assumes no responsibility or liability in connection with its use.

To obtain more information about estimating and remodeling, visit our website at www.RemodelMAX.com.

If you have any questions about how to use this manual or the information it contains, call us at 1-800-858-5629.

LABOR RATES USED IN THIS MANUAL

Carpenter - **$76.12**
Laborer - **$40.51**
Plumber - **$101.97**
Electrician - **$95.34**
Roofer - **$77.48**
Mason - **$66.21**
Concrete Finisher - **$54.06**
Painter - **$55.69**
Tile Mason - **$39.42**

Table of Contents

Table of Contents

Framing Demolition (continued) 3

General Demolition 4

Systems Demolition 5

Table of Contents

Table of Contents

Table of Contents

Roof Framing 11

Roofing and Gutters 12

Table of Contents

Exterior Doors 13

Wood Windows 14

Table of Contents

Wood Windows (continued) 14

Vinyl Windows 15

Aluminum Windows 16

Table of Contents

Skylights 17

Decks and Porches 18

Siding and Awnings 19

Table of Contents

Table of Contents

Bathroom Plumbing (continued) 22

Kitchen and Laundry Plumbing 23

HVAC - Heating, Ventilation, Air Conditioning 24

Table of Contents

Electrical 25

Appliances 26

Insulation 27

Table of Contents

Wall Coverings 28

Ceiling Coverings 29

Interior Doors 30

Table of Contents

Table of Contents

Interior Trim, Stairs, Accessories (cont.) 31

Cabinets and Countertops 32

Floor Covering 33

Table of Contents

Floor Covering (continued) 33

Exterior Painting 34

Table of Contents

Project Preparation

Plans and Permits

Description	Unit	Direct Labor	Direct Materials	Direct Total	Selling Price	Man-hours
PLANS WITH ON-SITE SURVEY, NO CONSULTATION						
Plans with on-site survey, project $4,000 - $6,000	EA	$740.18		$740.18	**$740.18**	9.724
Plans with on-site survey, project $6,000 - $8,000	EA	$888.23		$888.23	**$888.23**	11.669
Plans with on-site survey, project $8,000 - $10,000	EA	$1,036.28		$1,036.28	**$1,036.28**	13.614
Plans with on-site survey, project $10,000 - $12,000	EA	$1,184.33		$1,184.33	**$1,184.33**	15.559
Plans with on-site survey, project $12,000 - $14,000	EA	$1,233.65		$1,233.65	**$1,233.65**	16.207
Plans with on-site survey, project $14,000 - $16,000	EA	$1,283.05		$1,283.05	**$1,283.05**	16.856
Plans with on-site survey, project $18,000 - $20,000	EA	$1,332.38		$1,332.38	**$1,332.38**	17.504
Plans with on-site survey, project $20,000 - $25,000	EA	$1,431.10		$1,431.10	**$1,431.10**	18.801
Plans with on-site survey, project $25,000 - $30,000	EA	$1,603.82		$1,603.82	**$1,603.82**	21.070
Plans with on-site survey, project $30,000 - $35,000	EA	$1,801.19		$1,801.19	**$1,801.19**	23.663
Plans with on-site survey, project $35,000 - $40,000	EA	$2,047.89		$2,047.89	**$2,047.89**	26.904
Plans with on-site survey, project $40,000 - $50,000	EA	$2,294.67		$2,294.67	**$2,294.67**	30.146
Plans with on-site survey, project $50,000 - $60,000	EA	$2,541.37		$2,541.37	**$2,541.37**	33.387
Plans with on-site survey, project $60,000 - $70,000	EA	$2,788.14		$2,788.14	**$2,788.14**	36.629
Plans with on-site survey, project $70,000 - $80,000	EA	$3,034.84		$3,034.84	**$3,034.84**	39.870
Plans with on-site survey, project $80,000 - $90,000	EA	$3,281.62		$3,281.62	**$3,281.62**	43.112
Plans with on-site survey, project $90,000 - $100,000	EA	$3,528.32		$3,528.32	**$3,528.32**	46.353
PLANS, ON-SITE SURVEY, APPROVAL BY OWNER						
Plans, on-site survey, approval by owner, project $4,000 - $6,000	EA	$1,110.34		$1,110.34	**$1,110.34**	14.587
Plans, on-site survey, approval by owner, project $6,000 - $8,000	EA	$1,332.38		$1,332.38	**$1,332.38**	17.504
Plans, on-site survey, approval by owner, project $8,000 - $10,000	EA	$1,554.42		$1,554.42	**$1,554.42**	20.421
Plans, on-site survey, approval by owner, project $10,000 - $12,000	EA	$1,776.53		$1,776.53	**$1,776.53**	23.339
Plans, on-site survey, approval by owner, project $12,000 - $14,000	EA	$1,899.84		$1,899.84	**$1,899.84**	24.959
Plans, on-site survey, approval by owner, project $14,000 - $16,000	EA	$2,023.23		$2,023.23	**$2,023.23**	26.580
Plans, on-site survey, approval by owner, project $18,000 - $20,000	EA	$2,146.62		$2,146.62	**$2,146.62**	28.201
Plans, on-site survey, approval by owner, project $20,000 - $25,000	EA	$2,393.32		$2,393.32	**$2,393.32**	31.442
Plans, on-site survey, approval by owner, project $25,000 - $30,000	EA	$2,714.08		$2,714.08	**$2,714.08**	35.656
Plans, on-site survey, approval by owner, project $30,000 - $35,000	EA	$3,059.51		$3,059.51	**$3,059.51**	40.194
Plans, on-site survey, approval by owner, project $35,000 - $40,000	EA	$3,454.33		$3,454.33	**$3,454.33**	45.381
Plans, on-site survey, approval by owner, project $40,000 - $50,000	EA	$3,898.48		$3,898.48	**$3,898.48**	51.216
Plans, on-site survey, approval by owner, project $50,000 - $60,000	EA	$4,342.56		$4,342.56	**$4,342.56**	57.050
Plans, on-site survey, approval by owner, project $60,000 - $70,000	EA	$4,786.71		$4,786.71	**$4,786.71**	62.885
Plans, on-site survey, approval by owner, project $70,000 - $80,000	EA	$5,230.86		$5,230.86	**$5,230.86**	68.720
Plans, on-site survey, approval by owner, project $80,000 - $90,000	EA	$5,674.94		$5,674.94	**$5,674.94**	74.554
Plans, on-site survey, approval by owner, project $90,000 - $100,000	EA	$6,094.43		$6,094.43	**$6,094.43**	80.065

1

Project Preparation

Building permit Fees

Description	Unit	Direct Labor	Direct Materials	Direct Total	Selling Price	Man-hours
Building permit fee, project up to $1,000	EA		$66.00	$66.00	**$66.00**	
Building permit fee, project $1,000 - $2,000	EA		$88.00	$88.00	**$88.00**	
Building permit fee, project $2,000 - $3,000	EA		$110.00	$110.00	**$110.00**	
Building permit fee, project $3,000 - $4,000	EA		$132.00	$132.00	**$132.00**	
Building permit fee, project $4,000 - $6,000	EA		$165.00	$165.00	**$165.00**	
Building permit fee, project $6,000 - $8,000	EA		$198.00	$198.00	**$198.00**	
Building permit fee, project $8,000 - $10,000	EA		$231.00	$231.00	**$231.00**	
Building permit fee, project $10,000 - $12,000	EA		$264.00	$264.00	**$264.00**	
Building permit fee, project $12,000 - $14,000	EA		$297.00	$297.00	**$297.00**	
Building permit fee, project $14,000 - $16,000	EA		$330.00	$330.00	**$330.00**	
Building permit fee, project $16,000 - $18,000	EA		$363.00	$363.00	**$363.00**	
Building permit fee, project $18,000 - $20,000	EA		$396.00	$396.00	**$396.00**	
Building permit fee, project $20,000 - $25,000	EA		$462.00	$462.00	**$462.00**	
Building permit fee, project $25,000 - $30,000	EA		$528.00	$528.00	**$528.00**	
Building permit fee, project $30,000 - $35,000	EA		$594.00	$594.00	**$594.00**	
Building permit fee, project $35,000 - $40,000	EA		$660.00	$660.00	**$660.00**	
Building permit fee, project $40,000 - $45,000	EA		$726.00	$726.00	**$726.00**	
Building permit fee, project $45,000 - $50,000	EA		$781.00	$781.00	**$781.00**	
Building permit fee, project $50,000 - $60,000	EA		$869.00	$869.00	**$869.00**	
Building permit fee, project $60,000 - $70,000	EA		$968.00	$968.00	**$968.00**	
Building permit fee, project $70,000 - $80,000	EA		$1,067.00	$1,067.00	**$1,067.00**	
Building permit fee, project $80,000 - $90,000	EA		$1,166.00	$1,166.00	**$1,166.00**	
Building permit fee, project $90,000 - $100,000	EA		$1,232.00	$1,232.00	**$1,232.00**	

Surface Protection

Description	Unit	Direct Labor	Direct Materials	Direct Total	Selling Price	Man-hours
Cover contents with plastic sheeting	SF	$0.16	$0.09	$0.25	**$0.42**	0.004
Cover and mask floor with plastic sheeting	SF	$0.28	$0.12	$0.40	**$0.68**	0.007
Cover and mask floor with self-adhesive plastic film	SF	$0.57	$0.24	$0.81	**$1.35**	0.014
Mask and cover light fixture, average	EA	$6.72	$1.21	$7.93	**$13.25**	0.166
Mask and cover light fixture, large	EA	$13.49	$2.31	$15.80	**$26.39**	0.333

Project Preparation

Move Contents

Description	Unit	Direct Labor	Direct Materials	Direct Total	Selling Price	Man-hours
Move out then reset contents of room, average living room	EA	$81.02		$81.02	**$135.30**	2.000
Move out then reset contents of room, large living room	EA	$121.53		$121.53	**$202.95**	3.000
Move out then reset contents of room, average dining room	EA	$60.76		$60.76	**$101.47**	1.500
Move out then reset contents of room, large dining room	EA	$81.02		$81.02	**$135.30**	2.000
Move out then reset contents of room, average bedroom	EA	$60.76		$60.76	**$101.47**	1.500
Move out then reset contents of room, large bedroom	EA	$81.02		$81.02	**$135.30**	2.000
Move out then reset contents of room, refrigerator and range	EA	$60.76		$60.76	**$101.47**	1.500
Move out then reset contents of room, washer and dryer	EA	$60.76		$60.76	**$101.47**	1.500

Temporary Needs

Description	Unit	Direct Labor	Direct Materials	Direct Total	Selling Price	Man-hours
Power pole, 100 Amp, temporary	EA		$110.00	$110.00	**$183.70**	
Power pole, 200 Amp temporary	EA		$132.00	$132.00	**$220.44**	
Portable toilet	EA		$121.00	$121.00	**$202.07**	
Chain link fencing, 5' tall, temporary	LF	$2.55	$2.63	$5.18	**$8.65**	0.063
Plastic safety fencing, 4' tall, temporary	LF	$0.81	$0.94	$1.75	**$2.91**	0.020

Concrete Demolition

Driveway and Sidewalk Demolition

Description	Unit	Direct Labor	Direct Materials	Direct Total	Selling Price	Man-hours
DEMOLISH DRIVEWAY WITH AIR TOOLS, REINFORCED						
Demolish driveway with air tools, 4" thick, reinforced with wire mesh	SF	$2.63		$2.63	**$4.40**	0.065
Demolish driveway with air tools, 5" thick, reinforced with wire mesh	SF	$3.04		$3.04	**$5.07**	0.075
Demolish driveway with air tools, 6" thick, reinforced with wire mesh	SF	$3.44		$3.44	**$5.75**	0.085
DEMOLISH DRIVEWAY WITH AIR TOOLS, UNREINFORCED						
Demolish driveway with air tools, 4" thick, no reinforcement	SF	$1.82		$1.82	**$3.04**	0.045
Demolish driveway with air tools, 5" thick, no reinforcement	SF	$2.15		$2.15	**$3.59**	0.053
Demolish driveway with air tools, 6" thick, no reinforcement	SF	$2.35		$2.35	**$3.92**	0.058
DEMOLISH DRIVEWAY WITH MACHINE, REINFORCED						
Demolish driveway with machine, 4" thick, reinforced with wire mesh	SF	$2.33		$2.33	**$3.89**	0.032
Demolish driveway with machine, 5" thick, reinforced with wire mesh	SF	$2.70		$2.70	**$4.50**	0.037
Demolish driveway with machine, 6" thick, reinforced with wire mesh	SF	$2.99		$2.99	**$4.99**	0.041
DEMOLISH DRIVEWAY WITH MACHINE, UNREINFORCED						
Demolish driveway with machine, 4" thick, no reinforcement	SF	$1.60		$1.60	**$2.68**	0.022
Demolish driveway with machine, 5" thick, no reinforcement	SF	$1.82		$1.82	**$3.04**	0.025
Demolish driveway with machine, 6" thick, no reinforcement	SF	$2.04		$2.04	**$3.41**	0.028
DEMOLISH SIDEWALK WITH AIR TOOLS						
Demolish sidewalk with air tools, no reinforcement	SF	$1.78		$1.01	**$2.98**	0.044
Demolish sidewalk with air tools, reinforced with wire mesh	SF	$2.11		$1.50	**$3.52**	0.052
DEMOLISH BRICK SIDEWALK						
Demolish brick sidewalk by hand, in sand	SF	$0.57		$0.57	**$0.95**	0.014
Demolish brick sidewalk with air tools, in mortar bed	SF	$2.88		$2.88	**$4.80**	0.071

2

Concrete and Masonry Demolition

Slab Demolition

Description	Unit	Direct Labor	Direct Materials	Direct Total	Selling Price	Man-hours
DEMOLISH BASEMENT SLAB WITH AIR TOOLS, REINFORCED						
Demolish basement slab with air tools, 2" thick, mesh reinforced	SF	$2.55		$2.55	**$4.26**	0.063
Demolish basement slab with air tools, 4" thick, mesh reinforced	SF	$2.96		$2.96	**$4.94**	0.073
Demolish basement slab with air tools, 6" thick, mesh reinforced	SF	$3.52		$3.52	**$5.89**	0.087
DEMOLISH BASEMENT SLAB WITH AIR TOOLS, UNREINFORCED						
Demolish basement slab with air tools, 2" thick, no reinforcement	SF	$1.70		$1.70	**$2.84**	0.042
Demolish basement slab with air tools, 4" thick, no reinforcement	SF	$2.11		$2.11	**$3.52**	0.052
Demolish basement slab with air tools, 6" thick, no reinforcement	SF	$2.71		$2.71	**$4.53**	0.067
DEMOLISH EXTERIOR SLAB WITH AIR TOOLS, REINFORCED						
Demolish exterior slab with air tools, 4" thick, reinforced with wire mesh	SF	$2.63		$2.63	**$4.40**	0.065
Demolish exterior slab with air tools, 5" thick, reinforced with wire mesh	SF	$3.04		$3.04	**$5.07**	0.075
Demolish exterior slab with air tools, 6" thick, reinforced with wire mesh	SF	$3.44		$3.44	**$5.75**	0.085
DEMOLISH EXTERIOR SLAB WITH AIR TOOLS, UNREINFORCED						
Demolish exterior slab with air tools, 4" thick, no reinforcement	SF	$1.82		$1.82	**$3.04**	0.045
Demolish exterior slab with air tools, 5" thick, no reinforcement	SF	$2.15		$2.15	**$3.59**	0.053
Demolish exterior slab with air tools, 6" thick, no reinforcement	SF	$2.35		$2.35	**$3.92**	0.058
DEMOLISH SLAB AND STEPS						
Demolish suspended 6" slab and steps	SF	$4.05		$4.05	**$6.76**	0.100

Square or Round Footing Demolition

Description	Unit	Direct Labor	Direct Materials	Direct Total	Selling Price	Man-hours
DEMOLISH SQUARE/ROUND FOOTING 8"						
Demolish square/round footing, 8" by 12" deep	EA	$6.56		$6.56	**$10.96**	0.162
Demolish square/round footing, 8" by 24" deep	EA	$13.08		$13.08	**$21.85**	0.323
Demolish square/round footing, 8" by 36" deep	EA	$19.65		$19.65	**$32.81**	0.485
Demolish square/round footing, 8" by 48" deep	EA	$26.21		$26.21	**$43.77**	0.647
Demolish square/round footing, 8" by 60" deep	EA	$35.40		$35.40	**$59.13**	0.874
DEMOLISH SQUARE/ROUND FOOTING 10"						
Demolish square/round footing, 10" by 12" deep	EA	$8.02		$8.02	**$13.39**	0.198
Demolish square/round footing, 10" by 24" deep	EA	$16.00		$16.00	**$26.72**	0.395
Demolish square/round footing, 10" by 36" deep	EA	$24.02		$24.02	**$40.12**	0.593
Demolish square/round footing, 10" by 48" deep	EA	$32.04		$32.04	**$53.51**	0.791
Demolish square/round footing, 10" by 60" deep	EA	$43.26		$43.26	**$72.25**	1.068
DEMOLISH SQUARE/ROUND FOOTING 12"						
Demolish square/round footing, 12" by 12" deep	EA	$9.80		$9.80	**$16.37**	0.242
Demolish square/round footing, 12" by 24" deep	EA	$19.61		$19.61	**$32.74**	0.484
Demolish square/round footing, 12" by 36" deep	EA	$29.41		$29.41	**$49.11**	0.726
Demolish square/round footing, 12" by 48" deep	EA	$39.25		$39.25	**$65.55**	0.969
Demolish square/round footing, 12" by 60" deep	EA	$52.99		$52.99	**$88.49**	1.308

Concrete and Masonry Demolition

Footing Demolition

Description	Unit	Direct Labor	Direct Materials	Direct Total	Selling Price	Man-hours
DEMOLISH FOOTING WITH AIR TOOLS, 8" THICK						
Demolish footing with air tools, 8"T x 10"W, reinforced	LF	$5.35		$5.35	**$8.93**	0.132
Demolish footing with air tools, 8"T x 12"W, reinforced	LF	$5.71		$5.71	**$9.54**	0.141
Demolish footing with air tools, 8"T x 16"W, reinforced	LF	$7.21		$7.21	**$12.04**	0.178
Demolish footing with air tools, 8"T x 18"W, reinforced	LF	$7.82		$7.82	**$13.06**	0.193
Demolish footing with air tools, 8"T x 20"W, reinforced	LF	$9.48		$9.48	**$15.83**	0.234
DEMOLISH FOOTING WITH AIR TOOLS, 10" THICK						
Demolish footing with air tools, 10"T x 10"W, reinforced	LF	$6.40		$6.40	**$10.69**	0.158
Demolish footing with air tools, 10"T x 12"W, reinforced	LF	$6.85		$6.85	**$11.43**	0.169
Demolish footing with air tools, 10"T x 16"W, reinforced	LF	$8.67		$8.67	**$14.48**	0.214
Demolish footing with air tools, 10"T x 18"W, reinforced	LF	$9.40		$9.40	**$15.69**	0.232
Demolish footing with air tools, 10"T x 20"W, reinforced	LF	$11.38		$11.38	**$19.01**	0.281
DEMOLISH FOOTING WITH AIR TOOLS, 12" THICK						
Demolish footing with air tools, 12"T x 10"W, reinforced	LF	$7.09		$7.09	**$11.84**	0.175
Demolish footing with air tools, 12"T x 12"W, reinforced	LF	$7.58		$7.58	**$12.65**	0.187
Demolish footing with air tools, 12"T x 16"W, reinforced	LF	$9.60		$9.60	**$16.03**	0.237
Demolish footing with air tools, 12"T x 18"W, reinforced	LF	$10.41		$10.41	**$17.39**	0.257
Demolish footing with air tools, 12"T x 20"W, reinforced	LF	$12.60		$12.60	**$21.04**	0.311
DEMOLISH FOOTING WITH AIR TOOLS, 24" THICK						
Demolish footing with air tools, 24"T x 10"W, reinforced	LF	$13.33		$13.33	**$22.26**	0.329
Demolish footing with air tools, 24"T x 12"W, reinforced	LF	$14.26		$14.26	**$23.81**	0.352
Demolish footing with air tools, 24"T x 16"W, reinforced	LF	$18.03		$18.03	**$30.10**	0.445
Demolish footing with air tools, 24"T x 18"W, reinforced	LF	$19.57		$19.57	**$32.67**	0.483
Demolish footing with air tools, 24"T x 20"W, reinforced	LF	$23.70		$23.70	**$39.58**	0.585
Demolish footing with air tools, 24"T x 24"W, reinforced	LF	$27.26		$27.26	**$45.53**	0.673
DEMOLISH FOOTING WITH AIR TOOLS, 30" THICK						
Demolish footing with air tools, 30"T x 10"W, reinforced	LF	$15.35		$15.35	**$25.64**	0.379
Demolish footing with air tools, 30"T x 12"W, reinforced	LF	$16.37		$16.37	**$27.33**	0.404
Demolish footing with air tools, 30"T x 16"W, reinforced	LF	$20.74		$20.74	**$34.64**	0.512
Demolish footing with air tools, 30"T x 18"W, reinforced	LF	$22.48		$22.48	**$37.55**	0.555
Demolish footing with air tools, 30"T x 20"W, reinforced	LF	$27.26		$27.26	**$45.53**	0.673
Demolish footing with air tools, 30"T x 24"W, reinforced	LF	$31.35		$31.35	**$52.36**	0.774
DEMOLISH FOOTING WITH AIR TOOLS, 36" THICK						
Demolish footing with air tools, 36"T x 10"W, reinforced	LF	$16.28		$16.28	**$27.20**	0.402
Demolish footing with air tools, 36"T x 12"W, reinforced	LF	$17.38		$17.38	**$29.02**	0.429
Demolish footing with air tools, 36"T x 16"W, reinforced	LF	$22.00		$22.00	**$36.73**	0.543
Demolish footing with air tools, 36"T x 18"W, reinforced	LF	$23.86		$23.86	**$39.85**	0.589
Demolish footing with air tools, 36"T x 20"W, reinforced	LF	$28.92		$28.92	**$48.30**	0.714
Demolish footing with air tools, 36"T x 24"W, reinforced	LF	$33.26		$33.26	**$55.54**	0.821

Concrete and Masonry Demolition

Footing Demolition (continued)

Description	Unit	Direct Labor	Direct Materials	Direct Total	Selling Price	Man-hours
DEMOLISH FOOTING WITH AIR TOOLS, 42" THICK						
Demolish footing with air tools, 42"T x 12"W, reinforced	LF	$22.08		$22.08	**$36.87**	0.545
Demolish footing with air tools, 42"T x 16"W, reinforced	LF	$27.95		$27.95	**$46.68**	0.690
Demolish footing with air tools, 42"T x 18"W, reinforced	LF	$30.30		$30.30	**$50.60**	0.748
Demolish footing with air tools, 42"T x 20"W, reinforced	LF	$36.74		$36.74	**$61.36**	0.907
Demolish footing with air tools, 42"T x 24"W, reinforced	LF	$42.25		$42.25	**$70.56**	1.043
DEMOLISH FOOTING WITH AIR TOOLS, 48" THICK						
Demolish footing with air tools, 48"T x 12"W, reinforced	LF	$24.91		$24.91	**$41.60**	0.615
Demolish footing with air tools, 48"T x 16"W, reinforced	LF	$31.56		$31.56	**$52.70**	0.779
Demolish footing with air tools, 48"T x 18"W, reinforced	LF	$34.23		$34.23	**$57.16**	0.845
Demolish footing with air tools, 48"T x 20"W, reinforced	LF	$41.48		$41.48	**$69.27**	1.024
Demolish footing with air tools, 48"T x 24"W, reinforced	LF	$47.72		$47.72	**$79.69**	1.178
DEMOLISH FOOTING WITH AIR TOOLS, 60" THICK						
Demolish footing with air tools, 60"T x 12"W, reinforced	LF	$32.04		$32.04	**$53.51**	0.791
Demolish footing with air tools, 60"T x 16"W, reinforced	LF	$40.59		$40.59	**$67.78**	1.002
Demolish footing with air tools, 60"T x 18"W, reinforced	LF	$43.99		$43.99	**$73.47**	1.086
Demolish footing with air tools, 60"T x 20"W, reinforced	LF	$53.35		$53.35	**$89.09**	1.317
Demolish footing with air tools, 60"T x 24"W, reinforced	LF	$61.37		$61.37	**$102.49**	1.515

Concrete and Masonry Demolition

Pier Footing Demolition

Description	Unit	Direct Labor	Direct Materials	Direct Total	Selling Price	Man-hours
DEMOLISH PIER FOOTING WITH AIR TOOLS, 12" DEEP						
Demolish pier footing with air tools, 16"L x 16"W x 12"D, reinforced	EA	$15.43		$15.43	**$25.77**	0.381
Demolish pier footing with air tools, 24"L x 24"W x 12"D, reinforced	EA	$23.17		$23.17	**$38.70**	0.572
Demolish pier footing with air tools, 30"L x 30"W x 12"D, reinforced	EA	$28.96		$28.96	**$48.37**	0.715
Demolish pier footing with air tools, 36"L x 48"W x 12"D, reinforced	EA	$38.65		$38.65	**$64.54**	0.954
DEMOLISH PIER FOOTING WITH AIR TOOLS, 24" DEEP						
Demolish pier footing with air tools, 16"L x 16"W x 24"D, reinforced	EA	$29.37		$29.37	**$49.05**	0.725
Demolish pier footing with air tools, 24"L x 24"W x 24"D, reinforced	EA	$44.03		$44.03	**$73.54**	1.087
Demolish pier footing with air tools, 30"L x 30"W x 24"D, reinforced	EA	$55.05		$55.05	**$91.94**	1.359
Demolish pier footing with air tools, 36"L x 48"W x 24"D, reinforced	EA	$73.40		$73.40	**$122.58**	1.812
DEMOLISH PIER FOOTING WITH AIR TOOLS, 36" DEEP						
Demolish pier footing with air tools, 16"L x 16"W x 36"D, reinforced	EA	$38.65		$38.65	**$64.54**	0.954
Demolish pier footing with air tools, 24"L x 24"W x 36"D, reinforced	EA	$57.93		$57.93	**$96.74**	1.430
Demolish pier footing with air tools, 30"L x 30"W x 36"D, reinforced	EA	$72.43		$72.43	**$120.96**	1.788
Demolish pier footing with air tools, 36"L x 48"W x 36"D, reinforced	EA	$96.57		$96.57	**$161.28**	2.384
DEMOLISH PIER FOOTING WITH AIR TOOLS, 48" DEEP						
Demolish pier footing with air tools, 16"L x 16"W x 48"D, reinforced	EA	$54.08		$54.08	**$90.31**	1.335
Demolish pier footing with air tools, 24"L x 24"W x 48"D, reinforced	EA	$81.14		$81.14	**$135.50**	2.003
Demolish pier footing with air tools, 30"L x 30"W x 48"D, reinforced	EA	$101.39		$101.39	**$169.33**	2.503
Demolish pier footing with air tools, 36"L x 48"W x 48"D, reinforced	EA	$135.22		$135.22	**$225.81**	3.338
DEMOLISH PIER FOOTING WITH AIR TOOLS, 60" DEEP						
Demolish pier footing with air tools, 16"L x 16"W x 60"D, reinforced	EA	$61.82		$61.82	**$103.23**	1.526
Demolish pier footing with air tools, 24"L x 24"W x 60"D, reinforced	EA	$92.72		$92.72	**$154.85**	2.289
Demolish pier footing with air tools, 30"L x 30"W x 60"D, reinforced	EA	$115.90		$115.90	**$193.55**	2.861
Demolish pier footing with air tools, 36"L x 48"W x 60"D, reinforced	EA	$154.54		$154.54	**$258.08**	3.815

2

Concrete and Masonry Demolition

Block Wall Demolition

Description	Unit	Direct Labor	Direct Materials	Direct Total	Selling Price	Man-hours
DEMOLISH BLOCK WALL WITH AIR TOOLS, REINFORCED						
Demolish block wall with air tools, 4"W x 8"H x 16"L, vertically reinforced	SF	$2.84		$2.84	**$4.74**	0.070
Demolish block wall with air tools, 6"W x 8"H x 16"L, vertically reinforced	SF	$3.28		$3.28	**$5.48**	0.081
Demolish block wall with air tools, 8"W x 8"H x 16"L, vertically reinforced	SF	$3.61		$3.61	**$6.02**	0.089
Demolish block wall with air tools, 10"W x 8"H x 16"L, vertically reinforced	SF	$3.85		$3.85	**$6.43**	0.095
Demolish block wall with air tools, 12"W x 8"H x 16"L, vertically reinforced	SF	$4.17		$4.17	**$6.97**	0.103
DEMOLISH BLOCK WALL WITH AIR TOOLS, UNREINFORCED						
Demolish block wall with air tools, 4"W x 8"H x 16"L, no reinforcement	SF	$2.19		$2.19	**$3.65**	0.054
Demolish block wall with air tools, 6"W x 8"H x 16"L, no reinforcement	SF	$2.47		$2.47	**$4.13**	0.061
Demolish block wall with air tools, 8"W x 8"H x 16"L, no reinforcement	SF	$2.71		$2.71	**$4.53**	0.067
Demolish block wall with air tools, 10"W x 8"H x 16"L, no reinforcement	SF	$2.92		$2.92	**$4.87**	0.072
Demolish block wall with air tools, 12"W x 8"H x 16"L, no reinforcement	SF	$3.16		$3.16	**$5.28**	0.078
DEMOLISH BLOCK WALL BY HAND, UNREINFORCED						
Demolish block walls by hand, 4"W x 8"H x 16"L, no reinforcement	SF	$2.31		$2.31	**$3.86**	0.057
Demolish block walls by hand, 6"W x 8"H x 16"L, no reinforcement	SF	$2.55		$2.55	**$4.26**	0.063
Demolish block walls by hand, 8"W x 8"H x 16"L, no reinforcement	SF	$2.84		$2.84	**$4.74**	0.070
Demolish block walls by hand, 10"W x 8"H x 16"L, no reinforcement	SF	$3.44		$3.44	**$5.75**	0.085
Demolish block walls by hand, 12"W x 8"H x 16"L, no reinforcement	SF	$3.61		$3.61	**$6.02**	0.089
DEMOLISH SLUMP BLOCK WALL WITH AIR TOOLS						
Demolish concrete slump block wall with air tools, 4" thick	SF	$2.11		$2.11	**$3.52**	0.052
Demolish concrete slump block wall with air tools, 6" thick	SF	$2.35		$2.35	**$3.92**	0.058
Demolish concrete slump block wall with air tools, 8" thick	SF	$2.71		$2.71	**$4.53**	0.067
Demolish concrete slump block wall with air tools, 12" thick	SF	$3.04		$3.04	**$5.07**	0.075

Concrete Wall Demolition

Description	Unit	Direct Labor	Direct Materials	Direct Total	Selling Price	Man-hours
DEMOLISH CONCRETE WALL WITH AIR TOOLS, REINFORCED						
Demolish poured concrete wall with air tools, 8" thick, reinforced	SF	$5.71		$5.71	**$9.54**	0.141
Demolish poured concrete wall with air tools, 10" thick, reinforced	SF	$6.97		$6.97	**$11.64**	0.172
Demolish poured concrete wall with air tools, 12" thick, reinforced	SF	$8.55		$8.55	**$14.27**	0.211
DEMOLISH CONCRETE WALL WITH AIR TOOLS, UNREINFORCED						
Demolish poured concrete wall with air tools, 8" thick, no reinforcement	SF	$4.58		$4.58	**$7.64**	0.113
Demolish poured concrete wall with air tools, 10" thick, no reinforcement	SF	$5.59		$5.59	**$9.34**	0.138
Demolish poured concrete wall with air tools, 12" thick, no reinforcement	SF	$6.81		$6.81	**$11.37**	0.168

Concrete and Masonry Demolition

Masonry Wall, Column and Step Demolition

Description	Unit	Direct Labor	Direct Materials	Direct Total	Selling Price	Man-hours
DEMOLISH BRICK WALL BY HAND						
Demolish brick wall by hand, 4" thick	SF	$3.48		$3.48	**$5.82**	0.086
Demolish brick wall by hand, 8" thick	SF	$6.28		$6.28	**$10.49**	0.155
Demolish brick wall by hand, 12" thick	SF	$9.15		$9.15	**$15.29**	0.226
DEMOLISH BRICK WALL WITH AIR TOOLS						
Demolish brick wall with air tools, 4" thick	SF	$2.80		$2.80	**$4.67**	0.069
Demolish brick wall with air tools, 8" thick	SF	$5.02		$5.02	**$8.39**	0.124
Demolish brick wall with air tools, 12" thick	SF	$7.33		$7.33	**$12.24**	0.181
DEMOLISH BRICK AND BLOCK WALL WITH AIR TOOLS						
Demolish brick and block wall with air tools, 8" thick	SF	$3.44		$3.44	**$5.75**	0.085
Demolish brick and block wall with air tools, 12" thick	SF	$4.78		$4.78	**$7.98**	0.118
DEMOLISH ADOBE BRICK WALL WITH AIR TOOLS						
Demolish adobe brick wall with air tools, 4" thick	SF	$2.03		$2.03	**$3.38**	0.050
Demolish adobe brick wall with air tools, 6" thick	SF	$2.75		$2.75	**$4.60**	0.068
Demolish adobe brick wall with air tools, 8" thick	SF	$3.28		$3.28	**$5.48**	0.081
Demolish adobe brick wall with air tools, 10" thick	SF	$4.70		$4.70	**$7.85**	0.116
DEMOLISH STONE VENEER WITH AIR TOOLS						
Demolish stone veneer with air tools	SF	$6.44		$6.44	**$10.76**	0.159
DEMOLISH STUCCO AND LATH WITH AIR TOOLS						
Demolish stucco and wood lath with air tools	SF	$1.46		$1.46	**$2.44**	0.036
Demolish stucco and metal lath with air tools	SF	$1.86		$1.86	**$3.11**	0.046
DEMOLISH BRICK COLUMN WITH AIR TOOLS						
Demolish solid brick column with air tools, 8" x 8"	LF	$6.32		$6.32	**$10.55**	0.156
Demolish solid brick column with air tools, 12" x 12"	LF	$14.22		$14.22	**$23.75**	0.351
Demolish solid brick column with air tools, 16" x 16"	LF	$22.00		$22.00	**$36.73**	0.543
Demolish solid brick column with air tools, 20" x 20"	LF	$31.27		$31.27	**$52.23**	0.772
Demolish solid brick column with air tools, 24" x 24"	LF	$47.19		$47.19	**$78.81**	1.165
Demolish solid brick column with air tools, 28" x 28"	LF	$62.63		$62.63	**$104.59**	1.546
Demolish solid brick column with air tools, 32" x 32"	LF	$84.70		$84.70	**$141.46**	2.091
Demolish solid brick column with air tools, 36" x 36"	LF	$109.94		$109.94	**$183.60**	2.714
DEMOLISH MASONRY PLATFORM AND STEPS						
Demolish masonry platform & steps	SF	$7.33		$7.33	**$12.24**	0.181

2

Concrete and Masonry Demolition

Masonry Fireplace and Chimney Demolition

Description	Unit	Direct Labor	Direct Materials	Direct Total	Selling Price	Man-hours
DEMOLISH BRICK CHIMNEY, AIR TOOLS, EXTERIOR WALL						
Demolish brick chimney with air tools, exterior, to 20"x20"	LF	$23.70		$23.70	**$39.58**	0.585
Demolish brick chimney with air tools, exterior, to 24"x36"	LF	$51.20		$51.20	**$85.51**	1.264
Demolish brick chimney with air tools, exterior, to 30"x48"	LF	$85.35		$85.35	**$142.54**	2.107
DEMOLISH BRICK CHIMNEY, AIR TOOLS, INTERIOR WALL						
Demolish brick chimney, air tools, interior, to 20"x20", no patching	LF	$40.59		$40.59	**$67.78**	1.002
Demolish brick chimney, air tools, interior, to 24"x36", no patching	LF	$71.70		$71.70	**$119.74**	1.770
Demolish brick chimney, air tools, interior, to 30"x48", no patching	LF	$119.50		$119.50	**$199.57**	2.950
DEMOLISH BLOCK CHIMNEY, AIR TOOLS, EXTERIOR WALL						
Demolish block chimney with air tools, exterior, to 20"x20"	LF	$13.45		$13.45	**$22.46**	0.332
Demolish block chimney with air tools, exterior, to 24"x36"	LF	$29.04		$29.04	**$48.50**	0.717
Demolish block chimney with air tools, exterior, to 30"x48"	LF	$48.37		$48.37	**$80.77**	1.194
DEMOLISH BLOCK CHIMNEY, AIR TOOLS, INTERIOR WALL						
Demolish block chimney, air tools, interior, to 20"x20", no patching	LF	$23.62		$23.62	**$39.44**	0.583
Demolish block chimney, air tools, interior, to 24"x36", no patching	LF	$51.04		$51.04	**$85.24**	1.260
Demolish block chimney, air tools, interior, to 30"x48", no patching	LF	$85.07		$85.07	**$142.06**	2.100
DEMOLISH BRICK FIREPLACE AND HEARTH, EXTERIOR WALL						
Demolish fireplace and hearth, average size, exterior wall, no patching	EA	$283.56		$283.56	**$473.55**	7.000
Demolish fireplace and hearth, large size, exterior wall, no patching	EA	$364.58		$364.58	**$608.85**	9.000
DEMOLISH BRICK FIREPLACE AND HEARTH, INTERIOR WALL						
Demolish fireplace and hearth, average size, interior wall, no patching	EA	$405.09		$405.09	**$676.50**	10.000
Demolish fireplace and hearth, large size, interior wall, no patching	EA	$486.11		$486.11	**$811.80**	12.000

Framing Demolition

Wood Floor Joist Demolition

Description	Unit	Direct Labor	Direct Materials	Direct Total	Selling Price	Man-hours
DEMOLISH WOOD FLOOR JOISTS, 2" x 6"						
Demolish wood floor joists, 2" x 6" 12"oc	SF	$0.77		$0.77	**$1.29**	0.019
Demolish wood floor joists, 2" x 6" 16"oc	SF	$0.61		$0.61	**$1.01**	0.015
Demolish wood floor joists, 2" x 6" 24"oc	SF	$0.49		$0.49	**$0.81**	0.012
DEMOLISH WOOD FLOOR JOISTS, 2" x 8"						
Demolish wood floor joists, 2" x 8" 12"oc	SF	$0.81		$0.81	**$1.35**	0.020
Demolish wood floor joists, 2" x 8" 16"oc	SF	$0.65		$0.65	**$1.08**	0.016
Demolish wood floor joists, 2" x 8" 24"oc	SF	$0.53		$0.53	**$0.88**	0.013
DEMOLISH WOOD FLOOR JOISTS, 2" x 10"						
Demolish wood floor joists, 2" x 10" 12"oc	SF	$0.81		$0.81	**$1.35**	0.020
Demolish wood floor joists, 2" x 10" 16"oc	SF	$0.69		$0.69	**$1.15**	0.017
Demolish wood floor joists, 2" x 10" 24"oc	SF	$0.53		$0.53	**$0.88**	0.013
DEMOLISH WOOD FLOOR JOISTS, 2" x 12"						
Demolish wood floor joists, 2" x 12" 12"oc	SF	$0.85		$0.85	**$1.42**	0.021
Demolish wood floor joists, 2" x 12" 16"oc	SF	$0.73		$0.73	**$1.22**	0.018
Demolish wood floor joists, 2" x 12" 24"oc	SF	$0.57		$0.57	**$0.95**	0.014
DEMOLISH WOOD FLOOR JOISTS, 3" x 8"						
Demolish wood floor joists, 3" x 8" 12"oc	SF	$0.93		$0.93	**$1.56**	0.023
Demolish wood floor joists, 3" x 8" 16"oc	SF	$0.77		$0.77	**$1.29**	0.019
Demolish wood floor joists, 3" x 8" 24"oc	SF	$0.61		$0.61	**$1.01**	0.015
DEMOLISH WOOD FLOOR JOISTS, 3" x 10"						
Demolish wood floor joists, 3" x 10" 12"oc	SF	$1.01		$1.01	**$1.69**	0.025
Demolish wood floor joists, 3" x 10" 16"oc	SF	$0.85		$0.85	**$1.42**	0.021
Demolish wood floor joists, 3" x 10" 24"oc	SF	$0.69		$0.69	**$1.15**	0.017
DEMOLISH WOOD FLOOR JOISTS, 3" x 12"						
Demolish wood floor joists, 3" x 12" 12"oc	SF	$1.09		$1.09	**$1.83**	0.027
Demolish wood floor joists, 3" x 12" 16"oc	SF	$0.93		$0.93	**$1.56**	0.023
Demolish wood floor joists, 3" x 12" 24"oc	SF	$0.73		$0.73	**$1.22**	0.018

Framing Demolition

Wood I - Joist Demolition

Description	Unit	Direct Labor	Direct Materials	Direct Total	Selling Price	Man-hours
DEMOLISH WOOD FLOOR I-JOISTS, 9-1/2"						
Demolish I-joists, 9-1/2" 12"oc	SF	$0.69		$0.69	**$1.15**	0.017
Demolish I-joists, 9-1/2" 16"oc	SF	$0.61		$0.61	**$1.01**	0.015
Demolish I-joists, 9-1/2" 24"oc	SF	$0.49		$0.49	**$0.81**	0.012
DEMOLISH WOOD FLOOR I-JOISTS, 11-7/8"						
Demolish I-joists, 11-7/8" 12"oc	SF	$0.73		$0.73	**$1.22**	0.018
Demolish I-joists, 11-7/8" 16"oc	SF	$0.61		$0.61	**$1.01**	0.015
Demolish I-joists, 11-7/8" 24"oc	SF	$0.49		$0.49	**$0.81**	0.012
DEMOLISH WOOD FLOOR I-JOISTS, 14"						
Demolish I-joists, 14" 12"oc	SF	$0.77		$0.77	**$1.29**	0.019
Demolish I-joists, 14" 16"oc	SF	$0.65		$0.65	**$1.08**	0.016
Demolish I-joists, 14" 24"oc	SF	$0.53		$0.53	**$0.88**	0.013

Steel Floor Joist Demolition

Description	Unit	Direct Labor	Direct Materials	Direct Total	Selling Price	Man-hours
DEMOLISH STEEL FLOOR JOISTS, 8"						
Demolish steel joists, 8" 12"oc	SF	$0.73		$0.73	**$1.22**	0.018
Demolish steel joists, 8" 16"oc	SF	$0.61		$0.61	**$1.01**	0.015
Demolish steel joists, 8" 24"oc	SF	$0.49		$0.49	**$0.81**	0.012
DEMOLISH STEEL FLOOR JOISTS, 10"						
Demolish steel joists, 10" 12"oc	SF	$0.77		$0.77	**$1.29**	0.019
Demolish steel joists, 10" 16"oc	SF	$0.65		$0.65	**$1.08**	0.016
Demolish steel joists, 10" 24"oc	SF	$0.53		$0.53	**$0.88**	0.013
DEMOLISH STEEL FLOOR JOISTS, 12"						
Demolish steel joists, 12" 12"oc	SF	$0.81		$0.81	**$1.35**	0.020
Demolish steel joists, 12" 16"oc	SF	$0.69		$0.69	**$1.15**	0.017
Demolish steel joists, 12" 24"oc	SF	$0.53		$0.53	**$0.88**	0.013
DEMOLISH STEEL FLOOR JOISTS, 14"						
Demolish steel joists, 14" 12"oc	SF	$0.85		$0.85	**$1.42**	0.021
Demolish steel joists, 14" 16"oc	SF	$0.73		$0.73	**$1.22**	0.018
Demolish steel joists, 14" 24"oc	SF	$0.57		$0.57	**$0.95**	0.014

Framing Demolition

Floor Sheathing Demolition

Description	Unit	Direct Labor	Direct Materials	Direct Total	Selling Price	Man-hours
DEMOLISH FLOOR SHEATHING, STRIP						
Demolish subfloor, 1" x 8" strips, laid straight	SF	$0.93		$0.93	**$1.56**	0.023
Demolish subfloor, 1" x 8" strips, laid diagonally	SF	$1.05		$1.05	**$1.76**	0.026
DEMOLISH FLOOR SHEATHING, PLYWOOD, 5/8"						
Demolish subfloor, 5/8" plywood sheathing, nailed only	SF	$0.65		$0.65	**$1.08**	0.016
Demolish subfloor, 5/8" plywood sheathing, nailed & glued	SF	$0.81		$0.81	**$1.35**	0.020
DEMOLISH FLOOR SHEATHING, PLYWOOD, 3/4"						
Demolish subfloor, 3/4" plywood sheathing, nailed only	SF	$0.69		$0.69	**$1.15**	0.017
Demolish subfloor, 3/4" plywood sheathing, nailed & glued	SF	$0.85		$0.85	**$1.42**	0.021
DEMOLISH FLOOR SHEATHING, PLYWOOD, 1-1/8"						
Demolish subfloor, 1-1/8" plywood sheathing, nailed only	SF	$0.93		$0.93	**$1.56**	0.023
Demolish subfloor, 1-1/8" plywood sheathing, nailed & glued	SF	$1.09		$1.09	**$1.83**	0.027
DEMOLISH FLOOR UNDERLAYMENT, HARDBOARD						
Demolish subfloor, 0.215" hardboard sheathing, nailed only	SF	$0.49		$0.49	**$0.81**	0.012
Demolish subfloor, 0.215" hardboard sheathing, nailed & glued	SF	$0.65		$0.65	**$1.08**	0.016

Framing Demolition

Wall Framing Demolition

Description	Unit	Direct Labor	Direct Materials	Direct Total	Selling Price	Man-hours
DEMOLISH WOOD WALL FRAMING, 2" x 4", 8' HIGH						
Demolish wood wall framing, 8' high, 2" x 4" 12"oc	SF	$0.93		$0.93	**$1.56**	0.023
Demolish wood wall framing, 8' high, 2" x 4" 16"oc	SF	$0.81		$0.81	**$1.35**	0.020
Demolish wood wall framing, 8' high, 2" x 4" 24"oc	SF	$0.69		$0.69	**$1.15**	0.017
DEMOLISH WOOD WALL FRAMING, 2" x 4", 10' HIGH						
Demolish wood wall framing, 10' high, 2" x 4" 12"oc	SF	$0.77		$0.77	**$1.29**	0.019
Demolish wood wall framing, 10' high, 2" x 4" 16"oc	SF	$0.69		$0.69	**$1.15**	0.017
Demolish wood wall framing, 10' high, 2" x 4" 24"oc	SF	$0.53		$0.53	**$0.88**	0.013
DEMOLISH WOOD WALL FRAMING, 2" x 6", 8' HIGH						
Demolish wood wall framing, 8' high, 2" x 6" 12"oc	SF	$1.05		$1.05	**$1.76**	0.026
Demolish wood wall framing, 8' high, 2" x 6" 16"oc	SF	$0.93		$0.93	**$1.56**	0.023
Demolish wood wall framing, 8' high, 2" x 6" 24"oc	SF	$0.81		$0.81	**$1.35**	0.020
DEMOLISH WOOD WALL FRAMING, 2" x 6", 10' HIGH						
Demolish wood wall framing, 10' high, 2" x 6" 12"oc	SF	$0.85		$0.85	**$1.42**	0.021
Demolish wood wall framing, 10' high, 2" x 6" 16"oc	SF	$0.77		$0.77	**$1.29**	0.019
Demolish wood wall framing, 10' high, 2" x 6" 24"oc	SF	$0.65		$0.65	**$1.08**	0.016
DEMOLISH STEEL WALL FRAMING, 2" x 4", 8' HIGH						
Demolish steel wall framing, 8' high, up to 2" x 4" 12"oc	SF	$0.61		$0.61	**$1.01**	0.015
Demolish steel wall framing, 8' high, up to 2" x 4" 16"oc	SF	$0.57		$0.57	**$0.95**	0.014
Demolish steel wall framing, 8' high, up to 2" x 4" 24"oc	SF	$0.45		$0.45	**$0.74**	0.011
DEMOLISH STEEL WALL FRAMING, 2" x 4", 10' HIGH						
Demolish steel wall framing, 10' high, up to 2" x 4" 12"oc	SF	$0.49		$0.49	**$0.81**	0.012
Demolish steel wall framing, 10' high, up to 2" x 4" 16"oc	SF	$0.45		$0.45	**$0.74**	0.011
Demolish steel wall framing, 10' high, up to 2" x 4" 24"oc	SF	$0.36		$0.36	**$0.61**	0.009
DEMOLISH STEEL WALL FRAMING, 2" x 6", 8' HIGH						
Demolish steel wall framing, 8' high, up to 2" x 6" 12"oc	SF	$0.69		$0.69	**$1.15**	0.017
Demolish steel wall framing, 8' high, up to 2" x 6" 16"oc	SF	$0.61		$0.61	**$1.01**	0.015
Demolish steel wall framing, 8' high, up to 2" x 6" 24"oc	SF	$0.53		$0.53	**$0.88**	0.013
DEMOLISH STEEL WALL FRAMING, 2" x 6", 10' HIGH						
Demolish steel wall framing, 10' high, up to 2" x 6" 12"oc	SF	$0.57		$0.57	**$0.95**	0.014
Demolish steel wall framing, 10' high, up to 2" x 6" 16"oc	SF	$0.49		$0.49	**$0.81**	0.012
Demolish steel wall framing, 10' high, up to 2" x 6" 24"oc	SF	$0.45		$0.45	**$0.74**	0.011

Framing Demolition

Wall Sheathing Demolition

Description	Unit	Direct Labor	Direct Materials	Direct Total	Selling Price	Man-hours
DEMOLISH WALL SHEATHING, STRIP						
Demolish wall sheathing, 1" x 8" strips, laid straight	SF	$0.89		$0.89	**$1.49**	0.022
Demolish wall sheathing, 1" x 8" strips, laid diagonally	SF	$1.01		$1.01	**$1.69**	0.025
DEMOLISH WALL SHEATHING, PLYWOOD						
Demolish wall sheathing, 3/8" plywood	SF	$0.57		$0.57	**$0.95**	0.014
Demolish wall sheathing, 1/2" plywood	SF	$0.61		$0.61	**$1.01**	0.015
Demolish wall sheathing, 5/8" plywood	SF	$0.65		$0.65	**$1.08**	0.016
DEMOLISH WALL SHEATHING, FOAM BOARD						
Demolish wall sheathing, 1/2" polystyrene insulating board	SF	$0.16		$0.16	**$0.27**	0.004
Demolish wall sheathing, 3/4" polystyrene insulating board	SF	$0.16		$0.16	**$0.27**	0.004
Demolish wall sheathing, 1" polystyrene insulating board	SF	$0.20		$0.20	**$0.34**	0.005
Demolish wall sheathing, 1-1/2" polystyrene insulating board	SF	$0.24		$0.24	**$0.41**	0.006
Demolish wall sheathing, 2" polystyrene insulating board	SF	$0.28		$0.28	**$0.47**	0.007

Framing Demolition

Wood Ceiling Joist Demolition

Description	Unit	Direct Labor	Direct Materials	Direct Total	Selling Price	Man-hours
DEMOLISH WOOD CEILING JOISTS, 2" x 4"						
Demolish wood ceiling joists, 2" x 4" 12"oc	SF	$0.65		$0.65	**$1.08**	0.016
Demolish wood ceiling joists, 2" x 4" 16"oc	SF	$0.53		$0.53	**$0.88**	0.013
Demolish wood ceiling joists, 2" x 4" 24"oc	SF	$0.41		$0.41	**$0.68**	0.010
DEMOLISH WOOD CEILING JOISTS, 2" x 6"						
Demolish wood ceiling joists, 2" x 6" 12"oc	SF	$0.65		$0.65	**$1.08**	0.016
Demolish wood ceiling joists, 2" x 6" 16"oc	SF	$0.57		$0.57	**$0.95**	0.014
Demolish wood ceiling joists, 2" x 6" 24"oc	SF	$0.45		$0.45	**$0.74**	0.011
DEMOLISH WOOD CEILING JOISTS, 2" x 8"						
Demolish wood ceiling joists, 2" x 8" 12"oc	SF	$0.69		$0.69	**$1.15**	0.017
Demolish wood ceiling joists, 2" x 8" 16"oc	SF	$0.61		$0.61	**$1.01**	0.015
Demolish wood ceiling joists, 2" x 8" 24"oc	SF	$0.49		$0.49	**$0.81**	0.012
DEMOLISH WOOD CEILING JOISTS, 2" x 10"						
Demolish wood ceiling joists, 2" x 10" 12"oc	SF	$0.73		$0.73	**$1.22**	0.018
Demolish wood ceiling joists, 2" x 10" 16"oc	SF	$0.61		$0.61	**$1.01**	0.015
Demolish wood ceiling joists, 2" x 10" 24"oc	SF	$0.49		$0.49	**$0.81**	0.012
DEMOLISH WOOD CEILING JOISTS, 2" x 12"						
Demolish wood ceiling joists, 2" x 12" 12"oc	SF	$0.77		$0.77	**$1.29**	0.019
Demolish wood ceiling joists, 2" x 12" 16"oc	SF	$0.65		$0.65	**$1.08**	0.016
Demolish wood ceiling joists, 2" x 12" 24"oc	SF	$0.53		$0.53	**$0.88**	0.013
DEMOLISH WOOD CEILING JOISTS, 3" x 8"						
Demolish wood ceiling joists, 3" x 8" 12"oc	SF	$0.77		$0.77	**$1.29**	0.019
Demolish wood ceiling joists, 3" x 8" 16"oc	SF	$0.65		$0.65	**$1.08**	0.016
Demolish wood ceiling joists, 3" x 8" 24"oc	SF	$0.53		$0.53	**$0.88**	0.013
DEMOLISH WOOD CEILING JOISTS, 3" x 10"						
Demolish wood ceiling joists, 3" x 10" 12"oc	SF	$0.81		$0.81	**$1.35**	0.020
Demolish wood ceiling joists, 3" x 10" 16"oc	SF	$0.69		$0.69	**$1.15**	0.017
Demolish wood ceiling joists, 3" x 10" 24"oc	SF	$0.53		$0.53	**$0.88**	0.013
DEMOLISH WOOD CEILING JOISTS, 3" x 12"						
Demolish wood ceiling joists, 3" x 12" 12"oc	SF	$0.85		$0.85	**$1.42**	0.021
Demolish wood ceiling joists, 3" x 12" 16"oc	SF	$0.69		$0.69	**$1.15**	0.017
Demolish wood ceiling joists, 3" x 12" 24"oc	SF	$0.57		$0.57	**$0.95**	0.014

Framing Demolition

Wood Rafter and Truss Demolition

Description	Unit	Direct Labor	Direct Materials	Direct Total	Selling Price	Man-hours
DEMOLISH WOOD RAFTERS, 2" x 4"						
Demolish wood rafters, 2" x 4" 12"oc	SF	$0.89		$0.89	**$1.49**	0.022
Demolish wood rafters, 2" x 4" 16"oc	SF	$0.73		$0.73	**$1.22**	0.018
Demolish wood rafters, 2" x 4" 24"oc	SF	$0.61		$0.61	**$1.01**	0.015
DEMOLISH WOOD RAFTERS, 2" x 6"						
Demolish wood rafters, 2" x 6" 12"oc	SF	$0.93		$0.93	**$1.56**	0.023
Demolish wood rafters, 2" x 6" 16"oc	SF	$0.77		$0.77	**$1.29**	0.019
Demolish wood rafters, 2" x 6" 24"oc	SF	$0.61		$0.61	**$1.01**	0.015
DEMOLISH WOOD RAFTERS, 2" x 8"						
Demolish wood rafters, 2" x 8" 12"oc	SF	$0.97		$0.97	**$1.62**	0.024
Demolish wood rafters, 2" x 8" 16"oc	SF	$0.81		$0.81	**$1.35**	0.020
Demolish wood rafters, 2" x 8" 24"oc	SF	$0.65		$0.65	**$1.08**	0.016
DEMOLISH WOOD RAFTERS, 2" x 10"						
Demolish wood rafters, 2" x 10" 12"oc	SF	$1.01		$1.01	**$1.69**	0.025
Demolish wood rafters, 2" x 10" 16"oc	SF	$0.85		$0.85	**$1.42**	0.021
Demolish wood rafters, 2" x 10" 24"oc	SF	$0.69		$0.69	**$1.15**	0.017
DEMOLISH WOOD RAFTERS, 2" x 12"						
Demolish wood rafters, 2" x 12" 12"oc	SF	$1.09		$1.09	**$1.83**	0.027
Demolish wood rafters, 2" x 12" 16"oc	SF	$0.89		$0.89	**$1.49**	0.022
Demolish wood rafters, 2" x 12" 24"oc	SF	$0.73		$0.73	**$1.22**	0.018
DEMOLISH WOOD TRUSS						
Demolish wood truss, up to 26' span	EA	$42.82		$42.82	**$71.51**	1.057
Demolish wood truss, 26' to 30' span	EA	$49.42		$49.42	**$82.53**	1.220
Demolish wood truss, 30' to 36' span	EA	$59.26		$59.26	**$98.97**	1.463

Roof Sheathing Demolition

Description	Unit	Direct Labor	Direct Materials	Direct Total	Selling Price	Man-hours
DEMOLISH ROOF SHEATHING, STRIP						
Demolish roof sheathing, 1" x 8" strips, laid straight	SF	$0.89		$0.89	**$1.49**	0.022
Demolish roof sheathing, 1" x 8" strips, laid diagonally	SF	$1.01		$1.01	**$1.69**	0.025
DEMOLISH ROOF SHEATHING, PLYWOOD						
Demolish roof sheathing, 1/2" plywood	SF	$0.61		$0.61	**$1.01**	0.015
Demolish roof sheathing, 5/8" plywood	SF	$0.65		$0.61	**$1.08**	0.016
Demolish roof sheathing, 3/4" plywood	SF	$0.69		$0.65	**$1.15**	0.017

Framing Demolition

Column and Beam Demolition

Description	Unit	Direct Labor	Direct Materials	Direct Total	Selling Price	Man-hours
DEMOLISH STEEL BEAM						
Demolish steel I-beam, 6" x 4"	LF	$9.03		$9.03	**$15.09**	0.223
Demolish steel I-beam, 8" x 4"	LF	$9.60		$9.60	**$16.03**	0.237
Demolish steel I-beam, 10" x 4"	LF	$10.17		$10.17	**$16.98**	0.251
DEMOLISH WOOD BEAM, 2" THICK						
Demolish wood beam, 2" x 6"	LF	$0.69		$0.69	**$1.15**	0.017
Demolish wood beam, 2" x 8"	LF	$0.77		$0.77	**$1.29**	0.019
Demolish wood beam, 2" x 10"	LF	$0.81		$0.81	**$1.35**	0.020
Demolish wood beam, 2" x 12"	LF	$0.85		$0.85	**$1.42**	0.021
DEMOLISH WOOD BEAM, 3" THICK						
Demolish wood beam, 3" x 6", single or built-up	LF	$0.81		$0.81	**$1.35**	0.020
Demolish wood beam, 3" x 8", single or built-up	LF	$0.89		$0.89	**$1.49**	0.022
Demolish wood beam, 3" x 10", single or built-up	LF	$0.97		$0.97	**$1.62**	0.024
Demolish wood beam, 3" x 12", single or built-up	LF	$1.05		$1.05	**$1.76**	0.026
DEMOLISH WOOD BEAM, 4" THICK						
Demolish wood beam, 4" x 6", single or built-up	LF	$0.85		$0.85	**$1.42**	0.021
Demolish wood beam, 4" x 8", single or built-up	LF	$0.97		$0.97	**$1.62**	0.024
Demolish wood beam, 4" x 10", single or built-up	LF	$1.13		$1.13	**$1.89**	0.028
Demolish wood beam, 4" x 12", single or built-up	LF	$1.26		$1.26	**$2.10**	0.031
DEMOLISH WOOD BEAM, 6" THICK						
Demolish wood beam, 6" x 6", single or built-up	LF	$1.50		$1.50	**$2.50**	0.037
Demolish wood beam, 6" x 8", single or built-up	LF	$1.66		$1.66	**$2.77**	0.041
Demolish wood beam, 6" x 10", single or built-up	LF	$1.82		$1.82	**$3.04**	0.045
Demolish wood beam, 6" x 12", single or built-up	LF	$2.03		$2.03	**$3.38**	0.050
DEMOLISH WOOD COLUMN						
Demolish wood column, 4" x 4"	EA	$10.29		$10.29	**$17.18**	0.254
Demolish wood column, 4" x 6"	EA	$12.36		$12.36	**$20.63**	0.305
Demolish wood column, 4" x 8"	EA	$13.57		$13.57	**$22.66**	0.335
Demolish wood column, 6" x 6"	EA	$14.83		$14.83	**$24.76**	0.366
Demolish wood column, 6" x 8"	EA	$16.49		$16.49	**$27.53**	0.407
Demolish wood column, 6" x 10"	EA	$18.11		$18.11	**$30.24**	0.447
Demolish wood column, 8" x 8"	EA	$20.58		$20.58	**$34.37**	0.508
Demolish wood column, 8" x 10"	EA	$23.05		$23.05	**$38.49**	0.569
DEMOLISH STEEL COLUMN						
Demolish steel pipe column, 3" diameter	EA	$9.88		$9.88	**$16.51**	0.244
Demolish steel pipe column, 4" diameter	EA	$10.69		$10.69	**$17.86**	0.264
Demolish steel pipe column, 6" diameter	EA	$12.36		$12.36	**$20.63**	0.305
Demolish steel pipe column, 8" diameter	EA	$14.02		$14.02	**$23.41**	0.346

General Demolition

General Exterior Demolition

Description	Unit	Direct Labor	Direct Materials	Direct Total	Selling Price	Man-hours
DEMOLISH WOOD FASCIA						
Demolish wood fascia, 1" x 4"	LF	$0.61		$0.61	**$1.01**	0.015
Demolish wood fascia, 1" x 6"	LF	$0.69		$0.69	**$1.15**	0.017
Demolish wood fascia, 1" x 8"	LF	$0.73		$0.73	**$1.22**	0.018
DEMOLISH WOOD SOFFIT						
Demolish wood soffit, 6"	LF	$0.61		$0.61	**$1.01**	0.015
Demolish wood soffit, 12"	LF	$0.81		$0.81	**$1.35**	0.020
Demolish wood soffit, 24"	LF	$1.05		$1.05	**$1.76**	0.026
Demolish wood soffit, 36"	LF	$1.30		$1.30	**$2.16**	0.032
DEMOLISH WOOD FASCIA AND SOFFIT COMBINATION						
Demolish wood soffit and fascia, 6" overhang	LF	$0.97		$0.97	**$1.62**	0.024
Demolish wood soffit and fascia, 12" overhang	LF	$1.13		$1.13	**$1.89**	0.028
Demolish wood soffit and fascia, 24" overhang	LF	$1.38		$1.38	**$2.30**	0.034
Demolish wood soffit and fascia, 36" overhang	LF	$1.62		$1.62	**$2.71**	0.040
DEMOLISH METAL FASCIA AND SOFFIT COMBINATION						
Demolish metal soffit and fascia, 6" overhang	LF	$0.69		$0.69	**$1.15**	0.017
Demolish metal soffit and fascia, 12" overhang	LF	$0.85		$0.85	**$1.42**	0.021
Demolish metal soffit and fascia, 24" overhang	LF	$1.05		$1.05	**$1.76**	0.026
Demolish metal soffit and fascia, 36" overhang	LF	$1.26		$1.26	**$2.10**	0.031
DEMOLISH GUTTER AND DOWNSPOUT						
Remove metal or vinyl gutter	LF	$1.22		$1.22	**$2.03**	0.030
Remove wood gutter	LF	$1.62		$1.62	**$2.71**	0.040
Remove downspout	LF	$0.73		$0.73	**$1.22**	0.018
Remove gutter guard/screen	LF	$0.53		$0.53	**$0.88**	0.013

General Demolition

Siding Demolition

Description	Unit	Direct Labor	Direct Materials	Direct Total	Selling Price	Man-hours
DEMOLISH WOOD STRIP SIDING						
Demolish wood siding, 4"	SF	$1.13		$1.13	**$1.89**	0.028
Demolish wood siding, 6"	SF	$0.97		$0.97	**$1.62**	0.024
Demolish wood siding, 8"	SF	$0.85		$0.85	**$1.42**	0.021
Demolish wood siding, 10"	SF	$0.73		$0.73	**$1.22**	0.018
Demolish wood siding, 12"	SF	$0.61		$0.61	**$1.01**	0.015
DEMOLISH SHINGLE AND SHAKE SIDING						
Demolish wood shingle/shake siding, 16" long	SF	$0.65		$0.65	**$1.08**	0.016
Demolish wood shingle/shake siding, 18" long	SF	$0.57		$0.57	**$0.95**	0.014
Demolish wood shingle/shake siding, 24" long	SF	$0.49		$0.49	**$0.81**	0.012
DEMOLISH ALUMINUM AND VINYL SIDING						
Demolish aluminum/vinyl siding, 4"	SF	$0.97		$0.97	**$1.62**	0.024
Demolish aluminum/vinyl siding, 8"	SF	$0.65		$0.65	**$1.08**	0.016
Demolish aluminum/vinyl siding, 10"	SF	$0.61		$0.61	**$1.01**	0.015
DEMOLISH OTHER SIDING						
Demolish hardboard panel siding	SF	$0.32		$0.32	**$0.54**	0.008
Demolish plywood siding	SF	$0.49		$0.49	**$0.81**	0.012
Demolish wood board and batten siding	SF	$0.61		$0.61	**$1.01**	0.015
Demolish stone veneer with air tools	SF	$6.44		$6.44	**$10.76**	0.159
Demolish stucco and lath with air tools	SF	$1.46		$1.46	**$2.44**	0.036
Demolish stucco and metal lath with air tools	SF	$1.86		$1.86	**$3.11**	0.046

General Demolition

Roofing Demolition

Description	Unit	Direct Labor	Direct Materials	Direct Total	Selling Price	Man-hours
DEMOLISH ASPHALT/FIBERGLASS STRIP SHINGLES						
Demolish asphalt/fiberglass shingles, to 8/12 slope, 1 layer	SF	$0.60		$0.60	**$1.00**	0.008
Demolish asphalt/fiberglass shingles, over 8/12 slope, 1 layer	SF	$0.72		$0.72	**$1.20**	0.009
Demolish asphalt/fiberglass shingles, to 8/12 slope, 2 layers	SF	$0.90		$0.90	**$1.50**	0.012
Demolish asphalt/fiberglass shingles, over 8/12 slope, 2 layers	SF	$1.08		$1.08	**$1.80**	0.014
DEMOLISH MINERAL ROLL ROOFING						
Demolish mineral roll roofing, to 8/12 slope, 1 layer	SF	$0.38		$0.38	**$0.63**	0.005
Demolish mineral roll roofing, over 8/12 slope, 1 layer	SF	$0.50		$0.50	**$0.83**	0.006
Demolish mineral roll roofing, to 8/12 slope, 2 layers	SF	$0.57		$0.57	**$0.95**	0.007
Demolish mineral roll roofing, over 8/12 slope, 2 layers	SF	$0.75		$0.75	**$1.25**	0.010
DEMOLISH BUILT-UP ROOFING						
Demolish built-up roofing, with gravel, 3-ply	SF	$1.36		$1.36	**$2.26**	0.017
Demolish built-up roofing, without gravel, 3-ply	SF	$0.84		$0.84	**$1.40**	0.011
DEMOLISH MEMBRANE ROOFING						
Demolish rubber roofing, perimeter adhered	SF	$0.60		$0.60	**$1.00**	0.008
Demolish rubber roofing, fully adhered	SF	$0.76		$0.76	**$1.26**	0.010
Demolish modified bitumen roofing	SF	$0.58		$0.58	**$0.97**	0.007
DEMOLISH SLATE, CLAY AND METAL ROOFING						
Demolish slate roof, to 9/12 slope	SF	$1.16		$1.16	**$1.93**	0.015
Demolish slate roof, over 8/12 slope	SF	$1.30		$1.30	**$2.16**	0.017
Demolish clay tile roof, to 8/12 slope	SF	$1.20		$1.20	**$2.00**	0.015
Demolish clay tile roof, over 8/12 slope	SF	$1.33		$1.33	**$2.23**	0.017
Demolish metal roof, to 8/12 slope	SF	$1.08		$1.08	**$1.80**	0.014
Demolish metal roof, over 8/12 slope	SF	$1.22		$1.22	**$2.03**	0.016
Demolish steel tile roof, to 8/12 slope	SF	$0.84		$0.84	**$1.40**	0.011
Demolish steel tile roof, over 8/12 slope	SF	$0.98		$0.98	**$1.63**	0.013
DEMOLISH SHINGLE AND SHAKE ROOFING						
Demolish wood shingle/shake roof, 16" long, to 8/12 slope	SF	$0.88		$0.88	**$1.46**	0.011
Demolish wood shingle/shake roof, 18" long, to 8/12 slope	SF	$0.78		$0.78	**$1.30**	0.010
Demolish wood shingle/shake roof, 24" long, to 8/12 slope	SF	$0.68		$0.68	**$1.13**	0.009
Demolish wood shingle/shake roof, 16" long, over 8/12 slope	SF	$1.02		$1.02	**$1.70**	0.013
Demolish wood shingle/shake roof, 18" long, over 8/12 slope	SF	$0.92		$0.92	**$1.53**	0.012
Demolish wood shingle/shake roof, 24" long, over 8/12 slope	SF	$0.82		$0.82	**$1.37**	0.011

General Demolition

Roofing Demolition (continued)

Description	Unit	Direct Labor	Direct Materials	Direct Total	Selling Price	Man-hours
DEMOLISH ROOF SHEATHING, STRIP						
Demolish roof sheathing, 1" x 8" strips, laid straight	SF	$1.08		$1.08	**$1.81**	0.014
Demolish roof sheathing, 1" x 8" strips, laid diagonally	SF	$1.24		$1.24	**$2.07**	0.016
DEMOLISH ROOF SHEATHING, PLYWOOD						
Demolish roof sheathing, 1/2" plywood	SF	$0.77		$0.77	**$1.29**	0.010
Demolish roof sheathing, 5/8" plywood	SF	$0.77		$0.77	**$1.29**	0.010
Demolish roof sheathing, 3/4" plywood	SF	$0.85		$0.77	**$1.42**	0.011

Fencing Demolition

Description	Unit	Direct Labor	Direct Materials	Direct Total	Selling Price	Man-hours
DEMOLISH CHAIN LINK FENCE						
Demolish chain link fence and gates, up to 4' high, in concrete	LF	$4.09		$4.09	**$6.83**	0.101
Demolish chain link fence and gates, 4'-6' high, in concrete	LF	$4.74		$4.74	**$7.92**	0.117
DEMOLISH WOOD BOARD FENCE						
Demolish wood fence and gates, up to 4' high, in concrete	LF	$4.58		$4.58	**$7.64**	0.113
Demolish wood fence and gates, 4'-6' high, in concrete	LF	$5.43		$5.43	**$9.07**	0.134
Demolish wood fence and gates, up to 4' high, not in concrete	LF	$3.61		$3.61	**$6.02**	0.089
Demolish wood fence and gates, 4'-6' high, not in concrete	LF	$4.42		$4.42	**$7.37**	0.109
DEMOLISH WOOD RAIL FENCE						
Demolish post and rail fence, 2 rail	LF	$2.96		$2.96	**$4.94**	0.073
Demolish post and rail fence, 3 rail	LF	$3.28		$3.28	**$5.48**	0.081
DEMOLISH IRON FENCE						
Demolish iron fence and gates, up to 4' high, in concrete	LF	$4.58		$4.58	**$7.64**	0.113
Demolish iron fence and gates, 4'-6' high, in concrete	LF	$5.43		$5.43	**$9.07**	0.134

General Demolition

Deck and Porch Demolition

Description	Unit	Direct Labor	Direct Materials	Direct Total	Selling Price	Man-hours
DEMOLISH COMPLETE DECK						
Demolish deck surface, railing & framing up to 80SF	EA	$321.92		$321.92	**$537.61**	7.947
Demolish deck surface, railing & framing up to 160SF	EA	$445.03		$445.03	**$743.20**	10.986
Demolish deck surface, railing & framing up to 240SF	EA	$568.09		$568.09	**$948.72**	14.024
Demolish deck surface, railing & framing over 240SF	SF	$2.39		$2.39	**$3.99**	0.059
DEMOLISH DECK COMPONENTS						
Remove deck surface only, nailed	SF	$1.42		$1.42	**$2.37**	0.035
Remove deck surface only, screwed	SF	$1.58		$1.58	**$2.64**	0.039
Remove deck railing	LF	$0.97		$0.97	**$1.62**	0.024
DEMOLISH COMPLETE PORCH AND ROOF						
Demolish porch deck and roof structure up to 80SF	EA	$447.91		$447.91	**$748.00**	11.057
Demolish porch deck and roof structure up to 160SF	EA	$619.18		$619.18	**$1,034.02**	15.285
Demolish porch deck and roof structure up to 240SF	EA	$790.41		$790.41	**$1,319.98**	19.512
Demolish porch deck and roof structure over 240SF	SF	$3.28		$3.28	**$5.48**	0.081
DEMOLISH PORCH DECK STRUCTURE						
Demolish porch deck structure only, up to 80SF	EA	$230.54		$230.54	**$384.99**	5.691
Demolish porch deck structure only, up to 160SF	EA	$337.56		$337.56	**$563.72**	8.333
Demolish porch deck structure only, up to 240SF	EA	$444.62		$444.62	**$742.52**	10.976
Demolish porch deck structure only, over 240SF	SF	$1.86		$1.86	**$3.11**	0.046
DEMOLISH PORCH ROOF STRUCTURE						
Demolish porch roof structure only, up to 80SF	EA	$279.96		$279.96	**$467.53**	6.911
Demolish porch roof structure only, up to 160SF	EA	$386.98		$386.98	**$646.26**	9.553
Demolish porch roof structure only, up to 240SF	EA	$494.00		$494.00	**$824.99**	12.195
Demolish porch roof structure only, over 240SF	SF	$2.07		$2.07	**$3.45**	0.051
DEMOLISH PORCH COMPONENTS						
Remove porch screening	SF	$0.36		$0.36	**$0.61**	0.009
Remove tongue and groove porch flooring	SF	$0.97		$0.97	**$1.62**	0.024
Remove tongue and groove porch ceiling	SF	$0.97		$0.97	**$1.62**	0.024
Remove plywood porch ceiling	SF	$0.69		$0.69	**$1.15**	0.017
Remove porch railings & balusters	LF	$0.69		$0.69	**$1.15**	0.017

4

General Demolition

General Interior Demolition

Description	Unit	Direct Labor	Direct Materials	Direct Total	Selling Price	Man-hours
DEMOLISH INTERIOR TRIM						
Remove baseboard	LF	$0.41		$0.41	**$0.68**	0.010
Remove quarter round	LF	$0.12		$0.12	**$0.20**	0.003
Remove door or window moulding, 1 piece	LF	$0.49		$0.49	**$0.81**	0.012
Remove door or window moulding, 2 piece	LF	$0.61		$0.61	**$1.01**	0.015
Remove chair rail	LF	$0.36		$0.36	**$0.61**	0.009
Remove crown molding	LF	$0.53		$0.53	**$0.88**	0.013
Remove crown molding, multi-member	LF	$0.81		$0.81	**$1.35**	0.020
DEMOLISH BOOKCASES AND SHELVING						
Remove bookcase, 10" (SF = face area)	SF	$0.65		$0.65	**$1.08**	0.016
Remove bookcase, 12" (SF = face area)	SF	$0.73		$0.73	**$1.22**	0.018
Remove shelf and brackets, 12" (LF = length of shelf)	LF	$0.32		$0.32	**$0.54**	0.008
Remove shelf and brackets, 16" (LF = length of shelf)	LF	$0.41		$0.41	**$0.68**	0.010
Remove shelf and brackets, 24" (LF = length of shelf)	LF	$0.49		$0.49	**$0.81**	0.012

Ceiling Covering Demolition

Description	Unit	Direct Labor	Direct Materials	Direct Total	Selling Price	Man-hours
DEMOLISH GYPSUM AND PLASTER CEILING COVERING						
Remove gypsum drywall from ceiling	SF	$0.57		$0.57	**$0.95**	0.014
Remove plaster and gypsum lath ceiling	SF	$0.85		$0.85	**$1.42**	0.021
Remove plaster and wood lath from ceiling	SF	$1.01		$1.01	**$1.69**	0.025
Remove plaster and metal lath from ceiling	SF	$1.17		$1.17	**$1.96**	0.029
DEMOLISH TILE CEILING COVERING						
Remove ceiling tile, glued	SF	$0.77		$0.77	**$1.29**	0.019
Remove ceiling tile, stapled	SF	$0.53		$0.53	**$0.88**	0.013
Remove suspended ceiling, tiles and grid	SF	$0.65		$0.65	**$1.08**	0.016
Remove wood furring strips from ceiling	LF	$0.85		$0.85	**$1.42**	0.021
DEMOLISH WOOD CEILING COVERING						
Remove wood tongue and groove ceiling	SF	$0.97		$0.97	**$1.62**	0.024
Remove plywood ceiling	SF	$0.69		$0.69	**$1.15**	0.017

General Demolition

Door Demolition

Description	Unit	Direct Labor	Direct Materials	Direct Total	Selling Price	Man-hours
DEMOLISH SWINGING EXTERIOR DOORS						
Remove single exterior wood door	EA	$44.48		$44.48	**$74.28**	1.098
Remove double exterior wood door	EA	$62.59		$62.59	**$104.52**	1.545
Remove single exterior wood door with 1 sidelight	EA	$60.93		$60.93	**$101.75**	1.504
Remove single exterior wood door with 2 sidelights	EA	$74.09		$74.09	**$123.73**	1.829
Remove exterior door slab only	EA	$20.58		$20.58	**$34.37**	0.508
Remove single exterior steel door	EA	$65.87		$65.87	**$110.00**	1.626
Remove double exterior steel door	EA	$92.20		$92.20	**$153.97**	2.276
Remove storm combination door	EA	$29.65		$29.65	**$49.52**	0.732
DEMOLISH SLIDING EXTERIOR DOORS						
Remove exterior glass sliding doors, 2 lites wide	Set	$65.87		$65.87	**$110.00**	1.626
Remove exterior glass sliding doors, 3 lites wide	Set	$85.64		$85.64	**$143.01**	2.114
Remove exterior glass sliding doors, 4 lites wide	Set	$105.40		$105.40	**$176.02**	2.602
DEMOLISH GARAGE DOOR						
Remove single garage door	EA	$98.80		$98.80	**$165.00**	2.439
Remove double garage door	EA	$131.73		$131.73	**$220.00**	3.252
DEMOLISH SWINGING INTERIOR DOORS						
Remove single interior wood door	EA	$29.65		$29.65	**$49.52**	0.732
Remove double interior wood door	EA	$41.16		$41.16	**$68.73**	1.016
DEMOLISH SLIDING AND FOLDING INTERIOR DOORS						
Remove interior folding doors, 2 panels wide	Set	$31.27		$31.27	**$52.23**	0.772
Remove interior folding doors, 4 panels wide	Set	$44.48		$44.48	**$74.28**	1.098
Remove interior sliding doors, 2 panels wide	Set	$31.27		$31.27	**$52.23**	0.772
Remove interior sliding doors, 3 panels wide	Set	$39.54		$39.54	**$66.03**	0.976
Remove interior sliding doors, 4 panels wide	Set	$49.42		$49.42	**$82.53**	1.220
DEMOLISH EXTERIOR AWNING OR CANOPY						
Remove exterior awning or canopy	LF	$4.13		$4.13	**$6.90**	0.102

General Demolition

Window Demolition

Description	Unit	Direct Labor	Direct Materials	Direct Total	Selling Price	Man-hours
DEMOLISH WOOD WINDOW						
Remove small wood window in frame wall, to 12 SF	EA	$20.25		$20.25	**$33.82**	0.500
Remove medium wood window in frame wall, 12-25 SF	EA	$30.38		$30.38	**$50.74**	0.750
Remove large wood window in frame wall, over 25 SF	EA	$60.76		$60.76	**$101.47**	1.500
Remove small wood window in masonry wall, to 12 SF	EA	$24.31		$24.31	**$40.59**	0.600
Remove medium wood window in masonry wall, 12-25 SF	EA	$36.46		$36.46	**$60.88**	0.900
Remove large wood window in masonry wall, over 25 SF	EA	$72.92		$72.92	**$121.77**	1.800
DEMOLISH METAL OR VINYL WINDOW						
Remove small metal/vinyl window in frame wall, to 12 SF	EA	$17.22		$17.22	**$28.75**	0.425
Remove medium metal/vinyl window in frame wall, 12-25 SF	EA	$25.84		$25.84	**$43.16**	0.638
Remove largel metal/vinyl window in frame wall, over 25 SF	EA	$51.65		$51.65	**$86.25**	1.275
Remove small metal/vinyl window in masonry wall, to 12 SF	EA	$20.66		$20.66	**$34.50**	0.510
Remove medium metal/vinyl window in masonry wall, 12-25 SF	EA	$30.99		$30.99	**$51.75**	0.765
Remove large metal/vinyl window in masonry wall, over 25 SF	EA	$61.98		$61.98	**$103.50**	1.530
DEMOLISH IRON SECURITY GRILL						
Remove ornamental iron security grill, to 12 SF	EA	$20.25		$20.25	**$33.82**	0.500
Remove ornamental iron security grill, 12-25 SF	EA	$30.38		$30.38	**$50.74**	0.750
Remove ornamental iron security grill, over 25 SF	EA	$60.76		$60.76	**$101.47**	1.500
DEMOLISH SKYLIGHT						
Remove skylight and curb (LF = combined length of 4 sides of skylight)	LF	$7.29		$7.29	**$12.18**	0.180
Remove skylight only (LF = combined length of 4 sides of skylight)	LF	$3.16		$3.16	**$5.28**	0.078
DEMOLISH EXTERIOR AWNING OR CANOPY						
Remove exterior awning or canopy	LF	$4.13		$4.13	**$6.90**	0.102

General Demolition

Flooring Demolition

Description	Unit	Direct Labor	Direct Materials	Direct Total	Selling Price	Man-hours
DEMOLISH WOOD FLOORING						
Remove solid wood strip flooring, nailed	SF	$1.22		$1.22	**$2.03**	0.030
Remove solid wood strip flooring, glued	SF	$1.66		$1.66	**$2.77**	0.041
Remove solid wood flooring block (parquet), glued	SF	$1.34		$1.34	**$2.23**	0.033
Remove molding or trim for wood flooring	LF	$0.41		$0.41	**$0.68**	0.010
DEMOLISH CERAMIC FLOORING						
Demolish ceramic tile floor, set in thin-set, over wood	SF	$2.31		$2.31	**$3.86**	0.057
Demolish ceramic tile floor, set in thin-set, over concrete	SF	$3.20		$3.20	**$5.34**	0.079
Demolish ceramic tile floor, set in mortar, over wood	SF	$3.04		$3.04	**$5.07**	0.075
Demolish ceramic tile floor, set in mortar, over concrete	SF	$3.61		$3.61	**$6.02**	0.089
DEMOLISH MARBLE, GRANITE, STONE FLOORING						
Demolish marble, granite, stone floor, set in thin-set, over wood	SF	$2.63		$2.63	**$4.40**	0.065
Demolish marble, granite, stone floor, set in thin-set, over concrete	SF	$3.69		$3.69	**$6.16**	0.091
Demolish marble, granite, stone floor, set in mortar, over wood	SF	$3.48		$3.48	**$5.82**	0.086
Demolish marble, granite, stone floor, set in mortar, over concrete	SF	$4.17		$4.17	**$6.97**	0.103
DEMOLISH RESILIENT FLOORING						
Remove resilient sheet flooring, adhesive set	SF	$0.73		$0.73	**$1.22**	0.018
Remove resilient tile flooring, adhesive set	SF	$0.81		$0.81	**$1.35**	0.020
Remove cove base molding	LF	$0.28		$0.28	**$0.47**	0.007
DEMOLISH CARPETING						
Remove carpet, tack strips, padding	SF	$0.81		$0.81	**$1.35**	0.020
Remove adhesive set carpet	SF	$0.65		$0.65	**$1.08**	0.016
DEMOLISH SLEEPERS AND UNDERLAYMENT						
Remove sleepers and underlayment	SF	$0.81		$0.81	**$1.35**	0.020
Remove underlayment, nailed	SF	$0.57		$0.57	**$0.95**	0.014
Remove underlayment, nailed & glued	SF	$0.81		$0.81	**$1.35**	0.020

4

General Demolition

Wall Covering Demolition

Description	Unit	Direct Labor	Direct Materials	Direct Total	Selling Price	Man-hours
DEMOLISH GYPSUM AND PLASTER WALL COVERING						
Remove gypsum drywall from wall	SF	$0.45		$0.45	**$0.74**	0.011
Remove gypsum lath and plaster from wall	SF	$0.77		$0.77	**$1.29**	0.019
Remove wood lath and plaster from wall	SF	$0.93		$0.93	**$1.56**	0.023
Remove metal lath and plaster from wall	SF	$1.09		$1.09	**$1.83**	0.027
Remove plaster from masonry wall	SF	$1.78		$1.78	**$2.98**	0.044
DEMOLISH WOOD WALL COVERING						
Remove plywood paneling from wall	SF	$0.36		$0.36	**$0.61**	0.009
Remove solid wood paneling from wall	SF	$0.65		$0.65	**$1.08**	0.016
Remove furring strips from frame wall	LF	$0.85		$0.85	**$1.42**	0.021
Remove furring strips from masonry wall	LF	$1.17		$1.17	**$1.96**	0.029
DEMOLISH CERAMIC WALL COVERING						
Demolish ceramic tile wall in thin-set	SF	$1.54		$1.54	**$2.57**	0.038
Demolish ceramic tile wall in conventional mortar	SF	$2.07		$2.07	**$3.45**	0.051

Cabinet and Countertop Demolition

Description	Unit	Direct Labor	Direct Materials	Direct Total	Selling Price	Man-hours
DEMOLISH CABINETS						
Remove kitchen cabinets, base or wall	LF	$9.80		$9.80	**$16.37**	0.242
Remove kitchen cabinets, base or wall units	EA	$29.41		$29.41	**$49.11**	0.726
Remove medicine cabinet, flush mount	EA	$13.49		$13.49	**$22.53**	0.333
Remove medicine cabinet, recessed	EA	$20.25		$20.25	**$33.82**	0.500
DEMOLISH COUNTERTOPS						
Remove laminate countertop, no disconnect included	LF	$2.80		$2.80	**$4.67**	0.069
Remove solid surface countertop, no disconnect included	LF	$5.55		$5.55	**$9.27**	0.137
Remove stone countertop, no disconnect included	LF	$6.97		$6.97	**$11.64**	0.172
Remove tile countertop, no disconnect included	LF	$4.86		$4.86	**$8.12**	0.120

Systems Demolition

Plumbing Demolition

Description	Unit	Direct Labor	Direct Materials	Direct Total	Selling Price	Man-hours
DEMOLISH KITCHEN PLUMBING						
Sink, remove	EA	$76.48		$76.48	**$127.71**	0.750
Disposer, remove	EA	$101.97		$101.97	**$170.28**	1.000
Oven, gas, remove	EA	$76.48		$76.48	**$127.71**	0.750
Cooktop, gas, remove	EA	$76.48		$76.48	**$127.71**	0.750
Range, gas, remove	EA	$76.48		$76.48	**$127.71**	0.750
Dishwasher, remove	EA	$101.97		$101.97	**$170.28**	1.000
DEMOLISH LAUNDRY PLUMBING						
Dryer, gas, remove	EA	$76.48		$76.48	**$127.71**	0.750
Dryer, gas, remove, replace vent	EA	$152.95	$49.78	$202.73	**$338.55**	1.500
Washer, remove	EA	$101.97		$101.97	**$170.28**	1.000
Laundry Tub, remove	EA	$76.48		$76.48	**$127.71**	0.750
Remove gray box and valves	EA	$76.48		$76.48	**$127.71**	0.750
DEMOLISH BATHROOM PLUMBING						
Toilet, remove and use existing flange	EA	$76.48		$76.48	**$127.71**	0.750
Toilet, remove and replace flange	EA	$152.95	$13.53	$166.48	**$278.02**	1.500
Bidet, remove and use existing flange	EA	$76.48		$76.48	**$127.71**	0.750
Bidet, remove and replace flange	EA	$152.95	$13.53	$166.48	**$278.02**	1.500
Urinal, remove	EA	$76.48		$76.48	**$127.71**	0.750
DEMOLISH BATHROOM SINK PLUMBING						
Sink, pedestal or wall mount, remove	EA	$76.48		$76.48	**$127.71**	0.750
Vanity with single sink, remove all	EA	$152.95		$152.95	**$255.43**	1.500
Vanity with single sink, remove sink and faucets only	EA	$50.98		$50.98	**$85.14**	0.500
Vanity with double sink, remove all	EA	$203.93		$203.93	**$340.57**	2.000
Vanity with double sink, remove sinks and faucets only	EA	$101.97		$101.97	**$170.28**	1.000
DEMOLISH TUB, WHIRLPOOL AND SHOWER PLUMBING						
Tub, cast iron, remove	EA	$305.90		$305.90	**$510.85**	3.000
Tub, cast iron with fiberglass or acrylic surround, remove all	EA	$407.87		$407.87	**$681.14**	4.000
Tub, steel, remove	EA	$305.90		$305.90	**$510.85**	3.000
Tub, steel with fiberglass or acrylic surround, remove all	EA	$407.87		$407.87	**$681.14**	4.000
Tub, fiberglass or acrylic, remove	EA	$305.90		$305.90	**$510.85**	3.000
Tub, fiberglass or acrylic with fiberglass or acrylic surround, remove all	EA	$407.87		$407.87	**$681.14**	4.000
Shower with fiberglass or acrylic surround, remove all	EA	$407.87		$407.87	**$681.14**	4.000
Whirlpool spa only, remove	EA	$407.87		$407.87	**$681.14**	4.000
Whirlpool spa with fiberglass or acrylic surround, remove all	EA	$509.84		$509.84	**$851.42**	5.000

Systems Demolition

Plumbing Demolition (continued)

Description	Unit	Direct Labor	Direct Materials	Direct Total	Selling Price	Man-hours
DEMOLISH WATER HEATER PLUMBING						
Remove electric water heater	EA	$101.97		$101.97	**$170.28**	1.000
Remove gas water heater	EA	$152.95		$152.95	**$255.43**	1.500
DEMOLISH CERAMIC WALLS IN BATHROOM						
Demolish ceramic tile wall in thin-set	SF	$1.54		$1.54	**$2.57**	0.038
Demolish ceramic tile wall in conventional mortar	SF	$2.07		$2.07	**$3.45**	0.051

HVAC Demolition

Description	Unit	Direct Labor	Direct Materials	Direct Total	Selling Price	Man-hours
DEMOLISH HEATING UNIT						
Remove baseboard heating system	LF	$10.20		$10.20	**$17.03**	0.100
Remove baseboard radiators	LF	$21.11		$21.11	**$35.25**	0.207
Remove boiler	EA	$1,020.08		$1,020.08	**$1,703.53**	10.004
Remove gas furnace	EA	$305.90		$305.90	**$510.85**	3.000
Remove oil furnace	EA	$407.87		$407.87	**$681.14**	4.000
DEMOLISH HEATING AND DUCT SYSTEM						
Remove furnace and duct system, up to 1200 SF home	EA	$748.23		$748.23	**$1,249.55**	7.338
Remove furnace and duct system, 1200 SF to 1600 SF home	EA	$854.28		$854.28	**$1,426.65**	8.378
Remove furnace and duct system, 1600 SF to 2200 SF home	EA	$960.22		$960.22	**$1,603.57**	9.417
Remove furnace and duct system, 2200 SF to 2600 SF home	EA	$1,066.17		$1,066.17	**$1,780.50**	10.456
DEMOLISH SPLIT SYSTEM						
Remove split system, compressor/heat pump and air handler, 2 ton	EA	$529.82		$529.82	**$884.80**	5.196
Remove split system, compressor/heat pump and air handler, 3 ton	EA	$602.12		$602.12	**$1,005.53**	5.905
Remove split system, compressor/heat pump and air handler, 4 ton	EA	$644.43		$644.43	**$1,076.20**	6.320
DEMOLISH COMBINATION SYSTEM						
Remove heat pump/air conditioner, through wall unit, 2 ton	EA	$319.16		$319.16	**$532.99**	3.130
Remove heat pump/air conditioner, through wall unit, 3 ton	EA	$397.37		$397.37	**$663.60**	3.897
Remove heat pump/air conditioner, through wall unit, 4 ton	EA	$478.74		$478.74	**$799.49**	4.695
DEMOLISH DUCTWORK						
Remove 4" x 8" ductwork	LF	$2.75		$2.75	**$4.60**	0.068
Remove 6" x 8" ductwork	LF	$3.08		$3.08	**$5.14**	0.076
Remove 10" x 12" ductwork	LF	$3.85		$3.85	**$6.43**	0.095
Remove 6" round ductwork	LF	$2.03		$2.03	**$3.38**	0.050
Remove 8" flex ductwork	LF	$2.19		$2.19	**$3.65**	0.054

Systems Demolition

Electrical Demolition

Description	Unit	Direct Labor	Direct Materials	Direct Total	Selling Price	Man-hours
DEMOLISH ELECTRICAL FIXTURES						
Remove small ceiling fixture	EA	$23.84		$23.84	**$39.80**	0.250
Remove medium ceiling fixture	EA	$47.67		$47.67	**$79.61**	0.500
Remove large ceiling fixture	EA	$71.51		$71.51	**$119.41**	0.750
Remove recessed fixture	EA	$47.67		$47.67	**$79.61**	0.500
Remove 48" fluorescent fixture	EA	$23.84		$23.84	**$39.80**	0.250
Remove exterior light fixture	EA	$23.84		$23.84	**$39.80**	0.250
DEMOLISH ELECTRICAL OUTLETS						
Remove switch or duplex outlet	EA	$11.92		$11.92	**$19.90**	0.125
Remove 220 volt outlet	EA	$16.11		$16.11	**$26.91**	0.169
DEMOLISH FANS						
Remove attic fan	EA	$95.34		$95.34	**$159.22**	1.000
Remove bathroom exhaust fan	EA	$71.51		$71.51	**$119.41**	0.750
Remove whole house exhaust fan	EA	$143.01		$143.01	**$238.83**	1.500
Remove ceiling fan	EA	$71.51		$71.51	**$119.41**	0.750
DEMOLISH ELECTRIC BASEBOARD HEAT						
Remove baseboard electric heater, 4' to 6'	EA	$23.84		$23.84	**$39.80**	0.250
Remove baseboard electric heater, 8' to 10'	EA	$37.75		$37.75	**$63.05**	0.396
DEMOLISH ELECTRIC SERVICE						
Remove 60 amp service	EA	$95.34		$95.34	**$159.22**	1.000
Remove 100 amp service	EA	$143.01		$143.01	**$238.83**	1.500
Remove 150 amp service	EA	$190.68		$190.68	**$318.44**	2.000
DEMOLISH ELECTRIC WIRING AND CONDUIT						
Remove BX cable	LF	$1.24		$1.24	**$2.07**	0.013
Remove Romex wiring	LF	$0.76		$0.76	**$1.27**	0.008
Remove electrical metallic conduit, 1/2"	LF	$1.33		$1.33	**$2.23**	0.014
Remove electrical metallic conduit, 3/4"	LF	$1.72		$1.72	**$2.87**	0.018
Remove electrical metallic conduit, 1"	LF	$2.00		$2.00	**$3.34**	0.021
Remove PVC conduit, 1/2"	LF	$0.95		$0.95	**$1.59**	0.010
Remove PVC conduit, 3/4"	LF	$0.95		$0.95	**$1.59**	0.010
Remove PVC conduit, 1"	LF	$1.24		$1.24	**$2.07**	0.013

Excavation

General Excavation by Machine

Description	Unit	Direct Labor	Direct Materials	Direct Total	Selling Price	Man-hours
EXCAVATE BY MACHINE						
Excavation by machine, light soil	CY	$8.09		$8.09	**$13.50**	0.111
Excavation by machine, average soil	CY	$9.76		$9.76	**$16.30**	0.134
Excavation by machine, hard soil or loose rock	CY	$11.36		$11.36	**$18.98**	0.156
EXCAVATE TRENCH BY MACHINE, 1-1/2' DEEP						
Excavation, crawler mounted trencher, 1-1/2'D, light soil	LF	$1.82		$1.82	**$3.04**	0.025
Excavation, crawler mounted trencher, 1-1/2'D, average soil	LF	$2.11		$2.11	**$3.53**	0.029
Excavation, crawler mounted trencher, 1-1/2'D, hard soil or loose rock	LF	$2.55		$2.55	**$4.26**	0.035
EXCAVATE TRENCH BY MACHINE, 3' DEEP						
Excavation, crawler mounted trencher, 3'D, light soil	LF	$2.70		$2.70	**$4.50**	0.037
Excavation, crawler mounted trencher, 3'D, average soil	LF	$3.21		$3.21	**$5.35**	0.044
Excavation, crawler mounted trencher, 3'D, hard soil or loose rock	LF	$3.79		$3.79	**$6.33**	0.052
EXCAVATE TRENCH BY MACHINE, 5' DEEP						
Excavation, crawler mounted trencher, 5'D, light soil	LF	$3.64		$3.64	**$6.08**	0.050
Excavation, crawler mounted trencher, 5'D, average soil	LF	$4.30		$4.30	**$7.18**	0.059
Excavation, crawler mounted trencher, 5'D, hard soil or loose rock	LF	$5.10		$5.10	**$8.52**	0.070

General Excavation by Hand

Description	Unit	Direct Labor	Direct Materials	Direct Total	Selling Price	Man-hours
EXCAVATE BY HAND						
Excavation by hand, light soil	CY	$43.02		$43.02	**$71.84**	1.062
Excavation by hand, average soil	CY	$66.52		$66.52	**$111.08**	1.642
Excavation by hand, hard soil or loose rock	CY	$88.11		$88.11	**$147.14**	2.175
EXCAVATE TRENCH BY HAND, 1-1/2' DEEP						
Excavation, trench by hand, 1-1/2'D, light soil	LF	$3.24		$3.24	**$5.41**	0.080
Excavation, trench by hand, 1-1/2'D, average soil	LF	$5.02		$5.02	**$8.39**	0.124
Excavation, trench by hand, 1-1/2'D, hard soil or loose rock	LF	$6.68		$6.68	**$11.16**	0.165
EXCAVATE TRENCH BY HAND, 3' DEEP						
Excavation, trench by hand, 3'D, light soil	LF	$7.33		$7.33	**$12.24**	0.181
Excavation, trench by hand, 3'D, average soil	LF	$11.34		$11.34	**$18.94**	0.280
Excavation, trench by hand, 3'D, hard soil or loose rock	LF	$14.99		$14.99	**$25.03**	0.370
EXCAVATE TRENCH BY HAND, 5' DEEP						
Excavation, trench by hand, 5'D, light soil	LF	$13.04		$13.04	**$21.78**	0.322
Excavation, trench by hand, 5'D, average soil	LF	$20.17		$20.17	**$33.69**	0.498
Excavation, trench by hand, 5'D, hard soil or loose rock	LF	$26.70		$26.70	**$44.58**	0.659

Excavation

Continuous Footing Excavation by Hand

Description	Unit	Direct Labor	Direct Materials	Direct Total	Selling Price	Man-hours
EXCAVATE CONTINUOUS FOOTING BY HAND, 8" DEEP						
Excavation, continuous footing by hand, 8"D x 10"W	LF	$1.26		$1.26	**$2.10**	0.031
Excavation, continuous footing by hand, 8"D x 12"W	LF	$1.50		$1.50	**$2.50**	0.037
Excavation, continuous footing by hand, 8"D x 16"W	LF	$1.98		$1.98	**$3.31**	0.049
Excavation, continuous footing by hand, 8"D x 18"W	LF	$2.23		$2.23	**$3.72**	0.055
Excavation, continuous footing by hand, 8"D x 20"W	LF	$2.47		$2.47	**$4.13**	0.061
EXCAVATE CONTINUOUS FOOTING BY HAND, 10" DEEP						
Excavation, continuous footing by hand, 10"D x 10"W	LF	$1.70		$1.70	**$2.84**	0.042
Excavation, continuous footing by hand, 10"D x 12"W	LF	$2.07		$2.07	**$3.45**	0.051
Excavation, continuous footing by hand, 10"D x 16"W	LF	$2.75		$2.75	**$4.60**	0.068
Excavation, continuous footing by hand, 10"D x 18"W	LF	$3.08		$3.08	**$5.14**	0.076
Excavation, continuous footing by hand, 10"D x 20"W	LF	$3.40		$3.40	**$5.68**	0.084
EXCAVATE CONTINUOUS FOOTING BY HAND, 12" DEEP						
Excavation, continuous footing by hand, 12"D x 10"W	LF	$2.15		$2.15	**$3.59**	0.053
Excavation, continuous footing by hand, 12"D x 12"W	LF	$2.59		$2.59	**$4.33**	0.064
Excavation, continuous footing by hand, 12"D x 16"W	LF	$3.44		$3.44	**$5.75**	0.085
Excavation, continuous footing by hand, 12"D x 18"W	LF	$3.85		$3.85	**$6.43**	0.095
Excavation, continuous footing by hand, 12"D x 20"W	LF	$4.29		$4.29	**$7.17**	0.106
EXCAVATE CONTINUOUS FOOTING BY HAND, 24" DEEP						
Excavation, continuous footing by hand, 24"D x 10"W	LF	$4.50		$4.50	**$7.51**	0.111
Excavation, continuous footing by hand, 24"D x 12"W	LF	$5.39		$5.39	**$9.00**	0.133
Excavation, continuous footing by hand, 24"D x 16"W	LF	$7.17		$7.17	**$11.97**	0.177
Excavation, continuous footing by hand, 24"D x 18"W	LF	$8.06		$8.06	**$13.46**	0.199
Excavation, continuous footing by hand, 24"D x 20"W	LF	$8.95		$8.95	**$14.95**	0.221
Excavation, continuous footing by hand, 24"D x 24"W	LF	$10.73		$10.73	**$17.93**	0.265
EXCAVATE CONTINUOUS FOOTING BY HAND, 30" DEEP						
Excavation, continuous footing by hand, 30"D x 10"W	LF	$5.87		$5.87	**$9.81**	0.145
Excavation, continuous footing by hand, 30"D x 12"W	LF	$7.01		$7.01	**$11.70**	0.173
Excavation, continuous footing by hand, 30"D x 16"W	LF	$9.36		$9.36	**$15.63**	0.231
Excavation, continuous footing by hand, 30"D x 18"W	LF	$10.49		$10.49	**$17.52**	0.259
Excavation, continuous footing by hand, 30"D x 20"W	LF	$11.67		$11.67	**$19.48**	0.288
Excavation, continuous footing by hand, 30"D x 24"W	LF	$13.98		$13.98	**$23.34**	0.345
EXCAVATE CONTINUOUS FOOTING BY HAND, 36" DEEP						
Excavation, continuous footing by hand, 36"D x 10"W	LF	$7.33		$7.33	**$12.24**	0.181
Excavation, continuous footing by hand, 36"D x 12"W	LF	$8.75		$8.75	**$14.61**	0.216
Excavation, continuous footing by hand, 36"D x 16"W	LF	$11.67		$11.67	**$19.48**	0.288
Excavation, continuous footing by hand, 36"D x 18"W	LF	$13.08		$13.08	**$21.85**	0.323
Excavation, continuous footing by hand, 36"D x 20"W	LF	$14.54		$14.54	**$24.29**	0.359
Excavation, continuous footing by hand, 36"D x 24"W	LF	$17.54		$17.54	**$29.29**	0.433

Excavation

Continuous Footing by Hand (continued)

Description	Unit	Direct Labor	Direct Materials	Direct Total	Selling Price	Man-hours
EXCAVATE CONTINUOUS FOOTING BY HAND, 42" DEEP						
Excavation, continuous footing by hand, 42"D x 12"W	LF	$10.61		$10.61	**$17.72**	0.262
Excavation, continuous footing by hand, 42"D x 16"W	LF	$14.14		$14.14	**$23.61**	0.349
Excavation, continuous footing by hand, 42"D x 18"W	LF	$15.88		$15.88	**$26.52**	0.392
Excavation, continuous footing by hand, 42"D x 20"W	LF	$17.62		$17.62	**$29.43**	0.435
Excavation, continuous footing by hand, 42"D x 24"W	LF	$21.11		$21.11	**$35.25**	0.521
EXCAVATE CONTINUOUS FOOTING BY HAND, 48" DEEP						
Excavation, continuous footing by hand, 48"D x 12"W	LF	$12.60		$12.60	**$21.04**	0.311
Excavation, continuous footing by hand, 48"D x 16"W	LF	$16.73		$16.73	**$27.94**	0.413
Excavation, continuous footing by hand, 48"D x 18"W	LF	$18.80		$18.80	**$31.39**	0.464
Excavation, continuous footing by hand, 48"D x 20"W	LF	$20.90		$20.90	**$34.91**	0.516
Excavation, continuous footing by hand, 48"D x 24"W	LF	$25.03		$25.03	**$41.81**	0.618

Continuous Footing Excavation by Machine

Description	Unit	Direct Labor	Direct Materials	Direct Total	Selling Price	Man-hours
EXCAVATE CONTINUOUS FOOTING BY MACHINE, 12" DEEP						
Excavation, continuous footing by machine, 12"D x 10"W	LF	$0.44		$0.44	**$0.73**	0.006
Excavation, continuous footing by machine, 12"D x 12"W	LF	$0.58		$0.58	**$0.97**	0.008
Excavation, continuous footing by machine, 12"D x 16"W	LF	$0.73		$0.73	**$1.22**	0.010
Excavation, continuous footing by machine, 12"D x 18"W	LF	$0.80		$0.80	**$1.34**	0.011
Excavation, continuous footing by machine, 12"D x 20"W	LF	$0.95		$0.95	**$1.58**	0.013
EXCAVATE CONTINUOUS FOOTING BY MACHINE, 24" DEEP						
Excavation, continuous footing by machine, 24"D x 10"W	LF	$0.95		$0.95	**$1.58**	0.013
Excavation, continuous footing by machine, 24"D x 12"W	LF	$1.17		$1.17	**$1.95**	0.016
Excavation, continuous footing by machine, 24"D x 16"W	LF	$1.53		$1.53	**$2.55**	0.021
Excavation, continuous footing by machine, 24"D x 18"W	LF	$1.75		$1.75	**$2.92**	0.024
Excavation, continuous footing by machine, 24"D x 20"W	LF	$1.89		$1.89	**$3.16**	0.026
Excavation, continuous footing by machine, 24"D x 24"W	LF	$2.26		$2.26	**$3.77**	0.031
EXCAVATE CONTINUOUS FOOTING BY MACHINE, 30" DEEP						
Excavation, continuous footing by machine, 30"D x 10"W	LF	$1.24		$1.24	**$2.07**	0.017
Excavation, continuous footing by machine, 30"D x 12"W	LF	$1.53		$1.53	**$2.55**	0.021
Excavation, continuous footing by machine, 30"D x 16"W	LF	$1.97		$1.97	**$3.28**	0.027
Excavation, continuous footing by machine, 30"D x 18"W	LF	$2.26		$2.26	**$3.77**	0.031
Excavation, continuous footing by machine, 30"D x 20"W	LF	$2.48		$2.48	**$4.14**	0.034
Excavation, continuous footing by machine, 30"D x 24"W	LF	$2.99		$2.99	**$4.99**	0.041

Excavation

Continuous Footing by Machine (continued)

Description	Unit	Direct Labor	Direct Materials	Direct Total	Selling Price	Man-hours
EXCAVATE CONTINUOUS FOOTING BY MACHINE, 36" DEEP						
Excavation, continuous footing by machine, 36"D x 10"W	LF	$1.53		$1.53	**$2.55**	0.021
Excavation, continuous footing by machine, 36"D x 12"W	LF	$1.89		$1.89	**$3.16**	0.026
Excavation, continuous footing by machine, 36"D x 16"W	LF	$2.48		$2.48	**$4.14**	0.034
Excavation, continuous footing by machine, 36"D x 18"W	LF	$2.77		$2.77	**$4.62**	0.038
Excavation, continuous footing by machine, 36"D x 20"W	LF	$3.13		$3.13	**$5.23**	0.043
Excavation, continuous footing by machine, 36"D x 24"W	LF	$3.71		$3.71	**$6.20**	0.051
EXCAVATE CONTINUOUS FOOTING BY MACHINE, 42" DEEP						
Excavation, continuous footing by machine, 42"D x 12"W	LF	$2.26		$2.26	**$3.77**	0.031
Excavation, continuous footing by machine, 42"D x 16"W	LF	$2.99		$2.99	**$4.99**	0.041
Excavation, continuous footing by machine, 42"D x 18"W	LF	$3.35		$3.35	**$5.60**	0.046
Excavation, continuous footing by machine, 42"D x 20"W	LF	$3.71		$3.71	**$6.20**	0.051
Excavation, continuous footing by machine, 42"D x 24"W	LF	$4.52		$4.52	**$7.54**	0.062
EXCAVATE CONTINUOUS FOOTING BY MACHINE, 48" DEEP						
Excavation, continuous footing by machine, 48"D x 12"W	LF	$2.70		$2.70	**$4.50**	0.037
Excavation, continuous footing by machine, 48"D x 16"W	LF	$3.57		$3.57	**$5.96**	0.049
Excavation, continuous footing by machine, 48"D x 18"W	LF	$4.01		$4.01	**$6.69**	0.055
Excavation, continuous footing by machine, 48"D x 20"W	LF	$4.44		$4.44	**$7.42**	0.061
Excavation, continuous footing by machine, 48"D x 24"W	LF	$5.32		$5.32	**$8.88**	0.073
EXCAVATE CONTINUOUS FOOTING BY MACHINE, 60" DEEP						
Excavation, continuous footing by machine, 60"D x 16"W	LF	$4.59		$4.59	**$7.66**	0.063
Excavation, continuous footing by machine, 60"D x 18"W	LF	$5.10		$5.10	**$8.52**	0.070
Excavation, continuous footing by machine, 60"D x 20"W	LF	$5.68		$5.68	**$9.49**	0.078
Excavation, continuous footing by machine, 60"D x 24"W	LF	$6.85		$6.85	**$11.43**	0.094

Excavation

Pier Footing Excavation by Hand

Description	Unit	Direct Labor	Direct Materials	Direct Total	Selling Price	Man-hours
EXCAVATE PIER FOOTING BY HAND, 12" DEEP						
Excavation, pier footing by hand, 16"L x 16"W x 12"D	EA	$7.29		$7.29	**$12.18**	0.180
Excavation, pier footing by hand, 24"L x 24"W x 12"D	EA	$12.23		$12.23	**$20.43**	0.302
Excavation, pier footing by hand, 30"L x 30"W x 12"D	EA	$17.30		$17.30	**$28.89**	0.427
Excavation, pier footing by hand, 36"L x 48"W x 12"D	EA	$26.86		$26.86	**$44.85**	0.663
EXCAVATE PIER FOOTING BY HAND, 24" DEEP						
Excavation, pier footing by hand, 16"L x 16"W x 24"D	EA	$13.29		$13.29	**$22.19**	0.328
Excavation, pier footing by hand, 24"L x 24"W x 24"D	EA	$23.74		$23.74	**$39.64**	0.586
Excavation, pier footing by hand, 30"L x 30"W x 24"D	EA	$35.97		$35.97	**$60.07**	0.888
Excavation, pier footing by hand, 36"L x 48"W x 24"D	EA	$56.43		$56.43	**$94.24**	1.393
EXCAVATE PIER FOOTING BY HAND, 36" DEEP						
Excavation, pier footing by hand, 16"L x 16"W x 36"D	EA	$16.45		$16.45	**$27.47**	0.406
Excavation, pier footing by hand, 24"L x 24"W x 36"D	EA	$34.51		$34.51	**$57.64**	0.852
Excavation, pier footing by hand, 30"L x 30"W x 36"D	EA	$52.78		$52.78	**$88.15**	1.303
Excavation, pier footing by hand, 36"L x 48"W x 36"D	EA	$88.67		$88.67	**$148.09**	2.189
EXCAVATE PIER FOOTING BY HAND, 48" DEEP						
Excavation, pier footing by hand, 16"L x 16"W x 48"D	EA	$23.25		$23.25	**$38.83**	0.574
Excavation, pier footing by hand, 24"L x 24"W x 48"D	EA	$46.14		$46.14	**$77.05**	1.139
Excavation, pier footing by hand, 30"L x 30"W x 48"D	EA	$72.63		$72.63	**$121.30**	1.793
Excavation, pier footing by hand, 36"L x 48"W x 48"D	EA	$123.63		$123.63	**$206.47**	3.052
EXCAVATE PIER FOOTING BY HAND, 60" DEEP						
Excavation, pier footing by hand, 16"L x 16"W x 60"D	EA	$28.84		$28.84	**$48.17**	0.712
Excavation, pier footing by hand, 24"L x 24"W x 60"D	EA	$60.32		$60.32	**$100.73**	1.489
Excavation, pier footing by hand, 30"L x 30"W x 60"D	EA	$95.52		$95.52	**$159.52**	2.358
Excavation, pier footing by hand, 36"L x 48"W x 60"D	EA	$161.22		$161.22	**$269.25**	3.980

Pier Footing Excavation by Machine

Description	Unit	Direct Labor	Direct Materials	Direct Total	Selling Price	Man-hours
EXCAVATE PIER FOOTING BY MACHINE, 12" DEEP						
Excavation, pier footing by machine, 16"L x 16"W x 12"D	EA	$3.86		$3.86	**$6.45**	0.053
Excavation, pier footing by machine, 24"L x 24"W x 12"D	EA	$6.19		$6.19	**$10.34**	0.085
Excavation, pier footing by machine, 30"L x 30"W x 12"D	EA	$8.45		$8.45	**$14.11**	0.116
Excavation, pier footing by machine, 36"L x 48"W x 12"D	EA	$12.38		$12.38	**$20.68**	0.170
EXCAVATE PIER FOOTING BY MACHINE, 24" DEEP						
Excavation, pier footing by machine, 16"L x 16"W x 24"D	EA	$7.94		$7.94	**$13.26**	0.109
Excavation, pier footing by machine, 24"L x 24"W x 24"D	EA	$10.71		$10.71	**$17.88**	0.147
Excavation, pier footing by machine, 30"L x 30"W x 24"D	EA	$17.63		$17.63	**$29.44**	0.242
Excavation, pier footing by machine, 36"L x 48"W x 24"D	EA	$25.93		$25.93	**$43.31**	0.356

Excavation

Pier Footing by Machine (continued)

Description	Unit	Direct Labor	Direct Materials	Direct Total	Selling Price	Man-hours
EXCAVATE PIER FOOTING BY MACHINE, 36" DEEP						
Excavation, pier footing by machine, 16"L x 16"W x 36"D	EA	$10.12		$10.12	**$16.91**	0.139
Excavation, pier footing by machine, 24"L x 24"W x 36"D	EA	$17.70		$17.70	**$29.56**	0.243
Excavation, pier footing by machine, 30"L x 30"W x 36"D	EA	$21.20		$21.20	**$35.40**	0.291
Excavation, pier footing by machine, 36"L x 48"W x 36"D	EA	$40.72		$40.72	**$68.00**	0.559
EXCAVATE PIER FOOTING BY MACHINE, 48" DEEP						
Excavation, pier footing by machine, 16"L x 16"W x 48"D	EA	$16.61		$16.61	**$27.74**	0.228
Excavation, pier footing by machine, 24"L x 24"W x 48"D	EA	$20.98		$20.98	**$35.03**	0.288
Excavation, pier footing by machine, 30"L x 30"W x 48"D	EA	$29.57		$29.57	**$49.39**	0.406
Excavation, pier footing by machine, 36"L x 48"W x 48"D	EA	$56.82		$56.82	**$94.88**	0.780
EXCAVATE PIER FOOTING BY MACHINE, 60" DEEP						
Excavation, pier footing by machine, 16"L x 16"W x 60"D	EA	$21.56		$21.56	**$36.01**	0.296
Excavation, pier footing by machine, 24"L x 24"W x 60"D	EA	$28.77		$28.77	**$48.05**	0.395
Excavation, pier footing by machine, 30"L x 30"W x 60"D	EA	$38.61		$38.61	**$64.47**	0.530
Excavation, pier footing by machine, 36"L x 48"W x 60"D	EA	$74.08		$74.08	**$123.71**	1.017

Brush, Tree and Stump Removal

Description	Unit	Direct Labor	Direct Materials	Direct Total	Selling Price	Man-hours
REMOVE TREE BY HAND						
Tree removal by hand, up to 7" diameter trunk	EA	$60.76		$60.76	**$101.47**	1.500
Tree removal by hand, 8" to 12" diameter trunk	EA	$101.27		$101.27	**$169.12**	2.500
Tree removal by hand, 13" to 18" diameter trunk	EA	$141.78		$141.78	**$236.77**	3.500
Tree removal by hand, 19" to 24" diameter trunk	EA	$222.80		$222.80	**$372.07**	5.500
Tree removal by hand, 25" to 30" diameter trunk	EA	$283.56		$283.56	**$473.55**	7.000
REMOVE STUMP BY HAND						
Stump removal by hand, up to 7" diameter trunk	EA	$88.84		$88.84	**$148.36**	2.193
Stump removal by hand, 8" to 12" diameter trunk	EA	$116.71		$116.71	**$194.90**	2.881
Stump removal by hand, 13" to 18" diameter trunk	EA	$144.37		$144.37	**$241.10**	3.564
Stump removal by hand, 19" to 24" diameter trunk	EA	$172.24		$172.24	**$287.65**	4.252
Stump removal by hand, 25" to 30" diameter trunk	EA	$183.50		$183.50	**$306.45**	4.530
REMOVE BRUSH BY MACHINE						
Clear brush by machine, light growth	SF	$0.12		$0.12	**$0.20**	0.003
Clear brush by machine, medium growth	SF	$0.16		$0.16	**$0.27**	0.004
Clear brush by machine, heavy growth	SF	$0.24		$0.24	**$0.41**	0.006

Excavation

Hauling and Dumping

Description	Unit	Direct Labor	Direct Materials	Direct Total	Selling Price	Man-hours
LOAD TRUCK BY HAND						
Load truck by hand from piles, light soil	CY	$34.23		$34.23	**$57.16**	0.845
Load truck by hand from piles, average soil	CY	$52.90		$52.90	**$88.35**	1.306
Load truck by hand from piles, hard soil or loose rock	CY	$70.08		$70.08	**$117.03**	1.730
LOAD TRUCK BY MACHINE						
Load truck by machine from piles, light soil	CY	$3.93		$3.93	**$6.56**	0.097
Load truck by machine from piles, average soil	CY	$4.86		$4.86	**$8.12**	0.120
Load truck by machine from piles, hard soil or loose rock	CY	$5.67		$5.67	**$9.47**	0.140
HAUL BY DUMP TRUCK						
Haul by 3CY dump truck, less than 1 mile	CY	$10.95		$10.95	**$18.29**	0.319
Haul by 3CY dump truck, 2-3 miles	CY	$15.83		$15.83	**$26.44**	0.461
Haul by 3CY dump truck, 4-5 miles	CY	$23.69		$23.69	**$39.57**	0.690
Haul by 4CY dump truck, less than 1 mile	CY	$9.82		$9.82	**$16.40**	0.286
Haul by 4CY dump truck, 2-3 miles	CY	$15.38		$15.38	**$25.69**	0.448
Haul by 4CY dump truck, 4-5 miles	CY	$19.61		$19.61	**$32.74**	0.571
Haul by 5CY dump truck, less than 1 mile	CY	$8.62		$8.62	**$14.39**	0.251
Haul by 5CY dump truck, 2-3 miles	CY	$12.71		$12.71	**$21.22**	0.370
Haul by 5CY dump truck, 4-5 miles	CY	$18.58		$18.58	**$31.02**	0.541

Backfill and Grading

Description	Unit	Direct Labor	Direct Materials	Direct Total	Selling Price	Man-hours
STRIP TOPSOIL BY MACHINE						
Strip topsoil by machine, 4" deep	SF	$0.22		$0.22	**$0.36**	0.003
Strip topsoil by machine, 6" deep	SF	$0.29		$0.29	**$0.49**	0.004
PLACE SOIL						
Backfill by hand from piles, no compaction, medium soil	CF	$1.42		$1.42	**$2.37**	0.035
Compaction by hand, 4"-6" deep layer, medium soil	SF	$0.36		$0.36	**$0.61**	0.009
Compaction by vibrating plate, 12" deep layer, medium soil	SF	$0.49		$0.49	**$0.81**	0.012
Place topsoil and grade by hand from piles, 4" deep	SF	$0.57		$0.57	**$0.95**	0.014
Place topsoil and grade by hand from piles, 6" deep	SF	$0.73		$0.73	**$1.22**	0.018
Spread topsoil by machine, 4"-6" deep	SF	$0.12		$0.12	**$0.20**	0.003
SEED AND SOD						
Place sod, roll and water	SF	$0.81	$0.33	$1.14	**$1.90**	0.020
Seed, rake, water, tall fescue or equivalent	SF	$0.49	$0.09	$0.57	**$0.96**	0.012

Concrete

Continuous Footings, Chute Pour

> No forms or excavation included in price.
> 2 bar reinforcement included in price.

Description	Unit	Direct Labor	Direct Materials	Direct Total	Selling Price	Man-hours
CONTINUOUS FOOTINGS, CHUTE POUR, 8" DEEP						
Pour continuous footing by chute, reinforced, 8"D x 10"W	LF	$1.22	$3.55	$4.77	**$7.96**	0.030
Pour continuous footing by chute, reinforced, 8"D x 12"W	LF	$1.34	$4.12	$5.46	**$9.11**	0.033
Pour continuous footing by chute, reinforced, 8"D x 16"W	LF	$1.62	$5.25	$6.87	**$11.47**	0.040
Pour continuous footing by chute, reinforced, 8"D x 18"W	LF	$1.78	$5.81	$7.60	**$12.69**	0.044
Pour continuous footing by chute, reinforced, 8"D x 20"W	LF	$1.94	$6.39	$8.34	**$13.92**	0.048
CONTINUOUS FOOTINGS, CHUTE POUR, 10" DEEP						
Pour continuous footing by chute, reinforced, 10"D x 10"W	LF	$1.38	$4.26	$5.64	**$9.42**	0.034
Pour continuous footing by chute, reinforced, 10"D x 12"W	LF	$1.58	$4.97	$6.55	**$10.94**	0.039
Pour continuous footing by chute, reinforced, 10"D x 16"W	LF	$1.94	$6.38	$8.33	**$13.91**	0.048
Pour continuous footing by chute, reinforced, 10"D x 18"W	LF	$2.11	$7.09	$9.20	**$15.36**	0.052
Pour continuous footing by chute, reinforced, 10"D x 20"W	LF	$2.27	$7.81	$10.08	**$16.84**	0.056
CONTINUOUS FOOTINGS, CHUTE POUR, 12" DEEP						
Pour continuous footing by chute, reinforced, 12"D x 10"W	LF	$1.58	$4.97	$6.55	**$10.94**	0.039
Pour continuous footing by chute, reinforced, 12"D x 12"W	LF	$1.78	$5.82	$7.60	**$12.70**	0.044
Pour continuous footing by chute, reinforced, 12"D x 16"W	LF	$2.23	$7.52	$9.74	**$16.27**	0.055
Pour continuous footing by chute, reinforced, 12"D x 18"W	LF	$2.43	$8.36	$10.80	**$18.03**	0.060
Pour continuous footing by chute, reinforced, 12"D x 20"W	LF	$2.67	$9.23	$11.91	**$19.88**	0.066
CONTINUOUS FOOTINGS, CHUTE POUR, 24" DEEP						
Pour continuous footing by chute, reinforced, 24"D x 10"W	LF	$2.75	$9.41	$12.17	**$20.32**	0.068
Pour continuous footing by chute, reinforced, 24"D x 12"W	LF	$3.20	$11.11	$14.31	**$23.89**	0.079
Pour continuous footing by chute, reinforced, 24"D x 16"W	LF	$4.09	$14.50	$18.59	**$31.05**	0.101
Pour continuous footing by chute, reinforced, 24"D x 18"W	LF	$4.54	$16.19	$20.73	**$34.62**	0.112
Pour continuous footing by chute, reinforced, 24"D x 20"W	LF	$4.98	$17.93	$22.91	**$38.27**	0.123
Pour continuous footing by chute, reinforced, 24"D x 24"W	LF	$5.83	$21.36	$27.19	**$45.41**	0.144
CONTINUOUS FOOTINGS, CHUTE POUR, 30" DEEP						
Pour continuous footing by chute, reinforced, 30"D x 10"W	LF	$3.48	$11.84	$15.32	**$25.59**	0.086
Pour continuous footing by chute, reinforced, 30"D x 12"W	LF	$4.01	$13.96	$17.97	**$30.01**	0.099
Pour continuous footing by chute, reinforced, 30"D x 16"W	LF	$5.10	$18.20	$23.30	**$38.91**	0.126
Pour continuous footing by chute, reinforced, 30"D x 18"W	LF	$5.63	$20.32	$25.95	**$43.33**	0.139
Pour continuous footing by chute, reinforced, 30"D x 20"W	LF	$6.20	$22.49	$28.69	**$47.91**	0.153
Pour continuous footing by chute, reinforced, 30"D x 24"W	LF	$7.29	$26.77	$34.06	**$56.89**	0.180

Concrete

Continuous Footings, Chute Pour (cont.)

> No forms or excavation included in price.
> 2 bar reinforcement included in price.

Description	Unit	Direct Labor	Direct Materials	Direct Total	Selling Price	Man-hours
CONTINUOUS FOOTINGS, CHUTE POUR, 36" DEEP						
Pour continuous footing by chute, reinforced, 36"D x 10"W	LF	$4.09	$14.09	$18.18	**$30.36**	0.101
Pour continuous footing by chute, reinforced, 36"D x 12"W	LF	$4.74	$16.63	$21.37	**$35.69**	0.117
Pour continuous footing by chute, reinforced, 36"D x 16"W	LF	$6.04	$21.72	$27.75	**$46.35**	0.149
Pour continuous footing by chute, reinforced, 36"D x 18"W	LF	$6.68	$24.26	$30.95	**$51.68**	0.165
Pour continuous footing by chute, reinforced, 36"D x 20"W	LF	$7.37	$26.87	$34.24	**$57.18**	0.182
Pour continuous footing by chute, reinforced, 36"D x 24"W	LF	$8.67	$32.01	$40.68	**$67.93**	0.214
CONTINUOUS FOOTINGS, CHUTE POUR, 42" DEEP						
Pour continuous footing by chute, reinforced, 42"D x 12"W	LF	$5.51	$19.36	$24.87	**$41.54**	0.136
Pour continuous footing by chute, reinforced, 42"D x 16"W	LF	$7.05	$25.30	$32.35	**$54.02**	0.174
Pour continuous footing by chute, reinforced, 42"D x 18"W	LF	$7.78	$28.27	$36.04	**$60.19**	0.192
Pour continuous footing by chute, reinforced, 42"D x 20"W	LF	$8.55	$31.31	$39.85	**$66.56**	0.211
Pour continuous footing by chute, reinforced, 42"D x 24"W	LF	$10.05	$37.30	$47.35	**$79.07**	0.248
CONTINUOUS FOOTINGS, CHUTE POUR, 48" DEEP						
Pour continuous footing by chute, reinforced, 48"D x 12"W	LF	$6.36	$22.04	$28.40	**$47.42**	0.157
Pour continuous footing by chute, reinforced, 48"D x 16"W	LF	$8.10	$28.82	$36.92	**$61.66**	0.200
Pour continuous footing by chute, reinforced, 48"D x 18"W	LF	$8.99	$32.21	$41.20	**$68.81**	0.222
Pour continuous footing by chute, reinforced, 48"D x 20"W	LF	$9.84	$35.69	$45.53	**$76.03**	0.243
Pour continuous footing by chute, reinforced, 48"D x 24"W	LF	$11.59	$42.54	$54.12	**$90.39**	0.286
CONTINUOUS FOOTINGS, CHUTE POUR, 60" DEEP						
Pour continuous footing by chute, reinforced, 60"D x 12"W	LF	$8.02	$27.32	$35.34	**$59.02**	0.198
Pour continuous footing by chute, reinforced, 60"D x 16"W	LF	$10.17	$35.80	$45.97	**$76.77**	0.251
Pour continuous footing by chute, reinforced, 60"D x 18"W	LF	$11.26	$40.04	$51.30	**$85.68**	0.278
Pour continuous footing by chute, reinforced, 60"D x 20"W	LF	$12.36	$44.38	$56.74	**$94.75**	0.305
Pour continuous footing by chute, reinforced, 60"D x 24"W	LF	$14.54	$52.95	$67.49	**$112.71**	0.359

Concrete

Continuous Footings, Wheeled

> No forms or excavation included in price.
> 2 bar reinforcement included in price.

Description	Unit	Direct Labor	Direct Materials	Direct Total	Selling Price	Man-hours
CONTINUOUS FOOTINGS, WHEELED BY HAND, 8" DEEP						
Pour continuous footing, wheeled, reinforced, 8"D x 10"W	LF	$1.66	$3.55	$5.21	**$8.71**	0.041
Pour continuous footing, wheeled, reinforced, 8"D x 12"W	LF	$1.90	$4.12	$6.02	**$10.06**	0.047
Pour continuous footing, wheeled, reinforced, 8"D x 16"W	LF	$2.35	$5.25	$7.60	**$12.69**	0.058
Pour continuous footing, wheeled, reinforced, 8"D x 18"W	LF	$2.59	$5.81	$8.41	**$14.04**	0.064
Pour continuous footing, wheeled, reinforced, 8"D x 20"W	LF	$2.84	$6.39	$9.23	**$15.41**	0.070
CONTINUOUS FOOTINGS, WHEELED BY HAND, 10" DEEP						
Pour continuous footing, wheeled, reinforced, 10"D x 10"W	LF	$1.94	$4.26	$6.21	**$10.37**	0.048
Pour continuous footing, wheeled, reinforced, 10"D x 12"W	LF	$2.27	$4.97	$7.24	**$12.09**	0.056
Pour continuous footing, wheeled, reinforced, 10"D x 16"W	LF	$2.84	$6.38	$9.22	**$15.40**	0.070
Pour continuous footing, wheeled, reinforced, 10"D x 18"W	LF	$3.12	$7.09	$10.21	**$17.05**	0.077
Pour continuous footing, wheeled, reinforced, 10"D x 20"W	LF	$3.40	$7.81	$11.22	**$18.73**	0.084
CONTINUOUS FOOTINGS, WHEELED BY HAND, 12" DEEP						
Pour continuous footing, wheeled, reinforced, 12"D x 10"W	LF	$2.27	$4.97	$7.24	**$12.09**	0.056
Pour continuous footing, wheeled, reinforced, 12"D x 12"W	LF	$2.63	$5.82	$8.45	**$14.12**	0.065
Pour continuous footing, wheeled, reinforced, 12"D x 16"W	LF	$3.32	$7.52	$10.84	**$18.10**	0.082
Pour continuous footing, wheeled, reinforced, 12"D x 18"W	LF	$3.69	$8.36	$12.05	**$20.13**	0.091
Pour continuous footing, wheeled, reinforced, 12"D x 20"W	LF	$4.05	$9.23	$13.28	**$22.18**	0.100
CONTINUOUS FOOTINGS, WHEELED BY HAND, 24" DEEP						
Pour continuous footing, wheeled, reinforced, 24"D x 10"W	LF	$4.13	$9.41	$13.54	**$22.62**	0.102
Pour continuous footing, wheeled, reinforced, 24"D x 12"W	LF	$4.86	$11.11	$15.97	**$26.67**	0.120
Pour continuous footing, wheeled, reinforced, 24"D x 16"W	LF	$6.28	$14.50	$20.78	**$34.70**	0.155
Pour continuous footing, wheeled, reinforced, 24"D x 18"W	LF	$7.01	$16.19	$23.20	**$38.75**	0.173
Pour continuous footing, wheeled, reinforced, 24"D x 20"W	LF	$7.74	$17.93	$25.67	**$42.87**	0.191
Pour continuous footing, wheeled, reinforced, 24"D x 24"W	LF	$9.11	$21.36	$30.47	**$50.89**	0.225
CONTINUOUS FOOTINGS, WHEELED BY HAND, 30" DEEP						
Pour continuous footing, wheeled, reinforced, 30"D x 10"W	LF	$5.19	$11.84	$17.02	**$28.43**	0.128
Pour continuous footing, wheeled, reinforced, 30"D x 12"W	LF	$6.08	$13.96	$20.03	**$33.46**	0.150
Pour continuous footing, wheeled, reinforced, 30"D x 16"W	LF	$7.86	$18.20	$26.06	**$43.51**	0.194
Pour continuous footing, wheeled, reinforced, 30"D x 18"W	LF	$8.75	$20.32	$29.07	**$48.54**	0.216
Pour continuous footing, wheeled, reinforced, 30"D x 20"W	LF	$9.64	$22.49	$32.13	**$53.66**	0.238
Pour continuous footing, wheeled, reinforced, 30"D x 24"W	LF	$11.38	$26.77	$38.15	**$63.72**	0.281

Concrete

Continuous Footings, Wheeled (cont.)

> No forms or excavation included in price.
> 2 bar reinforcement included in price.

Description	Unit	Direct Labor	Direct Materials	Direct Total	Selling Price	Man-hours
CONTINUOUS FOOTINGS, WHEELED BY HAND, 36" DEEP						
Pour continuous footing, wheeled, reinforced, 36"D x 10"W	LF	$6.16	$14.09	$20.25	**$33.81**	0.152
Pour continuous footing, wheeled, reinforced, 36"D x 12"W	LF	$7.21	$16.63	$23.84	**$39.82**	0.178
Pour continuous footing, wheeled, reinforced, 36"D x 16"W	LF	$9.32	$21.72	$31.04	**$51.83**	0.230
Pour continuous footing, wheeled, reinforced, 36"D x 18"W	LF	$10.41	$24.26	$34.67	**$57.90**	0.257
Pour continuous footing, wheeled, reinforced, 36"D x 20"W	LF	$11.46	$26.87	$38.33	**$64.01**	0.283
Pour continuous footing, wheeled, reinforced, 36"D x 24"W	LF	$13.57	$32.01	$45.58	**$76.11**	0.335
CONTINUOUS FOOTINGS, WHEELED BY HAND, 42" DEEP						
Pour continuous footing, wheeled, reinforced, 42"D x 12"W	LF	$8.39	$19.36	$27.75	**$46.34**	0.207
Pour continuous footing, wheeled, reinforced, 42"D x 16"W	LF	$10.86	$25.30	$36.16	**$60.38**	0.268
Pour continuous footing, wheeled, reinforced, 42"D x 18"W	LF	$12.07	$28.27	$40.34	**$67.36**	0.298
Pour continuous footing, wheeled, reinforced, 42"D x 20"W	LF	$13.33	$31.31	$44.63	**$74.54**	0.329
Pour continuous footing, wheeled, reinforced, 42"D x 24"W	LF	$15.76	$37.30	$53.06	**$88.61**	0.389
CONTINUOUS FOOTINGS, WHEELED BY HAND, 48" DEEP						
Pour continuous footing, wheeled, reinforced, 48"D x 12"W	LF	$9.68	$22.04	$31.72	**$52.97**	0.239
Pour continuous footing, wheeled, reinforced, 48"D x 16"W	LF	$12.52	$28.82	$41.34	**$69.03**	0.309
Pour continuous footing, wheeled, reinforced, 48"D x 18"W	LF	$13.94	$32.21	$46.15	**$77.06**	0.344
Pour continuous footing, wheeled, reinforced, 48"D x 20"W	LF	$15.35	$35.69	$51.04	**$85.23**	0.379
Pour continuous footing, wheeled, reinforced, 48"D x 24"W	LF	$18.11	$42.54	$60.64	**$101.28**	0.447
CONTINUOUS FOOTINGS, WHEELED BY HAND, 60" DEEP						
Pour continuous footing, wheeled, reinforced, 60"D x 12"W	LF	$12.11	$27.32	$39.44	**$65.86**	0.299
Pour continuous footing, wheeled, reinforced, 60"D x 16"W	LF	$15.68	$35.80	$51.48	**$85.97**	0.387
Pour continuous footing, wheeled, reinforced, 60"D x 18"W	LF	$17.42	$40.04	$57.46	**$95.96**	0.430
Pour continuous footing, wheeled, reinforced, 60"D x 20"W	LF	$19.20	$44.38	$63.59	**$106.19**	0.474
Pour continuous footing, wheeled, reinforced, 60"D x 24"W	LF	$22.68	$52.95	$75.63	**$126.31**	0.560

Concrete

Continuous Footings, Pumped

> No forms or excavation included in price.
> 2 bar reinforcement included in price.

Description	Unit	Direct Labor	Direct Materials	Direct Total	Selling Price	Man-hours
CONTINUOUS FOOTINGS, PUMPED, 8" DEEP						
Pour continuous footing, pumped, reinforced, 8"D x 10"W	LF	$1.86	$3.55	$5.42	**$9.05**	0.046
Pour continuous footing, pumped, reinforced, 8"D x 12"W	LF	$2.15	$4.12	$6.27	**$10.46**	0.053
Pour continuous footing, pumped, reinforced, 8"D x 16"W	LF	$2.67	$5.25	$7.92	**$13.23**	0.066
Pour continuous footing, pumped, reinforced, 8"D x 18"W	LF	$2.96	$5.81	$8.77	**$14.65**	0.073
Pour continuous footing, pumped, reinforced, 8"D x 20"W	LF	$3.20	$6.39	$9.59	**$16.02**	0.079
CONTINUOUS FOOTINGS, PUMPED, 10" DEEP						
Pour continuous footing, pumped, reinforced, 10"D x 10"W	LF	$2.23	$4.26	$6.49	**$10.84**	0.055
Pour continuous footing, pumped, reinforced, 10"D x 12"W	LF	$2.55	$4.97	$7.52	**$12.56**	0.063
Pour continuous footing, pumped, reinforced, 10"D x 16"W	LF	$3.20	$6.38	$9.58	**$16.00**	0.079
Pour continuous footing, pumped, reinforced, 10"D x 18"W	LF	$3.52	$7.09	$10.61	**$17.73**	0.087
Pour continuous footing, pumped, reinforced, 10"D x 20"W	LF	$3.85	$7.81	$11.66	**$19.48**	0.095
CONTINUOUS FOOTINGS, PUMPED, 12" DEEP						
Pour continuous footing, pumped, reinforced, 12"D x 10"W	LF	$2.55	$4.97	$7.53	**$12.57**	0.063
Pour continuous footing, pumped, reinforced, 12"D x 12"W	LF	$2.96	$5.82	$8.78	**$14.66**	0.073
Pour continuous footing, pumped, reinforced, 12"D x 16"W	LF	$3.77	$7.52	$11.28	**$18.84**	0.093
Pour continuous footing, pumped, reinforced, 12"D x 18"W	LF	$4.13	$8.36	$12.50	**$20.87**	0.102
Pour continuous footing, pumped, reinforced, 12"D x 20"W	LF	$4.58	$9.23	$13.81	**$23.06**	0.113
CONTINUOUS FOOTINGS, PUMPED, 24" DEEP						
Pour continuous footing, pumped, reinforced, 24"D x 10"W	LF	$4.66	$9.41	$14.07	**$23.50**	0.115
Pour continuous footing, pumped, reinforced, 24"D x 12"W	LF	$5.51	$11.11	$16.62	**$27.75**	0.136
Pour continuous footing, pumped, reinforced, 24"D x 16"W	LF	$7.09	$14.50	$21.59	**$36.05**	0.175
Pour continuous footing, pumped, reinforced, 24"D x 18"W	LF	$7.90	$16.19	$24.09	**$40.24**	0.195
Pour continuous footing, pumped, reinforced, 24"D x 20"W	LF	$8.71	$17.93	$26.64	**$44.49**	0.215
Pour continuous footing, pumped, reinforced, 24"D x 24"W	LF	$10.29	$21.36	$31.65	**$52.85**	0.254
CONTINUOUS FOOTINGS, PUMPED, 30" DEEP						
Pour continuous footing, pumped, reinforced, 30"D x 10"W	LF	$5.87	$11.84	$17.71	**$29.58**	0.145
Pour continuous footing, pumped, reinforced, 30"D x 12"W	LF	$6.89	$13.96	$20.85	**$34.81**	0.170
Pour continuous footing, pumped, reinforced, 30"D x 16"W	LF	$8.87	$18.20	$27.07	**$45.21**	0.219
Pour continuous footing, pumped, reinforced, 30"D x 18"W	LF	$9.88	$20.32	$30.20	**$50.44**	0.244
Pour continuous footing, pumped, reinforced, 30"D x 20"W	LF	$10.90	$22.49	$33.39	**$55.75**	0.269
Pour continuous footing, pumped, reinforced, 30"D x 24"W	LF	$12.84	$26.77	$39.61	**$66.15**	0.317

Concrete

Continuous Footings, Pumped (cont.)

> No forms or excavation included in price.
> 2 bar reinforcement included in price.

Description	Unit	Direct Labor	Direct Materials	Direct Total	Selling Price	Man-hours
CONTINUOUS FOOTINGS, PUMPED, 36" DEEP						
Pour continuous footing, pumped, reinforced, 36"D x 10"W	LF	$6.93	$14.09	$21.01	**$35.09**	0.171
Pour continuous footing, pumped, reinforced, 36"D x 12"W	LF	$8.14	$16.63	$24.77	**$41.37**	0.201
Pour continuous footing, pumped, reinforced, 36"D x 16"W	LF	$10.53	$21.72	$32.25	**$53.86**	0.260
Pour continuous footing, pumped, reinforced, 36"D x 18"W	LF	$11.75	$24.26	$36.01	**$60.14**	0.290
Pour continuous footing, pumped, reinforced, 36"D x 20"W	LF	$12.96	$26.87	$39.83	**$66.52**	0.320
Pour continuous footing, pumped, reinforced, 36"D x 24"W	LF	$15.31	$32.01	$47.32	**$79.02**	0.378
CONTINUOUS FOOTINGS, PUMPED, 42" DEEP						
Pour continuous footing, pumped, reinforced, 42"D x 12"W	LF	$9.48	$19.36	$28.84	**$48.17**	0.234
Pour continuous footing, pumped, reinforced, 42"D x 16"W	LF	$12.27	$25.30	$37.57	**$62.75**	0.303
Pour continuous footing, pumped, reinforced, 42"D x 18"W	LF	$13.65	$28.27	$41.92	**$70.00**	0.337
Pour continuous footing, pumped, reinforced, 42"D x 20"W	LF	$15.07	$31.31	$46.38	**$77.45**	0.372
Pour continuous footing, pumped, reinforced, 42"D x 24"W	LF	$17.78	$37.30	$55.09	**$91.99**	0.439
CONTINUOUS FOOTINGS, PUMPED, 48" DEEP						
Pour continuous footing, pumped, reinforced, 48"D x 12"W	LF	$10.94	$22.04	$32.97	**$55.07**	0.270
Pour continuous footing, pumped, reinforced, 48"D x 16"W	LF	$14.14	$28.82	$42.96	**$71.74**	0.349
Pour continuous footing, pumped, reinforced, 48"D x 18"W	LF	$15.72	$32.21	$47.93	**$80.04**	0.388
Pour continuous footing, pumped, reinforced, 48"D x 20"W	LF	$17.34	$35.69	$53.02	**$88.55**	0.428
Pour continuous footing, pumped, reinforced, 48"D x 24"W	LF	$20.46	$42.54	$62.99	**$105.20**	0.505
CONTINUOUS FOOTINGS, PUMPED, 60" DEEP						
Pour continuous footing, pumped, reinforced, 60"D x 12"W	LF	$13.69	$27.32	$41.01	**$68.49**	0.338
Pour continuous footing, pumped, reinforced, 60"D x 16"W	LF	$17.70	$35.80	$53.50	**$89.35**	0.437
Pour continuous footing, pumped, reinforced, 60"D x 18"W	LF	$19.69	$40.04	$59.73	**$99.75**	0.486
Pour continuous footing, pumped, reinforced, 60"D x 20"W	LF	$21.71	$44.38	$66.10	**$110.38**	0.536
Pour continuous footing, pumped, reinforced, 60"D x 24"W	LF	$25.64	$52.95	$78.59	**$131.25**	0.633

Concrete

Pier Footings

> No forms or excavation included in price.
> 2 bar reinforcement included in price.

Description	Unit	Direct Labor	Direct Materials	Direct Total	Selling Price	Man-hours
PIER FOOTINGS, REINFORCED, 12" DEEP						
Pour pier footing, reinforced, 16"L x 16"W x 12"D	EA	$3.28	$10.88	$14.16	**$23.65**	0.081
Pour pier footing, reinforced, 24"L x 24"W x 12"D	EA	$7.41	$24.52	$31.93	**$53.32**	0.183
Pour pier footing, reinforced, 30"L x 30"W x 12"D	EA	$11.63	$38.29	$49.92	**$83.37**	0.287
Pour pier footing, reinforced, 36"L x 48"W x 12"D	EA	$22.28	$73.52	$95.80	**$159.99**	0.550
PIER FOOTINGS, REINFORCED, 24" DEEP						
Pour pier footing, reinforced, 16"L x 16"W x 24"D	EA	$7.25	$21.76	$29.02	**$48.46**	0.179
Pour pier footing, reinforced, 24"L x 24"W x 24"D	EA	$16.37	$49.03	$65.40	**$109.22**	0.404
Pour pier footing, reinforced, 30"L x 30"W x 24"D	EA	$25.52	$76.59	$102.11	**$170.52**	0.630
Pour pier footing, reinforced, 36"L x 48"W x 24"D	EA	$49.02	$147.04	$196.06	**$327.42**	1.210
PIER FOOTINGS, REINFORCED, 36" DEEP						
Pour pier footing, reinforced, 16"L x 16"W x 36"D	EA	$11.87	$32.65	$44.52	**$74.34**	0.293
Pour pier footing, reinforced, 24"L x 24"W x 36"D	EA	$26.74	$73.55	$100.29	**$167.48**	0.660
Pour pier footing, reinforced, 30"L x 30"W x 36"D	EA	$41.76	$114.88	$156.65	**$261.60**	1.031
Pour pier footing, reinforced, 36"L x 48"W x 36"D	EA	$80.21	$220.57	$300.77	**$502.29**	1.980
PIER FOOTINGS, REINFORCED, 48" DEEP						
Pour pier footing, reinforced, 16"L x 16"W x 48"D	EA	$17.14	$43.53	$60.66	**$101.31**	0.423
Pour pier footing, reinforced, 24"L x 24"W x 48"D	EA	$38.65	$98.07	$136.71	**$228.31**	0.954
Pour pier footing, reinforced, 30"L x 30"W x 48"D	EA	$60.36	$153.18	$213.54	**$356.60**	1.490
Pour pier footing, reinforced, 36"L x 48"W x 48"D	EA	$115.86	$294.09	$409.94	**$684.61**	2.860
PIER FOOTINGS, REINFORCED, 60" DEEP						
Pour pier footing, reinforced, 16"L x 16"W x 60"D	EA	$23.09	$54.41	$77.50	**$129.43**	0.570
Pour pier footing, reinforced, 24"L x 24"W x 60"D	EA	$52.01	$122.58	$174.60	**$291.58**	1.284
Pour pier footing, reinforced, 30"L x 30"W x 60"D	EA	$81.26	$191.47	$272.73	**$455.46**	2.006
Pour pier footing, reinforced, 36"L x 48"W x 60"D	EA	$156.00	$367.61	$523.61	**$874.43**	3.851

Concrete

Round Footings, Hand Dug

Description	Unit	Direct Labor	Direct Materials	Direct Total	Selling Price	Man-hours
ROUND FOOTINGS, HAND DUG, 8" DIAMETER						
Hand dig and pour 8" diameter pier footing, 12"D	EA	$10.01	$4.30	$14.30	**$23.88**	0.247
Hand dig and pour 8" diameter pier footing, 24"D	EA	$21.67	$8.59	$30.27	**$50.54**	0.535
Hand dig and pour 8" diameter pier footing, 36"D	EA	$33.34	$12.89	$46.23	**$77.20**	0.823
Hand dig and pour 8" diameter pier footing, 48"D	EA	$45.01	$17.19	$62.19	**$103.86**	1.111
Hand dig and pour 8" diameter pier footing, 60"D	EA	$59.95	$21.48	$81.44	**$136.00**	1.480
ROUND FOOTINGS, HAND DUG, 10" DIAMETER						
Hand dig and pour 10" diameter pier footing, 12"D	EA	$11.26	$5.33	$16.59	**$27.71**	0.278
Hand dig and pour 10" diameter pier footing, 24"D	EA	$24.39	$10.66	$35.05	**$58.53**	0.602
Hand dig and pour 10" diameter pier footing, 36"D	EA	$37.51	$15.99	$53.50	**$89.35**	0.926
Hand dig and pour 10" diameter pier footing, 48"D	EA	$50.60	$21.32	$71.92	**$120.10**	1.249
Hand dig and pour 10" diameter pier footing, 60"D	EA	$67.45	$26.65	$94.10	**$157.15**	1.665
ROUND FOOTINGS, HAND DUG, 12" DIAMETER						
Hand dig and pour 12" diameter pier footing, 12"D	EA	$12.52	$6.54	$19.06	**$31.83**	0.309
Hand dig and pour 12" diameter pier footing, 24"D	EA	$27.10	$13.09	$40.19	**$67.11**	0.669
Hand dig and pour 12" diameter pier footing, 36"D	EA	$41.64	$19.63	$61.27	**$102.32**	1.028
Hand dig and pour 12" diameter pier footing, 48"D	EA	$56.23	$26.17	$82.40	**$137.60**	1.388
Hand dig and pour 12" diameter pier footing, 60"D	EA	$74.94	$32.71	$107.66	**$179.78**	1.850

Round Footings, Dug with Power Auger

Description	Unit	Direct Labor	Direct Materials	Direct Total	Selling Price	Man-hours
ROUND FOOTINGS, DUG WITH POWER AUGER, 8" DIAMETER						
Dig with power auger and pour 8" diameter pier footing, 12"D	EA	$6.40	$4.30	$10.70	**$17.86**	0.158
Dig with power auger and pour 8" diameter pier footing, 24"D	EA	$12.76	$8.59	$21.35	**$35.66**	0.315
Dig with power auger and pour 8" diameter pier footing, 36"D	EA	$19.16	$12.89	$32.05	**$53.52**	0.473
Dig with power auger and pour 8" diameter pier footing, 48"D	EA	$25.56	$17.19	$42.75	**$71.39**	0.631
Dig with power auger and pour 8" diameter pier footing, 60"D	EA	$30.30	$21.48	$51.78	**$86.48**	0.748
ROUND FOOTINGS, DUG WITH POWER AUGER, 10" DIAMETER						
Dig with power auger and pour 10" diameter pier footing, 12"D	EA	$6.97	$5.33	$12.30	**$20.54**	0.172
Dig with power auger and pour 10" diameter pier footing, 24"D	EA	$13.98	$10.66	$24.64	**$41.14**	0.345
Dig with power auger and pour 10" diameter pier footing, 36"D	EA	$20.94	$15.99	$36.93	**$61.68**	0.517
Dig with power auger and pour 10" diameter pier footing, 48"D	EA	$27.91	$21.32	$49.23	**$82.22**	0.689
Dig with power auger and pour 10" diameter pier footing, 60"D	EA	$33.26	$26.65	$59.91	**$100.05**	0.821
ROUND FOOTINGS, DUG WITH POWER AUGER, 12" DIAMETER						
Dig with power auger and pour 12" diameter pier footing, 12"D	EA	$7.58	$6.54	$14.12	**$23.58**	0.187
Dig with power auger and pour 12" diameter pier footing, 24"D	EA	$15.15	$13.09	$28.24	**$47.15**	0.374
Dig with power auger and pour 12" diameter pier footing, 36"D	EA	$22.73	$19.63	$42.35	**$70.73**	0.561
Dig with power auger and pour 12" diameter pier footing, 48"D	EA	$28.64	$26.17	$54.81	**$91.53**	0.707
Dig with power auger and pour 12" diameter pier footing, 60"D	EA	$36.21	$32.71	$68.93	**$115.11**	0.894

Concrete

Monolithic Footing and Slab

> No forms or excavation included in price.
> 2 bar reinforcement included in price.

Description	Unit	Direct Labor	Direct Materials	Direct Total	Selling Price	Man-hours
MONOLITHIC SLAB, CHUTE POUR						
Pour monolithic slab by chute, 4" thick on existing footing	SF	$2.05	$2.38	$4.43	**$7.40**	0.038
MONOLITHIC FOOTING, CHUTE POUR						
Pour monolithic footing by chute, 12"D, 16"W at top, 8"W at bottom	LF	$2.23	$7.52	$9.75	**$16.28**	0.055
Pour monolithic footing by chute, 24"D, 16"W at top, 8"W at bottom	LF	$4.46	$15.05	$19.50	**$32.57**	0.110
Pour monolithic footing by chute, 36"D, 16"W at top, 8"W at bottom	LF	$6.52	$21.86	$28.38	**$47.39**	0.161
Pour monolithic footing by chute, 48"D, 16"W at top, 8"W at bottom	LF	$8.55	$29.02	$37.57	**$62.74**	0.211
Additional support footing by chute, 12"D x 12"W	LF	$1.78	$5.82	$7.60	**$12.70**	0.044
Additional support footing by chute, 24"D x 12"W	LF	$3.20	$11.11	$14.31	**$23.89**	0.079
MONOLITHIC SLAB, WHEELED BY HAND						
Pour monolithic slab, wheeled, 4" thick on existing footing	SF	$4.54	$2.38	$6.92	**$11.56**	0.084
MONOLITHIC FOOTING, WHEELED BY HAND						
Pour monolithic footing, wheeled, 12"D, 16"W at top, 8"W at bottom	LF	$3.08	$7.52	$10.60	**$17.71**	0.076
Pour monolithic footing, wheeled, 24"D, 16"W at top, 8"W at bottom	LF	$6.12	$15.05	$21.16	**$35.34**	0.151
Pour monolithic footing, wheeled, 36"D, 16"W at top, 8"W at bottom	LF	$8.99	$21.86	$30.85	**$51.52**	0.222
Pour monolithic footing, wheeled, 48"D, 16"W at top, 8"W at bottom	LF	$11.83	$29.02	$40.85	**$68.22**	0.292
Additional support footing, wheeled, 12"D x 12"W	LF	$2.47	$5.82	$8.29	**$13.85**	0.061
Additional support footing, wheeled, 24"D x 12"W	LF	$4.42	$11.11	$15.52	**$25.92**	0.109
MONOLITHIC SLAB, PUMPED						
Pour monolithic slab, pumped, 4" thick on existing footing	SF	$5.03	$2.38	$7.41	**$12.37**	0.093
MONOLITHIC FOOTING, PUMPED						
Pour monolithic footing, pumped, 12"D, 16"W at top, 8"W at bottom	LF	$3.48	$7.52	$11.01	**$18.38**	0.086
Pour monolithic footing, pumped, 24"D, 16"W at top, 8"W at bottom	LF	$6.93	$15.05	$21.97	**$36.70**	0.171
Pour monolithic footing, pumped, 36"D, 16"W at top, 8"W at bottom	LF	$10.13	$21.86	$31.98	**$53.41**	0.250
Pour monolithic footing, pumped, 48"D, 16"W at top, 8"W at bottom	LF	$13.37	$29.02	$42.39	**$70.79**	0.330
Additional support footing, pumped, 12"D x 12"W	LF	$2.80	$5.82	$8.62	**$14.39**	0.069
Additional support footing, pumped, 24"D x 12"W	LF	$5.02	$11.11	$16.13	**$26.94**	0.124

Concrete

Slabs within Existing Walls or Forms

> No forms or excavation included in price.

Description	Unit	Direct Labor	Direct Materials	Direct Total	Selling Price	Man-hours
SLAB, CHUTE POUR						
Pour slab by chute, 2" thick, existing forms/walls, no forms/excavation	SF	$1.78	$1.53	$3.31	**$5.53**	0.033
Pour slab by chute, 3" thick, existing forms/walls, no forms/excavation	SF	$1.89	$1.95	$3.85	**$6.42**	0.035
Pour slab by chute, 4" thick, existing forms/walls, no forms/excavation	SF	$2.05	$2.38	$4.43	**$7.40**	0.038
Pour slab by chute, 5" thick, existing forms/walls, no forms/excavation	SF	$2.16	$2.80	$4.97	**$8.30**	0.040
Pour slab by chute, 6" thick, existing forms/walls, no forms/excavation	SF	$2.32	$3.23	$5.56	**$9.28**	0.043
SLAB, WHEELED BY HAND						
Pour slab, wheeled, 2" thick, existing forms/walls, no forms/excavation	SF	$2.76	$1.53	$4.29	**$7.16**	0.051
Pour slab, wheeled, 3" thick, existing forms/walls, no forms/excavation	SF	$3.68	$1.95	$5.63	**$9.40**	0.068
Pour slab, wheeled, 4" thick, existing forms/walls, no forms/excavation	SF	$4.54	$2.38	$6.92	**$11.56**	0.084
Pour slab, wheeled, 5" thick, existing forms/walls, no forms/excavation	SF	$5.46	$2.80	$8.27	**$13.80**	0.101
Pour slab, wheeled, 6" thick, existing forms/walls, no forms/excavation	SF	$6.38	$3.23	$9.61	**$16.05**	0.118
SLAB, PUMPED						
Pour slab, pumped, 2" thick, existing forms/walls, no forms/excavation	SF	$2.97	$1.53	$4.50	**$7.52**	0.055
Pour slab, pumped, 3" thick, existing forms/walls, no forms/excavation	SF	$4.00	$1.95	$5.95	**$9.94**	0.074
Pour slab, pumped, 4" thick, existing forms/walls, no forms/excavation	SF	$4.97	$2.38	$7.35	**$12.28**	0.092
Pour slab, pumped, 5" thick, existing forms/walls, no forms/excavation	SF	$6.00	$2.80	$8.81	**$14.71**	0.111
Pour slab, pumped, 6" thick, existing forms/walls, no forms/excavation	SF	$7.03	$3.23	$10.26	**$17.13**	0.130

Concrete Steps and Slab

Description	Unit	Direct Labor	Direct Materials	Direct Total	Selling Price	Man-hours
SUSPENDED SLAB AND STEPS						
Suspended concrete slab for steps, up to 16 SF	EA	$341.09	$148.57	$489.65	**$817.72**	6.309
Suspended concrete slab for steps, 16 to 24 SF	EA	$454.78	$222.85	$677.63	**$1,131.64**	8.412
Suspended concrete slab for steps, 24 to 35 SF	EA	$636.71	$324.99	$961.69	**$1,606.03**	11.777
Suspended concrete slab for steps, over 35 SF	SF	$18.17	$9.29	$27.45	**$45.84**	0.336
Suspended step, 48" wide, per tread	EA	$159.16	$40.29	$199.45	**$333.09**	2.944
Suspended step, 60" wide, per tread	EA	$191.01	$50.36	$241.37	**$403.09**	3.533
Suspended step, 72" wide, per tread	EA	$219.66	$60.44	$280.10	**$467.76**	4.063
SLAB AND STEPS ON GRADE						
Concrete slab on grade for steps, up to 16 SF	EA	$306.97	$118.85	$425.83	**$711.13**	5.678
Concrete slab on grade for steps, 16 to 24 SF	EA	$409.32	$178.28	$587.59	**$981.28**	7.571
Concrete slab on grade for steps, 24 to 35 SF	EA	$573.02	$259.99	$833.01	**$1,391.13**	10.599
Concrete slab on grade for steps, over 35 SF	SF	$16.38	$7.43	$23.81	**$39.76**	0.303
Step on grade, 48" wide, per tread	EA	$143.27	$32.23	$175.50	**$293.09**	2.650
Step on grade, 60" wide, per tread	EA	$171.92	$40.29	$212.21	**$354.40**	3.180
Step on grade, 72" wide, per tread	EA	$197.71	$48.35	$246.06	**$410.92**	3.657

Concrete

Concrete Wall, Sectional Forms, Unreinforced

> No footing or excavation included in price.

Description	Unit	Direct Labor	Direct Materials	Direct Total	Selling Price	Man-hours
CONCRETE WALL BY CHUTE, UNREINFORCED, 8" THICK						
Set forms and pour walls by chute, 8"T x 24"H, unreinforced	LF	$17.84	$7.30	$25.14	**$41.98**	0.330
Set forms and pour walls by chute, 8"T x 36"H, unreinforced	LF	$27.30	$10.95	$38.25	**$63.87**	0.505
Set forms and pour walls by chute, 8"T x 48"H, unreinforced	LF	$36.38	$14.60	$50.98	**$85.14**	0.673
Set forms and pour walls by chute, 8"T x 60"H, unreinforced	LF	$45.47	$18.24	$63.71	**$106.40**	0.841
Set forms and pour walls by chute, 8"T x 72"H, unreinforced	LF	$54.55	$21.89	$76.44	**$127.66**	1.009
Set forms and pour walls by chute, 8"T x 84"H, unreinforced	LF	$63.69	$25.54	$89.23	**$149.01**	1.178
Set forms and pour walls by chute, 8"T x 96"H, unreinforced	LF	$72.77	$29.19	$101.96	**$170.27**	1.346
CONCRETE WALL BY CHUTE, UNREINFORCED, 10" THICK						
Set forms and pour walls by chute, 10"T x 24"H, unreinforced	LF	$18.27	$9.00	$27.27	**$45.54**	0.338
Set forms and pour walls by chute, 10"T x 36"H, unreinforced	LF	$28.11	$13.50	$41.61	**$69.49**	0.520
Set forms and pour walls by chute, 10"T x 48"H, unreinforced	LF	$37.52	$17.99	$55.51	**$92.71**	0.694
Set forms and pour walls by chute, 10"T x 60"H, unreinforced	LF	$46.87	$22.49	$69.37	**$115.84**	0.867
Set forms and pour walls by chute, 10"T x 72"H, unreinforced	LF	$56.28	$26.99	$83.27	**$139.06**	1.041
Set forms and pour walls by chute, 10"T x 84"H, unreinforced	LF	$65.63	$31.49	$97.12	**$162.20**	1.214
Set forms and pour walls by chute, 10"T x 96"H, unreinforced	LF	$75.04	$35.99	$111.03	**$185.42**	1.388
CONCRETE WALL BY CHUTE, UNREINFORCED, 12" THICK						
Set forms and pour walls by chute, 12"T x 24"H, unreinforced	LF	$18.76	$10.70	$29.46	**$49.19**	0.347
Set forms and pour walls by chute, 12"T x 36"H, unreinforced	LF	$28.98	$16.05	$45.02	**$75.19**	0.536
Set forms and pour walls by chute, 12"T x 48"H, unreinforced	LF	$38.66	$21.39	$60.05	**$100.28**	0.715
Set forms and pour walls by chute, 12"T x 60"H, unreinforced	LF	$48.28	$26.74	$75.02	**$125.28**	0.893
Set forms and pour walls by chute, 12"T x 72"H, unreinforced	LF	$57.96	$32.09	$90.05	**$150.38**	1.072
Set forms and pour walls by chute, 12"T x 84"H, unreinforced	LF	$67.63	$37.44	$105.07	**$175.47**	1.251
Set forms and pour walls by chute, 12"T x 96"H, unreinforced	LF	$77.26	$42.79	$120.04	**$200.47**	1.429

Concrete

Concrete Wall, Sectional, Unreinforced (cont.)

> No footing or excavation included in price.

CONCRETE WALL WHEELED BY HAND, UNREINFORCED, 8" THICK

Description	Unit	Direct Labor	Direct Materials	Direct Total	Selling Price	Man-hours
Set forms and pour walls, wheeled, 8"T x 24"H, unreinforced	LF	$21.46	$7.30	$28.76	**$48.03**	0.397
Set forms and pour walls, wheeled, 8"T x 36"H, unreinforced	LF	$34.06	$10.95	$45.01	**$75.16**	0.630
Set forms and pour walls, wheeled, 8"T x 48"H, unreinforced	LF	$45.36	$14.60	$59.95	**$100.12**	0.839
Set forms and pour walls, wheeled, 8"T x 60"H, unreinforced	LF	$56.71	$18.24	$74.96	**$125.18**	1.049
Set forms and pour walls, wheeled, 8"T x 72"H, unreinforced	LF	$68.07	$21.89	$89.96	**$150.23**	1.259
Set forms and pour walls, wheeled, 8"T x 84"H, unreinforced	LF	$79.42	$25.54	$104.96	**$175.28**	1.469
Set forms and pour walls, wheeled, 8"T x 96"H, unreinforced	LF	$90.72	$29.19	$119.91	**$200.25**	1.678

CONCRETE WALL WHEELED BY HAND, UNREINFORCED, 10" THICK

Description	Unit	Direct Labor	Direct Materials	Direct Total	Selling Price	Man-hours
Set forms and pour walls, wheeled, 10"T x 24"H, unreinforced	LF	$23.57	$9.00	$32.57	**$54.39**	0.436
Set forms and pour walls, wheeled, 10"T x 36"H, unreinforced	LF	$36.28	$13.50	$49.77	**$83.12**	0.671
Set forms and pour walls, wheeled, 10"T x 48"H, unreinforced	LF	$48.39	$17.99	$66.38	**$110.86**	0.895
Set forms and pour walls, wheeled, 10"T x 60"H, unreinforced	LF	$60.50	$22.49	$82.99	**$138.59**	1.119
Set forms and pour walls, wheeled, 10"T x 72"H, unreinforced	LF	$72.61	$26.99	$99.60	**$166.33**	1.343
Set forms and pour walls, wheeled, 10"T x 84"H, unreinforced	LF	$84.66	$31.49	$116.15	**$193.98**	1.566
Set forms and pour walls, wheeled, 10"T x 96"H, unreinforced	LF	$96.77	$35.99	$132.76	**$221.71**	1.790

CONCRETE WALL WHEELED BY HAND, UNREINFORCED, 12" THICK

Description	Unit	Direct Labor	Direct Materials	Direct Total	Selling Price	Man-hours
Set forms and pour walls, wheeled, 12"T x 24"H, unreinforced	LF	$25.30	$10.70	$36.00	**$60.12**	0.468
Set forms and pour walls, wheeled, 12"T x 36"H, unreinforced	LF	$39.09	$16.05	$55.13	**$92.07**	0.723
Set forms and pour walls, wheeled, 12"T x 48"H, unreinforced	LF	$52.12	$21.39	$73.51	**$122.76**	0.964
Set forms and pour walls, wheeled, 12"T x 60"H, unreinforced	LF	$65.15	$26.74	$91.89	**$153.45**	1.205
Set forms and pour walls, wheeled, 12"T x 72"H, unreinforced	LF	$78.18	$32.09	$110.27	**$184.14**	1.446
Set forms and pour walls, wheeled, 12"T x 84"H, unreinforced	LF	$91.21	$37.44	$128.64	**$214.84**	1.687
Set forms and pour walls, wheeled, 12"T x 96"H, unreinforced	LF	$104.23	$42.79	$147.02	**$245.53**	1.928

Concrete Wall, Sectional, Unreinforced (cont.)

> No footing or excavation included in price.

Description	Unit	Direct Labor	Direct Materials	Direct Total	Selling Price	Man-hours
CONCRETE WALL PUMPED, UNREINFORCED, 8" THICK						
Set forms and pour walls, pumped, 8"T x 24"H, unreinforced	LF	$23.19	$7.30	$30.49	**$50.92**	0.429
Set forms and pour walls, pumped, 8"T x 36"H, unreinforced	LF	$36.76	$10.95	$47.71	**$79.67**	0.680
Set forms and pour walls, pumped, 8"T x 48"H, unreinforced	LF	$48.98	$14.60	$63.58	**$106.17**	0.906
Set forms and pour walls, pumped, 8"T x 60"H, unreinforced	LF	$61.25	$18.24	$79.50	**$132.76**	1.133
Set forms and pour walls, pumped, 8"T x 72"H, unreinforced	LF	$73.47	$21.89	$95.36	**$159.26**	1.359
Set forms and pour walls, pumped, 8"T x 84"H, unreinforced	LF	$85.74	$25.54	$111.29	**$185.85**	1.586
Set forms and pour walls, pumped, 8"T x 96"H, unreinforced	LF	$98.02	$29.19	$127.21	**$212.44**	1.813
CONCRETE WALL PUMPED, UNREINFORCED, 10" THICK						
Set forms and pour walls, pumped, 10"T x 24"H, unreinforced	LF	$25.46	$9.00	$34.46	**$57.55**	0.471
Set forms and pour walls, pumped, 10"T x 36"H, unreinforced	LF	$39.20	$13.50	$52.69	**$88.00**	0.725
Set forms and pour walls, pumped, 10"T x 48"H, unreinforced	LF	$52.28	$17.99	$70.27	**$117.36**	0.967
Set forms and pour walls, pumped, 10"T x 60"H, unreinforced	LF	$65.31	$22.49	$87.80	**$146.63**	1.208
Set forms and pour walls, pumped, 10"T x 72"H, unreinforced	LF	$78.39	$26.99	$105.38	**$175.99**	1.450
Set forms and pour walls, pumped, 10"T x 84"H, unreinforced	LF	$91.48	$31.49	$122.97	**$205.35**	1.692
Set forms and pour walls, pumped, 10"T x 96"H, unreinforced	LF	$104.50	$35.99	$140.49	**$234.62**	1.933
CONCRETE WALL PUMPED, UNREINFORCED, 12" THICK						
Set forms and pour walls, pumped, 12"T x 24"H, unreinforced	LF	$27.30	$10.70	$38.00	**$63.46**	0.505
Set forms and pour walls, pumped, 12"T x 36"H, unreinforced	LF	$42.22	$16.05	$58.27	**$97.31**	0.781
Set forms and pour walls, pumped, 12"T x 48"H, unreinforced	LF	$56.28	$21.39	$77.67	**$129.71**	1.041
Set forms and pour walls, pumped, 12"T x 60"H, unreinforced	LF	$70.39	$26.74	$97.13	**$162.21**	1.302
Set forms and pour walls, pumped, 12"T x 72"H, unreinforced	LF	$84.45	$32.09	$116.54	**$194.62**	1.562
Set forms and pour walls, pumped, 12"T x 84"H, unreinforced	LF	$98.50	$37.44	$135.94	**$227.02**	1.822
Set forms and pour walls, pumped, 12"T x 96"H, unreinforced	LF	$112.61	$42.79	$155.40	**$259.52**	2.083

Concrete

Concrete Wall, Sectional Forms, Reinforced

> No footing or excavation included in price.

Description	Unit	Direct Labor	Direct Materials	Direct Total	Selling Price	Man-hours
CONCRETE WALL BY CHUTE, REINFORCED, 8" THICK						
Set forms and pour walls by chute, 8"T x 24"H, reinforced #3 24"oc	LF	$18.76	$9.91	$28.67	**$47.88**	0.347
Set forms and pour walls by chute, 8"T x 36"H, reinforced #3 24"oc	LF	$28.65	$14.87	$43.52	**$72.68**	0.530
Set forms and pour walls by chute, 8"T x 48"H, reinforced #3 24"oc	LF	$38.22	$19.82	$58.05	**$96.94**	0.707
Set forms and pour walls by chute, 8"T x 60"H, reinforced #3 24"oc	LF	$47.74	$24.78	$72.52	**$121.11**	0.883
Set forms and pour walls by chute, 8"T x 72"H, reinforced #3 24"oc	LF	$57.31	$29.74	$87.04	**$145.36**	1.060
Set forms and pour walls by chute, 8"T x 84"H, reinforced #3 24"oc	LF	$66.88	$34.69	$101.57	**$169.62**	1.237
Set forms and pour walls by chute, 8"T x 96"H, reinforced #3 24"oc	LF	$76.39	$39.65	$116.04	**$193.79**	1.413
CONCRETE WALL BY CHUTE, REINFORCED, 10" THICK						
Set forms and pour walls by chute, 10"T x 24"H, reinforced #3 24"oc	LF	$19.19	$11.61	$30.80	**$51.44**	0.355
Set forms and pour walls by chute, 10"T x 36"H, reinforced #3 24"oc	LF	$29.52	$17.42	$46.94	**$78.38**	0.546
Set forms and pour walls by chute, 10"T x 48"H, reinforced #3 24"oc	LF	$39.30	$23.22	$62.53	**$104.42**	0.727
Set forms and pour walls by chute, 10"T x 60"H, reinforced #3 24"oc	LF	$49.14	$29.03	$78.17	**$130.55**	0.909
Set forms and pour walls by chute, 10"T x 72"H, reinforced #3 24"oc	LF	$58.98	$34.84	$93.82	**$156.68**	1.091
Set forms and pour walls by chute, 10"T x 84"H, reinforced #3 24"oc	LF	$68.82	$40.64	$109.46	**$182.81**	1.273
Set forms and pour walls by chute, 10"T x 96"H, reinforced #3 24"oc	LF	$78.66	$46.45	$125.11	**$208.93**	1.455
CONCRETE WALL BY CHUTE, REINFORCED, 12" THICK						
Set forms and pour walls by chute, 12"T x 24"H, reinforced #3 24"oc	LF	$19.68	$13.31	$32.99	**$55.09**	0.364
Set forms and pour walls by chute, 12"T x 36"H, reinforced #3 24"oc	LF	$30.33	$19.97	$50.30	**$84.00**	0.561
Set forms and pour walls by chute, 12"T x 48"H, reinforced #3 24"oc	LF	$40.44	$26.62	$67.06	**$111.99**	0.748
Set forms and pour walls by chute, 12"T x 60"H, reinforced #3 24"oc	LF	$50.55	$33.28	$83.83	**$139.99**	0.935
Set forms and pour walls by chute, 12"T x 72"H, reinforced #3 24"oc	LF	$60.66	$39.93	$100.59	**$167.99**	1.122
Set forms and pour walls by chute, 12"T x 84"H, reinforced #3 24"oc	LF	$70.82	$46.59	$117.41	**$196.08**	1.310
Set forms and pour walls by chute, 12"T x 96"H, reinforced #3 24"oc	LF	$80.93	$53.25	$134.18	**$224.08**	1.497

Concrete

Concrete Wall, Sectional, Reinforced (cont.)

> No footing or excavation included in price.

Description	Unit	Direct Labor	Direct Materials	Direct Total	Selling Price	Man-hours
CONCRETE WALL WHEELED BY HAND, REINFORCED, 8" THICK						
Set forms and pour walls, wheeled, 8"T x 24"H, reinforced #3 24"oc	LF	$23.09	$9.91	$33.00	**$55.11**	0.427
Set forms and pour walls, wheeled, 8"T x 36"H, reinforced #3 24"oc	LF	$35.41	$14.87	$50.28	**$83.97**	0.655
Set forms and pour walls, wheeled, 8"T x 48"H, reinforced #3 24"oc	LF	$47.20	$19.82	$67.02	**$111.93**	0.873
Set forms and pour walls, wheeled, 8"T x 60"H, reinforced #3 24"oc	LF	$58.98	$24.78	$83.76	**$139.89**	1.091
Set forms and pour walls, wheeled, 8"T x 72"H, reinforced #3 24"oc	LF	$70.77	$29.74	$100.51	**$167.85**	1.309
Set forms and pour walls, wheeled, 8"T x 84"H, reinforced #3 24"oc	LF	$82.61	$34.69	$117.30	**$195.89**	1.528
Set forms and pour walls, wheeled, 8"T x 96"H, reinforced #3 24"oc	LF	$94.39	$39.65	$134.04	**$223.85**	1.746
CONCRETE WALL WHEELED BY HAND, REINFORCED, 10" THICK						
Set forms and pour walls, wheeled, 10"T x 24"H, reinforced #3 24"oc	LF	$24.49	$11.61	$36.10	**$60.29**	0.453
Set forms and pour walls, wheeled, 10"T x 36"H, reinforced #3 24"oc	LF	$37.68	$17.42	$55.10	**$92.02**	0.697
Set forms and pour walls, wheeled, 10"T x 48"H, reinforced #3 24"oc	LF	$50.23	$23.22	$73.45	**$122.66**	0.929
Set forms and pour walls, wheeled, 10"T x 60"H, reinforced #3 24"oc	LF	$62.77	$29.03	$91.80	**$153.30**	1.161
Set forms and pour walls, wheeled, 10"T x 72"H, reinforced #3 24"oc	LF	$75.31	$34.84	$110.15	**$183.94**	1.393
Set forms and pour walls, wheeled, 10"T x 84"H, reinforced #3 24"oc	LF	$87.85	$40.64	$128.49	**$214.59**	1.625
Set forms and pour walls, wheeled, 10"T x 96"H, reinforced #3 24"oc	LF	$100.40	$46.45	$146.84	**$245.23**	1.857
CONCRETE WALL WHEELED BY HAND, REINFORCED, 12" THICK						
Set forms and pour walls, wheeled, 12"T x 24"H, reinforced #3 24"oc	LF	$26.22	$13.31	$39.53	**$66.02**	0.485
Set forms and pour walls, wheeled, 12"T x 36"H, reinforced #3 24"oc	LF	$40.44	$19.97	$60.41	**$100.88**	0.748
Set forms and pour walls, wheeled, 12"T x 48"H, reinforced #3 24"oc	LF	$53.96	$26.62	$80.58	**$134.57**	0.998
Set forms and pour walls, wheeled, 12"T x 60"H, reinforced #3 24"oc	LF	$68.61	$33.28	$101.89	**$170.15**	1.269
Set forms and pour walls, wheeled, 12"T x 72"H, reinforced #3 24"oc	LF	$80.93	$39.93	$120.87	**$201.85**	1.497
Set forms and pour walls, wheeled, 12"T x 84"H, reinforced #3 24"oc	LF	$94.39	$46.59	$140.99	**$235.45**	1.746
Set forms and pour walls, wheeled, 12"T x 96"H, reinforced #3 24"oc	LF	$107.91	$53.25	$161.16	**$269.13**	1.996

Concrete

Concrete Wall, Sectional, Reinforced (cont.)

> No footing or excavation included in price.

Description	Unit	Direct Labor	Direct Materials	Direct Total	Selling Price	Man-hours
CONCRETE WALL PUMPED, REINFORCED, 8" THICK						
Set forms and pour walls, pumped, 8"T x 24"H, reinforced #3 24"oc	LF	$24.98	$9.91	$34.89	**$58.27**	0.462
Set forms and pour walls, pumped, 8"T x 36"H, reinforced #3 24"oc	LF	$38.22	$14.87	$53.09	**$88.66**	0.707
Set forms and pour walls, pumped, 8"T x 48"H, reinforced #3 24"oc	LF	$50.98	$19.82	$70.81	**$118.25**	0.943
Set forms and pour walls, pumped, 8"T x 60"H, reinforced #3 24"oc	LF	$63.69	$24.78	$88.47	**$147.74**	1.178
Set forms and pour walls, pumped, 8"T x 72"H, reinforced #3 24"oc	LF	$76.45	$29.74	$106.18	**$177.33**	1.414
Set forms and pour walls, pumped, 8"T x 84"H, reinforced #3 24"oc	LF	$89.20	$34.69	$123.90	**$206.91**	1.650
Set forms and pour walls, pumped, 8"T x 96"H, reinforced #3 24"oc	LF	$101.91	$39.65	$141.56	**$236.40**	1.885
CONCRETE WALL PUMPED, REINFORCED, 10" THICK						
Set forms and pour walls, pumped, 10"T x 24"H, reinforced #3 24"oc	LF	$26.44	$11.61	$38.05	**$63.54**	0.489
Set forms and pour walls, pumped, 10"T x 36"H, reinforced #3 24"oc	LF	$40.66	$17.41	$58.07	**$96.97**	0.752
Set forms and pour walls, pumped, 10"T x 48"H, reinforced #3 24"oc	LF	$54.23	$23.22	$77.45	**$129.34**	1.003
Set forms and pour walls, pumped, 10"T x 60"H, reinforced #3 24"oc	LF	$67.80	$29.03	$96.83	**$161.70**	1.254
Set forms and pour walls, pumped, 10"T x 72"H, reinforced #3 24"oc	LF	$81.31	$34.84	$116.15	**$193.97**	1.504
Set forms and pour walls, pumped, 10"T x 84"H, reinforced #3 24"oc	LF	$94.88	$40.64	$135.52	**$226.32**	1.755
Set forms and pour walls, pumped, 10"T x 96"H, reinforced #3 24"oc	LF	$108.45	$46.45	$154.90	**$258.68**	2.006
CONCRETE WALL PUMPED, REINFORCED, 12" THICK						
Set forms and pour walls, pumped, 12"T x 24"H, reinforced #3 24"oc	LF	$28.33	$13.31	$41.64	**$69.54**	0.524
Set forms and pour walls, pumped, 12"T x 36"H, reinforced #3 24"oc	LF	$43.68	$19.97	$63.65	**$106.30**	0.808
Set forms and pour walls, pumped, 12"T x 48"H, reinforced #3 24"oc	LF	$58.23	$26.62	$84.85	**$141.70**	1.077
Set forms and pour walls, pumped, 12"T x 60"H, reinforced #3 24"oc	LF	$74.07	$33.28	$107.35	**$179.27**	1.370
Set forms and pour walls, pumped, 12"T x 72"H, reinforced #3 24"oc	LF	$87.37	$39.93	$127.30	**$212.59**	1.616
Set forms and pour walls, pumped, 12"T x 84"H, reinforced #3 24"oc	LF	$101.96	$46.59	$148.55	**$248.09**	1.886
Set forms and pour walls, pumped, 12"T x 96"H, reinforced #3 24"oc	LF	$116.51	$53.25	$169.75	**$283.49**	2.155

Concrete

Driveways and Sidewalks

> No excavation included in price.

Description	Unit	Direct Labor	Direct Materials	Direct Total	Selling Price	Man-hours
CONCRETE DRIVEWAY						
Pour driveway slab, 3" thick, unreinforced, no excavation included	SF	$2.27	$2.15	$4.42	**$7.38**	0.042
Pour driveway slab, 4" thick, unreinforced, no excavation included	SF	$2.49	$2.62	$5.10	**$8.52**	0.046
Pour driveway slab, 6" thick, unreinforced, no excavation included	SF	$2.81	$3.55	$6.37	**$10.63**	0.052
Pour driveway slab, 3" thick, reinforced with wire mesh, no excavation	SF	$2.43	$2.45	$4.88	**$8.15**	0.045
Pour driveway slab, 4" thick, reinforced with wire mesh, no excavation	SF	$2.60	$2.91	$5.51	**$9.20**	0.048
Pour driveway slab, 6" thick, reinforced with wire mesh, no excavation	SF	$2.97	$4.09	$7.06	**$11.79**	0.055
Pour driveway apron, 4" thick, unreinforced, no excavation included	SF	$3.30	$2.61	$5.91	**$9.87**	0.061
Pour driveway apron, 4" thick, reinforced with wire mesh, no excavation	SF	$3.51	$2.91	$6.43	**$10.73**	0.065
ASPHALT DRIVEWAY						
Lay asphalt driveway, 6" stone base, 3" asphalt, no excavation included	SF	$1.97	$1.60	$3.56	**$5.95**	0.027
Lay asphalt driveway, 4" stone base, 2" asphalt, no excavation included	SF	$1.75	$1.16	$2.90	**$4.85**	0.024
CONCRETE SIDEWALK						
Pour concrete sidewalk, 4" thick, unreinforced, no excavation included	SF	$2.97	$2.62	$5.59	**$9.34**	0.055

Reinforcing

Description	Unit	Direct Labor	Direct Materials	Direct Total	Selling Price	Man-hours
STEEL BAR						
Place two #3 (3/8") steel rods to reinforce concrete footing	LF	$0.65	$0.62	$1.27	**$2.12**	0.012
Place two #4 (1/2") steel rods to reinforce concrete footing	LF	$0.70	$0.71	$1.42	**$2.36**	0.013
Place two #5 (5/8") steel rods to reinforce concrete footing	LF	$0.76	$0.94	$1.70	**$2.84**	0.014
Place three #3 (3/8") steel rods to reinforce concrete footing	LF	$0.87	$0.93	$1.80	**$3.00**	0.016
Place three #4 (1/2") steel rods to reinforce concrete footing	LF	$0.87	$1.07	$1.93	**$3.23**	0.016
Place three #5 (5/8") steel rods to reinforce concrete footing	LF	$0.92	$1.41	$2.33	**$3.90**	0.017
Place #3 (3/8") steel rods, 24"oc, to reinforce concrete wall	SF	$0.43	$0.62	$1.05	**$1.76**	0.008
Drill 6" deep into block foundation wall, install #4 (1/2") steel rod	EA	$7.79	$0.36	$8.14	**$13.60**	0.144
Drill 6" deep into brick foundation wall, install #4 (1/2") steel rod	EA	$8.81	$0.36	$9.17	**$15.31**	0.163
Drill 6" deep into concrete foundation wall, install #4 (1/2") steel rod	EA	$10.70	$0.36	$11.06	**$18.47**	0.198
STEEL MESH						
Place 6x6/10-10 wire mesh to reinforce concrete slab	SF	$0.11	$0.37	$0.48	**$0.80**	0.002
Place 6x6/6-6 wire mesh to reinforce concrete slab	SF	$0.16	$0.60	$0.77	**$1.28**	0.003

7

Concrete

Forms

Description	Unit	Direct Labor	Direct Materials	Direct Total	Selling Price	Man-hours
FORM, 1 TIME USE						
Place and wreck 2" x 4" forms for concrete work, 1 time use	LF	$1.46	$0.37	$1.83	**$3.06**	0.027
Place and wreck 2" x 6" forms for concrete work, 1 time use	LF	$1.73	$0.60	$2.33	**$3.90**	0.032
Place and wreck 2" x 8" forms for concrete work, 1 time use	LF	$2.00	$0.81	$2.81	**$4.70**	0.037
Place and wreck 2" x 12" forms for concrete work, 1 time use	LF	$2.27	$1.37	$3.64	**$6.08**	0.042
FORM, 3 TIME USE						
Place, wreck and clean 2" x 4" forms for concrete work, 3 time use	LF	$1.73	$0.16	$1.89	**$3.16**	0.032
Place, wreck and clean 2" x 6" forms for concrete work, 3 time use	LF	$2.00	$0.22	$2.22	**$3.71**	0.037
Place, wreck and clean 2" x 8" forms for concrete work, 3 time use	LF	$2.27	$0.30	$2.57	**$4.30**	0.042
Place, wreck and clean 2" x 12" forms for concrete work, 3 time use	LF	$2.54	$0.52	$3.06	**$5.12**	0.047
FORM, 6 TIME USE						
Place, wreck and clean 2" x 4" forms for concrete work, 6 time use	LF	$1.73	$0.09	$1.82	**$3.04**	0.032
Place, wreck and clean 2" x 6" forms for concrete work, 6 time use	LF	$2.00	$0.14	$2.14	**$3.57**	0.037
Place, wreck and clean 2" x 8" forms for concrete work, 6 time use	LF	$2.27	$0.19	$2.46	**$4.10**	0.042
Place, wreck and clean 2" x 12" forms for concrete work, 6 time use	LF	$2.54	$0.31	$2.85	**$4.77**	0.047

Concrete Cutting and Drilling

Description	Unit	Direct Labor	Direct Materials	Direct Total	Selling Price	Man-hours
CONCRETE CUTTING						
Foundation wall sawing, 8" thick	LF	$43.68		$43.68	**$72.95**	0.808
Foundation wall sawing, 10" thick	LF	$54.55		$54.55	**$91.10**	1.009
Foundation wall sawing, 12" thick	LF	$65.47		$65.47	**$109.34**	1.211
Concrete floor sawing, 4" thick	LF	$14.54		$14.54	**$24.29**	0.269
Concrete floor sawing, 6" thick	LF	$21.84		$21.84	**$36.48**	0.404
CONCRETE DRILLING						
Concrete core drilling, 1" diameter, 1" deep	EA	$5.46		$5.46	**$9.12**	0.101
Concrete core drilling, 2" diameter, 1" deep	EA	$8.16		$8.16	**$13.63**	0.151
Concrete core drilling, 3" diameter, 1" deep	EA	$10.92		$10.92	**$18.24**	0.202
Concrete core drilling, 4" diameter, 1" deep	EA	$13.62		$13.62	**$22.75**	0.252

Concrete

Concrete Finishes

Description	Unit	Direct Labor	Direct Materials	Direct Total	Selling Price	Man-hours
Surface sealer, silicon	SF	$0.50	$0.16	$0.66	**$1.11**	0.009
Epoxy finish, 1 coat with brush over concrete floor	SF	$0.45	$0.32	$0.77	**$1.28**	0.008
Epoxy finish, 2 coats with brush over concrete floor	SF	$0.84	$0.56	$1.39	**$2.32**	0.015
Epoxy finish, 1 coat with roller over concrete floor	SF	$0.39	$0.32	$0.71	**$1.19**	0.007
Epoxy finish, 2 coats with roller over concrete floor	SF	$0.67	$0.56	$1.22	**$2.05**	0.012
Epoxy finish, 1 coat with spray over concrete floor	SF	$0.22	$0.37	$0.60	**$1.00**	0.004
Epoxy finish, 2 coats with spray over concrete floor	SF	$0.39	$0.62	$1.01	**$1.69**	0.007
Non-slip aluminum oxide finish on concrete	SF	$0.61	$0.30	$0.91	**$1.52**	0.011
Apply overlay top coat, stamp polymer-modified concrete with pattern	SF	$7.30	$1.93	$9.22	**$15.41**	0.135
Stamp new concrete with finish	SF	$2.92	$0.00	$2.92	**$4.88**	0.054
Exposed aggregate finish	SF	$1.68	$0.27	$1.94	**$3.25**	0.031

Repair and Alteration

Description	Unit	Direct Labor	Direct Materials	Direct Total	Selling Price	Man-hours
Concrete epoxy patch repair	SF	$11.19	$6.42	$17.61	**$29.41**	0.207
Concrete epoxy crack repair	LF	$5.08	$3.21	$8.29	**$13.85**	0.094
Concrete edge repair	LF	$18.17	$2.14	$20.31	**$33.91**	0.336
Asphalt driveway crack repair	LF	$2.03	$0.43	$2.45	**$4.10**	0.050
Asphalt driveway cold-mix patch	SF	$10.13	$2.41	$12.53	**$20.93**	0.250
Asphalt driveway seal, 1coat	SF	$0.57	$0.21	$0.78	**$1.30**	0.014
Asphalt overlay 1-1/2" thick	SF	$0.95	$0.86	$1.80	**$3.01**	0.013
Asphalt cutting	LF	$2.16		$2.16	**$3.61**	0.040

Masonry

Concrete Block Wall

> No footing included in price.

Description	Unit	Direct Labor	Direct Materials	Direct Total	Selling Price	Man-hours
CONCRETE BLOCK WALL, STANDARD WEIGHT, REINFORCED						
Construct concrete block wall, 4"W x 8"H x 16"L, standard, reinforced	SF	$6.89	$2.91	$9.80	**$16.37**	0.104
Construct concrete block wall, 6"W x 8"H x 16"L, standard, reinforced	SF	$7.55	$3.19	$10.74	**$17.93**	0.114
Construct concrete block wall, 8"W x 8"H x 16"L, standard, reinforced	SF	$8.21	$3.43	$11.64	**$19.44**	0.124
Construct concrete block wall, 10"W x 8"H x 16"L, standard, reinforced	SF	$9.01	$3.68	$12.69	**$21.19**	0.136
Construct concrete block wall, 12"W x 8"H x 16"L, standard, reinforced	SF	$9.87	$3.85	$13.72	**$22.91**	0.149
CONCRETE BLOCK WALL, STANDARD WEIGHT, UNREINFORCED						
Construct concr block wall, 4"W x 8"H x 16"L, standard, unreinforced	SF	$6.29	$2.42	$8.71	**$14.55**	0.095
Construct concr block wall, 6"W x 8"H x 16"L, standard, unreinforced	SF	$6.95	$2.70	$9.65	**$16.12**	0.105
Construct concr block wall, 8"W x 8"H x 16"L, standard, unreinforced	SF	$7.61	$2.94	$10.55	**$17.62**	0.115
Construct concr block wall, 10"W x 8"H x 16"L, standard, unreinforced	SF	$8.41	$3.19	$11.60	**$19.37**	0.127
Construct concr block wall, 12"W x 8"H x 16"L, standard, unreinforced	SF	$9.27	$3.36	$12.63	**$21.09**	0.140
CONCRETE BLOCK WALL, LIGHTWEIGHT, REINFORCED						
Construct concrete block wall, 4"W x 8"H x 16"L, lightweight, reinforced	SF	$6.22	$2.74	$8.96	**$14.97**	0.094
Construct concrete block wall, 6"W x 8"H x 16"L, lightweight, reinforced	SF	$6.75	$3.01	$9.77	**$16.31**	0.102
Construct concrete block wall, 8"W x 8"H x 16"L, lightweight, reinforced	SF	$7.22	$3.25	$10.47	**$17.49**	0.109
Construct concrete block wall, 10"W x 8"H x 16"L, lightweight, reinforced	SF	$7.81	$3.51	$11.32	**$18.90**	0.118
Construct concrete block wall, 12"W x 8"H x 16"L, lightweight, reinforced	SF	$8.41	$3.67	$12.08	**$20.18**	0.127
CONCRETE BLOCK WALL, LIGHTWEIGHT, UNREINFORCED						
Construct concr block wall, 4"W x 8"H x 16"L, lightweight, unreinforced	SF	$5.63	$2.25	$7.88	**$13.15**	0.085
Construct concr block wall, 6"W x 8"H x 16"L, lightweight, unreinforced	SF	$6.16	$2.52	$8.68	**$14.50**	0.093
Construct concr block wall, 8"W x 8"H x 16"L, lightweight, unreinforced	SF	$6.69	$2.76	$9.45	**$15.78**	0.101
Construct concr block wall, 10"W x 8"H x 16"L, lightweight, unreinforced	SF	$7.22	$3.01	$10.23	**$17.09**	0.109
Construct concr block wall, 12"W x 8"H x 16"L, lightweight, unreinforced	SF	$7.81	$3.18	$10.99	**$18.35**	0.118

Description	Unit	Direct Labor	Direct Materials	Direct Total	Selling Price	Man-hours
CONCRETE SLUMP BLOCK WALL						
Construct concrete slump block wall, 6" x 4"x 16	SF	$7.68	$3.23	$10.91	**$18.22**	0.116
Construct concrete slump block wall, 6" x 6" x 16"	SF	$6.89	$3.02	$9.91	**$16.55**	0.104
Construct concrete slump block wall, 8" x 4" x 16"	SF	$8.01	$3.51	$11.52	**$19.25**	0.121
Construct concrete slump block wall, 8" x 6" x 16"	SF	$7.08	$3.30	$10.39	**$17.35**	0.107
Construct concrete slump block wall, 12" x 4" x 16"	SF	$8.81	$4.22	$13.02	**$21.75**	0.133
Construct concrete slump block wall, 12" x 6" x 16"	SF	$7.68	$4.00	$11.69	**$19.52**	0.116
DRAINPIPE						
Lay 4" plastic drainpipe in gravel, no excavation included	LF	$3.84	$1.93	$5.77	**$9.63**	0.058
SCAFFOLDING						
Additional charge for work above 1 story, per SF of work above 1 story	SF	$1.72		$1.72	**$2.88**	0.026

8

Masonry

Brick Wall

> No footing included in price.

Description	Unit	Direct Labor	Direct Materials	Direct Total	Selling Price	Man-hours
STANDARD BRICK WALL						
Construct standard brick wall (4x2-2/3x8), 4" thick	SF	$12.12	$3.66	$15.77	**$26.34**	0.183
Construct standard brick wall (4x2-2/3x8), 8" thick	SF	$22.31	$7.31	$29.62	**$49.47**	0.337
Construct standard brick wall (4x2-2/3x8), 12" thick	SF	$32.38	$10.97	$43.34	**$72.39**	0.489
ADOBE BRICK WALL						
Construct adobe brick wall, 4" x 4" x 16"	SF	$8.01	$1.85	$9.86	**$16.47**	0.121
Construct adobe brick wall, 6" x 4" x 16"	SF	$8.41	$2.68	$11.08	**$18.51**	0.127
Construct adobe brick wall, 8" x 4" x 16"	SF	$8.81	$3.58	$12.39	**$20.69**	0.133
Construct adobe brick wall, 12" x 4" x 16"	SF	$9.73	$5.18	$14.91	**$24.90**	0.147
CONCRETE SLUMP BRICK WALL						
Construct concrete slump brick wall, 4" x 4" x 8"	SF	$8.41	$6.06	$14.47	**$24.17**	0.127
Construct concrete slump brick wall, 4" x 4" x 12"	SF	$7.68	$5.82	$13.50	**$22.54**	0.116
DRAINPIPE						
Lay 4" plastic drainpipe in gravel, no excavation included	LF	$3.84	$1.93	$5.77	**$9.63**	0.058
SCAFFOLDING						
Additional charge for work above 1 story, per SF of work above 1 story	SF	$2.45		$2.45	**$4.09**	0.037

Brick and Block Wall

> No footing included in price.

Description	Unit	Direct Labor	Direct Materials	Direct Total	Selling Price	Man-hours
BRICK AND BLOCK WALL, UNREINFORCED						
Construct standard brick (4x2-2/3x8) & 4" block wall	SF	$19.00	$5.09	$24.10	**$40.24**	0.287
Construct standard brick (4x2-2/3x8) & 8" block wall	SF	$20.33	$5.40	$25.73	**$42.97**	0.307
BRICK AND BLOCK WALL, REINFORCED						
Construct standard brick (4x2-2/3x8) & 4" block wall, laterally reinforced	SF	$19.60	$5.49	$25.09	**$41.90**	0.296
Construct standard brick (4x2-2/3x8) & 8" block wall, laterally reinforced	SF	$20.92	$5.80	$26.72	**$44.63**	0.316
DRAINPIPE						
Lay 4" plastic drainpipe in gravel, no excavation included	LF	$3.84	$1.93	$5.77	**$9.63**	0.058
SCAFFOLDING						
Additional charge for work above 1 story, per SF of work above 1 story	SF	$2.45		$2.45	**$4.09**	0.037

Masonry

Brick Column

> No footing included in price.

Description	Unit	Direct Labor	Direct Materials	Direct Total	Selling Price	Man-hours
BRICK COLUMN						
Construct standard brick column, 12" x 12", solid interior	LF	$32.38	$10.97	$43.34	**$72.39**	0.489
Construct standard brick column, 16" x 12", solid interior	LF	$43.11	$14.59	$57.69	**$96.35**	0.651
Construct standard brick column, 20" x 12", solid interior	LF	$53.77	$18.20	$71.97	**$120.19**	0.812
Construct standard brick column, 24" x 12", solid interior	LF	$64.82	$21.93	$86.76	**$144.88**	0.979
Construct standard brick column, 16" x 16", solid interior	LF	$57.34	$19.40	$76.74	**$128.16**	0.866
Construct standard brick column, 20" x 16", solid interior	LF	$71.51	$24.21	$95.72	**$159.85**	1.080
Construct standard brick column, 24" x 16", solid interior	LF	$84.22	$29.17	$113.39	**$189.37**	1.272
Construct standard brick column, 28" x 16", solid interior	LF	$100.78	$34.10	$134.88	**$225.25**	1.522
Construct standard brick column, 20" x 20", solid interior	LF	$71.64	$24.25	$95.89	**$160.14**	1.082
Construct standard brick column, 24" x 20", solid interior	LF	$89.39	$30.26	$119.65	**$199.82**	1.350
Construct standard brick column, 28" x 20", solid interior	LF	$105.28	$36.46	$141.74	**$236.71**	1.590
Construct standard brick column, 32" x 20", solid interior	LF	$126.01	$42.63	$168.63	**$281.62**	1.903
Construct standard brick column, 24" x 24", solid interior	LF	$107.33	$36.31	$143.65	**$239.89**	1.621
Construct standard brick column, 28" x 24", solid interior	LF	$126.34	$43.75	$170.09	**$284.05**	1.908
Construct standard brick column, 32" x 24", solid interior	LF	$151.17	$51.15	$202.32	**$337.88**	2.283
Construct standard brick column, 36" x 24", solid interior	LF	$194.40	$65.80	$260.20	**$434.54**	2.936
SCAFFOLDING						
Additional charge for work above 1 story, per LF of work above 1 story	LF	$15.89		$15.89	**$26.54**	0.240

Block Column

> No footing included in price.

Description	Unit	Direct Labor	Direct Materials	Direct Total	Selling Price	Man-hours
BLOCK COLUMN						
Construct 16"x16" block column	LF	$40.13	$9.80	$49.93	**$83.38**	0.606
Construct 24"x24" block column	LF	$91.04	$19.61	$110.65	**$184.79**	1.375
Construct 32"x24" block column	LF	$120.44	$29.41	$149.85	**$250.25**	1.819
SCAFFOLDING						
Additional charge for work above 1 story, per LF of work above 1 story	LF	$15.89		$15.89	**$26.54**	0.240

Masonry

Brick Veneer

> Laid against existing wall or backer.

Description	Unit	Direct Labor	Direct Materials	Direct Total	Selling Price	Man-hours
Lay brick veneer, standard size (4x2-2/3x8)	SF	$12.12	$3.65	$15.77	**$26.34**	0.183
Lay brick veneer, economy size (4x4x8)	SF	$8.48	$2.84	$11.32	**$18.90**	0.128
Lay brick veneer, engineer size (4x3-1/5x8)	SF	$10.06	$4.21	$14.28	**$23.85**	0.152
Lay brick veneer, 6-inch jumbo size (6x4x12)	SF	$6.09	$4.47	$10.56	**$17.63**	0.092
Lay brick veneer, Norman size (4x2-2/3x12)	SF	$8.21	$3.63	$11.84	**$19.78**	0.124
Lay brick veneer, Norwegian size (4x3-1/5x12)	SF	$7.15	$2.84	$9.99	**$16.69**	0.108
Lay brick veneer, roman size (4x2x12)	SF	$10.66	$4.92	$15.58	**$26.01**	0.161
Lay brick veneer, SCR size (6x2-2/3x12)	SF	$8.48	$4.23	$12.70	**$21.21**	0.128
Lay brick veneer, utility size (4x4x12)	SF	$5.89	$3.31	$9.21	**$15.38**	0.089
Lay brick veneer, padre size (4x3x7-1/2)	SF	$9.40	$5.31	$14.71	**$24.57**	0.142
Lay brick veneer, large padre size (4x3x11-1/2)	SF	$8.21	$5.06	$13.27	**$22.16**	0.124
SCAFFOLDING						
Additional charge for work above 1 story, per SF of work above 1 story	SF	$1.99		$1.99	**$3.32**	0.030

Stone Veneer

Description	Unit	Direct Labor	Direct Materials	Direct Total	Selling Price	Man-hours
Install stone cast panels, 48" x 1/2" x 8', on existing structure/backer	SF	$4.17	$7.47	$11.64	**$19.44**	0.063
Install natural stone veneer, on existing structure/backer	SF	$27.41	$11.13	$38.54	**$64.37**	0.414
Install manufactured stone veneer, on existing structure/backer	SF	$15.49	$7.83	$23.33	**$38.95**	0.234

Stucco

Description	Unit	Direct Labor	Direct Materials	Direct Total	Selling Price	Man-hours
Install galvanized netting for stucco, 18 gauge, 15 lb felt	SF	$1.26	$0.69	$1.95	**$3.25**	0.019
Install Steel-Tex mesh for stucco, 15 lb felt	SF	$0.93	$1.14	$2.07	**$3.45**	0.014
Apply stucco over exterior masonry wall, 1 coat with float finish	SF	$3.64	$0.32	$3.96	**$6.62**	0.055
Apply stucco over exterior masonry wall, 2 coat with float finish	SF	$5.96	$0.54	$6.49	**$10.85**	0.090
Apply stucco over metal netting on exterior wall, 2 coat with float finish	SF	$6.95	$0.80	$7.75	**$12.95**	0.105
Apply stucco over metal netting on exterior wall, 3 coat with float finish	SF	$9.93	$1.28	$11.22	**$18.73**	0.150
Install 1" polystyrene board on existing surface, apply synthetic stucco	SF	$10.53	$3.16	$13.68	**$22.85**	0.159
Install 2" polystyrene board on existing surface, apply synthetic stucco	SF	$10.93	$3.53	$14.46	**$24.14**	0.165
Apply synthetic stucco to exterior masonry wall	SF	$7.55	$1.61	$9.15	**$15.29**	0.114
SCAFFOLDING						
Additional charge for work above 1 story, per SF of work above 1 story	SF	$1.72		$1.72	**$2.88**	0.026

Masonry

Chimneys

Description	Unit	Direct Labor	Direct Materials	Direct Total	Selling Price	Man-hours
BRICK CHIMNEY						
Construct 16" x 16" standard brick chimney, one 8" x 8" flue	LF	$94.36	$19.41	$113.76	**$189.98**	1.425
Construct 24" x 24" standard brick chimney, one 8" x 8" flue	LF	$159.64	$43.86	$203.51	**$339.86**	2.411
Construct 28" x 16" standard brick chimney, two 8" x 8" flues	LF	$123.16	$34.10	$157.26	**$262.63**	1.860
Construct 36" x 24" standard brick chimney, two 8" x 8" flues	LF	$226.12	$65.80	$291.92	**$487.50**	3.415
Construct 20" x 16" standard brick chimney, one 12" x 8" flue	LF	$102.57	$24.34	$126.91	**$211.94**	1.549
Construct 28" x 24" standard brick chimney, one 12" x 8" flue	LF	$175.34	$51.10	$226.44	**$378.15**	2.648
Construct 36" x 16" standard brick chimney, two 12" x 8" flues	LF	$139.18	$43.86	$183.05	**$305.69**	2.102
Construct 44" x 24" standard brick chimney, two 12" x 8" flues	LF	$260.09	$80.39	$340.47	**$568.59**	3.928
Construct 20" x 20" standard brick chimney, one 12" x 12" flue	LF	$110.64	$30.37	$141.02	**$235.50**	1.671
Construct 28" x 28" standard brick chimney, one 12" x 12" flue	LF	$191.03	$54.42	$245.44	**$409.89**	2.885
Construct 36" x 20" standard brick chimney, two 12" x 12" flues	LF	$152.89	$59.66	$212.55	**$354.95**	2.309
Construct 44" x 28" standard brick chimney, two 12" x 12" flues	LF	$264.06	$93.76	$357.82	**$597.56**	3.988
BLOCK CHIMNEY						
Construct block chimney, 8" x 8" flue	LF	$57.61	$13.70	$71.31	**$119.09**	0.870
Construct block chimney, 8" x 12" flue	LF	$64.56	$16.67	$81.23	**$135.65**	0.975
Construct block chimney, 12" x 12" flue	LF	$71.45	$19.64	$91.08	**$152.11**	1.079
SCAFFOLDING						
Additional charge for work above 1 story, per LF of work above 1 story	LF	$27.81		$27.81	**$46.44**	0.420

Fireplace

Description	Unit	Direct Labor	Direct Materials	Direct Total	Selling Price	Man-hours
Construct new brick fireplace, 36"W x 32"H x 18"D, chimney not included	EA	$2,118.85	$664.62	$2,783.47	**$4,648.39**	32.000
Construct new brick fireplace, 38"W x 36"H x 18"D, chimney not included	EA	$2,516.14	$747.69	$3,263.83	**$5,450.60**	38.000
Construct new brick fireplace, 42"W x 36"H x 20"D, chimney not included	EA	$3,112.06	$817.48	$3,929.54	**$6,562.33**	47.000
Construct new brick fireplace, 46"W x 48"H x 22"D, chimney not included	EA	$4,639.96	$1,060.06	$5,700.02	**$9,519.03**	70.075
Install damper in fireplace with no damper	EA	$662.14	$169.40	$831.54	**$1,388.67**	10.000
Face fireplace surround, brick	SF	$27.81	$5.82	$33.63	**$56.15**	0.420
Face fireplace surround, cultured stone	SF	$29.80	$8.80	$38.60	**$64.46**	0.450
Face fireplace surround, natural stone	SF	$51.65	$9.90	$61.55	**$102.78**	0.780
Construct fireplace hearth, brick	SF	$31.78	$8.31	$40.09	**$66.95**	0.480
Construct fireplace hearth, marble	SF	$39.73	$13.20	$52.93	**$88.39**	0.600
Construct fireplace hearth, ceramic tile	SF	$39.73	$24.20	$63.93	**$106.76**	0.600

8

Masonry

Patios and Walkways

Description	Unit	Direct Labor	Direct Materials	Direct Total	Selling Price	Man-hours
CONCRETE PAVERS						
Lay concrete pavers, 6" x 6", in sand on ground	SF	$4.94	$1.58	$6.52	**$10.89**	0.122
Lay concrete pavers, 6" x 6", in concrete bed on existing slab	SF	$9.93	$1.91	$11.84	**$19.78**	0.150
Lay concrete pavers, 6" x 12", in concrete bed on existing slab	SF	$8.74	$1.83	$10.57	**$17.65**	0.132
Lay concrete pavers, 12" x 12", in concrete bed on existing slab	SF	$7.55	$1.74	$9.29	**$15.52**	0.114
Lay concrete pavers, 12" x 18", in concrete bed on existing slab	SF	$6.16	$1.66	$7.82	**$13.06**	0.093
Lay round concrete stepping stones, 12" diameter	EA	$2.96	$3.16	$6.11	**$10.21**	0.073
Lay round concrete stepping stones, 18" diameter	EA	$3.97	$4.32	$8.29	**$13.84**	0.098
Lay round concrete stepping stones, 24" diameter	EA	$5.27	$6.48	$11.75	**$19.62**	0.130
BRICK PAVERS						
Lay standard paving brick, in sand on ground	SF	$5.27	$2.49	$7.76	**$12.96**	0.130
Lay standard paving brick, in concrete bed on existing slab	SF	$10.93	$2.91	$13.83	**$23.10**	0.165
Lay adobe brick paver, 6" x 12", in concrete bed on existing slab	SF	$8.74	$2.70	$11.44	**$19.11**	0.132
Lay adobe brick paver, 12" x 12", in concrete bed on existing slab	SF	$7.55	$2.41	$9.96	**$16.63**	0.114
SLATE AND FLAGSTONE PAVERS						
Lay flagstone, in sand on ground	SF	$9.56	$6.71	$16.27	**$27.17**	0.236
Lay flagstone, in concrete bed on existing slab	SF	$15.49	$7.26	$22.75	**$38.00**	0.234
Lay slate, in sand on ground	SF	$9.56	$8.36	$17.92	**$29.93**	0.236
Lay slate, in concrete bed on existing slab	SF	$15.49	$8.80	$24.29	**$40.57**	0.234

Glass Block

Description	Unit	Direct Labor	Direct Materials	Direct Total	Selling Price	Man-hours
Construct 6" x 6" x 4" thick glass block wall	SF	$35.36	$18.81	$54.17	**$90.46**	0.534
Construct 8" x 8" x 4" thick glass block wall	SF	$24.83	$16.17	$41.00	**$68.47**	0.375
Construct 12" x 12" x 4" thick glass block wall	SF	$15.49	$15.07	$30.56	**$51.04**	0.234
Construct 4" x 8" x 3" thick glass block wall	SF	$33.50	$13.42	$46.92	**$78.36**	0.506
Construct 6" x 8" x 3" thick glass block wall	SF	$28.01	$12.54	$40.55	**$67.72**	0.423

Coatings

Description	Unit	Direct Labor	Direct Materials	Direct Total	Selling Price	Man-hours
Apply waterproof paint, 2 coats	SF	$0.61	$0.18	$0.79	**$1.33**	0.011
Apply silicon paint with sprayer, 1 coat	SF	$0.28	$0.10	$0.37	**$0.63**	0.005
Apply parging, 1/2" thick, 2 coats	SF	$2.38	$0.43	$2.81	**$4.70**	0.036
Apply asphalt coating, 1 coat	SF	$0.65	$0.21	$0.86	**$1.44**	0.016
Apply asphalt coating, 2 coats	SF	$1.13	$0.37	$1.51	**$2.52**	0.028

Floor Framing

Wood Beams

Description	Unit	Direct Labor	Direct Materials	Direct Total	Selling Price	Man-hours
TRADITIONAL WOOD BEAMS, 2" THICK						
Install 2" x 8" single member beams	LF	$2.51	$1.15	$3.66	**$6.11**	0.033
Install 2" x 10" single member beam	LF	$2.59	$1.35	$3.94	**$6.58**	0.034
Install 2" x 12" single member beam	LF	$2.74	$1.93	$4.67	**$7.80**	0.036
TRADITIONAL WOOD BEAMS, 3" THICK						
Install 3" x 8" single member beam	LF	$2.74	$2.53	$5.27	**$8.81**	0.036
Install 3" x 10" single member beam	LF	$2.97	$3.14	$6.11	**$10.20**	0.039
Install 3" x 12" single member beam	LF	$3.20	$3.74	$6.94	**$11.59**	0.042
Install 3" x 14" single member beam	LF	$3.43	$4.52	$7.95	**$13.27**	0.045
TRADITIONAL WOOD BEAMS, 4" THICK						
Install 4" x 8" single member beam	LF	$3.12	$3.07	$6.19	**$10.34**	0.041
Install 4" x 10" single member beam	LF	$3.35	$3.80	$7.15	**$11.94**	0.044
Install 4" x 12" single member beam	LF	$3.65	$4.53	$8.19	**$13.67**	0.048
Install 4" x 14" single member beam	LF	$4.19	$5.51	$9.70	**$16.19**	0.055
TRADITIONAL WOOD BEAMS, 6" THICK						
Install 6" x 8" single member beam	LF	$4.72	$5.92	$10.64	**$17.76**	0.062
Install 6" x 10" single member beam	LF	$5.18	$7.49	$12.66	**$21.15**	0.068
Install 6" x 12" single member beam	LF	$5.56	$9.35	$14.90	**$24.89**	0.073
Install 6" x 14" single member beam	LF	$6.09	$10.88	$16.97	**$28.34**	0.080
TRADITIONAL WOOD BEAMS, MULTI-MEMBER						
Install 4"x8" multi-member wood beam	LF	$3.50	$2.30	$5.80	**$9.69**	0.046
Install 4"x10" multi-member wood beam	LF	$3.73	$2.70	$6.43	**$10.73**	0.049
Install 4"x12" multi-member wood beam	LF	$4.03	$3.86	$7.89	**$13.18**	0.053
Install 6"x8" multi-member wood beam	LF	$5.18	$3.45	$8.63	**$14.41**	0.068
Install 6"x10" multi-member wood beam	LF	$5.56	$4.05	$9.60	**$16.04**	0.073
Install 6"x12" multi-member wood beam	LF	$6.01	$5.79	$11.80	**$19.71**	0.079

Floor Framing

LVL and Glu-Lam Beams

Description	Unit	Direct Labor	Direct Materials	Direct Total	Selling Price	Man-hours
LVL BEAM						
Install LVL wood beam, 1-3/4"x9-1/4"	LF	$4.80	$4.55	$9.34	**$15.60**	0.063
Install LVL wood beam, 1-3/4"x11-7/8"	LF	$5.86	$5.67	$11.53	**$19.26**	0.077
Install LVL wood beam, 1-3/4"x14"	LF	$6.77	$7.02	$13.80	**$23.04**	0.089
Install LVL wood beam, 1-3/4"x16"	LF	$7.54	$7.81	$15.35	**$25.63**	0.099
Install LVL wood beam, two 1-3/4"x9-1/4"	LF	$8.60	$9.61	$18.22	**$30.42**	0.113
Install LVL wood beam, two 1-3/4 x11-7/8"	LF	$10.96	$12.02	$22.98	**$38.38**	0.144
Install LVL wood beam, two 1-3/4"x14"	LF	$13.02	$14.50	$27.51	**$45.95**	0.171
Install LVL wood beam, two 1-3/4"x16"	LF	$14.84	$16.44	$31.28	**$52.24**	0.195
Install LVL wood beam, three 1-3/4"x9-1/4"	LF	$12.41	$14.50	$26.90	**$44.93**	0.163
Install LVL wood beam, three 1-3/4"x11-7/8"	LF	$16.06	$18.05	$34.11	**$56.97**	0.211
Install LVL wood beam, three 1-3/4"x14"	LF	$19.26	$21.15	$40.40	**$67.47**	0.253
Install LVL wood beam, three 1-3/4"x16"	LF	$22.15	$24.33	$46.48	**$77.62**	0.291
GLU-LAM BEAM, 3-1/2" THICK						
Install glu-lam beams 9" deep 3-1/2 thick, 20' long	LF	$9.36	$13.14	$22.50	**$37.57**	0.123
Install glu-lam beams 10-1/2" deep 3-1/2 thick, 20' long	LF	$10.66	$15.23	$25.89	**$43.23**	0.140
Install glu-lam beams 12" deep 3-1/2 thick, 20' long	LF	$11.95	$16.97	$28.92	**$48.30**	0.157
Install glu-lam beams 13-1/2" deep 3-1/2 thick, 20' long	LF	$13.24	$18.83	$32.08	**$53.57**	0.174
Install glu-lam beams 15" deep 3-1/2 thick, 20' long	LF	$14.54	$20.69	$35.23	**$58.84**	0.191
Install glu-lam beams 16-1/2" deep 3-1/2 thick, 20' long	LF	$15.83	$22.55	$38.39	**$64.10**	0.208
Install glu-lam beams 18" deep 3-1/2 thick, 20' long	LF	$16.59	$24.41	$41.01	**$68.48**	0.218
GLU-LAM BEAM, 5-1/4" THICK						
Install glu-lam beams 12" deep 5-1/4 thick, 20' long	LF	$16.67	$20.69	$37.36	**$62.40**	0.219
Install glu-lam beams 13-1/2" deep 5-1/4 thick, 20' long	LF	$19.03	$22.90	$41.93	**$70.02**	0.250
Install glu-lam beams 15" deep 5-1/4 thick, 20' long	LF	$21.08	$25.23	$46.31	**$77.34**	0.277
Install glu-lam beams 16-1/2" deep 5-1/4 thick, 20' long	LF	$23.22	$27.55	$50.77	**$84.78**	0.305
Install glu-lam beams 18" deep 5-1/4 thick, 20' long	LF	$25.27	$29.88	$55.15	**$92.10**	0.332

Floor Framing

Wood Joists

Description	Unit	Direct Labor	Direct Materials	Direct Total	Selling Price	Man-hours
WOOD JOIST, 2" THICK						
Install 2" x 6", 12"oc, floor joists	SF	$2.59	$1.16	$3.75	**$6.26**	0.034
Install 2" x 6", 16"oc, floor joists	SF	$1.98	$0.89	$2.87	**$4.79**	0.026
Install 2" x 6", 24"oc, floor joists	SF	$1.29	$0.61	$1.90	**$3.18**	0.017
Install 2" x 8", 12"oc, floor joists	SF	$2.89	$1.64	$4.53	**$7.56**	0.038
Install 2" x 8", 16"oc, floor joists	SF	$2.21	$1.23	$3.44	**$5.75**	0.029
Install 2" x 8", 24"oc, floor joists	SF	$1.45	$0.84	$2.29	**$3.82**	0.019
Install 2" x 10", 12"oc, floor joists	SF	$3.20	$2.12	$5.32	**$8.89**	0.042
Install 2" x 10", 16"oc, floor joists	SF	$2.44	$1.61	$4.05	**$6.76**	0.032
Install 2" x 10", 24"oc, floor joists	SF	$1.60	$1.10	$2.70	**$4.50**	0.021
Install 2" x 12", 12"oc, floor joists	SF	$3.50	$2.60	$6.10	**$10.19**	0.046
Install 2" x 12", 16"oc, floor joists	SF	$2.59	$1.98	$4.57	**$7.62**	0.034
Install 2" x 12", 24"oc, floor joists	SF	$1.75	$1.34	$3.09	**$5.17**	0.023
WOOD JOIST, 3" THICK						
Install 3" x 8", 12"oc, floor joists	SF	$3.20	$3.27	$6.47	**$10.80**	0.042
Install 3" x 8", 16"oc, floor joists	SF	$2.44	$2.48	$4.91	**$8.21**	0.032
Install 3" x 8", 24"oc, floor joists	SF	$1.60	$1.68	$3.28	**$5.48**	0.021
Install 3" x 10", 12"oc, floor joists	SF	$3.50	$4.08	$7.58	**$12.66**	0.046
Install 3" x 10", 16"oc, floor joists	SF	$2.66	$3.09	$5.75	**$9.61**	0.035
Install 3" x 10", 24"oc, floor joists	SF	$1.75	$2.09	$3.84	**$6.41**	0.023
Install 3" x 12", 12"oc, floor joists	SF	$3.81	$4.89	$8.70	**$14.53**	0.050
Install 3" x 12", 16"oc, floor joists	SF	$2.89	$3.71	$6.60	**$11.03**	0.038
Install 3" x 12", 24"oc, floor joists	SF	$1.90	$2.53	$4.43	**$7.40**	0.025

I - Joists

Description	Unit	Direct Labor	Direct Materials	Direct Total	Selling Price	Man-hours
Install 9-1/2" I-joists, 12"oc	SF	$2.51	$2.16	$4.67	**$7.80**	0.033
Install 9-1/2" I-joists, 16"oc	SF	$2.21	$1.62	$3.82	**$6.39**	0.029
Install 9-1/2" I-joists, 24"oc	SF	$1.75	$1.08	$2.83	**$4.72**	0.023
Install 11-7/8" I-joists, 12"oc	SF	$2.74	$2.35	$5.09	**$8.50**	0.036
Install 11-7/8" I-joists, 16"oc	SF	$2.36	$1.76	$4.12	**$6.89**	0.031
Install 11-7/8" I-joists, 24"oc	SF	$1.90	$1.18	$3.08	**$5.14**	0.025
Install 14" I-joists, 12"oc	SF	$3.27	$3.43	$6.70	**$11.20**	0.043
Install 14" I-joists, 16"oc	SF	$2.82	$2.51	$5.33	**$8.89**	0.037
Install 14" I-joists, 24"oc	SF	$2.36	$1.13	$3.49	**$5.82**	0.031

Floor Framing

Floor Sheathing

Description	Unit	Direct Labor	Direct Materials	Direct Total	Selling Price	Man-hours
FLOOR SHEATHING, PLYWOOD						
Install plywood subfloor, 3/8"	SF	$1.22	$0.52	$1.74	**$2.90**	0.016
Install plywood subfloor, 1/2"	SF	$1.22	$0.58	$1.80	**$3.01**	0.016
Install plywood subfloor, 5/8"	SF	$1.29	$0.78	$2.07	**$3.46**	0.017
Install plywood subfloor, 3/4"	SF	$1.37	$0.98	$2.35	**$3.93**	0.018
Install plywood subfloor, 1-1/8"	SF	$1.37	$1.21	$2.58	**$4.30**	0.018
FLOOR SHEATHING, ORIENTED STRAND BOARD (OSB)						
Install oriented strand board subfloor, 3/8"	SF	$1.22	$0.45	$1.67	**$2.79**	0.016
Install oriented strand board subfloor, 1/2"	SF	$1.22	$0.54	$1.76	**$2.93**	0.016
Install oriented strand board subfloor, 5/8"	SF	$1.29	$0.69	$1.98	**$3.31**	0.017
Install oriented strand board subfloor, 3/4"	SF	$1.37	$0.84	$2.21	**$3.69**	0.018
FLOOR SHEATHING, TONGUE AND GROOVE PLYWOOD						
Install tongue and groove plywood subfloor, 5/8"	SF	$1.52	$0.95	$2.47	**$4.13**	0.020
Install tongue and groove plywood subfloor, 3/4"	SF	$1.60	$1.18	$2.77	**$4.63**	0.021
Install tongue and groove OSB subfloor, 5/8"	SF	$1.67	$0.80	$2.47	**$4.13**	0.022
Install tongue and groove OSB subfloor, 3/4"	SF	$1.75	$1.00	$2.75	**$4.60**	0.023
FLOOR SHEATHING, STRIP						
Install strip subfloor, straight, 1" x 6" or 1" x 8"	SF	$2.06	$1.21	$3.27	**$5.46**	0.027
Install strip subfloor, diagonal, 1" x 6" or 1" x 8"	SF	$2.36	$1.53	$3.89	**$6.50**	0.031

Columns

Description	Unit	Direct Labor	Direct Materials	Direct Total	Selling Price	Man-hours
STEEL COLUMNS						
Install steel pipe column, 3" diameter, 8' tall	EA	$18.88	$36.23	$55.10	**$92.02**	0.248
Install steel pipe column, 4" diameter, 8' tall	EA	$23.83	$47.09	$70.92	**$118.43**	0.313
Install steel pipe column, 6" diameter, 8' tall	EA	$33.64	$67.57	$101.22	**$169.03**	0.442
Install steel pipe column, 8" diameter, 8' tall	EA	$43.54	$89.30	$132.84	**$221.84**	0.572
WOOD COLUMNS						
Install wood column, 4" x 4"	LF	$5.56	$2.02	$7.58	**$12.65**	0.073
Install wood column, 4" x 6"	LF	$5.94	$3.04	$8.98	**$15.00**	0.078
Install wood column, 4" x 8"	LF	$6.47	$3.82	$10.29	**$17.19**	0.085
Install wood column, 6" x 6"	LF	$7.08	$6.38	$13.46	**$22.48**	0.093
Install wood column, 6" x 8"	LF	$7.61	$7.40	$15.02	**$25.08**	0.100
Install wood column, 6" x 10"	LF	$8.30	$8.81	$17.11	**$28.57**	0.109
Install wood column, 8" x 8"	LF	$8.98	$10.22	$19.20	**$32.06**	0.118

Floor Framing

Sleepers

Description	Unit	Direct Labor	Direct Materials	Direct Total	Selling Price	Man-hours
Install 2" x 3" sleepers on existing deck	SF	$1.22	$0.49	$1.71	**$2.86**	0.016
Install 2" x 4" sleepers on existing deck	SF	$1.22	$0.61	$1.83	**$3.05**	0.016
Install 2" x 6" sleepers on existing deck	SF	$1.29	$0.66	$1.96	**$3.27**	0.017
Install 2" x 3" sleepers on existing deck, pressure treated	SF	$1.22	$0.56	$1.78	**$2.97**	0.016
Install 2" x 4" sleepers on existing deck, pressure treated	SF	$1.22	$0.68	$1.90	**$3.17**	0.016
Install 2" x 6" sleepers on existing deck, pressure treated	SF	$1.29	$0.90	$2.20	**$3.67**	0.017

Wall Framing

Wood Wall Framing

Description	Unit	Direct Labor	Direct Materials	Direct Total	Selling Price	Man-hours
WOOD WALL FRAMING, 2" x 4", 8' TALL						
Install 2" x 4", 12"oc, wood frame wall, up to 8' tall	SF	$1.83	$0.73	$2.56	**$4.27**	0.024
Install 2" x 4", 16"oc, wood frame wall, up to 8' tall	SF	$1.60	$0.59	$2.19	**$3.66**	0.021
Install 2" x 4", 24"oc, wood frame wall, up to 8' tall	SF	$1.37	$0.46	$1.83	**$3.06**	0.018
WOOD WALL FRAMING, 2" x 4", 10' TALL						
Install 2" x 4", 12"oc, wood frame wall, up to 10' tall	SF	$1.52	$0.70	$2.23	**$3.72**	0.020
Install 2" x 4", 16"oc, wood frame wall, up to 10' tall	SF	$1.37	$0.57	$1.94	**$3.24**	0.018
Install 2" x 4", 24"oc, wood frame wall, up to 10' tall	SF	$1.14	$0.43	$1.57	**$2.63**	0.015
WOOD WALL FRAMING, 2" x 4", 12' TALL						
Install 2" x 4", 12"oc, wood frame wall, up to 12' tall	SF	$1.29	$0.67	$1.96	**$3.28**	0.017
Install 2" x 4", 16"oc, wood frame wall, up to 12' tall	SF	$1.14	$0.54	$1.68	**$2.81**	0.015
Install 2" x 4", 24"oc, wood frame wall, up to 12' tall	SF	$0.91	$0.41	$1.32	**$2.20**	0.012
WOOD WALL FRAMING, 2" x 6", 8' TALL						
Install 2" x 6", 12"oc, wood frame wall, up to 8' tall	SF	$1.98	$1.33	$3.31	**$5.52**	0.026
Install 2" x 6", 16"oc, wood frame wall, up to 8' tall	SF	$1.83	$1.08	$2.90	**$4.85**	0.024
Install 2" x 6", 24"oc, wood frame wall, up to 8' tall	SF	$1.60	$0.83	$2.42	**$4.05**	0.021
WOOD WALL FRAMING, 2" x 6", 10' TALL						
Install 2" x 6", 12"oc, wood frame wall, up to 10' tall	SF	$1.67	$1.26	$2.94	**$4.90**	0.022
Install 2" x 6", 16"oc, wood frame wall, up to 10' tall	SF	$1.52	$1.02	$2.54	**$4.25**	0.020
Install 2" x 6", 24"oc, wood frame wall, up to 10' tall	SF	$1.29	$0.77	$2.07	**$3.45**	0.017
WOOD WALL FRAMING, 2" x 6", 12' TALL						
Install 2" x 6", 12"oc, wood frame wall, up to 12' tall	SF	$1.52	$1.23	$2.75	**$4.59**	0.020
Install 2" x 6", 16"oc, wood frame wall, up to 12' tall	SF	$1.29	$0.98	$2.27	**$3.79**	0.017
Install 2" x 6", 24"oc, wood frame wall, up to 12' tall	SF	$1.07	$0.73	$1.79	**$3.00**	0.014
WOOD WALL FRAMING, 2" x 8", 8' TALL						
Install 2" x 8", 12"oc, wood frame wall, up to 8' tall	SF	$2.28	$1.86	$4.14	**$6.92**	0.030
Install 2" x 8", 16"oc, wood frame wall, up to 8' tall	SF	$1.98	$1.50	$3.48	**$5.81**	0.026
Install 2" x 8", 24"oc, wood frame wall, up to 8' tall	SF	$1.75	$1.15	$2.90	**$4.85**	0.023
WOOD WALL FRAMING, 2" x 8", 10' TALL						
Install 2" x 8", 12"oc, wood frame wall, up to 10' tall	SF	$1.90	$1.77	$3.67	**$6.14**	0.025
Install 2" x 8", 16"oc, wood frame wall, up to 10' tall	SF	$1.67	$1.42	$3.10	**$5.17**	0.022
Install 2" x 8", 24"oc, wood frame wall, up to 10' tall	SF	$1.37	$1.07	$2.44	**$4.07**	0.018
WOOD WALL FRAMING, 2" x 8", 12' TALL						
Install 2" x 8", 12"oc, wood frame wall, up to 12' tall	SF	$1.67	$1.73	$3.40	**$5.68**	0.022
Install 2" x 8", 16"oc, wood frame wall, up to 12' tall	SF	$1.45	$1.37	$2.82	**$4.70**	0.019
Install 2" x 8", 24"oc, wood frame wall, up to 12' tall	SF	$1.14	$1.01	$2.15	**$3.59**	0.015

Wall Framing

Wall Sheathing

Description	Unit	Direct Labor	Direct Materials	Direct Total	Selling Price	Man-hours
WALL SHEATHING, PLYWOOD						
Install plywood sheathing, 3/8"	SF	$1.29	$0.47	$1.76	**$2.95**	0.017
Install plywood sheathing, 1/2"	SF	$1.37	$0.53	$1.90	**$3.17**	0.018
Install plywood sheathing, 5/8"	SF	$1.37	$0.71	$2.08	**$3.47**	0.018
Install plywood sheathing, 3/4"	SF	$1.45	$0.89	$2.34	**$3.90**	0.019
Install plywood sheathing, 1/2", pressure treated	SF	$1.37	$0.77	$2.14	**$3.58**	0.018
Install plywood sheathing, 5/8", pressure treated	SF	$1.37	$1.03	$2.40	**$4.01**	0.018
Install plywood sheathing, 3/4", pressure treated	SF	$1.45	$1.30	$2.75	**$4.59**	0.019
WALL SHEATHING, ORIENTED STRAND BOARD (OSB)						
Install oriented strand board sheathing, 3/8"	SF	$1.29	$0.41	$1.71	**$2.85**	0.017
Install oriented strand board sheathing, 1/2"	SF	$1.37	$0.49	$1.86	**$3.11**	0.018
Install oriented strand board sheathing, 5/8"	SF	$1.37	$0.63	$2.00	**$3.34**	0.018
WALL SHEATHING, STRIP						
Install strip sheathing, straight, 1" x 6" or 1" x 8"	SF	$2.21	$1.10	$3.31	**$5.53**	0.029
Install strip sheathing, diagonal, 1" x 6" or 1" x 8"	SF	$2.51	$1.40	$3.91	**$6.52**	0.033
WALL SHEATHING, COMPOSITION BOARD						
Install asphalt composition sheathing, 1/2"	SF	$0.99	$0.34	$1.33	**$2.22**	0.013
WALL SHEATHING, FOAM BOARD						
Install foil faced foam sheathing, 1/2"	SF	$1.22	$0.30	$1.51	**$2.53**	0.016
Install foil faced foam sheathing, 5/8"	SF	$1.29	$0.34	$1.64	**$2.73**	0.017
Install foil faced foam sheathing, 3/4"	SF	$1.37	$0.40	$1.77	**$2.95**	0.018
Install foil faced foam sheathing, 1"	SF	$1.37	$0.45	$1.82	**$3.04**	0.018
Install foil faced foam sheathing, 2"	SF	$1.45	$0.79	$2.24	**$3.74**	0.019

Wall Framing

Columns

Description	Unit	Direct Labor	Direct Materials	Direct Total	Selling Price	Man-hours
STEEL COLUMNS						
Install steel pipe column, 3" diameter, 8' tall	EA	$18.88	$36.00	$54.88	**$91.65**	0.248
Install steel pipe column, 4" diameter, 8' tall	EA	$23.83	$47.00	$70.83	**$118.28**	0.313
Install steel pipe column, 6" diameter, 8' tall	EA	$33.64	$68.00	$101.64	**$169.75**	0.442
Install steel pipe column, 8" diameter, 8' tall	EA	$43.54	$89.00	$132.54	**$221.34**	0.572
WOOD COLUMNS						
Install wood column, 4" x 4"	LF	$5.56	$2.02	$7.58	**$12.65**	0.073
Install wood column, 4" x 6"	LF	$5.94	$3.04	$8.98	**$15.00**	0.078
Install wood column, 4" x 8"	LF	$6.47	$3.82	$10.29	**$17.19**	0.085
Install wood column, 6" x 6"	LF	$7.08	$6.38	$13.46	**$22.48**	0.093
Install wood column, 6" x 8"	LF	$7.61	$7.40	$15.02	**$25.08**	0.100
Install wood column, 6" x 10"	LF	$8.30	$8.81	$17.11	**$28.57**	0.109
Install wood column, 8" x 8"	LF	$8.98	$10.22	$19.20	**$32.06**	0.118
Install wood column, 8" x 10"	LF	$10.05	$13.08	$23.13	**$38.63**	0.132

Kneewall

Description	Unit	Direct Labor	Direct Materials	Direct Total	Selling Price	Man-hours
Install kneewall, 2" x4", 12"oc, 4' tall	LF	$14.23	$2.17	$16.40	**$27.39**	0.187
Install kneewall, 2" x4", 12"oc, 6' tall	LF	$17.89	$2.77	$20.66	**$34.49**	0.235
Install kneewall, 2" x4", 12"oc, 8' tall	LF	$21.62	$3.37	$24.99	**$41.74**	0.284
Install kneewall, 2" x4", 16"oc, 4' tall	LF	$10.66	$1.63	$12.28	**$20.51**	0.140
Install kneewall, 2" x4", 16"oc, 6' tall	LF	$13.40	$2.08	$15.47	**$25.84**	0.176
Install kneewall, 2" x4", 16"oc, 8' tall	LF	$16.21	$2.53	$18.74	**$31.30**	0.213
Install kneewall, 2" x4", 24"oc, 4' tall	LF	$8.53	$1.30	$9.83	**$16.41**	0.112
Install kneewall, 2" x4", 24"oc, 6' tall	LF	$10.73	$1.66	$12.39	**$20.70**	0.141
Install kneewall, 2" x4", 24"oc, 8' tall	LF	$12.94	$2.02	$14.96	**$24.99**	0.170

Wall Framing

Furring

Description	Unit	Direct Labor	Direct Materials	Direct Total	Selling Price	Man-hours
FURRING ON FRAME WALL						
Install furring on frame wall, 1" x 2", 12"oc	SF	$0.99	$0.16	$1.15	**$1.92**	0.013
Install furring on frame wall, 1" x 2", 16"oc	SF	$0.84	$0.12	$0.95	**$1.59**	0.011
Install furring on frame wall, 1" x 2", 24"oc	SF	$0.61	$0.08	$0.69	**$1.15**	0.008
Install furring on frame wall, 1" x 3", 12"oc	SF	$0.99	$0.19	$1.18	**$1.96**	0.013
Install furring on frame wall, 1" x 3", 16"oc	SF	$0.84	$0.14	$0.98	**$1.63**	0.011
Install furring on frame wall, 1" x 3", 24"oc	SF	$0.61	$0.09	$0.70	**$1.17**	0.008
FURRING ON MASONRY WALL						
Install furring on masonry wall, 1" x 2", 12"oc	SF	$1.60	$0.16	$1.76	**$2.94**	0.021
Install furring on masonry wall, 1" x 2", 16"oc	SF	$1.29	$0.12	$1.41	**$2.36**	0.017
Install furring on masonry wall, 1" x 2", 24"oc	SF	$0.99	$0.08	$1.07	**$1.79**	0.013
Install furring on masonry wall, 1" x 3", 12"oc	SF	$1.60	$0.19	$1.78	**$2.98**	0.021
Install furring on masonry wall, 1" x 3", 16"oc	SF	$1.29	$0.14	$1.43	**$2.39**	0.017
Install furring on masonry wall, 1" x 3", 24"oc	SF	$0.99	$0.09	$1.08	**$1.81**	0.013

Roof Framing

Wood Roof Framing

> Square footage is the actual measurement of the surface of the roof. Multiply soffit length by rake length to determine square footage of that portion of the roof.

Description	Unit	Direct Labor	Direct Materials	Direct Total	Selling Price	Man-hours
ROOF FRAMING, FLAT OR SHED ROOF						
Install 2" x 6", 12"oc, wood flat or shed roof framing	SF	$1.98	$1.25	$3.23	**$5.39**	0.026
Install 2" x 6", 16"oc, wood flat or shed roof framing	SF	$1.75	$0.95	$2.71	**$4.52**	0.023
Install 2" x 6", 24"oc, wood flat or shed roof framing	SF	$1.22	$0.68	$1.90	**$3.17**	0.016
Install 2" x 8", 12"oc, wood flat or shed roof framing	SF	$2.28	$1.73	$4.01	**$6.70**	0.030
Install 2" x 8", 16"oc, wood flat or shed roof framing	SF	$1.90	$1.32	$3.23	**$5.39**	0.025
Install 2" x 8", 24"oc, wood flat or shed roof framing	SF	$1.37	$0.94	$2.31	**$3.86**	0.018
Install 2" x 10", 12"oc, wood flat or shed roof framing	SF	$2.51	$2.04	$4.55	**$7.59**	0.033
Install 2" x 10", 16"oc, wood flat or shed roof framing	SF	$2.13	$1.56	$3.69	**$6.16**	0.028
Install 2" x 10", 24"oc, wood flat or shed roof framing	SF	$1.52	$1.11	$2.63	**$4.39**	0.020
Install 2" x 12", 12"oc, wood flat or shed roof framing	SF	$2.82	$2.42	$5.24	**$8.75**	0.037
Install 2" x 12", 16"oc, wood flat or shed roof framing	SF	$2.36	$1.85	$4.21	**$7.04**	0.031
Install 2" x 12", 24"oc, wood flat or shed roof framing	SF	$1.75	$1.32	$3.07	**$5.12**	0.023
ROOF FRAMING, GABLE ROOF						
Install 2" x 6", 12"oc, wood gable roof framing	SF	$2.13	$1.32	$3.45	**$5.76**	0.028
Install 2" x 6", 16"oc, wood gable roof framing	SF	$1.83	$1.01	$2.84	**$4.74**	0.024
Install 2" x 6", 24"oc, wood gable roof framing	SF	$1.29	$0.72	$2.01	**$3.36**	0.017
Install 2" x 8", 12"oc, wood gable roof framing	SF	$2.44	$1.83	$4.27	**$7.13**	0.032
Install 2" x 8", 16"oc, wood gable roof framing	SF	$2.06	$1.40	$3.46	**$5.77**	0.027
Install 2" x 8", 24"oc, wood gable roof framing	SF	$1.52	$0.99	$2.52	**$4.20**	0.020
Install 2" x 10", 12"oc, wood gable roof framing	SF	$2.66	$2.16	$4.82	**$8.05**	0.035
Install 2" x 10", 16"oc, wood gable roof framing	SF	$2.28	$1.65	$3.93	**$6.57**	0.030
Install 2" x 10", 24"oc, wood gable roof framing	SF	$1.67	$1.17	$2.85	**$4.75**	0.022
Install 2" x 12", 12"oc, wood gable roof framing	SF	$2.97	$2.54	$5.51	**$9.20**	0.039
Install 2" x 12", 16"oc, wood gable roof framing	SF	$2.51	$1.85	$4.36	**$7.28**	0.033
Install 2" x 12", 24"oc, wood gable roof framing	SF	$1.90	$1.38	$3.29	**$5.49**	0.025

11

Roof Framing

Wood Roof Framing

> Square footage is the actual measurement of the surface of the roof. Multiply fascia length by rake length to determine square footage of that portion of the roof.

Description	Unit	Direct Labor	Direct Materials	Direct Total	Selling Price	Man-hours
ROOF FRAMING, HIP ROOF						
Install 2" x 6", 12"oc, wood hip roof framing	SF	$3.04	$1.53	$4.58	**$7.65**	0.040
Install 2" x 6", 16"oc, wood hip roof framing	SF	$2.59	$1.17	$3.76	**$6.28**	0.034
Install 2" x 6", 24"oc, wood hip roof framing	SF	$1.83	$0.83	$2.66	**$4.44**	0.024
Install 2" x 8", 12"oc, wood hip roof framing	SF	$3.43	$2.13	$5.55	**$9.27**	0.045
Install 2" x 8", 16"oc, wood hip roof framing	SF	$2.89	$1.63	$4.52	**$7.55**	0.038
Install 2" x 8", 24"oc, wood hip roof framing	SF	$2.13	$1.16	$3.29	**$5.49**	0.028
Install 2" x 10", 12"oc, wood hip roof framing	SF	$3.73	$2.50	$6.23	**$10.41**	0.049
Install 2" x 10", 16"oc, wood hip roof framing	SF	$3.20	$1.92	$5.11	**$8.54**	0.042
Install 2" x 10", 24"oc, wood hip roof framing	SF	$2.36	$1.36	$3.72	**$6.21**	0.031
Install 2" x 12", 12"oc, wood hip roof framing	SF	$3.96	$2.84	$6.80	**$11.35**	0.052
Install 2" x 12", 16"oc, wood hip roof framing	SF	$3.35	$1.93	$5.28	**$8.82**	0.044
Install 2" x 12", 24"oc, wood hip roof framing	SF	$2.89	$1.59	$4.48	**$7.49**	0.038
ROOF FRAMING, GAMBREL ROOF						
Install 2" x 6", 12"oc, wood gambrel roof framing	SF	$3.27	$1.84	$5.11	**$8.54**	0.043
Install 2" x 6", 16"oc, wood gambrel roof framing	SF	$2.82	$1.41	$4.22	**$7.06**	0.037
Install 2" x 6", 24"oc, wood gambrel roof framing	SF	$2.06	$1.00	$3.05	**$5.10**	0.027
Install 2" x 8", 12"oc, wood gambrel roof framing	SF	$3.73	$2.55	$6.28	**$10.49**	0.049
Install 2" x 8", 16"oc, wood gambrel roof framing	SF	$3.20	$1.95	$5.15	**$8.60**	0.042
Install 2" x 8", 24"oc, wood gambrel roof framing	SF	$2.28	$1.39	$3.67	**$6.13**	0.030
Install 2" x 10", 12"oc, wood gambrel roof framing	SF	$4.11	$3.00	$7.11	**$11.88**	0.054
Install 2" x 10", 16"oc, wood gambrel roof framing	SF	$3.58	$2.30	$5.88	**$9.81**	0.047
Install 2" x 10", 24"oc, wood gambrel roof framing	SF	$2.59	$1.63	$4.22	**$7.05**	0.034
Install 2" x 12", 12"oc, wood gambrel roof framing	SF	$4.34	$3.35	$7.69	**$12.84**	0.057
Install 2" x 12", 16"oc, wood gambrel roof framing	SF	$3.73	$2.61	$6.34	**$10.60**	0.049
Install 2" x 12", 24"oc, wood gambrel roof framing	SF	$3.20	$1.91	$5.11	**$8.54**	0.042

Roof Framing

Wood Roof Trusses

> Square footage is the actual measurement of the surface of the roof. Multiply fascia length by rake length to determine square footage of that portion of the roof.

Description	Unit	Direct Labor	Direct Materials	Direct Total	Selling Price	Man-hours
WOOD ROOF TRUSS, FINK OR "W"						
Install fink or 'W' truss, with 2" x 4" chords, 16"oc	SF	$1.37	$3.26	$4.63	**$7.72**	0.018
Install fink or 'W' truss, with 2" x 4" chords, 24"oc	SF	$1.14	$2.15	$3.29	**$5.50**	0.015
Install fink or 'W' truss, with 2" x 6" chords, 16"oc	SF	$1.45	$3.91	$5.35	**$8.94**	0.019
Install fink or 'W' truss, with 2" x 6" chords, 24"oc	SF	$1.14	$2.58	$3.72	**$6.22**	0.015
WOOD ROOF TRUSS, SCISSOR						
Install scissors truss, with 2" x 4" chords, 16"oc	SF	$1.52	$3.72	$5.24	**$8.75**	0.020
Install scissors truss, with 2" x 4" chords, 24"oc	SF	$1.22	$2.45	$3.67	**$6.13**	0.016
Install scissors truss, with 2" x 6" chords, 16"oc	SF	$1.67	$4.46	$6.14	**$10.25**	0.022
Install scissors truss, with 2" x 6" chords, 24"oc	SF	$1.29	$2.94	$4.24	**$7.07**	0.017
WOOD ROOF TRUSS, ATTIC						
Install attic truss, with 2" x 4" chords, 16"oc	SF	$1.90	$3.95	$5.86	**$9.78**	0.025
Install attic truss, with 2" x 4" chords, 24"oc	SF	$1.52	$2.60	$4.13	**$6.89**	0.020
Install attic truss, with 2" x 6" chords, 16"oc	SF	$2.06	$4.74	$6.80	**$11.35**	0.027
Install attic truss, with 2" x 6" chords, 24"oc	SF	$1.60	$3.13	$4.73	**$7.89**	0.021
WOOD ROOF TRUSS, GAMBREL						
Install gambrel truss, with 2" x 4" chords, 16"oc	SF	$2.21	$5.12	$7.32	**$12.23**	0.029
Install gambrel truss, with 2" x 4" chords, 24"oc	SF	$1.83	$3.37	$5.20	**$8.68**	0.024
Install gambrel truss, with 2" x 6" chords, 16"oc	SF	$2.44	$6.14	$8.57	**$14.32**	0.032
Install gambrel truss, with 2" x 6" chords, 24"oc	SF	$1.90	$4.05	$5.95	**$9.93**	0.025

Roof Framing

Roof Sheathing

Description	Unit	Direct Labor	Direct Materials	Direct Total	Selling Price	Man-hours
ROOF SHEATHING, PLYWOOD						
Install plywood sheathing, 3/8"	SF	$1.29	$0.47	$1.76	**$2.95**	0.017
Install plywood sheathing, 1/2"	SF	$1.37	$0.53	$1.90	**$3.17**	0.018
Install plywood sheathing, 5/8"	SF	$1.45	$0.71	$2.15	**$3.59**	0.019
Install plywood sheathing, 3/4"	SF	$1.45	$0.89	$2.34	**$3.90**	0.019
ROOF SHEATHING, ORIENTED STRAND BOARD (OSB)						
Install oriented strand board sheathing, 3/8"	SF	$1.29	$0.41	$1.71	**$2.85**	0.017
Install oriented strand board sheathing, 1/2"	SF	$1.37	$0.49	$1.86	**$3.11**	0.018
Install oriented strand board sheathing, 5/8"	SF	$1.45	$0.63	$2.07	**$3.46**	0.019
Install oriented strand board sheathing, 3/4"	SF	$1.45	$0.76	$2.21	**$3.69**	0.019
ROOF SHEATHING, STRIP						
Install strip sheathing, straight, 1" x 6" or 1" x 8"	SF	$2.21	$1.10	$3.31	**$5.53**	0.029
Install strip sheathing, diagonal, 1" x 6" or 1" x 8"	SF	$2.59	$1.40	$3.98	**$6.65**	0.034
Install strip sheathing, 1" x 3", 5-1/2"oc	SF	$1.14	$0.58	$1.72	**$2.88**	0.015
Install strip sheathing, 1" x 3", 7-1/2"oc	SF	$0.84	$0.53	$1.37	**$2.29**	0.011

Ceiling Joists

Description	Unit	Direct Labor	Direct Materials	Direct Total	Selling Price	Man-hours
Install 2" x 4", 12"oc, ceiling joists	SF	$1.83	$0.52	$2.35	**$3.92**	0.024
Install 2" x 4", 16"oc, ceiling joists	SF	$1.37	$0.40	$1.77	**$2.96**	0.018
Install 2" x 4", 24"oc, ceiling joists	SF	$0.91	$0.28	$1.19	**$1.99**	0.012
Install 2" x 6", 12"oc, ceiling joists	SF	$1.98	$1.04	$3.02	**$5.05**	0.026
Install 2" x 6", 16"oc, ceiling joists	SF	$1.52	$0.80	$2.32	**$3.88**	0.020
Install 2" x 6", 24"oc, ceiling joists	SF	$0.99	$0.55	$1.54	**$2.57**	0.013
Install 2" x 8", 12"oc, ceiling joists	SF	$2.21	$1.47	$3.68	**$6.14**	0.029
Install 2" x 8", 16"oc, ceiling joists	SF	$1.67	$1.11	$2.78	**$4.65**	0.022
Install 2" x 8", 24"oc, ceiling joists	SF	$1.14	$0.76	$1.90	**$3.17**	0.015
Install 2" x 10", 12"oc, ceiling joists	SF	$2.44	$1.91	$4.35	**$7.26**	0.032
Install 2" x 10", 16"oc, ceiling joists	SF	$1.83	$1.45	$3.28	**$5.47**	0.024
Install 2" x 10", 24"oc, ceiling joists	SF	$1.22	$0.99	$2.21	**$3.69**	0.016
Install 2" x 12", 12"oc, ceiling joists	SF	$2.66	$2.34	$5.00	**$8.36**	0.035
Install 2" x 12", 16"oc, ceiling joists	SF	$1.98	$1.78	$3.76	**$6.28**	0.026
Install 2" x 12", 24"oc, ceiling joists	SF	$1.29	$1.21	$2.50	**$4.18**	0.017

Roof Framing

LVL and Glu-Lam

Description	Unit	Direct Labor	Direct Materials	Direct Total	Selling Price	Man-hours
LVL BEAM						
Install LVL wood beam, 1-3/4"x9-1/4"	LF	$4.80	$4.55	$9.34	**$15.60**	0.063
Install LVL wood beam, 1-3/4"x11-7/8"	LF	$5.86	$5.67	$11.53	**$19.26**	0.077
Install LVL wood beam, 1-3/4"x14"	LF	$6.77	$7.02	$13.80	**$23.04**	0.089
Install LVL wood beam, 1-3/4"x16"	LF	$7.54	$7.81	$15.35	**$25.63**	0.099
Install LVL wood beam, two 1-3/4"x9-1/4"	LF	$8.60	$9.61	$18.22	**$30.42**	0.113
Install LVL wood beam, two 1-3/4 x11-7/8"	LF	$10.96	$12.02	$22.98	**$38.38**	0.144
Install LVL wood beam, two 1-3/4"x14"	LF	$13.02	$14.50	$27.51	**$45.95**	0.171
Install LVL wood beam, two 1-3/4"x16"	LF	$14.84	$16.44	$31.28	**$52.24**	0.195
Install LVL wood beam, three 1-3/4"x9-1/4"	LF	$12.41	$14.50	$26.90	**$44.93**	0.163
Install LVL wood beam, three 1-3/4"x11-7/8"	LF	$16.06	$18.05	$34.11	**$56.97**	0.211
Install LVL wood beam, three 1-3/4"x14"	LF	$19.26	$21.15	$40.40	**$67.47**	0.253
Install LVL wood beam, three 1-3/4"x16"	LF	$22.15	$24.33	$46.48	**$77.62**	0.291
GLU-LAM BEAM, 3-1/2" THICK						
Install glu-lam beams 9" deep 3-1/2 thick, 20' long	LF	$9.36	$13.14	$22.50	**$37.57**	0.123
Install glu-lam beams 10-1/2" deep 3-1/2 thick, 20' long	LF	$10.66	$15.23	$25.89	**$43.23**	0.140
Install glu-lam beams 12" deep 3-1/2 thick, 20' long	LF	$11.95	$16.97	$28.92	**$48.30**	0.157
Install glu-lam beams 13-1/2" deep 3-1/2 thick, 20' long	LF	$13.24	$18.83	$32.08	**$53.57**	0.174
Install glu-lam beams 15" deep 3-1/2 thick, 20' long	LF	$14.54	$20.69	$35.23	**$58.84**	0.191
Install glu-lam beams 16-1/2" deep 3-1/2 thick, 20' long	LF	$15.83	$22.55	$38.39	**$64.10**	0.208
Install glu-lam beams 18" deep 3-1/2 thick, 20' long	LF	$16.59	$24.41	$41.01	**$68.48**	0.218
GLU-LAM BEAM, 5-1/4" THICK						
Install glu-lam beams 12" deep 5-1/4 thick, 20' long	LF	$16.67	$20.69	$37.36	**$62.40**	0.219
Install glu-lam beams 13-1/2" deep 5-1/4 thick, 20' long	LF	$19.03	$22.90	$41.93	**$70.02**	0.250
Install glu-lam beams 15" deep 5-1/4 thick, 20' long	LF	$21.08	$25.23	$46.31	**$77.34**	0.277
Install glu-lam beams 16-1/2" deep 5-1/4 thick, 20' long	LF	$23.22	$27.55	$50.77	**$84.78**	0.305
Install glu-lam beams 18" deep 5-1/4 thick, 20' long	LF	$25.27	$29.88	$55.15	**$92.10**	0.332

Roof Framing

Wood Beams

Description	Unit	Direct Labor	Direct Materials	Direct Total	Selling Price	Man-hours
TRADITIONAL WOOD BEAMS, 2" THICK						
Install 2" x 8" single member beams	LF	$2.51	$1.15	$3.66	**$6.11**	0.033
Install 2" x 10" single member beam	LF	$2.59	$1.35	$3.94	**$6.58**	0.034
Install 2" x 12" single member beam	LF	$2.74	$1.93	$4.67	**$7.80**	0.036
TRADITIONAL WOOD BEAMS, 3" THICK						
Install 3" x 8" single member beam	LF	$2.74	$2.53	$5.27	**$8.81**	0.036
Install 3" x 10" single member beam	LF	$2.97	$3.14	$6.11	**$10.20**	0.039
Install 3" x 12" single member beam	LF	$3.20	$3.74	$6.94	**$11.59**	0.042
Install 3" x 14" single member beam	LF	$3.43	$4.52	$7.95	**$13.27**	0.045
TRADITIONAL WOOD BEAMS, 4" THICK						
Install 4" x 8" single member beam	LF	$3.12	$3.07	$6.19	**$10.34**	0.041
Install 4" x 10" single member beam	LF	$3.35	$3.80	$7.15	**$11.94**	0.044
Install 4" x 12" single member beam	LF	$3.65	$4.53	$8.19	**$13.67**	0.048
Install 4" x 14" single member beam	LF	$4.19	$5.51	$9.70	**$16.19**	0.055
TRADITIONAL WOOD BEAMS, 6" THICK						
Install 6" x 8" single member beam	LF	$4.72	$5.92	$10.64	**$17.76**	0.062
Install 6" x 10" single member beam	LF	$5.18	$7.49	$12.66	**$21.15**	0.068
Install 6" x 12" single member beam	LF	$5.56	$9.35	$14.90	**$24.89**	0.073
Install 6" x 14" single member beam	LF	$6.09	$10.88	$16.97	**$28.34**	0.080
TRADITIONAL WOOD BEAMS, MULTI-MEMBER						
Install 4"x8" multi-member wood beam	LF	$3.50	$2.30	$5.80	**$9.69**	0.046
Install 4"x10" multi-member wood beam	LF	$3.73	$2.70	$6.43	**$10.73**	0.049
Install 4"x12" multi-member wood beam	LF	$4.03	$3.86	$7.89	**$13.18**	0.053
Install 6"x8" multi-member wood beam	LF	$5.18	$3.45	$8.63	**$14.41**	0.068
Install 6"x10" multi-member wood beam	LF	$5.56	$4.05	$9.60	**$16.04**	0.073
Install 6"x12" multi-member wood beam	LF	$6.01	$5.79	$11.80	**$19.71**	0.079

Roofing and Gutters

Fiberglass Shingle Roofing, Gable Roof

> **Square footage is the actual measurement of the surface of the roof. Multiply fascia length by rake length to determine square footage of that portion of the roof.**

Description	Unit	Direct Labor	Direct Materials	Direct Total	Selling Price	Man-hours
FIBERGLASS SHINGLES, GABLE ROOF, TRADITIONAL 3 TAB						
Install fiberglass shingles, 3 tab, 200lb, 20 year, to 8/12 slope, with felt	SF	$1.36	$0.90	$2.26	**$3.77**	0.017
Install fiberglass shingles, 3 tab, 200lb, 20 year, over 8/12 slope, felt	SF	$1.63	$0.90	$2.54	**$4.24**	0.021
Install fiberglass shingles, 3 tab, 200lb, 20 year, to 8/12 slope, no felt	SF	$1.16	$0.78	$1.93	**$3.23**	0.015
Install fiberglass shingles, 3 tab, 200lb, 20 year, over 8/12 slope, no felt	SF	$1.39	$0.78	$2.17	**$3.63**	0.018
Install fiberglass shingles, 3 tab, 225lb, 25 year, to 8/12 slope, with felt	SF	$1.36	$0.99	$2.34	**$3.91**	0.017
Install fiberglass shingles, 3 tab, 225lb, 25 year, over 8/12 slope, felt	SF	$1.63	$0.99	$2.62	**$4.38**	0.021
Install fiberglass shingles, 3 tab, 225lb, 25 year, to 8/12 slope, no felt	SF	$1.16	$0.88	$2.04	**$3.41**	0.015
Install fiberglass shingles, 3 tab, 225lb, 25 year, over 8/12 slope, no felt	SF	$1.39	$0.88	$2.28	**$3.80**	0.018
Install fiberglass shingles, 3 tab, 240lb, 30 year, to 8/12 slope, with felt	SF	$1.36	$1.24	$2.60	**$4.34**	0.017
Install fiberglass shingles, 3 tab, 240lb, 30 year, over 8/12 slope, felt	SF	$1.63	$1.24	$2.87	**$4.80**	0.021
Install fiberglass shingles, 3 tab, 240lb, 30 year, to 8/12 slope, no felt	SF	$1.16	$1.14	$2.29	**$3.83**	0.015
Install fiberglass shingles, 3 tab, 240lb, 30 year, over 8/12 slope, no felt	SF	$1.39	$1.14	$2.53	**$4.23**	0.018
FIBERGLASS SHINGLES, GABLE ROOF, LAMINATE SHINGLES						
Install fiberglass shingles, laminate, 240lb, 30 yr, to 8/12 slope, with felt	SF	$1.63	$1.85	$3.48	**$5.82**	0.021
Install fiberglass shingles, laminate, 240lb, 30 yr, over 8/12 slope, felt	SF	$1.99	$1.85	$3.84	**$6.42**	0.026
Install fiberglass shingles, laminate, 240lb, 30 yr, to 8/12 slope, no felt	SF	$1.43	$1.75	$3.18	**$5.31**	0.019
Install fiberglass shingles, laminate, 240lb, 30 yr, over 8/12 slope, no felt	SF	$1.75	$1.75	$3.50	**$5.84**	0.023
Install fiberglass shingles, laminate, 260lb, 40 yr, to 8/12 slope, with felt	SF	$1.89	$2.15	$4.04	**$6.74**	0.024
Install fiberglass shingles, laminate, 260lb, 40 yr, over 8/12 slope, felt	SF	$2.29	$2.15	$4.44	**$7.41**	0.030
Install fiberglass shingles, laminate, 260lb, 40 yr, to 8/12 slope, no felt	SF	$1.69	$2.04	$3.73	**$6.24**	0.022
Install fiberglass shingles, laminate, 260lb, 40 yr, over 8/12 slope, no felt	SF	$2.05	$2.04	$4.09	**$6.83**	0.026
Install fiberglass shingles, laminate, 300lb, 50 yr, to 8/12 slope, with felt	SF	$1.89	$2.61	$4.50	**$7.52**	0.024
Install fiberglass shingles, laminate, 300lb, 50 yr, over 8/12 slope, felt	SF	$2.29	$2.61	$4.90	**$8.18**	0.030
Install fiberglass shingles, laminate, 300lb, 50 yr, to 8/12 slope, no felt	SF	$1.69	$2.50	$4.20	**$7.01**	0.022
Install fiberglass shingles, laminate, 300lb, 50 yr, over 8/12 slope, no felt	SF	$2.05	$2.50	$4.56	**$7.61**	0.026
Install fiberglass shingles, laminate, 340lb, lifetime, to 8/12 slope, with felt	SF	$2.03	$3.81	$5.84	**$9.75**	0.026
Install fiberglass shingles, laminate, 340lb, lifetime, over 8/12 slope, felt	SF	$2.45	$3.81	$6.26	**$10.45**	0.032
Install fiberglass shingles, laminate, 340lb, lifetime, to 8/12 slope, no felt	SF	$1.83	$3.70	$5.53	**$9.24**	0.024
Install fiberglass shingle, laminate, 340, lifetime, over 8/12 slope, no felt	SF	$2.21	$3.70	$5.91	**$9.88**	0.029

12

Roofing and Gutters

Fiberglass Shingle Roofing, Hip Roof

> Square footage is the actual measurement of the surface of the roof. Multiply fascia length by rake length to determine square footage of that portion of the roof.

Description	Unit	Direct Labor	Direct Materials	Direct Total	Selling Price	Man-hours
FIBERGLASS SHINGLES, HIP ROOF, TRADITIONAL 3 TAB						
Install fiberglass shingles, 3 tab, 200lb, 20 year, to 8/12 slope, with felt	SF	$1.63	$0.99	$2.62	**$4.38**	0.021
Install fiberglass shingles, 3 tab, 200lb, 20 year, over 8/12 slope, felt	SF	$1.96	$0.99	$2.96	**$4.94**	0.025
Install fiberglass shingles, 3 tab, 200lb, 20 year, to 8/12 slope, no felt	SF	$1.39	$0.86	$2.24	**$3.75**	0.018
Install fiberglass shingles, 3 tab, 200lb, 20 year, over 8/12 slope, no felt	SF	$1.67	$0.86	$2.53	**$4.22**	0.022
Install fiberglass shingles, 3 tab, 225lb, 25 year, to 8/12 slope, with felt	SF	$1.63	$1.09	$2.71	**$4.53**	0.021
Install fiberglass shingles, 3 tab, 225lb, 25 year, over 8/12 slope, felt	SF	$1.96	$1.09	$3.05	**$5.09**	0.025
Install fiberglass shingles, 3 tab, 225lb, 25 year, to 8/12 slope, no felt	SF	$1.39	$0.97	$2.36	**$3.94**	0.018
Install fiberglass shingles, 3 tab, 225lb, 25 year, over 8/12 slope, no felt	SF	$1.67	$0.97	$2.65	**$4.42**	0.022
Install fiberglass shingles, 3 tab, 240lb, 30 year, to 8/12 slope, with felt	SF	$1.63	$1.36	$2.99	**$5.00**	0.021
Install fiberglass shingles, 3 tab, 240lb, 30 year, over 8/12 slope, felt	SF	$1.96	$1.36	$3.33	**$5.55**	0.025
Install fiberglass shingles, 3 tab, 240lb, 30 year, to 8/12 slope, no felt	SF	$1.39	$1.25	$2.64	**$4.40**	0.018
Install fiberglass shingles, 3 tab, 240lb, 30 year, over 8/12 slope, no felt	SF	$1.67	$1.25	$2.92	**$4.88**	0.022
FIBERGLASS SHINGLES, HIP ROOF, LAMINATE SHINGLES						
Install fiberglass shingles, laminate, 240lb, 30 yr, to 8/12 slope, with felt	SF	$1.96	$2.04	$4.00	**$6.67**	0.025
Install fiberglass shingles, laminate, 240lb, 30 yr, over 8/12 slope, felt	SF	$2.39	$2.04	$4.43	**$7.39**	0.031
Install fiberglass shingles, laminate, 240lb, 30 yr, to 8/12 slope, no felt	SF	$1.72	$1.92	$3.64	**$6.08**	0.022
Install fiberglass shingles, laminate, 240lb, 30 yr, over 8/12 slope, no felt	SF	$2.10	$1.92	$4.02	**$6.72**	0.027
Install fiberglass shingles, laminate, 260lb, 40 yr, to 8/12 slope, with felt	SF	$2.27	$2.36	$4.63	**$7.73**	0.029
Install fiberglass shingles, laminate, 260lb, 40 yr, over 8/12 slope, felt	SF	$2.75	$2.36	$5.11	**$8.53**	0.035
Install fiberglass shingles, laminate, 260lb, 40 yr, to 8/12 slope, no felt	SF	$2.03	$2.24	$4.28	**$7.14**	0.026
Install fiberglass shingles, laminate, 260lb, 40 yr, over 8/12 slope, no felt	SF	$2.46	$2.24	$4.71	**$7.86**	0.032
Install fiberglass shingles, laminate, 300lb, 50 yr, to 8/12 slope, with felt	SF	$2.27	$2.87	$5.14	**$8.58**	0.029
Install fiberglass shingles, laminate, 300lb, 50 yr, over 8/12 slope, felt	SF	$2.75	$2.87	$5.62	**$9.38**	0.035
Install fiberglass shingles, laminate, 300lb, 50 yr, to 8/12 slope, no felt	SF	$2.03	$2.75	$4.79	**$7.99**	0.026
Install fiberglass shingles, laminate, 300lb, 50 yr, over 8/12 slope, no felt	SF	$2.46	$2.75	$5.22	**$8.71**	0.032
Install fiberglass shingles, laminate, 340lb, lifetime, to 8/12 slope, with felt	SF	$2.44	$4.19	$6.63	**$11.07**	0.031
Install fiberglass shingles, laminate, 340lb, lifetime, over 8/12 slope, felt	SF	$2.94	$4.19	$7.13	**$11.90**	0.038
Install fiberglass shingles, laminate, 340lb, lifetime, to 8/12 slope, no felt	SF	$2.20	$4.07	$6.27	**$10.47**	0.028
Install fiberglass shingle, laminate, 340, lifetime, over 8/12 slope, no felt	SF	$2.65	$4.07	$6.73	**$11.23**	0.034

Roofing and Gutters

Fiberglass Shingle Roofing, Gambrel Roof

> Square footage is the actual measurement of the surface of the roof. Multiply fascia length by rake length to determine square footage of that portion of the roof.

Description	Unit	Direct Labor	Direct Materials	Direct Total	Selling Price	Man-hours
FIBERGLASS SHINGLES, GAMBREL ROOF, TRADITIONAL 3 TAB						
Install fiberglass shingles, 3 tab, 200lb, 20 year, to 8/12 slope, with felt	SF	$1.83	$0.90	$2.73	**$4.57**	0.024
Install fiberglass shingles, 3 tab, 200lb, 20 year, over 8/12 slope, felt	SF	$2.21	$0.90	$3.11	**$5.19**	0.028
Install fiberglass shingles, 3 tab, 200lb, 20 year, to 8/12 slope, no felt	SF	$1.56	$0.78	$2.34	**$3.91**	0.020
Install fiberglass shingles, 3 tab, 200lb, 20 year, over 8/12 slope, no felt	SF	$1.88	$0.78	$2.66	**$4.45**	0.024
Install fiberglass shingles, 3 tab, 225lb, 25 year, to 8/12 slope, with felt	SF	$1.83	$0.99	$2.82	**$4.71**	0.024
Install fiberglass shingles, 3 tab, 225lb, 25 year, over 8/12 slope, felt	SF	$2.21	$0.99	$3.19	**$5.33**	0.028
Install fiberglass shingles, 3 tab, 225lb, 25 year, to 8/12 slope, no felt	SF	$1.56	$0.88	$2.44	**$4.08**	0.020
Install fiberglass shingles, 3 tab, 225lb, 25 year, over 8/12 slope, no felt	SF	$1.88	$0.88	$2.77	**$4.62**	0.024
Install fiberglass shingles, 3 tab, 240lb, 30 year, to 8/12 slope, with felt	SF	$1.83	$1.24	$3.07	**$5.13**	0.024
Install fiberglass shingles, 3 tab, 240lb, 30 year, over 8/12 slope, felt	SF	$2.21	$1.24	$3.45	**$5.76**	0.028
Install fiberglass shingles, 3 tab, 240lb, 30 year, to 8/12 slope, no felt	SF	$1.56	$1.14	$2.70	**$4.50**	0.020
Install fiberglass shingles, 3 tab, 240lb, 30 year, over 8/12 slope, no felt	SF	$1.88	$1.14	$3.02	**$5.04**	0.024
FIBERGLASS SHINGLES, GAMBREL ROOF, LAMINATE SHINGLES						
Install fiberglass shingles, laminate, 240lb, 30 yr, to 8/12 slope, with felt	SF	$2.21	$1.85	$4.06	**$6.77**	0.028
Install fiberglass shingles, laminate, 240lb, 30 yr, over 8/12 slope, felt	SF	$2.69	$1.85	$4.54	**$7.58**	0.035
Install fiberglass shingles, laminate, 240lb, 30 yr, to 8/12 slope, no felt	SF	$1.94	$1.75	$3.68	**$6.15**	0.025
Install fiberglass shingles, laminate, 240lb, 30 yr, over 8/12 slope, no felt	SF	$2.37	$1.75	$4.11	**$6.87**	0.031
Install fiberglass shingles, laminate, 260lb, 40 yr, to 8/12 slope, with felt	SF	$2.56	$2.15	$4.70	**$7.85**	0.033
Install fiberglass shingles, laminate, 260lb, 40 yr, over 8/12 slope, felt	SF	$3.09	$2.15	$5.24	**$8.75**	0.040
Install fiberglass shingles, laminate, 260lb, 40 yr, to 8/12 slope, no felt	SF	$2.29	$2.04	$4.33	**$7.23**	0.030
Install fiberglass shingles, laminate, 260lb, 40 yr, over 8/12 slope, no felt	SF	$2.77	$2.04	$4.81	**$8.03**	0.036
Install fiberglass shingles, laminate, 300lb, 50 yr, to 8/12 slope, with felt	SF	$2.56	$2.61	$5.16	**$8.62**	0.033
Install fiberglass shingles, laminate, 300lb, 50 yr, over 8/12 slope, felt	SF	$3.09	$2.61	$5.70	**$9.52**	0.040
Install fiberglass shingles, laminate, 300lb, 50 yr, to 8/12 slope, no felt	SF	$2.29	$2.50	$4.79	**$8.00**	0.030
Install fiberglass shingles, laminate, 300lb, 50 yr, over 8/12 slope, no felt	SF	$2.77	$2.50	$5.27	**$8.81**	0.036
Install fiberglass shingles, laminate, 340lb, lifetime, to 8/12 slope, with felt	SF	$2.74	$3.81	$6.55	**$10.94**	0.035
Install fiberglass shingles, laminate, 340lb, lifetime, over 8/12 slope, felt	SF	$3.31	$3.81	$7.12	**$11.88**	0.043
Install fiberglass shingles, laminate, 340lb, lifetime, to 8/12 slope, no felt	SF	$2.47	$3.70	$6.18	**$10.31**	0.032
Install fiberglass shingle, laminate, 340, lifetime, over 8/12 slope, no felt	SF	$2.99	$3.70	$6.69	**$11.17**	0.039

Roofing and Gutters

Slate Roofing

> Square footage is the actual measurement of the surface of the roof. Multiply fascia length by rake length to determine square footage of that portion of the roof.

Description	Unit	Direct Labor	Direct Materials	Direct Total	Selling Price	Man-hours
SLATE ROOFING, GABLE ROOF						
Install slate roof, to 6/12 slope, economy	SF	$6.28	$5.12	$11.39	**$19.03**	0.081
Install slate roof, over 6/12 slope, economy	SF	$7.45	$5.12	$12.57	**$20.99**	0.096
Install slate roof, to 6/12 slope, average	SF	$6.28	$7.82	$14.10	**$23.54**	0.081
Install slate roof, over 6/12 slope, average	SF	$7.45	$7.82	$15.27	**$25.51**	0.096
Install slate roof, to 6/12 slope, premium	SF	$6.28	$9.55	$15.82	**$26.42**	0.081
Install slate roof, over 6/12 slope, premium	SF	$7.45	$9.55	$17.00	**$28.39**	0.096
SLATE ROOFING, HIP ROOF						
Install slate roof, to 6/12 slope, economy	SF	$7.53	$5.63	$13.16	**$21.98**	0.097
Install slate roof, over 6/12 slope, economy	SF	$8.94	$5.63	$14.57	**$24.34**	0.115
Install slate roof, to 6/12 slope, average	SF	$7.53	$8.60	$16.13	**$26.94**	0.097
Install slate roof, over 6/12 slope, average	SF	$8.94	$8.60	$17.55	**$29.30**	0.115
Install slate roof, to 6/12 slope, premium	SF	$7.53	$10.50	$18.03	**$30.11**	0.097
Install slate roof, over 6/12 slope, premium	SF	$8.94	$10.50	$19.44	**$32.47**	0.115
SLATE ROOFING, GAMBREL ROOF						
Install slate roof, to 6/12 slope, economy	SF	$8.47	$5.12	$13.59	**$22.70**	0.109
Install slate roof, over 6/12 slope, economy	SF	$10.06	$5.12	$15.18	**$25.35**	0.130
Install slate roof, to 6/12 slope, average	SF	$8.47	$7.82	$16.29	**$27.21**	0.109
Install slate roof, over 6/12 slope, average	SF	$10.06	$7.82	$17.88	**$29.86**	0.130
Install slate roof, to 6/12 slope, premium	SF	$8.47	$9.55	$18.02	**$30.09**	0.109
Install slate roof, over 6/12 slope, premium	SF	$10.06	$9.55	$19.61	**$32.74**	0.130

Roofing and Gutters

Cedar Shake Roofing

> Square footage is the actual measurement of the surface of the roof. Multiply fascia length by rake length to determine square footage of that portion of the roof.

Description	Unit	Direct Labor	Direct Materials	Direct Total	Selling Price	Man-hours
CEDAR SHAKE ROOFING, GABLE ROOF						
Install cedar shake roof, 24" long, 10" exposure, 1/2" to 3/4" thick	SF	$3.23	$2.33	$5.56	**$9.28**	0.042
Install cedar shake roof, 24" long, 10" exp, 1/2" to 3/4" thick, fire resistant	SF	$3.23	$3.09	$6.32	**$10.55**	0.042
Install cedar shake roof, 24" long, 10" exposure, 3/4" to 5/4" thick	SF	$3.69	$2.65	$6.34	**$10.59**	0.048
Install cedar shake roof, 24" long, 10" exp, 3/4" to 5/4" thick, fire resistant	SF	$3.69	$3.41	$7.10	**$11.85**	0.048
CEDAR SHAKE ROOFING, HIP ROOF						
Install cedar shake roof, 24" long, 10" exposure, 1/2" to 3/4" thick	SF	$3.87	$2.56	$6.44	**$10.75**	0.050
Install cedar shake roof, 24" long, 10" exp, 1/2" to 3/4" thick, fire resistant	SF	$3.87	$3.40	$7.27	**$12.14**	0.050
Install cedar shake roof, 24" long, 10" exposure, 3/4" to 5/4" thick	SF	$4.42	$2.92	$7.34	**$12.26**	0.057
Install cedar shake roof, 24" long, 10" exp, 3/4" to 5/4" thick, fire resistant	SF	$4.42	$3.75	$8.18	**$13.66**	0.057
CEDAR SHAKE ROOFING, GAMBREL ROOF						
Install cedar shake roof, 24" long, 10" exposure, 1/2" to 3/4" thick	SF	$4.36	$2.33	$6.69	**$11.17**	0.056
Install cedar shake roof, 24" long, 10" exp, 1/2" to 3/4" thick, fire resistant	SF	$4.36	$3.09	$7.44	**$12.43**	0.056
Install cedar shake roof, 24" long, 10" exposure, 3/4" to 5/4" thick	SF	$4.98	$2.65	$7.63	**$12.74**	0.064
Install cedar shake roof, 24" long, 10" exp, 3/4" to 5/4" thick, fire resistant	SF	$4.98	$3.41	$8.39	**$14.01**	0.064

Roofing and Gutters

Cedar Shingle Roofing

> Square footage is the actual measurement of the surface of the roof. Multiply fascia length by rake length to determine square footage of that portion of the roof.

Description	Unit	Direct Labor	Direct Materials	Direct Total	Selling Price	Man-hours
CEDAR SHINGLE ROOFING, GABLE ROOF						
Install cedar shingle roof, 16" long, 5" exposure, #1 perfections	SF	$2.99	$2.93	$5.92	**$9.88**	0.039
Install cedar shingle roof, 16", 5" exp, #1 perfections, fire resistant	SF	$2.99	$3.79	$6.78	**$11.32**	0.039
Install cedar shingle roof, 18" long, 5-1/2" exposure, #1 perfections	SF	$2.73	$3.26	$5.99	**$10.00**	0.035
Install cedar shingle roof, 18", 5-1/2" exp, #1 perfections, fire resistant	SF	$2.73	$4.06	$6.79	**$11.34**	0.035
Install cedar shingle roof, 24" long, 7-1/2" exposure, #1 perfections	SF	$2.03	$3.07	$5.10	**$8.52**	0.026
Install cedar shingle roof, 24", 7-1/2" exp, #1 perfections, fire resistant	SF	$2.03	$3.83	$5.87	**$9.80**	0.026
CEDAR SHINGLE ROOFING, HIP ROOF						
Install cedar shingle roof, 16" long, 5" exposure, #1 perfections	SF	$3.59	$3.22	$6.81	**$11.37**	0.046
Install cedar shingle roof, 16", 5" exp, #1 perfections, fire resistant	SF	$3.59	$4.17	$7.76	**$12.95**	0.046
Install cedar shingle roof, 18" long, 5-1/2" exposure, #1 perfections	SF	$3.28	$3.58	$6.86	**$11.46**	0.042
Install cedar shingle roof, 18", 5-1/2" exp, #1 perfections, fire resistant	SF	$3.28	$4.47	$7.74	**$12.93**	0.042
Install cedar shingle roof, 24" long, 7-1/2" exposure, #1 perfections	SF	$2.44	$3.38	$5.82	**$9.71**	0.031
Install cedar shingle roof, 24", 7-1/2" exp, #1 perfections, fire resistant	SF	$2.44	$3.03	$5.47	**$9.13**	0.031
CEDAR SHINGLE ROOFING, GAMBREL ROOF						
Install cedar shingle roof, 16" long, 5" exposure, #1 perfections	SF	$4.04	$2.93	$6.96	**$11.63**	0.052
Install cedar shingle roof, 16", 5" exp, #1 perfections, fire resistant	SF	$4.04	$3.79	$7.83	**$13.07**	0.052
Install cedar shingle roof, 18" long, 5-1/2" exposure, #1 perfections	SF	$3.69	$3.26	$6.94	**$11.60**	0.048
Install cedar shingle roof, 18", 5-1/2" exp, #1 perfections, fire resistant	SF	$3.69	$4.06	$7.75	**$12.94**	0.048
Install cedar shingle roof, 24" long, 7-1/2" exposure, #1 perfections	SF	$2.74	$3.07	$5.82	**$9.71**	0.035
Install cedar shingle roof, 24", 7-1/2" exp, #1 perfections, fire resistant	SF	$2.74	$2.75	$5.50	**$9.18**	0.035

Roofing and Gutters

Fiber-Cement, Concrete, Clay, Metal Roofing

> Square footage is the actual measurement of the surface of the roof. Multiply fascia length by rake length to determine square footage of that portion of the roof.

Description	Unit	Direct Labor	Direct Materials	Direct Total	Selling Price	Man-hours
FIBER-CEMENT ROOFING						
Install fiber-cement roof, 15-3/4 x 10-5/8, 2" lap	SF	$3.51	$3.22	$6.73	**$11.23**	0.045
Install fiber-cement roof, 15-3/4 x 10-5/8, 3" lap	SF	$3.65	$3.51	$7.15	**$11.95**	0.047
Install fiber-cement roof, 15-3/4 x 10-5/8, 4" lap	SF	$3.79	$3.80	$7.58	**$12.66**	0.049
Install fiber-cement roof, 23-5/8 x 11-78, 2" lap	SF	$2.97	$3.11	$6.07	**$10.14**	0.038
Install fiber-cement roof, 23-5/8 x 11-78, 3" lap	SF	$3.11	$3.28	$6.39	**$10.66**	0.040
Install fiber-cement roof, 23-5/8 x 11-78, 4" lap	SF	$3.25	$3.39	$6.64	**$11.09**	0.042
Install concrete tile roof, 16-1/2 x 13x1/2	SF	$2.79	$1.73	$4.52	**$7.54**	0.036
CLAY TILE ROOFING						
Install Spanish tile roof, 11"oc, 15"exposure	SF	$6.76	$3.43	$10.18	**$17.00**	0.087
Install mission tile roof (barrel), 10-3/4"oc	SF	$7.75	$4.35	$12.10	**$20.20**	0.100
METAL ROOFING						
Install copper roof, 20 oz, flat seam	SF	$8.47	$9.09	$17.55	**$29.32**	0.109
Install copper roof, 20 oz, standing seam	SF	$8.47	$9.89	$18.36	**$30.66**	0.109
Install galvanized steel roof, 26 gauge, flat seam	SF	$6.97	$2.13	$9.10	**$15.20**	0.090
Install galvanized steel roof, 26 gauge, standing seam	SF	$6.97	$2.59	$9.56	**$15.97**	0.090
Install copper shingle roof	SF	$4.48	$6.33	$10.81	**$18.05**	0.058
Install steel tile roof, granular coated	SF	$2.99	$3.62	$6.61	**$11.04**	0.039
Install aluminum shingle roof	SF	$2.39	$2.65	$5.04	**$8.41**	0.031
Install galvanized tin shingle roof	SF	$2.39	$1.84	$4.23	**$7.07**	0.031

12

Roofing and Gutters

Single Ply and Built-Up Roofing

Description	Unit	Direct Labor	Direct Materials	Direct Total	Selling Price	Man-hours
BUILT-UP ROOFING						
Install 2 ply built-up roof with gravel	SF	$1.83	$0.72	$2.55	**$4.26**	0.024
Install 2 ply built-up roof no gravel	SF	$1.39	$0.38	$1.76	**$2.95**	0.018
Install 3 ply built-up roof with gravel	SF	$2.48	$0.82	$3.30	**$5.51**	0.032
Install 3 ply built-up roof no gravel	SF	$2.30	$0.54	$2.83	**$4.73**	0.030
Install 4 ply built-up roof with gravel	SF	$2.87	$0.92	$3.79	**$6.33**	0.037
Install 4 ply built-up roof no gravel	SF	$2.44	$0.65	$3.09	**$5.16**	0.031
Mop 1 coat over existing surface with no gravel	SF	$0.28	$0.10	$0.38	**$0.64**	0.004
Remove gravel, mop 1 coat, replace old gravel	SF	$0.72	$0.16	$0.88	**$1.46**	0.009
Mop 2 layers of felt over existing surface with no gravel	SF	$1.06	$0.27	$1.34	**$2.23**	0.014
Remove gravel, mop 2 layers of felt, replace old gravel	SF	$1.53	$0.33	$1.86	**$3.11**	0.020
SINGLE PLY ROOFING						
Apply rubber membrane roof, fully adhered	SF	$2.79	$1.44	$4.23	**$7.06**	0.036
Apply rubber membrane roof, edge adhered	SF	$2.19	$1.38	$3.57	**$5.97**	0.028
Install modified bitumen roof	SF	$2.39	$1.04	$3.43	**$5.72**	0.031

Cupolas and Weathervanes

Description	Unit	Direct Labor	Direct Materials	Direct Total	Selling Price	Man-hours
Install redwood cupola, 24" x 24" x 25" tall	EA	$114.18	$242.00	$356.18	**$481.08**	1.500
Install redwood cupola, 30" x 30" x 30" tall	EA	$114.18	$308.00	$422.18	**$560.28**	1.500
Install redwood cupola, 35" x 35" x 33" tall	EA	$114.18	$429.00	$543.18	**$705.48**	1.500
Install aluminum weathervane, 18" tall	EA	$38.06	$55.00	$93.06	**$129.56**	0.500
Install aluminum weathervane, 24" tall	EA	$38.06	$72.00	$110.06	**$149.96**	0.500
Install aluminum weathervane, 36" tall	EA	$38.06	$110.00	$148.06	**$195.56**	0.500

Roofing and Gutters

Roof Flashing, Ventilation, Felt, Drip Edge

Description	Unit	Direct Labor	Direct Materials	Direct Total	Selling Price	Man-hours
ROOFING FELT						
Install roofing felt, 15lb	SF	$0.20	$0.06	$0.25	**$0.42**	0.003
Install roofing felt, 30lb	SF	$0.20	$0.12	$0.31	**$0.52**	0.003
DRIP EDGE						
Install aluminum drip edge	LF	$1.70	$0.46	$2.16	**$3.61**	0.022
Install copper drip edge	LF	$2.25	$2.12	$4.36	**$7.29**	0.029
FLASHING						
Flash chimney, aluminum, small (24" x 24")	EA	$155.42	$25.30	$180.72	**$301.81**	2.006
Flash chimney, aluminum, average (32" x 36")	EA	$217.17	$35.65	$252.82	**$422.22**	2.803
Flash chimney, aluminum, large (32" x 60")	EA	$269.01	$43.70	$312.71	**$522.22**	3.472
Flash chimney, copper, small (24" x 24")	EA	$191.30	$82.80	$274.10	**$457.74**	2.469
Flash chimney, copper, average (32" x 36")	EA	$267.07	$115.00	$382.07	**$638.06**	3.447
Flash chimney, copper, large (32" x 60")	EA	$320.84	$142.60	$463.44	**$773.95**	4.141
Install aluminum stepflashing in open joints	LF	$14.26	$2.35	$16.60	**$27.73**	0.184
Install aluminum stepflashing on wood sheathing	LF	$15.26	$2.53	$17.79	**$29.71**	0.197
Install copper stepflashing in open joints	LF	$16.27	$8.05	$24.32	**$40.62**	0.210
Install copper stepflashing on wood sheathing	LF	$17.20	$8.28	$25.48	**$42.55**	0.222
Flash valleys, aluminum	LF	$3.56	$2.53	$6.09	**$10.18**	0.046
Flash valleys, copper	LF	$5.19	$9.43	$14.62	**$24.42**	0.067
Cut joint for flashing in soft mortar	LF	$5.73		$5.73	**$9.57**	0.074
Cut joint for flashing in hard mortar	LF	$9.92		$9.92	**$16.56**	0.128
Flash plumbing vent, aluminum	EA	$28.90	$11.50	$40.40	**$67.47**	0.373
Flash plumbing vent, copper	EA	$34.87	$37.95	$72.82	**$121.60**	0.450
VENTILATION						
Install continuous ridge vent, aluminum, cut roofing and install	LF	$9.45	$4.01	$13.47	**$22.49**	0.122
Install continuous ridge vent, shingle over style, cut roofing and install	LF	$12.16	$3.67	$15.83	**$26.44**	0.157
Install continuous ridge vent, aluminum, installation only	LF	$4.49	$4.01	$8.51	**$14.21**	0.058
Install continuous ridge vent, shingle over style, installation only	LF	$7.21	$3.67	$10.87	**$18.16**	0.093

12

Roofing and Gutters

Roofing Demolition

Description	Unit	Direct Labor	Direct Materials	Direct Total	Selling Price	Man-hours
DEMOLISH ASPHALT/FIBERGLASS STRIP SHINGLES						
Demolish asphalt/fiberglass shingles, to 8/12 slope, 1 layer	SF	$0.60		$0.60	**$1.00**	0.008
Demolish asphalt/fiberglass shingles, over 8/12 slope, 1 layer	SF	$0.72		$0.72	**$1.20**	0.009
Demolish asphalt/fiberglass shingles, to 8/12 slope, 2 layers	SF	$0.90		$0.90	**$1.50**	0.012
Demolish asphalt/fiberglass shingles, over 8/12 slope, 2 layers	SF	$1.08		$1.08	**$1.80**	0.014
DEMOLISH MINERAL ROLL ROOFING						
Demolish mineral roll roofing, to 8/12 slope, 1 layer	SF	$0.38		$0.38	**$0.63**	0.005
Demolish mineral roll roofing, over 8/12 slope, 1 layer	SF	$0.50		$0.50	**$0.83**	0.006
Demolish mineral roll roofing, to 8/12 slope, 2 layers	SF	$0.57		$0.57	**$0.95**	0.007
Demolish mineral roll roofing, over 8/12 slope, 2 layers	SF	$0.75		$0.75	**$1.25**	0.010
DEMOLISH BUILT-UP ROOFING						
Demolish built-up roofing, with gravel, 3-ply	SF	$1.36		$1.36	**$2.26**	0.017
Demolish built-up roofing, without gravel, 3-ply	SF	$0.84		$0.84	**$1.40**	0.011
DEMOLISH MEMBRANE ROOFING						
Demolish rubber roofing, perimeter adhered	SF	$0.60		$0.60	**$1.00**	0.008
Demolish rubber roofing, fully adhered	SF	$0.76		$0.76	**$1.26**	0.010
Demolish modified bitumen roofing	SF	$0.58		$0.58	**$0.97**	0.007
DEMOLISH SLATE, CLAY, AND METAL ROOFING						
Demolish slate roof, to 9/12 slope	SF	$1.16		$1.16	**$1.93**	0.015
Demolish slate roof, over 8/12 slope	SF	$1.30		$1.30	**$2.16**	0.017
Demolish clay tile roof, to 8/12 slope	SF	$1.20		$1.20	**$2.00**	0.015
Demolish clay tile roof, over 8/12 slope	SF	$1.33		$1.33	**$2.23**	0.017
Demolish metal roof, to 8/12 slope	SF	$1.08		$1.08	**$1.80**	0.014
Demolish metal roof, over 8/12 slope	SF	$1.22		$1.22	**$2.03**	0.016
Demolish steel tile roof, to 8/12 slope	SF	$0.84		$0.84	**$1.40**	0.011
Demolish steel tile roof, over 8/12 slope	SF	$0.98		$0.98	**$1.63**	0.013
DEMOLISH SHINGLE AND SHAKE ROOFING						
Demolish wood shingle/shake roof, 16" long, to 8/12 slope	SF	$0.88		$0.88	**$1.46**	0.011
Demolish wood shingle/shake roof, 18" long, to 8/12 slope	SF	$0.78		$0.78	**$1.30**	0.010
Demolish wood shingle/shake roof, 24" long, to 8/12 slope	SF	$0.68		$0.68	**$1.13**	0.009
Demolish wood shingle/shake roof, 16" long, over 8/12 slope	SF	$1.02		$1.02	**$1.70**	0.013
Demolish wood shingle/shake roof, 18" long, over 8/12 slope	SF	$0.92		$0.92	**$1.53**	0.012
Demolish wood shingle/shake roof, 24" long, over 8/12 slope	SF	$0.82		$0.82	**$1.37**	0.011

Roofing and Gutters

Roof Sheathing

Description	Unit	Direct Labor	Direct Materials	Direct Total	Selling Price	Man-hours
ROOF SHEATHING, PLYWOOD						
Install plywood sheathing, 3/8"	SF	$1.08	$0.47	$1.56	**$2.60**	0.014
Install plywood sheathing, 1/2"	SF	$1.08	$0.53	$1.61	**$2.70**	0.014
Install plywood sheathing, 5/8"	SF	$1.16	$0.71	$1.87	**$3.12**	0.015
Install plywood sheathing, 3/4"	SF	$1.16	$0.89	$2.05	**$3.43**	0.015
ROOF SHEATHING, ORIENTED STRAND BOARD (OSB)						
Install oriented strand board sheathing, 3/8"	SF	$1.08	$0.41	$1.50	**$2.50**	0.014
Install oriented strand board sheathing, 1/2"	SF	$1.08	$0.49	$1.57	**$2.63**	0.014
Install oriented strand board sheathing, 5/8"	SF	$1.16	$0.63	$1.79	**$2.99**	0.015
Install oriented strand board sheathing, 3/4"	SF	$1.16	$0.76	$1.93	**$3.22**	0.015
ROOF SHEATHING, STRIP						
Install strip sheathing, straight, 1" x 6" or 1" x 8"	SF	$1.78	$1.10	$2.89	**$4.82**	0.023
Install strip sheathing, diagonal, 1" x 6" or 1" x 8"	SF	$2.09	$1.40	$3.49	**$5.82**	0.027
Install strip sheathing, 1" x 3", 5-1/2"oc	SF	$0.93	$0.58	$1.51	**$2.52**	0.012
Install strip sheathing, 1" x 3", 7-1/2"oc	SF	$0.70	$0.53	$1.23	**$2.06**	0.009

Roof Insulation

Description	Unit	Direct Labor	Direct Materials	Direct Total	Selling Price	Man-hours
Install roof insulation, fiberglass board, 3/4"	SF	$0.54	$0.44	$0.98	**$1.64**	0.007
Install roof insulation, fiberglass board, 1-1/8"	SF	$0.62	$0.55	$1.17	**$1.95**	0.008
Install roof insulation, fiberglass board, 1-1/2"	SF	$0.77	$0.81	$1.59	**$2.65**	0.010
Install roof insulation, perlite board, 1"	SF	$0.54	$0.55	$1.09	**$1.82**	0.007
Install roof insulation, perlite board, 1-1/2"	SF	$0.62	$0.77	$1.39	**$2.32**	0.008
Install roof insulation, perlite board, 2-1/2"	SF	$0.77	$1.21	$1.98	**$3.31**	0.010
Install roof insulation, perlite board, 4"	SF	$1.01	$1.94	$2.94	**$4.92**	0.013
Install roof insulation, polystyrene board, 1"	SF	$0.46	$0.50	$0.96	**$1.60**	0.006
Install roof insulation, polystyrene board, 1-1/2"	SF	$0.54	$0.61	$1.15	**$1.92**	0.007
Install roof insulation, polystyrene board, 2"	SF	$0.62	$0.77	$1.39	**$2.32**	0.008
Install roof insulation, urethane board, 3/4"	SF	$0.39	$0.53	$0.92	**$1.53**	0.005
Install roof insulation, urethane board, 1"	SF	$0.39	$0.66	$1.05	**$1.75**	0.005
Install roof insulation, urethane board, 1-1/2"	SF	$0.46	$0.94	$1.40	**$2.34**	0.006
Install roof insulation, urethane board, 2"	SF	$0.54	$1.27	$1.81	**$3.02**	0.007
Install roof insulation, composition board, 1-1/2"	SF	$0.62	$1.10	$1.72	**$2.87**	0.008
Install roof insulation, composition board, 2"	SF	$0.85	$2.15	$3.00	**$5.01**	0.011
Install roof insulation, composition board, 2-1/2"	SF	$1.01	$3.03	$4.03	**$6.73**	0.013

12

Roofing and Gutters

Gutters and Downspouts

Description	Unit	Direct Labor	Direct Materials	Direct Total	Selling Price	Man-hours
GUTTERS AND DOWNSPOUTS, ALUMINUM						
Install 5" seamless aluminum guttering	LF	$10.20	$1.84	$12.04	**$20.11**	0.134
Install 6" seamless aluminum guttering	LF	$13.40	$2.65	$16.04	**$26.79**	0.176
Install 5" component aluminum guttering	LF	$7.00	$1.90	$8.90	**$14.86**	0.092
Install 6" component aluminum guttering	LF	$7.92	$2.76	$10.68	**$17.83**	0.104
Install 2" x 3" aluminum downspout	LF	$7.00	$1.55	$8.56	**$14.29**	0.092
Install 3" x 4" aluminum downspout	LF	$7.92	$2.53	$10.45	**$17.45**	0.104
GUTTERS AND DOWNSPOUTS, COPPER						
Install 5" component copper guttering	LF	$8.60	$6.04	$14.64	**$24.45**	0.113
Install 6" component copper guttering	LF	$9.74	$8.45	$18.20	**$30.39**	0.128
Install 2" x 3" copper downspout	LF	$8.30	$5.52	$13.82	**$23.07**	0.109
Install 3" x 4" copper downspout	LF	$9.29	$8.45	$17.74	**$29.62**	0.122
GUTTERS AND DOWNSPOUTS, GALVANIZED STEEL						
Install 5" component galvanized steel guttering	LF	$7.38	$2.36	$9.74	**$16.27**	0.097
Install 6" component galvanized steel guttering	LF	$8.30	$3.22	$11.52	**$19.23**	0.109
Install 2" x 3" galvanized steel downspout	LF	$7.38	$1.67	$9.05	**$15.12**	0.097
Install 3" x 4" galvanized steel downspout	LF	$8.30	$2.70	$11.00	**$18.37**	0.109
GUTTERS AND DOWNSPOUTS, VINYL						
Install 5" component vinyl guttering	LF	$6.09	$1.38	$7.46	**$12.47**	0.080
Install 2"x3" vinyl downspout	LF	$6.09	$1.16	$7.24	**$12.10**	0.080

Exterior Doors

Labor Costs to Install Exterior Doors

> Labor costs do not include materials such as door slab, jamb, casings or other trim.

Description	Unit	Direct Labor	Direct Materials	Direct Total	Selling Price	Man-hours
LABOR TO INSTALL FIELD HUNG DOORS						
Install field exterior hung door, jamb, sill, threshold, mould 2 sides	EA	$304.47		$304.47	**$508.47**	4.000
Install double field hung door, jamb, sill, threshold, mould 2 sides	Set	$456.71		$456.71	**$762.71**	6.000
Install field hung exterior door, jamb, sill, threshold, no moulding	EA	$228.36		$228.36	**$381.35**	3.000
Install double field hung door, jamb, sill, threshold, no moulding	Set	$361.56		$361.56	**$603.81**	4.750
Install new exterior door slab in existing jamb	EA	$114.18		$114.18	**$190.68**	1.500
LABOR TO INSTALL PRE-HUNG DOORS						
Install exterior pre-hung door	EA	$114.18		$114.18	**$190.68**	1.500
Install double unit exterior pre-hung door	Set	$152.24		$152.24	**$254.24**	2.000
Install pre-hung metal exterior door	EA	$152.24		$152.24	**$254.24**	2.000
LABOR TO INSTALL DOORS WITH SIDELIGHTS						
Install single door with 2 sidelights unit in prepared opening	EA	$380.59		$380.59	**$635.59**	5.000
Install double door with 2 sidelights unit in prepared opening	EA	$494.77		$494.77	**$826.27**	6.500
Install sidelight in existing frame	EA	$76.12		$76.12	**$127.12**	1.000
LABOR TO INSTALL SLIDING DOORS						
Install wood sliding patio door or atrium unit, 2 panels wide	EA	$304.47		$304.47	**$508.47**	4.000
Install wood sliding patio door or atrium unit, 3 panels wide	EA	$437.68		$437.68	**$730.93**	5.750
Install aluminum sliding patio door unit, 2 panels wide	EA	$266.41		$266.41	**$444.91**	3.500
Install aluminum sliding patio door unit, 3 panels wide	EA	$361.56		$361.56	**$603.81**	4.750
LABOR TO INSTALL GARAGE DOORS						
Install single width garage door, exterior mould	EA	$380.59		$380.59	**$635.59**	5.000
Install double width garage door, exterior mould	EA	$570.89		$570.89	**$953.38**	7.500
LABOR TO INSTALL SCREEN, STORM AND SECURITY DOORS						
Install wood or aluminum screen door	EA	$76.12		$76.12	**$127.12**	1.000
Install storm/combination door	EA	$114.18		$114.18	**$190.68**	1.500
Install ornamental iron security door	EA	$266.41		$266.41	**$444.91**	3.500

Exterior Doors

Labor Costs to Remove Exterior Doors

Description	Unit	Direct Labor	Direct Materials	Direct Total	Selling Price	Man-hours
LABOR TO REMOVE DOORS						
Remove single exterior wood door	EA	$57.09		$57.09	**$95.34**	0.750
Remove double exterior wood door	EA	$95.15		$95.15	**$158.90**	1.250
Remove exterior door slab only	EA	$38.06		$38.06	**$63.56**	0.500
Remove single exterior steel door	EA	$95.15		$95.15	**$158.90**	1.250
Remove double exterior steel door	EA	$133.21		$133.21	**$222.46**	1.750
Remove single exterior wood door unit with 1 sidelight	EA	$95.15		$95.15	**$158.90**	1.250
Remove single exterior wood door unit with 2 sidelights	EA	$114.18		$114.18	**$190.68**	1.500
Remove exterior glass sliding doors, 2 lites wide	Set	$114.18		$114.18	**$190.68**	1.500
Remove exterior glass sliding doors, 3 lites wide	Set	$152.24		$152.24	**$254.24**	2.000
Remove exterior glass sliding doors, 4 lites wide	Set	$190.30		$190.30	**$317.79**	2.500
Remove single garage door	EA	$190.30		$190.30	**$317.79**	2.500
Remove double garage door	EA	$266.41		$266.41	**$444.91**	3.500
Remove storm combination door	EA	$57.09		$57.09	**$95.34**	0.750
Remove exterior awning or canopy	LF	$6.17		$6.17	**$10.30**	0.081

Create Door Opening in Existing Wall

Description	Unit	Direct Labor	Direct Materials	Direct Total	Selling Price	Man-hours
Create door opening up to 4' wide in frame wall	EA	$608.95	$37.20	$646.15	**$1,079.07**	8.000
Create door opening up to 8' wide in frame wall	EA	$761.18	$51.15	$812.33	**$1,356.60**	10.000
Create door opening up to 12' wide in frame wall	EA	$989.54	$69.75	$1,059.29	**$1,769.01**	13.000
Create door opening up to 4' wide in brick veneer wall	EA	$723.13	$37.20	$760.33	**$1,269.74**	9.500
Create door opening up to 8' wide in brick veneer wall	EA	$932.45	$51.15	$983.60	**$1,642.61**	12.250
Create door opening up to 12' wide in brick veneer wall	EA	$1,141.78	$69.75	$1,211.53	**$2,023.25**	15.000
Create door opening up to 4' wide in brick and block wall	EA	$780.21	$37.20	$817.41	**$1,365.08**	10.250
Create door opening up to 8' wide in brick and block wall	EA	$1,008.57	$51.15	$1,059.72	**$1,769.73**	13.250
Create door opening up to 12' wide in brick and block wall	EA	$1,236.93	$69.75	$1,306.68	**$2,182.15**	16.250
Create door opening up to 4' wide in stucco wall	EA	$685.07	$37.20	$722.27	**$1,206.18**	9.000
Create door opening up to 8' wide in stucco wall	EA	$894.39	$51.15	$945.54	**$1,579.06**	11.750
Create door opening up to 12' wide in stucco wall	EA	$1,103.72	$69.75	$1,173.47	**$1,959.69**	14.500

Exterior Doors

Door Entrances

Description	Unit	Direct Labor	Direct Materials	Direct Total	Selling Price	Man-hours
DOOR ENTRANCES						
Install entrance frame, plain with 1 sidelight, door slab not included	EA	$228.36	$258.00	$486.36	**$690.95**	3.000
Install entrance frame, plain with 2 sidelights, door slab not included	EA	$266.41	$314.00	$580.41	**$821.71**	3.500
Install entrance frame, plain, 2 pilasters, 2 sidelights, slab not included	EA	$304.47	$375.00	$679.47	**$958.47**	4.000
Install entrance, colonial, no pediment, 1 door, door slab not included	EA	$190.30	$282.00	$472.30	**$656.19**	2.500
Install entrance, colonial, pediment, 1 door, door slab not included	EA	$228.36	$330.00	$558.36	**$777.35**	3.000
Install entrance, colonial, arched pediment, 1 door, slab not included	EA	$228.36	$500.00	$728.36	**$981.35**	3.000
Install entrance, colonial, no pediment, 2 door, door slabs not included	EA	$304.47	$380.00	$684.47	**$964.47**	4.000
Install entrance, colonial, pediment, 2 door, door slabs not included	EA	$342.53	$533.00	$875.53	**$1,211.63**	4.500
Install entrance, colonial, arched pediment, 2 door, slab not included	EA	$342.53	$706.00	$1,048.53	**$1,419.23**	4.500

Door Locks and Accessories

Description	Unit	Direct Labor	Direct Materials	Direct Total	Selling Price	Man-hours
Install exterior knob lockset, premium quality	EA	$53.13	$118.00	$171.13	**$230.33**	0.698
Install exterior knob lockset, average quality	EA	$53.13	$90.00	$143.13	**$196.73**	0.698
Install exterior knob lockset, economy quality	EA	$53.13	$50.00	$103.13	**$148.73**	0.698
Install exterior handle lockset, premium quality	EA	$53.13	$134.00	$187.13	**$249.53**	0.698
Install exterior handle lockset, average quality	EA	$53.13	$106.00	$159.13	**$215.93**	0.698
Install exterior handle lockset, economy quality	EA	$53.13	$62.00	$115.13	**$163.13**	0.698
Install deadbolt, premium quality	EA	$53.13	$90.00	$143.13	**$196.73**	0.698
Install deadbolt, average quality	EA	$53.13	$62.00	$115.13	**$163.13**	0.698
Install deadbolt, economy quality	EA	$53.13	$39.00	$92.13	**$135.53**	0.698
Install aluminum threshold	LF	$9.36	$4.61	$13.98	**$21.17**	0.123
Install oak threshold	LF	$9.36	$4.93	$14.29	**$21.55**	0.123
Install exterior wood door sill, 8/4 x 8 deep	LF	$15.60	$11.93	$27.53	**$40.37**	0.205
Install exterior wood door sill, 8/4 x 10 deep	LF	$19.71	$14.83	$34.54	**$50.72**	0.259
Install aluminum kickplate, 8 x 30	EA	$36.38	$20.00	$56.38	**$84.76**	0.478
Install brass kickplate, 8 x 30	EA	$36.38	$27.00	$63.38	**$93.16**	0.478
Install stainless steel kickplate, 8 x 30	EA	$36.38	$32.00	$68.38	**$99.16**	0.478
Install interlocking weatherstripping on single exterior door	EA	$61.66	$67.00	$128.66	**$183.37**	0.810
Install door sweep on single exterior door	EA	$30.83	$8.00	$38.83	**$61.08**	0.405

Exterior Doors

Jamb and Casing for Field Hung Door

> Material Costs only. Labor is included in 'Labor to Install Field Hung Door' item.

Description	Unit	Direct Labor	Direct Materials	Direct Total	Selling Price	Man-hours
JAMB ONLY, UP TO 36" WIDE						
Paint grade pine jambs, no trim or casings, up to 36", 5/4 x 4-9/16 deep	EA		$42.85	$42.85	**$71.56**	
Paint grade pine jambs, no trim or casings, up to 36", 5/4 x 5-3/16 deep	EA		$52.28	$52.28	**$87.31**	
Paint grade pine jambs, no trim or casings, up to 36", 5/4 x 6-9/16 deep	EA		$59.96	$59.96	**$100.14**	
Stain grade pine jambs, no trim or casings, up to 36", 5/4 x 4-9/16 deep	EA		$60.05	$60.05	**$100.28**	
Stain grade pine jambs, no trim or casings, up to 36", 5/4 x 5-3/16 deep	EA		$71.35	$71.35	**$119.15**	
Stain grade pine jambs, no trim or casings, up to 36", 5/4 x 6-9/16 deep	EA		$79.86	$79.86	**$133.37**	
Solid oak jambs, no trim or casings, up to 36", 5/4 x 4-9/16 deep	EA		$64.69	$64.69	**$108.03**	
Solid oak jambs, no trim or casings, up to 36", 5/4 x 5-3/16 deep	EA		$75.83	$75.83	**$126.64**	
Solid oak jambs, no trim or casings, up to 36", 5/4 x 6-9/16 deep	EA		$87.13	$87.13	**$145.50**	
JAMB, CASING AND TRIM, UP TO 36" WIDE						
Paint grade pine jambs, trim and casing, up to 36", 5/4 x 4-9/16 deep	EA		$77.92	$77.92	**$130.13**	
Paint grade pine jambs, trim and casing, up to 36", 5/4 x 5-3/16 deep	EA		$90.62	$90.62	**$151.33**	
Paint grade pine jambs, trim and casing, up to 36", 5/4 x 6-9/16 deep	EA		$101.59	$101.59	**$169.66**	
Stain grade pine jambs, trim and casing, up to 36", 5/4 x 4-9/16 deep	EA		$87.54	$87.54	**$146.20**	
Stain grade pine jambs, trim and casing, up to 36", 5/4 x 5-3/16 deep	EA		$100.29	$100.29	**$167.48**	
Stain grade pine jambs, trim and casing, up to 36", 5/4 x 6-9/16 deep	EA		$114.29	$114.29	**$190.87**	
Solid oak jambs, trim and casing, up to 36", 5/4 x 4-9/16 deep	EA		$109.95	$109.95	**$183.61**	
Solid oak jambs, trim and casing, up to 36", 5/4 x 5-3/16 deep	EA		$124.22	$124.22	**$207.45**	
Solid oak jambs, trim and casing, up to 36", 5/4 x 6-9/16 deep	EA		$140.69	$140.69	**$234.95**	
JAMB ONLY, 36" TO 60" WIDE						
Paint grade pine jambs, no trim or casings, 36" to 60", 5/4 x 4-9/16 deep	EA		$51.59	$51.59	**$86.16**	
Paint grade pine jambs, no trim or casings, 36" to 60", 5/4 x 5-3/16 deep	EA		$59.83	$59.83	**$99.92**	
Paint grade pine jambs, no trim or casings, 36" to 60", 5/4 x 6-9/16 deep	EA		$69.35	$69.35	**$115.81**	
Stain grade pine jambs, no trim or casings, 36" to 60", 5/4 x 4-9/16 deep	EA		$68.55	$68.55	**$114.47**	
Stain grade pine jambs, no trim or casings, 36" to 60", 5/4 x 5-3/16 deep	EA		$77.18	$77.18	**$128.89**	
Stain grade pine jambs, no trim or casings, 36" to 60", 5/4 x 6-9/16 deep	EA		$87.00	$87.00	**$145.30**	
Solid oak jambs, no trim or casings, 36" to 60", 5/4 x 4-9/16 deep	EA		$72.19	$72.19	**$120.55**	
Solid oak jambs, no trim or casings, 36" to 60", 5/4 x 5-3/16 deep	EA		$81.30	$81.30	**$135.78**	
Solid oak jambs, no trim or casings, 36" to 60", 5/4 x 6-9/16 deep	EA		$91.42	$91.42	**$152.68**	

Exterior Doors

Jamb and Casing for Field Hung Door (cont.)

> Material Costs only. Labor is included in 'Labor to Install Field Hung Door' item.

Description	Unit	Direct Labor	Direct Materials	Direct Total	Selling Price	Man-hours
JAMB, CASING AND TRIM, 36" TO 60" WIDE						
Paint grade pine jambs, trim and casing, 36" to 60", 5/4 x 4-9/16 deep	EA		$85.74	$85.74	**$143.19**	
Paint grade pine jambs, trim and casing, 36" to 60", 5/4 x 5-3/16 deep	EA		$98.06	$98.06	**$163.76**	
Paint grade pine jambs, trim and casing, 36" to 60", 5/4 x 6-9/16 deep	EA		$108.92	$108.92	**$181.90**	
Stain grade pine jambs, trim and casing, 36" to 60", 5/4 x 4-9/16 deep	EA		$99.19	$99.19	**$165.65**	
Stain grade pine jambs, trim and casing, 36" to 60", 5/4 x 5-3/16 deep	EA		$112.98	$112.98	**$188.68**	
Stain grade pine jambs, trim and casing, 36" to 60", 5/4 x 6-9/16 deep	EA		$126.67	$126.67	**$211.55**	
Solid oak jambs, trim and casing, 36" to 60", 5/4 x 4-9/16 deep	EA		$122.83	$122.83	**$205.13**	
Solid oak jambs, trim and casing, 36" to 60", 5/4 x 5-3/16 deep	EA		$137.27	$137.27	**$229.24**	
Solid oak jambs, trim and casing, 36" to 60", 5/4 x 6-9/16 deep	EA		$153.35	$153.35	**$256.10**	

Field Hung Flush Wood Doors

> Material Costs only. Select labor item from 'Labor Costs to Install Doors' section.

Description	Unit	Direct Labor	Direct Materials	Direct Total	Selling Price	Man-hours
Exterior flush particle core door in existing jamb, 2-6 x 6-8	EA		$83.00	$83.00	**$99.60**	
Exterior flush particle core door in existing jamb, 2-8 x 6-8	EA		$88.00	$88.00	**$105.60**	
Exterior flush particle core door in existing jamb, 3-0 x 6-8	EA		$95.00	$95.00	**$114.00**	
Exterior flush particle core door in existing jamb, 3-0 x 7-0	EA		$106.00	$106.00	**$127.20**	
Exterior flush solid core door in existing jamb, 2-6 x 6-8	EA		$121.00	$121.00	**$145.20**	
Exterior flush solid core door in existing jamb, 2-8 x 6-8	EA		$128.00	$128.00	**$153.60**	
Exterior flush solid core door in existing jamb, 3-0 x 6-8	EA		$136.00	$136.00	**$163.20**	
Exterior flush solid core door in existing jamb, 3-0 x 7-0	EA		$150.00	$150.00	**$180.00**	

Exterior Doors

Field Hung Panel Wood Doors

> Material Costs only. Select labor item from 'Labor Costs to Install Doors' section.

Description	Unit	Direct Labor	Direct Materials	Direct Total	Selling Price	Man-hours
FIELD HUNG PANEL WOOD DOORS, FIR/PINE						
Exterior 2 raised panel fir/pine door in existing jamb, 2-8 x 6-8	EA		$261.00	$261.00	**$313.20**	
Exterior 2 raised panel fir/pine door in existing jamb, 3-0 x 6-8	EA		$272.00	$272.00	**$326.40**	
Exterior 2 raised panel fir/pine door in existing jamb, 3-0 x 7-0	EA		$310.00	$310.00	**$372.00**	
Exterior 6 raised panel fir/pine door in existing jamb, 2-8 x 6-8	EA		$273.00	$273.00	**$327.60**	
Exterior 6 raised panel fir/pine door in existing jamb, 3-0 x 6-8	EA		$284.00	$284.00	**$340.80**	
Exterior 6 raised panel fir/pine door in existing jamb, 3-0 x 7-0			$323.00	$323.00	**$387.60**	
	EA					
Exterior 8 raised panel fir/pine door in existing jamb, 2-8 x 6-8	EA		$286.00	$286.00	**$343.20**	
Exterior 8 raised panel fir/pine door in existing jamb, 3-0 x 6-8	EA		$298.00	$298.00	**$357.60**	
Exterior 8 raised panel fir/pine door in existing jamb, 3-0 x 7-0	EA		$340.00	$340.00	**$408.00**	
FIELD HUNG PANEL WOOD DOORS, OAK						
Exterior 2 raised panel oak door in existing jamb, 2-8 x 6-8	EA		$326.00	$326.00	**$391.20**	
Exterior 2 raised panel oak door in existing jamb, 3-0 x 6-8	EA		$339.00	$339.00	**$406.80**	
Exterior 2 raised panel oak door in existing jamb, 3-0 x 7-0	EA		$387.00	$387.00	**$464.40**	
Exterior 6 raised panel oak door in existing jamb, 2-8 x 6-8	EA		$341.00	$341.00	**$409.20**	
Exterior 6 raised panel oak door in existing jamb, 3-0 x 6-8	EA		$355.00	$355.00	**$426.00**	
Exterior 6 raised panel oak door in existing jamb, 3-0 x 7-0	EA		$404.00	$404.00	**$484.80**	
Exterior 8 raised panel oak door in existing jamb, 2-8 x 6-8	EA		$358.00	$358.00	**$429.60**	
Exterior 8 raised panel oak door in existing jamb, 3-0 x 6-8	EA		$372.00	$372.00	**$446.40**	
Exterior 8 raised panel oak door in existing jamb, 3-0 x 7-0	EA		$425.00	$425.00	**$510.00**	

Exterior Doors

Field Hung Panel Wood Doors with Glass

> Material Costs only. Select labor item from 'Labor Costs to Install Doors' section.

Description	Unit	Direct Labor	Direct Materials	Direct Total	Selling Price	Man-hours
Exterior fir/pine door with full beveled oval lite in existing jamb, 2-8 x 6-8	EA		$1,098.00	$1,098.00	**$1,317.60**	
Exterior fir/pine door with full beveled oval lite in existing jamb, 3-0 x 6-8	EA		$1,170.00	$1,170.00	**$1,404.00**	
Exterior fir/pine door with 2 half beveled lites in existing jamb, 2-8 x 6-8	EA		$823.00	$823.00	**$987.60**	
Exterior fir/pine door with 2 half beveled lites in existing jamb, 3-0 x 6-8	EA		$877.00	$877.00	**$1,052.40**	
Exterior oak door with full beveled oval lite in existing jamb, 2-8 x 6-8	EA		$1,372.00	$1,372.00	**$1,646.40**	
Exterior oak door with full beveled oval lite in existing jamb, 3-0 x 6-8	EA		$1,462.00	$1,462.00	**$1,754.40**	
Exterior oak door with 2 half door beveled lites in existing jamb, 2-8 x 6-8	EA		$1,029.00	$1,029.00	**$1,234.80**	
Exterior oak door with 2 half door beveled lites in existing jamb, 3-0 x 6-8	EA		$1,096.00	$1,096.00	**$1,315.20**	
Exterior 1 raised panel fir/pine door with 1 lite in existing jamb, 2-8 x 6-8	EA		$286.00	$286.00	**$343.20**	
Exterior 1 raised panel fir/pine door with 1 lite in existing jamb, 3-0 x 6-8	EA		$307.00	$307.00	**$368.40**	
Exterior 1 raised panel fir/pine door with 4 lites in existing jamb, 2-8 x 6-8	EA		$307.00	$307.00	**$368.40**	
Exterior 1 raised panel fir/pine door with 4 lites in existing jamb, 3-0 x 6-8	EA		$330.00	$330.00	**$396.00**	
Exterior 1 raised panel fir/pine door with 6 lites in existing jamb, 2-8 x 6-8	EA		$314.00	$314.00	**$376.80**	
Exterior 1 raised panel fir/pine door with 6 lites in existing jamb, 3-0 x 6-8	EA		$338.00	$338.00	**$405.60**	

Field Hung French Wood Doors

> Material Costs only. Select labor item from 'Labor Costs to Install Doors' section.

Description	Unit	Direct Labor	Direct Materials	Direct Total	Selling Price	Man-hours
Exterior fir/pine french door with 5 lites in existing jamb, 2-0 x 6-8	EA		$127.00	$127.00	**$152.40**	
Exterior fir/pine french door with 5 lites in existing jamb, 2-4 x 6-8	EA		$136.00	$136.00	**$163.20**	
Exterior fir/pine french door with 5 lites in existing jamb, 2-6 x 6-8	EA		$142.00	$142.00	**$170.40**	
Exterior fir/pine french door with 5 lites in existing jamb, 2-8 x 6-8	EA		$148.00	$148.00	**$177.60**	
Exterior fir/pine french door with 5 lites in existing jamb, 3-0 x 6-8	EA		$155.00	$155.00	**$186.00**	
Exterior fir/pine french door with 2 rows of 5 lites in existing jamb, 2-0 x 6-8	EA		$167.00	$167.00	**$200.40**	
Exterior fir/pine french door with 2 rows of 5 lites in existing jamb, 2-4 x 6-8	EA		$176.00	$176.00	**$211.20**	
Exterior fir/pine french door with 2 rows of 5 lites in existing jamb, 2-6 x 6-8	EA		$184.00	$184.00	**$220.80**	
Exterior fir/pine french door with 2 rows of 5 lites in existing jamb, 2-8 x 6-8	EA		$192.00	$192.00	**$230.40**	
Exterior fir/pine french door with 2 rows of 5 lites in existing jamb, 3-0 x 6-8	EA		$200.00	$200.00	**$240.00**	
Exterior fir/pine french door with 3 rows of 5 lites in existing jamb, 2-6 x 6-8	EA		$224.00	$224.00	**$268.80**	
Exterior fir/pine french door with 3 rows of 5 lites in existing jamb, 2-8 x 6-8	EA		$234.00	$234.00	**$280.80**	
Exterior fir/pine french door with 3 rows of 5 lites in existing jamb, 3-0 x 6-8	EA		$251.00	$251.00	**$301.20**	

Exterior Doors

Pre-Hung Flush Wood Doors

➤ No removal of old door included.

Description	Unit	Direct Labor	Direct Materials	Direct Total	Selling Price	Man-hours
Exterior pre-hung flush particle core door unit, 2-6 x 6-8	EA	$114.18	$169.00	$283.18	**$393.48**	1.500
Exterior pre-hung flush particle core door unit, 2-8 x 6-8	EA	$114.18	$178.00	$292.18	**$404.28**	1.500
Exterior pre-hung flush particle core door unit, 3-0 x 6-8	EA	$114.18	$186.00	$300.18	**$413.88**	1.500
Exterior pre-hung flush particle core door unit, 3-0 x 7-0	EA	$114.18	$206.00	$320.18	**$437.88**	1.500
Exterior pre-hung flush solid core door unit, 2-6 x 6-8	EA	$114.18	$232.00	$346.18	**$469.08**	1.500
Exterior pre-hung flush solid core door unit, 2-8 x 6-8	EA	$114.18	$242.00	$356.18	**$481.08**	1.500
Exterior pre-hung flush solid core door unit, 3-0 x 6-8	EA	$114.18	$252.00	$366.18	**$493.08**	1.500
Exterior pre-hung flush solid core door unit, 3-0 x 7-0	EA	$114.18	$270.00	$384.18	**$514.68**	1.500

Pre-Hung French Wood Doors

➤ No removal of old door included.

Description	Unit	Direct Labor	Direct Materials	Direct Total	Selling Price	Man-hours
Exterior pre-hung fir/pine french door unit with 5 lites, 2-0 x 6-8	EA	$114.18	$197.00	$311.18	**$427.08**	1.500
Exterior pre-hung fir/pine french door unit with 5 lites, 2-4 x 6-8	EA	$114.18	$211.00	$325.18	**$443.88**	1.500
Exterior pre-hung fir/pine french door unit with 5 lites, 2-6 x 6-8	EA	$114.18	$220.00	$334.18	**$454.68**	1.500
Exterior pre-hung fir/pine french door unit with 5 lites, 2-8 x 6-8	EA	$114.18	$229.00	$343.18	**$465.48**	1.500
Exterior pre-hung fir/pine french door unit with 5 lites, 3-0 x 6-8	EA	$114.18	$240.00	$354.18	**$478.68**	1.500
Exterior pre-hung fir/pine french door unit with 2 rows of 5 lites, 2-0 x 6-8	EA	$114.18	$239.00	$353.18	**$477.48**	1.500
Exterior pre-hung fir/pine french door unit with 2 rows of 5 lites, 2-4 x 6-8	EA	$114.18	$252.00	$366.18	**$493.08**	1.500
Exterior pre-hung fir/pine french door unit with 2 rows of 5 lites, 2-6 x 6-8	EA	$114.18	$264.00	$378.18	**$507.48**	1.500
Exterior pre-hung fir/pine french door unit with 2 rows of 5 lites, 2-8 x 6-8	EA	$114.18	$274.00	$388.18	**$519.48**	1.500
Exterior pre-hung fir/pine french door unit with 2 rows of 5 lites, 3-0 x 6-8	EA	$114.18	$285.00	$399.18	**$532.68**	1.500
Exterior pre-hung fir/pine french door unit with 3 rows of 5 lites, 2-6 x 6-8	EA	$114.18	$298.00	$412.18	**$548.28**	1.500
Exterior pre-hung fir/pine french door unit with 3 rows of 5 lites, 2-8 x 6-8	EA	$114.18	$311.00	$425.18	**$563.88**	1.500
Exterior pre-hung fir/pine french door unit with 3 rows of 5 lites, 3-0 x 6-8	EA	$114.18	$334.00	$448.18	**$591.48**	1.500

Exterior Doors

Pre-Hung Panel Wood Doors

> No removal of old door included.

Description	Unit	Direct Labor	Direct Materials	Direct Total	Selling Price	Man-hours
PRE-HUNG PANEL WOOD DOORS, FIR/PINE						
Exterior pre-hung 2 raised panel fir/pine door unit, 2-8 x 6-8	EA	$114.18	$339.00	$453.18	**$597.48**	1.500
Exterior pre-hung 2 raised panel fir/pine door unit, 3-0 x 6-8	EA	$114.18	$353.00	$467.18	**$614.28**	1.500
Exterior pre-hung 2 raised panel fir/pine door unit, 3-0 x 7-0	EA	$114.18	$402.00	$516.18	**$673.08**	1.500
Exterior pre-hung 2 raised panel fir/pine double door unit, 6-0 x 6-8	Set	$152.24	$684.00	$836.24	**$1,075.04**	2.000
Exterior pre-hung 6 raised panel fir/pine door unit, 2-8 x 6-8	EA	$114.18	$355.00	$469.18	**$616.68**	1.500
Exterior pre-hung 6 raised panel fir/pine door unit, 3-0 x 6-8	EA	$114.18	$369.00	$483.18	**$633.48**	1.500
Exterior pre-hung 6 raised panel fir/pine door unit, 3-0 x 7-0	EA	$114.18	$420.00	$534.18	**$694.68**	1.500
Exterior pre-hung 6 raised panel fir/pine double door unit, 6-0 x 6-8	Set	$152.24	$715.00	$867.24	**$1,112.24**	2.000
Exterior pre-hung 8 raised panel fir/pine door unit, 2-8 x 6-8	EA	$114.18	$372.00	$486.18	**$637.08**	1.500
Exterior pre-hung 8 raised panel fir/pine door unit, 3-0 x 6-8	EA	$114.18	$387.00	$501.18	**$655.08**	1.500
Exterior pre-hung 8 raised panel fir/pine door unit, 3-0 x 7-0	EA	$114.18	$442.00	$556.18	**$721.08**	1.500
Exterior pre-hung 8 raised panel fir/pine double door unit, 6-0 x 6-8	Set	$152.24	$752.00	$904.24	**$1,156.64**	2.000
PRE-HUNG PANEL WOOD DOORS, OAK						
Exterior pre-hung 2 raised panel oak door unit, 2-8 x 6-8	EA	$114.18	$506.00	$620.18	**$797.88**	1.500
Exterior pre-hung 2 raised panel oak door unit, 3-0 x 6-8	EA	$114.18	$526.00	$640.18	**$821.88**	1.500
Exterior pre-hung 2 raised panel oak door unit, 3-0 x 7-0	EA	$114.18	$600.00	$714.18	**$910.68**	1.500
Exterior pre-hung 2 raised panel oak double door unit, 6-0 x 6-8	Set	$152.24	$1,008.00	$1,160.24	**$1,463.84**	2.000
Exterior pre-hung 6 raised panel oak door unit, 2-8 x 6-8	EA	$114.18	$529.00	$643.18	**$825.48**	1.500
Exterior pre-hung 6 raised panel oak door unit, 3-0 x 6-8	EA	$114.18	$550.00	$664.18	**$850.68**	1.500
Exterior pre-hung 6 raised panel oak door unit, 3-0 x 7-0	EA	$114.18	$627.00	$741.18	**$943.08**	1.500
Exterior pre-hung 6 raised panel oak double door unit, 6-0 x 6-8	Set	$152.24	$1,055.00	$1,207.24	**$1,520.24**	2.000
Exterior pre-hung 8 raised panel oak door unit, 2-8 x 6-8	EA	$114.18	$555.00	$669.18	**$856.68**	1.500
Exterior pre-hung 8 raised panel oak door unit, 3-0 x 6-8	EA	$114.18	$577.00	$691.18	**$883.08**	1.500
Exterior pre-hung 8 raised panel oak door unit, 3-0 x 7-0	EA	$114.18	$658.00	$772.18	**$980.28**	1.500
Exterior pre-hung 8 raised panel oak double door unit, 6-0 x 6-8	Set	$152.24	$1,109.00	$1,261.24	**$1,585.04**	2.000

Exterior Doors

Pre-Hung Panel Wood Doors with Glass

> No removal of old door included.

Description	Unit	Direct Labor	Direct Materials	Direct Total	Selling Price	Man-hours
Exterior pre-hung 1 raised panel fir/pine door unit with 1 lite, 2-8 x 6-8	EA	$114.18	$371.00	$485.18	**$635.88**	1.500
Exterior pre-hung 1 raised panel fir/pine door unit with 1 lite, 3-0 x 6-8	EA	$114.18	$399.00	$513.18	**$669.48**	1.500
Exterior pre-hung 1 raised panel fir/pine door unit with 4 lite, 2-8 x 6-8	EA	$114.18	$399.00	$513.18	**$669.48**	1.500
Exterior pre-hung 1 raised panel fir/pine door unit with 4 lite, 3-0 x 6-8	EA	$114.18	$429.00	$543.18	**$705.48**	1.500
Exterior pre-hung 1 raised panel fir/pine door unit with 6 lite, 2-8 x 6-8	EA	$114.18	$408.00	$522.18	**$680.28**	1.500
Exterior pre-hung 1 raised panel fir/pine door unit with 6 lite, 3-0 x 6-8	EA	$114.18	$439.00	$553.18	**$717.48**	1.500

Wood Sidelights

> Material Costs only. Select labor item from 'Labor Costs to Install Doors' section.

Description	Unit	Direct Labor	Direct Materials	Direct Total	Selling Price	Man-hours
WOOD SIDELIGHTS, FIR/PINE, BEVELED LITES						
Entrance sidelight, fir/pine, 1 beveled leaded lite, 1-0 x 6-8	EA		$435.00	$435.00	**$522.00**	
Entrance sidelight, fir/pine, 1 beveled leaded lite, 1-2 x 6-8	EA		$456.00	$456.00	**$547.20**	
Entrance sidelight, fir/pine, 6 beveled lites, 1-0 x 6-8	EA		$335.00	$335.00	**$402.00**	
Entrance sidelight, fir/pine, 6 beveled lites, 1-2 x 6-8	EA		$351.00	$351.00	**$421.20**	
WOOD SIDELIGHTS, OAK, BEVELED LITES						
Entrance sidelight, oak, 1 beveled leaded lite, 1-0 x 6-8	EA		$526.00	$526.00	**$631.20**	
Entrance sidelight, oak, 1 beveled leaded lite, 1-2 x 6-8	EA		$570.00	$570.00	**$684.00**	
Entrance sidelight, oak, 6 beveled lites, 1-0 x 6-8	EA		$405.00	$405.00	**$486.00**	
Entrance sidelight, oak, 6 beveled lites, 1-2 x 6-8	EA		$438.00	$438.00	**$525.60**	
WOOD FRENCH SIDELIGHTS						
French sidelight, pine/fir, 5 lites, 1-0 x 6-8	EA		$191.00	$191.00	**$229.20**	
French sidelight, pine/fir, 5 lites, 1-2 x 6-8	EA		$200.00	$200.00	**$240.00**	
French sidelight, pine/fir, 5 lites, 1-4 x 6-8	EA		$214.00	$214.00	**$256.80**	
French sidelight, pine/fir, 5 lites, 1-6 x 6-8	EA		$227.00	$227.00	**$272.40**	
WOOD SIDELIGHTS, PLAIN LITES						
Entrance sidelight, fir/pine, 6 plain lites, 1-0 x 6-8	EA		$188.00	$188.00	**$225.60**	
Entrance sidelight, fir/pine, 6 plain lites, 1-2 x 6-8	EA		$198.00	$198.00	**$237.60**	
Entrance sidelight, oak, 6 plain lites, 1-0 x 6-8	EA		$235.00	$235.00	**$282.00**	
Entrance sidelight, oak, 6 plain lites, 1-2 x 6-8	EA		$247.00	$247.00	**$296.40**	

Exterior Doors

Pre-Hung Metal Doors

> No removal of old door included.

Description	Unit	Direct Labor	Direct Materials	Direct Total	Selling Price	Man-hours
PRE-HUNG FLUSH METAL DOORS						
Exterior pre-hung flush steel door unit, 2-6 x 6-8	EA	$152.24	$257.00	$409.24	**$562.64**	2.000
Exterior pre-hung flush steel door unit, 2-8 x 6-8	EA	$152.24	$273.00	$425.24	**$581.84**	2.000
Exterior pre-hung flush steel door unit, 3-0 x 6-8	EA	$152.24	$280.00	$432.24	**$590.24**	2.000
Exterior pre-hung flush steel door unit, 3-0 x 7-0	EA	$152.24	$328.00	$480.24	**$647.84**	2.000
PRE-HUNG PANEL METAL DOORS						
Exterior pre-hung 6 panel steel door unit, 2-6 x 6-8	EA	$152.24	$270.00	$422.24	**$578.24**	2.000
Exterior pre-hung 6 panel steel door unit, 2-8 x 6-8	EA	$152.24	$286.00	$438.24	**$597.44**	2.000
Exterior pre-hung 6 panel steel door unit, 3-0 x 6-8	EA	$152.24	$294.00	$446.24	**$607.04**	2.000
Exterior pre-hung 6 panel steel door unit, 3-0 x 7-0	EA	$152.24	$344.00	$496.24	**$667.04**	2.000
PRE-HUNG PANEL METAL DOORS WITH GLASS						
Exterior pre-hung 1 panel 1 lite steel door unit, 2-6 x 6-8	EA	$152.24	$312.00	$464.24	**$628.64**	2.000
Exterior pre-hung 1 panel 1 lite steel door unit, 2-8 x 6-8	EA	$152.24	$326.00	$478.24	**$645.44**	2.000
Exterior pre-hung 1 panel 1 lite steel door unit, 3-0 x 6-8	EA	$152.24	$339.00	$491.24	**$661.04**	2.000
Exterior pre-hung 1 panel 9 lite steel door unit, 2-8 x 6-8	EA	$152.24	$365.00	$517.24	**$692.24**	2.000
Exterior pre-hung 1 panel 9 lite steel door unit, 3-0 x 6-8	EA	$152.24	$404.00	$556.24	**$739.04**	2.000
Exterior pre-hung 1 panel 1 fan lite steel door unit, 2-8 x 6-8	EA	$152.24	$405.00	$557.24	**$740.24**	2.000
Exterior pre-hung 1 panel 1 fan lite steel door unit, 3-0 x 6-8	EA	$152.24	$414.00	$566.24	**$751.04**	2.000
Exterior pre-hung 4 panel 1 lite steel door unit, 2-6 x 6-8	EA	$152.24	$312.00	$464.24	**$628.64**	2.000
Exterior pre-hung 4 panel 1 lite steel door unit, 2-8 x 6-8	EA	$152.24	$326.00	$478.24	**$645.44**	2.000
Exterior pre-hung 4 panel 1 lite steel door unit, 3-0 x 6-8	EA	$152.24	$339.00	$491.24	**$661.04**	2.000
Exterior pre-hung 4 panel 9 lite steel door unit, 2-8 x 6-8	EA	$152.24	$365.00	$517.24	**$692.24**	2.000
Exterior pre-hung 4 panel 9 lite steel door unit, 3-0 x 6-8	EA	$152.24	$404.00	$556.24	**$739.04**	2.000
Exterior pre-hung 4 panel 1 fan lite steel door unit, 2-8 x 6-8	EA	$152.24	$405.00	$557.24	**$740.24**	2.000
Exterior pre-hung 4 panel 1 fan lite steel door unit, 3-0 x 6-8	EA	$152.24	$414.00	$566.24	**$751.04**	2.000
PRE-HUNG FRENCH METAL DOORS						
Exterior pre-hung steel french door unit, 2 rows of 5 lites, 2-6 x 6-8	EA	$152.24	$444.00	$596.24	**$787.04**	2.000
Exterior pre-hung steel french door unit, 2 rows of 5 lites, 2-8 x 6-8	EA	$152.24	$452.00	$604.24	**$796.64**	2.000
Exterior pre-hung steel french door unit, 2 rows of 5 lites, 3-0 x 6-8	EA	$152.24	$464.00	$616.24	**$811.04**	2.000
Exterior pre-hung steel french door unit, 3 rows of 5 lites, 2-6 x 6-8	EA	$152.24	$470.00	$622.24	**$818.24**	2.000
Exterior pre-hung steel french door unit, 3 rows of 5 lites, 2-8 x 6-8	EA	$152.24	$479.00	$631.24	**$829.04**	2.000
Exterior pre-hung steel french door unit, 3 rows of 5 lites, 3-0 x 6-8	EA	$152.24	$489.00	$641.24	**$841.04**	2.000

Exterior Doors

Sliding Exterior Wood Doors

> No removal of old door included.

Description	Unit	Direct Labor	Direct Materials	Direct Total	Selling Price	Man-hours
SLIDING EXTERIOR WOOD DOORS, 2 PANEL						
Exterior fir/pine sliding glass door, 2 panel, 5-0 x 6-8, economy grade	EA	$304.47	$609.00	$913.47	**$1,239.27**	4.000
Exterior fir/pine sliding glass door, 2 panel, 6-0 x 6-8, economy grade	EA	$304.47	$701.00	$1,005.47	**$1,349.67**	4.000
Exterior fir/pine sliding glass door, 2 panel, 8-0 x 6-8, economy grade	EA	$304.47	$824.00	$1,128.47	**$1,497.27**	4.000
Exterior fir/pine sliding glass door, 2 panel, 5-0 x 6-8, insulated glass	EA	$304.47	$975.00	$930.68	**$1,678.47**	4.000
Exterior fir/pine sliding glass door, 2 panel, 6-0 x 6-8, insulated glass	EA	$304.47	$1,089.00	$1,030.56	**$1,815.27**	4.000
Exterior fir/pine sliding glass door, 2 panel, 8-0 x 6-8, insulated glass	EA	$304.47	$1,278.00	$1,250.43	**$2,042.07**	4.000
Exterior fir/pine sliding door, 2 panel, 5-0 x 6-8, insulated, clad	Ea	$304.47	$1,434.00	$1,738.47	**$2,229.27**	4.000
Exterior fir/pine sliding door, 2 panel, 6-0 x 6-8, insulated, clad	EA	$304.47	$1,631.00	$1,935.47	**$2,465.67**	4.000
Exterior fir/pine sliding door, 2 panel, 8-0 x 6-8, insulated, clad	EA	$304.47	$1,917.00	$2,221.47	**$2,808.87**	4.000
SLIDING EXTERIOR WOOD DOORS, 3 PANEL						
Exterior fir/pine sliding glass door, 3 panel, 9-0 x 6-8, economy grade	EA	$437.68	$997.00	$1,434.68	**$1,927.33**	5.750
Exterior fir/pine sliding glass door, 3 panel, 10-0 x 6-8, economy grade	EA	$437.68	$1,057.00	$1,494.68	**$1,999.33**	5.750
Exterior fir/pine sliding glass door, 3 panel, 12-0 x 6-8, economy grade	EA	$437.68	$1,259.00	$1,696.68	**$2,241.73**	5.750
Exterior fir/pine sliding glass door, 3 panel, 9-0 x 6-8, insulated glass	EA	$437.68	$1,577.00	$2,014.68	**$2,623.33**	5.750
Exterior fir/pine sliding glass door, 3 panel, 10-0 x 6-8, insulated glass	EA	$437.68	$1,780.00	$2,217.68	**$2,866.93**	5.750
Exterior fir/pine sliding glass door, 3 panel, 12-0 x 6-8, insulated glass	EA	$437.68	$2,022.00	$2,459.68	**$3,157.33**	5.750
Exterior fir/pine sliding door, 3 panel, 9-0 x 6-8, insulated, clad	EA	$437.68	$2,269.00	$2,706.68	**$3,453.73**	5.750
Exterior fir/pine sliding door, 3 panel, 10-0 x 6-8, insulated, clad	EA	$437.68	$2,391.00	$2,828.68	**$3,600.13**	5.750
Exterior fir/pine sliding door, 3 panel, 12-0 x 6-8, insulated, clad	EA	$437.68	$2,737.00	$3,174.68	**$4,015.33**	5.750
SLIDING EXTERIOR FRENCH DOORS						
Exterior fir/pine sliding french door, 2 rows of 5 lites, 2 panel, 5-0 x 6-8	EA	$304.47	$2,027.00	$2,331.47	**$2,940.87**	4.000
Exterior fir/pine sliding french door, 2 rows of 5 lites, 2 panel, 6-0 x 6-8	EA	$304.47	$2,207.00	$2,511.47	**$3,156.87**	4.000
Exterior fir/pine sliding french door, 2 rows of 5 lites, 2 panel, 8-0 x 6-8	EA	$304.47	$2,391.00	$2,695.47	**$3,377.67**	4.000
Exterior fir/pine sliding french door, 3 rows of 5 lites, 2 panel, 5-0 x 6-8	EA	$304.47	$2,407.00	$2,711.47	**$3,396.87**	4.000
Exterior fir/pine sliding french door, 3 rows of 5 lites, 2 panel, 6-0 x 6-8	EA	$304.47	$2,608.00	$2,912.47	**$3,638.07**	4.000
Exterior fir/pine sliding french door, 3 rows of 5 lites, 2 panel, 8-0 x 6-8	EA	$304.47	$2,821.00	$3,125.47	**$3,893.67**	4.000

Exterior Doors

Sliding Exterior Aluminum Doors

> No removal of old door included.

Description	Unit	Direct Labor	Direct Materials	Direct Total	Selling Price	Man-hours
SLIDING EXTERIOR ALUMINUM DOORS						
Exterior aluminum sliding glass door, 2 panel, 5-0 x 6-8, economy grade	EA	$266.41	$455.00	$721.41	**$990.91**	3.500
Exterior aluminum sliding glass door, 2 panel, 6-0 x 6-8, economy grade	EA	$266.41	$496.00	$762.41	**$1,040.11**	3.500
Exterior aluminum sliding glass door, 2 panel, 8-0 x 6-8, economy grade	EA	$266.41	$569.00	$835.41	**$1,127.71**	3.500
Exterior aluminum sliding glass door, 2 panel, 5-0 x 6-8, insulated glass	EA	$266.41	$722.00	$988.41	**$1,311.31**	3.500
Exterior aluminum sliding glass door, 2 panel, 6-0 x 6-8, insulated glass	EA	$266.41	$793.00	$1,059.41	**$1,396.51**	3.500
Exterior aluminum sliding glass door, 2 panel, 8-0 x 6-8, insulated glass	EA	$266.41	$977.00	$1,243.41	**$1,617.31**	3.500
Exterior aluminum sliding glass door, 3 panel, 9-0 x 6-8, economy grade	EA	$361.56	$720.00	$1,081.56	**$1,467.81**	4.750
Exterior aluminum sliding glass door, 3 panel, 10-0 x 6-8, economy grade	EA	$361.56	$829.00	$1,190.56	**$1,598.61**	4.750
Exterior aluminum sliding glass door, 3 panel, 12-0 x 6-8, economy grade	EA	$361.56	$919.00	$1,280.56	**$1,706.61**	4.750
Exterior aluminum sliding glass door, 4 panel, 12-0 x 6-8, economy grade	EA	$361.56	$1,016.00	$1,377.56	**$1,823.01**	4.750
Exterior aluminum sliding glass door, 3 panel, 9-0 x 6-8, insulated glass	EA	$361.56	$1,206.00	$1,567.56	**$2,051.01**	4.750
Exterior aluminum sliding glass door, 3 panel, 10-0 x 6-8, insulated glass	EA	$361.56	$1,394.00	$1,755.56	**$2,276.61**	4.750
Exterior aluminum sliding glass door, 3 panel, 12-0 x 6-8, insulated glass	EA	$361.56	$1,487.00	$1,848.56	**$2,388.21**	4.750
Exterior aluminum sliding glass door, 4 panel, 12-0 x 6-8, insulated glass	EA	$361.56	$1,651.00	$2,012.56	**$2,585.01**	4.750

Exterior Wood Atrium Doors

> No removal of old door included.

Description	Unit	Direct Labor	Direct Materials	Direct Total	Selling Price	Man-hours
Exterior wood atrium door, 1 door, 1 fixed panel, 5-0 x 6-8, economy	EA	$304.47	$525.00	$829.47	**$1,138.47**	4.000
Exterior wood atrium door, 1 door, 1 fixed panel, 6-0 x 6-8, economy	EA	$304.47	$584.00	$888.47	**$1,209.27**	4.000
Exterior wood atrium door, 1 door, 1 fixed panel, 7-0 x 6-8, economy	EA	$304.47	$649.00	$953.47	**$1,287.27**	4.000
Exterior wood atrium door, 2 door, 1 fixed panel, 8-0 x 6-8, economy	EA	$437.68	$745.00	$1,182.68	**$1,624.93**	5.750
Exterior wood atrium door, 2 door, 1 fixed panel, 9-0 x 6-8, economy	EA	$437.68	$800.00	$1,237.68	**$1,690.93**	5.750
Ext. wood atrium door, 1 door, 1 fixed panel, 5-0 x 6-8, insulated glass	EA	$304.47	$853.00	$1,157.47	**$1,532.07**	4.000
Ext. wood atrium door, 1 door, 1 fixed panel, 6-0 x 6-8, insulated glass	EA	$304.47	$949.00	$1,253.47	**$1,647.27**	4.000
Ext. wood atrium door, 1 door, 1 fixed panel, 7-0 x 6-8, insulated glass	EA	$304.47	$1,054.00	$1,358.47	**$1,773.27**	4.000
Ext. wood atrium door, 2 door, 1 fixed panel, 8-0 x 6-8, insulated glass	EA	$437.68	$1,211.00	$1,648.68	**$2,184.13**	5.750
Ext. wood atrium door, 2 door, 1 fixed panel, 9-0 x 6-8, insulated glass	EA	$437.68	$1,300.00	$1,737.68	**$2,290.93**	5.750
Atrium door, 1 door, 1 fixed panel, 5-0 x 6-8, insul glass, alum/vinyl clad	EA	$304.47	$998.00	$1,302.47	**$1,706.07**	4.000
Atrium door, 1 door, 1 fixed panel, 6-0 x 6-8, insul glass, alum/vinyl clad	EA	$304.47	$1,049.00	$1,353.47	**$1,767.27**	4.000
Atrium door, 1 door, 1 fixed panel, 7-0 x 6-8, insul glass, alum/vinyl clad	EA	$304.47	$1,111.00	$1,415.47	**$1,841.67**	4.000
Atrium door, 2 door, 1 fixed panel, 8-0 x 6-8, insul glass, alum/vinyl clad	EA	$437.68	$1,293.00	$1,730.68	**$2,282.53**	5.750
Atrium door, 2 door, 1 fixed panel, 9-0 x 6-8, insul glass, alum/vinyl clad	EA	$437.68	$1,401.00	$1,838.68	**$2,412.13**	5.750

Exterior Doors

Garage Doors, Sectional Type

> No removal of old door included.

Description	Unit	Direct Labor	Direct Materials	Direct Total	Selling Price	Man-hours
Wood garage door, sectional, 8' x 7', includes hardware	EA	$380.59	$426.00	$806.59	**$1,146.79**	5.000
Wood garage door, sectional, 9' x 7', includes hardware	EA	$380.59	$448.00	$828.59	**$1,173.19**	5.000
Wood garage door, sectional, 16' x 7', includes hardware	EA	$570.89	$706.00	$1,276.89	**$1,800.58**	7.500
Steel garage door, sectional, 8' x 7', includes hardware	EA	$380.59	$560.00	$940.59	**$1,307.59**	5.000
Steel garage door, sectional, 9' x 7', includes hardware	EA	$380.59	$582.00	$962.59	**$1,333.99**	5.000
Steel garage door, sectional, 16' x 7', includes hardware	EA	$570.89	$918.00	$1,488.89	**$2,054.98**	7.500
Fiberglass garage door, sectional, 8' x 7', includes hardware	EA	$380.59	$493.00	$873.59	**$1,227.19**	5.000
Fiberglass garage door, sectional, 9' x 7', includes hardware	EA	$380.59	$515.00	$895.59	**$1,253.59**	5.000
Fiberglass garage door, sectional, 16' x 7, includes hardware	EA	$570.89	$840.00	$1,410.89	**$1,961.38**	7.500
Aluminum frame, foam/plastic garage door, sectional, 8' x 7', hardware	EA	$380.59	$650.00	$1,030.59	**$1,415.59**	5.000
Aluminum frame, foam/plastic garage door, sectional, 9' x 7', hardware	EA	$380.59	$697.00	$1,077.59	**$1,471.99**	5.000
Aluminum frame, foam/plastic garage door, sectional, 16' x 7', hardware	EA	$570.89	$1,098.00	$1,668.89	**$2,270.98**	7.500

Garage Doors, Jamb Type

> No removal of old door included.

Description	Unit	Direct Labor	Direct Materials	Direct Total	Selling Price	Man-hours
Wood garage door, jamb type, 8' x 7', includes hardware	EA	$380.59	$342.00	$722.59	**$1,045.99**	5.000
Wood garage door, jamb type, 9' x 7', includes hardware	EA	$380.59	$392.00	$772.59	**$1,105.99**	5.000
Wood garage door, jamb type, 16' x 7', includes hardware	EA	$570.89	$700.00	$1,270.89	**$1,793.38**	7.500
Steel garage door, jamb type, 8' x 7', includes hardware	EA	$380.59	$302.00	$682.59	**$997.99**	5.000
Steel garage door, jamb type, 9' x 7', includes hardware	EA	$380.59	$336.00	$716.59	**$1,038.79**	5.000
Steel garage door, jamb type, 16' x 7', includes hardware	EA	$570.89	$582.00	$1,152.89	**$1,651.78**	7.500
Fiberglass garage door, jamb type, 8' x 7', includes hardware	EA	$380.59	$353.00	$733.59	**$1,059.19**	5.000
Fiberglass garage door, jamb type, 9' x 7', includes hardware	EA	$380.59	$403.00	$783.59	**$1,119.19**	5.000
Fiberglass garage door, jamb type, 16' x 7, includes hardware	EA	$570.89	$706.00	$1,276.89	**$1,800.58**	7.500
Aluminum frame, foam/plastic garage door, jamb type, 8' x 7', hardware	EA	$380.59	$381.00	$761.59	**$1,092.79**	5.000
Aluminum frame, foam/plastic garage door, jamb type, 9' x 7', hardware	EA	$380.59	$420.00	$800.59	**$1,139.59**	5.000
Aluminum frame, foam/plastic garage door, jamb type, 16' x 7', hardware	EA	$570.89	$672.00	$1,242.89	**$1,759.78**	7.500

Exterior Doors

Garage Door Operators

Description	Unit	Direct Labor	Direct Materials	Direct Total	Selling Price	Man-hours
Install garage door opener, chain drive, 1/4 hp, one transmitter	EA	$304.47	$187.00	$491.47	**$732.87**	4.000
Install garage door opener, chain drive, 1/3 hp, one transmitter	EA	$304.47	$209.00	$513.47	**$759.27**	4.000
Install garage door opener, direct drive, 1/3 hp, one transmitter	EA	$304.47	$231.00	$535.47	**$785.67**	4.000
Install garage door opener, chain drive, 1/2 hp, one transmitter	EA	$304.47	$264.00	$568.47	**$825.27**	4.000
Install garage door opener, direct drive, 1/2 hp, one transmitter	EA	$304.47	$286.00	$590.47	**$851.67**	4.000
Additional garage door opener transmitters	EA		$39.00	$39.00	**$46.80**	

Screen, Storm and Security Doors

> No removal of old door included.

Description	Unit	Direct Labor	Direct Materials	Direct Total	Selling Price	Man-hours
Exterior fir/pine screen door, full screen, 2-6 x 6-8	EA	$76.12	$113.00	$189.12	**$262.72**	1.000
Exterior fir/pine screen door, full screen, 2-8 x 6-8	EA	$76.12	$124.00	$200.12	**$275.92**	1.000
Exterior fir/pine screen door, full screen, 3-0 x 6-8	EA	$76.12	$136.00	$212.12	**$290.32**	1.000
Exterior fir/pine screen door, half screen, 2-6 x 6-8	EA	$76.12	$151.00	$227.12	**$308.32**	1.000
Exterior fir/pine screen door, half screen, 2-8 x 6-8	EA	$76.12	$166.00	$242.12	**$326.32**	1.000
Exterior fir/pine screen door, half screen, 3-0 x 6-8	EA	$76.12	$180.00	$256.12	**$343.12**	1.000
Exterior aluminum screen door, half screen, 2-6 x 6-8	EA	$76.12	$134.00	$210.12	**$287.92**	1.000
Exterior aluminum screen door, half screen, 2-8 x 6-8	EA	$76.12	$140.00	$216.12	**$295.12**	1.000
Exterior aluminum screen door, half screen, 3-0 x 6-8	EA	$76.12	$146.00	$222.12	**$302.32**	1.000
Exterior aluminum glass storm door, full view, screen insert	EA	$114.18	$246.00	$360.18	**$485.88**	1.500
Exterior aluminum glass storm door, half view, screen insert	EA	$114.18	$224.00	$338.18	**$459.48**	1.500
Exterior aluminum self-storing combination glass/screen door	EA	$114.18	$291.00	$405.18	**$539.88**	1.500
Exterior ornamental iron security door, 2-8 x 6-8	EA	$266.41	$474.00	$740.41	**$1,013.71**	3.500
Exterior ornamental iron security door, 3-0 x 6-8	EA	$266.41	$559.00	$825.41	**$1,115.71**	3.500

Wood Windows

Labor Costs to Install Wood Windows

> Labor costs do not include materials such as sash, frame, casings or other trim.

Description	Unit	Direct Labor	Direct Materials	Direct Total	Selling Price	Man-hours
LABOR TO INSTALL SINGLE/DOUBLE HUNG WINDOWS						
Install wood double hung window, up to 15 SF, medium	Set	$95.15		$95.15	**$158.90**	1.250
Install wood double hung window, over 15 SF, large	Set	$152.24		$152.24	**$254.24**	2.000
LABOR TO INSTALL AWNING WINDOWS						
Install wood awning window, 1 lite wide	EA	$76.12		$76.12	**$127.12**	1.000
Install wood awning window, 2 lites wide	EA	$133.21		$133.21	**$222.46**	1.750
Install wood awning window, 3 lites wide	EA	$190.30		$190.30	**$317.79**	2.500
LABOR TO INSTALL CASEMENT WINDOWS						
Install wood casement window, 1 venting, up to 48 high	Set	$76.12		$76.12	**$127.12**	1.000
Install wood casement window, 1 venting, over 48 high	Set	$114.18		$114.18	**$190.68**	1.500
Install wood casement window, 2 venting, up to 48 high	Set	$114.18		$114.18	**$190.68**	1.500
Install wood casement window, 2 venting, over 48 high	Set	$152.24		$152.24	**$254.24**	2.000
LABOR TO INSTALL SLIDING WINDOWS						
Install wood sliding window, up to 48 wide	EA	$133.21		$133.21	**$222.46**	1.750
Install wood sliding window, over 48 wide	EA	$228.36		$228.36	**$381.35**	3.000
LABOR TO INSTALL SPECIALTY AND PICTURE WINDOWS						
Install wood picture window, up to 48 high	Set	$114.18		$114.18	**$190.68**	1.500
Install wood picture window, over 48 high	Set	$152.24		$152.24	**$254.24**	2.000
Install wood picture window with flankers, up to 48 high	Set	$190.30		$190.30	**$317.79**	2.500
Install wood picture window with flankers, over 48 high	Set	$228.36		$228.36	**$381.35**	3.000
Install wood rectangular transom window	EA	$133.21		$133.21	**$222.46**	1.750
Install wood round, half round, window	EA	$133.21		$133.21	**$222.46**	1.750

Labor Costs to Remove Wood Windows

Description	Unit	Direct Labor	Direct Materials	Direct Total	Selling Price	Man-hours
LABOR TO REMOVE WOOD WINDOWS						
Remove small wood window in frame wall, to 12 SF	EA	$38.06		$38.06	**$63.56**	0.500
Remove medium wood window in frame wall, 12-25 SF	EA	$57.09		$57.09	**$95.34**	0.750
Remove large wood window in frame wall, over 25 SF	EA	$95.15		$95.15	**$158.90**	1.250
Remove small wood window in masonry wall, to 12 SF	EA	$57.09		$57.09	**$95.34**	0.750
Remove medium wood window in masonry wall, 12-25 SF	EA	$76.12		$76.12	**$127.12**	1.000
Remove large wood window in masonry wall, over 25 SF	EA	$114.18		$114.18	**$190.68**	1.500
Remove exterior awning or canopy	LF	$6.17		$6.17	**$10.30**	0.081

Wood Windows

Create Window Opening in Existing Wall

Description	Unit	Direct Labor	Direct Materials	Direct Total	Selling Price	Man-hours
Create small window opening up to 12 SF in frame wall	EA	$456.71	$22.09	$478.80	**$799.59**	6.000
Create medium window opening 12-25 SF in frame wall	EA	$608.95	$37.20	$646.15	**$1,079.07**	8.000
Create large window opening over 25 SF in frame wall	EA	$837.30	$44.18	$881.48	**$1,472.07**	11.000
Create small window opening up to 12 SF in brick veneer wall	EA	$551.86	$22.09	$573.95	**$958.49**	7.250
Create medium window opening 12-25 SF in brick veneer wall	EA	$723.13	$37.20	$760.33	**$1,269.74**	9.500
Create large window opening over 25 SF in brick veneer wall	EA	$989.54	$44.18	$1,033.72	**$1,726.30**	13.000
Create small window opening up to 12 SF in brick and block wall	EA	$608.95	$22.09	$631.04	**$1,053.83**	8.000
Create medium window opening 12-25 SF in brick and block wall	EA	$780.21	$37.20	$817.41	**$1,365.08**	10.250
Create large window opening over 25 SF in brick and block wall	EA	$1,065.66	$44.18	$1,109.83	**$1,853.42**	14.000
Create small window opening up to 12 SF in stucco wall	EA	$532.83	$22.09	$554.92	**$926.71**	7.000
Create medium window opening 12-25 SF in stucco wall	EA	$704.10	$37.20	$741.30	**$1,237.96**	9.250
Create large window opening over 25 SF in stucco wall	EA	$951.48	$44.18	$995.66	**$1,662.75**	12.500

Wood Windows

Double Hung, Single Glazed Wood Window

➤ No removal of old window included.

Description	Unit	Direct Labor	Direct Materials	Direct Total	Selling Price	Man-hours
Double hung, single glaze, wood window, 1-8 x 3-2	EA	$95.15	$103.00	$198.15	**$282.50**	1.250
Double hung, single glaze, wood window, 1-8 x 3-10	EA	$95.15	$107.00	$202.15	**$287.30**	1.250
Double hung, single glaze, wood window, 1-8 x 4-2	EA	$95.15	$112.00	$207.15	**$293.30**	1.250
Double hung, single glaze, wood window, 1-8 x 4-6	EA	$95.15	$117.00	$212.15	**$299.30**	1.250
Double hung, single glaze, wood window, 2-0 x 3-2	EA	$95.15	$107.00	$202.15	**$287.30**	1.250
Double hung, single glaze, wood window, 2-0 x 3-10	EA	$95.15	$111.00	$206.15	**$292.10**	1.250
Double hung, single glaze, wood window, 2-0 x 4-2	EA	$95.15	$113.00	$208.15	**$294.50**	1.250
Double hung, single glaze, wood window, 2-0 x 4-6	EA	$95.15	$117.00	$212.15	**$299.30**	1.250
Double hung, single glaze, wood window, 2-0 x 5-2	EA	$95.15	$129.00	$224.15	**$313.70**	1.250
Double hung, single glaze, wood window, 2-4 x 3-2	EA	$95.15	$111.00	$206.15	**$292.10**	1.250
Double hung, single glaze, wood window, 2-4 x 3-10	EA	$95.15	$116.00	$211.15	**$298.10**	1.250
Double hung, single glaze, wood window, 2-4 x 4-2	EA	$95.15	$118.00	$213.15	**$300.50**	1.250
Double hung, single glaze, wood window, 2-4 x 4-6	EA	$95.15	$128.00	$223.15	**$312.50**	1.250
Double hung, single glaze, wood window, 2-4 x 5-2	EA	$95.15	$137.00	$232.15	**$323.30**	1.250
Double hung, single glaze, wood window, 2-8 x 3-2	EA	$95.15	$120.00	$215.15	**$302.90**	1.250
Double hung, single glaze, wood window, 2-8 x 3-10	EA	$95.15	$124.00	$219.15	**$307.70**	1.250
Double hung, single glaze, wood window, 2-8 x 4-2	EA	$95.15	$133.00	$228.15	**$318.50**	1.250
Double hung, single glaze, wood window, 2-8 x 4-6	EA	$95.15	$143.00	$238.15	**$330.50**	1.250
Double hung, single glaze, wood window, 2-8 x 5-2	EA	$95.15	$153.00	$248.15	**$342.50**	1.250
Double hung, single glaze, wood window, 2-8 x 5-6	EA	$95.15	$166.00	$261.15	**$358.10**	1.250
Double hung, single glaze, wood window, 2-8 x 6-2	EA	$152.24	$183.00	$335.24	**$473.84**	2.000
Double hung, single glaze, wood window, 3-0 x 3-10	EA	$95.15	$133.00	$228.15	**$318.50**	1.250
Double hung, single glaze, wood window, 3-0 x 4-2	EA	$95.15	$152.00	$247.15	**$341.30**	1.250
Double hung, single glaze, wood window, 3-0 x 4-6	EA	$95.15	$161.00	$256.15	**$352.10**	1.250
Double hung, single glaze, wood window, 3-0 x 5-2	EA	$152.24	$176.00	$328.24	**$465.44**	2.000
Double hung, single glaze, wood window, 3-0 x 5-6	EA	$152.24	$187.00	$339.24	**$478.64**	2.000
Double hung, single glaze, wood window, 3-0 x 6-2	EA	$152.24	$200.00	$352.24	**$494.24**	2.000
Double hung, single glaze, wood window, 3-4 x 3-10	EA	$95.15	$139.00	$234.15	**$325.70**	1.250
Double hung, single glaze, wood window, 3-4 x 4-2	EA	$95.15	$158.00	$253.15	**$348.50**	1.250
Double hung, single glaze, wood window, 3-4 x 4-6	EA	$152.24	$170.00	$322.24	**$458.24**	2.000
Double hung, single glaze, wood window, 3-4 x 5-2	EA	$152.24	$193.00	$345.24	**$485.84**	2.000
Double hung, single glaze, wood window, 3-4 x 5-6	EA	$152.24	$209.00	$361.24	**$505.04**	2.000
Double hung, single glaze, wood window, 3-4 x 6-2	EA	$152.24	$224.00	$376.24	**$523.04**	2.000
Double hung, single glaze, wood window, 3-8 x 4-2	EA	$152.24	$166.00	$318.24	**$453.44**	2.000
Double hung, single glaze, wood window, 3-8 x 4-6	EA	$152.24	$182.00	$334.24	**$472.64**	2.000
Double hung, single glaze, wood window, 3-8 x 5-2	EA	$152.24	$210.00	$362.24	**$506.24**	2.000
Double hung, single glaze, wood window, 3-8 x 5-6	EA	$152.24	$232.00	$384.24	**$532.64**	2.000
Double hung, single glaze, wood window, 3-8 x 6-2	EA	$152.24	$252.00	$404.24	**$556.64**	2.000

Wood Windows

Double Hung, Insulated Glass Wood Window

➤ No removal of old window included.

Description	Unit	Direct Labor	Direct Materials	Direct Total	Selling Price	Man-hours
Double hung, double glaze, wood window, 1-8 x 3-2	EA	$95.15	$209.00	$304.15	**$409.70**	1.250
Double hung, insulated glass, wood window, 1-8 x 3-10	EA	$95.15	$211.00	$306.15	**$412.10**	1.250
Double hung, insulated glass, wood window, 1-8 x 4-2	EA	$95.15	$219.00	$314.15	**$421.70**	1.250
Double hung, insulated glass, wood window, 1-8 x 4-6	EA	$95.15	$225.00	$320.15	**$428.90**	1.250
Double hung, insulated glass, wood window, 2-0 x 3-2	EA	$95.15	$211.00	$306.15	**$412.10**	1.250
Double hung, insulated glass, wood window, 2-0 x 3-10	EA	$95.15	$219.00	$314.15	**$421.70**	1.250
Double hung, insulated glass, wood window, 2-0 x 4-2	EA	$95.15	$225.00	$320.15	**$428.90**	1.250
Double hung, insulated glass, wood window, 2-0 x 4-6	EA	$95.15	$240.00	$335.15	**$446.90**	1.250
Double hung, insulated glass, wood window, 2-0 x 5-2	EA	$95.15	$246.00	$341.15	**$454.10**	1.250
Double hung, insulated glass, wood window, 2-4 x 3-2	EA	$95.15	$200.00	$295.15	**$398.90**	1.250
Double hung, insulated glass, wood window, 2-4 x 3-10	EA	$95.15	$218.00	$313.15	**$420.50**	1.250
Double hung, insulated glass, wood window, 2-4 x 4-2	EA	$95.15	$225.00	$320.15	**$428.90**	1.250
Double hung, insulated glass, wood window, 2-4 x 4-6	EA	$95.15	$232.00	$327.15	**$437.30**	1.250
Double hung, insulated glass, wood window, 2-4 x 5-2	EA	$95.15	$246.00	$341.15	**$454.10**	1.250
Double hung, insulated glass, wood window, 2-8 x 3-2	EA	$95.15	$232.00	$327.15	**$437.30**	1.250
Double hung, insulated glass, wood window, 2-8 x 3-10	EA	$95.15	$246.00	$341.15	**$454.10**	1.250
Double hung, insulated glass, wood window, 2-8 x 4-2	EA	$95.15	$260.00	$355.15	**$470.90**	1.250
Double hung, insulated glass, wood window, 2-8 x 4-6	EA	$95.15	$274.00	$369.15	**$487.70**	1.250
Double hung, insulated glass, wood window, 2-8 x 5-2	EA	$95.15	$286.00	$381.15	**$502.10**	1.250
Double hung, insulated glass, wood window, 2-8 x 5-6	EA	$95.15	$300.00	$395.15	**$518.90**	1.250
Double hung, insulated glass, wood window, 2-8 x 6-2	EA	$152.24	$314.00	$466.24	**$631.04**	2.000
Double hung, insulated glass, wood window, 3-0 x 3-10	EA	$95.15	$277.00	$372.15	**$491.30**	1.250
Double hung, insulated glass, wood window, 3-0 x 4-2	EA	$95.15	$291.00	$386.15	**$508.10**	1.250
Double hung, insulated glass, wood window, 3-0 x 4-6	EA	$95.15	$300.00	$395.15	**$518.90**	1.250
Double hung, insulated glass, wood window, 3-0 x 5-2	EA	$152.24	$314.00	$466.24	**$631.04**	2.000
Double hung, insulated glass, wood window, 3-0 x 5-6	EA	$152.24	$328.00	$480.24	**$647.84**	2.000
Double hung, insulated glass, wood window, 3-0 x 6-2	EA	$152.24	$344.00	$496.24	**$667.04**	2.000
Double hung, insulated glass, wood window, 3-4 x 3-10	EA	$95.15	$305.00	$400.15	**$524.90**	1.250
Double hung, insulated glass, wood window, 3-4 x 4-2	EA	$95.15	$319.00	$414.15	**$541.70**	1.250
Double hung, insulated glass, wood window, 3-4 x 4-6	EA	$152.24	$335.00	$487.24	**$656.24**	2.000
Double hung, insulated glass, wood window, 3-4 x 5-2	EA	$152.24	$348.00	$500.24	**$671.84**	2.000
Double hung, insulated glass, wood window, 3-4 x 5-6	EA	$152.24	$363.00	$515.24	**$689.84**	2.000
Double hung, insulated glass, wood window, 3-4 x 6-2	EA	$152.24	$381.00	$533.24	**$711.44**	2.000
Double hung, insulated glass, wood window, 3-8 x 4-2	EA	$152.24	$336.00	$488.24	**$657.44**	2.000
Double hung, insulated glass, wood window, 3-8 x 4-6	EA	$152.24	$350.00	$502.24	**$674.24**	2.000
Double hung, insulated glass, wood window, 3-8 x 5-2	EA	$152.24	$365.00	$517.24	**$692.24**	2.000
Double hung, insulated glass, wood window, 3-8 x 5-6	EA	$152.24	$380.00	$532.24	**$710.24**	2.000
Double hung, insulated glass, wood window, 3-8 x 6-2	EA	$152.24	$397.00	$549.24	**$730.64**	2.000

Wood Windows

Double Hung, Insulated Glass, Alum/Vinyl Clad Wood Window, PREMIUM GRADE

> No removal of old window included.

Description	Unit	Direct Labor	Direct Materials	Direct Total	Selling Price	Man-hours
Double hung, insulated glass, clad wood window, 1-8 x 3-2, premium	EA	$95.15	$316.00	$411.15	**$538.10**	1.250
Double hung, insulated glass, clad wood window, 1-8 x 3-10, premium	EA	$95.15	$319.00	$414.15	**$541.70**	1.250
Double hung, insulated glass, clad wood window, 1-8 x 4-2, premium	EA	$95.15	$319.00	$414.15	**$541.70**	1.250
Double hung, insulated glass, clad wood window, 1-8 x 4-6, premium	EA	$95.15	$329.00	$424.15	**$553.70**	1.250
Double hung, insulated glass, clad wood window, 2-0 x 3-2, premium	EA	$95.15	$319.00	$414.15	**$541.70**	1.250
Double hung, insulated glass, clad wood window, 2-0 x 3-10, premium	EA	$95.15	$321.00	$416.15	**$544.10**	1.250
Double hung, insulated glass, clad wood window, 2-0 x 4-2, premium	EA	$95.15	$324.00	$419.15	**$547.70**	1.250
Double hung, insulated glass, clad wood window, 2-0 x 4-6, premium	EA	$95.15	$349.00	$444.15	**$577.70**	1.250
Double hung, insulated glass, clad wood window, 2-0 x 5-2, premium	EA	$95.15	$363.00	$458.15	**$594.50**	1.250
Double hung, insulated glass, clad wood window, 2-4 x 3-2, premium	EA	$95.15	$362.00	$457.15	**$593.30**	1.250
Double hung, insulated glass, clad wood window, 2-4 x 3-10, premium	EA	$95.15	$386.00	$481.15	**$622.10**	1.250
Double hung, insulated glass, clad wood window, 2-4 x 4-2, premium	EA	$95.15	$398.00	$493.15	**$636.50**	1.250
Double hung, insulated glass, clad wood window, 2-4 x 4-6, premium	EA	$95.15	$407.00	$502.15	**$647.30**	1.250
Double hung, insulated glass, clad wood window, 2-4 x 5-2, premium	EA	$95.15	$411.00	$506.15	**$652.10**	1.250
Double hung, insulated glass, clad wood window, 2-8 x 3-10, premium	EA	$95.15	$394.00	$489.15	**$631.70**	1.250
Double hung, insulated glass, clad wood window, 2-8 x 4-2, premium	EA	$95.15	$424.00	$519.15	**$667.70**	1.250
Double hung, insulated glass, clad wood window, 2-8 x 4-6, premium	EA	$95.15	$437.00	$532.15	**$683.30**	1.250
Double hung, insulated glass, clad wood window, 2-8 x 5-2, premium	EA	$95.15	$458.00	$553.15	**$708.50**	1.250
Double hung, insulated glass, clad wood window, 2-8 x 5-6, premium	EA	$95.15	$479.00	$574.15	**$733.70**	1.250
Double hung, insulated glass, clad wood window, 3-0 x 3-10, premium	EA	$95.15	$440.00	$535.15	**$686.90**	1.250
Double hung, insulated glass, clad wood window, 3-0 x 4-2, premium	EA	$95.15	$469.00	$564.15	**$721.70**	1.250
Double hung, insulated glass, clad wood window, 3-0 x 4-6, premium	EA	$95.15	$479.00	$574.15	**$733.70**	1.250
Double hung, insulated glass, clad wood window, 3-0 x 5-2, premium	EA	$152.24	$502.00	$654.24	**$856.64**	2.000
Double hung, insulated glass, clad wood window, 3-0 x 5-6, premium	EA	$152.24	$528.00	$680.24	**$887.84**	2.000
Double hung, insulated glass, clad wood window, 3-4 x 4-2, premium	EA	$95.15	$512.00	$607.15	**$773.30**	1.250
Double hung, insulated glass, clad wood window, 3-4 x 4-6, premium	EA	$152.24	$531.00	$683.24	**$891.44**	2.000
Double hung, insulated glass, clad wood window, 3-4 x 5-2, premium	EA	$152.24	$554.00	$706.24	**$919.04**	2.000
Double hung, insulated glass, clad wood window, 3-4 x 5-6, premium	EA	$152.24	$577.00	$729.24	**$946.64**	2.000
Double hung, insulated glass, clad wood window, 3-4 x 6-2, premium	EA	$152.24	$614.00	$766.24	**$991.04**	2.000
Double hung, insulated glass, clad wood window, 3-8 x 4-2, premium	EA	$152.24	$544.00	$696.24	**$907.04**	2.000
Double hung, insulated glass, clad wood window, 3-8 x 4-6, premium	EA	$152.24	$564.00	$716.24	**$931.04**	2.000
Double hung, insulated glass, clad wood window, 3-8 x 5-2, premium	EA	$152.24	$587.00	$739.24	**$958.64**	2.000
Double hung, insulated glass, clad wood window, 3-8 x 5-6, premium	EA	$152.24	$613.00	$765.24	**$989.84**	2.000
Double hung, insulated glass, clad wood window, 3-8 x 6-2, premium	EA	$152.24	$652.00	$804.24	**$1,036.64**	2.000

Wood Windows

Double Hung, Insulated Glass, Alum/Vinyl Clad Wood Window, AVERAGE GRADE

> No removal of old window included.

Description	Unit	Direct Labor	Direct Materials	Direct Total	Selling Price	Man-hours
Double hung, insulated glass, clad wood window, 1-8 x 3-2, average	EA	$95.15	$287.00	$382.15	**$503.30**	1.250
Double hung, insulated glass, clad wood window, 1-8 x 3-10, average	EA	$95.15	$290.00	$385.15	**$506.90**	1.250
Double hung, insulated glass, clad wood window, 1-8 x 4-2, average	EA	$95.15	$290.00	$385.15	**$506.90**	1.250
Double hung, insulated glass, clad wood window, 1-8 x 4-6, average	EA	$95.15	$299.00	$394.15	**$517.70**	1.250
Double hung, insulated glass, clad wood window, 2-0 x 3-2, average	EA	$95.15	$290.00	$385.15	**$506.90**	1.250
Double hung, insulated glass, clad wood window, 2-0 x 3-10, average	EA	$95.15	$292.00	$387.15	**$509.30**	1.250
Double hung, insulated glass, clad wood window, 2-0 x 4-2, average	EA	$95.15	$295.00	$390.15	**$512.90**	1.250
Double hung, insulated glass, clad wood window, 2-0 x 4-6, average	EA	$95.15	$317.00	$412.15	**$539.30**	1.250
Double hung, insulated glass, clad wood window, 2-0 x 5-2, average	EA	$95.15	$330.00	$425.15	**$554.90**	1.250
Double hung, insulated glass, clad wood window, 2-4 x 3-2, average	EA	$95.15	$329.00	$424.15	**$553.70**	1.250
Double hung, insulated glass, clad wood window, 2-4 x 3-10, average	EA	$95.15	$351.00	$446.15	**$580.10**	1.250
Double hung, insulated glass, clad wood window, 2-4 x 4-2, average	EA	$95.15	$361.00	$456.15	**$592.10**	1.250
Double hung, insulated glass, clad wood window, 2-4 x 4-6, average	EA	$95.15	$370.00	$465.15	**$602.90**	1.250
Double hung, insulated glass, clad wood window, 2-4 x 5-2, average	EA	$95.15	$373.00	$468.15	**$606.50**	1.250
Double hung, insulated glass, clad wood window, 2-8 x 3-10, average	EA	$95.15	$358.00	$453.15	**$588.50**	1.250
Double hung, insulated glass, clad wood window, 2-8 x 4-2, average	EA	$95.15	$385.00	$480.15	**$620.90**	1.250
Double hung, insulated glass, clad wood window, 2-8 x 4-6, average	EA	$95.15	$397.00	$492.15	**$635.30**	1.250
Double hung, insulated glass, clad wood window, 2-8 x 5-2, average	EA	$95.15	$416.00	$511.15	**$658.10**	1.250
Double hung, insulated glass, clad wood window, 2-8 x 5-6, average	EA	$95.15	$435.00	$530.15	**$680.90**	1.250
Double hung, insulated glass, clad wood window, 3-0 x 3-10, average	EA	$95.15	$400.00	$495.15	**$638.90**	1.250
Double hung, insulated glass, clad wood window, 3-0 x 4-2, average	EA	$95.15	$427.00	$522.15	**$671.30**	1.250
Double hung, insulated glass, clad wood window, 3-0 x 4-6, average	EA	$95.15	$435.00	$530.15	**$680.90**	1.250
Double hung, insulated glass, clad wood window, 3-0 x 5-2, average	EA	$152.24	$456.00	$608.24	**$801.44**	2.000
Double hung, insulated glass, clad wood window, 3-0 x 5-6, average	EA	$152.24	$480.00	$632.24	**$830.24**	2.000
Double hung, insulated glass, clad wood window, 3-4 x 4-2, average	EA	$95.15	$465.00	$560.15	**$716.90**	1.250
Double hung, insulated glass, clad wood window, 3-4 x 4-6, average	EA	$152.24	$483.00	$635.24	**$833.84**	2.000
Double hung, insulated glass, clad wood window, 3-4 x 5-2, average	EA	$152.24	$504.00	$656.24	**$859.04**	2.000
Double hung, insulated glass, clad wood window, 3-4 x 5-6, average	EA	$152.24	$524.00	$676.24	**$883.04**	2.000
Double hung, insulated glass, clad wood window, 3-4 x 6-2, average	EA	$152.24	$558.00	$710.24	**$923.84**	2.000
Double hung, insulated glass, clad wood window, 3-8 x 4-2, average	EA	$152.24	$495.00	$647.24	**$848.24**	2.000
Double hung, insulated glass, clad wood window, 3-8 x 4-6, average	EA	$152.24	$512.00	$664.24	**$868.64**	2.000
Double hung, insulated glass, clad wood window, 3-8 x 5-2, average	EA	$152.24	$533.00	$685.24	**$893.84**	2.000
Double hung, insulated glass, clad wood window, 3-8 x 5-6, average	EA	$152.24	$557.00	$709.24	**$922.64**	2.000
Double hung, insulated glass, clad wood window, 3-8 x 6-2, average	EA	$152.24	$592.00	$744.24	**$964.64**	2.000

Wood Windows

Double Hung, Insulated Glass, Alum/Vinyl Clad Wood Window, ECONOMY GRADE

> No removal of old window included.

Description	Unit	Direct Labor	Direct Materials	Direct Total	Selling Price	Man-hours
Double hung, insulated glass, clad wood window, 1-8 x 3-10, economy	EA	$95.15	$252.00	$347.15	**$461.30**	1.250
Double hung, insulated glass, clad wood window, 1-8 x 4-2, economy	EA	$95.15	$252.00	$347.15	**$461.30**	1.250
Double hung, insulated glass, clad wood window, 1-8 x 4-6, economy	EA	$95.15	$260.00	$355.15	**$470.90**	1.250
Double hung, insulated glass, clad wood window, 2-0 x 3-10, economy	EA	$95.15	$254.00	$349.15	**$463.70**	1.250
Double hung, insulated glass, clad wood window, 2-0 x 4-2, economy	EA	$95.15	$256.00	$351.15	**$466.10**	1.250
Double hung, insulated glass, clad wood window, 2-0 x 4-6, economy	EA	$95.15	$276.00	$371.15	**$490.10**	1.250
Double hung, insulated glass, clad wood window, 2-0 x 5-2, economy	EA	$95.15	$287.00	$382.15	**$503.30**	1.250
Double hung, insulated glass, clad wood window, 2-4 x 3-2, economy	EA	$95.15	$286.00	$381.15	**$502.10**	1.250
Double hung, insulated glass, clad wood window, 2-4 x 3-10, economy	EA	$95.15	$305.00	$400.15	**$524.90**	1.250
Double hung, insulated glass, clad wood window, 2-4 x 4-2, economy	EA	$95.15	$314.00	$409.15	**$535.70**	1.250
Double hung, insulated glass, clad wood window, 2-4 x 4-6, economy	EA	$95.15	$322.00	$417.15	**$545.30**	1.250
Double hung, insulated glass, clad wood window, 2-4 x 5-2, economy	EA	$95.15	$325.00	$420.15	**$548.90**	1.250
Double hung, insulated glass, clad wood window, 2-8 x 3-10, economy	EA	$95.15	$312.00	$407.15	**$533.30**	1.250
Double hung, insulated glass, clad wood window, 2-8 x 4-2, economy	EA	$95.15	$335.00	$430.15	**$560.90**	1.250
Double hung, insulated glass, clad wood window, 2-8 x 4-6, economy	EA	$95.15	$345.00	$440.15	**$572.90**	1.250
Double hung, insulated glass, clad wood window, 2-8 x 5-2, economy	EA	$95.15	$362.00	$457.15	**$593.30**	1.250
Double hung, insulated glass, clad wood window, 2-8 x 5-6, economy	EA	$95.15	$379.00	$474.15	**$613.70**	1.250
Double hung, insulated glass, clad wood window, 3-0 x 3-10, economy	EA	$95.15	$348.00	$443.15	**$576.50**	1.250
Double hung, insulated glass, clad wood window, 3-0 x 4-2, economy	EA	$95.15	$371.00	$466.15	**$604.10**	1.250
Double hung, insulated glass, clad wood window, 3-0 x 4-6, economy	EA	$95.15	$379.00	$474.15	**$613.70**	1.250
Double hung, insulated glass, clad wood window, 3-0 x 5-2, economy	EA	$152.24	$397.00	$549.24	**$730.64**	2.000
Double hung, insulated glass, clad wood window, 3-0 x 5-6, economy	EA	$152.24	$417.00	$569.24	**$754.64**	2.000
Double hung, insulated glass, clad wood window, 3-4 x 4-2, economy	EA	$95.15	$404.00	$499.15	**$643.70**	1.250
Double hung, insulated glass, clad wood window, 3-4 x 4-6, economy	EA	$152.24	$420.00	$572.24	**$758.24**	2.000
Double hung, insulated glass, clad wood window, 3-4 x 5-2, economy	EA	$152.24	$438.00	$590.24	**$779.84**	2.000
Double hung, insulated glass, clad wood window, 3-4 x 5-6, economy	EA	$152.24	$456.00	$608.24	**$801.44**	2.000
Double hung, insulated glass, clad wood window, 3-4 x 6-2, economy	EA	$152.24	$486.00	$638.24	**$837.44**	2.000
Double hung, insulated glass, clad wood window, 3-8 x 4-2, economy	EA	$152.24	$430.00	$582.24	**$770.24**	2.000
Double hung, insulated glass, clad wood window, 3-8 x 4-6, economy	EA	$152.24	$446.00	$598.24	**$789.44**	2.000
Double hung, insulated glass, clad wood window, 3-8 x 5-2, economy	EA	$152.24	$464.00	$616.24	**$811.04**	2.000
Double hung, insulated glass, clad wood window, 3-8 x 5-6, economy	EA	$152.24	$484.00	$636.24	**$835.04**	2.000
Double hung, insulated glass, clad wood window, 3-8 x 6-2, economy	EA	$152.24	$515.00	$667.24	**$872.24**	2.000

Wood Windows

Awning, Insulated Glass Wood Window

> No removal of old window included.

Description	Unit	Direct Labor	Direct Materials	Direct Total	Selling Price	Man-hours
AWNING, INSULATED GLASS, WOOD WINDOW, 1 WIDE						
Awning, insulated glass, wood window, 1 wide, 2-0 x 1-6	EA	$76.12	$146.00	$222.12	**$302.32**	1.000
Awning, insulated glass, wood window, 1 wide, 2-0 x 2-0	EA	$76.12	$162.00	$238.12	**$321.52**	1.000
Awning, insulated glass, wood window, 1 wide, 2-0 x 2-6	EA	$76.12	$179.00	$255.12	**$341.92**	1.000
Awning, insulated glass, wood window, 1 wide, 2-0 x 3-0	EA	$76.12	$201.00	$277.12	**$368.32**	1.000
Awning, insulated glass, wood window, 1 wide, 3-0 x 1-6	EA	$76.12	$166.00	$242.12	**$326.32**	1.000
Awning, insulated glass, wood window, 1 wide, 3-0 x 2-0	EA	$76.12	$187.00	$263.12	**$351.52**	1.000
Awning, insulated glass, wood window, 1 wide, 3-0 x 2-6	EA	$76.12	$197.00	$273.12	**$363.52**	1.000
Awning, insulated glass, wood window, 1 wide, 3-0 x 3-0	EA	$76.12	$245.00	$321.12	**$421.12**	1.000
Awning, insulated glass, wood window, 1 wide, 3-6 x 1-6	EA	$76.12	$182.00	$258.12	**$345.52**	1.000
Awning, insulated glass, wood window, 1 wide, 3-6 x 2-0	EA	$76.12	$204.00	$280.12	**$371.92**	1.000
Awning, insulated glass, wood window, 1 wide, 3-6 x 2-6	EA	$76.12	$213.00	$289.12	**$382.72**	1.000
Awning, insulated glass, wood window, 1 wide, 3-6 x 3-0	EA	$76.12	$230.00	$306.12	**$403.12**	1.000
Awning, insulated glass, wood window, 1 wide, 4-0 x 1-6	EA	$76.12	$197.00	$273.12	**$363.52**	1.000
Awning, insulated glass, wood window, 1 wide, 4-0 x 2-0	EA	$76.12	$219.00	$295.12	**$389.92**	1.000
Awning, insulated glass, wood window, 1 wide, 4-0 x 2-6	EA	$76.12	$236.00	$312.12	**$410.32**	1.000
Awning, insulated glass, wood window, 1 wide, 4-0 x 3-0	EA	$76.12	$264.00	$340.12	**$443.92**	1.000
Awning, insulated glass, wood window, 1 wide, 4-6 x 1-6	EA	$76.12	$221.00	$297.12	**$392.32**	1.000
Awning, insulated glass, wood window, 1 wide, 4-6 x 2-0	EA	$76.12	$238.00	$314.12	**$412.72**	1.000
Awning, insulated glass, wood window, 1 wide, 4-6 x 2-6	EA	$76.12	$267.00	$343.12	**$447.52**	1.000
Awning, insulated glass, wood window, 1 wide, 4-6 x 3-0	EA	$76.12	$310.00	$386.12	**$499.12**	1.000
AWNING, INSULATED GLASS, WOOD WINDOW, 2 WIDE						
Awning, insulated glass, wood window, 2 wide, 4-0 x 1-6	EA	$133.21	$308.00	$441.21	**$592.06**	1.750
Awning, insulated glass, wood window, 2 wide, 4-0 x 2-0	EA	$133.21	$341.00	$474.21	**$631.66**	1.750
Awning, insulated glass, wood window, 2 wide, 4-0 x 2-6	EA	$133.21	$358.00	$491.21	**$652.06**	1.750
Awning, insulated glass, wood window, 2 wide, 4-0 x 3-0	EA	$133.21	$377.00	$510.21	**$674.86**	1.750
Awning, insulated glass, wood window, 2 wide, 4-0 x 3-6	EA	$133.21	$402.00	$535.21	**$704.86**	1.750
Awning, insulated glass, wood window, 2 wide, 6-0 x 1-6	EA	$133.21	$354.00	$487.21	**$647.26**	1.750
Awning, insulated glass, wood window, 2 wide, 6-0 x 2-0	EA	$133.21	$394.00	$527.21	**$695.26**	1.750
Awning, insulated glass, wood window, 2 wide, 6-0 x 2-6	EA	$133.21	$418.00	$551.21	**$724.06**	1.750
Awning, insulated glass, wood window, 2 wide, 6-0 x 3-0	EA	$133.21	$445.00	$578.21	**$756.46**	1.750
Awning, insulated glass, wood window, 2 wide, 6-0 x 3-6	EA	$133.21	$473.00	$606.21	**$790.06**	1.750
Awning, insulated glass, wood window, 2 wide, 7-0 x 1-6	EA	$133.21	$388.00	$521.21	**$688.06**	1.750
Awning, insulated glass, wood window, 2 wide, 7-0 x 2-0	EA	$133.21	$429.00	$562.21	**$737.26**	1.750
Awning, insulated glass, wood window, 2 wide, 7-0 x 2-6	EA	$133.21	$452.00	$585.21	**$764.86**	1.750
Awning, insulated glass, wood window, 2 wide, 7-0 x 3-0	EA	$133.21	$473.00	$606.21	**$790.06**	1.750
Awning, insulated glass, wood window, 2 wide, 7-0 x 3-6	EA	$133.21	$501.00	$634.21	**$823.66**	1.750

Wood Windows

Awning, Insulated Glass Wood Window

> No removal of old window included.

Description	Unit	Direct Labor	Direct Materials	Direct Total	Selling Price	Man-hours
AWNING, INSULATED GLASS, WOOD WINDOW, 2 WIDE (cont.)						
Awning, insulated glass, wood window, 2 wide, 8-0 x 1-6	EA	$133.21	$416.00	$549.21	**$721.66**	1.750
Awning, insulated glass, wood window, 2 wide, 8-0 x 2-0	EA	$133.21	$459.00	$592.21	**$773.26**	1.750
Awning, insulated glass, wood window, 2 wide, 8-0 x 2-6	EA	$133.21	$495.00	$628.21	**$816.46**	1.750
Awning, insulated glass, wood window, 2 wide, 8-0 x 3-0	EA	$133.21	$522.00	$655.21	**$848.86**	1.750
Awning, insulated glass, wood window, 2 wide, 8-0 x 3-6	EA	$133.21	$551.00	$684.21	**$883.66**	1.750
AWNING, INSULATED GLASS, WOOD WINDOW, 3 WIDE						
Awning, insulated glass, wood window, 3 wide, 6-0 x 2-0	EA	$190.30	$515.00	$705.30	**$935.79**	2.500
Awning, insulated glass, wood window, 3 wide, 6-0 x 2-6	EA	$190.30	$541.00	$731.30	**$966.99**	2.500
Awning, insulated glass, wood window, 3 wide, 6-0 x 3-0	EA	$190.30	$565.00	$755.30	**$995.79**	2.500
Awning, insulated glass, wood window, 3 wide, 6-0 x 3-6	EA	$190.30	$592.00	$782.30	**$1,028.19**	2.500
Awning, insulated glass, wood window, 3 wide, 9-0 x 2-0	EA	$190.30	$615.00	$805.30	**$1,055.79**	2.500
Awning, insulated glass, wood window, 3 wide, 9-0 x 2-6	EA	$190.30	$651.00	$841.30	**$1,098.99**	2.500
Awning, insulated glass, wood window, 3 wide, 9-0 x 3-0	EA	$190.30	$685.00	$875.30	**$1,139.79**	2.500
Awning, insulated glass, wood window, 3 wide, 9-0 x 3-6	EA	$190.30	$721.00	$911.30	**$1,182.99**	2.500
Awning, insulated glass, wood window, 3 wide, 10-0 x 2-0	EA	$190.30	$656.00	$846.30	**$1,104.99**	2.500
Awning, insulated glass, wood window, 3 wide, 10-0 x 2-6	EA	$190.30	$691.00	$881.30	**$1,146.99**	2.500
Awning, insulated glass, wood window, 3 wide, 10-0 x 3-0	EA	$190.30	$725.00	$915.30	**$1,187.79**	2.500
Awning, insulated glass, wood window, 3 wide, 10-0 x 3-6	EA	$190.30	$761.00	$951.30	**$1,230.99**	2.500
Awning, insulated glass, wood window, 3 wide, 12-0 x 2-0	EA	$190.30	$703.00	$893.30	**$1,161.39**	2.500
Awning, insulated glass, wood window, 3 wide, 12-0 x 2-6	EA	$190.30	$759.00	$949.30	**$1,228.59**	2.500
Awning, insulated glass, wood window, 3 wide, 12-0 x 3-0	EA	$190.30	$821.00	$1,011.30	**$1,302.99**	2.500
Awning, insulated glass, wood window, 3 wide, 12-0 x 3-6	EA	$190.30	$886.00	$1,076.30	**$1,380.99**	2.500

Awning, Insulated Glass, Aluminum/Vinyl Clad Wood Window, PREMIUM GRADE

> No removal of old window included.

Description	Unit	Direct Labor	Direct Materials	Direct Total	Selling Price	Man-hours
AWNING, INSULATED GLASS, CLAD, 1 WIDE, PREMIUM						
Awning, insulated glass, clad wood window, 1 wide, 2-0 x 1-6, premium	EA	$76.12	$222.00	$298.12	**$393.52**	1.000
Awning, insulated glass, clad wood window, 1 wide, 2-0 x 2-0, premium	EA	$76.12	$247.00	$323.12	**$423.52**	1.000
Awning, insulated glass, clad wood window, 1 wide, 2-0 x 2-6, premium	EA	$76.12	$273.00	$349.12	**$454.72**	1.000
Awning, insulated glass, clad wood window, 1 wide, 2-0 x 3-0, premium	EA	$76.12	$305.00	$236.00	**$493.12**	1.000
Awning, insulated glass, clad wood window, 1 wide, 3-0 x 1-6, premium	EA	$76.12	$253.00	$329.12	**$430.72**	1.000
Awning, insulated glass, clad wood window, 1 wide, 3-0 x 2-0, premium	EA	$76.12	$285.00	$361.12	**$469.12**	1.000
Awning, insulated glass, clad wood window, 1 wide, 3-0 x 2-6, premium	EA	$76.12	$299.00	$375.12	**$485.92**	1.000
Awning, insulated glass, clad wood window, 1 wide, 3-0 x 3-0, premium	EA	$76.12	$373.00	$236.00	**$574.72**	1.000

Wood Windows

Awning, Insulated Glass, Aluminum/Vinyl Clad Wood Window, PREMIUM GRADE

➤ No removal of old window included.

Description	Unit	Direct Labor	Direct Materials	Direct Total	Selling Price	Man-hours
AWNING, INSULATED GLASS, CLAD, 1 WIDE, PREMIUM (cont.)						
Awning, insulated glass, clad wood window, 1 wide, 3-6 x 1-6, premium	EA	$76.12	$277.00	$353.12	**$459.52**	1.000
Awning, insulated glass, clad wood window, 1 wide, 3-6 x 2-0, premium	EA	$76.12	$310.00	$386.12	**$499.12**	1.000
Awning, insulated glass, clad wood window, 1 wide, 3-6 x 2-6, premium	EA	$76.12	$323.00	$399.12	**$514.72**	1.000
Awning, insulated glass, clad wood window, 1 wide, 3-6 x 3-0, premium	EA	$76.12	$350.00	$226.00	**$547.12**	1.000
Awning, insulated glass, clad wood window, 1 wide, 4-0 x 1-6, premium	EA	$76.12	$299.00	$375.12	**$485.92**	1.000
Awning, insulated glass, clad wood window, 1 wide, 4-0 x 2-0, premium	EA	$76.12	$333.00	$409.12	**$526.72**	1.000
Awning, insulated glass, clad wood window, 1 wide, 4-0 x 2-6, premium	EA	$76.12	$359.00	$435.12	**$557.92**	1.000
Awning, insulated glass, clad wood window, 1 wide, 4-0 x 3-0, premium	EA	$76.12	$402.00	$259.00	**$609.52**	1.000
Awning, insulated glass, clad wood window, 1 wide, 4-6 x 1-6, premium	EA	$76.12	$336.00	$412.12	**$530.32**	1.000
Awning, insulated glass, clad wood window, 1 wide, 4-6 x 2-0, premium	EA	$76.12	$362.00	$438.12	**$561.52**	1.000
Awning, insulated glass, clad wood window, 1 wide, 4-6 x 2-6, premium	EA	$76.12	$406.00	$482.12	**$614.32**	1.000
Awning, insulated glass, clad wood window, 1 wide, 4-6 x 3-0, premium	EA	$76.12	$472.00	$548.12	**$693.52**	1.000
AWNING, INSULATED GLASS, CLAD, 2 WIDE, PREMIUM						
Awning, insulated glass, clad wood window, 2 wide, 4-0 x 1-6, premium	EA	$133.21	$468.00	$601.21	**$784.06**	1.750
Awning, insulated glass, clad wood window, 2 wide, 4-0 x 2-0, premium	EA	$133.21	$518.00	$651.21	**$844.06**	1.750
Awning, insulated glass, clad wood window, 2 wide, 4-0 x 2-6, premium	EA	$133.21	$544.00	$677.21	**$875.26**	1.750
Awning, insulated glass, clad wood window, 2 wide, 4-0 x 3-0, premium	EA	$133.21	$573.00	$706.21	**$910.06**	1.750
Awning, insulated glass, clad wood window, 2 wide, 4-0 x 3-6, premium	EA	$133.21	$612.00	$745.21	**$956.86**	1.750
Awning, insulated glass, clad wood window, 2 wide, 6-0 x 1-6, premium	EA	$133.21	$538.00	$671.21	**$868.06**	1.750
Awning, insulated glass, clad wood window, 2 wide, 6-0 x 2-0, premium	EA	$133.21	$599.00	$732.21	**$941.26**	1.750
Awning, insulated glass, clad wood window, 2 wide, 6-0 x 2-6, premium	EA	$133.21	$636.00	$769.21	**$985.66**	1.750
Awning, insulated glass, clad wood window, 2 wide, 6-0 x 3-0, premium	EA	$133.21	$676.00	$809.21	**$1,033.66**	1.750
Awning, insulated glass, clad wood window, 2 wide, 6-0 x 3-6, premium	EA	$133.21	$719.00	$852.21	**$1,085.26**	1.750
Awning, insulated glass, clad wood window, 2 wide, 7-0 x 1-6, premium	EA	$133.21	$591.00	$724.21	**$931.66**	1.750
Awning, insulated glass, clad wood window, 2 wide, 7-0 x 2-0, premium	EA	$133.21	$652.00	$785.21	**$1,004.86**	1.750
Awning, insulated glass, clad wood window, 2 wide, 7-0 x 2-6, premium	EA	$133.21	$687.00	$820.21	**$1,046.86**	1.750
Awning, insulated glass, clad wood window, 2 wide, 7-0 x 3-0, premium	EA	$133.21	$719.00	$852.21	**$1,085.26**	1.750
Awning, insulated glass, clad wood window, 2 wide, 7-0 x 3-6, premium	EA	$133.21	$762.00	$895.21	**$1,136.86**	1.750
Awning, insulated glass, clad wood window, 2 wide, 8-0 x 1-6, premium	EA	$133.21	$633.00	$766.21	**$982.06**	1.750
Awning, insulated glass, clad wood window, 2 wide, 8-0 x 2-0, premium	EA	$133.21	$699.00	$832.21	**$1,061.26**	1.750
Awning, insulated glass, clad wood window, 2 wide, 8-0 x 2-6, premium	EA	$133.21	$753.00	$886.21	**$1,126.06**	1.750
Awning, insulated glass, clad wood window, 2 wide, 8-0 x 3-0, premium	EA	$133.21	$794.00	$927.21	**$1,175.26**	1.750
Awning, insulated glass, clad wood window, 2 wide, 8-0 x 3-6, premium	EA	$133.21	$839.00	$972.21	**$1,229.26**	1.750

Wood Windows

Awning, Insulated Glass, Aluminum/Vinyl Clad Wood Window, PREMIUM GRADE

> No removal of old window included.

Description	Unit	Direct Labor	Direct Materials	Direct Total	Selling Price	Man-hours
AWNING, INSULATED GLASS, CLAD, 3 WIDE, PREMIUM						
Awning, insulated glass, clad wood window, 3 wide, 6-0 x 2-0, premium	EA	$190.30	$784.00	$974.30	**$1,258.59**	2.500
Awning, insulated glass, clad wood window, 3 wide, 6-0 x 2-6, premium	EA	$190.30	$823.00	$1,013.30	**$1,305.39**	2.500
Awning, insulated glass, clad wood window, 3 wide, 6-0 x 3-0, premium	EA	$190.30	$860.00	$1,050.30	**$1,349.79**	2.500
Awning, insulated glass, clad wood window, 3 wide, 6-0 x 3-6, premium	EA	$190.30	$900.00	$1,090.30	**$1,397.79**	2.500
Awning, insulated glass, clad wood window, 3 wide, 9-0 x 2-0, premium	EA	$190.30	$935.00	$1,125.30	**$1,439.79**	2.500
Awning, insulated glass, clad wood window, 3 wide, 9-0 x 2-6, premium	EA	$190.30	$990.00	$1,180.30	**$1,505.79**	2.500
Awning, insulated glass, clad wood window, 3 wide, 9-0 x 3-0, premium	EA	$190.30	$1,042.00	$1,232.30	**$1,568.19**	2.500
Awning, insulated glass, clad wood window, 3 wide, 9-0 x 3-6, premium	EA	$190.30	$1,096.00	$1,286.30	**$1,632.99**	2.500
Awning, insulated glass, clad wood window, 3 wide, 10-0 x 2-0, premium	EA	$190.30	$998.00	$1,188.30	**$1,515.39**	2.500
Awning, insulated glass, clad wood window, 3 wide, 10-0 x 2-6, premium	EA	$190.30	$1,051.00	$1,241.30	**$1,578.99**	2.500
Awning, insulated glass, clad wood window, 3 wide, 10-0 x 3-0, premium	EA	$190.30	$1,102.00	$1,292.30	**$1,640.19**	2.500
Awning, insulated glass, clad wood window, 3 wide, 10-0 x 3-6, premium	EA	$190.30	$1,157.00	$1,347.30	**$1,706.19**	2.500
Awning, insulated glass, clad wood window, 3 wide, 12-0 x 2-0, premium	EA	$190.30	$1,069.00	$1,259.30	**$1,600.59**	2.500
Awning, insulated glass, clad wood window, 3 wide, 12-0 x 2-6, premium	EA	$190.30	$1,154.00	$1,344.30	**$1,702.59**	2.500
Awning, insulated glass, clad wood window, 3 wide, 12-0 x 3-0, premium	EA	$190.30	$1,248.00	$1,438.30	**$1,815.39**	2.500
Awning, insulated glass, clad wood window, 3 wide, 12-0 x 3-6, premium	EA	$190.30	$1,348.00	$1,538.30	**$1,935.39**	2.500

Awning, Insulated Glass, Aluminum/Vinyl Clad Wood Window, AVERAGE GRADE

> No removal of old window included.

Description	Unit	Direct Labor	Direct Materials	Direct Total	Selling Price	Man-hours
AWNING, INSULATED GLASS, CLAD, 1 WIDE, AVERAGE						
Awning, insulated glass, clad wood window, 1 wide, 2-0 x 1-6, average	EA	$76.12	$193.00	$269.12	**$358.72**	1.000
Awning, insulated glass, clad wood window, 1 wide, 2-0 x 2-0, average	EA	$76.12	$215.00	$291.12	**$385.12**	1.000
Awning, insulated glass, clad wood window, 1 wide, 2-0 x 2-6, average	EA	$76.12	$237.00	$313.12	**$411.52**	1.000
Awning, insulated glass, clad wood window, 1 wide, 2-0 x 3-0, average	EA	$76.12	$265.00	$236.00	**$445.12**	1.000
Awning, insulated glass, clad wood window, 1 wide, 3-0 x 1-6, average	EA	$76.12	$220.00	$296.12	**$391.12**	1.000
Awning, insulated glass, clad wood window, 1 wide, 3-0 x 2-0, average	EA	$76.12	$248.00	$324.12	**$424.72**	1.000
Awning, insulated glass, clad wood window, 1 wide, 3-0 x 2-6, average	EA	$76.12	$260.00	$336.12	**$439.12**	1.000
Awning, insulated glass, clad wood window, 1 wide, 3-0 x 3-0, average	EA	$76.12	$324.00	$236.00	**$515.92**	1.000
Awning, insulated glass, clad wood window, 1 wide, 3-6 x 1-6, average	EA	$76.12	$241.00	$317.12	**$416.32**	1.000
Awning, insulated glass, clad wood window, 1 wide, 3-6 x 2-0, average	EA	$76.12	$269.00	$345.12	**$449.92**	1.000
Awning, insulated glass, clad wood window, 1 wide, 3-6 x 2-6, average	EA	$76.12	$281.00	$357.12	**$464.32**	1.000
Awning, insulated glass, clad wood window, 1 wide, 3-6 x 3-0, average	EA	$76.12	$304.00	$226.00	**$491.92**	1.000
Awning, insulated glass, clad wood window, 1 wide, 4-0 x 1-6, average	EA	$76.12	$260.00	$336.12	**$439.12**	1.000
Awning, insulated glass, clad wood window, 1 wide, 4-0 x 2-0, average	EA	$76.12	$289.00	$365.12	**$473.92**	1.000
Awning, insulated glass, clad wood window, 1 wide, 4-0 x 2-6, average	EA	$76.12	$312.00	$388.12	**$501.52**	1.000
Awning, insulated glass, clad wood window, 1 wide, '4-0 x 3-0, average	EA	$76.12	$349.00	$259.00	**$545.92**	1.000

Wood Windows

Awning, Insulated Glass, Aluminum/Vinyl Clad Wood Window, AVERAGE GRADE

> No removal of old window included.

Description	Unit	Direct Labor	Direct Materials	Direct Total	Selling Price	Man-hours
AWNING, INSULATED GLASS, CLAD, 1 WIDE, AVERAGE (cont.)						
Awning, insulated glass, clad wood window, 1 wide, 4-6 x 1-6, average	EA	$76.12	$292.00	$368.12	**$477.52**	1.000
Awning, insulated glass, clad wood window, 1 wide, 4-6 x 2-0, average	EA	$76.12	$315.00	$391.12	**$505.12**	1.000
Awning, insulated glass, clad wood window, 1 wide, 4-6 x 2-6, average	EA	$76.12	$353.00	$429.12	**$550.72**	1.000
Awning, insulated glass, clad wood window, 1 wide, 4-6 x 3-0, average	EA	$76.12	$411.00	$487.12	**$620.32**	1.000
AWNING, INSULATED GLASS, CLAD, 2 WIDE, AVERAGE						
Awning, insulated glass, clad wood window, 2 wide, 4-0 x 1-6, average	EA	$133.21	$407.00	$540.21	**$710.86**	1.750
Awning, insulated glass, clad wood window, 2 wide, 4-0 x 2-0, average	EA	$133.21	$451.00	$584.21	**$763.66**	1.750
Awning, insulated glass, clad wood window, 2 wide, 4-0 x 2-6, average	EA	$133.21	$473.00	$606.21	**$790.06**	1.750
Awning, insulated glass, clad wood window, 2 wide, 4-0 x 3-0, average	EA	$133.21	$499.00	$632.21	**$821.26**	1.750
Awning, insulated glass, clad wood window, 2 wide, 4-0 x 3-6, average	EA	$133.21	$532.00	$665.21	**$860.86**	1.750
Awning, insulated glass, clad wood window, 2 wide, 6-0 x 1-6, average	EA	$133.21	$468.00	$601.21	**$784.06**	1.750
Awning, insulated glass, clad wood window, 2 wide, 6-0 x 2-0, average	EA	$133.21	$521.00	$654.21	**$847.66**	1.750
Awning, insulated glass, clad wood window, 2 wide, 6-0 x 2-6, average	EA	$133.21	$553.00	$686.21	**$886.06**	1.750
Awning, insulated glass, clad wood window, 2 wide, 6-0 x 3-0, average	EA	$133.21	$588.00	$721.21	**$928.06**	1.750
Awning, insulated glass, clad wood window, 2 wide, 6-0 x 3-6, average	EA	$133.21	$625.00	$758.21	**$972.46**	1.750
Awning, insulated glass, clad wood window, 2 wide, 7-0 x 1-6, average	EA	$133.21	$514.00	$647.21	**$839.26**	1.750
Awning, insulated glass, clad wood window, 2 wide, 7-0 x 2-0, average	EA	$133.21	$567.00	$700.21	**$902.86**	1.750
Awning, insulated glass, clad wood window, 2 wide, 7-0 x 2-6, average	EA	$133.21	$598.00	$731.21	**$940.06**	1.750
Awning, insulated glass, clad wood window, 2 wide, 7-0 x 3-0, average	EA	$133.21	$625.00	$758.21	**$972.46**	1.750
Awning, insulated glass, clad wood window, 2 wide, 7-0 x 3-6, average	EA	$133.21	$663.00	$796.21	**$1,018.06**	1.750
Awning, insulated glass, clad wood window, 2 wide, 8-0 x 1-6, average	EA	$133.21	$550.00	$683.21	**$882.46**	1.750
Awning, insulated glass, clad wood window, 2 wide, 8-0 x 2-0, average	EA	$133.21	$607.00	$740.21	**$950.86**	1.750
Awning, insulated glass, clad wood window, 2 wide, 8-0 x 2-6, average	EA	$133.21	$655.00	$788.21	**$1,008.46**	1.750
Awning, insulated glass, clad wood window, 2 wide, 8-0 x 3-0, average	EA	$133.21	$691.00	$824.21	**$1,051.66**	1.750
Awning, insulated glass, clad wood window, 2 wide, 8-0 x 3-6, average	EA	$133.21	$729.00	$862.21	**$1,097.26**	1.750
AWNING, INSULATED GLASS, CLAD, 3 WIDE, AVERAGE						
Awning, insulated glass, clad wood window, 3 wide, 6-0 x 2-0, average	EA	$190.30	$682.00	$872.30	**$1,136.19**	2.500
Awning, insulated glass, clad wood window, 3 wide, 6-0 x 2-6, average	EA	$190.30	$715.00	$905.30	**$1,175.79**	2.500
Awning, insulated glass, clad wood window, 3 wide, 6-0 x 3-0, average	EA	$190.30	$748.00	$938.30	**$1,215.39**	2.500
Awning, insulated glass, clad wood window, 3 wide, 6-0 x 3-6, average	EA	$190.30	$783.00	$973.30	**$1,257.39**	2.500
Awning, insulated glass, clad wood window, 3 wide, 9-0 x 2-0, average	EA	$190.30	$813.00	$1,003.30	**$1,293.39**	2.500
Awning, insulated glass, clad wood window, 3 wide, 9-0 x 2-6, average	EA	$190.30	$861.00	$1,051.30	**$1,350.99**	2.500
Awning, insulated glass, clad wood window, 3 wide, 9-0 x 3-0, average	EA	$190.30	$906.00	$1,096.30	**$1,404.99**	2.500
Awning, insulated glass, clad wood window, 3 wide, 9-0 x 3-6, average	EA	$190.30	$953.00	$1,143.30	**$1,461.39**	2.500

Wood Windows

Awning, Insulated Glass, Aluminum/Vinyl Clad Wood Window, AVERAGE GRADE

> No removal of old window included.

Description	Unit	Direct Labor	Direct Materials	Direct Total	Selling Price	Man-hours
AWNING, INSULATED GLASS, CLAD, 3 WIDE, AVERAGE (cont.)						
Awning, insulated glass, clad wood window, 3 wide, 10-0 x 2-0, average	EA	$190.30	$868.00	$1,058.30	**$1,359.39**	2.500
Awning, insulated glass, clad wood window, 3 wide, 10-0 x 2-6, average	EA	$190.30	$914.00	$1,104.30	**$1,414.59**	2.500
Awning, insulated glass, clad wood window, 3 wide, 10-0 x 3-0, average	EA	$190.30	$958.00	$1,148.30	**$1,467.39**	2.500
Awning, insulated glass, clad wood window, 3 wide, 10-0 x 3-6, average	EA	$190.30	$1,006.00	$1,196.30	**$1,524.99**	2.500
Awning, insulated glass, clad wood window, 3 wide, 12-0 x 2-0, average	EA	$190.30	$929.00	$1,119.30	**$1,432.59**	2.500
Awning, insulated glass, clad wood window, 3 wide, 12-0 x 2-6, average	EA	$190.30	$1,004.00	$1,194.30	**$1,522.59**	2.500
Awning, insulated glass, clad wood window, 3 wide, 12-0 x 3-0, average	EA	$190.30	$1,085.00	$1,275.30	**$1,619.79**	2.500
Awning, insulated glass, clad wood window, 3 wide, 12-0 x 3-6, average	EA	$190.30	$1,172.00	$1,362.30	**$1,724.19**	2.500

Awning, Insulated Glass, Aluminum/Vinyl Clad Wood Window, ECONOMY GRADE

> No removal of old window included.

Description	Unit	Direct Labor	Direct Materials	Direct Total	Selling Price	Man-hours
AWNING, INSULATED GLASS, CLAD, 1 WIDE, ECONOMY						
Awning, insulated glass, clad wood window, 1 wide, 2-0 x 1-6, economy	EA	$76.12	$168.00	$244.12	**$328.72**	1.000
Awning, insulated glass, clad wood window, 1 wide, 2-0 x 2-0, economy	EA	$76.12	$187.00	$263.12	**$351.52**	1.000
Awning, insulated glass, clad wood window, 1 wide, 2-0 x 2-6, economy	EA	$76.12	$206.00	$282.12	**$374.32**	1.000
Awning, insulated glass, clad wood window, 1 wide, 2-0 x 3-0, economy	EA	$76.12	$231.00	$236.00	**$404.32**	1.000
Awning, insulated glass, clad wood window, 1 wide, 3-0 x 1-6, economy	EA	$76.12	$191.00	$267.12	**$356.32**	1.000
Awning, insulated glass, clad wood window, 1 wide, 3-0 x 2-0, economy	EA	$76.12	$216.00	$292.12	**$386.32**	1.000
Awning, insulated glass, clad wood window, 1 wide, 3-0 x 2-6, economy	EA	$76.12	$226.00	$302.12	**$398.32**	1.000
Awning, insulated glass, clad wood window, 1 wide, 3-0 x 3-0, economy	EA	$76.12	$282.00	$236.00	**$465.52**	1.000
Awning, insulated glass, clad wood window, 1 wide, 3-6 x 1-6, economy	EA	$76.12	$210.00	$286.12	**$379.12**	1.000
Awning, insulated glass, clad wood window, 1 wide, 3-6 x 2-0, economy	EA	$76.12	$234.00	$310.12	**$407.92**	1.000
Awning, insulated glass, clad wood window, 1 wide, 3-6 x 2-6, economy	EA	$76.12	$245.00	$321.12	**$421.12**	1.000
Awning, insulated glass, clad wood window, 1 wide, 3-6 x 3-0, economy	EA	$76.12	$264.00	$226.00	**$443.92**	1.000
Awning, insulated glass, clad wood window, 1 wide, 4-0 x 1-6, economy	EA	$76.12	$226.00	$302.12	**$398.32**	1.000
Awning, insulated glass, clad wood window, 1 wide, 4-0 x 2-0, economy	EA	$76.12	$252.00	$328.12	**$429.52**	1.000
Awning, insulated glass, clad wood window, 1 wide, 4-0 x 2-6, economy	EA	$76.12	$271.00	$347.12	**$452.32**	1.000
Awning, insulated glass, clad wood window, 1 wide, 4-0 x 3-0, economy	EA	$76.12	$304.00	$259.00	**$491.92**	1.000
Awning, insulated glass, clad wood window, 1 wide, 4-6 x 1-6, economy	EA	$76.12	$254.00	$330.12	**$431.92**	1.000
Awning, insulated glass, clad wood window, 1 wide, 4-6 x 2-0, economy	EA	$76.12	$274.00	$350.12	**$455.92**	1.000
Awning, insulated glass, clad wood window, 1 wide, 4-6 x 2-6, economy	EA	$76.12	$307.00	$383.12	**$495.52**	1.000
Awning, insulated glass, clad wood window, 1 wide, 4-6 x 3-0, economy	EA	$76.12	$357.00	$433.12	**$555.52**	1.000

Wood Windows

Awning, Insulated Glass, Aluminum/Vinyl Clad Wood Window, ECONOMY GRADE

> No removal of old window included.

Description	Unit	Direct Labor	Direct Materials	Direct Total	Selling Price	Man-hours
AWNING, INSULATED GLASS, CLAD, 2 WIDE, ECONOMY						
Awning, insulated glass, clad wood window, 2 wide, 4-0 x 1-6, economy	EA	$133.21	$354.00	$487.21	**$647.26**	1.750
Awning, insulated glass, clad wood window, 2 wide, 4-0 x 2-0, economy	EA	$133.21	$392.00	$525.21	**$692.86**	1.750
Awning, insulated glass, clad wood window, 2 wide, 4-0 x 2-6, economy	EA	$133.21	$411.00	$544.21	**$715.66**	1.750
Awning, insulated glass, clad wood window, 2 wide, 4-0 x 3-0, economy	EA	$133.21	$434.00	$567.21	**$743.26**	1.750
Awning, insulated glass, clad wood window, 2 wide, 4-0 x 3-6, economy	EA	$133.21	$463.00	$596.21	**$778.06**	1.750
Awning, insulated glass, clad wood window, 2 wide, 6-0 x 1-6, economy	EA	$133.21	$407.00	$540.21	**$710.86**	1.750
Awning, insulated glass, clad wood window, 2 wide, 6-0 x 2-0, economy	EA	$133.21	$453.00	$586.21	**$766.06**	1.750
Awning, insulated glass, clad wood window, 2 wide, 6-0 x 2-6, economy	EA	$133.21	$481.00	$614.21	**$799.66**	1.750
Awning, insulated glass, clad wood window, 2 wide, 6-0 x 3-0, economy	EA	$133.21	$511.00	$644.21	**$835.66**	1.750
Awning, insulated glass, clad wood window, 2 wide, 6-0 x 3-6, economy	EA	$133.21	$544.00	$677.21	**$875.26**	1.750
Awning, insulated glass, clad wood window, 2 wide, 7-0 x 1-6, economy	EA	$133.21	$447.00	$580.21	**$758.86**	1.750
Awning, insulated glass, clad wood window, 2 wide, 7-0 x 2-0, economy	EA	$133.21	$493.00	$626.21	**$814.06**	1.750
Awning, insulated glass, clad wood window, 2 wide, 7-0 x 2-6, economy	EA	$133.21	$520.00	$653.21	**$846.46**	1.750
Awning, insulated glass, clad wood window, 2 wide, 7-0 x 3-0, economy	EA	$133.21	$544.00	$677.21	**$875.26**	1.750
Awning, insulated glass, clad wood window, 2 wide, 7-0 x 3-6, economy	EA	$133.21	$576.00	$709.21	**$913.66**	1.750
Awning, insulated glass, clad wood window, 2 wide, 8-0 x 1-6, economy	EA	$133.21	$478.00	$611.21	**$796.06**	1.750
Awning, insulated glass, clad wood window, 2 wide, 8-0 x 2-0, economy	EA	$133.21	$528.00	$661.21	**$856.06**	1.750
Awning, insulated glass, clad wood window, 2 wide, 8-0 x 2-6, economy	EA	$133.21	$570.00	$703.21	**$906.46**	1.750
Awning, insulated glass, clad wood window, 2 wide, 8-0 x 3-0, economy	EA	$133.21	$600.00	$733.21	**$942.46**	1.750
Awning, insulated glass, clad wood window, 2 wide, 8-0 x 3-6, economy	EA	$133.21	$634.00	$767.21	**$983.26**	1.750
AWNING, INSULATED GLASS, CLAD, 3 WIDE, ECONOMY						
Awning, insulated glass, clad wood window, 3 wide, 6-0 x 2-0, economy	EA	$190.30	$593.00	$783.30	**$1,029.39**	2.500
Awning, insulated glass, clad wood window, 3 wide, 6-0 x 2-6, economy	EA	$190.30	$622.00	$812.30	**$1,064.19**	2.500
Awning, insulated glass, clad wood window, 3 wide, 6-0 x 3-0, economy	EA	$190.30	$650.00	$840.30	**$1,097.79**	2.500
Awning, insulated glass, clad wood window, 3 wide, 6-0 x 3-6, economy	EA	$190.30	$680.00	$870.30	**$1,133.79**	2.500
Awning, insulated glass, clad wood window, 3 wide, 9-0 x 2-0, economy	EA	$190.30	$707.00	$897.30	**$1,166.19**	2.500
Awning, insulated glass, clad wood window, 3 wide, 9-0 x 2-6, economy	EA	$190.30	$749.00	$939.30	**$1,216.59**	2.500
Awning, insulated glass, clad wood window, 3 wide, 9-0 x 3-0, economy	EA	$190.30	$788.00	$978.30	**$1,263.39**	2.500
Awning, insulated glass, clad wood window, 3 wide, 9-0 x 3-6, economy	EA	$190.30	$829.00	$1,019.30	**$1,312.59**	2.500
Awning, insulated glass, clad wood window, 3 wide, 10-0 x 2-0, economy	EA	$190.30	$755.00	$945.30	**$1,223.79**	2.500
Awning, insulated glass, clad wood window, 3 wide, 10-0 x 2-6, economy	EA	$190.30	$795.00	$985.30	**$1,271.79**	2.500
Awning, insulated glass, clad wood window, 3 wide, 10-0 x 3-0, economy	EA	$190.30	$833.00	$1,023.30	**$1,317.39**	2.500
Awning, insulated glass, clad wood window, 3 wide, 10-0 x 3-6, economy	EA	$190.30	$875.00	$1,065.30	**$1,367.79**	2.500

Wood Windows

Awning, Insulated Glass, Aluminum/Vinyl Clad Wood Window, ECONOMY GRADE

> No removal of old window included.

Description	Unit	Direct Labor	Direct Materials	Direct Total	Selling Price	Man-hours
AWNING, INSULATED GLASS, CLAD, 3 WIDE, ECONOMY (cont.)						
Awning, insulated glass, clad wood window, 3 wide, 12-0 x 2-0, economy	EA	$190.30	$808.00	$998.30	**$1,287.39**	2.500
Awning, insulated glass, clad wood window, 3 wide, 12-0 x 2-6, economy	EA	$190.30	$873.00	$1,063.30	**$1,365.39**	2.500
Awning, insulated glass, clad wood window, 3 wide, 12-0 x 3-0, economy	EA	$190.30	$944.00	$1,134.30	**$1,450.59**	2.500
Awning, insulated glass, clad wood window, 3 wide, 12-0 x 3-6, economy	EA	$190.30	$1,019.00	$1,209.30	**$1,540.59**	2.500

Casement, Insulated Glass, Wood Window

> No removal of old window included.

Description	Unit	Direct Labor	Direct Materials	Direct Total	Selling Price	Man-hours
CASEMENT, INSULATED GLASS WOOD WINDOW						
Casement, insulated glass, wood window, 1 venting, 1-6 x 2-6	EA	$76.12	$173.00	$249.12	**$334.72**	1.000
Casement, insulated glass, wood window, 1 venting, 1-6 x 3-0	EA	$76.12	$188.00	$264.12	**$352.72**	1.000
Casement, insulated glass, wood window, 1 venting, 1-6 x 3-6	EA	$76.12	$207.00	$283.12	**$375.52**	1.000
Casement, insulated glass, wood window, 1 venting, 1-6 x 4-0	EA	$76.12	$234.00	$310.12	**$407.92**	1.000
Casement, insulated glass, wood window, 1 venting, 1-6 x 4-6	EA	$114.18	$255.00	$369.18	**$496.68**	1.500
Casement, insulated glass, wood window, 1 venting, 1-6 x 5-0	EA	$114.18	$282.00	$396.18	**$529.08**	1.500
Casement, insulated glass, wood window, 1 venting, 1-6 x 5-6	EA	$114.18	$303.00	$417.18	**$554.28**	1.500
Casement, insulated glass, wood window, 1 venting, 1-8 x 2-6	EA	$76.12	$180.00	$256.12	**$343.12**	1.000
Casement, insulated glass, wood window, 1 venting, 1-8 x 3-0	EA	$76.12	$194.00	$270.12	**$359.92**	1.000
Casement, insulated glass, wood window, 1 venting, 1-8 x 3-6	EA	$76.12	$213.00	$289.12	**$382.72**	1.000
Casement, insulated glass, wood window, 1 venting, 1-8 x 4-0	EA	$76.12	$234.00	$310.12	**$407.92**	1.000
Casement, insulated glass, wood window, 1 venting, 1-8 x 4-6	EA	$114.18	$261.00	$375.18	**$503.88**	1.500
Casement, insulated glass, wood window, 1 venting, 1-8 x 5-0	EA	$114.18	$288.00	$402.18	**$536.28**	1.500
Casement, insulated glass, wood window, 1 venting, 1-8 x 5-6	EA	$114.18	$316.00	$430.18	**$569.88**	1.500
Casement, insulated glass, wood window, 1 venting, 2-0 x 2-6	EA	$76.12	$201.00	$277.12	**$368.32**	1.000
Casement, insulated glass, wood window, 1 venting, 2-0 x 3-0	EA	$76.12	$213.00	$289.12	**$382.72**	1.000
Casement, insulated glass, wood window, 1 venting, 2-0 x 3-6	EA	$76.12	$228.00	$304.12	**$400.72**	1.000
Casement, insulated glass, wood window, 1 venting, 2-0 x 4-0	EA	$76.12	$255.00	$331.12	**$433.12**	1.000
Casement, insulated glass, wood window, 1 venting, 2-0 x 4-6	EA	$114.18	$286.00	$400.18	**$533.88**	1.500
Casement, insulated glass, wood window, 1 venting, 2-0 x 5-0	EA	$114.18	$303.00	$417.18	**$554.28**	1.500
Casement, insulated glass, wood window, 1 venting, 2-0 x 5-6	EA	$114.18	$343.00	$457.18	**$602.28**	1.500
Casement, insulated glass, wood window, 1 venting, 2-6 x 2-6	EA	$76.12	$228.00	$304.12	**$400.72**	1.000
Casement, insulated glass, wood window, 1 venting, 2-6 x 3-0	EA	$76.12	$241.00	$317.12	**$416.32**	1.000
Casement, insulated glass, wood window, 1 venting, 2-6 x 3-6	EA	$76.12	$255.00	$331.12	**$433.12**	1.000
Casement, insulated glass, wood window, 1 venting, 2-6 x 4-0	EA	$76.12	$294.00	$370.12	**$479.92**	1.000
Casement, insulated glass, wood window, 1 venting, 2-6 x 4-6	EA	$114.18	$323.00	$437.18	**$578.28**	1.500
Casement, insulated glass, wood window, 1 venting, 2-6 x 5-0	EA	$114.18	$351.00	$465.18	**$611.88**	1.500
Casement, insulated glass, wood window, 1 venting, 2-6 x 5-6	EA	$114.18	$388.00	$502.18	**$656.28**	1.500

Wood Windows

Casement, Insulated Glass, Aluminum/Vinyl Clad Wood Window, PREMIUM GRADE

> No removal of old window included.

Description	Unit	Direct Labor	Direct Materials	Direct Total	Selling Price	Man-hours
CASEMENT, INSULATED GLASS, CLAD WINDOW, PREMIUM						
Casement, insulated glass, clad window, 1 venting, 1-6 x 2-6, premium	EA	$76.12	$237.00	$313.12	**$411.52**	1.000
Casement, insulated glass, clad window, 1 venting, 1-6 x 3-0, premium	EA	$76.12	$256.00	$332.12	**$434.32**	1.000
Casement, insulated glass, clad window, 1 venting, 1-6 x 3-6, premium	EA	$76.12	$283.00	$359.12	**$466.72**	1.000
Casement, insulated glass, clad window, 1 venting, 1-6 x 4-0, premium	EA	$76.12	$320.00	$396.12	**$511.12**	1.000
Casement, insulated glass, clad window, 1 venting, 1-6 x 4-6, premium	EA	$114.18	$348.00	$462.18	**$608.28**	1.500
Casement, insulated glass, clad window, 1 venting, 1-6 x 5-0, premium	EA	$114.18	$386.00	$500.18	**$653.88**	1.500
Casement, insulated glass, clad window, 1 venting, 1-6 x 5-6, premium	EA	$114.18	$414.00	$528.18	**$687.48**	1.500
Casement, insulated glass, clad window, 1 venting, 1-8 x 2-6, premium	EA	$76.12	$246.00	$322.12	**$422.32**	1.000
Casement, insulated glass, clad window, 1 venting, 1-8 x 3-0, premium	EA	$76.12	$265.00	$341.12	**$445.12**	1.000
Casement, insulated glass, clad window, 1 venting, 1-8 x 3-6, premium	EA	$76.12	$292.00	$368.12	**$477.52**	1.000
Casement, insulated glass, clad window, 1 venting, 1-8 x 4-0, premium	EA	$76.12	$320.00	$396.12	**$511.12**	1.000
Casement, insulated glass, clad window, 1 venting, 1-8 x 4-6, premium	EA	$114.18	$357.00	$471.18	**$619.08**	1.500
Casement, insulated glass, clad window, 1 venting, 1-8 x 5-0, premium	EA	$114.18	$394.00	$508.18	**$663.48**	1.500
Casement, insulated glass, clad window, 1 venting, 1-8 x 5-6, premium	EA	$114.18	$432.00	$546.18	**$709.08**	1.500
Casement, insulated glass, clad window, 1 venting, 2-0 x 2-6, premium	EA	$76.12	$274.00	$350.12	**$455.92**	1.000
Casement, insulated glass, clad window, 1 venting, 2-0 x 3-0, premium	EA	$76.12	$292.00	$368.12	**$477.52**	1.000
Casement, insulated glass, clad window, 1 venting, 2-0 x 3-6, premium	EA	$76.12	$311.00	$387.12	**$500.32**	1.000
Casement, insulated glass, clad window, 1 venting, 2-0 x 4-0, premium	EA	$76.12	$348.00	$424.12	**$544.72**	1.000
Casement, insulated glass, clad window, 1 venting, 2-0 x 4-6, premium	EA	$114.18	$391.00	$505.18	**$659.88**	1.500
Casement, insulated glass, clad window, 1 venting, 2-0 x 5-0, premium	EA	$114.18	$414.00	$528.18	**$687.48**	1.500
Casement, insulated glass, clad window, 1 venting, 2-0 x 5-6, premium	EA	$114.18	$469.00	$583.18	**$753.48**	1.500
Casement, insulated glass, clad window, 1 venting, 2-6 x 2-6, premium	EA	$76.12	$311.00	$387.12	**$500.32**	1.000
Casement, insulated glass, clad window, 1 venting, 2-6 x 3-0, premium	EA	$76.12	$329.00	$405.12	**$521.92**	1.000
Casement, insulated glass, clad window, 1 venting, 2-6 x 3-6, premium	EA	$76.12	$348.00	$424.12	**$544.72**	1.000
Casement, insulated glass, clad window, 1 venting, 2-6 x 4-0, premium	EA	$76.12	$402.00	$478.12	**$609.52**	1.000
Casement, insulated glass, clad window, 1 venting, 2-6 x 4-6, premium	EA	$114.18	$442.00	$556.18	**$721.08**	1.500
Casement, insulated glass, clad window, 1 venting, 2-6 x 5-0, premium	EA	$114.18	$479.00	$593.18	**$765.48**	1.500
Casement, insulated glass, clad window, 1 venting, 2-6 x 5-6, premium	EA	$114.18	$531.00	$645.18	**$827.88**	1.500

Wood Windows

Casement, Insulated Glass, Aluminum/Vinyl Clad Wood Window, AVERAGE GRADE

> No removal of old window included.

Description	Unit	Direct Labor	Direct Materials	Direct Total	Selling Price	Man-hours
CASEMENT, INSULATED GLASS, CLAD WINDOW, AVERAGE						
Casement, insulated glass, clad window, 1 venting, 1-6 x 2-6, average	EA	$76.12	$215.00	$291.12	**$385.12**	1.000
Casement, insulated glass, clad window, 1 venting, 1-6 x 3-0, average	EA	$76.12	$233.00	$309.12	**$406.72**	1.000
Casement, insulated glass, clad window, 1 venting, 1-6 x 3-6, average	EA	$76.12	$257.00	$333.12	**$435.52**	1.000
Casement, insulated glass, clad window, 1 venting, 1-6 x 4-0, average	EA	$76.12	$291.00	$367.12	**$476.32**	1.000
Casement, insulated glass, clad window, 1 venting, 1-6 x 4-6, average	EA	$114.18	$317.00	$431.18	**$571.08**	1.500
Casement, insulated glass, clad window, 1 venting, 1-6 x 5-0, average	EA	$114.18	$351.00	$465.18	**$611.88**	1.500
Casement, insulated glass, clad window, 1 venting, 1-6 x 5-6, average	EA	$114.18	$376.00	$490.18	**$641.88**	1.500
Casement, insulated glass, clad window, 1 venting, 1-8 x 2-6, average	EA	$76.12	$224.00	$300.12	**$395.92**	1.000
Casement, insulated glass, clad window, 1 venting, 1-8 x 3-0, average	EA	$76.12	$241.00	$317.12	**$416.32**	1.000
Casement, insulated glass, clad window, 1 venting, 1-8 x 3-6, average	EA	$76.12	$265.00	$341.12	**$445.12**	1.000
Casement, insulated glass, clad window, 1 venting, 1-8 x 4-0, average	EA	$76.12	$291.00	$367.12	**$476.32**	1.000
Casement, insulated glass, clad window, 1 venting, 1-8 x 4-6, average	EA	$114.18	$325.00	$439.18	**$580.68**	1.500
Casement, insulated glass, clad window, 1 venting, 1-8 x 5-0, average	EA	$114.18	$359.00	$473.18	**$621.48**	1.500
Casement, insulated glass, clad window, 1 venting, 1-8 x 5-6, average	EA	$114.18	$392.00	$506.18	**$661.08**	1.500
Casement, insulated glass, clad window, 1 venting, 2-0 x 2-6, average	EA	$76.12	$249.00	$325.12	**$425.92**	1.000
Casement, insulated glass, clad window, 1 venting, 2-0 x 3-0, average	EA	$76.12	$265.00	$341.12	**$445.12**	1.000
Casement, insulated glass, clad window, 1 venting, 2-0 x 3-6, average	EA	$76.12	$283.00	$359.12	**$466.72**	1.000
Casement, insulated glass, clad window, 1 venting, 2-0 x 4-0, average	EA	$76.12	$317.00	$393.12	**$507.52**	1.000
Casement, insulated glass, clad window, 1 venting, 2-0 x 4-6, average	EA	$114.18	$355.00	$469.18	**$616.68**	1.500
Casement, insulated glass, clad window, 1 venting, 2-0 x 5-0, average	EA	$114.18	$376.00	$490.18	**$641.88**	1.500
Casement, insulated glass, clad window, 1 venting, 2-0 x 5-6, average	EA	$114.18	$426.00	$540.18	**$701.88**	1.500
Casement, insulated glass, clad window, 1 venting, 2-6 x 2-6, average	EA	$76.12	$283.00	$359.12	**$466.72**	1.000
Casement, insulated glass, clad window, 1 venting, 2-6 x 3-0, average	EA	$76.12	$299.00	$375.12	**$485.92**	1.000
Casement, insulated glass, clad window, 1 venting, 2-6 x 3-6, average	EA	$76.12	$317.00	$393.12	**$507.52**	1.000
Casement, insulated glass, clad window, 1 venting, 2-6 x 4-0, average	EA	$76.12	$365.00	$441.12	**$565.12**	1.000
Casement, insulated glass, clad window, 1 venting, 2-6 x 4-6, average	EA	$114.18	$402.00	$516.18	**$673.08**	1.500
Casement, insulated glass, clad window, 1 venting, 2-6 x 5-0, average	EA	$114.18	$436.00	$550.18	**$713.88**	1.500
Casement, insulated glass, clad window, 1 venting, 2-6 x 5-6, average	EA	$114.18	$482.00	$596.18	**$769.08**	1.500

Wood Windows

Casement, Insulated Glass, Aluminum/Vinyl Clad Wood Window, ECONOMY GRADE

> No removal of old window included.

Description	Unit	Direct Labor	Direct Materials	Direct Total	Selling Price	Man-hours
CASEMENT, INSULATED GLASS, CLAD WINDOW, ECONOMY						
Casement, insulated glass, clad window, 1 venting, 1-6 x 2-6, economy	EA	$76.12	$196.00	$272.12	**$362.32**	1.000
Casement, insulated glass, clad window, 1 venting, 1-6 x 3-0, economy	EA	$76.12	$212.00	$288.12	**$381.52**	1.000
Casement, insulated glass, clad window, 1 venting, 1-6 x 3-6, economy	EA	$76.12	$234.00	$310.12	**$407.92**	1.000
Casement, insulated glass, clad window, 1 venting, 1-6 x 4-0, economy	EA	$76.12	$265.00	$341.12	**$445.12**	1.000
Casement, insulated glass, clad window, 1 venting, 1-6 x 4-6, economy	EA	$114.18	$288.00	$402.18	**$536.28**	1.500
Casement, insulated glass, clad window, 1 venting, 1-6 x 5-0, economy	EA	$114.18	$319.00	$433.18	**$573.48**	1.500
Casement, insulated glass, clad window, 1 venting, 1-6 x 5-6, economy	EA	$114.18	$342.00	$456.18	**$601.08**	1.500
Casement, insulated glass, clad window, 1 venting, 1-8 x 2-6, economy	EA	$76.12	$203.00	$279.12	**$370.72**	1.000
Casement, insulated glass, clad window, 1 venting, 1-8 x 3-0, economy	EA	$76.12	$219.00	$295.12	**$389.92**	1.000
Casement, insulated glass, clad window, 1 venting, 1-8 x 3-6, economy	EA	$76.12	$241.00	$317.12	**$416.32**	1.000
Casement, insulated glass, clad window, 1 venting, 1-8 x 4-0, economy	EA	$76.12	$265.00	$341.12	**$445.12**	1.000
Casement, insulated glass, clad window, 1 venting, 1-8 x 4-6, economy	EA	$114.18	$295.00	$409.18	**$544.68**	1.500
Casement, insulated glass, clad window, 1 venting, 1-8 x 5-0, economy	EA	$114.18	$326.00	$440.18	**$581.88**	1.500
Casement, insulated glass, clad window, 1 venting, 1-8 x 5-6, economy	EA	$114.18	$357.00	$471.18	**$619.08**	1.500
Casement, insulated glass, clad window, 1 venting, 2-0 x 2-6, economy	EA	$76.12	$227.00	$303.12	**$399.52**	1.000
Casement, insulated glass, clad window, 1 venting, 2-0 x 3-0, economy	EA	$76.12	$241.00	$317.12	**$416.32**	1.000
Casement, insulated glass, clad window, 1 venting, 2-0 x 3-6, economy	EA	$76.12	$257.00	$333.12	**$435.52**	1.000
Casement, insulated glass, clad window, 1 venting, 2-0 x 4-0, economy	EA	$76.12	$288.00	$364.12	**$472.72**	1.000
Casement, insulated glass, clad window, 1 venting, 2-0 x 4-6, economy	EA	$114.18	$323.00	$437.18	**$578.28**	1.500
Casement, insulated glass, clad window, 1 venting, 2-0 x 5-0, economy	EA	$114.18	$342.00	$456.18	**$601.08**	1.500
Casement, insulated glass, clad window, 1 venting, 2-0 x 5-6, economy	EA	$114.18	$387.00	$501.18	**$655.08**	1.500
Casement, insulated glass, clad window, 1 venting, 2-6 x 2-6, economy	EA	$76.12	$257.00	$333.12	**$435.52**	1.000
Casement, insulated glass, clad window, 1 venting, 2-6 x 3-0, economy	EA	$76.12	$272.00	$348.12	**$453.52**	1.000
Casement, insulated glass, clad window, 1 venting, 2-6 x 3-6, economy	EA	$76.12	$288.00	$364.12	**$472.72**	1.000
Casement, insulated glass, clad window, 1 venting, 2-6 x 4-0, economy	EA	$76.12	$332.00	$408.12	**$525.52**	1.000
Casement, insulated glass, clad window, 1 venting, 2-6 x 4-6, economy	EA	$114.18	$365.00	$479.18	**$628.68**	1.500
Casement, insulated glass, clad window, 1 venting, 2-6 x 5-0, economy	EA	$114.18	$396.00	$510.18	**$665.88**	1.500
Casement, insulated glass, clad window, 1 venting, 2-6 x 5-6, economy	EA	$114.18	$439.00	$553.18	**$717.48**	1.500

Wood Windows

Slider, Insulated Glass, Wood Window

> No removal of old window included.

Description	Unit	Direct Labor	Direct Materials	Direct Total	Selling Price	Man-hours
SLIDER, INSULATED GLASS WOOD WINDOW						
Slider, insulated glass, wood window, 3-0 x 2-0	EA	$133.21	$269.00	$402.21	**$545.26**	1.750
Slider, insulated glass, wood window, 3-0 x 2-6	EA	$133.21	$277.00	$410.21	**$554.86**	1.750
Slider, insulated glass, wood window, 3-0 x 3-0	EA	$133.21	$274.00	$407.21	**$551.26**	1.750
Slider, insulated glass, wood window, 3-0 x 3-6	EA	$133.21	$282.00	$415.21	**$560.86**	1.750
Slider, insulated glass, wood window, 3-0 x 4-0	EA	$133.21	$292.00	$425.21	**$572.86**	1.750
Slider, insulated glass, wood window, 3-0 x 4-6	EA	$133.21	$301.00	$434.21	**$583.66**	1.750
Slider, insulated glass, wood window, 3-0 x 5-0	EA	$133.21	$312.00	$445.21	**$596.86**	1.750
Slider, insulated glass, wood window, 4-0 x 2-0	EA	$133.21	$308.00	$441.21	**$592.06**	1.750
Slider, insulated glass, wood window, 4-0 x 2-6	EA	$133.21	$316.00	$449.21	**$601.66**	1.750
Slider, insulated glass, wood window, 4-0 x 3-0	EA	$133.21	$323.00	$456.21	**$610.06**	1.750
Slider, insulated glass, wood window, 4-0 x 3-6	EA	$133.21	$331.00	$464.21	**$619.66**	1.750
Slider, insulated glass, wood window, 4-0 x 4-0	EA	$133.21	$339.00	$472.21	**$629.26**	1.750
Slider, insulated glass, wood window, 4-0 x 4-6	EA	$133.21	$349.00	$482.21	**$641.26**	1.750
Slider, insulated glass, wood window, 4-0 x 5-0	EA	$133.21	$361.00	$494.21	**$655.66**	1.750
Slider, insulated glass, wood window, 5-0 x 2-0	EA	$228.36	$344.00	$572.36	**$794.15**	3.000
Slider, insulated glass, wood window, 5-0 x 2-6	EA	$228.36	$356.00	$584.36	**$808.55**	3.000
Slider, insulated glass, wood window, 5-0 x 3-0	EA	$228.36	$369.00	$597.36	**$824.15**	3.000
Slider, insulated glass, wood window, 5-0 x 3-6	EA	$228.36	$380.00	$608.36	**$837.35**	3.000
Slider, insulated glass, wood window, 5-0 x 4-0	EA	$228.36	$393.00	$621.36	**$852.95**	3.000
Slider, insulated glass, wood window, 5-0 x 4-6	EA	$228.36	$405.00	$633.36	**$867.35**	3.000
Slider, insulated glass, wood window, 5-0 x 5-0	EA	$228.36	$414.00	$642.36	**$878.15**	3.000
Slider, insulated glass, wood window, 6-0 x 2-0	EA	$228.36	$502.00	$730.36	**$983.75**	3.000
Slider, insulated glass, wood window, 6-0 x 2-6	EA	$228.36	$512.00	$740.36	**$995.75**	3.000
Slider, insulated glass, wood window, 6-0 x 3-0	EA	$228.36	$524.00	$752.36	**$1,010.15**	3.000
Slider, insulated glass, wood window, 6-0 x 3-6	EA	$228.36	$533.00	$761.36	**$1,020.95**	3.000
Slider, insulated glass, wood window, 6-0 x 4-0	EA	$228.36	$543.00	$771.36	**$1,032.95**	3.000
Slider, insulated glass, wood window, 6-0 x 4-6	EA	$228.36	$555.00	$783.36	**$1,047.35**	3.000
Slider, insulated glass, wood window, 6-0 x 5-0	EA	$228.36	$564.00	$792.36	**$1,058.15**	3.000

Wood Windows

Slider, Insulated Glass, Aluminum/Vinyl Clad Wood Window, PREMIUM GRADE

> No removal of old window included.

Description	Unit	Direct Labor	Direct Materials	Direct Total	Selling Price	Man-hours
SLIDER, INSULATED GLASS, CLAD WINDOW, PREMIUM						
Slider, insulated glass, clad wood window, 3-0 x 2-0, premium	EA	$133.21	$402.00	$535.21	**$704.86**	1.750
Slider, insulated glass, clad wood window, 3-0 x 2-6, premium	EA	$133.21	$414.00	$547.21	**$719.26**	1.750
Slider, insulated glass, clad wood window, 3-0 x 3-0, premium	EA	$133.21	$410.00	$543.21	**$714.46**	1.750
Slider, insulated glass, clad wood window, 3-0 x 3-6, premium	EA	$133.21	$421.00	$554.21	**$727.66**	1.750
Slider, insulated glass, clad wood window, 3-0 x 4-0, premium	EA	$133.21	$437.00	$570.21	**$746.86**	1.750
Slider, insulated glass, clad wood window, 3-0 x 4-6, premium	EA	$133.21	$450.00	$583.21	**$762.46**	1.750
Slider, insulated glass, clad wood window, 3-0 x 5-0, premium	EA	$133.21	$466.00	$599.21	**$781.66**	1.750
Slider, insulated glass, clad wood window, 4-0 x 2-0, premium	EA	$133.21	$460.00	$593.21	**$774.46**	1.750
Slider, insulated glass, clad wood window, 4-0 x 2-6, premium	EA	$133.21	$472.00	$605.21	**$788.86**	1.750
Slider, insulated glass, clad wood window, 4-0 x 3-0, premium	EA	$133.21	$483.00	$616.21	**$802.06**	1.750
Slider, insulated glass, clad wood window, 4-0 x 3-6, premium	EA	$133.21	$495.00	$628.21	**$816.46**	1.750
Slider, insulated glass, clad wood window, 4-0 x 4-0, premium	EA	$133.21	$506.00	$639.21	**$829.66**	1.750
Slider, insulated glass, clad wood window, 4-0 x 4-6, premium	EA	$133.21	$522.00	$655.21	**$848.86**	1.750
Slider, insulated glass, clad wood window, 4-0 x 5-0, premium	EA	$133.21	$539.00	$672.21	**$869.26**	1.750
Slider, insulated glass, clad wood window, 5-0 x 2-0, premium	EA	$228.36	$514.00	$742.36	**$998.15**	3.000
Slider, insulated glass, clad wood window, 5-0 x 2-6, premium	EA	$228.36	$532.00	$760.36	**$1,019.75**	3.000
Slider, insulated glass, clad wood window, 5-0 x 3-0, premium	EA	$228.36	$551.00	$779.36	**$1,042.55**	3.000
Slider, insulated glass, clad wood window, 5-0 x 3-6, premium	EA	$228.36	$568.00	$796.36	**$1,062.95**	3.000
Slider, insulated glass, clad wood window, 5-0 x 4-0, premium	EA	$228.36	$588.00	$816.36	**$1,086.95**	3.000
Slider, insulated glass, clad wood window, 5-0 x 4-6, premium	EA	$228.36	$605.00	$833.36	**$1,107.35**	3.000
Slider, insulated glass, clad wood window, 5-0 x 5-0, premium	EA	$228.36	$619.00	$847.36	**$1,124.15**	3.000
Slider, insulated glass, clad wood window, 6-0 x 2-0, premium	EA	$228.36	$750.00	$978.36	**$1,281.35**	3.000
Slider, insulated glass, clad wood window, 6-0 x 2-6, premium	EA	$228.36	$766.00	$994.36	**$1,300.55**	3.000
Slider, insulated glass, clad wood window, 6-0 x 3-0, premium	EA	$228.36	$783.00	$1,011.36	**$1,320.95**	3.000
Slider, insulated glass, clad wood window, 6-0 x 3-6, premium	EA	$228.36	$796.00	$1,024.36	**$1,336.55**	3.000
Slider, insulated glass, clad wood window, 6-0 x 4-0, premium	EA	$228.36	$812.00	$1,040.36	**$1,355.75**	3.000
Slider, insulated glass, clad wood window, 6-0 x 4-6, premium	EA	$228.36	$829.00	$1,057.36	**$1,376.15**	3.000
Slider, insulated glass, clad wood window, 6-0 x 5-0, premium	EA	$228.36	$843.00	$1,071.36	**$1,392.95**	3.000

Wood Windows

Slider, Insulated Glass, Aluminum/Vinyl Clad Wood Window, AVERAGE GRADE

> No removal of old window included.

Description	Unit	Direct Labor	Direct Materials	Direct Total	Selling Price	Man-hours
SLIDER, INSULATED GLASS, CLAD WINDOW, AVERAGE						
Slider, insulated glass, clad wood window, 3-0 x 2-0, average	EA	$133.21	$350.00	$483.21	**$642.46**	1.750
Slider, insulated glass, clad wood window, 3-0 x 2-6, average	EA	$133.21	$360.00	$493.21	**$654.46**	1.750
Slider, insulated glass, clad wood window, 3-0 x 3-0, average	EA	$133.21	$356.00	$489.21	**$649.66**	1.750
Slider, insulated glass, clad wood window, 3-0 x 3-6, average	EA	$133.21	$366.00	$499.21	**$661.66**	1.750
Slider, insulated glass, clad wood window, 3-0 x 4-0, average	EA	$133.21	$380.00	$513.21	**$678.46**	1.750
Slider, insulated glass, clad wood window, 3-0 x 4-6, average	EA	$133.21	$392.00	$525.21	**$692.86**	1.750
Slider, insulated glass, clad wood window, 3-0 x 5-0, average	EA	$133.21	$405.00	$538.21	**$708.46**	1.750
Slider, insulated glass, clad wood window, 4-0 x 2-0, average	EA	$133.21	$400.00	$533.21	**$702.46**	1.750
Slider, insulated glass, clad wood window, 4-0 x 2-6, average	EA	$133.21	$410.00	$543.21	**$714.46**	1.750
Slider, insulated glass, clad wood window, 4-0 x 3-0, average	EA	$133.21	$420.00	$553.21	**$726.46**	1.750
Slider, insulated glass, clad wood window, 4-0 x 3-6, average	EA	$133.21	$430.00	$563.21	**$738.46**	1.750
Slider, insulated glass, clad wood window, 4-0 x 4-0, average	EA	$133.21	$440.00	$573.21	**$750.46**	1.750
Slider, insulated glass, clad wood window, 4-0 x 4-6, average	EA	$133.21	$454.00	$587.21	**$767.26**	1.750
Slider, insulated glass, clad wood window, 4-0 x 5-0, average	EA	$133.21	$469.00	$602.21	**$785.26**	1.750
Slider, insulated glass, clad wood window, 5-0 x 2-0, average	EA	$228.36	$447.00	$675.36	**$917.75**	3.000
Slider, insulated glass, clad wood window, 5-0 x 2-6, average	EA	$228.36	$462.00	$690.36	**$935.75**	3.000
Slider, insulated glass, clad wood window, 5-0 x 3-0, average	EA	$228.36	$479.00	$707.36	**$956.15**	3.000
Slider, insulated glass, clad wood window, 5-0 x 3-6, average	EA	$228.36	$494.00	$722.36	**$974.15**	3.000
Slider, insulated glass, clad wood window, 5-0 x 4-0, average	EA	$228.36	$511.00	$739.36	**$994.55**	3.000
Slider, insulated glass, clad wood window, 5-0 x 4-6, average	EA	$228.36	$526.00	$754.36	**$1,012.55**	3.000
Slider, insulated glass, clad wood window, 5-0 x 5-0, average	EA	$228.36	$538.00	$766.36	**$1,026.95**	3.000
Slider, insulated glass, clad wood window, 6-0 x 2-0, average	EA	$228.36	$652.00	$880.36	**$1,163.75**	3.000
Slider, insulated glass, clad wood window, 6-0 x 2-6, average	EA	$228.36	$666.00	$894.36	**$1,180.55**	3.000
Slider, insulated glass, clad wood window, 6-0 x 3-0, average	EA	$228.36	$681.00	$909.36	**$1,198.55**	3.000
Slider, insulated glass, clad wood window, 6-0 x 3-6, average	EA	$228.36	$693.00	$921.36	**$1,212.95**	3.000
Slider, insulated glass, clad wood window, 6-0 x 4-0, average	EA	$228.36	$706.00	$934.36	**$1,228.55**	3.000
Slider, insulated glass, clad wood window, 6-0 x 4-6, average	EA	$228.36	$721.00	$949.36	**$1,246.55**	3.000
Slider, insulated glass, clad wood window, 6-0 x 5-0, average	EA	$228.36	$733.00	$961.36	**$1,260.95**	3.000

Wood Windows

Slider, Insulated Glass, Aluminum/Vinyl Clad Wood Window, ECONOMY GRADE

> No removal of old window included.

Description	Unit	Direct Labor	Direct Materials	Direct Total	Selling Price	Man-hours
SLIDER, INSULATED GLASS, CLAD WINDOW, ECONOMY						
Slider, insulated glass, clad wood window, 3-0 x 2-0, economy	EA	$133.21	$304.00	$437.21	**$587.26**	1.750
Slider, insulated glass, clad wood window, 3-0 x 2-6, economy	EA	$133.21	$313.00	$446.21	**$598.06**	1.750
Slider, insulated glass, clad wood window, 3-0 x 3-0, economy	EA	$133.21	$310.00	$443.21	**$594.46**	1.750
Slider, insulated glass, clad wood window, 3-0 x 3-6, economy	EA	$133.21	$319.00	$452.21	**$605.26**	1.750
Slider, insulated glass, clad wood window, 3-0 x 4-0, economy	EA	$133.21	$330.00	$463.21	**$618.46**	1.750
Slider, insulated glass, clad wood window, 3-0 x 4-6, economy	EA	$133.21	$341.00	$474.21	**$631.66**	1.750
Slider, insulated glass, clad wood window, 3-0 x 5-0, economy	EA	$133.21	$352.00	$485.21	**$644.86**	1.750
Slider, insulated glass, clad wood window, 4-0 x 2-0, economy	EA	$133.21	$348.00	$481.21	**$640.06**	1.750
Slider, insulated glass, clad wood window, 4-0 x 2-6, economy	EA	$133.21	$357.00	$490.21	**$650.86**	1.750
Slider, insulated glass, clad wood window, 4-0 x 3-0, economy	EA	$133.21	$365.00	$498.21	**$660.46**	1.750
Slider, insulated glass, clad wood window, 4-0 x 3-6, economy	EA	$133.21	$374.00	$507.21	**$671.26**	1.750
Slider, insulated glass, clad wood window, 4-0 x 4-0, economy	EA	$133.21	$383.00	$516.21	**$682.06**	1.750
Slider, insulated glass, clad wood window, 4-0 x 4-6, economy	EA	$133.21	$395.00	$528.21	**$696.46**	1.750
Slider, insulated glass, clad wood window, 4-0 x 5-0, economy	EA	$133.21	$408.00	$541.21	**$712.06**	1.750
Slider, insulated glass, clad wood window, 5-0 x 2-0, economy	EA	$228.36	$389.00	$617.36	**$848.15**	3.000
Slider, insulated glass, clad wood window, 5-0 x 2-6, economy	EA	$228.36	$402.00	$630.36	**$863.75**	3.000
Slider, insulated glass, clad wood window, 5-0 x 3-0, economy	EA	$228.36	$417.00	$645.36	**$881.75**	3.000
Slider, insulated glass, clad wood window, 5-0 x 3-6, economy	EA	$228.36	$430.00	$658.36	**$897.35**	3.000
Slider, insulated glass, clad wood window, 5-0 x 4-0, economy	EA	$228.36	$444.00	$672.36	**$914.15**	3.000
Slider, insulated glass, clad wood window, 5-0 x 4-6, economy	EA	$228.36	$458.00	$686.36	**$930.95**	3.000
Slider, insulated glass, clad wood window, 5-0 x 5-0, economy	EA	$228.36	$468.00	$696.36	**$942.95**	3.000
Slider, insulated glass, clad wood window, 6-0 x 2-0, economy	EA	$228.36	$567.00	$795.36	**$1,061.75**	3.000
Slider, insulated glass, clad wood window, 6-0 x 2-6, economy	EA	$228.36	$579.00	$807.36	**$1,076.15**	3.000
Slider, insulated glass, clad wood window, 6-0 x 3-0, economy	EA	$228.36	$592.00	$820.36	**$1,091.75**	3.000
Slider, insulated glass, clad wood window, 6-0 x 3-6, economy	EA	$228.36	$602.00	$830.36	**$1,103.75**	3.000
Slider, insulated glass, clad wood window, 6-0 x 4-0, economy	EA	$228.36	$614.00	$842.36	**$1,118.15**	3.000
Slider, insulated glass, clad wood window, 6-0 x 4-6, economy	EA	$228.36	$627.00	$855.36	**$1,133.75**	3.000
Slider, insulated glass, clad wood window, 6-0 x 5-0, economy	EA	$228.36	$637.00	$865.36	**$1,145.75**	3.000

Wood Windows

Wood Picture Window, Single Glazed

> No removal of old window included.

Description	Unit	Direct Labor	Direct Materials	Direct Total	Selling Price	Man-hours
WOOD PICTURE WINDOW, SINGLE GLAZED						
Picture window, single glaze, wood, 3-0 x 3-0	EA	$114.18	$138.00	$252.18	**$356.28**	1.500
Picture window, single glaze, wood, 3-0 x 4-0	EA	$114.18	$170.00	$284.18	**$394.68**	1.500
Picture window, single glaze, wood, 3-0 x 5-0	EA	$152.24	$212.00	$364.24	**$508.64**	2.000
Picture window, single glaze, wood, 3-6 x 3-0	EA	$114.18	$157.00	$271.18	**$379.08**	1.500
Picture window, single glaze, wood, 3-6 x 4-0	EA	$114.18	$193.00	$307.18	**$422.28**	1.500
Picture window, single glaze, wood, 3-6 x 5-0	EA	$152.24	$234.00	$386.24	**$535.04**	2.000
Picture window, single glaze, wood, 4-0 x 3-0	EA	$114.18	$170.00	$284.18	**$394.68**	1.500
Picture window, single glaze, wood, 4-0 x 4-0	EA	$114.18	$226.00	$340.18	**$461.88**	1.500
Picture window, single glaze, wood, 4-0 x 5-0	EA	$152.24	$256.00	$408.24	**$561.44**	2.000
Picture window, single glaze, wood, 4-6 x 3-0	EA	$114.18	$192.00	$306.18	**$421.08**	1.500
Picture window, single glaze, wood, 4-6 x 4-0	EA	$114.18	$246.00	$360.18	**$485.88**	1.500
Picture window, single glaze, wood, 4-6 x 5-0	EA	$152.24	$291.00	$443.24	**$603.44**	2.000
Picture window, single glaze, wood, 5-0 x 3-0	EA	$114.18	$212.00	$326.18	**$445.08**	1.500
Picture window, single glaze, wood, 5-0 x 4-0	EA	$114.18	$257.00	$371.18	**$499.08**	1.500
Picture window, single glaze, wood, 5-0 x 5-0	EA	$152.24	$315.00	$467.24	**$632.24**	2.000
Picture window, single glaze, wood, 5-6 x 3-0	EA	$114.18	$229.00	$343.18	**$465.48**	1.500
Picture window, single glaze, wood, 5-6 x 4-0	EA	$114.18	$295.00	$409.18	**$544.68**	1.500
Picture window, single glaze, wood, 5-6 x 5-0	EA	$152.24	$340.00	$492.24	**$662.24**	2.000

Wood Picture Window, Insulated Glass

> No removal of old window included.

Description	Unit	Direct Labor	Direct Materials	Direct Total	Selling Price	Man-hours
WOOD PICTURE WINDOW, INSULATED GLASS						
Picture window, insulated glass, wood, 3-0 x 3-0	EA	$114.18	$197.00	$311.18	**$427.08**	1.500
Picture window, insulated glass, wood, 3-0 x 3-6	EA	$114.18	$224.00	$338.18	**$459.48**	1.500
Picture window, insulated glass, wood, 3-0 x 4-0	EA	$114.18	$243.00	$357.18	**$482.28**	1.500
Picture window, insulated glass, wood, 3-0 x 4-2	EA	$152.24	$308.00	$460.24	**$623.84**	2.000
Picture window, insulated glass, wood, 3-0 x 4-6	EA	$152.24	$277.00	$429.24	**$586.64**	2.000
Picture window, insulated glass, wood, 3-0 x 5-0	EA	$152.24	$303.00	$455.24	**$617.84**	2.000
Picture window, insulated glass, wood, 3-0 x 5-6	EA	$152.24	$327.00	$479.24	**$646.64**	2.000
Picture window, insulated glass, wood, 3-6 x 3-0	EA	$114.18	$224.00	$338.18	**$459.48**	1.500
Picture window, insulated glass, wood, 3-6 x 3-6	EA	$114.18	$263.00	$377.18	**$506.28**	1.500
Picture window, insulated glass, wood, 3-6 x 4-0	EA	$114.18	$276.00	$390.18	**$521.88**	1.500
Picture window, insulated glass, wood, 3-6 x 4-2	EA	$152.24	$283.00	$435.24	**$593.84**	2.000
Picture window, insulated glass, wood, 3-6 x 4-6	EA	$152.24	$314.00	$466.24	**$631.04**	2.000
Picture window, insulated glass, wood, 3-6 x 5-0	EA	$152.24	$334.00	$486.24	**$655.04**	2.000
Picture window, insulated glass, wood, 3-6 x 5-6	EA	$152.24	$375.00	$527.24	**$704.24**	2.000

Wood Windows

Wood Picture Window, Insulated Glass

> No removal of old window included.

Description	Unit	Direct Labor	Direct Materials	Direct Total	Selling Price	Man-hours
WOOD PICTURE WINDOW, INSULATED GLASS (cont.)						
Picture window, insulated glass, wood, 4-0 x 3-0	EA	$114.18	$243.00	$357.18	**$482.28**	1.500
Picture window, insulated glass, wood, 4-0 x 3-6	EA	$114.18	$276.00	$390.18	**$521.88**	1.500
Picture window, insulated glass, wood, 4-0 x 4-0	EA	$114.18	$323.00	$437.18	**$578.28**	1.500
Picture window, insulated glass, wood, 4-0 x 4-2	EA	$152.24	$352.00	$504.24	**$676.64**	2.000
Picture window, insulated glass, wood, 4-0 x 4-6	EA	$152.24	$352.00	$504.24	**$676.64**	2.000
Picture window, insulated glass, wood, 4-0 x 5-0	EA	$152.24	$366.00	$518.24	**$693.44**	2.000
Picture window, insulated glass, wood, 4-0 x 5-6	EA	$152.24	$422.00	$574.24	**$760.64**	2.000
Picture window, insulated glass, wood, 4-6 x 3-0	EA	$114.18	$274.00	$388.18	**$519.48**	1.500
Picture window, insulated glass, wood, 4-6 x 3-6	EA	$114.18	$314.00	$428.18	**$567.48**	1.500
Picture window, insulated glass, wood, 4-6 x 4-0	EA	$114.18	$352.00	$466.18	**$613.08**	1.500
Picture window, insulated glass, wood, 4-6 x 4-2	EA	$152.24	$357.00	$509.24	**$682.64**	2.000
Picture window, insulated glass, wood, 4-6 x 4-6	EA	$152.24	$378.00	$530.24	**$707.84**	2.000
Picture window, insulated glass, wood, 4-6 x 5-0	EA	$152.24	$415.00	$567.24	**$752.24**	2.000
Picture window, insulated glass, wood, 4-6 x 5-6	EA	$152.24	$451.00	$603.24	**$795.44**	2.000
Picture window, insulated glass, wood, 5-0 x 3-0	EA	$114.18	$303.00	$417.18	**$554.28**	1.500
Picture window, insulated glass, wood, 5-0 x 3-6	EA	$114.18	$336.00	$450.18	**$593.88**	1.500
Picture window, insulated glass, wood, 5-0 x 4-0	EA	$114.18	$367.00	$481.18	**$631.08**	1.500
Picture window, insulated glass, wood, 5-0 x 4-2	EA	$152.24	$384.00	$536.24	**$715.04**	2.000
Picture window, insulated glass, wood, 5-0 x 4-6	EA	$152.24	$415.00	$567.24	**$752.24**	2.000
Picture window, insulated glass, wood, 5-0 x 5-0	EA	$152.24	$450.00	$602.24	**$794.24**	2.000
Picture window, insulated glass, wood, 5-0 x 5-6	EA	$152.24	$485.00	$637.24	**$836.24**	2.000
Picture window, insulated glass, wood, 5-6 x 3-0	EA	$114.18	$327.00	$441.18	**$583.08**	1.500
Picture window, insulated glass, wood, 5-6 x 3-6	EA	$114.18	$374.00	$488.18	**$639.48**	1.500
Picture window, insulated glass, wood, 5-6 x 4-0	EA	$114.18	$422.00	$536.18	**$697.08**	1.500
Picture window, insulated glass, wood, 5-6 x 4-2	EA	$152.24	$428.00	$580.24	**$767.84**	2.000
Picture window, insulated glass, wood, 5-6 x 4-6	EA	$152.24	$451.00	$603.24	**$795.44**	2.000
Picture window, insulated glass, wood, 5-6 x 5-0	EA	$152.24	$485.00	$637.24	**$836.24**	2.000
Picture window, insulated glass, wood, 5-6 x 5-6	EA	$152.24	$524.00	$676.24	**$883.04**	2.000

Wood Windows

Wood Picture Window, Insulated Glass, Aluminum/Vinyl Clad, PREMIUM GRADE

> No removal of old window included.

Description	Unit	Direct Labor	Direct Materials	Direct Total	Selling Price	Man-hours
WOOD PICTURE WINDOW, INSUL. GLASS, CLAD, PREMIUM						
Picture window, insulated glass, clad wood, 3-0 x 3-0, premium	EA	$114.18	$274.00	$388.18	**$519.48**	1.500
Picture window, insulated glass, clad wood, 3-0 x 3-6, premium	EA	$114.18	$311.00	$425.18	**$563.88**	1.500
Picture window, insulated glass, clad wood, 3-0 x 4-0, premium	EA	$114.18	$338.00	$452.18	**$596.28**	1.500
Picture window, insulated glass, clad wood, 3-0 x 4-2, premium	EA	$152.24	$428.00	$580.24	**$767.84**	2.000
Picture window, insulated glass, clad wood, 3-0 x 4-6, premium	EA	$152.24	$385.00	$537.24	**$716.24**	2.000
Picture window, insulated glass, clad wood, 3-0 x 5-0, premium	EA	$152.24	$421.00	$573.24	**$759.44**	2.000
Picture window, insulated glass, clad wood, 3-0 x 5-6, premium	EA	$152.24	$455.00	$607.24	**$800.24**	2.000
Picture window, insulated glass, clad wood, 3-6 x 3-0, premium	EA	$114.18	$311.00	$425.18	**$563.88**	1.500
Picture window, insulated glass, clad wood, 3-6 x 3-6, premium	EA	$114.18	$365.00	$479.18	**$628.68**	1.500
Picture window, insulated glass, clad wood, 3-6 x 4-0, premium	EA	$114.18	$383.00	$497.18	**$650.28**	1.500
Picture window, insulated glass, clad wood, 3-6 x 4-2, premium	EA	$152.24	$395.00	$547.24	**$728.24**	2.000
Picture window, insulated glass, clad wood, 3-6 x 4-6, premium	EA	$152.24	$437.00	$589.24	**$778.64**	2.000
Picture window, insulated glass, clad wood, 3-6 x 5-0, premium	EA	$152.24	$464.00	$616.24	**$811.04**	2.000
Picture window, insulated glass, clad wood, 3-6 x 5-6, premium	EA	$152.24	$522.00	$674.24	**$880.64**	2.000
Picture window, insulated glass, clad wood, 4-0 x 3-0, premium	EA	$114.18	$338.00	$452.18	**$596.28**	1.500
Picture window, insulated glass, clad wood, 4-0 x 3-6, premium	EA	$114.18	$383.00	$497.18	**$650.28**	1.500
Picture window, insulated glass, clad wood, 4-0 x 4-0, premium	EA	$114.18	$450.00	$564.18	**$730.68**	1.500
Picture window, insulated glass, clad wood, 4-0 x 4-2, premium	EA	$152.24	$490.00	$642.24	**$842.24**	2.000
Picture window, insulated glass, clad wood, 4-0 x 4-6, premium	EA	$152.24	$490.00	$642.24	**$842.24**	2.000
Picture window, insulated glass, clad wood, 4-0 x 5-0, premium	EA	$152.24	$509.00	$661.24	**$865.04**	2.000
Picture window, insulated glass, clad wood, 4-0 x 5-6, premium	EA	$152.24	$587.00	$739.24	**$958.64**	2.000
Picture window, insulated glass, clad wood, 4-6 x 3-0, premium	EA	$114.18	$382.00	$496.18	**$649.08**	1.500
Picture window, insulated glass, clad wood, 4-6 x 3-6, premium	EA	$114.18	$437.00	$551.18	**$715.08**	1.500
Picture window, insulated glass, clad wood, 4-6 x 4-0, premium	EA	$114.18	$490.00	$604.18	**$778.68**	1.500
Picture window, insulated glass, clad wood, 4-6 x 4-2, premium	EA	$152.24	$505.00	$657.24	**$860.24**	2.000
Picture window, insulated glass, clad wood, 4-6 x 4-6, premium	EA	$152.24	$526.00	$678.24	**$885.44**	2.000
Picture window, insulated glass, clad wood, 4-6 x 5-0, premium	EA	$152.24	$578.00	$730.24	**$947.84**	2.000
Picture window, insulated glass, clad wood, 4-6 x 5-6, premium	EA	$152.24	$628.00	$780.24	**$1,007.84**	2.000

Wood Windows

Wood Picture Window, Insulated Glass, Aluminum/Vinyl Clad, PREMIUM GRADE

> No removal of old window included.

Description	Unit	Direct Labor	Direct Materials	Direct Total	Selling Price	Man-hours
PICTURE WINDOW, INSUL. GLASS, CLAD, PREMIUM (cont.)						
Picture window, insulated glass, clad wood, 5-0 x 3-0, premium	EA	$114.18	$421.00	$535.18	**$695.88**	1.500
Picture window, insulated glass, clad wood, 5-0 x 3-6, premium	EA	$114.18	$468.00	$582.18	**$752.28**	1.500
Picture window, insulated glass, clad wood, 5-0 x 4-0, premium	EA	$114.18	$511.00	$625.18	**$803.88**	1.500
Picture window, insulated glass, clad wood, 5-0 x 4-2, premium	EA	$152.24	$538.00	$690.24	**$899.84**	2.000
Picture window, insulated glass, clad wood, 5-0 x 4-6, premium	EA	$152.24	$578.00	$730.24	**$947.84**	2.000
Picture window, insulated glass, clad wood, 5-0 x 5-0, premium	EA	$152.24	$626.00	$778.24	**$1,005.44**	2.000
Picture window, insulated glass, clad wood, 5-0 x 5-6, premium	EA	$152.24	$675.00	$827.24	**$1,064.24**	2.000
Picture window, insulated glass, clad wood, 5-6 x 3-0, premium	EA	$114.18	$455.00	$569.18	**$736.68**	1.500
Picture window, insulated glass, clad wood, 5-6 x 3-6, premium	EA	$114.18	$520.00	$634.18	**$814.68**	1.500
Picture window, insulated glass, clad wood, 5-6 x 4-0, premium	EA	$114.18	$587.00	$701.18	**$895.08**	1.500
Picture window, insulated glass, clad wood, 5-6 x 4-2, premium	EA	$152.24	$605.00	$757.24	**$980.24**	2.000
Picture window, insulated glass, clad wood, 5-6 x 4-6, premium	EA	$152.24	$628.00	$780.24	**$1,007.84**	2.000
Picture window, insulated glass, clad wood, 5-6 x 5-0, premium	EA	$152.24	$675.00	$827.24	**$1,064.24**	2.000
Picture window, insulated glass, clad wood, 5-6 x 5-6, premium	EA	$152.24	$729.00	$881.24	**$1,129.04**	2.000

Wood Picture Window, Insulated Glass, Aluminum/Vinyl Clad, AVERAGE GRADE

> No removal of old window included.

Description	Unit	Direct Labor	Direct Materials	Direct Total	Selling Price	Man-hours
WOOD PICTURE WINDOW, INSUL. GLASS, CLAD, AVERAGE						
Picture window, insulated glass, clad wood, 3-0 x 3-0, average	EA	$114.18	$249.00	$363.18	**$489.48**	1.500
Picture window, insulated glass, clad wood, 3-0 x 3-6, average	EA	$114.18	$283.00	$397.18	**$530.28**	1.500
Picture window, insulated glass, clad wood, 3-0 x 4-0, average	EA	$114.18	$308.00	$422.18	**$560.28**	1.500
Picture window, insulated glass, clad wood, 3-0 x 4-2, average	EA	$152.24	$389.00	$541.24	**$721.04**	2.000
Picture window, insulated glass, clad wood, 3-0 x 4-6, average	EA	$152.24	$350.00	$502.24	**$674.24**	2.000
Picture window, insulated glass, clad wood, 3-0 x 5-0, average	EA	$152.24	$383.00	$535.24	**$713.84**	2.000
Picture window, insulated glass, clad wood, 3-0 x 5-6, average	EA	$152.24	$414.00	$566.24	**$751.04**	2.000
Picture window, insulated glass, clad wood, 3-6 x 3-0, average	EA	$114.18	$283.00	$397.18	**$530.28**	1.500
Picture window, insulated glass, clad wood, 3-6 x 3-6, average	EA	$114.18	$332.00	$446.18	**$589.08**	1.500
Picture window, insulated glass, clad wood, 3-6 x 4-0, average	EA	$114.18	$349.00	$463.18	**$609.48**	1.500
Picture window, insulated glass, clad wood, 3-6 x 4-2, average	EA	$152.24	$371.00	$523.24	**$699.44**	2.000
Picture window, insulated glass, clad wood, 3-6 x 4-6, average	EA	$152.24	$398.00	$550.24	**$731.84**	2.000
Picture window, insulated glass, clad wood, 3-6 x 5-0, average	EA	$152.24	$422.00	$574.24	**$760.64**	2.000
Picture window, insulated glass, clad wood, 3-6 x 5-6, average	EA	$152.24	$475.00	$627.24	**$824.24**	2.000

Wood Windows

Wood Picture Window, Insulated Glass, Aluminum/Vinyl Clad, AVERAGE GRADE

> No removal of old window included.

Description	Unit	Direct Labor	Direct Materials	Direct Total	Selling Price	Man-hours
PICTURE WINDOW, INSUL. GLASS, CLAD, AVERAGE (cont.)						
Picture window, insulated glass, clad wood, 4-0 x 3-0, average	EA	$114.18	$308.00	$422.18	**$560.28**	1.500
Picture window, insulated glass, clad wood, 4-0 x 3-6, average	EA	$114.18	$349.00	$463.18	**$609.48**	1.500
Picture window, insulated glass, clad wood, 4-0 x 4-0, average	EA	$114.18	$409.00	$523.18	**$681.48**	1.500
Picture window, insulated glass, clad wood, 4-0 x 4-2, average	EA	$152.24	$445.00	$597.24	**$788.24**	2.000
Picture window, insulated glass, clad wood, 4-0 x 4-6, average	EA	$152.24	$445.00	$597.24	**$788.24**	2.000
Picture window, insulated glass, clad wood, 4-0 x 5-0, average	EA	$152.24	$463.00	$615.24	**$809.84**	2.000
Picture window, insulated glass, clad wood, 4-0 x 5-6, average	EA	$152.24	$533.00	$685.24	**$893.84**	2.000
Picture window, insulated glass, clad wood, 4-6 x 3-0, average	EA	$114.18	$347.00	$461.18	**$607.08**	1.500
Picture window, insulated glass, clad wood, 4-6 x 3-6, average	EA	$114.18	$398.00	$512.18	**$668.28**	1.500
Picture window, insulated glass, clad wood, 4-6 x 4-0, average	EA	$114.18	$445.00	$559.18	**$724.68**	1.500
Picture window, insulated glass, clad wood, 4-6 x 4-2, average	EA	$152.24	$458.00	$610.24	**$803.84**	2.000
Picture window, insulated glass, clad wood, 4-6 x 4-6, average	EA	$152.24	$478.00	$630.24	**$827.84**	2.000
Picture window, insulated glass, clad wood, 4-6 x 5-0, average	EA	$152.24	$525.00	$677.24	**$884.24**	2.000
Picture window, insulated glass, clad wood, 4-6 x 5-6, average	EA	$152.24	$571.00	$723.24	**$939.44**	2.000
Picture window, insulated glass, clad wood, 5-0 x 3-0, average	EA	$114.18	$383.00	$497.18	**$650.28**	1.500
Picture window, insulated glass, clad wood, 5-0 x 3-6, average	EA	$114.18	$425.00	$539.18	**$700.68**	1.500
Picture window, insulated glass, clad wood, 5-0 x 4-0, average	EA	$114.18	$465.00	$579.18	**$748.68**	1.500
Picture window, insulated glass, clad wood, 5-0 x 4-2, average	EA	$152.24	$477.00	$629.24	**$826.64**	2.000
Picture window, insulated glass, clad wood, 5-0 x 4-6, average	EA	$152.24	$525.00	$677.24	**$884.24**	2.000
Picture window, insulated glass, clad wood, 5-0 x 5-0, average	EA	$152.24	$569.00	$721.24	**$937.04**	2.000
Picture window, insulated glass, clad wood, 5-0 x 5-6, average	EA	$152.24	$614.00	$766.24	**$991.04**	2.000
Picture window, insulated glass, clad wood, 5-6 x 3-0, average	EA	$114.18	$414.00	$528.18	**$687.48**	1.500
Picture window, insulated glass, clad wood, 5-6 x 3-6, average	EA	$114.18	$473.00	$587.18	**$758.28**	1.500
Picture window, insulated glass, clad wood, 5-6 x 4-0, average	EA	$114.18	$533.00	$647.18	**$830.28**	1.500
Picture window, insulated glass, clad wood, 5-6 x 4-2, average	EA	$152.24	$542.00	$694.24	**$904.64**	2.000
Picture window, insulated glass, clad wood, 5-6 x 4-6, average	EA	$152.24	$571.00	$723.24	**$939.44**	2.000
Picture window, insulated glass, clad wood, 5-6 x 5-0, average	EA	$152.24	$614.00	$766.24	**$991.04**	2.000
Picture window, insulated glass, clad wood, 5-6 x 5-6, average	EA	$152.24	$663.00	$815.24	**$1,049.84**	2.000

Wood Windows

Wood Picture Window, Insulated Glass, Aluminum/Vinyl Clad, ECONOMY GRADE

> No removal of old window included.

Description	Unit	Direct Labor	Direct Materials	Direct Total	Selling Price	Man-hours
WOOD PICTURE WINDOW, INSUL. GLASS, CLAD, ECONOMY						
Picture window, insulated glass, clad wood, 3-0 x 3-0, economy	EA	$114.18	$226.00	$340.18	**$461.88**	1.500
Picture window, insulated glass, clad wood, 3-0 x 3-6, economy	EA	$114.18	$257.00	$371.18	**$499.08**	1.500
Picture window, insulated glass, clad wood, 3-0 x 4-0, economy	EA	$114.18	$280.00	$394.18	**$526.68**	1.500
Picture window, insulated glass, clad wood, 3-0 x 4-2, economy	EA	$152.24	$354.00	$506.24	**$679.04**	2.000
Picture window, insulated glass, clad wood, 3-0 x 4-6, economy	EA	$152.24	$318.00	$470.24	**$635.84**	2.000
Picture window, insulated glass, clad wood, 3-0 x 5-0, economy	EA	$152.24	$348.00	$500.24	**$671.84**	2.000
Picture window, insulated glass, clad wood, 3-0 x 5-6, economy	EA	$152.24	$376.00	$528.24	**$705.44**	2.000
Picture window, insulated glass, clad wood, 3-6 x 3-0, economy	EA	$114.18	$257.00	$371.18	**$499.08**	1.500
Picture window, insulated glass, clad wood, 3-6 x 3-6, economy	EA	$114.18	$302.00	$416.18	**$553.08**	1.500
Picture window, insulated glass, clad wood, 3-6 x 4-0, economy	EA	$114.18	$317.00	$431.18	**$571.08**	1.500
Picture window, insulated glass, clad wood, 3-6 x 4-2, economy	EA	$152.24	$327.00	$479.24	**$646.64**	2.000
Picture window, insulated glass, clad wood, 3-6 x 4-6, economy	EA	$152.24	$361.00	$513.24	**$687.44**	2.000
Picture window, insulated glass, clad wood, 3-6 x 5-0, economy	EA	$152.24	$384.00	$536.24	**$715.04**	2.000
Picture window, insulated glass, clad wood, 3-6 x 5-6, economy	EA	$152.24	$431.00	$583.24	**$771.44**	2.000
Picture window, insulated glass, clad wood, 4-0 x 3-0, economy	EA	$114.18	$280.00	$394.18	**$526.68**	1.500
Picture window, insulated glass, clad wood, 4-0 x 3-6, economy	EA	$114.18	$317.00	$431.18	**$571.08**	1.500
Picture window, insulated glass, clad wood, 4-0 x 4-0, economy	EA	$114.18	$372.00	$486.18	**$637.08**	1.500
Picture window, insulated glass, clad wood, 4-0 x 4-2, economy	EA	$152.24	$405.00	$557.24	**$740.24**	2.000
Picture window, insulated glass, clad wood, 4-0 x 4-6, economy	EA	$152.24	$405.00	$557.24	**$740.24**	2.000
Picture window, insulated glass, clad wood, 4-0 x 5-0, economy	EA	$152.24	$421.00	$573.24	**$759.44**	2.000
Picture window, insulated glass, clad wood, 4-0 x 5-6, economy	EA	$152.24	$485.00	$637.24	**$836.24**	2.000
Picture window, insulated glass, clad wood, 4-6 x 3-0, economy	EA	$114.18	$315.00	$429.18	**$568.68**	1.500
Picture window, insulated glass, clad wood, 4-6 x 3-6, economy	EA	$114.18	$361.00	$475.18	**$623.88**	1.500
Picture window, insulated glass, clad wood, 4-6 x 4-0, economy	EA	$114.18	$405.00	$519.18	**$676.68**	1.500
Picture window, insulated glass, clad wood, 4-6 x 4-2, economy	EA	$152.24	$414.00	$566.24	**$751.04**	2.000
Picture window, insulated glass, clad wood, 4-6 x 4-6, economy	EA	$152.24	$434.00	$586.24	**$775.04**	2.000
Picture window, insulated glass, clad wood, 4-6 x 5-0, economy	EA	$152.24	$478.00	$630.24	**$827.84**	2.000
Picture window, insulated glass, clad wood, 4-6 x 5-6, economy	EA	$152.24	$519.00	$671.24	**$877.04**	2.000

Wood Windows

Wood Picture Window, Insulated Glass, Aluminum/Vinyl Clad, ECONOMY GRADE

> No removal of old window included.

Description	Unit	Direct Labor	Direct Materials	Direct Total	Selling Price	Man-hours
PICTURE WINDOW, INSUL. GLASS, CLAD, ECONOMY (cont.)						
Picture window, insulated glass, clad wood, 5-0 x 3-0, economy	EA	$114.18	$348.00	$462.18	**$608.28**	1.500
Picture window, insulated glass, clad wood, 5-0 x 3-6, economy	EA	$114.18	$387.00	$501.18	**$655.08**	1.500
Picture window, insulated glass, clad wood, 5-0 x 4-0, economy	EA	$114.18	$422.00	$536.18	**$697.08**	1.500
Picture window, insulated glass, clad wood, 5-0 x 4-2, economy	EA	$152.24	$433.00	$585.24	**$773.84**	2.000
Picture window, insulated glass, clad wood, 5-0 x 4-6, economy	EA	$152.24	$478.00	$630.24	**$827.84**	2.000
Picture window, insulated glass, clad wood, 5-0 x 5-0, economy	EA	$152.24	$518.00	$670.24	**$875.84**	2.000
Picture window, insulated glass, clad wood, 5-0 x 5-6, economy	EA	$152.24	$558.00	$710.24	**$923.84**	2.000
Picture window, insulated glass, clad wood, 5-6 x 3-0, economy	EA	$114.18	$376.00	$490.18	**$641.88**	1.500
Picture window, insulated glass, clad wood, 5-6 x 3-6, economy	EA	$114.18	$430.00	$544.18	**$706.68**	1.500
Picture window, insulated glass, clad wood, 5-6 x 4-0, economy	EA	$114.18	$485.00	$599.18	**$772.68**	1.500
Picture window, insulated glass, clad wood, 5-6 x 4-2, economy	EA	$152.24	$382.00	$534.24	**$712.64**	2.000
Picture window, insulated glass, clad wood, 5-6 x 4-6, economy	EA	$152.24	$519.00	$671.24	**$877.04**	2.000
Picture window, insulated glass, clad wood, 5-6 x 5-0, economy	EA	$152.24	$558.00	$710.24	**$923.84**	2.000
Picture window, insulated glass, clad wood, 5-6 x 5-6, economy	EA	$152.24	$602.00	$754.24	**$976.64**	2.000

Rectangular Fixed, Insulated Glass, Aluminum/Vinyl Clad, Wood Window

> No removal of old window included.

Description	Unit	Direct Labor	Direct Materials	Direct Total	Selling Price	Man-hours
Rectangular fixed window, insulated glass, clad wood, 2-0 x 1-0	EA	$133.21	$191.00	$324.21	**$451.66**	1.750
Rectangular fixed window, insulated glass, clad wood, 2-6 x 1-0	EA	$133.21	$201.00	$334.21	**$463.66**	1.750
Rectangular fixed window, insulated glass, clad wood, 3-0 x 1-0	EA	$133.21	$229.00	$362.21	**$497.26**	1.750
Rectangular fixed window, insulated glass, clad wood, 3-6 x 1-0	EA	$133.21	$251.00	$384.21	**$523.66**	1.750
Rectangular fixed window, insulated glass, clad wood, 4-0 x 1-0	EA	$133.21	$282.00	$415.21	**$560.86**	1.750
Rectangular fixed window, insulated glass, clad wood, 5-0 x 1-0	EA	$133.21	$328.00	$461.21	**$616.06**	1.750
Rectangular fixed window, insulated glass, clad wood, 6-0 x 1-0	EA	$133.21	$397.00	$530.21	**$698.86**	1.750
Rectangular fixed window, insulated glass, clad wood, 2-0 x 2-0	EA	$133.21	$226.00	$359.21	**$493.66**	1.750
Rectangular fixed window, insulated glass, clad wood, 2-6 x 2-0	EA	$133.21	$235.00	$368.21	**$504.46**	1.750
Rectangular fixed window, insulated glass, clad wood, 3-0 x 2-0	EA	$133.21	$269.00	$402.21	**$545.26**	1.750
Rectangular fixed window, insulated glass, clad wood, 3-6 x 2-0	EA	$133.21	$283.00	$416.21	**$562.06**	1.750
Rectangular fixed window, insulated glass, clad wood, 4-0 x 2-0	EA	$133.21	$319.00	$452.21	**$605.26**	1.750
Rectangular fixed window, insulated glass, clad wood, 5-0 x 2-0	EA	$133.21	$353.00	$486.21	**$646.06**	1.750
Rectangular fixed window, insulated glass, clad wood, 6-0 x 2-0	EA	$133.21	$385.00	$518.21	**$684.46**	1.750

Wood Windows

Round and Half Round, Insulated Glass, Aluminum/Vinyl Clad, Wood Window

> No removal of old window included.

Description	Unit	Direct Labor	Direct Materials	Direct Total	Selling Price	Man-hours
Round window, insulated glass, clad wood, 2-0 x 2-0	EA	$133.21	$362.00	$495.21	**$656.86**	1.750
Round window, insulated glass, clad wood, 2-6 x 2-6	EA	$133.21	$408.00	$541.21	**$712.06**	1.750
Round window, insulated glass, clad wood, 3-0 x 3-0	EA	$133.21	$520.00	$653.21	**$846.46**	1.750
Half round window, insulated glass, clad wood, 2-0 x 1-0	EA	$133.21	$325.00	$458.21	**$612.46**	1.750
Half round window, insulated glass, clad wood, 2-6 x 1-3	EA	$133.21	$359.00	$492.21	**$653.26**	1.750
Half round window, insulated glass, clad wood, 3-0 x 1-6	EA	$133.21	$416.00	$549.21	**$721.66**	1.750
Half round window, insulated glass, clad wood, 3-6 x 1-9	EA	$133.21	$491.00	$624.21	**$811.66**	1.750
Half round window, insulated glass, clad wood, 4-0 x 2-0	EA	$133.21	$549.00	$682.21	**$881.26**	1.750

Wood Window Glazing

Description	Unit	Direct Labor	Direct Materials	Direct Total	Selling Price	Man-hours
Remove old glass from wood sash, reglaze with 3/16" float, 8" x 12"	EA	$30.45	$4.54	$34.98	**$58.42**	0.400
Remove old glass from wood sash, reglaze with 3/16" float, 12" x 16"	EA	$33.57	$7.44	$41.01	**$68.49**	0.441
Remove old glass from wood sash, reglaze with 3/16" float, 14" x 20"	EA	$39.28	$9.89	$49.16	**$82.10**	0.516
Remove old glass from wood sash, reglaze with 3/16" float, 16" x 24"	EA	$42.25	$12.62	$54.87	**$91.63**	0.555
Remove old glass from wood sash, reglaze with 3/16" float, 24" x 26"	EA	$51.00	$18.45	$69.45	**$115.98**	0.670
Remove old glass from wood sash, reglaze with 3/16" float, 36" x 24"	EA	$54.35	$24.32	$78.67	**$131.38**	0.714
Remove glass from wood sash, reglaze with 1/8" tempered, 8" x 12"	EA	$30.45	$6.81	$37.25	**$62.21**	0.400
Remove glass from wood sash, reglaze with 1/8" tempered, 12" x 16"	EA	$33.57	$11.16	$44.73	**$74.70**	0.441
Remove glass from wood sash, reglaze with 1/8" tempered, 14" x 20"	EA	$39.28	$14.83	$54.11	**$90.36**	0.516
Remove glass from wood sash, reglaze with 1/8" tempered, 16" x 24"	EA	$42.25	$18.93	$61.18	**$102.16**	0.555
Remove glass from wood sash, reglaze with 1/8" tempered, 24" x 26"	EA	$51.00	$27.68	$78.68	**$131.39**	0.670
Remove glass from wood sash, reglaze with 1/8" tempered, 36" x 24"	EA	$54.35	$36.48	$90.83	**$151.69**	0.714
Remove old glass from wood sash, reglaze with 1/4" float, 8" x 12"	EA	$30.45	$5.90	$36.35	**$60.70**	0.400
Remove old glass from wood sash, reglaze with 1/4" float, 12" x 16"	EA	$33.57	$9.67	$43.24	**$72.21**	0.441
Remove old glass from wood sash, reglaze with 1/4" float, 14" x 20"	EA	$39.28	$12.85	$52.13	**$87.05**	0.516
Remove old glass from wood sash, reglaze with 1/4" float, 16" x 24"	EA	$42.25	$16.41	$58.65	**$97.95**	0.555
Remove old glass from wood sash, reglaze with 1/4" float, 24" x 26"	EA	$51.00	$23.99	$74.99	**$125.23**	0.670
Remove old glass from wood sash, reglaze with 1/4" float, 36" x 24"	EA	$54.35	$31.62	$85.97	**$143.56**	0.714
Remove glass from wood sash, reglaze with 3/8" wire glass, 8" x 12"	EA	$36.61	$11.43	$48.05	**$80.24**	0.481
Remove glass from wood sash, reglaze with 3/8" wire glass, 12" x 16"	EA	$40.27	$18.75	$59.02	**$98.56**	0.529
Remove glass from wood sash, reglaze with 3/8" wire glass, 14" x 20"	EA	$47.12	$24.91	$72.03	**$120.29**	0.619
Remove glass from wood sash, reglaze with 3/8" wire glass, 16" x 24"	EA	$50.69	$31.80	$82.50	**$137.77**	0.666
Remove glass from wood sash, reglaze with 3/8" wire glass, 24" x 26"	EA	$61.20	$46.50	$107.70	**$179.86**	0.804
Remove glass from wood sash, reglaze with 3/8" wire glass, 36" x 24"	EA	$65.23	$61.29	$126.52	**$211.29**	0.857

Vinyl Windows

Labor Costs to Install Vinyl Windows

> Labor costs do not include materials such as sash, frame, casings or other trim.

Description	Unit	Direct Labor	Direct Materials	Direct Total	Selling Price	Man-hours
LABOR TO INSTALL SINGLE/DOUBLE HUNG WINDOWS						
Install vinyl double hung window, up to 15 SF, medium	Set	$76.12		$76.12	**$127.12**	1.000
Install vinyl double hung window, over 15 SF, large	Set	$121.79		$121.79	**$203.39**	1.600
LABOR TO INSTALL AWNING WINDOWS						
Install vinyl awning window, 1 lite wide	EA	$60.89		$60.89	**$101.69**	0.800
Install vinyl awning window, 2 lites wide	EA	$106.57		$106.57	**$177.97**	1.400
Install vinyl awning window, 3 lites wide	EA	$152.24		$152.24	**$254.24**	2.000
LABOR TO INSTALL CASEMENT WINDOWS						
Install vinyl casement window, 1 venting, up to 48 high	Set	$60.89		$60.89	**$101.69**	0.800
Install vinyl casement window, 1 venting, over 48 high	Set	$91.34		$91.34	**$152.54**	1.200
Install vinyl casement window, 2 venting, up to 48 high	Set	$91.34		$91.34	**$152.54**	1.200
Install vinyl casement window, 2 venting, over 48 high	Set	$121.79		$121.79	**$203.39**	1.600
LABOR TO INSTALL SLIDING WINDOWS						
Install vinyl sliding window, up to 48 wide	EA	$106.57		$106.57	**$177.97**	1.400
Install vinyl sliding window, over 48 wide	EA	$182.68		$182.68	**$305.08**	2.400
LABOR TO INSTALL SPECIALTY AND PICTURE WINDOWS						
Install vinyl picture window, up to 48 high	Set	$95.15		$95.15	**$158.90**	1.250
Install vinyl picture window, over 48 high	Set	$133.21		$133.21	**$222.46**	1.750
Install vinyl picture window with flankers, up to 48 high	Set	$152.24		$152.24	**$254.24**	2.000
Install vinyl picture window with flankers, over 48 high	Set	$182.68		$182.68	**$305.08**	2.400
Install vinyl rectangular transom window	EA	$106.57		$106.57	**$177.97**	1.400
Install vinyl round, half round, window	EA	$106.57		$106.57	**$177.97**	1.400

Labor Costs to Remove Vinyl Windows

Description	Unit	Direct Labor	Direct Materials	Direct Total	Selling Price	Man-hours
LABOR TO REMOVE VINYL WINDOWS						
Remove small vinyl window in frame wall, to 12 SF	EA	$38.06		$38.06	**$63.56**	0.500
Remove average vinyl window in frame wall, 12-25 SF	EA	$57.09		$57.09	**$95.34**	0.750
Remove large vinyl window in frame wall, over 25 SF	EA	$76.12		$76.12	**$127.12**	1.000
Remove small vinyl window in masonry wall, to 12 SF	EA	$57.09		$57.09	**$95.34**	0.750
Remove average vinyl window in masonry wall, 12-25 SF	EA	$76.12		$76.12	**$127.12**	1.000
Remove large vinyl window in masonry wall, over 25 SF	EA	$95.15		$95.15	**$158.90**	1.250
Remove exterior awning or canopy	LF	$6.17		$6.17	**$10.30**	0.081

Vinyl Windows

Create Window Opening in Existing Wall

Description	Unit	Direct Labor	Direct Materials	Direct Total	Selling Price	Man-hours
Create small window opening up to 12 SF in frame wall	EA	$456.71	$22.09	$478.80	**$799.59**	6.000
Create medium window opening 12-25 SF in frame wall	EA	$608.95	$37.20	$646.15	**$1,079.07**	8.000
Create large window opening over 25 SF in frame wall	EA	$837.30	$44.18	$881.48	**$1,472.07**	11.000
Create small window opening up to 12 SF in brick veneer wall	EA	$551.86	$22.09	$573.95	**$958.49**	7.250
Create medium window opening 12-25 SF in brick veneer wall	EA	$723.13	$37.20	$760.33	**$1,269.74**	9.500
Create large window opening over 25 SF in brick veneer wall	EA	$989.54	$44.18	$1,033.72	**$1,726.30**	13.000
Create small window opening up to 12 SF in brick and block wall	EA	$608.95	$22.09	$631.04	**$1,053.83**	8.000
Create medium window opening 12-25 SF in brick and block wall	EA	$780.21	$37.20	$817.41	**$1,365.08**	10.250
Create large window opening over 25 SF in brick and block wall	EA	$1,065.66	$44.18	$1,109.83	**$1,853.42**	14.000
Create small window opening up to 12 SF in stucco wall	EA	$532.83	$22.09	$554.92	**$926.71**	7.000
Create medium window opening 12-25 SF in stucco wall	EA	$704.10	$37.20	$741.30	**$1,237.96**	9.250
Create large window opening over 25 SF in stucco wall	EA	$951.48	$44.18	$995.66	**$1,662.75**	12.500

Vinyl Windows

Single Hung, Insulated Glass Vinyl Window

> No removal of old window included.

Description	Unit	Direct Labor	Direct Materials	Direct Total	Selling Price	Man-hours
Single hung, insulated glass, vinyl window, 2-0 x 3-0	EA	$76.12	$185.00	$261.12	**$349.12**	1.000
Single hung, insulated glass, vinyl window, 2-0 x 3-6	EA	$76.12	$196.00	$272.12	**$362.32**	1.000
Single hung, insulated glass, vinyl window, 2-0 x 4-0	EA	$76.12	$209.00	$285.12	**$377.92**	1.000
Single hung, insulated glass, vinyl window, 2-0 x 4-6	EA	$76.12	$221.00	$297.12	**$392.32**	1.000
Single hung, insulated glass, vinyl window, 2-0 x 5-0	EA	$76.12	$233.00	$309.12	**$406.72**	1.000
Single hung, insulated glass, vinyl window, 2-0 x 5-6	EA	$76.12	$246.00	$322.12	**$422.32**	1.000
Single hung, insulated glass, vinyl window, 2-6 x 3-0	EA	$76.12	$199.00	$275.12	**$365.92**	1.000
Single hung, insulated glass, vinyl window, 2-6 x 3-6	EA	$76.12	$211.00	$287.12	**$380.32**	1.000
Single hung, insulated glass, vinyl window, 2-6 x 4-0	EA	$76.12	$223.00	$299.12	**$394.72**	1.000
Single hung, insulated glass, vinyl window, 2-6 x 4-6	EA	$76.12	$236.00	$312.12	**$410.32**	1.000
Single hung, insulated glass, vinyl window, 2-6 x 5-0	EA	$76.12	$247.00	$323.12	**$423.52**	1.000
Single hung, insulated glass, vinyl window, 2-6 x 5-6	EA	$76.12	$260.00	$336.12	**$439.12**	1.000
Single hung, insulated glass, vinyl window, 3-0 x 3-0	EA	$76.12	$213.00	$289.12	**$382.72**	1.000
Single hung, insulated glass, vinyl window, 3-0 x 3-6	EA	$76.12	$225.00	$301.12	**$397.12**	1.000
Single hung, insulated glass, vinyl window, 3-0 x 4-0	EA	$76.12	$237.00	$313.12	**$411.52**	1.000
Single hung, insulated glass, vinyl window, 3-0 x 4-6	EA	$76.12	$249.00	$325.12	**$425.92**	1.000
Single hung, insulated glass, vinyl window, 3-0 x 5-0	EA	$76.12	$261.00	$337.12	**$440.32**	1.000
Single hung, insulated glass, vinyl window, 3-0 x 5-6	EA	$121.79	$273.00	$394.79	**$530.99**	1.600
Single hung, insulated glass, vinyl window, 3-6 x 3-0	EA	$76.12	$229.00	$305.12	**$401.92**	1.000
Single hung, insulated glass, vinyl window, 3-6 x 3-6	EA	$76.12	$240.00	$316.12	**$415.12**	1.000
Single hung, insulated glass, vinyl window, 3-6 x 4-0	EA	$76.12	$250.00	$326.12	**$427.12**	1.000
Single hung, insulated glass, vinyl window, 3-6 x 4-6	EA	$121.79	$263.00	$384.79	**$518.99**	1.600
Single hung, insulated glass, vinyl window, 3-6 x 5-0	EA	$121.79	$275.00	$396.79	**$533.39**	1.600
Single hung, insulated glass, vinyl window, 3-6 x 5-6	EA	$121.79	$287.00	$408.79	**$547.79**	1.600

Vinyl Windows

Double Hung, Insulated Glass Vinyl Window

> No removal of old window included.

Description	Unit	Direct Labor	Direct Materials	Direct Total	Selling Price	Man-hours
Double hung, insulated glass, vinyl window, 2-0 x 3-0	EA	$76.12	$229.00	$305.12	**$401.92**	1.000
Double hung, insulated glass, vinyl window, 2-0 x 3-6	EA	$76.12	$244.00	$320.12	**$419.92**	1.000
Double hung, insulated glass, vinyl window, 2-0 x 4-0	EA	$76.12	$257.00	$333.12	**$435.52**	1.000
Double hung, insulated glass, vinyl window, 2-0 x 4-6	EA	$76.12	$272.00	$348.12	**$453.52**	1.000
Double hung, insulated glass, vinyl window, 2-0 x 5-0	EA	$76.12	$286.00	$362.12	**$470.32**	1.000
Double hung, insulated glass, vinyl window, 2-0 x 5-6	EA	$76.12	$299.00	$375.12	**$485.92**	1.000
Double hung, insulated glass, vinyl window, 2-6 x 3-0	EA	$76.12	$248.00	$324.12	**$424.72**	1.000
Double hung, insulated glass, vinyl window, 2-6 x 3-6	EA	$76.12	$261.00	$337.12	**$440.32**	1.000
Double hung, insulated glass, vinyl window, 2-6 x 4-0	EA	$76.12	$275.00	$351.12	**$457.12**	1.000
Double hung, insulated glass, vinyl window, 2-6 x 4-6	EA	$76.12	$290.00	$366.12	**$475.12**	1.000
Double hung, insulated glass, vinyl window, 2-6 x 5-0	EA	$76.12	$303.00	$379.12	**$490.72**	1.000
Double hung, insulated glass, vinyl window, 2-6 x 5-6	EA	$76.12	$316.00	$392.12	**$506.32**	1.000
Double hung, insulated glass, vinyl window, 3-0 x 3-0	EA	$76.12	$267.00	$343.12	**$447.52**	1.000
Double hung, insulated glass, vinyl window, 3-0 x 3-6	EA	$76.12	$279.00	$355.12	**$461.92**	1.000
Double hung, insulated glass, vinyl window, 3-0 x 4-0	EA	$76.12	$292.00	$368.12	**$477.52**	1.000
Double hung, insulated glass, vinyl window, 3-0 x 4-6	EA	$76.12	$307.00	$383.12	**$495.52**	1.000
Double hung, insulated glass, vinyl window, 3-0 x 5-0	EA	$76.12	$322.00	$398.12	**$513.52**	1.000
Double hung, insulated glass, vinyl window, 3-0 x 5-6	EA	$121.79	$335.00	$456.79	**$605.39**	1.600
Double hung, insulated glass, vinyl window, 3-6 x 3-0	EA	$76.12	$283.00	$359.12	**$466.72**	1.000
Double hung, insulated glass, vinyl window, 3-6 x 3-6	EA	$76.12	$295.00	$371.12	**$481.12**	1.000
Double hung, insulated glass, vinyl window, 3-6 x 4-0	EA	$76.12	$310.00	$386.12	**$499.12**	1.000
Double hung, insulated glass, vinyl window, 3-6 x 4-6	EA	$121.79	$324.00	$445.79	**$592.19**	1.600
Double hung, insulated glass, vinyl window, 3-6 x 5-0	EA	$121.79	$339.00	$460.79	**$610.19**	1.600
Double hung, insulated glass, vinyl window, 3-6 x 5-6	EA	$121.79	$354.00	$475.79	**$628.19**	1.600

Vinyl Windows

Awning, Insulated Glass Vinyl Window

> No removal of old window included.

Description	Unit	Direct Labor	Direct Materials	Direct Total	Selling Price	Man-hours
AWNING, INSULATED GLASS, VINYL WINDOW, 1 WIDE						
Awning, insulated glass, vinyl window, 1 wide, 2-0 x 1-6	EA	$60.89	$150.00	$210.89	**$281.69**	0.800
Awning, insulated glass, vinyl window, 1 wide, 2-0 x 2-0	EA	$60.89	$166.00	$226.89	**$300.89**	0.800
Awning, insulated glass, vinyl window, 1 wide, 2-0 x 2-6	EA	$60.89	$173.00	$233.89	**$309.29**	0.800
Awning, insulated glass, vinyl window, 1 wide, 3-0 x 1-6	EA	$60.89	$170.00	$230.89	**$305.69**	0.800
Awning, insulated glass, vinyl window, 1 wide, 3-0 x 2-0	EA	$60.89	$192.00	$252.89	**$332.09**	0.800
Awning, insulated glass, vinyl window, 1 wide, 3-0 x 2-6	EA	$60.89	$202.00	$262.89	**$344.09**	0.800
Awning, insulated glass, vinyl window, 1 wide, 3-6 x 1-6	EA	$60.89	$187.00	$247.89	**$326.09**	0.800
Awning, insulated glass, vinyl window, 1 wide, 3-6 x 2-0	EA	$60.89	$208.00	$268.89	**$351.29**	0.800
Awning, insulated glass, vinyl window, 1 wide, 3-6 x 2-6	EA	$60.89	$218.00	$278.89	**$363.29**	0.800
Awning, insulated glass, vinyl window, 1 wide, 4-0 x 1-6	EA	$60.89	$202.00	$262.89	**$344.09**	0.800
Awning, insulated glass, vinyl window, 1 wide, 4-0 x 2-0	EA	$60.89	$224.00	$284.89	**$370.49**	0.800
Awning, insulated glass, vinyl window, 1 wide, 4-0 x 2-6	EA	$60.89	$241.00	$301.89	**$390.89**	0.800
AWNING, INSULATED GLASS, VINYL WINDOW, 2 WIDE						
Awning, insulated glass, vinyl window, 2 wide, 6-0 x 2-0	EA	$106.57	$404.00	$510.57	**$662.77**	1.400
Awning, insulated glass, vinyl window, 2 wide, 6-0 x 2-4	EA	$106.57	$421.00	$527.57	**$683.17**	1.400
Awning, insulated glass, vinyl window, 2 wide, 6-0 x 2-8	EA	$106.57	$440.00	$546.57	**$705.97**	1.400
Awning, insulated glass, vinyl window, 2 wide, 6-8 x 2-0	EA	$106.57	$445.00	$551.57	**$711.97**	1.400
Awning, insulated glass, vinyl window, 2 wide, 6-8 x 2-4	EA	$106.57	$467.00	$573.57	**$738.37**	1.400
Awning, insulated glass, vinyl window, 2 wide, 6-8 x 2-8	EA	$106.57	$488.00	$594.57	**$763.57**	1.400
AWNING, INSULATED GLASS, VINYL WINDOW, 3 WIDE						
Awning, insulated glass, vinyl window, 3 wide, 9-0 x 2-0	EA	$152.24	$629.00	$781.24	**$1,009.04**	2.000
Awning, insulated glass, vinyl window, 3 wide, 9-0 x 2-4	EA	$152.24	$664.00	$816.24	**$1,051.04**	2.000
Awning, insulated glass, vinyl window, 3 wide, 9-0 x 2-8	EA	$152.24	$699.00	$851.24	**$1,093.04**	2.000
Awning, insulated glass, vinyl window, 3 wide, 10-0 x 2-0	EA	$152.24	$673.00	$825.24	**$1,061.84**	2.000
Awning, insulated glass, vinyl window, 3 wide, 10-0 x 2-4	EA	$152.24	$712.00	$864.24	**$1,108.64**	2.000
Awning, insulated glass, vinyl window, 3 wide, 10-0 x 2-8	EA	$152.24	$751.00	$903.24	**$1,155.44**	2.000

Vinyl Windows

Casement, Insulated Glass Vinyl Window

> No removal of old window included.

Description	Unit	Direct Labor	Direct Materials	Direct Total	Selling Price	Man-hours
CASEMENT, INSULATED GLASS, VINYL WINDOW						
Casement, insulated glass, vinyl window, 1 venting, 1-8 x 2-0	EA	$60.89	$141.00	$201.89	**$270.89**	0.800
Casement, insulated glass, vinyl window, 1 venting, 1-8 x 2-6	EA	$60.89	$168.00	$228.89	**$303.29**	0.800
Casement, insulated glass, vinyl window, 1 venting, 1-8 x 3-0	EA	$60.89	$194.00	$254.89	**$334.49**	0.800
Casement, insulated glass, vinyl window, 1 venting, 1-8 x 3-6	EA	$60.89	$222.00	$282.89	**$368.09**	0.800
Casement, insulated glass, vinyl window, 1 venting, 1-8 x 4-0	EA	$60.89	$248.00	$308.89	**$399.29**	0.800
Casement, insulated glass, vinyl window, 1 venting, 1-8 x 4-6	EA	$91.34	$275.00	$366.34	**$482.54**	1.200
Casement, insulated glass, vinyl window, 1 venting, 1-8 x 5-0	EA	$91.34	$302.00	$393.34	**$514.94**	1.200
Casement, insulated glass, vinyl window, 1 venting, 1-8 x 5-6	EA	$91.34	$329.00	$420.34	**$547.34**	1.200
Casement, insulated glass, vinyl window, 1 venting, 2-0 x 2-0	EA	$60.89	$160.00	$220.89	**$293.69**	0.800
Casement, insulated glass, vinyl window, 1 venting, 2-0 x 2-6	EA	$60.89	$184.00	$244.89	**$322.49**	0.800
Casement, insulated glass, vinyl window, 1 venting, 2-0 x 3-0	EA	$60.89	$208.00	$268.89	**$351.29**	0.800
Casement, insulated glass, vinyl window, 1 venting, 2-0 x 3-6	EA	$60.89	$232.00	$292.89	**$380.09**	0.800
Casement, insulated glass, vinyl window, 1 venting, 2-0 x 4-0	EA	$60.89	$256.00	$316.89	**$408.89**	0.800
Casement, insulated glass, vinyl window, 1 venting, 2-0 x 4-6	EA	$91.34	$280.00	$371.34	**$488.54**	1.200
Casement, insulated glass, vinyl window, 1 venting, 2-0 x 5-0	EA	$91.34	$305.00	$396.34	**$518.54**	1.200
Casement, insulated glass, vinyl window, 1 venting, 2-0 x 5-6	EA	$91.34	$330.00	$421.34	**$548.54**	1.200
Casement, insulated glass, vinyl window, 1 venting, 2-6 x 2-0	EA	$60.89	$193.00	$253.89	**$333.29**	0.800
Casement, insulated glass, vinyl window, 1 venting, 2-6 x 2-6	EA	$60.89	$217.00	$277.89	**$362.09**	0.800
Casement, insulated glass, vinyl window, 1 venting, 2-6 x 3-0	EA	$60.89	$241.00	$301.89	**$390.89**	0.800
Casement, insulated glass, vinyl window, 1 venting, 2-6 x 3-6	EA	$60.89	$265.00	$325.89	**$419.69**	0.800
Casement, insulated glass, vinyl window, 1 venting, 2-6 x 4-0	EA	$60.89	$290.00	$350.89	**$449.69**	0.800
Casement, insulated glass, vinyl window, 1 venting, 2-6 x 4-6	EA	$91.34	$314.00	$405.34	**$529.34**	1.200
Casement, insulated glass, vinyl window, 1 venting, 2-6 x 5-0	EA	$91.34	$338.00	$429.34	**$558.14**	1.200
Casement, insulated glass, vinyl window, 1 venting, 2-6 x 5-6	EA	$91.34	$362.00	$453.34	**$586.94**	1.200

Vinyl Windows

Slider, Insulated Glass Vinyl Window

> No removal of old window included.

Description	Unit	Direct Labor	Direct Materials	Direct Total	Selling Price	Man-hours
SLIDING, INSULATED GLASS, VINYL WINDOW						
Slider, insulated glass, vinyl window, 3-0 x 2-0	EA	$106.57	$211.00	$317.57	**$431.17**	1.400
Slider, insulated glass, vinyl window, 3-0 x 2-6	EA	$106.57	$228.00	$334.57	**$451.57**	1.400
Slider, insulated glass, vinyl window, 3-0 x 3-0	EA	$106.57	$259.00	$365.57	**$488.77**	1.400
Slider, insulated glass, vinyl window, 3-0 x 3-6	EA	$106.57	$258.00	$364.57	**$487.57**	1.400
Slider, insulated glass, vinyl window, 3-0 x 4-0	EA	$106.57	$279.00	$385.57	**$512.77**	1.400
Slider, insulated glass, vinyl window, 3-0 x 4-6	EA	$106.57	$301.00	$407.57	**$539.17**	1.400
Slider, insulated glass, vinyl window, 3-0 x 5-0	EA	$106.57	$328.00	$434.57	**$571.57**	1.400
Slider, insulated glass, vinyl window, 4-0 x 2-0	EA	$106.57	$232.00	$338.57	**$456.37**	1.400
Slider, insulated glass, vinyl window, 4-0 x 2-6	EA	$106.57	$266.00	$372.57	**$497.17**	1.400
Slider, insulated glass, vinyl window, 4-0 x 3-0	EA	$106.57	$290.00	$396.57	**$525.97**	1.400
Slider, insulated glass, vinyl window, 4-0 x 3-6	EA	$106.57	$309.00	$415.57	**$548.77**	1.400
Slider, insulated glass, vinyl window, 4-0 x 4-0	EA	$106.57	$330.00	$436.57	**$573.97**	1.400
Slider, insulated glass, vinyl window, 4-0 x 4-6	EA	$106.57	$351.00	$457.57	**$599.17**	1.400
Slider, insulated glass, vinyl window, 4-0 x 5-0	EA	$106.57	$391.00	$497.57	**$647.17**	1.400
Slider, insulated glass, vinyl window, 5-0 x 2-0	EA	$182.68	$290.00	$472.68	**$653.08**	2.400
Slider, insulated glass, vinyl window, 5-0 x 2-6	EA	$182.68	$321.00	$503.68	**$690.28**	2.400
Slider, insulated glass, vinyl window, 5-0 x 3-0	EA	$182.68	$334.00	$516.68	**$705.88**	2.400
Slider, insulated glass, vinyl window, 5-0 x 3-6	EA	$182.68	$382.00	$564.68	**$763.48**	2.400
Slider, insulated glass, vinyl window, 5-0 x 4-0	EA	$182.68	$405.00	$587.68	**$791.08**	2.400
Slider, insulated glass, vinyl window, 5-0 x 4-6	EA	$182.68	$430.00	$612.68	**$821.08**	2.400
Slider, insulated glass, vinyl window, 5-0 x 5-0	EA	$182.68	$472.00	$654.68	**$871.48**	2.400
Slider, insulated glass, vinyl window, 6-0 x 2-0	EA	$182.68	$325.00	$507.68	**$695.08**	2.400
Slider, insulated glass, vinyl window, 6-0 x 2-6	EA	$182.68	$368.00	$550.68	**$746.68**	2.400
Slider, insulated glass, vinyl window, 6-0 x 3-0	EA	$182.68	$420.00	$602.68	**$809.08**	2.400
Slider, insulated glass, vinyl window, 6-0 x 3-6	EA	$182.68	$465.00	$647.68	**$863.08**	2.400
Slider, insulated glass, vinyl window, 6-0 x 4-0	EA	$182.68	$528.00	$710.68	**$938.68**	2.400
Slider, insulated glass, vinyl window, 6-0 x 4-6	EA	$182.68	$574.00	$756.68	**$993.88**	2.400
Slider, insulated glass, vinyl window, 6-0 x 5-0	EA	$182.68	$632.00	$814.68	**$1,063.48**	2.400

Vinyl Windows

Picture Window, Insulated Glass, Vinyl

> No removal of old window included.

Description	Unit	Direct Labor	Direct Materials	Direct Total	Selling Price	Man-hours
PICTURE WINDOW, INSULATED GLASS, VINYL						
Picture window, insulated glass, vinyl, 3-0 x 2-0	EA	$95.15	$164.00	$259.15	**$355.70**	1.250
Picture window, insulated glass, vinyl, 3-0 x 2-6	EA	$95.15	$179.00	$274.15	**$373.70**	1.250
Picture window, insulated glass, vinyl, 3-0 x 3-0	EA	$95.15	$193.00	$288.15	**$390.50**	1.250
Picture window, insulated glass, vinyl, 3-0 x 3-6	EA	$95.15	$210.00	$305.15	**$410.90**	1.250
Picture window, insulated glass, vinyl, 3-0 x 4-0	EA	$95.15	$227.00	$322.15	**$431.30**	1.250
Picture window, insulated glass, vinyl, 3-0 x 4-6	EA	$133.21	$242.00	$375.21	**$512.86**	1.750
Picture window, insulated glass, vinyl, 3-0 x 5-0	EA	$133.21	$257.00	$390.21	**$530.86**	1.750
Picture window, insulated glass, vinyl, 3-0 x 5-6	EA	$133.21	$273.00	$406.21	**$550.06**	1.750
Picture window, insulated glass, vinyl, 3-6 x 2-0	EA	$95.15	$179.00	$274.15	**$373.70**	1.250
Picture window, insulated glass, vinyl, 3-6 x 2-6	EA	$95.15	$196.00	$291.15	**$394.10**	1.250
Picture window, insulated glass, vinyl, 3-6 x 3-0	EA	$95.15	$215.00	$310.15	**$416.90**	1.250
Picture window, insulated glass, vinyl, 3-6 x 3-6	EA	$95.15	$233.00	$328.15	**$438.50**	1.250
Picture window, insulated glass, vinyl, 3-6 x 4-0	EA	$95.15	$251.00	$346.15	**$460.10**	1.250
Picture window, insulated glass, vinyl, 3-6 x 4-6	EA	$133.21	$270.00	$403.21	**$546.46**	1.750
Picture window, insulated glass, vinyl, 3-6 x 5-0	EA	$133.21	$287.00	$420.21	**$566.86**	1.750
Picture window, insulated glass, vinyl, 3-6 x 5-6	EA	$133.21	$303.00	$436.21	**$586.06**	1.750
Picture window, insulated glass, vinyl, 4-0 x 2-0	EA	$95.15	$202.00	$297.15	**$401.30**	1.250
Picture window, insulated glass, vinyl, 4-0 x 2-6	EA	$95.15	$221.00	$316.15	**$424.10**	1.250
Picture window, insulated glass, vinyl, 4-0 x 3-0	EA	$95.15	$239.00	$334.15	**$445.70**	1.250
Picture window, insulated glass, vinyl, 4-0 x 3-6	EA	$95.15	$259.00	$354.15	**$469.70**	1.250
Picture window, insulated glass, vinyl, 4-0 x 4-0	EA	$95.15	$279.00	$374.15	**$493.70**	1.250
Picture window, insulated glass, vinyl, 4-0 x 4-6	EA	$133.21	$299.00	$432.21	**$581.26**	1.750
Picture window, insulated glass, vinyl, 4-0 x 5-0	EA	$133.21	$317.00	$450.21	**$602.86**	1.750
Picture window, insulated glass, vinyl, 4-0 x 5-6	EA	$133.21	$340.00	$473.21	**$630.46**	1.750
Picture window, insulated glass, vinyl, 5-0 x 2-0	EA	$95.15	$248.00	$343.15	**$456.50**	1.250
Picture window, insulated glass, vinyl, 5-0 x 2-6	EA	$95.15	$274.00	$369.15	**$487.70**	1.250
Picture window, insulated glass, vinyl, 5-0 x 3-0	EA	$95.15	$299.00	$394.15	**$517.70**	1.250
Picture window, insulated glass, vinyl, 5-0 x 3-6	EA	$95.15	$323.00	$418.15	**$546.50**	1.250
Picture window, insulated glass, vinyl, 5-0 x 4-0	EA	$95.15	$349.00	$444.15	**$577.70**	1.250
Picture window, insulated glass, vinyl, 5-0 x 4-6	EA	$133.21	$374.00	$507.21	**$671.26**	1.750
Picture window, insulated glass, vinyl, 5-0 x 5-0	EA	$133.21	$398.00	$531.21	**$700.06**	1.750
Picture window, insulated glass, vinyl, 5-0 x 5-6	EA	$133.21	$426.00	$559.21	**$733.66**	1.750

Vinyl Windows

Picture Window, Insulated Glass, Vinyl

> No removal of old window included.

Description	Unit	Direct Labor	Direct Materials	Direct Total	Selling Price	Man-hours
PICTURE WINDOW, INSULATED GLASS, VINYL (continued)						
Picture window, insulated glass, vinyl, 6-0 x 2-0	EA	$133.21	$316.00	$449.21	**$601.66**	1.750
Picture window, insulated glass, vinyl, 6-0 x 2-6	EA	$133.21	$345.00	$478.21	**$636.46**	1.750
Picture window, insulated glass, vinyl, 6-0 x 3-0	EA	$133.21	$374.00	$507.21	**$671.26**	1.750
Picture window, insulated glass, vinyl, 6-0 x 3-6	EA	$133.21	$404.00	$537.21	**$707.26**	1.750
Picture window, insulated glass, vinyl, 6-0 x 4-0	EA	$133.21	$434.00	$567.21	**$743.26**	1.750
Picture window, insulated glass, vinyl, 6-0 x 4-6	EA	$133.21	$463.00	$596.21	**$778.06**	1.750
Picture window, insulated glass, vinyl, 6-0 x 5-0	EA	$133.21	$495.00	$628.21	**$816.46**	1.750
Picture window, insulated glass, vinyl, 6-0 x 5-6	EA	$133.21	$380.00	$513.21	**$678.46**	1.750

Rectangular Fixed, Insulated Glass, Vinyl Window

> No removal of old window included.

Description	Unit	Direct Labor	Direct Materials	Direct Total	Selling Price	Man-hours
Rectangular fixed window, insulated glass, vinyl, 2-0 x 1-0	EA	$106.57	$133.00	$239.57	**$337.57**	1.400
Rectangular fixed window, insulated glass, vinyl, 2-6 x 1-0	EA	$106.57	$151.00	$257.57	**$359.17**	1.400
Rectangular fixed window, insulated glass, vinyl, 3-0 x 1-0	EA	$106.57	$173.00	$279.57	**$385.57**	1.400
Rectangular fixed window, insulated glass, vinyl, 3-6 x 1-0	EA	$106.57	$190.00	$296.57	**$405.97**	1.400
Rectangular fixed window, insulated glass, vinyl, 4-0 x 1-0	EA	$106.57	$213.00	$319.57	**$433.57**	1.400
Rectangular fixed window, insulated glass, vinyl, 5-0 x 1-0	EA	$106.57	$249.00	$355.57	**$476.77**	1.400
Rectangular fixed window, insulated glass, vinyl, 6-0 x 1-0	EA	$106.57	$301.00	$407.57	**$539.17**	1.400
Rectangular fixed window, insulated glass, vinyl, 2-0 x 1-6	EA	$106.57	$155.00	$261.57	**$363.97**	1.400
Rectangular fixed window, insulated glass, vinyl, 2-6 x 1-6	EA	$106.57	$181.00	$287.57	**$395.17**	1.400
Rectangular fixed window, insulated glass, vinyl, 3-0 x 1-6	EA	$106.57	$207.00	$313.57	**$426.37**	1.400
Rectangular fixed window, insulated glass, vinyl, 3-6 x 1-6	EA	$106.57	$228.00	$334.57	**$451.57**	1.400
Rectangular fixed window, insulated glass, vinyl, 4-0 x 1-6	EA	$106.57	$255.00	$361.57	**$483.97**	1.400
Rectangular fixed window, insulated glass, vinyl, 5-0 x 1-6	EA	$106.57	$298.00	$404.57	**$535.57**	1.400
Rectangular fixed window, insulated glass, vinyl, 6-0 x 1-6	EA	$106.57	$361.00	$467.57	**$611.17**	1.400

Vinyl Windows

Round and Half Round, Insulated Glass, Vinyl Window

> No removal of old window included.

Description	Unit	Direct Labor	Direct Materials	Direct Total	Selling Price	Man-hours
Round window, insulated glass, vinyl, 2-0 x 2-0	EA	$106.57	$301.00	$407.57	**$539.17**	1.400
Round window, insulated glass, vinyl, 2-6 x 2-6	EA	$106.57	$359.00	$465.57	**$608.77**	1.400
Round window, insulated glass, vinyl, 3-0 x 3-0	EA	$106.57	$443.00	$549.57	**$709.57**	1.400
Half round window, insulated glass, vinyl, 2-0 x 1-0	EA	$106.57	$257.00	$363.57	**$486.37**	1.400
Half round window, insulated glass, vinyl, 2-6 x 1-3	EA	$106.57	$310.00	$416.57	**$549.97**	1.400
Half round window, insulated glass, vinyl, 3-0 x 1-6	EA	$106.57	$371.00	$477.57	**$623.17**	1.400
Half round window, insulated glass, vinyl, 3-6 x 1-9	EA	$106.57	$410.00	$516.57	**$669.97**	1.400
Half round window, insulated glass, vinyl, 4-0 x 2-0	EA	$106.57	$465.00	$571.57	**$735.97**	1.400

Vinyl Window Glazing

Description	Unit	Direct Labor	Direct Materials	Direct Total	Selling Price	Man-hours
Remove old glass, reglaze double-pane thermal window, up to 9 SF	EA	$57.09	$92.12	$149.21	**$249.18**	0.750
Remove old glass, reglaze double-pane thermal window, 10 SF to 16 SF	EA	$76.12	$155.35	$231.47	**$386.56**	1.000
Remove old glass, reglaze double-pane thermal window, 17 SF to 24 SF	EA	$114.18	$233.57	$347.75	**$580.75**	1.500
Remove old glass, reglaze double-pane thermal window, 25 SF to 30 SF	EA	$133.21	$298.60	$431.80	**$721.11**	1.750

Aluminum Windows

Labor Costs to Install Aluminum Windows

> Labor costs do not include materials such as sash, frame, casings or other trim.

Description	Unit	Direct Labor	Direct Materials	Direct Total	Selling Price	Man-hours
LABOR TO INSTALL SINGLE/DOUBLE HUNG WINDOWS						
Install aluminum double hung window, up to 15 SF, medium	Set	$76.12		$76.12	**$127.12**	1.000
Install aluminum double hung window, over 15 SF, large	Set	$114.18		$114.18	**$190.68**	1.500
LABOR TO INSTALL AWNING WINDOWS						
Install aluminum awning window, up to 48 high	EA	$76.12		$76.12	**$127.12**	1.000
Install aluminum awning window, over 48 high	EA	$114.18		$114.18	**$190.68**	1.500
LABOR TO INSTALL CASEMENT WINDOWS						
Install aluminum casement window, 1 venting, up to 48 high	Set	$57.09		$57.09	**$95.34**	0.750
Install aluminum casement window, 1 venting, over 48 high	Set	$95.15		$95.15	**$158.90**	1.250
Install aluminum casement window, 2 venting, up to 48 high	Set	$95.15		$95.15	**$158.90**	1.250
Install aluminum casement window, 2 venting, over 48 high	Set	$133.21		$133.21	**$222.46**	1.750
LABOR TO INSTALL SLIDING WINDOWS						
Install aluminum sliding window, up to 48 wide	EA	$114.18		$114.18	**$190.68**	1.500
Install aluminum sliding window, over 48 wide	EA	$171.27		$171.27	**$286.02**	2.250
LABOR TO INSTALL SPECIALTY AND PICTURE WINDOWS						
Install aluminum picture window, up to 48 high	Set	$76.12		$76.12	**$127.12**	1.000
Install aluminum picture window, over 48 high	Set	$114.18		$114.18	**$190.68**	1.500
Install aluminum picture window with flankers, up to 48 high	Set	$152.24		$152.24	**$254.24**	2.000
Install aluminum picture window with flankers, over 48 high	Set	$190.30		$190.30	**$317.79**	2.500

Labor Costs to Remove Aluminum Windows

Description	Unit	Direct Labor	Direct Materials	Direct Total	Selling Price	Man-hours
LABOR TO REMOVE ALUMINUM WINDOWS						
Remove small aluminum window in frame wall, to 12 SF	EA	$38.06		$38.06	**$63.56**	0.500
Remove average aluminum window in frame wall, 12-25 SF	EA	$57.09		$57.09	**$95.34**	0.750
Remove large aluminum window in frame wall, over 25 SF	EA	$76.12		$76.12	**$127.12**	1.000
Remove small aluminum window in masonry wall, to 12 SF	EA	$57.09		$57.09	**$95.34**	0.750
Remove average aluminum window in masonry wall, 12-25 SF	EA	$76.12		$76.12	**$127.12**	1.000
Remove large aluminum window in masonry wall, over 25 SF	EA	$95.15		$95.15	**$158.90**	1.250
Remove exterior awning or canopy	LF	$6.17		$6.17	**$10.30**	0.081

Aluminum Windows

Create Window Opening in Existing Wall

Description	Unit	Direct Labor	Direct Materials	Direct Total	Selling Price	Man-hours
Create small window opening up to 12 SF in frame wall	EA	$456.71	$22.09	$478.80	**$799.59**	6.000
Create medium window opening 12-25 SF in frame wall	EA	$608.95	$37.20	$646.15	**$1,079.07**	8.000
Create large window opening over 25 SF in frame wall	EA	$837.30	$44.18	$881.48	**$1,472.07**	11.000
Create small window opening up to 12 SF in brick veneer wall	EA	$551.86	$22.09	$573.95	**$958.49**	7.250
Create medium window opening 12-25 SF in brick veneer wall	EA	$723.13	$37.20	$760.33	**$1,269.74**	9.500
Create large window opening over 25 SF in brick veneer wall	EA	$989.54	$44.18	$1,033.72	**$1,726.30**	13.000
Create small window opening up to 12 SF in brick and block wall	EA	$608.95	$22.09	$631.04	**$1,053.83**	8.000
Create medium window opening 12-25 SF in brick and block wall	EA	$780.21	$37.20	$817.41	**$1,365.08**	10.250
Create large window opening over 25 SF in brick and block wall	EA	$1,065.66	$44.18	$1,109.83	**$1,853.42**	14.000
Create small window opening up to 12 SF in stucco wall	EA	$532.83	$22.09	$554.92	**$926.71**	7.000
Create medium window opening 12-25 SF in stucco wall	EA	$704.10	$37.20	$741.30	**$1,237.96**	9.250
Create large window opening over 25 SF in stucco wall	EA	$951.48	$44.18	$995.66	**$1,662.75**	12.500

Aluminum Windows

Single Hung, Single Glaze Aluminum Window

> No removal of old window included.

Description	Unit	Direct Labor	Direct Materials	Direct Total	Selling Price	Man-hours
Single hung, single glaze, aluminum window, 2-0 x 3-0	EA	$76.12	$74.00	$150.12	**$215.92**	1.000
Single hung, single glaze, aluminum window, 2-0 x 4-0	EA	$76.12	$84.00	$160.12	**$227.92**	1.000
Single hung, single glaze, aluminum window, 2-0 x 5-0	EA	$76.12	$93.00	$169.12	**$238.72**	1.000
Single hung, single glaze, aluminum window, 2-8 x 3-0	EA	$76.12	$82.00	$158.12	**$225.52**	1.000
Single hung, single glaze, aluminum window, 2-8 x 4-0	EA	$76.12	$91.00	$167.12	**$236.32**	1.000
Single hung, single glaze, aluminum window, 2-8 x 5-0	EA	$76.12	$102.00	$178.12	**$249.52**	1.000
Single hung, single glaze, aluminum window, 3-0 x 3-0	EA	$76.12	$85.00	$161.12	**$229.12**	1.000
Single hung, single glaze, aluminum window, 3-0 x 4-0	EA	$76.12	$95.00	$171.12	**$241.12**	1.000
Single hung, single glaze, aluminum window, 3-0 x 5-0	EA	$76.12	$104.00	$180.12	**$251.92**	1.000
Single hung, single glaze, aluminum window, 3-8 x 3-0	EA	$114.18	$94.00	$208.18	**$303.48**	1.500
Single hung, single glaze, aluminum window, 3-8 x 4-0	EA	$114.18	$103.00	$217.18	**$314.28**	1.500
Single hung, single glaze, aluminum window, 3-8 x 5-0	EA	$114.18	$115.00	$229.18	**$328.68**	1.500

Aluminum Windows

Single Hung, Insulated Glass Alum. Window

> No removal of old window included.

Description	Unit	Direct Labor	Direct Materials	Direct Total	Selling Price	Man-hours
Single hung, insulated glass, aluminum window, 2-0 x 3-0	EA	$76.12	$102.00	$178.12	**$249.52**	1.000
Single hung, insulated glass, aluminum window, 2-0 x 3-6	EA	$76.12	$108.00	$184.12	**$256.72**	1.000
Single hung, insulated glass, aluminum window, 2-0 x 4-0	EA	$76.12	$115.00	$191.12	**$265.12**	1.000
Single hung, insulated glass, aluminum window, 2-0 x 4-6	EA	$76.12	$121.00	$197.12	**$272.32**	1.000
Single hung, insulated glass, aluminum window, 2-0 x 5-0	EA	$76.12	$128.00	$204.12	**$280.72**	1.000
Single hung, insulated glass, aluminum window, 2-0 x 5-6	EA	$76.12	$135.00	$211.12	**$289.12**	1.000
Single hung, insulated glass, aluminum window, 2-8 x 3-0	EA	$76.12	$111.00	$187.12	**$260.32**	1.000
Single hung, insulated glass, aluminum window, 2-8 x 3-6	EA	$76.12	$118.00	$194.12	**$268.72**	1.000
Single hung, insulated glass, aluminum window, 2-8 x 4-0	EA	$76.12	$126.00	$202.12	**$278.32**	1.000
Single hung, insulated glass, aluminum window, 2-8 x 4-6	EA	$76.12	$132.00	$208.12	**$285.52**	1.000
Single hung, insulated glass, aluminum window, 2-8 x 5-0	EA	$76.12	$141.00	$217.12	**$296.32**	1.000
Single hung, insulated glass, aluminum window, 2-8 x 5-6	EA	$76.12	$147.00	$223.12	**$303.52**	1.000
Single hung, insulated glass, aluminum window, 3-0 x 3-0	EA	$76.12	$117.00	$193.12	**$267.52**	1.000
Single hung, insulated glass, aluminum window, 3-0 x 3-6	EA	$76.12	$124.00	$200.12	**$275.92**	1.000
Single hung, insulated glass, aluminum window, 3-0 x 4-0	EA	$76.12	$130.00	$206.12	**$283.12**	1.000
Single hung, insulated glass, aluminum window, 3-0 x 4-6	EA	$76.12	$137.00	$213.12	**$291.52**	1.000
Single hung, insulated glass, aluminum window, 3-0 x 5-0	EA	$76.12	$143.00	$219.12	**$298.72**	1.000
Single hung, insulated glass, aluminum window, 3-0 x 5-6	EA	$114.18	$150.00	$264.18	**$370.68**	1.500
Single hung, insulated glass, aluminum window, 3-8 x 3-0	EA	$76.12	$129.00	$205.12	**$281.92**	1.000
Single hung, insulated glass, aluminum window, 3-8 x 3-6	EA	$76.12	$135.00	$211.12	**$289.12**	1.000
Single hung, insulated glass, aluminum window, 3-8 x 4-0	EA	$76.12	$143.00	$219.12	**$298.72**	1.000
Single hung, insulated glass, aluminum window, 3-8 x 4-6	EA	$114.18	$149.00	$263.18	**$369.48**	1.500
Single hung, insulated glass, aluminum window, 3-8 x 5-0	EA	$114.18	$157.00	$271.18	**$379.08**	1.500
Single hung, insulated glass, aluminum window, 3-8 x 5-6	EA	$114.18	$169.00	$283.18	**$393.48**	1.500

Aluminum Windows

Double Hung, Single Glaze Alum. Window

> No removal of old window included.

Description	Unit	Direct Labor	Direct Materials	Direct Total	Selling Price	Man-hours
Double hung, single glaze, aluminum window, 2-0 x 3-0	EA	$76.12	$93.00	$169.12	**$238.72**	1.000
Double hung, single glaze, aluminum window, 2-0 x 4-0	EA	$76.12	$105.00	$181.12	**$253.12**	1.000
Double hung, single glaze, aluminum window, 2-0 x 5-0	EA	$76.12	$117.00	$193.12	**$267.52**	1.000
Double hung, single glaze, aluminum window, 2-8 x 3-0	EA	$76.12	$102.00	$178.12	**$249.52**	1.000
Double hung, single glaze, aluminum window, 2-8 x 4-0	EA	$76.12	$114.00	$190.12	**$263.92**	1.000
Double hung, single glaze, aluminum window, 2-8 x 5-0	EA	$76.12	$127.00	$203.12	**$279.52**	1.000
Double hung, single glaze, aluminum window, 3-0 x 3-0	EA	$76.12	$106.00	$182.12	**$254.32**	1.000
Double hung, single glaze, aluminum window, 3-0 x 4-0	EA	$76.12	$118.00	$194.12	**$268.72**	1.000
Double hung, single glaze, aluminum window, 3-0 x 5-0	EA	$76.12	$130.00	$206.12	**$283.12**	1.000
Double hung, single glaze, aluminum window, 3-8 x 3-0	EA	$76.12	$118.00	$194.12	**$268.72**	1.000
Double hung, single glaze, aluminum window, 3-8 x 4-0	EA	$76.12	$129.00	$205.12	**$281.92**	1.000
Double hung, single glaze, aluminum window, 3-8 x 5-0	EA	$114.18	$143.00	$257.18	**$362.28**	1.500

Aluminum Windows

Double Hung, Insulated Glass Alum. Window

> No removal of old window included.

Description	Unit	Direct Labor	Direct Materials	Direct Total	Selling Price	Man-hours
Double hung, insulated glass, aluminum window, 2-0 x 3-0	EA	$76.12	$127.00	$203.12	**$279.52**	1.000
Double hung, insulated glass, aluminum window, 2-0 x 3-6	EA	$76.12	$135.00	$211.12	**$289.12**	1.000
Double hung, insulated glass, aluminum window, 2-0 x 4-0	EA	$76.12	$144.00	$220.12	**$299.92**	1.000
Double hung, insulated glass, aluminum window, 2-0 x 4-6	EA	$76.12	$152.00	$228.12	**$309.52**	1.000
Double hung, insulated glass, aluminum window, 2-0 x 5-0	EA	$76.12	$160.00	$236.12	**$319.12**	1.000
Double hung, insulated glass, aluminum window, 2-0 x 5-6	EA	$76.12	$169.00	$245.12	**$329.92**	1.000
Double hung, insulated glass, aluminum window, 2-8 x 3-0	EA	$76.12	$139.00	$215.12	**$293.92**	1.000
Double hung, insulated glass, aluminum window, 2-8 x 3-6	EA	$76.12	$148.00	$224.12	**$304.72**	1.000
Double hung, insulated glass, aluminum window, 2-8 x 4-0	EA	$76.12	$157.00	$233.12	**$315.52**	1.000
Double hung, insulated glass, aluminum window, 2-8 x 4-6	EA	$76.12	$165.00	$241.12	**$325.12**	1.000
Double hung, insulated glass, aluminum window, 2-8 x 5-0	EA	$76.12	$176.00	$252.12	**$338.32**	1.000
Double hung, insulated glass, aluminum window, 2-8 x 5-6	EA	$76.12	$183.00	$259.12	**$346.72**	1.000
Double hung, insulated glass, aluminum window, 3-0 x 3-0	EA	$76.12	$146.00	$222.12	**$302.32**	1.000
Double hung, insulated glass, aluminum window, 3-0 x 3-6	EA	$76.12	$155.00	$231.12	**$313.12**	1.000
Double hung, insulated glass, aluminum window, 3-0 x 4-0	EA	$76.12	$163.00	$239.12	**$322.72**	1.000
Double hung, insulated glass, aluminum window, 3-0 x 4-6	EA	$76.12	$171.00	$247.12	**$332.32**	1.000
Double hung, insulated glass, aluminum window, 3-0 x 5-0	EA	$76.12	$179.00	$255.12	**$341.92**	1.000
Double hung, insulated glass, aluminum window, 3-0 x 5-6	EA	$114.18	$188.00	$302.18	**$416.28**	1.500
Double hung, insulated glass, aluminum window, 3-8 x 3-0	EA	$76.12	$161.00	$237.12	**$320.32**	1.000
Double hung, insulated glass, aluminum window, 3-8 x 3-6	EA	$76.12	$169.00	$245.12	**$329.92**	1.000
Double hung, insulated glass, aluminum window, 3-8 x 4-0	EA	$76.12	$179.00	$255.12	**$341.92**	1.000
Double hung, insulated glass, aluminum window, 3-8 x 4-6	EA	$114.18	$187.00	$301.18	**$415.08**	1.500
Double hung, insulated glass, aluminum window, 3-8 x 5-0	EA	$114.18	$196.00	$310.18	**$425.88**	1.500
Double hung, insulated glass, aluminum window, 3-8 x 5-6	EA	$114.18	$211.00	$325.18	**$443.88**	1.500

Aluminum Windows

Awning, Insulated Glass Aluminum Window

> No removal of old window included.

Description	Unit	Direct Labor	Direct Materials	Direct Total	Selling Price	Man-hours
Awning, insulated glass, aluminum window, 2-0 x 2-0	EA	$76.12	$102.00	$178.12	**$249.52**	1.000
Awning, insulated glass, aluminum window, 2-0 x 3-0	EA	$76.12	$112.00	$188.12	**$261.52**	1.000
Awning, insulated glass, aluminum window, 2-0 x 4-0	EA	$76.12	$147.00	$223.12	**$303.52**	1.000
Awning, insulated glass, aluminum window, 2-0 x 5-0	EA	$114.18	$157.00	$271.18	**$379.08**	1.500
Awning, insulated glass, aluminum window, 2-0 x 6-0	EA	$114.18	$174.00	$288.18	**$399.48**	1.500
Awning, insulated glass, aluminum window, 3-0 x 2-0	EA	$76.12	$107.00	$183.12	**$255.52**	1.000
Awning, insulated glass, aluminum window, 3-0 x 3-0	EA	$76.12	$132.00	$208.12	**$285.52**	1.000
Awning, insulated glass, aluminum window, 3-0 x 4-0	EA	$76.12	$157.00	$233.12	**$315.52**	1.000
Awning, insulated glass, aluminum window, 3-0 x 5-0	EA	$114.18	$189.00	$303.18	**$417.48**	1.500
Awning, insulated glass, aluminum window, 3-0 x 6-0	EA	$114.18	$214.00	$328.18	**$447.48**	1.500
Awning, insulated glass, aluminum window, 4-0 x 2-0	EA	$76.12	$132.00	$208.12	**$285.52**	1.000
Awning, insulated glass, aluminum window, 4-0 x 3-0	EA	$76.12	$149.00	$225.12	**$305.92**	1.000
Awning, insulated glass, aluminum window, 4-0 x 4-0	EA	$76.12	$189.00	$265.12	**$353.92**	1.000
Awning, insulated glass, aluminum window, 4-0 x 5-0	EA	$114.18	$204.00	$318.18	**$435.48**	1.500
Awning, insulated glass, aluminum window, 4-0 x 6-0	EA	$114.18	$258.00	$372.18	**$500.28**	1.500

Casement, Insulated Glass Alum. Window

> No removal of old window included.

Description	Unit	Direct Labor	Direct Materials	Direct Total	Selling Price	Man-hours
Casement, insulated glass, aluminum window, 1 venting, 1-8 x 2-0	EA	$57.09	$113.00	$170.09	**$230.94**	0.750
Casement, insulated glass, aluminum window, 1 venting, 1-8 x 2-6	EA	$57.09	$134.00	$191.09	**$256.14**	0.750
Casement, insulated glass, aluminum window, 1 venting, 1-8 x 3-0	EA	$57.09	$155.00	$212.09	**$281.34**	0.750
Casement, insulated glass, aluminum window, 1 venting, 1-8 x 3-6	EA	$57.09	$177.00	$234.09	**$307.74**	0.750
Casement, insulated glass, aluminum window, 1 venting, 1-8 x 4-0	EA	$57.09	$199.00	$256.09	**$334.14**	0.750
Casement, insulated glass, aluminum window, 1 venting, 1-8 x 4-6	EA	$95.15	$220.00	$315.15	**$422.90**	1.250
Casement, insulated glass, aluminum window, 1 venting, 1-8 x 5-0	EA	$95.15	$242.00	$337.15	**$449.30**	1.250
Casement, insulated glass, aluminum window, 1 venting, 1-8 x 5-6	EA	$95.15	$263.00	$358.15	**$474.50**	1.250
Casement, insulated glass, aluminum window, 1 venting, 2-6 x 2-0	EA	$57.09	$154.00	$211.09	**$280.14**	0.750
Casement, insulated glass, aluminum window, 1 venting, 2-6 x 2-6	EA	$57.09	$174.00	$231.09	**$304.14**	0.750
Casement, insulated glass, aluminum window, 1 venting, 2-6 x 3-0	EA	$57.09	$193.00	$250.09	**$326.94**	0.750
Casement, insulated glass, aluminum window, 1 venting, 2-6 x 3-6	EA	$57.09	$212.00	$269.09	**$349.74**	0.750
Casement, insulated glass, aluminum window, 1 venting, 2-6 x 4-0	EA	$57.09	$232.00	$289.09	**$373.74**	0.750
Casement, insulated glass, aluminum window, 1 venting, 2-6 x 4-6	EA	$95.15	$251.00	$346.15	**$460.10**	1.250
Casement, insulated glass, aluminum window, 1 venting, 2-6 x 5-0	EA	$95.15	$270.00	$365.15	**$482.90**	1.250
Casement, insulated glass, aluminum window, 1 venting, 2-6 x 5-6	EA	$95.15	$289.00	$384.15	**$505.70**	1.250

Aluminum Windows

Slider, Insulated Glass Aluminum Window

> No removal of old window included.

Description	Unit	Direct Labor	Direct Materials	Direct Total	Selling Price	Man-hours
Slider, insulated glass, aluminum window, 3-0 x 2-0	EA	$114.18	$116.00	$230.18	**$329.88**	1.500
Slider, insulated glass, aluminum window, 3-0 x 2-6	EA	$114.18	$126.00	$240.18	**$341.88**	1.500
Slider, insulated glass, aluminum window, 3-0 x 3-0	EA	$114.18	$142.00	$256.18	**$361.08**	1.500
Slider, insulated glass, aluminum window, 3-0 x 3-6	EA	$114.18	$142.00	$256.18	**$361.08**	1.500
Slider, insulated glass, aluminum window, 3-0 x 4-0	EA	$114.18	$153.00	$267.18	**$374.28**	1.500
Slider, insulated glass, aluminum window, 3-0 x 4-6	EA	$114.18	$166.00	$280.18	**$389.88**	1.500
Slider, insulated glass, aluminum window, 3-0 x 5-0	EA	$114.18	$180.00	$294.18	**$406.68**	1.500
Slider, insulated glass, aluminum window, 4-0 x 2-0	EA	$114.18	$128.00	$242.18	**$344.28**	1.500
Slider, insulated glass, aluminum window, 4-0 x 2-6	EA	$114.18	$146.00	$260.18	**$365.88**	1.500
Slider, insulated glass, aluminum window, 4-0 x 3-0	EA	$114.18	$160.00	$274.18	**$382.68**	1.500
Slider, insulated glass, aluminum window, 4-0 x 3-6	EA	$114.18	$170.00	$284.18	**$394.68**	1.500
Slider, insulated glass, aluminum window, 4-0 x 4-0	EA	$114.18	$181.00	$295.18	**$407.88**	1.500
Slider, insulated glass, aluminum window, 4-0 x 4-6	EA	$114.18	$193.00	$307.18	**$422.28**	1.500
Slider, insulated glass, aluminum window, 4-0 x 5-0	EA	$114.18	$215.00	$329.18	**$448.68**	1.500
Slider, insulated glass, aluminum window, 5-0 x 2-0	EA	$171.27	$160.00	$331.27	**$478.02**	2.250
Slider, insulated glass, aluminum window, 5-0 x 2-6	EA	$171.27	$177.00	$348.27	**$498.42**	2.250
Slider, insulated glass, aluminum window, 5-0 x 3-0	EA	$171.27	$184.00	$355.27	**$506.82**	2.250
Slider, insulated glass, aluminum window, 5-0 x 3-6	EA	$171.27	$210.00	$381.27	**$538.02**	2.250
Slider, insulated glass, aluminum window, 5-0 x 4-0	EA	$171.27	$223.00	$394.27	**$553.62**	2.250
Slider, insulated glass, aluminum window, 5-0 x 4-6	EA	$171.27	$236.00	$407.27	**$569.22**	2.250
Slider, insulated glass, aluminum window, 5-0 x 5-0	EA	$171.27	$260.00	$431.27	**$598.02**	2.250
Slider, insulated glass, aluminum window, 6-0 x 2-0	EA	$171.27	$178.00	$349.27	**$499.62**	2.250
Slider, insulated glass, aluminum window, 6-0 x 2-6	EA	$171.27	$203.00	$374.27	**$529.62**	2.250
Slider, insulated glass, aluminum window, 6-0 x 3-0	EA	$171.27	$231.00	$402.27	**$563.22**	2.250
Slider, insulated glass, aluminum window, 6-0 x 3-6	EA	$171.27	$255.00	$426.27	**$592.02**	2.250
Slider, insulated glass, aluminum window, 6-0 x 4-0	EA	$171.27	$290.00	$461.27	**$634.02**	2.250
Slider, insulated glass, aluminum window, 6-0 x 4-6	EA	$171.27	$316.00	$487.27	**$665.22**	2.250
Slider, insulated glass, aluminum window, 6-0 x 5-0	EA	$171.27	$348.00	$519.27	**$703.62**	2.250

Aluminum Windows

Picture Window, Insulated Glass, Aluminum

> No removal of old window included.

Description	Unit	Direct Labor	Direct Materials	Direct Total	Selling Price	Man-hours
Picture window, insulated glass, aluminum, 3-0 x 2-0	EA	$76.12	$131.00	$207.12	**$284.32**	1.000
Picture window, insulated glass, aluminum, 3-0 x 3-0	EA	$76.12	$154.00	$230.12	**$311.92**	1.000
Picture window, insulated glass, aluminum, 3-0 x 4-0	EA	$76.12	$181.00	$257.12	**$344.32**	1.000
Picture window, insulated glass, aluminum, 3-0 x 5-0	EA	$114.18	$206.00	$320.18	**$437.88**	1.500
Picture window, insulated glass, aluminum, 4-0 x 2-0	EA	$76.12	$162.00	$238.12	**$321.52**	1.000
Picture window, insulated glass, aluminum, 4-0 x 3-0	EA	$76.12	$191.00	$267.12	**$356.32**	1.000
Picture window, insulated glass, aluminum, 4-0 x 4-0	EA	$76.12	$223.00	$299.12	**$394.72**	1.000
Picture window, insulated glass, aluminum, 4-0 x 5-0	EA	$114.18	$254.00	$368.18	**$495.48**	1.500
Picture window, insulated glass, aluminum, 5-0 x 2-0	EA	$76.12	$199.00	$275.12	**$365.92**	1.000
Picture window, insulated glass, aluminum, 5-0 x 3-0	EA	$76.12	$239.00	$315.12	**$413.92**	1.000
Picture window, insulated glass, aluminum, 5-0 x 4-0	EA	$76.12	$279.00	$355.12	**$461.92**	1.000
Picture window, insulated glass, aluminum, 5-0 x 5-0	EA	$114.18	$319.00	$433.18	**$573.48**	1.500
Picture window, insulated glass, aluminum, 6-0 x 2-0	EA	$76.12	$252.00	$328.12	**$429.52**	1.000
Picture window, insulated glass, aluminum, 6-0 x 3-0	EA	$76.12	$299.00	$375.12	**$485.92**	1.000
Picture window, insulated glass, aluminum, 6-0 x 4-0	EA	$76.12	$347.00	$423.12	**$543.52**	1.000
Picture window, insulated glass, aluminum, 6-0 x 5-0	EA	$114.18	$396.00	$510.18	**$665.88**	1.500

Skylights

Labor Costs for Skylights

> Labor costs do not include materials such as sash, frame, casings or other trim.

Description	Unit	Direct Labor	Direct Materials	Direct Total	Selling Price	Man-hours
LABOR TO INSTALL SKYLIGHTS						
Install step-flashed unit (LF = combined length of 4 sides of skylight)	LF	$25.42		$25.42	**$42.46**	0.334
Install self-flashing unit (LF = combined length of 4 sides of skylight)	LF	$16.90		$16.90	**$28.22**	0.222
Install manufacturer curb kit (LF = combined length of 4 sides of skylight)	LF	$9.51		$9.51	**$15.89**	0.125
Build curb, existing opening (LF = combined length of 4 sides of skylight)	LF	$14.39	$5.01	$19.40	**$32.39**	0.189
LABOR TO REMOVE SKYLIGHTS						
Remove skylight and curb (LF = combined length of 4 sides of skylight)	LF	$10.88		$10.88	**$18.18**	0.143
Remove skylight only (LF = combined length of 4 sides of skylight)	LF	$6.62		$6.62	**$11.06**	0.087
LABOR TO INSTALL SKYLIGHT SHADES						
Install manual shades, up to 27" wide	EA	$38.06		$38.06	**$63.56**	0.500
Install manual shades, 27" to 38" wide	EA	$57.09		$57.09	**$95.34**	0.750
Install manual shades, over 39" wide	EA	$76.12		$76.12	**$127.12**	1.000
Install electric shades, up to 27" wide, electrical wiring not included	EA	$76.12		$76.12	**$127.12**	1.000
Install electric shades, 27" to 38" wide, electrical wiring not included	EA	$95.15		$95.15	**$158.90**	1.250
Install electric shades, over 39" wide, electrical wiring not included	EA	$114.18		$114.18	**$190.68**	1.500

Create Opening for Skylight

Description	Unit	Direct Labor	Direct Materials	Direct Total	Selling Price	Man-hours
Create opening in shingled roof	EA	$304.47	$21.55	$326.03	**$544.46**	4.000
Create opening in slate roof	EA	$456.71	$75.02	$531.73	**$887.98**	6.000
Create opening in clay tile roof	EA	$608.95	$104.35	$713.29	**$1,191.20**	8.000
Create opening in concrete tile roof	EA	$608.95	$75.02	$683.96	**$1,142.22**	8.000
Create opening in built-up roof, not including curb	EA	$380.59	$25.97	$406.56	**$678.96**	5.000

Skylights

Self-Flashed Skylights

> Material Costs only. Select labor item from 'Labor Costs for Skylights' section.

Description	Unit	Direct Labor	Direct Materials	Direct Total	Selling Price	Man-hours
SELF-FLASHED SKYLIGHTS, FIXED						
Skylight, fixed lite, self-flash, tempered Low-E glass, 23-1/4 x 23-7/16	EA		$185.00	$185.00	**$222.00**	
Skylight, fixed lite, self-flash, tempered Low-E glass, 23-1/4 x 30-1/2	EA		$218.00	$218.00	**$261.60**	
Skylight, fixed lite, self-flash, tempered Low-E glass, 23-1/4 x 46-1/4	EA		$232.00	$232.00	**$278.40**	
Skylight, fixed lite, self-flash, tempered Low-E glass, 30-9/16 x 30-1/2	EA		$230.00	$230.00	**$276.00**	
Skylight, fixed lite, self-flash, tempered Low-E glass, 30-9/16 x 46-1/4	EA		$280.00	$280.00	**$336.00**	
Skylight, fixed lite, self-flash, tempered Low-E glass, 47-1/4 x 46-1/4	EA		$353.00	$353.00	**$423.60**	
Skylight, fixed lite, self-flash, laminated Low-E glass, 23-1/4 x 23-7/16	EA		$207.00	$207.00	**$248.40**	
Skylight, fixed lite, self-flash, laminated Low-E glass, 23-1/4 x 30-1/2	EA		$249.00	$249.00	**$298.80**	
Skylight, fixed lite, self-flash, laminated Low-E glass, 23-1/4 x 46-1/4	EA		$271.00	$271.00	**$325.20**	
Skylight, fixed lite, self-flash, laminated Low-E glass, 30-9/16 x 30-1/2	EA		$267.00	$267.00	**$320.40**	
Skylight, fixed lite, self-flash, laminated Low-E glass, 30-9/16 x 46-1/4	EA		$327.00	$327.00	**$392.40**	
Skylight, fixed lite, self-flash, laminated Low-E glass, 47-1/4 x 46-1/4	EA		$420.00	$420.00	**$504.00**	
Blinds, manual, for fixed lite skylight size 23-1/4 x 23-7/16	EA		$95.00	$95.00	**$114.00**	
Blinds, manual, for fixed lite skylight size 23-1/4 x 30-1/2	EA		$101.00	$101.00	**$121.20**	
Blinds, manual, for fixed lite skylight size 23-1/4 x 46-1/4	EA		$108.00	$108.00	**$129.60**	
Blinds, manual, for fixed lite skylight size 30-9/16 x 30-1/2	EA		$114.00	$114.00	**$136.80**	
Blinds, manual, for fixed lite skylight size 30-9/16 x 46-1/4	EA		$123.00	$123.00	**$147.60**	
Blinds, manual, for fixed lite skylight size 47-1/4 x 46-1/4	EA		$146.00	$146.00	**$175.20**	
SELF-FLASHED SKYLIGHTS, MANUAL VENT						
Skylight, manual, self-flash, tempered Low-E glass, 23-1/4 x 23-7/16	EA		$347.00	$347.00	**$416.40**	
Skylight, manual, self-flash, tempered Low-E glass, 23-1/4 x 30-1/2	EA		$391.00	$391.00	**$469.20**	
Skylight, manual, self-flash, tempered Low-E glass, 23-1/4 x 46-1/4	EA		$402.00	$402.00	**$482.40**	
Skylight, manual, self-flash, tempered Low-E glass, 30-9/16 x 30-1/2	EA		$375.00	$375.00	**$450.00**	
Skylight, manual, self-flash, tempered Low-E glass, 30-9/16 x 46-1/4	EA		$442.00	$442.00	**$530.40**	
Skylight, manual, self-flash, tempered Low-E glass, 47-1/4 x 46-1/4	EA		$569.00	$569.00	**$682.80**	
Skylight, manual, self-flash, laminated Low-E glass, 23-1/4 x 23-7/16	EA		$377.00	$377.00	**$452.40**	
Skylight, manual, self-flash, laminated Low-E glass, 23-1/4 x 30-1/2	EA		$420.00	$420.00	**$504.00**	
Skylight, manual, self-flash, laminated Low-E glass, 23-1/4 x 46-1/4	EA		$448.00	$448.00	**$537.60**	
Skylight, manual, self-flash, laminated Low-E glass, 30-9/16 x 30-1/2	EA		$426.00	$426.00	**$511.20**	
Skylight, manual, self-flash, laminated Low-E glass, 30-9/16 x 46-1/4	EA		$521.00	$521.00	**$625.20**	
Skylight, manual, self-flash, laminated Low-E glass, 47-1/4 x 46-1/4	EA		$633.00	$633.00	**$759.60**	

Skylights

Self-Flashed Skylights

> Material Costs only. Select labor item from 'Labor Costs for Skylights' section.

Description	Unit	Direct Labor	Direct Materials	Direct Total	Selling Price	Man-hours
SELF-FLASHED SKYLIGHTS, MANUAL VENT (continued)						
Blinds, manual, for manual vent skylight size 23-1/4 x 23-7/16	EA		$95.00	$95.00	**$114.00**	
Blinds, manual, for manual vent skylight size 23-1/4 x 30-1/2	EA		$101.00	$101.00	**$121.20**	
Blinds, manual, for manual vent skylight size 23-1/4 x 46-1/4	EA		$108.00	$108.00	**$129.60**	
Blinds, manual, for manual vent skylight size 30-9/16 x 30-1/2	EA		$114.00	$114.00	**$136.80**	
Blinds, manual, for manual vent skylight size 30-9/16 x 46-1/4	EA		$123.00	$123.00	**$147.60**	
Blinds, manual, for manual vent skylight size 47-1/4 x 46-1/4	EA		$146.00	$146.00	**$175.20**	
SELF-FLASHED SKYLIGHTS, ELECTRIC VENT						
Skylight, electric, self-flash, tempered Low-E glass, 23-1/4 x 23-7/16	EA		$666.00	$666.00	**$799.20**	
Skylight, electric, self-flash, tempered Low-E glass, 23-1/4 x 30-1/2	EA		$725.00	$725.00	**$870.00**	
Skylight, electric, self-flash, tempered Low-E glass, 23-1/4 x 46-1/4	EA		$772.00	$772.00	**$926.40**	
Skylight, electric, self-flash, tempered Low-E glass, 30-9/16 x 30-1/2	EA		$755.00	$755.00	**$906.00**	
Skylight, electric, self-flash, tempered Low-E glass, 30-9/16 x 46-1/4	EA		$825.00	$825.00	**$990.00**	
Skylight, electric, self-flash, tempered Low-E glass, 47-1/4 x 46-1/4	EA		$965.00	$965.00	**$1,158.00**	
Skylight, electric, self-flash, laminated Low-E glass, 23-1/4 x 23-7/16	EA		$717.00	$717.00	**$860.40**	
Skylight, electric, self-flash, laminated Low-E glass, 23-1/4 x 30-1/2	EA		$759.00	$759.00	**$910.80**	
Skylight, electric, self-flash, laminated Low-E glass, 23-1/4 x 46-1/4	EA		$805.00	$805.00	**$966.00**	
Skylight, electric, self-flash, laminated Low-E glass, 30-9/16 x 30-1/2	EA		$790.00	$790.00	**$948.00**	
Skylight, electric, self-flash, laminated Low-E glass, 30-9/16 x 46-1/4	EA		$887.00	$887.00	**$1,064.40**	
Skylight, electric, self-flash, laminated Low-E glass, 47-1/4 x 46-1/4	EA		$1,027.00	$1,027.00	**$1,232.40**	
Blinds, electric, for electric vent skylight size 23-1/4 x 23-7/16	EA		$269.00	$269.00	**$322.80**	
Blinds, electric, for electric vent skylight size 23-1/4 x 30-1/2	EA		$274.00	$274.00	**$328.80**	
Blinds, electric, for electric vent skylight size 23-1/4 x 46-1/4	EA		$280.00	$280.00	**$336.00**	
Blinds, electric, for electric vent skylight size 30-9/16 x 30-1/2	EA		$284.00	$284.00	**$340.80**	
Blinds, electric, for electric vent skylight size 30-9/16 x 46-1/4	EA		$291.00	$291.00	**$349.20**	
Blinds, electric, for electric vent skylight size 47-1/4 x 46-1/4	EA		$316.00	$316.00	**$379.20**	

Skylights

Curb Mounted Skylights with Flashing

> Material Costs only. Select labor item from 'Labor Costs for Skylights' section.

Description	Unit	Direct Labor	Direct Materials	Direct Total	Selling Price	Man-hours
CURB MOUNTED SKYLIGHTS, FIXED						
Skylight, fixed lite, curb mount, tempered Low-E glass, 18-1/4 x 34-1/4	EA		$183.00	$183.00	**$219.60**	
Skylight, fixed lite, curb mount, tempered Low-E glass, 18-1/4 x 49-3/4	EA		$200.00	$200.00	**$240.00**	
Skylight, fixed lite, curb mount, tempered Low-E glass, 26-1/4 x 26-1/4	EA		$184.00	$184.00	**$220.80**	
Skylight, fixed lite, curb mount, tempered Low-E glass, 26-1/4 x 34-1/4	EA		$209.00	$209.00	**$250.80**	
Skylight, fixed lite, curb mount, tempered Low-E glass, 26-1/4 x 38-1/4	EA		$220.00	$220.00	**$264.00**	
Skylight, fixed lite, curb mount, tempered Low-E glass, 26-1/4 x 50-1/4	EA		$232.00	$232.00	**$278.40**	
Skylight, fixed lite, curb mount, tempered Low-E glass, 34-1/4 x 34-1/4	EA		$256.00	$256.00	**$307.20**	
Skylight, fixed lite, curb mount, tempered Low-E glass, 34-1/4 x 50-1/4	EA		$330.00	$330.00	**$396.00**	
Skylight, fixed lite, curb mount, tempered Low-E glass, 38-1/4 x 38-1/4	EA		$316.00	$316.00	**$379.20**	
Skylight, fixed lite, curb mount, tempered Low-E glass, 50-1/4 x 50-1/4	EA		$363.00	$363.00	**$435.60**	
Skylight, fixed lite, curb mount, laminated Low-E glass, 18-1/4 x 34-1/4	EA		$207.00	$207.00	**$248.40**	
Skylight, fixed lite, curb mount, laminated Low-E glass, 18-1/4 x 49-3/4	EA		$216.00	$216.00	**$259.20**	
Skylight, fixed lite, curb mount, laminated Low-E glass, 26-1/4 x 26-1/4	EA		$208.00	$208.00	**$249.60**	
Skylight, fixed lite, curb mount, laminated Low-E glass, 26-1/4 x 34-1/4	EA		$233.00	$233.00	**$279.60**	
Skylight, fixed lite, curb mount, laminated Low-E glass, 26-1/4 x 38-1/4	EA		$243.00	$243.00	**$291.60**	
Skylight, fixed lite, curb mount, laminated Low-E glass, 26-1/4 x 50-1/4	EA		$254.00	$254.00	**$304.80**	
Skylight, fixed lite, curb mount, laminated Low-E glass, 34-1/4 x 34-1/4	EA		$286.00	$286.00	**$343.20**	
Skylight, fixed lite, curb mount, laminated Low-E glass, 34-1/4 x 50-1/4	EA		$360.00	$360.00	**$432.00**	
Skylight, fixed lite, curb mount, laminated Low-E glass, 38-1/4 x 38-1/4	EA		$338.00	$338.00	**$405.60**	
Skylight, fixed lite, curb mount, laminated Low-E glass, 50-1/4 x 50-1/4	EA		$395.00	$395.00	**$474.00**	
Blinds, manual, for fixed lite skylight size 18-1/4 x 34-1/4	EA		$95.00	$95.00	**$114.00**	
Blinds, manual, for fixed lite skylight size 18-1/4 x 49-3/4	EA		$101.00	$101.00	**$121.20**	
Blinds, manual, for fixed lite skylight size 26-1/4 x 26-1/4	EA		$106.00	$106.00	**$127.20**	
Blinds, manual, for fixed lite skylight size 26-1/4 x 34-1/4	EA		$112.00	$112.00	**$134.40**	
Blinds, manual, for fixed lite skylight size 26-1/4 x 38-1/4	EA		$119.00	$119.00	**$142.80**	
Blinds, manual, for fixed lite skylight size 26-1/4 x 50-1/4	EA		$123.00	$123.00	**$147.60**	
Blinds, manual, for fixed lite skylight size 34-1/4 x 34-1/4	EA		$128.00	$128.00	**$153.60**	
Blinds, manual, for fixed lite skylight size 34-1/4 x 50-1/4	EA		$132.00	$132.00	**$158.40**	
Blinds, manual, for fixed lite skylight size 38-1/4 x 38-1/4	EA		$130.00	$130.00	**$156.00**	
Blinds, manual, for fixed lite skylight size 50-1/4 x 50-1/4	EA		$159.00	$159.00	**$190.80**	

Skylights

Curb Mounted Skylights with Flashing

> Material Costs only. Select labor item from 'Labor Costs for Skylights' section.

Description	Unit	Direct Labor	Direct Materials	Direct Total	Selling Price	Man-hours
CURB MOUNTED SKYLIGHTS, MANUAL VENT						
Skylight, manual vent, curb mount, tempered Low-E, 26-1/4 x 26-1/4	EA		$383.00	$383.00	**$459.60**	
Skylight, manual vent, curb mount, tempered Low-E, 26-1/4 x 38-1/4	EA		$438.00	$438.00	**$525.60**	
Skylight, manual vent, curb mount, tempered Low-E, 26-1/4 x 50-1/4	EA		$463.00	$463.00	**$555.60**	
Skylight, manual vent, curb mount, tempered Low-E, 34-1/4 x 34-1/4	EA		$495.00	$495.00	**$594.00**	
Skylight, manual vent, curb mount, tempered Low-E, 34-1/4 x 50-1/4	EA		$580.00	$580.00	**$696.00**	
Skylight, manual vent, curb mount, tempered Low-E, 38-1/4 x 38-1/4	EA		$567.00	$567.00	**$680.40**	
Skylight, manual vent, curb mount, tempered Low-E, 50-1/4 x 50-1/4	EA		$715.00	$715.00	**$858.00**	
Skylight, manual vent, curb mount, laminated Low-E, 26-1/4 x 26-1/4	EA		$402.00	$402.00	**$482.40**	
Skylight, manual vent, curb mount, laminated Low-E, 26-1/4 x 38-1/4	EA		$461.00	$461.00	**$553.20**	
Skylight, manual vent, curb mount, laminated Low-E, 26-1/4 x 50-1/4	EA		$501.00	$501.00	**$601.20**	
Skylight, manual vent, curb mount, laminated Low-E, 34-1/4 x 34-1/4	EA		$534.00	$534.00	**$640.80**	
Skylight, manual vent, curb mount, laminated Low-E, 34-1/4 x 50-1/4	EA		$622.00	$622.00	**$746.40**	
Skylight, manual vent, curb mount, laminated Low-E, 38-1/4 x 38-1/4	EA		$606.00	$606.00	**$727.20**	
Skylight, manual vent, curb mount, laminated Low-E, 50-1/4 x 50-1/4	EA		$762.00	$762.00	**$914.40**	
Blinds, manual, for manual vent skylight size 26-1/4 x 26-1/4	EA		$106.00	$106.00	**$127.20**	
Blinds, manual, for manual vent skylight size 26-1/4 x 38-1/4	EA		$119.00	$119.00	**$142.80**	
Blinds, manual, for manual vent skylight size 26-1/4 x 50-1/4	EA		$123.00	$123.00	**$147.60**	
Blinds, manual, for manual vent skylight size 34-1/4 x 34-1/4	EA		$128.00	$128.00	**$153.60**	
Blinds, manual, for manual vent skylight size 34-1/4 x 50-1/4	EA		$132.00	$132.00	**$158.40**	
Blinds, manual, for manual vent skylight size 38-1/4 x 38-1/4	EA		$130.00	$130.00	**$156.00**	
Blinds, manual, for manual vent skylight size 50-1/4 x 50-1/4	EA		$159.00	$159.00	**$190.80**	

Skylights

Curb Mounted Skylights with Flashing

> **Material Costs only. Select labor item from 'Labor Costs for Skylights' section.**

Description	Unit	Direct Labor	Direct Materials	Direct Total	Selling Price	Man-hours
CURB MOUNTED SKYLIGHTS, ELECTRIC VENT						
Skylight, electric vent, curb mount, tempered Low-E, 26-1/4 x 26-1/4	EA		$699.00	$699.00	**$838.80**	
Skylight, electric vent, curb mount, tempered Low-E, 26-1/4 x 38-1/4	EA		$803.00	$803.00	**$963.60**	
Skylight, electric vent, curb mount, tempered Low-E, 26-1/4 x 50-1/4	EA		$843.00	$843.00	**$1,011.60**	
Skylight, electric vent, curb mount, tempered Low-E, 34-1/4 x 34-1/4	EA		$857.00	$857.00	**$1,028.40**	
Skylight, electric vent, curb mount, tempered Low-E, 34-1/4 x 50-1/4	EA		$906.00	$906.00	**$1,087.20**	
Skylight, electric vent, curb mount, tempered Low-E, 38-1/4 x 38-1/4	EA		$885.00	$885.00	**$1,062.00**	
Skylight, electric vent, curb mount, tempered Low-E, 50-1/4 x 50-1/4	EA		$1,035.00	$1,035.00	**$1,242.00**	
Skylight, electric vent, curb mount, laminated Low-E, 26-1/4 x 26-1/4	EA		$732.00	$732.00	**$878.40**	
Skylight, electric vent, curb mount, laminated Low-E, 26-1/4 x 38-1/4	EA		$849.00	$849.00	**$1,018.80**	
Skylight, electric vent, curb mount, laminated Low-E, 26-1/4 x 50-1/4	EA		$889.00	$889.00	**$1,066.80**	
Skylight, electric vent, curb mount, laminated Low-E, 34-1/4 x 34-1/4	EA		$903.00	$903.00	**$1,083.60**	
Skylight, electric vent, curb mount, laminated Low-E, 34-1/4 x 50-1/4	EA		$961.00	$961.00	**$1,153.20**	
Skylight, electric vent, curb mount, laminated Low-E, 38-1/4 x 38-1/4	EA		$949.00	$949.00	**$1,138.80**	
Skylight, electric vent, curb mount, laminated Low-E, 50-1/4 x 50-1/4	EA		$1,110.00	$1,110.00	**$1,332.00**	
Blinds, electric, for electric vent skylight size 26-1/4 x 26-1/4	EA		$318.00	$318.00	**$381.60**	
Blinds, electric, for electric vent skylight size 26-1/4 x 38-1/4	EA		$324.00	$324.00	**$388.80**	
Blinds, electric, for electric vent skylight size 26-1/4 x 50-1/4	EA		$329.00	$329.00	**$394.80**	
Blinds, electric, for electric vent skylight size 34-1/4 x 34-1/4	EA		$342.00	$342.00	**$410.40**	
Blinds, electric, for electric vent skylight size 34-1/4 x 50-1/4	EA		$353.00	$353.00	**$423.60**	
Blinds, electric, for electric vent skylight size 38-1/4 x 38-1/4	EA		$347.00	$347.00	**$416.40**	
Blinds, electric, for electric vent skylight size 50-1/4 x 50-1/4	EA		$375.00	$375.00	**$450.00**	

Skylights

Deck Mount Skylight, Flashing Not Included

> Material Costs only. Select labor item from 'Labor Costs for Skylights' section.

Description	Unit	Direct Labor	Direct Materials	Direct Total	Selling Price	Man-hours
DECK MOUNTED SKYLIGHTS, FIXED						
Skylight, fixed, deck mount, tempered Low-E glass, 15-1/4 x 46-1/4	EA		$162.00	$162.00	**$194.40**	
Skylight, fixed, deck mount, tempered Low-E glass, 21-1/2 x 27-3/8	EA		$141.00	$141.00	**$169.20**	
Skylight, fixed, deck mount, tempered Low-E glass, 21-1/2 x 38-3/8	EA		$168.00	$168.00	**$201.60**	
Skylight, fixed, deck mount, tempered Low-E glass, 21-1/2 x 46-1/4	EA		$190.00	$190.00	**$228.00**	
Skylight, fixed, deck mount, tempered Low-E glass, 21-1/2 x 54-15/16	EA		$209.00	$209.00	**$250.80**	
Skylight, fixed, deck mount, tempered Low-E glass, 21-1/2 x 70-3/4	EA		$280.00	$280.00	**$336.00**	
Skylight, fixed, deck mount, tempered Low-E glass, 30-9/16 x 30-1/2	EA		$175.00	$175.00	**$210.00**	
Skylight, fixed, deck mount, tempered Low-E glass, 30-9/16 x 38-3/8	EA		$194.00	$194.00	**$232.80**	
Skylight, fixed, deck mount, tempered Low-E glass, 30-9/16 x 46-1/4	EA		$226.00	$226.00	**$271.20**	
Skylight, fixed, deck mount, tempered Low-E glass, 30-9/16 x 54-15/16	EA		$252.00	$252.00	**$302.40**	
Skylight, fixed, deck mount, tempered Low-E glass, 44-3/4 x 27-3/8	EA		$212.00	$212.00	**$254.40**	
Skylight, fixed, deck mount, tempered Low-E glass, 44-3/4 x 46-1/4	EA		$282.00	$282.00	**$338.40**	
Skylight, fixed, deck mount, laminated Low-E glass, 15-1/4 x 46-1/4	EA		$195.00	$195.00	**$234.00**	
Skylight, fixed, deck mount, laminated Low-E glass, 21-1/2 x 27-3/8	EA		$159.00	$159.00	**$190.80**	
Skylight, fixed, deck mount, laminated Low-E glass, 21-1/2 x 38-3/8	EA		$202.00	$202.00	**$242.40**	
Skylight, fixed, deck mount, laminated Low-E glass, 21-1/2 x 46-1/4	EA		$226.00	$226.00	**$271.20**	
Skylight, fixed, deck mount, laminated Low-E glass, 21-1/2 x 54-15/16	EA		$244.00	$244.00	**$292.80**	
Skylight, fixed, deck mount, laminated Low-E glass, 21-1/2 x 70-3/4	EA		$310.00	$310.00	**$372.00**	
Skylight, fixed, deck mount, laminated Low-E glass, 30-9/16 x 30-1/2	EA		$213.00	$213.00	**$255.60**	
Skylight, fixed, deck mount, laminated Low-E glass, 30-9/16 x 38-3/8	EA		$240.00	$240.00	**$288.00**	
Skylight, fixed, deck mount, laminated Low-E glass, 30-9/16 x 46-1/4	EA		$273.00	$273.00	**$327.60**	
Skylight, fixed, deck mount, laminated Low-E glass, 30-9/16 x 54-15/16	EA		$306.00	$306.00	**$367.20**	
Skylight, fixed, deck mount, laminated Low-E glass, 44-3/4 x 27-3/8	EA		$253.00	$253.00	**$303.60**	
Skylight, fixed, deck mount, laminated Low-E glass, 44-3/4 x 46-1/4	EA		$353.00	$353.00	**$423.60**	
Blinds, manual, for fixed lite skylight size 21-1/2 x 27-3/8	EA		$106.00	$106.00	**$127.20**	
Blinds, manual, for fixed lite skylight size 21-1/2 x 38-3/8	EA		$119.00	$119.00	**$142.80**	
Blinds, manual, for fixed lite skylight size 21-1/2 x 46-1/4	EA		$123.00	$123.00	**$147.60**	
Blinds, manual, for fixed lite skylight size 21-1/2 x 54-15/16	EA		$136.00	$136.00	**$163.20**	
Blinds, manual, for fixed lite skylight size 21-1/2 x 70-3/4	EA		$149.00	$149.00	**$178.80**	
Blinds, manual, for fixed lite skylight size 30-9/16 x 30-1/2	EA		$128.00	$128.00	**$153.60**	
Blinds, manual, for fixed lite skylight size 30-9/16 x 38-3/8	EA		$130.00	$130.00	**$156.00**	
Blinds, manual, for fixed lite skylight size 30-9/16 x 46-1/4	EA		$136.00	$136.00	**$163.20**	
Blinds, manual, for fixed lite skylight size 30-9/16 x 54-15/16	EA		$149.00	$149.00	**$178.80**	
Blinds, manual, for fixed lite skylight size 44-3/4 x 27-3/8	EA		$136.00	$136.00	**$163.20**	
Blinds, manual, for fixed lite skylight size 44-3/4 x 46-1/4	EA		$159.00	$159.00	**$190.80**	

Skylights

Deck Mount Skylight, Flashing Not Included

> Material Costs only. Select labor item from 'Labor Costs for Skylights' section.

Description	Unit	Direct Labor	Direct Materials	Direct Total	Selling Price	Man-hours
DECK MOUNTED SKYLIGHTS, MANUAL VENT						
Skylight, manual vent, deck mount, tempered Low-E, 21-1/2 x 27-3/8	EA		$320.00	$320.00	**$384.00**	
Skylight, manual vent, deck mount, tempered Low-E, 21-1/2 x 38-3/8	EA		$347.00	$347.00	**$416.40**	
Skylight, manual vent, deck mount, tempered Low-E, 21-1/2 x 46-1/4	EA		$377.00	$377.00	**$452.40**	
Skylight, manual vent, deck mount, tempered Low-E, 21-1/2 x 54-15/16	EA		$410.00	$410.00	**$492.00**	
Skylight, manual vent, deck mount, tempered Low-E, 30-9/16 x 38-3/8	EA		$380.00	$380.00	**$456.00**	
Skylight, manual vent, deck mount, tempered Low-E, 30-9/16 x 46-1/4	EA		$409.00	$409.00	**$490.80**	
Skylight, manual vent, deck mount, tempered Low-E, 30-9/16 x 54-15/16	EA		$458.00	$458.00	**$549.60**	
Skylight, manual vent, deck mount, tempered Low-E, 44-3/4 x 27-3/8	EA		$424.00	$424.00	**$508.80**	
Skylight, manual vent, deck mount, tempered Low-E, 44-3/4 x 46-1/4	EA		$510.00	$510.00	**$612.00**	
Skylight, manual vent, deck mount, laminated Low-E, 21-1/2 x 27-3/8	EA		$338.00	$338.00	**$405.60**	
Skylight, manual vent, deck mount, laminated Low-E, 21-1/2 x 38-3/8	EA		$376.00	$376.00	**$451.20**	
Skylight, manual vent, deck mount, laminated Low-E, 21-1/2 x 46-1/4	EA		$409.00	$409.00	**$490.80**	
Skylight, manual vent, deck mount, laminated Low-E, 21-1/2 x 54-15/16	EA		$433.00	$433.00	**$519.60**	
Skylight, manual vent, deck mount, laminated Low-E, 30-9/16 x 38-3/8	EA		$430.00	$430.00	**$516.00**	
Skylight, manual vent, deck mount, laminated Low-E, 30-9/16 x 46-1/4	EA		$468.00	$468.00	**$561.60**	
Skylight, manual vent, deck mount, laminated Low-E, 30-9/16 x 54-15/16	EA		$516.00	$516.00	**$619.20**	
Skylight, manual vent, deck mount, laminated Low-E, 44-3/4 x 27-3/8	EA		$454.00	$454.00	**$544.80**	
Skylight, manual vent, deck mount, laminated Low-E, 44-3/4 x 46-1/4	EA		$573.00	$573.00	**$687.60**	
Blinds, manual, for manual vent skylight size 21-1/2 x 27-3/8	EA		$106.00	$106.00	**$127.20**	
Blinds, manual, for manual vent skylight size 21-1/2 x 38-3/8	EA		$119.00	$119.00	**$142.80**	
Blinds, manual, for manual vent skylight size 21-1/2 x 46-1/4	EA		$123.00	$123.00	**$147.60**	
Blinds, manual, for manual vent skylight size 21-1/2 x 54-15/16	EA		$136.00	$136.00	**$163.20**	
Blinds, manual, for manual vent skylight size 30-9/16 x 38-3/8	EA		$130.00	$130.00	**$156.00**	
Blinds, manual, for manual vent skylight size 30-9/16 x 46-1/4	EA		$136.00	$136.00	**$163.20**	
Blinds, manual, for manual vent skylight size 30-9/16 x 54-15/16	EA		$149.00	$149.00	**$178.80**	
Blinds, manual, for manual vent skylight size 44-3/4 x 27-3/8	EA		$136.00	$136.00	**$163.20**	
Blinds, manual, for manual vent skylight size 44-3/4 x 46-1/4	EA		$159.00	$159.00	**$190.80**	

Skylights

Deck Mount Skylight, Flashing Not Included > Material Costs only. Select labor item from 'Labor Costs for Skylights' section.

Description	Unit	Direct Labor	Direct Materials	Direct Total	Selling Price	Man-hours
DECK MOUNTED SKYLIGHTS, ELECTRIC VENT						
Skylight, electric vent, deck mount, tempered Low-E, 21-1/2 x 27-3/8	EA		$641.00	$641.00	**$769.20**	
Skylight, electric vent, deck mount, tempered Low-E, 21-1/2 x 38-3/8	EA		$692.00	$692.00	**$830.40**	
Skylight, electric vent, deck mount, tempered Low-E, 21-1/2 x 46-1/4	EA		$740.00	$740.00	**$888.00**	
Skylight, electric vent, deck mount, tempered Low-E, 21-1/2 x 54-15/16	EA		$786.00	$786.00	**$943.20**	
Skylight, electric vent, deck mount, tempered Low-E, 30-9/16 x 38-3/8	EA		$760.00	$760.00	**$912.00**	
Skylight, electric vent, deck mount, tempered Low-E, 30-9/16 x 46-1/4	EA		$784.00	$784.00	**$940.80**	
Skylight, electric vent, deck mount, tempered Low-E, 30-9/16 x 54-15/16	EA		$837.00	$837.00	**$1,004.40**	
Skylight, electric vent, deck mount, tempered Low-E, 44-3/4 x 27-3/8	EA		$791.00	$791.00	**$949.20**	
Skylight, electric vent, deck mount, tempered Low-E, 44-3/4 x 46-1/4	EA		$902.00	$902.00	**$1,082.40**	
Skylight, electric vent, deck mount, laminated Low-E, 21-1/2 x 27-3/8	EA		$668.00	$668.00	**$801.60**	
Skylight, electric vent, deck mount, laminated Low-E, 21-1/2 x 38-3/8	EA		$721.00	$721.00	**$865.20**	
Skylight, electric vent, deck mount, laminated Low-E, 21-1/2 x 46-1/4	EA		$776.00	$776.00	**$931.20**	
Skylight, electric vent, deck mount, laminated Low-E, 21-1/2 x 54-15/16	EA		$821.00	$821.00	**$985.20**	
Skylight, electric vent, deck mount, laminated Low-E, 30-9/16 x 38-3/8	EA		$806.00	$806.00	**$967.20**	
Skylight, electric vent, deck mount, laminated Low-E, 30-9/16 x 46-1/4	EA		$848.00	$848.00	**$1,017.60**	
Skylight, electric vent, deck mount, laminated Low-E, 30-9/16 x 54-15/16	EA		$899.00	$899.00	**$1,078.80**	
Skylight, electric vent, deck mount, laminated Low-E, 44-3/4 x 27-3/8	EA		$855.00	$855.00	**$1,026.00**	
Skylight, electric vent, deck mount, laminated Low-E, 44-3/4 x 46-1/4	EA		$983.00	$983.00	**$1,179.60**	
Blinds, electric, for electric vent skylight size 21-1/2 x 27-3/8	EA		$273.00	$273.00	**$327.60**	
Blinds, electric, for electric vent skylight size 21-1/2 x 38-3/8	EA		$282.00	$282.00	**$338.40**	
Blinds, electric, for electric vent skylight size 21-1/2 x 46-1/4	EA		$287.00	$287.00	**$344.40**	
Blinds, electric, for electric vent skylight size 21-1/2 x 54-15/16	EA		$299.00	$299.00	**$358.80**	
Blinds, electric, for electric vent skylight size 30-9/16 x 38-3/8	EA		$293.00	$293.00	**$351.60**	
Blinds, electric, for electric vent skylight size 30-9/16 x 46-1/4	EA		$299.00	$299.00	**$358.80**	
Blinds, electric, for electric vent skylight size 30-9/16 x 54-15/16	EA		$312.00	$312.00	**$374.40**	
Blinds, electric, for electric vent skylight size 44-3/4 x 27-3/8	EA		$299.00	$299.00	**$358.80**	
Blinds, electric, for electric vent skylight size 44-3/4 x 46-1/4	EA		$320.00	$320.00	**$384.00**	

Skylights

Deck Mount Skylight Flashing Kits

> Material Costs only. Select labor item from 'Labor Costs for Skylights' section.

Description	Unit	Direct Labor	Direct Materials	Direct Total	Selling Price	Man-hours
Flashing system, step flashing, 15-1/4 x 46-1/4	EA		$56.00	$56.00	**$67.20**	
Flashing system, step flashing, 21-1/2 x 27-3/8	EA		$60.00	$60.00	**$72.00**	
Flashing system, step flashing, 21-1/2 x 38-3/8	EA		$60.00	$60.00	**$72.00**	
Flashing system, step flashing, 21-1/2 x 46-1/4	EA		$60.00	$60.00	**$72.00**	
Flashing system, step flashing, 21-1/2 x 54-15/16	EA		$73.00	$73.00	**$87.60**	
Flashing system, step flashing, 21-1/2 x 70-3/4	EA		$73.00	$73.00	**$87.60**	
Flashing system, step flashing, 30-9/16 x 30-1/2	EA		$66.00	$66.00	**$79.20**	
Flashing system, step flashing, 30-9/16 x 38-3/8	EA		$66.00	$66.00	**$79.20**	
Flashing system, step flashing, 30-9/16 x 46-1/4	EA		$66.00	$66.00	**$79.20**	
Flashing system, step flashing, 30-9/16 x 54-15/16	EA		$66.00	$66.00	**$79.20**	
Flashing system, step flashing, 44-3/4 x 27-3/8	EA		$73.00	$73.00	**$87.60**	
Flashing system, step flashing, 44-3/4 x 46-1/4	EA		$73.00	$73.00	**$87.60**	
Flashing system, copper step flashing, 15-1/4 x 46-1/4	EA		$112.00	$112.00	**$134.40**	
Flashing system, copper step flashing, 21-1/2 x 27-3/8	EA		$121.00	$121.00	**$145.20**	
Flashing system, copper step flashing, 21-1/2 x 38-3/8	EA		$121.00	$121.00	**$145.20**	
Flashing system, copper step flashing, 21-1/2 x 46-1/4	EA		$121.00	$121.00	**$145.20**	
Flashing system, copper step flashing, 21-1/2 x 54-15/16	EA		$146.00	$146.00	**$175.20**	
Flashing system, copper step flashing, 21-1/2 x 70-3/4	EA		$146.00	$146.00	**$175.20**	
Flashing system, copper step flashing, 30-9/16 x 30-1/2	EA		$132.00	$132.00	**$158.40**	
Flashing system, copper step flashing, 30-9/16 x 38-3/8	EA		$132.00	$132.00	**$158.40**	
Flashing system, copper step flashing, 30-9/16 x 46-1/4	EA		$132.00	$132.00	**$158.40**	
Flashing system, copper step flashing, 30-9/16 x 54-15/16	EA		$132.00	$132.00	**$158.40**	
Flashing system, copper step flashing, 44-3/4 x 27-3/8	EA		$146.00	$146.00	**$175.20**	
Flashing system, copper step flashing, 44-3/4 x 46-1/4	EA		$146.00	$146.00	**$175.20**	

Skylights

Deck Mount Skylight Flashing Kits

> Material Costs only. Select labor item from 'Labor Costs for Skylights' section.

Description	Unit	Direct Labor	Direct Materials	Direct Total	Selling Price	Man-hours
Flashing system, metal roof flashing, 15-1/4 x 46-1/4	EA		$177.00	$177.00	**$212.40**	
Flashing system, metal roof flashing, 21-1/2 x 27-3/8	EA		$177.00	$177.00	**$212.40**	
Flashing system, metal roof flashing, 21-1/2 x 38-3/8	EA		$189.00	$189.00	**$226.80**	
Flashing system, metal roof flashing, 21-1/2 x 46-1/4	EA		$197.00	$197.00	**$236.40**	
Flashing system, metal roof flashing, 21-1/2 x 54-15/16	EA		$209.00	$209.00	**$250.80**	
Flashing system, metal roof flashing, 21-1/2 x 70-3/4	EA		$228.00	$228.00	**$273.60**	
Flashing system, metal roof flashing, 30-9/16 x 30-1/2	EA		$205.00	$205.00	**$246.00**	
Flashing system, metal roof flashing, 30-9/16 x 38-3/8	EA		$206.00	$206.00	**$247.20**	
Flashing system, metal roof flashing, 30-9/16 x 46-1/4	EA		$215.00	$215.00	**$258.00**	
Flashing system, metal roof flashing, 30-9/16 x 54-15/16	EA		$223.00	$223.00	**$267.60**	
Flashing system, metal roof flashing, 44-3/4 x 27-3/8	EA		$222.00	$222.00	**$266.40**	
Flashing system, metal roof flashing, 44-3/4 x 46-1/4	EA		$239.00	$239.00	**$286.80**	
Roof curb kit, 15-1/4 x 46-1/4	EA		$254.00	$254.00	**$304.80**	
Roof curb kit, 21-1/2 x 27-3/8	EA		$254.00	$254.00	**$304.80**	
Roof curb kit, 21-1/2 x 38-3/8	EA		$278.00	$278.00	**$333.60**	
Roof curb kit, 21-1/2 x 46-1/4	EA		$297.00	$297.00	**$356.40**	
Roof curb kit, 21-1/2 x 54-15/16	EA		$316.00	$316.00	**$379.20**	
Roof curb kit, 21-1/2 x 70-3/4	EA		$385.00	$385.00	**$462.00**	
Roof curb kit, 30-9/16 x 30-1/2	EA		$295.00	$295.00	**$354.00**	
Roof curb kit, 30-9/16 x 38-3/8	EA		$297.00	$297.00	**$356.40**	
Roof curb kit, 30-9/16 x 46-1/4	EA		$319.00	$319.00	**$382.80**	
Roof curb kit, 30-9/16 x 54-15/16	EA		$338.00	$338.00	**$405.60**	
Roof curb kit, 44-3/4 x 27-3/8	EA		$300.00	$300.00	**$360.00**	
Roof curb kit, 44-3/4 x 46-1/4	EA		$349.00	$349.00	**$418.80**	

Decks and Porches

Deck Framing

Description	Unit	Direct Labor	Direct Materials	Direct Total	Selling Price	Man-hours
POSTS						
Install pressure treated posts, 4 x 4, 8' tall, in concrete	EA	$38.06	$33.36	$71.41	**$119.26**	0.500
Install pressure treated posts, 6 x 6, 8' tall, in concrete	EA	$57.09	$46.70	$103.79	**$173.32**	0.750
Install cedar posts, 4 x 4, 8' tall, in concrete	EA	$38.06	$28.76	$66.82	**$111.59**	0.500
Install cedar posts, 6 x 6, 8' tall, in concrete	EA	$57.09	$60.55	$117.64	**$196.46**	0.750
Install redwood posts, 4 x 4, 8' tall, in concrete	EA	$38.06	$26.96	$65.02	**$108.59**	0.500
Install redwood posts, 6 x 6, 8' tall, in concrete	EA	$57.09	$51.36	$108.45	**$181.11**	0.750
JOISTS						
Install joists, pres. treated, doubled all sides, 2x6, 16"oc, up to 50 SF	SF	$4.11	$2.34	$6.45	**$10.77**	0.054
Install joists, pres. treated, doubled all sides, 2x6, 16"oc, up to 80 SF	SF	$3.35	$1.82	$5.17	**$8.63**	0.044
Install joists, pres. treated, doubled all sides, 2x6, 16"oc, up to 120 SF	SF	$2.97	$1.53	$4.50	**$7.51**	0.039
Install joists, pres. treated, doubled all sides, 2x6, 16"oc, up to 180 SF	SF	$2.66	$1.34	$4.00	**$6.68**	0.035
Install joists, pres. treated, doubled all sides, 2x6, 16"oc, over 180 SF	SF	$2.59	$1.29	$3.88	**$6.48**	0.034
Install joists, pres. treated, doubled all sides, 2x8, 16"oc, up to 50 SF	SF	$4.34	$2.57	$6.91	**$11.54**	0.057
Install joists, pres. treated, doubled all sides, 2x8, 16"oc, up to 80 SF	SF	$3.50	$2.00	$5.50	**$9.19**	0.046
Install joists, pres. treated, doubled all sides, 2x8, 16"oc, up to 120 SF	SF	$3.12	$1.68	$4.80	**$8.02**	0.041
Install joists, pres. treated, doubled all sides, 2x8, 16"oc, up to 180 SF	SF	$2.82	$1.47	$4.29	**$7.16**	0.037
Install joists, pres. treated, doubled all sides, 2x8, 16"oc, over 180 SF	SF	$2.74	$1.42	$4.16	**$6.95**	0.036
Install joists, pres. treated, doubled all sides, 2x10, 16"oc, up to 50 SF	SF	$4.57	$3.04	$7.61	**$12.70**	0.060
Install joists, pres. treated, doubled all sides, 2x10, 16"oc, up to 80 SF	SF	$3.73	$2.36	$6.09	**$10.18**	0.049
Install joists, pres. treated, doubled all sides, 2x10, 16"oc, up to 120 SF	SF	$3.20	$1.99	$5.18	**$8.66**	0.042
Install joists, pres. treated, doubled all sides, 2x10, 16"oc, up to 180 SF	SF	$2.89	$1.74	$4.63	**$7.73**	0.038
Install joists, pres. treated, doubled all sides, 2x10, 16"oc, over 180 SF	SF	$2.82	$1.68	$4.50	**$7.51**	0.037
Install joists, pres. treated, doubled all sides, 2x12, 16"oc, up to 50 SF	SF	$4.80	$3.98	$8.77	**$14.65**	0.063
Install joists, pres. treated, doubled all sides, 2x12, 16"oc, up to 80 SF	SF	$3.88	$3.09	$6.97	**$11.64**	0.051
Install joists, pres. treated, doubled all sides, 2x12, 16"oc, up to 120 SF	SF	$3.35	$2.60	$5.95	**$9.93**	0.044
Install joists, pres. treated, doubled all sides, 2x12, 16"oc, up to 180 SF	SF	$3.04	$2.27	$5.32	**$8.88**	0.040
Install joists, pres. treated, doubled all sides, 2x12, 16"oc, over 180 SF	SF	$2.97	$2.20	$5.17	**$8.63**	0.039
DECK BAND						
Install deck band, cedar, 1 x 10	LF	$2.59	$2.65	$5.24	**$8.75**	0.034
Install deck band, cedar, 1 x 12	LF	$2.59	$3.41	$5.99	**$10.01**	0.034
Install deck band, redwood, 1 x 10	LF	$2.59	$2.57	$5.16	**$8.61**	0.034
Install deck band, redwood, 1 x 12	LF	$2.59	$3.21	$5.80	**$9.68**	0.034

18

Decks and Porches

Deck Surface

Description	Unit	Direct Labor	Direct Materials	Direct Total	Selling Price	Man-hours
DECK SURFACE, NAILED						
Install deck surface, pressure treated, 5/4 x 6, straight, nailed	SF	$2.13	$2.79	$4.92	**$8.22**	0.028
Install deck surface, pressure treated, 2 x 6, straight, nailed	SF	$2.28	$3.17	$5.45	**$9.11**	0.030
Install deck surface, pressure treated, 5/4 x 6, diagonal, nailed	SF	$2.66	$3.54	$6.21	**$10.37**	0.035
Install deck surface, pressure treated, 2 x 6, diagonal, nailed	SF	$2.89	$4.00	$6.90	**$11.51**	0.038
Install deck surface, cedar, 5/4 x 6, straight, nailed	SF	$2.13	$4.11	$6.24	**$10.42**	0.028
Install deck surface, cedar, 2 x 6, straight, nailed	SF	$2.28	$4.66	$6.94	**$11.59**	0.030
Install deck surface, cedar, 5/4 x 6, diagonal, nailed	SF	$2.66	$5.21	$7.88	**$13.15**	0.035
Install deck surface, cedar, 2 x 6, diagonal, nailed	SF	$2.89	$5.89	$8.78	**$14.66**	0.038
Install deck surface, redwood, 5/4 x 6, straight, nailed	SF	$2.13	$4.13	$6.26	**$10.46**	0.028
Install deck surface, redwood, 2 x 6, straight, nailed	SF	$2.28	$4.68	$6.97	**$11.64**	0.030
Install deck surface, redwood, 5/4 x 6, diagonal, nailed	SF	$2.66	$5.24	$7.90	**$13.20**	0.035
Install deck surface, redwood, 2 x 6, diagonal, nailed	SF	$2.89	$5.92	$8.81	**$14.71**	0.038
DECK SURFACE, SCREWED						
Install deck surface, pressure treated, 5/4 x 6, straight, screwed	SF	$2.74	$2.86	$5.60	**$9.35**	0.036
Install deck surface, pressure treated, 2 x 6, straight, screwed	SF	$2.89	$3.24	$6.13	**$10.23**	0.038
Install deck surface, pressure treated, 5/4 x 6, diagonal, screwed	SF	$3.35	$3.61	$6.96	**$11.62**	0.044
Install deck surface, pressure treated, 2 x 6, diagonal, screwed	SF	$3.50	$4.07	$7.57	**$12.64**	0.046
Install deck surface, cedar, 5/4 x 6, straight, screwed	SF	$2.74	$4.17	$6.91	**$11.54**	0.036
Install deck surface, cedar, 2 x 6, straight, screwed	SF	$2.89	$4.72	$7.61	**$12.71**	0.038
Install deck surface, cedar, 5/4 x 6, diagonal, screwed	SF	$3.35	$5.27	$8.62	**$14.40**	0.044
Install deck surface, cedar, 2 x 6, diagonal, screwed	SF	$3.50	$5.95	$9.45	**$15.78**	0.046
Install deck surface, redwood, 5/4 x 6, straight, screwed	SF	$2.74	$4.18	$6.92	**$11.56**	0.036
Install deck surface, redwood, 2 x 6, straight, screwed	SF	$2.89	$4.74	$7.63	**$12.74**	0.038
Install deck surface, redwood, 5/4 x 6, diagonal, screwed	SF	$3.35	$5.29	$8.64	**$14.43**	0.044
Install deck surface, redwood, 2 x 6, diagonal, screwed	SF	$3.50	$5.97	$9.47	**$15.81**	0.046

Decks and Porches

Deck Surface

Description	Unit	Direct Labor	Direct Materials	Direct Total	Selling Price	Man-hours
DECK SURFACE, CONCEALED SCREWS						
Install deck surface, pressure treated, 5/4 x 6, straight, concealed screws	SF	$4.19	$3.79	$7.98	**$13.33**	0.055
Install deck surface, pressure treated, 2 x 6, straight, concealed screws	SF	$4.34	$4.17	$8.51	**$14.21**	0.057
Install deck surface, pressure treated, 5/4 x 6, diagonal, concealed screws	SF	$4.80	$4.54	$9.34	**$15.60**	0.063
Install deck surface, pressure treated, 2 x 6, diagonal, concealed screws	SF	$4.95	$5.00	$9.95	**$16.62**	0.065
Install deck surface, cedar, 5/4 x 6, straight, concealed screws	SF	$4.19	$5.02	$9.20	**$15.37**	0.055
Install deck surface, cedar, 2 x 6, straight, concealed screws	SF	$4.34	$5.57	$9.91	**$16.54**	0.057
Install deck surface, cedar, 5/4 x 6, diagonal, concealed screws	SF	$4.80	$6.12	$10.91	**$18.23**	0.063
Install deck surface, cedar, 2 x 6, diagonal, concealed screws	SF	$4.95	$6.79	$11.74	**$19.61**	0.065
Install deck surface, redwood, 5/4 x 6, straight, concealed screws	SF	$4.19	$4.90	$9.09	**$15.17**	0.055
Install deck surface, redwood, 2 x 6, straight, concealed screws	SF	$4.34	$5.45	$9.79	**$16.35**	0.057
Install deck surface, redwood, 5/4 x 6, diagonal, concealed screws	SF	$4.80	$6.01	$10.80	**$18.04**	0.063
Install deck surface, redwood, 2 x 6, diagonal, concealed screws	SF	$4.95	$6.69	$11.64	**$19.43**	0.065

18

Decks and Porches

Deck Railing

Description	Unit	Direct Labor	Direct Materials	Direct Total	Selling Price	Man-hours
DECK RAILING, RAIL STYLE, NO PICKETS						
Install deck railing, rail style, no pickets, pres. treated, 42" tall, economy	LF	$7.99	$5.67	$13.66	**$22.82**	0.105
Install deck railing, rail style, no pickets, pres. treated, 42" tall, average	LF	$9.97	$8.82	$18.79	**$31.39**	0.131
Install deck railing, rail style, no pickets, pres. treated, 42" tall, premium	LF	$12.64	$14.72	$27.35	**$45.68**	0.166
Install deck railing, rail style, no pickets, cedar, 42" tall, economy	LF	$7.99	$8.34	$16.33	**$27.27**	0.105
Install deck railing, rail style, no pickets, cedar, 42" tall, average	LF	$9.97	$12.97	$22.94	**$38.32**	0.131
Install deck railing, rail style, no pickets, cedar, 42" tall, premium	LF	$12.64	$21.64	$34.28	**$57.24**	0.166
Install deck railing, rail style, no pickets, redwood, 42" tall, economy	LF	$7.99	$8.38	$16.37	**$27.35**	0.105
Install deck railing, rail style, no pickets, redwood, 42" tall, average	LF	$9.97	$13.04	$23.01	**$38.43**	0.131
Install deck railing, rail style, no pickets, redwood, 42" tall, premium	LF	$12.64	$21.76	$34.39	**$57.44**	0.166
DECK RAILING WITH PICKETS						
Install deck railing with pickets, pressure treated, 42" tall, economy	LF	$11.95	$8.55	$20.50	**$34.23**	0.157
Install deck railing with pickets, pressure treated, 42" tall, average	LF	$13.85	$13.82	$27.67	**$46.21**	0.182
Install deck railing with pickets, pressure treated, 42" tall, premium	LF	$17.13	$23.98	$41.11	**$68.65**	0.225
Install deck railing with pickets, cedar, 42" tall, economy	LF	$11.95	$12.57	$24.52	**$40.95**	0.157
Install deck railing with pickets, cedar, 42" tall, average	LF	$13.85	$20.32	$34.17	**$57.07**	0.182
Install deck railing with pickets, cedar, 42" tall, premium	LF	$17.13	$35.26	$52.39	**$87.49**	0.225
Install deck railing with pickets, redwood, 42" tall, economy	LF	$11.95	$12.64	$24.59	**$41.06**	0.157
Install deck railing with pickets, redwood, 42" tall, average	LF	$13.85	$20.43	$34.28	**$57.25**	0.182
Install deck railing with pickets, redwood, 42" tall, premium	LF	$17.13	$35.45	$52.58	**$87.81**	0.225

Decks and Porches

Deck Steps

Description	Unit	Direct Labor	Direct Materials	Direct Total	Selling Price	Man-hours
Install pressure treated step with open risers, 4' wide	EA	$38.06	$10.17	$48.23	**$80.55**	0.500
Install pressure treated step with treated risers, 4' wide	EA	$57.09	$13.26	$70.35	**$117.48**	0.750
Install cedar step with open riser, 4' wide	EA	$38.06	$12.51	$50.57	**$84.45**	0.500
Install cedar step with cedar riser, 4' wide	EA	$57.09	$16.47	$73.56	**$122.84**	0.750
Install redwood step with open riser, 4' wide	EA	$38.06	$13.63	$51.69	**$86.32**	0.500
Install redwood step with redwood riser, 4' wide	EA	$57.09	$17.75	$74.84	**$124.98**	0.750

Lattice

Description	Unit	Direct Labor	Direct Materials	Direct Total	Selling Price	Man-hours
Install fir/pine lattice, 1/4" x 1-1/4"	SF	$2.13	$0.38	$2.51	**$4.20**	0.028
Install fir/pine lattice, 1/4" x 1-5/8"	SF	$2.13	$0.42	$2.56	**$4.27**	0.028
Install fir/pine lattice, 1/4" x 2-1/2"	SF	$2.13	$0.66	$2.79	**$4.66**	0.028
Install fir/pine lattice, 1/4" x 3-1/2"	SF	$2.13	$0.81	$2.94	**$4.91**	0.028
Install redwood lattice, 5/16" x 1-1/4"	SF	$2.13	$0.41	$2.54	**$4.24**	0.028
Install redwood lattice, 5/16" x 1-5/8"	SF	$2.13	$0.45	$2.58	**$4.31**	0.028
Install redwood lattice, 5/16" x 2-1/2"	SF	$2.13	$0.66	$2.80	**$4.67**	0.028
Install redwood lattice, 5/16" x 3-1/2"	SF	$2.13	$0.80	$2.93	**$4.89**	0.028

Decks and Porches

Porches

Description	Unit	Direct Labor	Direct Materials	Direct Total	Selling Price	Man-hours
PORCH CEILING						
Install porch ceiling, pine V-joint, 1 x 6	SF	$3.73	$3.80	$7.52	**$12.57**	0.049
Install porch ceiling, redwood V-joint, 1 x 6	SF	$3.73	$7.29	$11.02	**$18.41**	0.049
Install porch ceiling, fir plywood, 3/8"	SF	$2.36	$2.15	$4.50	**$7.52**	0.031
Install porch ceiling, interlocking vinyl	SF	$2.36	$1.97	$4.33	**$7.23**	0.031
PORCH FLOORING						
Install porch flooring, pine tongue and groove, 3/4 x 4	SF	$3.58	$3.83	$7.41	**$12.37**	0.047
PORCH SCREENING						
Install aluminum screening, 2 x 4 framing	SF	$3.50	$1.49	$4.99	**$8.33**	0.046
PORCH RAILING						
Install iron porch railing, economy	LF	$12.71	$12.57	$25.28	**$42.23**	0.167
Install iron porch railing, average	LF	$12.71	$15.75	$28.46	**$47.53**	0.167
Install iron porch railing, premium	LF	$12.71	$23.60	$36.31	**$60.63**	0.167
PORCH POSTS						
Install fir/pine post, 4" x 4", with 1" x 6" wrap, 8' tall	EA	$76.12	$49.29	$125.41	**$209.43**	1.000
Install redwood post, 4" x 4", with 1" x 6" wrap, 8' tall	EA	$76.12	$94.56	$170.68	**$285.03**	1.000
Install fir/pine turned post, 4" x 4", 8' tall	EA	$76.12	$98.00	$174.12	**$290.78**	1.000
Install fir/pine turned post, 5" x 5", 8' tall	EA	$76.12	$131.00	$207.12	**$345.89**	1.000
Install fir/pine round colonial post, 8" diameter, 8' tall	EA	$228.36	$278.00	$506.36	**$845.61**	3.000
Install fir/pine round colonial post, 10" diameter, 8' tall	EA	$228.36	$334.00	$562.36	**$939.13**	3.000
Install fir/pine round colonial post, 12" diameter, 8' tall	EA	$304.47	$386.00	$690.47	**$1,153.09**	4.000
Install fir/pine round colonial post, 14" diameter, 8' tall	EA	$304.47	$494.00	$798.47	**$1,333.45**	4.000

Siding and Awnings

Beveled Wood Siding

> Includes necessary trim.

Description	Unit	Direct Labor	Direct Materials	Direct Total	Selling Price	Man-hours
BEVELED CEDAR SIDING						
Install cedar clear bevel siding, 1/2" x 4", 2-3/4" exposure	SF	$3.96	$2.47	$6.43	**$10.73**	0.052
Install cedar clear bevel siding, 1/2" x 6", 4-3/4" exposure	SF	$3.20	$2.34	$5.54	**$9.24**	0.042
Install cedar clear bevel siding, 1/2" x 8", 6-3/4" exposure	SF	$2.74	$2.09	$4.83	**$8.06**	0.036
Install cedar clear bevel siding, 3/4" x 8", 6-3/4" exposure	SF	$2.82	$2.14	$4.96	**$8.28**	0.037
Install cedar clear bevel siding, 5/8" x 10", 8-3/4" exposure	SF	$2.13	$2.12	$4.25	**$7.10**	0.028
Install cedar clear bevel siding, 3/4" x 10", 8-3/4" exposure	SF	$2.21	$2.17	$4.38	**$7.32**	0.029
Install cedar clear bevel siding, 3/4" x 12", 10-3/4" exposure	SF	$1.83	$2.07	$3.89	**$6.50**	0.024
BEVELED REDWOOD SIDING						
Install redwood clear bevel siding, 1/2" x 4", 2-3/4" exposure	SF	$3.96	$3.33	$7.29	**$12.18**	0.052
Install redwood clear bevel siding, 1/2" x 6", 4-3/4" exposure	SF	$3.20	$3.16	$6.35	**$10.61**	0.042
Install redwood clear bevel siding, 5/8" x 8", 6-3/4" exposure	SF	$2.74	$2.82	$5.56	**$9.28**	0.036
Install redwood clear bevel siding, 3/4" x 8", 6-3/4" exposure	SF	$2.82	$2.89	$5.71	**$9.53**	0.037
Install redwood clear bevel siding, 5/8" x 10", 8-3/4" exposure	SF	$2.13	$2.86	$4.99	**$8.34**	0.028
Install redwood clear bevel siding, 3/4" x 10", 8-3/4" exposure	SF	$2.21	$2.94	$5.14	**$8.59**	0.029
Install redwood clear bevel siding, 3/4" x 12", 10-3/4" exposure	SF	$1.83	$2.82	$4.64	**$7.75**	0.024

Tongue and Groove Wood Siding

> Includes necessary trim.

Description	Unit	Direct Labor	Direct Materials	Direct Total	Selling Price	Man-hours
TONGUE AND GROOVE CEDAR SIDING						
Install cedar tongue & groove clear siding, 1" x 4"	SF	$4.41	$2.62	$7.04	**$11.75**	0.058
Install cedar tongue & groove clear siding, 1" x 6"	SF	$3.58	$2.43	$6.01	**$10.04**	0.047
Install cedar tongue & groove clear siding, 1" x 8"	SF	$2.97	$2.36	$5.33	**$8.90**	0.039
Install cedar tongue & groove clear siding, 1" x 10"	SF	$2.28	$2.25	$4.54	**$7.58**	0.030
TONGUE AND GROOVE REDWOOD SIDING						
Install redwood tongue & groove clear siding, 1" x 4"	SF	$4.41	$3.51	$7.92	**$13.23**	0.058
Install redwood tongue & groove clear siding, 1" x 6"	SF	$3.58	$3.28	$6.86	**$11.45**	0.047
Install redwood tongue & groove clear siding, 1" x 8"	SF	$2.97	$3.20	$6.17	**$10.30**	0.039
Install redwood tongue & groove clear siding, 1" x 10"	SF	$2.28	$3.02	$5.31	**$8.86**	0.030
TONGUE AND GROOVE PINE/FIR SIDING						
Install pine/fir tongue & groove clear siding, 1" x 4"	SF	$4.41	$3.07	$7.49	**$12.50**	0.058
Install pine/fir tongue & groove clear siding, 1" x 6"	SF	$3.58	$2.77	$6.34	**$10.59**	0.047
Install pine/fir tongue & groove clear siding, 1" x 8"	SF	$2.97	$2.61	$5.58	**$9.31**	0.039
Install pine/fir tongue & groove clear siding, 1" x 10"	SF	$2.28	$2.46	$4.75	**$7.93**	0.030
Additional charge for work above 1 story, per SF of work above 1 story	SF	$0.23		$0.23	**$0.38**	0.003

19

Siding and Awnings

Board and Batten Wood Siding

> Includes necessary trim.

Description	Unit	Direct Labor	Direct Materials	Direct Total	Selling Price	Man-hours
BOARD AND BATTEN SIDING, CEDAR						
Install cedar board & batten siding, 1" x 8"	SF	$3.20	$1.89	$5.09	**$8.49**	0.042
Install cedar board & batten siding, 1" x 10"	SF	$2.82	$1.80	$4.62	**$7.71**	0.037
Install cedar board & batten siding, 1" x 12"	SF	$2.44	$1.71	$4.15	**$6.93**	0.032
BOARD AND BATTEN SIDING, REDWOOD						
Install redwood board & batten siding, 1" x 8"	SF	$3.20	$2.56	$5.75	**$9.61**	0.042
Install redwood board & batten siding, 1" x 10"	SF	$2.82	$2.42	$5.24	**$8.74**	0.037
Install redwood board & batten siding, 1" x 12"	SF	$2.44	$2.30	$4.74	**$7.91**	0.032
BOARD AND BATTEN SIDING, PINE/FIR						
Install pine/fir board & batten siding, 1" x 8"	SF	$3.20	$2.23	$5.43	**$9.07**	0.042
Install pine/fir board & batten siding, 1" x 10"	SF	$2.82	$2.11	$5.05	**$8.23**	0.037
Install pine/fir board & batten siding, 1" x 12"	SF	$2.44	$1.99	$4.55	**$7.38**	0.032

Wood Lap Siding

> Includes necessary trim.

Description	Unit	Direct Labor	Direct Materials	Direct Total	Selling Price	Man-hours
WOOD LAP SIDING, CEDAR						
Install cedar lap siding, 6"W, rough sawn	SF	$3.58	$1.59	$5.17	**$8.63**	0.047
Install cedar lap siding, 8"W, rough sawn	SF	$2.97	$1.43	$4.40	**$7.35**	0.039
Install cedar lap siding, 12"W, rough sawn	SF	$1.98	$1.31	$3.29	**$5.49**	0.026
Install cedar lap siding, 6"W, smooth	SF	$3.58	$1.96	$5.54	**$9.25**	0.047
Install cedar lap siding, 8"W, smooth	SF	$2.97	$1.76	$4.73	**$7.90**	0.039
Install cedar lap siding, 12"W, smooth	SF	$1.98	$1.61	$3.59	**$6.00**	0.026
WOOD LAP SIDING, REDWOOD						
Install redwood lap siding, 6"W, rough sawn	SF	$3.58	$2.16	$5.74	**$9.58**	0.047
Install redwood lap siding, 8"W, rough sawn	SF	$2.97	$1.94	$4.91	**$8.20**	0.039
Install redwood lap siding, 12"W, rough sawn	SF	$1.98	$1.77	$3.75	**$6.27**	0.026
Install redwood lap siding, 6"W, smooth	SF	$3.58	$2.66	$6.23	**$10.41**	0.047
Install redwood lap siding, 8"W, smooth	SF	$2.97	$2.39	$5.36	**$8.95**	0.039
Install redwood lap siding, 12"W, smooth	SF	$1.98	$2.18	$4.16	**$6.95**	0.026
WOOD LAP SIDING, PINE/FIR						
Install pine/fir lap siding, 6"W, rough sawn	SF	$3.58	$1.82	$5.39	**$9.01**	0.047
Install pine/fir lap siding, 8"W, rough sawn	SF	$2.97	$1.63	$4.60	**$7.69**	0.039
Install pine/fir lap siding, 12"W, rough sawn	SF	$1.98	$1.49	$3.47	**$5.80**	0.026
Install pine/fir lap siding, 6"W, smooth	SF	$3.58	$2.23	$5.81	**$9.71**	0.047
Install pine/fir lap siding, 8"W, smooth	SF	$2.97	$2.01	$4.98	**$8.32**	0.039
Install pine/fir lap siding, 12"W, smooth	SF	$1.98	$1.84	$3.82	**$6.37**	0.026
Additional charge for work above 1 story, per SF of work above 1 story	SF	$0.23		$0.23	**$0.38**	0.003

Siding and Awnings

Cedar Shake Siding

> Includes necessary trim.

Description	Unit	Direct Labor	Direct Materials	Direct Total	Selling Price	Man-hours
Install cedar shake siding, 24" long, 1/2"-3/4" thick, 8-1/2" exposure	SF	$2.82	$2.14	$4.95	**$8.27**	0.037
Install cedar shake siding, 24" long, 1/2"-3/4" thick, 10" exposure	SF	$2.59	$1.79	$4.38	**$7.31**	0.034
Install cedar shake siding, 24" long, 1/2"-3/4" thick, 11-1/2" exposure	SF	$2.36	$1.39	$3.75	**$6.27**	0.031
Install cedar shake, 24" long, 1/2"-3/4" thick, fire retardant, 8-1/2" exp	SF	$2.82	$3.21	$6.03	**$10.07**	0.037
Install cedar shake, 24" long, 1/2"-3/4" thick, fire retardant, 10" exp	SF	$2.59	$2.67	$5.26	**$8.78**	0.034
Install cedar shake, 24" long, 1/2"-3/4" thick, fire retardant, 11-1/2" exp	SF	$2.36	$2.11	$4.47	**$7.46**	0.031
Additional charge for work above 1 story, per SF of work above 1 story	SF	$0.38		$0.38	**$0.64**	0.005

Cedar Shingle Siding

> Includes necessary trim.

Description	Unit	Direct Labor	Direct Materials	Direct Total	Selling Price	Man-hours
Install cedar shingle siding, 16" long, 5" exposure	SF	$3.58	$1.86	$5.44	**$9.08**	0.047
Install cedar shingle siding, 16" long, 7-1/2" exposure	SF	$3.04	$1.62	$4.67	**$7.80**	0.040
Install cedar shingle siding, 16" long, fire retardant, 5" exp	SF	$3.58	$2.81	$6.38	**$10.66**	0.047
Install cedar shingle siding, 16" long, fire retardant, 7-1/2" exp	SF	$3.04	$2.43	$5.48	**$9.14**	0.040
Install cedar shingle siding, 18" long, #1 perfections, 5-1/2"exposure	SF	$3.35	$2.23	$5.58	**$9.32**	0.044
Install cedar shingle siding, 18" long, #1 perfections, 7-1/2"exposure	SF	$2.74	$1.64	$4.38	**$7.31**	0.036
Install cedar shingle siding, 18" long, #1 perfections, 8-1/2"exposure	SF	$2.59	$1.45	$4.04	**$6.75**	0.034
Install cedar shingle, 18" long, #1 perfections, fire retardant, 5-1/2"exp	SF	$3.35	$3.22	$6.57	**$10.96**	0.044
Install cedar shingle, 18" long, #1 perfections, fire retardant, 7-1/2"exp	SF	$2.74	$2.42	$5.16	**$8.61**	0.036
Install cedar shingle, 18" long, #1 perfections, fire retardant, 8-1/2"exp	SF	$2.59	$2.10	$4.69	**$7.83**	0.034
Install cedar shingle siding, 24" long, #1 perfections, 8-1/2"exposure	SF	$3.12	$2.57	$5.69	**$9.50**	0.041
Install cedar shingle siding, 24" long, #1 perfections, 10"exposure	SF	$2.66	$1.88	$4.54	**$7.59**	0.035
Install cedar shingle siding, 24" long, #1 perfections, 11-1/2"exposure	SF	$2.44	$1.67	$4.10	**$6.85**	0.032
Install cedar shingle, 24" long, #1 perfections, fire retardant, 8-1/2"exp	SF	$3.12	$3.70	$6.82	**$11.39**	0.041
Install cedar shingle, 24" long, #1 perfections, fire retardant, 10"exp	SF	$2.66	$2.78	$5.44	**$9.09**	0.035
Install cedar shingle, 24" long, #1 perfections, fire retardant, 11-1/2"exp	SF	$2.44	$2.42	$4.85	**$8.10**	0.032
Additional charge for work above 1 story, per SF of work above 1 story	SF	$0.38		$0.38	**$0.64**	0.005

19

Siding and Awnings

Plywood Siding

> Includes necessary trim.

Description	Unit	Direct Labor	Direct Materials	Direct Total	Selling Price	Man-hours
Install pine/fir plywood, 3/8" thick T1-11, 4' x 8'	SF	$1.45	$0.93	$2.38	**$3.97**	0.019
Install pine/fir plywood, 5/8" thick T1-11, 4' x 8'	SF	$1.60	$1.14	$2.74	**$4.57**	0.021
Install cedar plywood, 3/8" thick T1-11, 4' x 8'	SF	$1.45	$0.71	$2.16	**$3.60**	0.019
Install cedar plywood, 5/8" thick T1-11, 4' x 8'	SF	$1.60	$0.87	$2.47	**$4.13**	0.021
Install redwood plywood, 3/8" thick T1-11, 4' x 8'	SF	$1.45	$0.89	$2.34	**$3.90**	0.019
Install redwood plywood, 5/8" thick T1-11, 4' x 8'	SF	$1.60	$1.11	$2.71	**$4.52**	0.021
Additional charge for work above 1 story, per SF of work above 1 story	SF	$0.15		$0.15	**$0.25**	0.002

Hardboard Siding

> Includes necessary trim.

Description	Unit	Direct Labor	Direct Materials	Direct Total	Selling Price	Man-hours
Install hardboard siding, rough sawn/primed	SF	$1.60	$1.34	$2.94	**$4.91**	0.021
Install hardboard siding, rough sawn/prefinished	SF	$1.60	$1.55	$3.15	**$5.26**	0.021
Install hardboard siding, stucco/primed	SF	$1.60	$1.74	$3.34	**$5.57**	0.021
Install hardboard siding, stucco/prefinished	SF	$1.60	$1.90	$3.50	**$5.85**	0.021
Install hardboard strip siding, 1/2" x 12", smooth finish	SF	$1.98	$1.74	$3.72	**$6.21**	0.026
Install hardboard strip siding, 1/2" x 12", textured finish	SF	$1.98	$2.05	$4.03	**$6.72**	0.026
Install hardboard strip siding, 1/2" x 12", wood grain finish	SF	$1.98	$2.19	$4.17	**$6.96**	0.026
Additional charge for work above 1 story, per SF of work above 1 story	SF	$0.23		$0.23	**$0.38**	0.003

Fiber-Cement Siding

> Includes necessary trim.

Description	Unit	Direct Labor	Direct Materials	Direct Total	Selling Price	Man-hours
Install fiber-cement siding, 6-1/4"W, 5" exposure	SF	$3.58	$1.42	$5.00	**$8.34**	0.047
Install fiber-cement siding, 8-1/4"W, 7" exposure	SF	$2.97	$1.39	$4.36	**$7.28**	0.039
Install fiber-cement siding, 9-1/2"W, 8-1/4" exposure	SF	$2.74	$1.38	$4.12	**$6.87**	0.036
Install fiber-cement siding, 12"W, 10-3/4" exposure	SF	$2.13	$1.32	$3.45	**$5.76**	0.028
Install fiber-cement siding, 4' x 8' panels	SF	$1.60	$1.32	$2.92	**$4.87**	0.021
Additional charge for work above 1 story, per SF of work above 1 story	SF	$0.23		$0.23	**$0.38**	0.003

Siding and Awnings

Aluminum Siding

> Includes necessary trim.

Description	Unit	Direct Labor	Direct Materials	Direct Total	Selling Price	Man-hours
Install aluminum siding, 8"	SF	$2.06	$1.71	$3.76	**$6.28**	0.027
Install aluminum siding, 8" double 4	SF	$2.06	$1.76	$3.82	**$6.37**	0.027
Install aluminum siding, 10"	SF	$1.90	$1.60	$3.50	**$5.84**	0.025
Install aluminum siding, 10" double 5	SF	$1.90	$1.65	$3.55	**$5.93**	0.025
Install aluminum siding, 12" vertical board	SF	$1.75	$1.54	$3.29	**$5.50**	0.023
Additional charge for work above 1 story, per SF of work above 1 story	SF	$0.23		$0.23	**$0.38**	0.003

Vinyl Siding

> Includes necessary trim.

Description	Unit	Direct Labor	Direct Materials	Direct Total	Selling Price	Man-hours
Install vinyl siding, 8"	SF	$2.06	$1.27	$3.32	**$5.54**	0.027
Install vinyl siding, 8" double 4	SF	$2.06	$1.32	$3.38	**$5.64**	0.027
Install vinyl siding, 10"	SF	$1.90	$1.16	$3.06	**$5.11**	0.025
Install vinyl siding, 10" double 5	SF	$1.90	$1.21	$3.11	**$5.20**	0.025
Additional charge for work above 1 story, per SF of work above 1 story	SF	$0.23		$0.23	**$0.38**	0.003

Formed Resin Siding

> Includes necessary trim.

Description	Unit	Direct Labor	Direct Materials	Direct Total	Selling Price	Man-hours
Install formed resin siding panels, hand-split shake, 41-3/8" x 18-3/4"	SF	$3.35	$2.69	$6.04	**$10.08**	0.044
Install formed resin siding panels, hand-laid brick, 44-1/4" x 18-5/8"	SF	$3.35	$2.83	$6.18	**$10.32**	0.044
Install formed resin siding panels, hand-cut stone, 44-1/4" x 18-5/8"	SF	$3.35	$2.83	$6.18	**$10.32**	0.044
Install formed resin siding panels, rough sawn cedar, 59-1/4" x 15"	SF	$3.35	$2.92	$6.27	**$10.46**	0.044
Additional charge for work above 1 story, per SF of work above 1 story	SF	$0.23		$0.23	**$0.38**	0.003

Stone Veneer

> Includes necessary trim.

Description	Unit	Direct Labor	Direct Materials	Direct Total	Selling Price	Man-hours
Install stone cast panels, 48" x 1/2" x 8', on existing structure/backer	SF	$4.17	$7.47	$11.64	**$19.44**	0.063
Install natural stone veneer, on existing structure/backer	SF	$27.41	$11.13	$38.54	**$64.37**	0.414
Install manufactured stone veneer, on existing structure/backer	SF	$15.49	$7.83	$23.33	**$38.95**	0.234

19

Siding and Awnings

Stucco

> On existing backer or structure.

Description	Unit	Direct Labor	Direct Materials	Direct Total	Selling Price	Man-hours
Install galvanized netting for stucco, 18 gauge, 15 lb felt	SF	$1.26	$0.69	$1.95	**$3.25**	0.019
Install Steel-Tex mesh for stucco, 15 lb felt	SF	$0.93	$1.14	$2.07	**$3.45**	0.014
Apply stucco over exterior masonry wall, 1 coat with float finish	SF	$3.64	$0.32	$3.96	**$6.62**	0.055
Apply stucco over exterior masonry wall, 2 coat with float finish	SF	$5.96	$0.54	$6.49	**$10.85**	0.090
Apply stucco over metal netting on exterior wall, 2 coat with float finish	SF	$6.95	$0.80	$7.75	**$12.95**	0.105
Apply stucco over metal netting on exterior wall, 3 coat with float finish	SF	$9.93	$1.28	$11.22	**$18.73**	0.150
Install 1" polystyrene board on existing structure, apply synthetic stucco	SF	$10.53	$3.16	$13.68	**$22.85**	0.159
Install 2" polystyrene board on existing structure, apply synthetic stucco	SF	$10.93	$3.53	$14.46	**$24.14**	0.165
Apply synthetic stucco to exterior masonry wall	SF	$7.55	$1.61	$9.15	**$15.29**	0.114
Additional charge for work above 1 story, per SF of work above 1 story	SF	$0.40		$0.40	**$0.66**	0.006

House Wrap

Description	Unit	Direct Labor	Direct Materials	Direct Total	Selling Price	Man-hours
Install tear-proof plastic house wrap	SF	$0.23	$0.11	$0.34	**$0.57**	0.003
Install rosin coated sheathing paper	SF	$0.23	$0.02	$0.25	**$0.42**	0.003

Siding and Awnings

Awnings and Canopies

Description	Unit	Direct Labor	Direct Materials	Direct Total	Selling Price	Man-hours
DOOR CANOPY, ALUMINUM						
Install aluminum door canopy, 4' wide, 36" deep	EA	$92.56	$227.00	$319.56	**$533.67**	1.216
Install aluminum door canopy, 5' wide, 36" deep	EA	$123.39	$254.00	$377.39	**$630.24**	1.621
Install aluminum door canopy, 6' wide, 36" deep	EA	$148.05	$275.00	$423.05	**$706.49**	1.945
Install aluminum door canopy, 6' wide, 42" deep	EA	$172.71	$360.00	$532.71	**$889.63**	2.269
Install aluminum door canopy, 6' wide, 48" deep	EA	$197.38	$377.00	$574.38	**$959.21**	2.593
Install aluminum door canopy, 8' wide, 42" deep	EA	$234.37	$420.00	$654.37	**$1,092.80**	3.079
Install aluminum door canopy, 8' wide, 48" deep	EA	$271.44	$515.00	$786.44	**$1,313.35**	3.566
WINDOW AWNING, ALUMINUM						
Install aluminum window awning, 4' wide, 36" high	EA	$92.56	$76.00	$168.56	**$281.50**	1.216
Install aluminum window awning, 6' wide, 36" high	EA	$123.39	$91.00	$214.39	**$358.03**	1.621
Install aluminum window awning, 6' wide, 48" high	EA	$141.88	$116.00	$257.88	**$430.67**	1.864
Install aluminum window awning, 9' wide, 48" high	EA	$209.71	$157.00	$366.71	**$612.40**	2.755
WINDOW AWNING, FABRIC						
Install waterproof fabric window awning, 3' wide, 30" high, tube frame	EA	$61.66	$75.00	$136.66	**$228.22**	0.810
Install waterproof fabric window awning, 4' wide, 30" high, tube frame	EA	$73.99	$90.00	$163.99	**$273.86**	0.972
Install waterproof fabric window awning, 5' wide, 30" high, tube frame	EA	$92.56	$103.00	$195.56	**$326.59**	1.216
Install waterproof fabric window awning, 6' wide, 30" high, tube frame	EA	$111.06	$114.00	$225.06	**$375.84**	1.459
Install waterproof fabric window awning, 8' wide, 30" high, tube frame	EA	$148.05	$128.00	$276.05	**$461.00**	1.945
SECURITY AWNING, ALUMINUM						
Install aluminum roll-up security awning, 3' wide	EA	$123.39	$154.00	$277.39	**$463.24**	1.621
Install aluminum roll-up security awning, 4' wide	EA	$154.22	$198.00	$352.22	**$588.20**	2.026
Install aluminum roll-up security awning, 6' wide	EA	$185.04	$265.00	$450.04	**$751.57**	2.431
Install aluminum roll-up security awning, 9' wide	EA	$246.70	$419.00	$665.70	**$1,111.72**	3.241

Exterior Trim

Fascia and Soffit, Wood

Description	Unit	Direct Labor	Direct Materials	Direct Total	Selling Price	Man-hours
Install fir/pine fascia, 1" x 4"	LF	$3.20	$0.70	$3.90	**$6.51**	0.042
Install fir/pine fascia, 1" x 6"	LF	$3.35	$0.91	$4.26	**$7.11**	0.044
Install fir/pine fascia, 1" x 8"	LF	$3.43	$1.03	$4.46	**$7.45**	0.045
Install fir/pine fascia, 1" x 10"	LF	$3.58	$1.39	$4.96	**$8.29**	0.047
Install cedar fascia, 1" x 4"	LF	$3.20	$0.60	$3.80	**$6.34**	0.042
Install cedar fascia, 1" x 6"	LF	$3.35	$0.78	$4.13	**$6.89**	0.044
Install cedar fascia, 1" x 8"	LF	$3.43	$0.89	$4.31	**$7.20**	0.045
Install redwood fascia, 1" x 4"	LF	$3.20	$0.80	$4.00	**$6.68**	0.042
Install redwood fascia, 1" x 6"	LF	$3.35	$1.04	$4.39	**$7.33**	0.044
Install redwood fascia, 1" x 8"	LF	$3.43	$1.18	$4.61	**$7.69**	0.045
Install fir/pine soffit, 1" x 6"	LF	$3.43	$0.91	$4.34	**$7.24**	0.045
Install fir/pine soffit, 1" x 8"	LF	$3.58	$1.03	$4.61	**$7.70**	0.047
Install fir/pine soffit, 1" x 10"	LF	$3.73	$1.39	$5.12	**$8.54**	0.049
Install fir/pine soffit, 1" x 12"	LF	$3.88	$1.68	$5.56	**$9.28**	0.051
Install fir plywood soffit, 3/8" x 12"	LF	$3.73	$1.62	$5.35	**$8.93**	0.049
Install fir plywood soffit, 3/8" x 16"	LF	$3.96	$2.16	$6.11	**$10.21**	0.052
Install fir plywood soffit, 3/8" x 18"	LF	$4.19	$2.43	$6.62	**$11.05**	0.055
Install fir plywood soffit, 3/8" x 24"	LF	$4.72	$3.23	$7.95	**$13.28**	0.062
Install fir plywood soffit, 3/8" x 30"	LF	$5.40	$4.05	$9.45	**$15.79**	0.071
Install fir plywood soffit, 3/8" x 36"	LF	$6.17	$4.85	$11.02	**$18.40**	0.081

Lattice, Wood

Description	Unit	Direct Labor	Direct Materials	Direct Total	Selling Price	Man-hours
Install fir/pine lattice, 1/4" x 1-1/4"	SF	$2.13	$0.38	$2.51	**$4.20**	0.028
Install fir/pine lattice, 1/4" x 1-5/8"	SF	$2.13	$0.42	$2.56	**$4.27**	0.028
Install fir/pine lattice, 1/4" x 2-1/2"	SF	$2.13	$0.66	$2.79	**$4.66**	0.028
Install fir/pine lattice, 1/4" x 3-1/2"	SF	$2.13	$0.81	$2.94	**$4.91**	0.028
Install redwood lattice, 5/16" x 1-1/4"	SF	$2.13	$0.34	$2.47	**$4.13**	0.028
Install redwood lattice, 5/16" x 1-5/8"	SF	$2.13	$0.38	$2.51	**$4.19**	0.028
Install redwood lattice, 5/16" x 2-1/2"	SF	$2.13	$0.59	$2.72	**$4.54**	0.028
Install redwood lattice, 5/16" x 3-1/2"	SF	$2.13	$0.72	$2.85	**$4.76**	0.028

20

Exterior Trim

Exterior Trim, Aluminum and Vinyl

Description	Unit	Direct Labor	Direct Materials	Direct Total	Selling Price	Man-hours
Wrap small window with aluminum	EA	$38.06	$8.78	$46.84	**$78.22**	0.500
Wrap medium window with aluminum	EA	$63.18	$11.91	$75.09	**$125.40**	0.830
Wrap large window with aluminum	EA	$76.12	$15.05	$91.17	**$152.25**	1.000
Wrap single door with aluminum	EA	$63.18	$10.34	$73.52	**$122.78**	0.830
Install vinyl fascia, 4"	LF	$1.90	$0.99	$2.89	**$4.83**	0.025
Install vinyl fascia, 6"	LF	$2.06	$1.18	$3.23	**$5.40**	0.027
Install vinyl fascia, 8"	LF	$2.21	$1.36	$3.57	**$5.96**	0.029
Install vinyl soffit, 8"	LF	$2.74	$2.00	$4.74	**$7.92**	0.036
Install vinyl soffit, 12"	LF	$2.82	$2.83	$5.64	**$9.42**	0.037
Install vinyl soffit, 18"	LF	$2.97	$3.23	$6.20	**$10.36**	0.039
Install vinyl soffit, 24"	LF	$3.04	$3.64	$6.69	**$11.17**	0.040
Install aluminum fascia, 4"	LF	$1.90	$0.88	$2.78	**$4.65**	0.025
Install aluminum fascia, 6"	LF	$2.06	$1.07	$3.12	**$5.21**	0.027
Install aluminum fascia, 8"	LF	$2.21	$1.25	$3.46	**$5.78**	0.029
Install aluminum soffit, 8"	LF	$2.74	$1.69	$4.43	**$7.41**	0.036
Install aluminum soffit, 12"	LF	$2.82	$2.43	$5.25	**$8.76**	0.037
Install aluminum soffit, 18"	LF	$2.97	$3.21	$6.18	**$10.32**	0.039
Install aluminum soffit, 24"	LF	$3.04	$3.93	$6.97	**$11.64**	0.040

Wood Posts

Description	Unit	Direct Labor	Direct Materials	Direct Total	Selling Price	Man-hours
Install fir/pine post, 4" x 4", with 1" x 6" wrap, 8' tall	EA	$76.12	$49.29	$125.41	**$209.43**	1.000
Install redwood post, 4" x 4", with 1" x 6" wrap, 8' tall	EA	$76.12	$94.56	$170.68	**$285.03**	1.000
Install fir/pine turned post, 4" x 4", 8' tall	EA	$76.12	$98.00	$174.12	**$290.78**	1.000
Install fir/pine turned post, 5" x 5", 8' tall	EA	$76.12	$131.00	$207.12	**$345.89**	1.000
Install fir/pine round colonial post, 8" diameter, 8' tall	EA	$228.36	$278.00	$506.36	**$845.61**	3.000
Install fir/pine round colonial post, 10" diameter, 8' tall	EA	$228.36	$334.00	$562.36	**$939.13**	3.000
Install fir/pine round colonial post, 12" diameter, 8' tall	EA	$304.47	$386.00	$690.47	**$1,153.09**	4.000
Install fir/pine round colonial post, 14" diameter, 8' tall	EA	$304.47	$494.00	$798.47	**$1,333.45**	4.000

Exterior Trim

Non-Wood Posts

Description	Unit	Direct Labor	Direct Materials	Direct Total	Selling Price	Man-hours
Install aluminum round colonial post, 8" diameter, 8' tall	EA	$152.24	$162.00	$314.24	**$524.78**	2.000
Install aluminum round colonial post, 8" diameter, 10' tall	EA	$152.24	$191.00	$343.24	**$573.21**	2.000
Install aluminum round colonial post, 10" diameter, 8' tall	EA	$190.30	$190.00	$380.30	**$635.09**	2.500
Install aluminum round colonial post, 10" diameter, 10' tall	EA	$190.30	$223.00	$413.30	**$690.20**	2.500
Install aluminum round colonial post, 10" diameter, 16' tall	EA	$304.47	$355.00	$659.47	**$1,101.32**	4.000
Install aluminum round colonial post, 12" diameter, 8' tall	EA	$228.36	$318.00	$546.36	**$912.41**	3.000
Install aluminum round colonial post, 12" diameter, 10' tall	EA	$228.36	$366.00	$594.36	**$992.57**	3.000
Install aluminum round colonial post, 12" diameter, 16' tall	EA	$342.53	$618.00	$960.53	**$1,604.09**	4.500
Install permacast round plain post, 8" diameter, 8' tall	EA	$152.24	$147.00	$299.24	**$499.73**	2.000
Install permacast round fluted post, 8" diameter, 8' tall	EA	$152.24	$193.00	$345.24	**$576.55**	2.000
Install permacast round plain post, 10" diameter, 8' tall	EA	$190.30	$196.00	$386.30	**$645.11**	2.500
Install permacast round fluted post, 10" diameter, 8' tall	EA	$190.30	$254.00	$444.30	**$741.97**	2.500
Install permacast round plain post, 12" diameter, 8' tall	EA	$209.33	$305.00	$514.33	**$858.92**	2.750
Install permacast round fluted post, 12" diameter, 8' tall	EA	$209.33	$395.00	$604.33	**$1,009.22**	2.750

Exterior Trim

Wood Shutters

Description	Unit	Direct Labor	Direct Materials	Direct Total	Selling Price	Man-hours
WOOD SHUTTERS, RAISED PANEL						
Install fir/pine shutters with raised panels, 1'-3" wide x 6'-9" tall	Pair	$114.18	$66.00	$180.18	**$300.90**	1.500
Install fir/pine shutters with raised panels, 1'-6" wide x 6'-9" tall	Pair	$114.18	$77.00	$191.18	**$319.27**	1.500
Install fir/pine shutters with raised panels, 12" wide x 2'-1" tall	Pair	$76.12	$35.00	$111.12	**$185.57**	1.000
Install fir/pine shutters with raised panels, 12" wide x 3'-1" tall	Pair	$76.12	$37.00	$113.12	**$188.91**	1.000
Install fir/pine shutters with raised panels, 12" wide x 4'-1" tall	Pair	$76.12	$43.00	$119.12	**$198.93**	1.000
Install fir/pine shutters with raised panels, 12" wide x 5'-1" tall	Pair	$76.12	$53.00	$129.12	**$215.63**	1.000
Install fir/pine shutters with raised panels, 12" wide x 6'-1" tall	Pair	$76.12	$62.00	$138.12	**$230.66**	1.000
Install fir/pine shutters with raised panels, 18" wide x 2'-1" tall	Pair	$76.12	$42.00	$118.12	**$197.26**	1.000
Install fir/pine shutters with raised panels, 18" wide x 3' 1" tall	Pair	$76.12	$44.00	$120.12	**$200.60**	1.000
Install fir/pine shutters with raised panels, 18" wide x 4'-1" tall	Pair	$76.12	$53.00	$129.12	**$215.63**	1.000
Install fir/pine shutters with raised panels, 18" wide x 5'-1" tall	Pair	$76.12	$62.00	$138.12	**$230.66**	1.000
Install fir/pine shutters with raised panels, 18" wide x 6'-1" tall	Pair	$76.12	$74.00	$150.12	**$250.70**	1.000
WOOD SHUTTERS, FIXED SLATS						
Install fir/pine shutters with fixed slats, 1'-3" wide x 6'-9" tall	Pair	$114.18	$108.00	$222.18	**$371.04**	1.500
Install fir/pine shutters with fixed slats, 1'-6" wide x 6'-9" tall	Pair	$114.18	$127.00	$241.18	**$402.77**	1.500
Install fir/pine shutters with fixed slats, 12" wide x 2'-1" tall	Pair	$76.12	$53.00	$129.12	**$215.63**	1.000
Install fir/pine shutters with fixed slats, 12" wide x 3'-1" tall	Pair	$76.12	$56.00	$132.12	**$220.64**	1.000
Install fir/pine shutters with fixed slats, 12" wide x 4'-1" tall	Pair	$76.12	$65.00	$141.12	**$235.67**	1.000
Install fir/pine shutters with fixed slats, 12" wide x 5'-1" tall	Pair	$76.12	$79.00	$155.12	**$259.05**	1.000
Install fir/pine shutters with fixed slats, 12" wide x 6'-1" tall	Pair	$76.12	$92.00	$168.12	**$280.76**	1.000
Install fir/pine shutters with fixed slats, 18" wide x 2'-1" tall	Pair	$76.12	$63.00	$139.12	**$232.33**	1.000
Install fir/pine shutters with fixed slats, 18" wide x 3'-1" tall	Pair	$76.12	$66.00	$142.12	**$237.34**	1.000
Install fir/pine shutters with fixed slats, 18" wide x 4'-1" tall	Pair	$76.12	$79.00	$155.12	**$259.05**	1.000
Install fir/pine shutters with fixed slats, 18" wide x 5'-1" tall	Pair	$76.12	$92.00	$168.12	**$280.76**	1.000
Install fir/pine shutters with fixed slats, 18" wide x 6'-1" tall	Pair	$76.12	$111.00	$187.12	**$312.49**	1.000

Exterior Trim

Polystyrene Shutters

Description	Unit	Direct Labor	Direct Materials	Direct Total	Selling Price	Man-hours
Install molded polystyrene shutters, 12" wide x 3'-3" tall	Pair	$57.09	$30.00	$87.09	**$145.44**	0.750
Install molded polystyrene shutters, 16" wide x 3'-3" tall	Pair	$57.09	$34.00	$91.09	**$152.12**	0.750
Install molded polystyrene shutters, 18" wide x 3'-3" tall	Pair	$57.09	$36.00	$93.09	**$155.46**	0.750
Install molded polystyrene shutters, 12" wide x 4'-7" tall	Pair	$57.09	$41.00	$98.09	**$163.81**	0.750
Install molded polystyrene shutters, 16" wide x 4'-7" tall	Pair	$57.09	$46.00	$103.09	**$172.16**	0.750
Install molded polystyrene shutters, 18" wide x 4'-7" tall	Pair	$57.09	$50.00	$107.09	**$178.84**	0.750
Install molded polystyrene shutters, 16" wide x 5'-3" tall	Pair	$57.09	$50.00	$107.09	**$178.84**	0.750
Install molded polystyrene shutters, 18" wide x 5'-3" tall	Pair	$57.09	$53.00	$110.09	**$183.85**	0.750
Install molded polystyrene shutters, 16" wide x 6'-3" tall	Pair	$57.09	$54.00	$111.09	**$185.52**	0.750
Install molded polystyrene shutters, 18" wide x 6'-3" tall	Pair	$57.09	$59.00	$116.09	**$193.87**	0.750
Install molded polystyrene shutters, 16" wide x 6'-9" tall	Pair	$57.09	$58.00	$115.09	**$192.20**	0.750
Install molded polystyrene shutters, 18" wide x 6'-9" tall	Pair	$57.09	$66.00	$123.09	**$205.56**	0.750

Cupolas and Weathervanes

Description	Unit	Direct Labor	Direct Materials	Direct Total	Selling Price	Man-hours
Install redwood cupola, 24" x 24" x 25" tall	EA	$114.18	$242.00	$356.18	**$594.82**	1.500
Install redwood cupola, 30" x 30" x 30" tall	EA	$114.18	$308.00	$422.18	**$705.04**	1.500
Install redwood cupola, 35" x 35" x 33" tall	EA	$114.18	$429.00	$543.18	**$907.11**	1.500
Install aluminum weathervane, 18" tall	EA	$38.06	$55.00	$93.06	**$155.41**	0.500
Install aluminum weathervane, 24" tall	EA	$38.06	$72.00	$110.06	**$183.80**	0.500
Install aluminum weathervane, 36" tall	EA	$38.06	$110.00	$148.06	**$247.26**	0.500

Exterior Trim

Vents

Description	Unit	Direct Labor	Direct Materials	Direct Total	Selling Price	Man-hours
Install redwood louver vent, round, 24" diameter	EA	$76.12	$112.00	$188.12	**$314.16**	1.000
Install redwood louver vent, half round, 30" x 15"	EA	$76.12	$144.00	$220.12	**$367.60**	1.000
Install redwood louver vent, rectangular, 16" x 24"	EA	$76.12	$87.00	$163.12	**$272.41**	1.000
Install metal louver vent, gable, 12"	EA	$50.77	$46.00	$96.77	**$161.61**	0.667
Install metal louver vent, gable, 16"	EA	$50.77	$55.00	$105.77	**$176.64**	0.667
Install metal louver vent, gable, 20"	EA	$50.77	$66.00	$116.77	**$195.01**	0.667
Install metal louver vent, rectangular, 6" x 14"	EA	$38.06	$14.00	$52.06	**$86.94**	0.500
Install metal louver vent, rectangular, 8" x 16"	EA	$38.06	$22.00	$60.06	**$100.30**	0.500
Install metal louver vent, rectangular, 15" x 21"	EA	$50.77	$25.00	$75.77	**$126.54**	0.667
Install metal louver vent, rectangular, 24" x 30"	EA	$50.77	$37.00	$87.77	**$146.58**	0.667
Install metal louver vent, rectangular, 27" x 33"	EA	$50.77	$46.00	$96.77	**$161.61**	0.667
Install metal louver vent, round, 12" diameter	EA	$50.77	$24.00	$74.77	**$124.87**	0.667
Install metal louver vent, round, 14" diameter	EA	$50.77	$26.00	$76.77	**$128.21**	0.667
Install metal louver vent, round, 16" diameter	EA	$50.77	$28.00	$78.77	**$131.55**	0.667
Install metal louver vent, round, 18" diameter	EA	$50.77	$33.00	$83.77	**$139.90**	0.667
Install metal louver vent, round, 24" diameter	EA	$50.77	$55.00	$105.77	**$176.64**	0.667
Install metal louver vent, half round, 18" x 9"	EA	$76.12	$24.00	$100.12	**$167.20**	1.000
Install metal louver vent, half round, 24" x 12"	EA	$76.12	$32.00	$108.12	**$180.56**	1.000
Install vinyl louver vent, gable, 12"	EA	$50.77	$35.00	$85.77	**$143.24**	0.667
Install vinyl louver vent, gable, 16"	EA	$50.77	$45.00	$95.77	**$159.94**	0.667
Install vinyl louver vent, gable, 20"	EA	$50.77	$57.00	$107.77	**$179.98**	0.667
Install vinyl louver vent, rectangular, 6" x 14"	EA	$38.06	$12.00	$50.06	**$83.60**	0.500
Install vinyl louver vent, rectangular, 8" x 16"	EA	$38.06	$18.00	$56.06	**$93.62**	0.500
Install vinyl louver vent, rectangular, 15" x 21"	EA	$50.77	$22.00	$72.77	**$121.53**	0.667
Install vinyl louver vent, rectangular, 24" x 30"	EA	$50.77	$35.00	$85.77	**$143.24**	0.667
Install vinyl louver vent, rectangular, 27" x 33"	EA	$50.77	$44.00	$94.77	**$158.27**	0.667
Install soffit vent, aluminum, 1"	EA	$2.51	$0.83	$3.34	**$5.57**	0.033
Install soffit vent, aluminum, 2"	EA	$2.51	$1.65	$4.16	**$6.95**	0.033
Install soffit vent, aluminum, 3"	EA	$2.51	$2.48	$4.99	**$8.33**	0.033
Install soffit vent, aluminum, 8" x 12"	EA	$25.35	$10.40	$35.74	**$59.69**	0.333
Install foundation vent, galvanized, 6" x 14"	EA	$25.35	$3.08	$28.43	**$47.47**	0.333
Install foundation vent, galvanized, 8" x 14"	EA	$25.35	$3.52	$28.87	**$48.21**	0.333

General Plumbing

Water Heaters

Description	Unit	Direct Labor	Direct Materials	Direct Total	Selling Price	Man-hours
GAS WATER HEATERS						
Remove gas water heater	EA	$152.95		$152.95	**$255.43**	1.500
Install gas water heater, 30 gallon	EA	$407.87	$363.00	$770.87	**$1,116.74**	4.000
Install gas water heater, 40 gallon	EA	$407.87	$418.00	$825.87	**$1,182.74**	4.000
Install gas water heater, 50 gallon	EA	$458.85	$473.00	$931.85	**$1,333.88**	4.500
Install gas water heater, 75 gallon	EA	$458.85	$693.00	$1,151.85	**$1,597.88**	4.500
ELECTRIC WATER HEATERS						
Remove electric water heater	EA	$101.97		$101.97	**$170.28**	1.000
Install electric water heater, 30 gallon	EA	$280.41	$363.00	$643.41	**$903.88**	2.750
Install electric water heater, 40 gallon	EA	$280.41	$418.00	$698.41	**$969.88**	2.750
Install electric water heater, 52 gallon	EA	$305.90	$473.00	$778.90	**$1,078.45**	3.000
Install electric water heater, 82 gallon	EA	$305.90	$693.00	$998.90	**$1,342.45**	3.000

Hot Water Baseboard Heat

Description	Unit	Direct Labor	Direct Materials	Direct Total	Selling Price	Man-hours
Radiator, baseboard, 1/2" element, 8' section	EA	$305.90	$83.00	$388.90	**$610.45**	3.000
Radiator, baseboard, 3/4" element, 8' section	EA	$305.90	$135.00	$440.90	**$672.85**	3.000
Radiator, baseboard, 1/2" element, 16' section	EA	$509.84	$158.00	$667.84	**$1,041.02**	5.000
Radiator, baseboard, 3/4" element, 16' section	EA	$509.84	$264.00	$773.84	**$1,168.22**	5.000
Radiator, baseboard, copper element, 8' section	EA	$305.90	$270.00	$575.90	**$834.85**	3.000
Radiator, baseboard, copper element, 16' section	EA	$509.84	$528.00	$1,037.84	**$1,485.02**	5.000

21

General Plumbing

Boilers

Description	Unit	Direct Labor	Direct Materials	Direct Total	Selling Price	Man-hours
GAS FIRED BOILERS						
Install cast iron gas fired boiler, 80,000 BTU	EA	$815.74	$1,650.00	$2,465.74	**$3,342.28**	8.000
Install cast iron gas fired boiler, 100,000 BTU	EA	$815.74	$1,870.00	$2,685.74	**$3,606.28**	8.000
Install cast iron gas fired boiler, 130,000 BTU	EA	$815.74	$2,090.00	$2,905.74	**$3,870.28**	8.000
Install steel gas fired boiler, 80,000 BTU	EA	$815.74	$2,530.00	$3,345.74	**$4,398.28**	8.000
Install steel gas fired boiler, 100,000 BTU	EA	$815.74	$2,860.00	$3,675.74	**$4,794.28**	8.000
Install steel gas fired boiler, 130,000 BTU	EA	$815.74	$3,190.00	$4,005.74	**$5,190.28**	8.000
OIL FIRED BOILERS						
Install cast iron oil fired boiler, 110,000 BTU	EA	$815.74	$1,760.00	$2,575.74	**$3,474.28**	8.000
Install cast iron oil fired boiler, 130,000 BTU	EA	$815.74	$2,035.00	$2,850.74	**$3,804.28**	8.000
Install cast iron oil fired boiler, 170,000 BTU	EA	$815.74	$2,200.00	$3,015.74	**$4,002.28**	8.000
Install steel oil fired boiler, 110,000 BTU	EA	$815.74	$2,970.00	$3,785.74	**$4,926.28**	8.000
Install steel oil fired boiler, 130,000 BTU	EA	$815.74	$3,300.00	$4,115.74	**$5,322.28**	8.000
Install steel oil fired boiler, 170,000 BTU	EA	$815.74	$3,630.00	$4,445.74	**$5,718.28**	8.000
ELECTRIC FIRED BOILERS						
Install electric fired boiler, 40,000 BTU	EA	$917.70	$3,300.00	$4,217.70	**$5,492.56**	9.000
Install electric fired boiler, 82,000 BTU	EA	$917.70	$3,630.00	$4,547.70	**$5,888.56**	9.000
Install electric fired boiler, 109,000 BTU	EA	$917.70	$3,960.00	$4,877.70	**$6,284.56**	9.000

Bathroom Plumbing

Bathroom Plumbing Rough-In, Open Walls and Open Ceiling Below

> **Supply and waste rough-in as needed, including cut-off valves and flanges.**

Description	Unit	Direct Labor	Direct Materials	Direct Total	Selling Price	Man-hours
BATHROOM ROUGH-IN, OPEN WALLS AND OPEN CEILING						
Cut channel in concrete slab for waste	LF	$39.87		$39.87	**$66.58**	0.391
Over 5 feet from stack, ADD per LF	LF	$50.98	$9.13	$60.11	**$100.39**	0.500
Toilet rough-in, open walls and ceiling	EA	$713.77	$98.45	$812.22	**$1,356.41**	7.000
Bidet rough-in, open walls and ceiling	EA	$713.77	$98.45	$812.22	**$1,356.41**	7.000
Urinal rough-in, open walls and ceiling	EA	$407.87	$76.23	$484.10	**$808.44**	4.000
Sink rough-in, single bowl, open walls and ceiling	EA	$611.80	$76.23	$688.03	**$1,149.01**	6.000
Sink rough-in, double bowl, open walls and ceiling	EA	$815.74	$117.15	$932.89	**$1,557.92**	8.000
Tub rough-in, open walls and ceiling	EA	$611.80	$76.23	$688.03	**$1,149.01**	6.000
Tub with shower rough-in, open walls and ceiling	EA	$815.74	$95.15	$910.89	**$1,521.18**	8.000
Shower rough-in, open walls and ceiling	EA	$713.77	$84.04	$797.81	**$1,332.34**	7.000
Whirlpool spa rough-in, open walls and ceiling	EA	$713.77	$76.23	$790.00	**$1,319.30**	7.000
Electrical installation for whirlpool spa, open walls and ceiling	EA	$356.88	$41.80	$398.68	**$665.80**	3.500
Deduct for 2 fixtures roughed-in at same time	EA	-$254.92		-$254.92	**-$425.71**	-2.500
Deduct for 3 fixtures roughed-in at same time	EA	-$407.87		-$407.87	**-$681.14**	-4.000
Deduct for 4 fixtures roughed-in at same time	EA	-$509.84		-$509.84	**-$851.42**	-5.000

Bathroom Plumbing

Bathroom Plumbing Rough-In, Finished Walls and Open Ceiling Below

> Supply and waste rough-in as needed, including cut-off valves and flanges. No patching included.

Description	Unit	Direct Labor	Direct Materials	Direct Total	Selling Price	Man-hours
BATHROOM ROUGH-IN, FINISHED WALLS AND OPEN CEILING						
Cut channel in concrete slab for waste	LF	$39.87		$39.87	**$66.58**	0.391
Over 5 feet from stack, ADD per LF	LF	$50.98	$9.13	$60.11	**$100.39**	0.500
Toilet rough-in, finished walls, open ceiling	EA	$815.74	$98.45	$914.19	**$1,526.69**	8.000
Bidet rough-in, finished walls, open ceiling	EA	$815.74	$98.45	$914.19	**$1,526.69**	8.000
Urinal rough-in, finished walls, open ceiling	EA	$509.84	$76.23	$586.07	**$978.73**	5.000
Sink rough-in, single bowl, finished walls, open ceiling	EA	$713.77	$76.23	$790.00	**$1,319.30**	7.000
Sink rough-in, double bowl, finished walls, open ceiling	EA	$917.70	$117.15	$1,034.85	**$1,728.21**	9.000
Tub rough-in, finished walls, open ceiling	EA	$611.80	$76.23	$688.03	**$1,149.01**	6.000
Tub with shower rough-in, finished walls, open ceiling	EA	$917.70	$95.15	$1,012.85	**$1,691.47**	9.000
Shower rough-in , finished walls, open ceiling	EA	$815.74	$84.04	$899.78	**$1,502.63**	8.000
Whirlpool spa rough-in, finished walls, open ceiling	EA	$713.77	$76.23	$790.00	**$1,319.30**	7.000
Electrical installation for whirlpool spa, finished walls, open ceiling	EA	$382.38	$41.80	$424.18	**$708.37**	3.750
Deduct for 2 fixtures roughed-in at same time	EA	-$305.90		-$305.90	**-$510.85**	-3.000
Deduct for 3 fixtures roughed-in at same time	EA	-$458.85		-$458.85	**-$766.28**	-4.500
Deduct for 4 fixtures roughed-in at same time	EA	-$560.82		-$560.82	**-$936.57**	-5.500

Bathroom Plumbing

Bathroom Plumbing Rough-In, Finished Walls and Finished Ceiling Below

> Supply and waste rough-in as needed, including cut-off valves and flanges. No patching included.

Description	Unit	Direct Labor	Direct Materials	Direct Total	Selling Price	Man-hours
BATHROOM ROUGH-IN, FINISHED WALLS AND CEILING						
Cut channel in concrete slab for waste	LF	$39.87		$39.87	**$66.58**	0.391
Over 5 feet from stack, ADD per LF	LF	$76.48	$9.13	$85.61	**$142.96**	0.750
Toilet rough-in, finished walls and ceiling	EA	$917.70	$98.45	$1,016.15	**$1,696.98**	9.000
Bidet rough-in, finished walls and ceiling	EA	$917.70	$98.45	$1,016.15	**$1,696.98**	9.000
Urinal rough-in, finished walls and ceiling	EA	$611.80	$76.23	$688.03	**$1,149.01**	6.000
Sink rough-in, single bowl, finished walls and ceiling	EA	$815.74	$76.23	$891.97	**$1,489.58**	8.000
Sink rough-in, double bowl, finished walls and ceiling	EA	$1,019.67	$117.15	$1,136.82	**$1,898.49**	10.000
Tub rough-in, finished walls and ceiling	EA	$713.77	$76.23	$790.00	**$1,319.30**	7.000
Tub with shower rough-in, finished walls and ceiling	EA	$1,019.67	$95.15	$1,114.82	**$1,861.75**	10.000
Shower rough-in, finished walls and ceiling	EA	$917.70	$84.04	$1,001.74	**$1,672.91**	9.000
Whirlpool spa rough-in, finished walls and ceiling	EA	$815.74	$76.23	$891.97	**$1,489.58**	8.000
Electrical installation for whirlpool spa, finished walls and ceiling	EA	$484.34	$41.80	$526.14	**$878.66**	4.750
Deduct for 2 fixtures roughed-in at same time	EA	-$382.38		-$382.38	**-$638.57**	-3.750
Deduct for 3 fixtures roughed-in at same time	EA	-$535.33		-$535.33	**-$894.00**	-5.250
Deduct for 4 fixtures roughed-in at same time	EA	-$637.29		-$637.29	**-$1,064.28**	-6.250

Bathroom Plumbing

Remove Existing Fixture, Location Ready for New Fixture

Description	Unit	Direct Labor	Direct Materials	Direct Total	Selling Price	Man-hours
REMOVE EXISTING FIXTURE, LOCATION READY FOR NEW						
Toilet, remove and use existing flange	EA	$76.48		$76.48	**$127.71**	0.750
Toilet, remove and replace flange	EA	$152.95	$13.53	$166.48	**$278.02**	1.500
Bidet, remove and use existing flange	EA	$76.48		$76.48	**$127.71**	0.750
Bidet, remove and replace flange	EA	$152.95	$13.53	$166.48	**$278.02**	1.500
Urinal, remove	EA	$76.48		$76.48	**$127.71**	0.750
Sink, pedestal or wall mount, remove	EA	$76.48		$76.48	**$127.71**	0.750
Vanity with single sink, remove all	EA	$152.95		$152.95	**$255.43**	1.500
Vanity with single sink, remove sink and faucets only	EA	$50.98		$50.98	**$85.14**	0.500
Vanity with double sink, remove all	EA	$203.93		$203.93	**$340.57**	2.000
Vanity with double sink, remove sinks and faucets only	EA	$101.97		$101.97	**$170.28**	1.000
Tub, cast iron, remove	EA	$305.90		$305.90	**$510.85**	3.000
Tub, cast iron with fiberglass or acrylic surround, remove all	EA	$407.87		$407.87	**$681.14**	4.000
Tub, steel, remove	EA	$305.90		$305.90	**$510.85**	3.000
Tub, steel with fiberglass or acrylic surround, remove all	EA	$407.87		$407.87	**$681.14**	4.000
Tub, fiberglass or acrylic, remove	EA	$305.90		$305.90	**$510.85**	3.000
Tub, fiberglass or acrylic with fiberglass or acrylic surround, remove all	EA	$407.87		$407.87	**$681.14**	4.000
Shower with fiberglass or acrylic surround, remove all	EA	$407.87		$407.87	**$681.14**	4.000
Shower receptor (pan), remove	EA	$203.93		$203.93	**$340.57**	2.000
Whirlpool spa only, remove	EA	$407.87		$407.87	**$681.14**	4.000
Whirlpool spa with fiberglass or acrylic surround, remove all	EA	$509.84		$509.84	**$851.42**	5.000
Demolish ceramic tile wall in thin-set	SF	$2.04		$2.04	**$3.41**	0.020
Demolish ceramic tile wall in conventional mortar	SF	$2.75		$2.75	**$4.60**	0.027

Bathroom Plumbing

Install New Fixture in Prepared Location

> Install new fixture to cut-off valve and stubbed out or flanged waste.

Description	Unit	Direct Labor	Direct Materials	Direct Total	Selling Price	Man-hours
INSTALL FIXTURE IN PREPARED LOCATION						
Toilet, install	EA	$152.95		$152.95	**$255.43**	1.500
Bidet, install	EA	$152.95		$152.95	**$255.43**	1.500
Urinal, install	EA	$152.95		$152.95	**$255.43**	1.500
Sink and faucet, pedestal or wall mount, install	EA	$152.95		$152.95	**$255.43**	1.500
Vanity and top with single sink and faucet, install all	EA	$305.90		$305.90	**$510.85**	3.000
Vanity with single sink, install sink and faucets only	EA	$152.95		$152.95	**$255.43**	1.500
Vanity and top with double sink and faucets, install all	EA	$509.84		$509.84	**$851.42**	5.000
Vanity with double sink, install sinks and faucets only	EA	$305.90		$305.90	**$510.85**	3.000
Tub and faucet, cast iron, install	EA	$407.87		$407.87	**$681.14**	4.000
Tub, faucet, diverter, head, cast iron with fiberglass or acrylic surround	EA	$713.77		$713.77	**$1,191.99**	7.000
Tub and faucet, steel, install	EA	$407.87		$407.87	**$681.14**	4.000
Tub, faucet, diverter, head, steel with fiberglass or acrylic surround	EA	$713.77		$713.77	**$1,191.99**	7.000
Tub and faucet, fiberglass or acrylic, install	EA	$407.87		$407.87	**$681.14**	4.000
Tub, faucet, diverter, head, fiberglass or acrylic with surround	EA	$713.77		$713.77	**$1,191.99**	7.000
Shower, faucet and head with fiberglass or acrylic surround	EA	$611.80		$611.80	**$1,021.71**	6.000
Faucet and head for shower, install, no surround	EA	$203.93		$203.93	**$340.57**	2.000
Shower receptor (pan), install	EA	$254.92		$254.92	**$425.71**	2.500
Whirlpool spa and faucet only, install	EA	$611.80		$611.80	**$1,021.71**	6.000
Whirlpool spa and faucet with fiberglass or acrylic surround	EA	$815.74		$815.74	**$1,362.28**	8.000

Bathroom Plumbing

Toilet

> Installed in prepared location. No removal or rough-in included.

Description	Unit	Direct Labor	Direct Materials	Direct Total	Selling Price	Man-hours
Toilet. 1 piece, round, premium	EA	$152.95	$648.00	$800.95	**$1,033.03**	1.500
Toilet. 1 piece, round, pressure assist, premium	EA	$203.93	$946.00	$1,149.93	**$1,475.77**	2.000
Toilet. 1 piece, elongated, premium	EA	$152.95	$782.00	$934.95	**$1,193.83**	1.500
Toilet. 1 piece, elongated, pressure assist, premium	EA	$203.93	$1,091.00	$1,294.93	**$1,649.77**	2.000
Toilet. 2 piece, round, average	EA	$152.95	$288.00	$440.95	**$601.03**	1.500
Toilet. 2 piece, round, pressure assist, average	EA	$203.93	$421.00	$624.93	**$845.77**	2.000
Toilet. 2 piece, elongated, average	EA	$152.95	$440.00	$592.95	**$783.43**	1.500
Toilet. 2 piece, elongated, pressure assist, average	EA	$203.93	$578.00	$781.93	**$1,034.17**	2.000
Toilet. 2 piece, round, average, economy	EA	$152.95	$155.00	$307.95	**$441.43**	1.500
Toilet. 2 piece, elongated, economy	EA	$152.95	$253.00	$405.95	**$559.03**	1.500
Toilet. 2 piece, elongated, tall, average	EA	$152.95	$514.00	$666.95	**$872.23**	1.500
Toilet. 2 piece, elongated, tall, economy	EA	$152.95	$356.00	$508.95	**$682.63**	1.500

Bidet

> Installed in prepared location. No removal or rough-in included.

Description	Unit	Direct Labor	Direct Materials	Direct Total	Selling Price	Man-hours
Bidet, premium	EA	$152.95	$668.00	$820.95	**$1,057.03**	1.500
Bidet, average	EA	$152.95	$527.00	$679.95	**$887.83**	1.500
Bidet, economy	EA	$152.95	$380.00	$532.95	**$711.43**	1.500

Urinal

> Installed in prepared location. No removal or rough-in included.

Description	Unit	Direct Labor	Direct Materials	Direct Total	Selling Price	Man-hours
Urinal, premium	EA	$152.95	$623.00	$775.95	**$1,003.03**	1.500
Urinal, average	EA	$152.95	$531.00	$683.95	**$892.63**	1.500
Urinal, economy	EA	$152.95	$311.00	$463.95	**$628.63**	1.500

Bathroom Plumbing

Bathtub

> Fixture costs only. See 'Install New Fixture' section for labor costs.

Description	Unit	Direct Labor	Direct Materials	Direct Total	Selling Price	Man-hours
Bathtub, cast iron, premium	EA		$968.00	$968.00	**$1,161.60**	
Bathtub, cast iron, average	EA		$649.00	$649.00	**$778.80**	
Bathtub, cast iron, economy	EA		$413.00	$413.00	**$495.60**	
Bathtub, steel, premium	EA		$748.00	$748.00	**$897.60**	
Bathtub, steel, average	EA		$468.00	$468.00	**$561.60**	
Bathtub, steel, economy	EA		$248.00	$248.00	**$297.60**	
Bathtub, acrylic, premium	EA		$836.00	$836.00	**$1,003.20**	
Bathtub, acrylic, average	EA		$677.00	$677.00	**$812.40**	
Bathtub, acrylic, economy	EA		$369.00	$369.00	**$442.80**	
Bathtub/shower one piece combination, acrylic, premium	EA		$1,078.00	$1,078.00	**$1,293.60**	
Bathtub/shower one piece combination, acrylic, average	EA		$858.00	$858.00	**$1,029.60**	

Shower

> Install shower, faucet/diverter in prepared location. No removal or rough-in included.

Description	Unit	Direct Labor	Direct Materials	Direct Total	Selling Price	Man-hours
Shower unit, acrylic, 32" x 32", 72" tall (faucet/diverter not included)	EA	$611.80	$523.00	$1,134.80	**$1,649.31**	6.000
Shower unit, acrylic, 36" x 36", 72" tall (faucet/diverter not included)	EA	$611.80	$594.00	$1,205.80	**$1,734.51**	6.000
Shower unit, acrylic, 42" x 34", 72" tall (faucet/diverter not included)	EA	$611.80	$649.00	$1,260.80	**$1,800.51**	6.000
Shower unit, acrylic, 48" x 35", 72" tall (faucet/diverter not included)	EA	$611.80	$688.00	$1,299.80	**$1,847.31**	6.000
Shower unit, acrylic, 54" x 35", 72" tall (faucet/diverter not included)	EA	$611.80	$781.00	$1,392.80	**$1,958.91**	6.000
Shower unit, neo-angle, 36" x 36", 72" tall (faucet/diverter not included)	EA	$611.80	$578.00	$1,189.80	**$1,715.31**	6.000
Shower unit, neo-angle, 40" x 40", 72" tall (faucet/diverter not included)	EA	$611.80	$761.00	$1,372.80	**$1,934.91**	6.000

Shower Receptor (Pan)

> Installed in prepared location. No removal or rough-in included.

Description	Unit	Direct Labor	Direct Materials	Direct Total	Selling Price	Man-hours
Acrylic shower stall receptor, 32" x 32"	EA	$254.92	$123.00	$377.92	**$573.31**	2.500
Acrylic shower stall receptor, 32" x 48"	EA	$254.92	$172.00	$426.92	**$632.11**	2.500
Acrylic shower stall receptor, 34" x 48"	EA	$254.92	$175.00	$429.92	**$635.71**	2.500
Acrylic shower stall receptor, 34" x 60"	EA	$254.92	$218.00	$472.92	**$687.31**	2.500
Acrylic shower stall receptor, 36" x 36", neo angle	EA	$254.92	$155.00	$409.92	**$611.71**	2.500
Acrylic shower stall receptor, 38" x 38", neo angle	EA	$254.92	$182.00	$436.92	**$644.11**	2.500

Bathroom Plumbing

Whirlpool Spa or Bath

> Fixture costs only. See 'Install New Fixture' section for labor costs.

Description	Unit	Direct Labor	Direct Materials	Direct Total	Selling Price	Man-hours
Whirlpool spa, acrylic, open sides, corner, 60" x 60" x 20" deep	EA		$2,063.00	$2,063.00	**$2,475.60**	
Whirlpool spa, acrylic, open sides, 60" x 30" x 17" deep	EA		$1,403.00	$1,403.00	**$1,683.60**	
Whirlpool spa, acrylic, open sides, 62" x 42" x 18" deep	EA		$2,046.00	$2,046.00	**$2,455.20**	
Whirlpool spa, acrylic, open sides, 66" x 42" x 20" deep	EA		$2,195.00	$2,195.00	**$2,634.00**	
Whirlpool spa, acrylic, open sides, 72" x 42" x 20" deep	EA		$2,965.00	$2,965.00	**$3,558.00**	
Whirlpool spa, acrylic, open sides, 72" x 48" x 20" deep	EA		$3,905.00	$3,905.00	**$4,686.00**	
Whirlpool spa, acrylic, open sides, 72" x 54" x 28" deep	EA		$5,335.00	$5,335.00	**$6,402.00**	
Whirlpool bath, acrylic, integral apron, 60" x 32" x 18" deep	EA		$2,063.00	$2,063.00	**$2,475.60**	
Whirlpool bath, acrylic, integral apron, 60" x 34" x 20" deep	EA		$3,185.00	$3,185.00	**$3,822.00**	
Whirlpool bath, acrylic, integral apron, 68" x 38" x 20" deep	EA		$3,988.00	$3,988.00	**$4,785.60**	
Whirlpool bath, acrylic, integral apron, 72" x 42" x 22" deep	EA		$4,565.00	$4,565.00	**$5,478.00**	
Whirlpool bath, cast iron, integral apron, 60" x 32" x 18" deep	EA		$3,410.00	$3,410.00	**$4,092.00**	
Whirlpool bath, cast iron, integral apron, 60" x 34" x 20" deep	EA		$5,143.00	$5,143.00	**$6,171.60**	
Whirlpool bath, cast iron, integral apron, 68" x 38" x 20" deep	EA		$6,028.00	$6,028.00	**$7,233.60**	
Whirlpool bath, cast iron, integral apron, 72" x 42" x 22" deep	EA		$7,464.00	$7,464.00	**$8,956.80**	

Sink, Bathtub and Shower Faucets

> Fixture costs only. See 'Install New Fixture' section for labor costs.

Description	Unit	Direct Labor	Direct Materials	Direct Total	Selling Price	Man-hours
Sink faucet, single lever control, premium	EA		$275.00	$275.00	**$330.00**	
Sink faucet, single lever control, average	EA		$187.00	$187.00	**$224.40**	
Sink faucet, single lever control, economy	EA		$110.00	$110.00	**$132.00**	
Sink faucet, single unit, 2 handle control, premium	EA		$275.00	$275.00	**$330.00**	
Sink faucet, single unit, 2 handle control, average	EA		$154.00	$154.00	**$184.80**	
Sink faucet, single unit, 2 handle control, economy	EA		$88.00	$88.00	**$105.60**	
Sink faucet, 3 piece unit, 2 handle control and spout, premium	EA		$352.00	$352.00	**$422.40**	
Sink faucet, 3 piece unit, 2 handle control and spout, average	EA		$209.00	$209.00	**$250.80**	
Sink faucet, 3 piece unit, 2 handle control and spout, economy	EA		$132.00	$132.00	**$158.40**	
Shower control set, single control, head, spout, premium	EA		$308.00	$308.00	**$369.60**	
Shower control set, single control, head, spout, average	EA		$209.00	$209.00	**$250.80**	
Shower control set, single control, head, spout, economy	EA		$143.00	$143.00	**$171.60**	
Shower control set, 3 handle control, head, spout, premium	EA		$352.00	$352.00	**$422.40**	
Shower control set, 3 handle control, head, spout, average	EA		$220.00	$220.00	**$264.00**	
Shower control set, 3 handle control, head, spout, economy	EA		$165.00	$165.00	**$198.00**	

Bathroom Plumbing

Sink

> Fixture costs only. See 'Install New Fixture' section for labor costs.

Description	Unit	Direct Labor	Direct Materials	Direct Total	Selling Price	Man-hours
PEDESTAL SINK						
Pedestal sink, 22" x 18", premium	EA		$330.00	$330.00	**$396.00**	
Pedestal sink, 24" x 18", premium	EA		$352.00	$352.00	**$422.40**	
Pedestal sink, 24" x 20", premium	EA		$374.00	$374.00	**$448.80**	
Pedestal sink, 25" x 20", premium	EA		$396.00	$396.00	**$475.20**	
Pedestal sink, 27" x 20", premium	EA		$440.00	$440.00	**$528.00**	
Pedestal sink, 30" x 20", premium	EA		$484.00	$484.00	**$580.80**	
Pedestal sink, 22" x 18", average	EA		$204.00	$204.00	**$244.80**	
Pedestal sink, 24" x 18", average	EA		$220.00	$220.00	**$264.00**	
Pedestal sink, 24" x 20", average	EA		$237.00	$237.00	**$284.40**	
Pedestal sink, 25" x 20", average	EA		$253.00	$253.00	**$303.60**	
Pedestal sink, 27" x 20", average	EA		$286.00	$286.00	**$343.20**	
Pedestal sink, 30" x 20", average	EA		$319.00	$319.00	**$382.80**	
Pedestal sink, 22" x 18", economy	EA		$121.00	$121.00	**$145.20**	
Pedestal sink, 24" x 18", economy	EA		$132.00	$132.00	**$158.40**	
Pedestal sink, 24" x 20", economy	EA		$143.00	$143.00	**$171.60**	
Pedestal sink, 25" x 20", economy	EA		$154.00	$154.00	**$184.80**	
Pedestal sink, 27" x 20", economy	EA		$176.00	$176.00	**$211.20**	
Pedestal sink, 30" x 20", economy	EA		$198.00	$198.00	**$237.60**	
WALL-HUNG SINK						
Wall-hung sink, 13" x 13", premium	EA		$264.00	$264.00	**$316.80**	
Wall-hung sink, 13" x 16", premium	EA		$286.00	$286.00	**$343.20**	
Wall-hung sink, 19" x 17", premium	EA		$308.00	$308.00	**$369.60**	
Wall-hung sink, 21" x 18", premium	EA		$330.00	$330.00	**$396.00**	
Wall-hung sink, 24" x 19", premium	EA		$374.00	$374.00	**$448.80**	
Wall-hung sink, 13" x 13", average	EA		$165.00	$165.00	**$198.00**	
Wall-hung sink, 13" x 16", average	EA		$182.00	$182.00	**$218.40**	
Wall-hung sink, 19" x 17", average	EA		$209.00	$209.00	**$250.80**	
Wall-hung sink, 21" x 18", average	EA		$226.00	$226.00	**$271.20**	
Wall-hung sink, 24" x 19", average	EA		$259.00	$259.00	**$310.80**	
Wall-hung sink, 13" x 13", economy	EA		$88.00	$88.00	**$105.60**	
Wall-hung sink, 13" x 16", economy	EA		$99.00	$99.00	**$118.80**	
Wall-hung sink, 19" x 17", economy	EA		$110.00	$110.00	**$132.00**	
Wall-hung sink, 21" x 18", economy	EA		$121.00	$121.00	**$145.20**	
Wall-hung sink, 24" x 19", economy	EA		$143.00	$143.00	**$171.60**	

Sink (cont.)

> Fixture costs only. See 'Install New Fixture' section for labor costs.

Description	Unit	Direct Labor	Direct Materials	Direct Total	Selling Price	Man-hours
VANITY SELF RIM SINK						
Bathroom vanity sink, self rim, 20" x 17", premium	EA		$308.00	$308.00	**$369.60**	
Bathroom vanity sink, self rim, 22" x 19", premium	EA		$330.00	$330.00	**$396.00**	
Bathroom vanity sink, self rim, 24" x 19", premium	EA		$352.00	$352.00	**$422.40**	
Bathroom vanity sink, self rim, 26" x 20", premium	EA		$374.00	$374.00	**$448.80**	
Bathroom vanity sink, self rim, 19" diameter, premium	EA		$286.00	$286.00	**$343.20**	
Bathroom vanity sink, self rim, 20" x 17", average	EA		$204.00	$204.00	**$244.80**	
Bathroom vanity sink, self rim, 22" x 19", average	EA		$220.00	$220.00	**$264.00**	
Bathroom vanity sink, self rim, 24" x 19", average	EA		$237.00	$237.00	**$284.40**	
Bathroom vanity sink, self rim, 26" x 20", average	EA		$253.00	$253.00	**$303.60**	
Bathroom vanity sink, self rim, 19" diameter, average	EA		$187.00	$187.00	**$224.40**	
Bathroom vanity sink, self rim, 20" x 17", economy	EA		$132.00	$132.00	**$158.40**	
Bathroom vanity sink, self rim, 22" x 19", economy	EA		$143.00	$143.00	**$171.60**	
Bathroom vanity sink, self rim, 24" x 19", economy	EA		$154.00	$154.00	**$184.80**	
Bathroom vanity sink, self rim, 26" x 20", economy	EA		$176.00	$176.00	**$211.20**	
Bathroom vanity sink, self rim, 19" diameter, economy	EA		$110.00	$110.00	**$132.00**	
VANITY UNDERCOUNTER SINK						
Bathroom vanity sink, undercounter, 17" x 14", premium	EA		$330.00	$330.00	**$396.00**	
Bathroom vanity sink, undercounter, 18" x 12", premium	EA		$352.00	$352.00	**$422.40**	
Bathroom vanity sink, undercounter, 21" x 12", premium	EA		$374.00	$374.00	**$448.80**	
Bathroom vanity sink, undercounter, 19" x 15", premium	EA		$396.00	$396.00	**$475.20**	
Bathroom vanity sink, undercounter, 16" diameter, premium	EA		$330.00	$330.00	**$396.00**	
Bathroom vanity sink, undercounter, 17" x 14", average	EA		$187.00	$187.00	**$224.40**	
Bathroom vanity sink, undercounter, 18" x 12", average	EA		$204.00	$204.00	**$244.80**	
Bathroom vanity sink, undercounter, 21" x 12", average	EA		$220.00	$220.00	**$264.00**	
Bathroom vanity sink, undercounter, 19" x 15", average	EA		$253.00	$253.00	**$303.60**	
Bathroom vanity sink, undercounter, 16" diameter, average	EA		$187.00	$187.00	**$224.40**	
Bathroom vanity sink, undercounter, 17" x 14", economy	EA		$121.00	$121.00	**$145.20**	
Bathroom vanity sink, undercounter, 18" x 12", economy	EA		$132.00	$132.00	**$158.40**	
Bathroom vanity sink, undercounter, 21" x 12", economy	EA		$143.00	$143.00	**$171.60**	
Bathroom vanity sink, undercounter, 19" x 15", economy	EA		$165.00	$165.00	**$198.00**	
Bathroom vanity sink, undercounter, 16" diameter, economy	EA		$121.00	$121.00	**$145.20**	

Bathroom Plumbing

Vanity

> Fixture costs only. See 'Install New Fixture' section for labor costs.

Description	Unit	Direct Labor	Direct Materials	Direct Total	Selling Price	Man-hours
Vanity, 20" x 16", 1 door, premium	EA		$363.00	$363.00	**$435.60**	
Vanity, 20" x 16", 1 door, average	EA		$231.00	$231.00	**$277.20**	
Vanity, 20" x 16", 1 door, economy	EA		$143.00	$143.00	**$171.60**	
Vanity, corner, 22" x 22", 1 door, premium	EA		$396.00	$396.00	**$475.20**	
Vanity, corner, 22" x 22", 1 door, average	EA		$264.00	$264.00	**$316.80**	
Vanity, corner, 22" x 22", 1 door, economy	EA		$176.00	$176.00	**$211.20**	
Vanity, 25" x 19", 1 door, premium	EA		$418.00	$418.00	**$501.60**	
Vanity, 25" x 19", 1 door, average	EA		$286.00	$286.00	**$343.20**	
Vanity, 25" x 19", 1 door, economy	EA		$187.00	$187.00	**$224.40**	
Vanity, 31" x 19", 2 door, premium	EA		$462.00	$462.00	**$554.40**	
Vanity, 31" x 19", 2 door, average	EA		$308.00	$308.00	**$369.60**	
Vanity, 31" x 19", 2 door, economy	EA		$209.00	$209.00	**$250.80**	
Vanity, 35" x 19", 2 door, premium	EA		$495.00	$495.00	**$594.00**	
Vanity, 35" x 19", 2 door, average	EA		$352.00	$352.00	**$422.40**	
Vanity, 35" x 19", 2 door, economy	EA		$231.00	$231.00	**$277.20**	
Vanity, 37" x 19", 2 door, 3 drawer, premium	EA		$550.00	$550.00	**$660.00**	
Vanity, 37" x 19", 2 door, 3 drawer, average	EA		$440.00	$440.00	**$528.00**	
Vanity, 37" x 19", 2 door, 3 drawer, economy	EA		$286.00	$286.00	**$343.20**	
Vanity, 49" x 19", 2 door, 3 drawer, premium	EA		$638.00	$638.00	**$765.60**	
Vanity, 49" x 19", 2 door, 3 drawer, average	EA		$495.00	$495.00	**$594.00**	
Vanity, 49" x 19", 2 door, 3 drawer, economy	EA		$319.00	$319.00	**$382.80**	
Vanity, 60" x 19", 2 door, 3 drawer, premium	EA		$748.00	$748.00	**$897.60**	
Vanity, 60" x 19", 2 door, 3 drawer, average	EA		$583.00	$583.00	**$699.60**	
Vanity, 60" x 19", 2 door, 3 drawer, economy	EA		$363.00	$363.00	**$435.60**	

Bathroom Plumbing

Vanity Top

> Fixture costs only. See 'Install New Fixture' section for labor costs.

Description	Unit	Direct Labor	Direct Materials	Direct Total	Selling Price	Man-hours
Cultured marble vanity top with integral sink, 25" x 19"	EA		$110.00	$110.00	**$132.00**	
Cultured marble vanity top with integral sink, 31" x 19"	EA		$132.00	$132.00	**$158.40**	
Cultured marble vanity top with integral sink, 35" x 19"	EA		$154.00	$154.00	**$184.80**	
Cultured marble vanity top with integral sink, 37" x 19"	EA		$165.00	$165.00	**$198.00**	
Laminate vanity top, 25" x 19"	EA		$72.00	$72.00	**$86.40**	
Laminate vanity top, 31" x 19"	EA		$83.00	$83.00	**$99.60**	
Laminate vanity top, 35" x 19"	EA		$94.00	$94.00	**$112.80**	
Laminate vanity top, 37" x 19"	EA		$99.00	$99.00	**$118.80**	
Laminate vanity top, 49" x 19"	EA		$138.00	$138.00	**$165.60**	
Laminate vanity top, 60" x 19"	EA		$165.00	$165.00	**$198.00**	
Granite vanity top, 25" x 19"	EA		$264.00	$264.00	**$316.80**	
Granite vanity top, 31" x 19"	EA		$297.00	$297.00	**$356.40**	
Granite vanity top, 35" x 19"	EA		$330.00	$330.00	**$396.00**	
Granite vanity top, 37" x 19"	EA		$352.00	$352.00	**$422.40**	
Granite vanity top, 49" x 19"	EA		$396.00	$396.00	**$475.20**	
Granite vanity top, 60" x 19"	EA		$440.00	$440.00	**$528.00**	
Solid surface vanity top, 25" x 19"	EA		$303.00	$303.00	**$363.60**	
Solid surface vanity top, 31" x 19"	EA		$341.00	$341.00	**$409.20**	
Solid surface vanity top, 35" x 19"	EA		$380.00	$380.00	**$456.00**	
Solid surface vanity top, 37" x 19"	EA		$407.00	$407.00	**$488.40**	
Solid surface vanity top, 49" x 19"	EA		$457.00	$457.00	**$548.40**	
Solid surface vanity top, 60" x 19"	EA		$506.00	$506.00	**$607.20**	

Bathroom Plumbing

Install or Remove Tub or Shower Doors

> Does not include cost of door, track or frame.

Description	Unit	Direct Labor	Direct Materials	Direct Total	Selling Price	Man-hours
Install folding tub or shower door	EA	$152.24		$152.24	**$254.24**	2.000
Install sliding tub or shower door	EA	$228.36		$228.36	**$381.35**	3.000
Install swinging tub or shower door	EA	$190.30		$190.30	**$317.79**	2.500
Remove tub or shower door	EA	$76.12		$76.12	**$127.12**	1.000

Shower Doors

> Includes installation only. No removal of old door.

Description	Unit	Direct Labor	Direct Materials	Direct Total	Selling Price	Man-hours
SHOWER DOOR, FOLDING						
Shower door, folding, aluminum, tempered, 30" to 32" x 72", premium	EA	$152.24	$539.00	$691.24	**$901.04**	2.000
Shower door, folding, aluminum, tempered, 32" to 36" x 72", premium	EA	$152.24	$561.00	$713.24	**$927.44**	2.000
Shower door, folding, aluminum, tempered, 36" to 42" x 72", premium	EA	$152.24	$583.00	$735.24	**$953.84**	2.000
Shower door, folding, aluminum, tempered, 42" to 48" x 72", premium	EA	$152.24	$605.00	$757.24	**$980.24**	2.000
Shower door, folding, aluminum, tempered, 30" to 32" x 72", average	EA	$152.24	$352.00	$504.24	**$676.64**	2.000
Shower door, folding, aluminum, tempered, 32" to 36" x 72", average	EA	$152.24	$369.00	$521.24	**$697.04**	2.000
Shower door, folding, aluminum, tempered, 36" to 42" x 72", average	EA	$152.24	$385.00	$537.24	**$716.24**	2.000
Shower door, folding, aluminum, tempered, 42" to 48" x 72", average	EA	$152.24	$402.00	$554.24	**$736.64**	2.000
Shower door, folding, aluminum, tempered, 30" to 32" x 72", economy	EA	$152.24	$220.00	$372.24	**$518.24**	2.000
Shower door, folding, aluminum, tempered, 32" to 36" x 72", economy	EA	$152.24	$231.00	$383.24	**$531.44**	2.000
Shower door, folding, aluminum, tempered, 36" to 42" x 72", economy	EA	$152.24	$242.00	$394.24	**$544.64**	2.000
Shower door, folding, aluminum, tempered, 42" to 48" x 72", economy	EA	$152.24	$253.00	$405.24	**$557.84**	2.000
SHOWER DOOR, PIVOT OR SWINGING						
Shower door, pivot, aluminum, tempered, 26" to 28" x 72", premium	EA	$190.30	$440.00	$630.30	**$845.79**	2.500
Shower door, pivot, aluminum, tempered, 28" to 32" x 72", premium	EA	$190.30	$462.00	$652.30	**$872.19**	2.500
Shower door, pivot, aluminum, tempered, 32" to 36" x 72", premium	EA	$190.30	$484.00	$674.30	**$898.59**	2.500
Shower door, pivot, aluminum, tempered, 36" to 42" x 72", premium	EA	$190.30	$506.00	$696.30	**$924.99**	2.500
Shower door, pivot, aluminum, tempered, 42" to 48" x 72", premium	EA	$190.30	$528.00	$718.30	**$951.39**	2.500
Shower door, pivot, aluminum, tempered, 26" to 28" x 72", average	EA	$190.30	$264.00	$454.30	**$634.59**	2.500
Shower door, pivot, aluminum, tempered, 28" to 32" x 72", average	EA	$190.30	$281.00	$471.30	**$654.99**	2.500
Shower door, pivot, aluminum, tempered, 32" to 36" x 72", average	EA	$190.30	$297.00	$487.30	**$674.19**	2.500
Shower door, pivot, aluminum, tempered, 36" to 42" x 72", average	EA	$190.30	$314.00	$504.30	**$694.59**	2.500
Shower door, pivot, aluminum, tempered, 42" to 48" x 72", average	EA	$190.30	$330.00	$520.30	**$713.79**	2.500
Shower door, pivot, aluminum, tempered, 26" to 28" x 72", economy	EA	$190.30	$132.00	$322.30	**$476.19**	2.500
Shower door, pivot, aluminum, tempered, 28" to 32" x 72", economy	EA	$190.30	$143.00	$333.30	**$489.39**	2.500
Shower door, pivot, aluminum, tempered, 32" to 36" x 72", economy	EA	$190.30	$154.00	$344.30	**$502.59**	2.500
Shower door, pivot, aluminum, tempered, 36" to 42" x 72", economy	EA	$190.30	$165.00	$355.30	**$515.79**	2.500
Shower door, pivot, aluminum, tempered, 42" to 48" x 72", economy	EA	$190.30	$176.00	$366.30	**$528.99**	2.500

Bathroom Plumbing

Shower Doors (cont.)

> Includes installation only. No removal of old door.

Description	Unit	Direct Labor	Direct Materials	Direct Total	Selling Price	Man-hours
SHOWER DOOR, BYPASS OR SLIDING						
Shower door, bypass, aluminum, tempered, 40" to 46" x 72", premium	EA	$228.36	$638.00	$866.36	**$1,146.95**	3.000
Shower door, bypass, aluminum, tempered, 46" to 52" x 72", premium	EA	$228.36	$660.00	$888.36	**$1,173.35**	3.000
Shower door, bypass, aluminum, tempered, 52" to 58" x 72", premium	EA	$228.36	$682.00	$910.36	**$1,199.75**	3.000
Shower door, bypass, aluminum, tempered, 58" to 64" x 72", premium	EA	$228.36	$704.00	$932.36	**$1,226.15**	3.000
Shower door, bypass, aluminum, tempered, 40" to 46" x 72", average	EA	$228.36	$363.00	$591.36	**$816.95**	3.000
Shower door, bypass, aluminum, tempered, 46" to 52" x 72", average	EA	$228.36	$380.00	$608.36	**$837.35**	3.000
Shower door, bypass, aluminum, tempered, 52" to 58" x 72", average	EA	$228.36	$396.00	$624.36	**$856.55**	3.000
Shower door, bypass, aluminum, tempered, 58" to 64" x 72", average	EA	$228.36	$413.00	$641.36	**$876.95**	3.000
Shower door, bypass, aluminum, tempered, 40" to 46" x 72", economy	EA	$228.36	$253.00	$481.36	**$684.95**	3.000
Shower door, bypass, aluminum, tempered, 46" to 52" x 72", economy	EA	$228.36	$264.00	$492.36	**$698.15**	3.000
Shower door, bypass, aluminum, tempered, 52" to 58" x 72", economy	EA	$228.36	$275.00	$503.36	**$711.35**	3.000
Shower door, bypass, aluminum, tempered, 58" to 64" x 72", economy	EA	$228.36	$286.00	$514.36	**$724.55**	3.000

Description	Unit	Direct Labor	Direct Materials	Direct Total	Selling Price	Man-hours
SHOWER DOOR, NEO ANGLE						
Shower door, pivot, aluminum, tempered, neo angle, premium	EA	$190.30	$825.00	$1,015.30	**$1,307.79**	2.500
Shower door, pivot, aluminum, tempered, neo angle, average	EA	$190.30	$578.00	$768.30	**$1,011.39**	2.500
Shower door, pivot, aluminum, tempered, neo angle, economy	EA	$190.30	$418.00	$608.30	**$819.39**	2.500

Bathroom Plumbing

Bathtub Doors

> Includes installation only. No removal of old door.

Description	Unit	Direct Labor	Direct Materials	Direct Total	Selling Price	Man-hours
BATHTUB DOOR, FOLDING						
Bathtub door, folding, aluminum, tempered, 56" to 58" x 57", premium	EA	$152.24	$473.00	$625.24	**$821.84**	2.000
Bathtub door, folding, aluminum, tempered, 58" to 60" x 57", premium	EA	$152.24	$495.00	$647.24	**$848.24**	2.000
Bathtub door, folding, aluminum, tempered, 60" to 63" x 57", premium	EA	$152.24	$517.00	$669.24	**$874.64**	2.000
Bathtub door, folding, aluminum, tempered, 63" to 66" x 57", premium	EA	$152.24	$539.00	$691.24	**$901.04**	2.000
Bathtub door, folding, aluminum, tempered, 66" to 69" x 57", premium	EA	$152.24	$561.00	$713.24	**$927.44**	2.000
Bathtub door, folding, aluminum, tempered, 69" to 72" x 57", premium	EA	$152.24	$583.00	$735.24	**$953.84**	2.000
Bathtub door, folding, aluminum, tempered, 56" to 58" x 57", average	EA	$152.24	$319.00	$471.24	**$637.04**	2.000
Bathtub door, folding, aluminum, tempered, 58" to 60" x 57", average	EA	$152.24	$336.00	$488.24	**$657.44**	2.000
Bathtub door, folding, aluminum, tempered, 60" to 63" x 57", average	EA	$152.24	$352.00	$504.24	**$676.64**	2.000
Bathtub door, folding, aluminum, tempered, 63" to 66" x 57", average	EA	$152.24	$369.00	$521.24	**$697.04**	2.000
Bathtub door, folding, aluminum, tempered, 66" to 69" x 57", average	EA	$152.24	$385.00	$537.24	**$716.24**	2.000
Bathtub door, folding, aluminum, tempered, 69" to 72" x 57", average	EA	$152.24	$402.00	$554.24	**$736.64**	2.000
Bathtub door, folding, aluminum, tempered, 56" to 58" x 57", economy	EA	$152.24	$198.00	$350.24	**$491.84**	2.000
Bathtub door, folding, aluminum, tempered, 58" to 60" x 57", economy	EA	$152.24	$209.00	$361.24	**$505.04**	2.000
Bathtub door, folding, aluminum, tempered, 60" to 63" x 57", economy	EA	$152.24	$220.00	$372.24	**$518.24**	2.000
Bathtub door, folding, aluminum, tempered, 63" to 66" x 57", economy	EA	$152.24	$231.00	$383.24	**$531.44**	2.000
Bathtub door, folding, aluminum, tempered, 66" to 69" x 57", economy	EA	$152.24	$242.00	$394.24	**$544.64**	2.000
Bathtub door, folding, aluminum, tempered, 69" to 72" x 57", economy	EA	$152.24	$253.00	$405.24	**$557.84**	2.000
BATHTUB DOOR, BYPASS OR SLIDING						
Bathtub door, bypass, aluminum, tempered, 56" to 58" x 57", premium	EA	$228.36	$594.00	$822.36	**$1,094.15**	3.000
Bathtub door, bypass, aluminum, tempered, 58" to 60" x 57", premium	EA	$228.36	$616.00	$844.36	**$1,120.55**	3.000
Bathtub door, bypass, aluminum, tempered, 60" to 63" x 57", premium	EA	$228.36	$638.00	$866.36	**$1,146.95**	3.000
Bathtub door, bypass, aluminum, tempered, 63" to 66" x 57", premium	EA	$228.36	$660.00	$888.36	**$1,173.35**	3.000
Bathtub door, bypass, aluminum, tempered, 66" to 69" x 57", premium	EA	$228.36	$682.00	$910.36	**$1,199.75**	3.000
Bathtub door, bypass, aluminum, tempered, 69" to 72" x 57", premium	EA	$228.36	$704.00	$932.36	**$1,226.15**	3.000
Bathtub door, bypass, aluminum, tempered, 56" to 58" x 57", average	EA	$228.36	$374.00	$602.36	**$830.15**	3.000
Bathtub door, bypass, aluminum, tempered, 58" to 60" x 57", average	EA	$228.36	$391.00	$619.36	**$850.55**	3.000
Bathtub door, bypass, aluminum, tempered, 60" to 63" x 57", average	EA	$228.36	$407.00	$635.36	**$869.75**	3.000
Bathtub door, bypass, aluminum, tempered, 63" to 66" x 57", average	EA	$228.36	$424.00	$652.36	**$890.15**	3.000
Bathtub door, bypass, aluminum, tempered, 66" to 69" x 57", average	EA	$228.36	$440.00	$668.36	**$909.35**	3.000
Bathtub door, bypass, aluminum, tempered, 69" to 72" x 57", average	EA	$228.36	$457.00	$685.36	**$929.75**	3.000
Bathtub door, bypass, aluminum, tempered, 56" to 58" x 57", economy	EA	$228.36	$231.00	$459.36	**$658.55**	3.000
Bathtub door, bypass, aluminum, tempered, 58" to 60" x 57", economy	EA	$228.36	$242.00	$470.36	**$671.75**	3.000
Bathtub door, bypass, aluminum, tempered, 60" to 63" x 57", economy	EA	$228.36	$253.00	$481.36	**$684.95**	3.000
Bathtub door, bypass, aluminum, tempered, 63" to 66" x 57", economy	EA	$228.36	$264.00	$492.36	**$698.15**	3.000
Bathtub door, bypass, aluminum, tempered, 66" to 69" x 57", economy	EA	$228.36	$275.00	$503.36	**$711.35**	3.000
Bathtub door, bypass, aluminum, tempered, 69" to 72" x 57", economy	EA	$228.36	$286.00	$514.36	**$724.55**	3.000

Kitchen and Laundry Plumbing

Kitchen and Laundry Rough-In, Open Walls and Open Ceiling Below

> Supply and waste rough-in, including cut-off valves as needed.

Description	Unit	Direct Labor	Direct Materials	Direct Total	Selling Price	Man-hours
ROUGH-IN, OPEN WALLS AND OPEN CEILING						
Cut channel in concrete slab for waste	LF	$39.87		$39.87	**$66.58**	0.391
Over 5 feet from stack, ADD per LF	LF	$50.98	$9.13	$60.11	**$100.39**	0.500
Sink rough-in, open walls and ceiling	EA	$611.80	$76.23	$688.03	**$1,149.01**	6.000
Disposer rough-in, includes electric & switch, open walls and ceiling	EA	$407.87	$43.62	$451.48	**$753.98**	4.000
Dishwasher rough-in, including electric, open walls and ceiling	EA	$407.87	$24.57	$432.44	**$722.18**	4.000
Oven rough-in, gas, including electric, open walls and ceiling	EA	$509.84	$49.87	$559.71	**$934.71**	5.000
Cooktop rough-in, gas, including electric, open walls and ceiling	EA	$509.84	$49.87	$559.71	**$934.71**	5.000
Range rough-in, gas, including electric, open walls and ceiling	EA	$509.84	$49.87	$559.71	**$934.71**	5.000
Dryer rough-in, gas, includes electric & vent, open walls and ceiling	EA	$509.84	$93.87	$603.71	**$1,008.19**	5.000
Gray box rough-in, open walls and ceiling	EA	$611.80	$102.56	$714.37	**$1,192.99**	6.000
Laundry tub rough-in, open walls and ceiling	EA	$611.80	$76.23	$688.03	**$1,149.01**	6.000
Deduct for 2 fixtures roughed-in at same time	EA	-$203.93		-$203.93	**-$340.57**	-2.000
Deduct for 3 fixtures roughed-in at same time	EA	-$326.29		-$326.29	**-$544.91**	-3.200
Deduct for 4 fixtures roughed-in at same time	EA	-$407.87		-$407.87	**-$681.14**	-4.000

23

Kitchen and Laundry Plumbing

Kitchen and Laundry Rough-In, Finished Walls and Open Ceiling Below

> Supply and waste rough-in, including cut-off valves as needed. No Patching.

Description	Unit	Direct Labor	Direct Materials	Direct Total	Selling Price	Man-hours
ROUGH-IN, FINISHED WALLS AND OPEN CEILING						
Cut channel in concrete slab for waste	LF	$39.87		$39.87	**$66.58**	0.391
Over 5 feet from stack, ADD per LF	LF	$50.98	$9.13	$60.11	**$100.39**	0.500
Sink rough-in, finished walls, open ceiling	EA	$713.77	$76.23	$790.00	**$1,319.30**	7.000
Disposer rough-in, includes electric & switch, finished walls, open ceiling	EA	$509.84	$43.62	$553.45	**$924.26**	5.000
Dishwasher rough-in, including electric, finished walls, open ceiling	EA	$458.85	$24.57	$483.43	**$807.32**	4.500
Oven rough-in, gas, including electric, finished walls, open ceiling	EA	$560.82	$49.87	$610.69	**$1,019.86**	5.500
Cooktop rough-in, gas, including electric, finished walls, open ceiling	EA	$560.82	$49.87	$610.69	**$1,019.86**	5.500
Range rough-in, gas, including electric, finished walls, open ceiling	EA	$560.82	$49.87	$610.69	**$1,019.86**	5.500
Dryer rough-in, gas, includes electric & vent, finished walls, open ceiling	EA	$560.82	$93.87	$654.69	**$1,093.34**	5.500
Gray box rough-in, finished walls, open ceiling	EA	$713.77	$102.56	$816.33	**$1,363.28**	7.000
Laundry tub rough-in, finished walls, open ceiling	EA	$713.77	$76.23	$790.00	**$1,319.30**	7.000
Deduct for 2 fixtures roughed-in at same time	EA	-$254.92		-$254.92	**-$425.71**	-2.500
Deduct for 3 fixtures roughed-in at same time	EA	-$377.28		-$377.28	**-$630.05**	-3.700
Deduct for 4 fixtures roughed-in at same time	EA	-$458.85		-$458.85	**-$766.28**	-4.500

Kitchen and Laundry Plumbing

Kitchen and Laundry Rough-In, Finished Walls and Finished Ceiling Below

> Supply and waste rough-in, including cut-off valves as needed. No Patching.

Description	Unit	Direct Labor	Direct Materials	Direct Total	Selling Price	Man-hours
ROUGH-IN, FINISHED WALLS AND FINISHED CEILING						
Cut channel in concrete slab for waste	LF	$39.87		$39.87	**$66.58**	0.391
Over 5 feet from stack, ADD per LF	LF	$76.48	$9.13	$85.61	**$142.96**	0.750
Sink rough-in, finished walls and ceiling	EA	$815.74	$76.23	$891.97	**$1,489.58**	8.000
Disposer rough-in, includes electric& switch, finished walls and ceiling	EA	$509.84	$43.62	$553.45	**$924.26**	5.000
Dishwasher rough-in, including electric, finished walls and ceiling	EA	$458.85	$24.57	$483.43	**$807.32**	4.500
Oven rough-in, gas, including electric, finished walls and ceiling	EA	$662.79	$49.87	$712.66	**$1,190.14**	6.500
Cooktop rough-in, gas, including electric, finished walls and ceiling	EA	$662.79	$49.87	$712.66	**$1,190.14**	6.500
Range rough-in, including electric, gas, finished walls and ceiling	EA	$662.79	$49.87	$712.66	**$1,190.14**	6.500
Dryer rough-in, gas, includes electric & vent, finished walls and ceiling	EA	$662.79	$93.87	$756.66	**$1,263.62**	6.500
Gray box rough-in, finished walls and ceiling	EA	$815.74	$102.56	$918.30	**$1,533.56**	8.000
Laundry tub rough-in, finished walls and ceiling	EA	$815.74	$76.23	$891.97	**$1,489.58**	8.000
Deduct for 2 fixtures roughed-in at same time	EA	-$305.90		-$305.90	**-$510.85**	-3.000
Deduct for 3 fixtures roughed-in at same time	EA	-$428.26		-$428.26	**-$715.20**	-4.200
Deduct for 4 fixtures roughed-in at same time	EA	-$509.84		-$509.84	**-$851.42**	-5.000

23

Kitchen and Laundry Plumbing

Remove Existing Fixture, Location Ready for New Fixture

Description	Unit	Direct Labor	Direct Materials	Direct Total	Selling Price	Man-hours
REMOVE EXISTING FIXTURE, LOCATION READY FOR NEW						
Sink and faucet, remove	EA	$76.48		$76.48	**$127.71**	0.750
Disposer, remove	EA	$101.97		$101.97	**$170.28**	1.000
Dishwasher, remove	EA	$101.97		$101.97	**$170.28**	1.000
Oven, gas, remove	EA	$76.48		$76.48	**$127.71**	0.750
Cooktop, gas, remove	EA	$76.48		$76.48	**$127.71**	0.750
Range, gas, remove	EA	$76.48		$76.48	**$127.71**	0.750
Dryer, gas, remove	EA	$76.48		$76.48	**$127.71**	0.750
Dryer, gas, remove, replace vent	EA	$152.95	$49.78	$202.73	**$338.55**	1.500
Washer, remove	EA	$60.76		$60.76	**$101.47**	1.500
Laundry tub and faucet, remove	EA	$76.48		$76.48	**$127.71**	0.750

Install New Fixture in Prepared Location

> Install new fixture to cut-off valve and stubbed out waste or gray box.

Description	Unit	Direct Labor	Direct Materials	Direct Total	Selling Price	Man-hours
Sink and faucet, install	EA	$203.93		$203.93	**$340.57**	2.000
Disposer, install	EA	$152.95		$152.95	**$255.43**	1.500
Dishwasher, install	EA	$152.95		$152.95	**$255.43**	1.500
Oven, gas, install	EA	$203.93		$203.93	**$340.57**	2.000
Cooktop, gas, install	EA	$203.93		$203.93	**$340.57**	2.000
Range, gas, install	EA	$203.93		$203.93	**$340.57**	2.000
Dryer, gas, install	EA	$203.93		$203.93	**$340.57**	2.000
Washer, install	EA	$81.02		$81.02	**$135.30**	2.000
Laundry tub and faucet, install	EA	$203.93		$203.93	**$340.57**	2.000

Kitchen and Laundry Plumbing

Kitchen Sink, Stainless Steel

> Fixture costs only. See 'Install New Fixture' section for labor costs.

Description	Unit	Direct Labor	Direct Materials	Direct Total	Selling Price	Man-hours
Kitchen sink, stainless steel, 1 bowl, 25" x 22", economy	EA		$108.00	$108.00	**$129.60**	
Kitchen sink, stainless steel, 1 bowl, 25" x 22", average	EA		$176.00	$176.00	**$211.20**	
Kitchen sink, stainless steel, 1 bowl, 25" x 22", premium	EA		$325.00	$325.00	**$390.00**	
Kitchen sink, stainless steel, 2 bowls, 33" x 22", economy	EA		$151.00	$151.00	**$181.20**	
Kitchen sink, stainless steel, 2 bowls, 33" x 22", average	EA		$248.00	$248.00	**$297.60**	
Kitchen sink, stainless steel, 2 bowls, 33" x 22", premium	EA		$465.00	$465.00	**$558.00**	
Kitchen sink, stainless steel, 2 bowls, 42" x 22", economy	EA		$242.00	$242.00	**$290.40**	
Kitchen sink, stainless steel, 2 bowls, 42" x 22", average	EA		$369.00	$369.00	**$442.80**	
Kitchen sink, stainless steel, 2 bowls, 42" x 22", premium	EA		$596.00	$596.00	**$715.20**	
Kitchen sink, stainless steel, 2 bowls, 43" x 22", economy	EA		$358.00	$358.00	**$429.60**	
Kitchen sink, stainless steel, 2 bowls, 43" x 22", average	EA		$484.00	$484.00	**$580.80**	
Kitchen sink, stainless steel, 2 bowls, 43" x 22", premium	EA		$707.00	$707.00	**$848.40**	

Kitchen Sink, Enameled Steel

> Fixture costs only. See 'Install New Fixture' section for labor costs.

Description	Unit	Direct Labor	Direct Materials	Direct Total	Selling Price	Man-hours
Kitchen sink, enameled steel, 1 bowl, 25" x 22", economy	EA		$259.00	$259.00	**$310.80**	
Kitchen sink, enameled steel, 1 bowl, 25" x 22", average	EA		$365.00	$365.00	**$438.00**	
Kitchen sink, enameled steel, 1 bowl, 25" x 22", premium	EA		$538.00	$538.00	**$645.60**	
Kitchen sink, enameled steel, 2 bowls, 33" x 22", economy	EA		$286.00	$286.00	**$343.20**	
Kitchen sink, enameled steel, 2 bowls, 33" x 22", average	EA		$428.00	$428.00	**$513.60**	
Kitchen sink, enameled steel, 2 bowls, 33" x 22", premium	EA		$622.00	$622.00	**$746.40**	
Kitchen sink, enameled steel, 2 bowls, 38" x 22", economy	EA		$386.00	$386.00	**$463.20**	
Kitchen sink, enameled steel, 2 bowls, 38" x 22", average	EA		$574.00	$574.00	**$688.80**	
Kitchen sink, enameled steel, 2 bowls, 38" x 22", premium	EA		$919.00	$919.00	**$1,102.80**	

23

Kitchen and Laundry Plumbing

Kitchen Sink, Cast Iron

> Fixture costs only. See 'Install New Fixture' section for labor costs.

Description	Unit	Direct Labor	Direct Materials	Direct Total	Selling Price	Man-hours
Kitchen sink, enameled cast iron, 1 bowl, 31" x 21", economy	EA		$248.00	$248.00	**$297.60**	
Kitchen sink, enameled cast iron, 1 bowl, 31" x 21", average	EA		$424.00	$424.00	**$508.80**	
Kitchen sink, enameled cast iron, 1 bowl, 31" x 21", premium	EA		$688.00	$688.00	**$825.60**	
Kitchen sink, enameled cast iron, 2 bowls, 33" x 22", economy	EA		$303.00	$303.00	**$363.60**	
Kitchen sink, enameled cast iron, 2 bowls, 33" x 22", average	EA		$523.00	$523.00	**$627.60**	
Kitchen sink, enameled cast iron, 2 bowls, 33" x 22", premium	EA		$935.00	$935.00	**$1,122.00**	
Kitchen sink, enameled cast iron, 2 bowls, 43" x 22", economy	EA		$468.00	$468.00	**$561.60**	
Kitchen sink, enameled cast iron, 2 bowls, 43" x 22", average	EA		$798.00	$798.00	**$957.60**	
Kitchen sink, enameled cast iron, 2 bowls, 43" x 22", premium	EA		$1,265.00	$1,265.00	**$1,518.00**	
Kitchen sink, enameled cast iron, 3 bowls, 48" x 22", economy	EA		$638.00	$638.00	**$765.60**	
Kitchen sink, enameled cast iron, 3 bowls, 48" x 22", average	EA		$952.00	$952.00	**$1,142.40**	
Kitchen sink, enameled cast iron, 3 bowls, 48" x 22", premium	EA		$1,419.00	$1,419.00	**$1,702.80**	

Kitchen Faucets

> Fixture costs only. See 'Install New Fixture' section for labor costs.

Description	Unit	Direct Labor	Direct Materials	Direct Total	Selling Price	Man-hours
Sink faucet, kitchen, premium	EA		$418.00	$418.00	**$501.60**	
Sink faucet, kitchen, average	EA		$198.00	$198.00	**$237.60**	
Sink faucet, kitchen, economy	EA		$110.00	$110.00	**$132.00**	

Kitchen and Laundry Plumbing

Disposer

> Install in prepared location. No removal or rough-in included.

Description	Unit	Direct Labor	Direct Materials	Direct Total	Selling Price	Man-hours
Disposer, 1/3 HP, economy	EA	$152.95	$94.00	$246.95	**$368.23**	1.500
Disposer, 1/3 HP, average	EA	$152.95	$122.00	$274.95	**$401.83**	1.500
Disposer, 1/3 HP, premium	EA	$152.95	$171.00	$323.95	**$460.63**	1.500
Disposer, 1/2 HP, economy	EA	$152.95	$142.00	$294.95	**$425.83**	1.500
Disposer, 1/2 HP, average	EA	$152.95	$166.00	$318.95	**$454.63**	1.500
Disposer, 1/2 HP, premium	EA	$152.95	$220.00	$372.95	**$519.43**	1.500
Disposer, 3/4 HP, economy	EA	$152.95	$172.00	$324.95	**$461.83**	1.500
Disposer, 3/4 HP, average	EA	$152.95	$243.00	$395.95	**$547.03**	1.500
Disposer, 3/4 HP, premium	EA	$152.95	$392.00	$544.95	**$725.83**	1.500
Disposer, 1 HP, economy	EA	$152.95	$302.00	$454.95	**$617.83**	1.500
Disposer, 1 HP, average	EA	$152.95	$380.00	$532.95	**$711.43**	1.500
Disposer, 1 HP, premium	EA	$152.95	$439.00	$591.95	**$782.23**	1.500

Dishwasher

> Install in prepared location. No removal or rough-in included.

Description	Unit	Direct Labor	Direct Materials	Direct Total	Selling Price	Man-hours
Dishwasher, economy	EA	$152.95	$348.00	$500.95	**$673.03**	1.500
Dishwasher, average	EA	$152.95	$589.00	$741.95	**$962.23**	1.500
Dishwasher, premium	EA	$152.95	$1,068.00	$1,220.95	**$1,537.03**	1.500

23

Kitchen and Laundry Plumbing

Range

> Install in prepared location. No removal or rough-in included.

Description	Unit	Direct Labor	Direct Materials	Direct Total	Selling Price	Man-hours
Range, gas, economy	EA	$203.93	$578.00	$781.93	**$1,034.17**	2.000
Range, gas, average	EA	$203.93	$825.00	$1,028.93	**$1,330.57**	2.000
Range, gas, premium	EA	$203.93	$1,458.00	$1,661.93	**$2,090.17**	2.000
Range, commercial, gas, 30"	EA	$407.87	$4,252.00	$4,659.87	**$5,783.54**	4.000
Range, commercial, gas, 36"	EA	$407.87	$4,792.00	$5,199.87	**$6,431.54**	4.000
Range, commercial, gas, 48"	EA	$407.87	$5,715.00	$6,122.87	**$7,539.14**	4.000

Cooktop

> Install in prepared location. No removal or rough-in included.

Description	Unit	Direct Labor	Direct Materials	Direct Total	Selling Price	Man-hours
Cooktop, gas, economy	EA	$203.93	$422.00	$625.93	**$846.97**	2.000
Cooktop, gas, average	EA	$203.93	$538.00	$741.93	**$986.17**	2.000
Cooktop, gas, premium	EA	$203.93	$866.00	$1,069.93	**$1,379.77**	2.000

Oven

> Install in prepared location. No removal or rough-in included.

Description	Unit	Direct Labor	Direct Materials	Direct Total	Selling Price	Man-hours
Wall oven, single, gas, economy	EA	$203.93	$419.00	$622.93	**$843.37**	2.000
Wall oven, single, gas, average	EA	$203.93	$572.00	$775.93	**$1,026.97**	2.000
Wall oven, single, gas, premium	EA	$203.93	$842.00	$1,045.93	**$1,350.97**	2.000
Wall oven, double, gas, economy	EA	$356.88	$572.00	$928.88	**$1,282.40**	3.500
Wall oven, double, gas, average	EA	$356.88	$906.00	$1,262.88	**$1,683.20**	3.500
Wall oven, double, gas, premium	EA	$356.88	$1,236.00	$1,592.88	**$2,079.20**	3.500

Kitchen and Laundry Plumbing

Washer and Dryer

> Install in prepared location.
> No removal or rough-in included.

Description	Unit	Direct Labor	Direct Materials	Direct Total	Selling Price	Man-hours
Clothes washer, economy	EA	$81.02	$355.00	$436.02	**$561.30**	2.000
Clothes washer, average	EA	$81.02	$595.00	$676.02	**$849.30**	2.000
Clothes washer, premium	EA	$81.02	$1,099.00	$1,180.02	**$1,454.10**	2.000
Clothes dryer, gas, economy	EA	$203.93	$356.00	$559.93	**$767.77**	2.000
Clothes dryer, gas, average	EA	$203.93	$600.00	$803.93	**$1,060.57**	2.000
Clothes dryer, gas, premium	EA	$203.93	$1,078.00	$1,281.93	**$1,634.17**	2.000

Laundry Tub and Faucets

> Install in prepared location.
> No removal or rough-in included.

Description	Unit	Direct Labor	Direct Materials	Direct Total	Selling Price	Man-hours
Laundry tub, single tub, economy (faucet not included, select below)	EA	$203.93	$72.00	$275.93	**$426.97**	2.000
Laundry tub, double tub, economy (faucet not included, select below)	EA	$203.93	$121.00	$324.93	**$485.77**	2.000
Laundry tub, single tub, average (faucet not included, select below)	EA	$203.93	$121.00	$324.93	**$485.77**	2.000
Laundry tub, double tub, average (faucet not included, select below)	EA	$203.93	$209.00	$412.93	**$591.37**	2.000
Laundry tub, single tub, premium (faucet not included, select below)	EA	$203.93	$259.00	$462.93	**$651.37**	2.000
Laundry tub, double tub, premium (faucet not included, select below)	EA	$203.93	$429.00	$632.93	**$855.37**	2.000
Laundry faucet, premium	EA		$165.00	$165.00	**$198.00**	
Laundry faucet, average	EA		$88.00	$88.00	**$105.60**	
Laundry faucet, economy	EA		$55.00	$55.00	**$66.00**	

Forced Air Furnace

> No ductwork Included. See 'System Demolition' for removal of old system.

Description	Unit	Direct Labor	Direct Materials	Direct Total	Selling Price	Man-hours
FORCE AIR FURNACE, GAS FIRED						
Install gas fired forced air furnace, 50,000 BTU, AFUE 80%	EA	$407.87	$704.00	$710.00	**$1,525.94**	4.000
Install gas fired forced air furnace, 75,000 BTU, AFUE 80%	EA	$407.87	$907.00	$750.00	**$1,769.54**	4.000
Install gas fired forced air furnace, 100,000 BTU, AFUE 80%	EA	$407.87	$949.00	$845.00	**$1,819.94**	4.000
Install gas fired forced air furnace, 125,000 BTU, AFUE 80%	EA	$509.84	$1,031.00	$890.00	**$2,088.62**	5.000
Install gas fired forced air furnace, 150,000 BTU, AFUE 80%	EA	$509.84	$1,319.00	$920.00	**$2,434.22**	5.000
Install gas fired forced air furnace, 50,000 BTU, AFUE 92%	EA	$407.87	$810.00	$1,540.00	**$1,653.14**	4.000
Install gas fired forced air furnace, 75,000 BTU, AFUE 92%	EA	$407.87	$1,042.00	$1,650.00	**$1,931.54**	4.000
Install gas fired forced air furnace, 100,000 BTU, AFUE 92%	EA	$407.87	$1,090.00	$1,760.00	**$1,989.14**	4.000
Install gas fired forced air furnace, 125,000 BTU, AFUE 92%	EA	$509.84	$1,185.00	$1,890.00	**$2,273.42**	5.000
Install gas fired forced air furnace, 150,000 BTU, AFUE 92%	EA	$509.84	$1,517.00	$2,090.00	**$2,671.82**	5.000
Install gas fired wall furnace, direct vent, 15,000 BTU	EA	$305.90	$655.00	$960.90	**$1,296.85**	3.000
Install gas fired wall furnace, direct vent, 25,000 BTU	EA	$305.90	$704.00	$1,009.90	**$1,355.65**	3.000
Install gas fired wall furnace, direct vent, 35,000 BTU	EA	$407.87	$829.00	$1,236.87	**$1,675.94**	4.000
Install gas fired wall furnace, direct vent, 50,000 BTU	EA	$407.87	$891.00	$1,298.87	**$1,750.34**	4.000
FORCE AIR FURNACE, ELECTRIC FIRED						
Install electric fired forced air furnace, 30,000 BTU	EA	$407.87	$688.00	$1,095.87	**$1,506.74**	4.000
Install electric fired forced air furnace, 60,000 BTU	EA	$407.87	$858.00	$1,265.87	**$1,710.74**	4.000
Install electric fired forced air furnace, 75,000 BTU	EA	$407.87	$968.00	$1,375.87	**$1,842.74**	4.000
Install electric fired forced air furnace, 90,000 BTU	EA	$484.34	$1,062.00	$1,546.34	**$2,083.25**	4.750
Install electric fired forced air furnace, 100,000 BTU	EA	$484.34	$1,238.00	$1,722.34	**$2,294.45**	4.750
Install electric fired forced air furnace, 120,000 BTU	EA	$484.34	$1,397.00	$1,881.34	**$2,485.25**	4.750
FORCE AIR FURNACE, OIL FIRED						
Install oil fired forced air furnace, 67,000 BTU, AFUE 80%	EA	$407.87	$1,089.00	$1,345.00	**$1,987.94**	4.000
Install oil fired forced air furnace, 112,000 BTU, AFUE 80%	EA	$407.87	$1,293.00	$1,385.00	**$2,232.74**	4.000
Install oil fired forced air furnace, 134,000 BTU, AFUE 80%	EA	$484.34	$1,293.00	$1,520.00	**$2,360.45**	4.750
Install oil fired forced air furnace, 151,000 BTU, AFUE 80%	EA	$484.34	$1,529.00	$1,746.00	**$2,643.65**	4.750

HVAC (Heating, Ventilation, Air Conditioning)

Boilers

See 'System Demolition' for removal of old system.

Description	Unit	Direct Labor	Direct Materials	Direct Total	Selling Price	Man-hours
BOILER, GAS FIRED						
Install cast iron gas fired boiler, 80,000 BTU	EA	$815.74	$1,650.00	$2,465.74	**$3,342.28**	8.000
Install cast iron gas fired boiler, 100,000 BTU	EA	$815.74	$1,870.00	$2,685.74	**$3,606.28**	8.000
Install cast iron gas fired boiler, 130,000 BTU	EA	$815.74	$2,090.00	$2,905.74	**$3,870.28**	8.000
Install steel gas fired boiler, 80,000 BTU	EA	$815.74	$2,530.00	$3,345.74	**$4,398.28**	8.000
Install steel gas fired boiler, 100,000 BTU	EA	$815.74	$2,860.00	$3,675.74	**$4,794.28**	8.000
Install steel gas fired boiler, 130,000 BTU	EA	$815.74	$3,190.00	$4,005.74	**$5,190.28**	8.000
BOILER, ELECTRIC FIRED						
Install electric fired boiler, 40,000 BTU	EA	$917.70	$3,300.00	$4,217.70	**$5,492.56**	9.000
Install electric fired boiler, 82,000 BTU	EA	$917.70	$3,630.00	$4,547.70	**$5,888.56**	9.000
Install electric fired boiler, 109,000 BTU	EA	$917.70	$3,960.00	$4,877.70	**$6,284.56**	9.000
BOILER, OIL FIRED						
Install cast iron oil fired boiler, 110,000 BTU	EA	$815.74	$1,760.00	$2,575.74	**$3,474.28**	8.000
Install cast iron oil fired boiler, 130,000 BTU	EA	$815.74	$2,035.00	$2,850.74	**$3,804.28**	8.000
Install cast iron oil fired boiler, 170,000 BTU	EA	$815.74	$2,200.00	$3,015.74	**$4,002.28**	8.000
Install steel oil fired boiler, 110,000 BTU	EA	$815.74	$2,970.00	$3,785.74	**$4,926.28**	8.000
Install steel oil fired boiler, 130,000 BTU	EA	$815.74	$3,300.00	$4,115.74	**$5,322.28**	8.000
Install steel oil fired boiler, 170,000 BTU	EA	$815.74	$3,630.00	$4,445.74	**$5,718.28**	8.000

Electric Baseboard Heat

Within 15' of power source. No patching included.

Description	Unit	Direct Labor	Direct Materials	Direct Total	Selling Price	Man-hours
ELECTRIC BASEBOARD HEAT, RADIANT						
Install electric baseboard, 1000W, 4' long, within 15' of power	EA	$190.68	$119.00	$309.68	**$461.24**	2.000
Install electric baseboard, 1500W, 6' long, within 15' of power	EA	$238.35	$163.00	$401.35	**$593.64**	2.500
Install electric baseboard, 2000W, 8' long, within 15' of power	EA	$286.02	$207.00	$493.02	**$726.05**	3.000
Install electric baseboard, 2500W, 10' long, within 15' of power	EA	$333.69	$251.00	$584.69	**$858.46**	3.500
ELECTRIC BASEBOARD HEAT, RECIRCULATING HOT WATER						
Install electric hot water baseboard, 750W, 4' long, within 15' of power	EA	$190.68	$182.00	$372.68	**$536.84**	2.000
Install electric hot water baseboard, 1000W, 5' long, within 15' of power	EA	$214.52	$209.00	$423.52	**$609.04**	2.250
Install electric hot water baseboard, 1380W, 6' long, within 15' of power	EA	$238.35	$237.00	$475.35	**$682.44**	2.500
Install electric hot water baseboard, 1500W, 7' long, within 15' of power	EA	$262.19	$270.00	$532.19	**$761.85**	2.750
Install electric hot water baseboard, 2000W, 8' long, within 15' of power	EA	$286.02	$292.00	$578.02	**$828.05**	3.000

HVAC (Heating, Ventilation, Air Conditioning)

Hot Water Baseboard Heat

> Within 10' of hot water source. See 'System Demolition' for removal of old system.

Description	Unit	Direct Labor	Direct Materials	Direct Total	Selling Price	Man-hours
Radiator, baseboard, 1/2" element, 8' section	EA	$305.90	$99.00	$404.90	**$629.65**	3.000
Radiator, baseboard, 3/4" element, 8' section	EA	$305.90	$152.00	$457.90	**$693.25**	3.000
Radiator, baseboard, 1/2" element, 16' section	EA	$509.84	$175.00	$684.84	**$1,061.42**	5.000
Radiator, baseboard, 3/4" element, 16' section	EA	$509.84	$281.00	$790.84	**$1,188.62**	5.000
Radiator, baseboard, copper element, 8' section	EA	$305.90	$296.00	$601.90	**$866.05**	3.000
Radiator, baseboard, copper element, 16' section	EA	$509.84	$545.00	$1,054.84	**$1,505.42**	5.000

Heat Pump

> Existing power source. See 'System Demolition' for removal of old system.

Description	Unit	Direct Labor	Direct Materials	Direct Total	Selling Price	Man-hours
SPLIT SYSTEM, 12 Seer						
Install heat pump and handler, split system, 1.5 ton, 12 Seer	EA	$1,070.65	$1,918.00	$2,988.65	**$4,089.59**	10.500
Install heat pump and handler, split system, 2.0 ton, 12 Seer	EA	$1,070.65	$1,967.00	$3,037.65	**$4,148.39**	10.500
Install heat pump and handler, split system, 2.5 ton, 12 Seer	EA	$1,070.65	$2,209.00	$3,279.65	**$4,438.79**	10.500
Install heat pump and handler, split system, 3.0 ton, 12 Seer	EA	$1,172.62	$2,381.00	$3,553.62	**$4,815.48**	11.500
Install heat pump and handler, split system, 3.5 ton, 12 Seer	EA	$1,172.62	$2,584.00	$3,756.62	**$5,059.08**	11.500
Install heat pump and handler, split system, 4.0 ton, 12 Seer	EA	$1,172.62	$2,983.00	$4,155.62	**$5,537.88**	11.500
Install heat pump and handler, split system, 5.0 ton, 12 Seer	EA	$1,172.62	$3,267.00	$4,439.62	**$5,878.68**	11.500
SPLIT SYSTEM, 14 Seer						
Install heat pump and handler, split system, 1.5 ton, 14 Seer	EA	$1,070.65	$3,157.00	$4,227.65	**$5,576.39**	10.500
Install heat pump and handler, split system, 2.0 ton, 14 Seer	EA	$1,070.65	$3,367.00	$4,437.65	**$5,828.39**	10.500
Install heat pump and handler, split system, 2.5 ton, 14 Seer	EA	$1,070.65	$3,665.00	$4,735.65	**$6,185.99**	10.500
Install heat pump and handler, split system, 3.0 ton, 14 Seer	EA	$1,172.62	$3,814.00	$4,986.62	**$6,535.08**	11.500
Install heat pump and handler, split system, 3.5 ton, 14 Seer	EA	$1,172.62	$4,156.00	$5,328.62	**$6,945.48**	11.500
Install heat pump and handler, split system, 4.0 ton, 14 Seer	EA	$1,172.62	$5,027.00	$6,199.62	**$7,990.68**	11.500
Install heat pump and handler, split system, 5.0 ton, 14 Seer	EA	$1,172.62	$5,183.00	$6,355.62	**$8,177.88**	11.500
SELF CONTAINED SYSTEM, 12 Seer (heat pump and air handler one unit)						
Install self contained heat pump package, 1.5 ton, 12 Seer	EA	$917.70	$2,622.00	$3,539.70	**$4,678.96**	9.000
Install self contained heat pump package, 2.0 ton, 12 Seer	EA	$917.70	$2,706.00	$3,623.70	**$4,779.76**	9.000
Install self contained heat pump package, 2.5 ton, 12 Seer	EA	$1,019.67	$2,802.00	$3,821.67	**$5,065.25**	10.000
Install self contained heat pump package, 3.0 ton, 12 Seer	EA	$1,019.67	$3,111.00	$4,130.67	**$5,436.05**	10.000
Install self contained heat pump package, 3.5 ton, 12 Seer	EA	$1,019.67	$3,627.00	$4,646.67	**$6,055.25**	10.000
Install self contained heat pump package, 4.0 ton, 12 Seer	EA	$1,019.67	$3,953.00	$4,972.67	**$6,446.45**	10.000

HVAC (Heating, Ventilation, Air Conditioning)

Air Conditioning

> Existing power source. See 'System Demolition' for removal of old system.

Description	Unit	Direct Labor	Direct Materials	Direct Total	Selling Price	Man-hours
CONDENSER AND COIL, EXISTING AIR HANDLER, 12 Seer						
Install air conditioning condenser and coil, 2.0 ton, 12 Seer	EA	$764.75	$1,736.00	$2,500.75	**$3,360.34**	7.500
Install air conditioning condenser and coil, 2.5 ton, 12 Seer	EA	$764.75	$1,829.00	$2,593.75	**$3,471.94**	7.500
Install air conditioning condenser and coil, 3.0 ton, 12 Seer	EA	$866.72	$2,029.00	$2,895.72	**$3,882.22**	8.500
Install air conditioning condenser and coil, 3.5 ton, 12 Seer	EA	$866.72	$2,181.00	$3,047.72	**$4,064.62**	8.500
Install air conditioning condenser and coil, 4.0 ton, 12 Seer	EA	$866.72	$2,390.00	$3,256.72	**$4,315.42**	8.500
Install air conditioning condenser and coil, 5.0 ton, 12 Seer	EA	$866.72	$2,763.00	$3,629.72	**$4,763.02**	8.500
CONDENSER AND COIL, EXISTING AIR HANDLER, 14 Seer						
Install air conditioning condenser and coil, 2.0 ton, 14 Seer	EA	$764.75	$2,194.00	$2,958.75	**$3,909.94**	7.500
Install air conditioning condenser and coil, 2.5 ton, 14 Seer	EA	$764.75	$2,482.00	$3,246.75	**$4,255.54**	7.500
Install air conditioning condenser and coil, 3.0 ton, 14 Seer	EA	$866.72	$2,708.00	$3,574.72	**$4,697.02**	8.500
Install air conditioning condenser and coil, 3.5 ton, 14 Seer	EA	$866.72	$2,945.00	$3,811.72	**$4,981.42**	8.500
Install air conditioning condenser and coil, 4.0 ton, 14 Seer	EA	$866.72	$3,751.00	$4,617.72	**$5,948.62**	8.500
Install air conditioning condenser and coil, 5.0 ton, 14 Seer	EA	$866.72	$4,105.00	$4,971.72	**$6,373.42**	8.500
SELF CONTAINED SYSTEM, 12 Seer (condenser and air handler one unit)						
Install self contained air conditioning package, 1.5 ton, 12 Seer	EA	$764.75	$2,054.00	$2,818.75	**$3,741.94**	7.500
Install self contained air conditioning package, 2.0 ton, 12 Seer	EA	$764.75	$2,082.00	$2,846.75	**$3,775.54**	7.500
Install self contained air conditioning package, 2.5 ton, 12 Seer	EA	$764.75	$2,238.00	$3,002.75	**$3,962.74**	7.500
Install self contained air conditioning package, 3.0 ton, 12 Seer	EA	$866.72	$2,443.00	$3,309.72	**$4,379.02**	8.500
Install self contained air conditioning package, 3.5 ton, 12 Seer	EA	$866.72	$2,767.00	$3,633.72	**$4,767.82**	8.500
Install self contained air conditioning package, 4.0 ton, 12 Seer	EA	$866.72	$3,208.00	$4,074.72	**$5,297.02**	8.500
Install self contained air conditioning package, 5.0 ton, 12 Seer	EA	$866.72	$3,776.00	$4,642.72	**$5,978.62**	8.500

HVAC (Heating, Ventilation, Air Conditioning)

Masonry Chimney

Description	Unit	Direct Labor	Direct Materials	Direct Total	Selling Price	Man-hours
Construct 16" x 16" standard brick chimney, one 8" x 8" flue	LF	$94.36	$19.41	$113.76	**$189.98**	1.425
Construct 24" x 24" standard brick chimney, one 8" x 8" flue	LF	$159.64	$43.86	$203.51	**$339.86**	2.411
Construct 28" x 16" standard brick chimney, two 8" x 8" flues	LF	$123.16	$34.10	$157.26	**$262.63**	1.860
Construct 36" x 24" standard brick chimney, two 8" x 8" flues	LF	$226.12	$65.80	$291.92	**$487.50**	3.415
Construct 20" x 16" standard brick chimney, one 12" x 8" flue	LF	$102.57	$24.34	$126.91	**$211.94**	1.549
Construct 28" x 24" standard brick chimney, one 12" x 8" flue	LF	$175.34	$51.10	$226.44	**$378.15**	2.648
Construct 36" x 16" standard brick chimney, two 12" x 8" flues	LF	$139.18	$43.86	$183.05	**$305.69**	2.102
Construct 44" x 24" standard brick chimney, two 12" x 8" flues	LF	$260.09	$80.39	$340.47	**$568.59**	3.928
Construct 20" x 20" standard brick chimney, one 12" x 12" flue	LF	$110.64	$30.37	$141.02	**$235.50**	1.671
Construct 28" x 28" standard brick chimney, one 12" x 12" flue	LF	$191.03	$54.42	$245.44	**$409.89**	2.885
Construct 36" x 20" standard brick chimney, two 12" x 12" flues	LF	$152.89	$59.66	$212.55	**$354.95**	2.309
Construct 44" x 28" standard brick chimney, two 12" x 12" flues	LF	$264.06	$93.76	$357.82	**$597.56**	3.988
Construct block chimney, 8" x 8" flue	LF	$57.61	$13.70	$71.31	**$119.09**	0.870
Construct block chimney, 8" x 12" flue	LF	$64.56	$16.67	$81.23	**$135.65**	0.975
Construct block chimney, 12" x 12" flue	LF	$71.45	$19.64	$91.08	**$152.11**	1.079
Additional charge for scaffolding, per LF of work done using scaffold	LF	$31.78		$31.78	**$53.08**	0.480

Masonry Fireplaces

Description	Unit	Direct Labor	Direct Materials	Direct Total	Selling Price	Man-hours
Construct new brick fireplace, 36"W x 32"H x 18"D, chimney not included	EA	$2,118.85	$664.62	$2,783.47	**$4,648.39**	32.000
Construct new brick fireplace, 38"W x 36"H x 18"D, chimney not included	EA	$2,516.14	$747.69	$3,263.83	**$5,450.60**	38.000
Construct new brick fireplace, 42"W x 36"H x 20"D, chimney not included	EA	$2,913.42	$817.48	$3,730.90	**$6,230.60**	44.000
Construct new brick fireplace, 46"W x 48"H x 22"D, chimney not included	EA	$3,641.78	$1,060.06	$4,701.84	**$7,852.07**	55.000
Install damper in fireplace with no damper	EA	$529.71	$169.40	$699.11	**$1,167.52**	8.000
Face fireplace surround, brick	SF	$27.81	$5.82	$33.63	**$56.15**	0.420
Face fireplace surround, cultured stone	SF	$29.80	$8.80	$38.60	**$64.46**	0.450
Face fireplace surround, natural stone	SF	$51.65	$9.90	$61.55	**$102.78**	0.780
Construct fireplace hearth, brick	SF	$31.78	$8.31	$40.09	**$66.95**	0.480
Construct fireplace hearth, marble	SF	$39.73	$13.20	$52.93	**$88.39**	0.600
Construct fireplace hearth, ceramic tile	SF	$39.73	$24.20	$63.93	**$106.76**	0.600

HVAC (Heating, Ventilation, Air Conditioning)

Bathroom Fans, Lights, Heaters

> Within 10' of power source.
> No patching included.

Description	Unit	Direct Labor	Direct Materials	Direct Total	Selling Price	Man-hours
BATHROOM LIGHT						
Install bathroom light and switch, open ceiling and walls, economy	EA	$190.68	$82.50	$273.18	**$456.21**	2.000
Install bathroom light and switch, open ceiling and walls, average	EA	$190.68	$104.50	$295.18	**$492.95**	2.000
Install bathroom light and switch, open ceiling and walls, premium	EA	$190.68	$137.50	$328.18	**$548.06**	2.000
Install bathroom light and switch, finished ceiling and walls, economy	EA	$381.36	$82.50	$463.86	**$774.65**	4.000
Install bathroom light and switch, finished ceiling and walls, average	EA	$381.36	$104.50	$485.86	**$811.39**	4.000
Install bathroom light and switch, finished ceiling and walls, premium	EA	$381.36	$137.50	$518.86	**$866.50**	4.000
BATHROOM LIGHT AND FAN						
Install bathroom light with fan & switch, open ceiling and walls, economy	EA	$190.68	$104.50	$295.18	**$492.95**	2.000
Install bathroom light with fan & switch, open ceiling and walls, average	EA	$190.68	$137.50	$328.18	**$548.06**	2.000
Install bathroom light with fan & switch, open ceiling and walls, premium	EA	$190.68	$181.50	$372.18	**$621.54**	2.000
Install bathroom light with fan & switch, finished ceiling/walls, economy	EA	$381.36	$104.50	$485.86	**$811.39**	4.000
Install bathroom light with fan & switch, finished ceiling/walls, average	EA	$381.36	$137.50	$518.86	**$866.50**	4.000
Install bathroom light with fan & switch, finished ceiling/walls, premium	EA	$381.36	$181.50	$562.86	**$939.98**	4.000
BATHROOM LIGHT, FAN AND HEATER						
Install bathroom light, fan, heater, switch, open ceiling/walls, economy	EA	$190.68	$159.50	$350.18	**$584.80**	2.000
Install bathroom light, fan, heater, switch, open ceiling/walls, average	EA	$190.68	$209.00	$399.68	**$667.47**	2.000
Install bathroom light, fan, heater, switch, open ceiling/walls, premium	EA	$190.68	$269.50	$460.18	**$768.50**	2.000
Install bathroom light, fan, heater, switch, finished ceiling/walls, economy	EA	$381.36	$159.50	$540.86	**$903.24**	4.000
Install bathroom light, fan, heater, switch, finished ceiling/walls, average	EA	$381.36	$209.00	$590.36	**$985.90**	4.000
Install bathroom light, fan, heater, switch, finished ceiling/walls, premium	EA	$381.36	$269.50	$650.86	**$1,086.94**	4.000

HVAC (Heating, Ventilation, Air Conditioning)

Bathroom Wall Heaters

> Within 10' of power source. No patching included.

Description	Unit	Direct Labor	Direct Materials	Direct Total	Selling Price	Man-hours
BATHROOM WALL HEATER, FORCED AIR HEAT						
Install wall heater, forced air, 1250W, open walls, economy	EA	$143.01	$192.50	$335.51	**$560.30**	1.500
Install wall heater, forced air, 1250W, open walls, average	EA	$143.01	$220.00	$363.01	**$606.23**	1.500
Install wall heater, forced air, 1250W, open walls, premium	EA	$143.01	$275.00	$418.01	**$698.08**	1.500
Install wall heater, forced air, 1250W, finished walls, economy	EA	$286.02	$192.50	$478.52	**$799.13**	3.000
Install wall heater, forced air, 1250W, finished walls, average	EA	$286.02	$220.00	$506.02	**$845.05**	3.000
Install wall heater, forced air, 1250W, finished walls, premium	EA	$286.02	$275.00	$561.02	**$936.90**	3.000
Install wall heater, forced air, 1500W, open walls, economy	EA	$143.01	$225.50	$368.51	**$615.41**	1.500
Install wall heater, forced air, 1500W, open walls, average	EA	$143.01	$253.00	$396.01	**$661.34**	1.500
Install wall heater, forced air, 1500W, open walls, premium	EA	$143.01	$308.00	$451.01	**$753.19**	1.500
Install wall heater, forced air, 1500W, finished walls, economy	EA	$286.02	$225.50	$511.52	**$854.24**	3.000
Install wall heater, forced air, 1500W, finished walls, average	EA	$286.02	$253.00	$539.02	**$900.16**	3.000
Install wall heater, forced air, 1500W, finished walls, premium	EA	$286.02	$308.00	$594.02	**$992.01**	3.000
BATHROOM WALL HEATER, RADIANT HEAT						
Install wall heater, radiant heat, 1250W, open walls, economy	EA	$143.01	$159.50	$302.51	**$505.19**	1.500
Install wall heater, radiant heat, 1250W, open walls, average	EA	$143.01	$187.00	$330.01	**$551.12**	1.500
Install wall heater, radiant heat, 1250W, open walls, premium	EA	$143.01	$247.50	$390.51	**$652.15**	1.500
Install wall heater, radiant heat, 1250W, finished walls, economy	EA	$286.02	$159.50	$445.52	**$744.02**	3.000
Install wall heater, radiant heat, 1250W, finished walls, average	EA	$286.02	$187.00	$473.02	**$789.94**	3.000
Install wall heater, radiant heat, 1250W, finished walls, premium	EA	$286.02	$247.50	$533.52	**$890.98**	3.000
Install wall heater, radiant heat, 1500W, open walls, economy	EA	$143.01	$192.50	$335.51	**$560.30**	1.500
Install wall heater, radiant heat, 1500W, open walls, average	EA	$143.01	$220.00	$363.01	**$606.23**	1.500
Install wall heater, radiant heat, 1500W, open walls, premium	EA	$143.01	$275.00	$418.01	**$698.08**	1.500
Install wall heater, radiant heat, 1500W, finished walls, economy	EA	$286.02	$192.50	$478.52	**$799.13**	3.000
Install wall heater, radiant heat, 1500W, finished walls, average	EA	$286.02	$220.00	$506.02	**$845.05**	3.000
Install wall heater, radiant heat, 1500W, finished walls, premium	EA	$286.02	$275.00	$561.02	**$936.90**	3.000

HVAC (Heating, Ventilation, Air Conditioning)

Fans

> Within 10' of power source.
> No patching included.

Description	Unit	Direct Labor	Direct Materials	Direct Total	Selling Price	Man-hours
WHOLE HOUSE FAN						
Install whole house fan, 30" diameter	EA	$214.52	$528.00	$742.52	**$991.84**	2.250
Install whole house fan, 36" diameter	EA	$238.35	$583.00	$821.35	**$1,097.64**	2.500
Install whole house fan, 42" diameter	EA	$262.19	$660.00	$922.19	**$1,229.85**	2.750
Install whole house fan, 48" diameter	EA	$286.02	$792.00	$1,078.02	**$1,428.05**	3.000
CEILING FAN						
Install ceiling fan, existing wiring, economy	EA	$71.51	$192.50	$264.01	**$350.41**	0.750
Install ceiling fan, existing wiring, average	EA	$71.51	$286.00	$357.51	**$462.61**	0.750
Install ceiling fan, existing wiring, economy	EA	$71.51	$434.50	$506.01	**$640.81**	0.750
Install ceiling fan, new wiring, no switch, open ceiling & walls, economy	EA	$238.35	$220.00	$458.35	**$662.04**	2.500
Install ceiling fan, new wiring, no switch, open ceiling & walls, average	EA	$238.35	$313.50	$551.85	**$774.24**	2.500
Install ceiling fan, new wiring, no switch, open ceiling & walls, premium	EA	$238.35	$462.00	$700.35	**$952.44**	2.500
Install ceiling fan, new wiring, no switch, finished ceiling/walls, economy	EA	$381.36	$220.00	$601.36	**$900.87**	4.000
Install ceiling fan, new wiring, no switch, finished ceiling/walls, average	EA	$381.36	$313.50	$694.86	**$1,013.07**	4.000
Install ceiling fan, new wiring, no switch, finished ceiling/walls, premium	EA	$381.36	$462.00	$843.36	**$1,191.27**	4.000
Install ceiling fan, new wiring and switch, open ceiling & walls, economy	EA	$286.02	$236.50	$522.52	**$761.45**	3.000
Install ceiling fan, new wiring and switch, open ceiling & walls, average	EA	$286.02	$330.00	$616.02	**$873.65**	3.000
Install ceiling fan, new wiring and switch, open ceiling & walls, premium	EA	$286.02	$478.50	$764.52	**$1,051.85**	3.000
Install ceiling fan, new wiring and switch, finished ceiling/walls, economy	EA	$429.03	$236.50	$665.53	**$1,000.28**	4.500
Install ceiling fan, new wiring and switch, finished ceiling/walls, average	EA	$429.03	$330.00	$759.03	**$1,112.48**	4.500
Install ceiling fan, new wiring and switch, finished ceiling/walls, premium	EA	$429.03	$478.50	$907.53	**$1,290.68**	4.500
GABLE EXHAUST FAN						
Install gable fan, economy	EA	$190.68	$121.00	$311.68	**$463.64**	2.000
Install gable fan, average	EA	$190.68	$198.00	$388.68	**$556.04**	2.000
Install gable fan, premium	EA	$190.68	$275.00	$465.68	**$648.44**	2.000

Electrical

Outlets and Switches

> Within 10' of power source.
> No patching included.

Description	Unit	Direct Labor	Direct Materials	Direct Total	Selling Price	Man-hours
OUTLETS AND SWITCHES, 110 V						
Install box and duplex outlet, open walls, within 10' of power	EA	$47.67	$13.75	$61.42	**$102.57**	0.500
Install box and duplex outlet, finished walls, within 10' of power	EA	$143.01	$13.75	$156.76	**$261.79**	1.500
Install box and switch, open walls, within 10' of power	EA	$47.67	$13.75	$61.42	**$102.57**	0.500
Install box and switch, finished walls, within 10' of power	EA	$143.01	$13.75	$156.76	**$261.79**	1.500
Install 3 way switch set, open walls, within 10' of power	EA	$166.85	$36.30	$203.15	**$339.25**	1.750
Install 3 way switch set, finished walls, within 10' of power	EA	$381.36	$36.30	$417.66	**$697.49**	4.000
Install ceiling box, open walls, within 10' of power	EA	$47.67	$13.75	$61.42	**$102.57**	0.500
Install ceiling box, finished walls, within 10' of power	EA	$143.01	$13.75	$156.76	**$261.79**	1.500
Install ceiling box and wall switch, open walls, within 10' of power	EA	$166.85	$30.25	$197.10	**$329.15**	1.750
Install ceiling box and wall switch, finished walls, within 10' of power	EA	$381.36	$30.25	$411.61	**$687.39**	4.000
Install GFIC outlet in existing box	EA	$47.67	$13.20	$60.87	**$101.65**	0.500
OUTLETS, 220 V						
Install 220 V outlet, within 15' of power, open walls	EA	$166.85	$35.20	$202.05	**$337.42**	1.750
Install 220 V outlet, within 25' of power, open walls	EA	$238.35	$46.20	$284.55	**$475.20**	2.500
Install 220 V outlet, within 35' of power, open walls	EA	$309.86	$57.20	$367.06	**$612.98**	3.250
Install 220 V outlet, within 15' of power, finished walls	EA	$357.53	$35.20	$392.73	**$655.85**	3.750
Install 220 V outlet, within 25' of power, finished walls	EA	$524.37	$35.20	$559.57	**$934.48**	5.500
Install 220 V outlet, within 35' of power, finished walls	EA	$619.71	$35.20	$654.91	**$1,093.70**	6.500

Electrical

Kitchen and Laundry Appliance Outlets

> Within 15' of power source. No patching included.

Description	Unit	Direct Labor	Direct Materials	Direct Total	Selling Price	Man-hours
TRASH COMPACTOR OUTLET						
Install trash compactor electric outlet, open walls and ceiling	EA	$95.34	$24.57	$119.91	**$200.26**	1.000
Install trash compactor electric outlet, finished walls, open ceiling	EA	$143.01	$24.57	$167.58	**$279.87**	1.500
Install trash compactor electric outlet, finished walls and ceiling	EA	$190.68	$24.57	$215.25	**$359.47**	2.000
REFRIGERATOR OUTLET						
Install refrigerator wall outlet, open walls and ceiling	EA	$95.34	$24.57	$119.91	**$200.26**	1.000
Install refrigerator wall outlet, finished walls, open ceiling	EA	$143.01	$24.57	$167.58	**$279.87**	1.500
Install refrigerator wall outlet, finished walls and ceiling	EA	$190.68	$24.57	$215.25	**$359.47**	2.000
OVEN OUTLET						
Install oven electric outlet, 30 amp, open walls and ceiling	EA	$166.85	$53.64	$220.48	**$368.20**	1.750
Install oven electric outlet, 30 amp, finished walls, open ceiling	EA	$262.19	$53.64	$315.82	**$527.42**	2.750
Install oven electric outlet, 30 amp, finished walls and ceiling	EA	$333.69	$53.64	$387.33	**$646.83**	3.500
COOKTOP OUTLET						
Install cooktop electric outlet, 30 amp, open walls and ceiling	EA	$166.85	$53.64	$220.48	**$368.20**	1.750
Install cooktop electric outlet, 30 amp, finished walls, open ceiling	EA	$262.19	$53.64	$315.82	**$527.42**	2.750
Install cooktop electric outlet, 30 amp, finished walls and ceiling	EA	$333.69	$53.64	$387.33	**$646.83**	3.500
RANGE OUTLET						
Install range electric outlet, 50 amp, open walls and ceiling	EA	$166.85	$53.64	$220.48	**$368.20**	1.750
Install range electric outlet, 50 amp, finished walls, open ceiling	EA	$262.19	$53.64	$315.82	**$527.42**	2.750
Install range electric outlet, 50 amp, finished walls and ceiling	EA	$333.69	$53.64	$387.33	**$646.83**	3.500
HOOD OUTLET						
Install hood & fan outlet, open walls and ceiling	EA	$95.34	$24.57	$119.91	**$200.26**	1.000
Install hood & fan outlet, finished walls, open ceiling	EA	$143.01	$24.57	$167.58	**$279.87**	1.500
Install hood & fan outlet, finished walls and ceiling	EA	$190.68	$24.57	$215.25	**$359.47**	2.000
DRYER OUTLET						
Install dryer electric outlet, 40 amp, open walls, open ceiling	EA	$166.85	$53.64	$220.48	**$368.20**	1.750
Install dryer electric outlet, 40 amp, finished walls, open ceiling	EA	$262.19	$53.64	$315.82	**$527.42**	2.750
Install dryer electric outlet, 40 amp, finished walls and ceiling	EA	$333.69	$53.64	$387.33	**$646.83**	3.500

Electrical

Recessed Lighting

> Within 10' of power source.
> No patching included.

Description	Unit	Direct Labor	Direct Materials	Direct Total	Selling Price	Man-hours
Install recessed fixture, 8" frame, open wall, within 10' power, economy	EA	$71.51	$41.80	$113.31	**$189.22**	0.750
Install recessed fixture, 8" frame, open wall, within 10' power, average	EA	$71.51	$58.30	$129.81	**$216.77**	0.750
Install recessed fixture, 8" frame, open wall, within 10' power, premium	EA	$71.51	$74.80	$146.31	**$244.33**	0.750
Install recessed fixture, 10" frame, open wall, within 10' power, economy	EA	$71.51	$52.80	$124.31	**$207.59**	0.750
Install recessed fixture, 10" frame, open wall, within 10' power, average	EA	$71.51	$69.30	$140.81	**$235.14**	0.750
Install recessed fixture, 10" frame, open wall, within 10' power, premium	EA	$71.51	$85.80	$157.31	**$262.70**	0.750
Install recessed fixture, 12" frame, open wall, within 10' power, economy	EA	$71.51	$63.80	$135.31	**$225.96**	0.750
Install recessed fixture, 12" frame, open wall, within 10' power, average	EA	$71.51	$80.30	$151.81	**$253.51**	0.750
Install recessed fixture, 12" frame, open wall, within 10' power, premium	EA	$71.51	$96.80	$168.31	**$281.07**	0.750
Install recessed fixture, 8" frame, finish wall, within 10' power, economy	EA	$190.68	$41.80	$232.48	**$388.24**	2.000
Install recessed fixture, 8" frame, finish wall, within 10' power, average	EA	$190.68	$58.30	$248.98	**$415.80**	2.000
Install recessed fixture, 8" frame, finish wall, within 10' power, premium	EA	$190.68	$74.80	$265.48	**$443.35**	2.000
Install recessed fixture, 10" frame, finish wall, within 10' power, economy	EA	$190.68	$52.80	$243.48	**$406.61**	2.000
Install recessed fixture, 10" frame, finish wall, within 10' power, average	EA	$190.68	$69.30	$259.98	**$434.17**	2.000
Install recessed fixture, 10" frame, finish wall, within 10' power, premium	EA	$190.68	$85.80	$276.48	**$461.72**	2.000
Install recessed fixture, 12" frame, finish wall, within 10' power, economy	EA	$190.68	$63.80	$254.48	**$424.98**	2.000
Install recessed fixture, 12" frame, finish wall, within 10' power, average	EA	$190.68	$80.30	$270.98	**$452.54**	2.000
Install recessed fixture, 12" frame, finish wall, within 10' power, premium	EA	$190.68	$96.80	$287.48	**$480.09**	2.000

Electrical

Fluorescent Lighting

> Within 10' of power source.
> No patching included.

Description	Unit	Direct Labor	Direct Materials	Direct Total	Selling Price	Man-hours
FLUORESCENT UNDERCOUNTER LIGHTING						
Install under-cabinet fluorescent lights, 18" x 5" x 2"	EA	$47.67	$27.50	$75.17	**$125.53**	0.500
Install under-cabinet fluorescent lights, 24" x 5" x 2"	EA	$47.67	$33.00	$80.67	**$134.72**	0.500
Install under-cabinet fluorescent lights, 36" x 5" x 2"	EA	$71.51	$38.50	$110.01	**$183.71**	0.750
Install under-cabinet fluorescent lights, 48" x 5" x 2"	EA	$71.51	$44.00	$115.51	**$192.89**	0.750
FLUORESCENT CEILING LIGHTING						
Install ceiling fluorescent fixture in existing box, acrylic diffuser, 2' x 2'	EA	$95.34	$93.50	$188.84	**$315.36**	1.000
Install ceiling fluorescent fixture in existing box, acrylic diffuser, 4' long	EA	$95.34	$55.00	$150.34	**$251.07**	1.000
Install ceiling fluorescent fixture in existing box, acrylic diffuser, 6' long	EA	$95.34	$77.00	$172.34	**$287.81**	1.000
Install ceiling fluorescent fixture in existing box, acrylic diffuser, 8' long	EA	$95.34	$99.00	$194.34	**$324.55**	1.000
Install fluorescent ceiling fixture in existing box, 8" diameter	EA	$71.51	$41.80	$113.31	**$189.22**	0.750
Install fluorescent ceiling fixture in existing box, 12" diameter	EA	$71.51	$52.80	$124.31	**$207.59**	0.750
Install fluorescent ceiling fixture in existing box, 16" diameter	EA	$71.51	$71.50	$143.01	**$238.82**	0.750
FLUORESCENT GRID CEILING LIGHTING						
Install fixture in grid ceiling within 10' of power, 2' x 2', economy	EA	$119.18	$77.00	$196.18	**$327.61**	1.250
Install fixture in grid ceiling within 10' of power, 2' x 2', average	EA	$119.18	$121.00	$240.18	**$401.09**	1.250
Install fixture in grid ceiling within 10' of power, 2' x 2', premium	EA	$119.18	$154.00	$273.18	**$456.20**	1.250
Install fixture in grid ceiling within 10' of power, 2' x 4', economy	EA	$166.85	$99.00	$265.85	**$443.96**	1.750
Install fixture in grid ceiling within 10' of power, 2' x 4', average	EA	$166.85	$143.00	$309.85	**$517.44**	1.750
Install fixture in grid ceiling within 10' of power, 2' x 4', premium	EA	$166.85	$176.00	$342.85	**$572.55**	1.750

Electrical

Incandescent Lighting

> Within 10' of power source. No patching included.

Description	Unit	Direct Labor	Direct Materials	Direct Total	Selling Price	Man-hours
INCANDESCENT HANGING LIGHTING						
Install hanging light in existing box, economy	EA	$95.34	$88.00	$183.34	**$306.18**	1.000
Install hanging light in existing box, average	EA	$95.34	$154.00	$249.34	**$416.40**	1.000
Install hanging light in existing box, premium	EA	$95.34	$308.00	$403.34	**$673.58**	1.000
INCANDESCENT CEILING LIGHTING						
Install ceiling light in existing box, economy	EA	$71.51	$44.00	$115.51	**$192.89**	0.750
Install ceiling light in existing box, average	EA	$71.51	$88.00	$159.51	**$266.37**	0.750
Install ceiling light in existing box, premium	EA	$71.51	$154.00	$225.51	**$376.59**	0.750
INCANDESCENT WALL LIGHTING						
Install wall sconce in existing box, economy	EA	$95.34	$55.00	$150.34	**$251.07**	1.000
Install wall sconce in existing box, average	EA	$95.34	$82.50	$177.84	**$296.99**	1.000
Install wall sconce in existing box, premium	EA	$95.34	$110.00	$205.34	**$342.92**	1.000

Exterior Lighting

> Within 10' of power source. No patching included.

Description	Unit	Direct Labor	Direct Materials	Direct Total	Selling Price	Man-hours
Install outdoor flood, single lamp, within 10' of power source	EA	$166.85	$35.20	$202.05	**$337.42**	1.750
Install outdoor flood, dual lamp, within 10' of power source	EA	$166.85	$44.00	$210.85	**$352.11**	1.750
Install outdoor flood, dual lamp/motion sensor, within 10' of power	EA	$166.85	$88.00	$254.85	**$425.59**	1.750
Install outdoor flood, triple lamp, within 10' of power source	EA	$166.85	$52.80	$219.65	**$366.81**	1.750
Install incandescent porch ceiling fixture in existing box, economy	EA	$71.51	$41.80	$71.51	**$189.22**	0.750
Install incandescent porch ceiling fixture in existing box, average	EA	$71.51	$63.80	$113.31	**$225.96**	0.750
Install incandescent porch ceiling fixture in existing box, premium	EA	$71.51	$96.80	$135.31	**$281.07**	0.750
Install incandescent porch wall fixture in existing box, economy	EA	$71.51	$49.50	$71.51	**$202.08**	0.750
Install incandescent porch wall fixture in existing box, average	EA	$71.51	$71.50	$143.01	**$238.82**	0.750
Install incandescent porch wall fixture in existing box, premium	EA	$71.51	$93.50	$165.01	**$275.56**	0.750

Electrical

Bathroom Fans, Lights, Heaters

> Within 10' of power source. No patching included.

Description	Unit	Direct Labor	Direct Materials	Direct Total	Selling Price	Man-hours
BATHROOM LIGHT						
Install bathroom light and wall switch, open ceiling and walls, economy	EA	$190.68	$82.50	$273.18	**$456.21**	2.000
Install bathroom light and wall switch, open ceiling and walls, average	EA	$190.68	$104.50	$295.18	**$492.95**	2.000
Install bathroom light and wall switch, open ceiling and walls, premium	EA	$190.68	$137.50	$328.18	**$548.06**	2.000
Install bathroom light & wall switch, finished ceiling and walls, economy	EA	$381.36	$82.50	$463.86	**$774.65**	4.000
Install bathroom light & wall switch, finished ceiling and walls, average	EA	$381.36	$104.50	$485.86	**$811.39**	4.000
Install bathroom light & wall switch, finished ceiling and walls, premium	EA	$381.36	$137.50	$518.86	**$866.50**	4.000
BATHROOM LIGHT AND FAN						
Install bathroom light/fan and wall switch, open ceiling/walls, economy	EA	$190.68	$104.50	$295.18	**$492.95**	2.000
Install bathroom light/fan and wall switch, open ceiling/walls, average	EA	$190.68	$137.50	$328.18	**$548.06**	2.000
Install bathroom light/fan and wall switch, open ceiling/walls, premium	EA	$190.68	$181.50	$372.18	**$621.54**	2.000
Install bathroom light/fan & wall switch, finished ceiling/walls, economy	EA	$381.36	$104.50	$485.86	**$811.39**	4.000
Install bathroom light/fan & wall switch, finished ceiling/walls, average	EA	$381.36	$137.50	$518.86	**$866.50**	4.000
Install bathroom light/fan & wall switch, finished ceiling/walls, premium	EA	$381.36	$181.50	$562.86	**$939.98**	4.000
BATHROOM LIGHT, FAN AND HEATER						
Install bathroom light/fan/heater, switch, open ceiling/walls, economy	EA	$190.68	$159.50	$350.18	**$584.80**	2.000
Install bathroom light/fan/heater, switch, open ceiling/walls, average	EA	$190.68	$209.00	$399.68	**$667.47**	2.000
Install bathroom light/fan/heater, switch, open ceiling/walls, premium	EA	$190.68	$269.50	$460.18	**$768.50**	2.000
Install bathroom light/fan/heater, switch, finished ceiling/walls, economy	EA	$381.36	$159.50	$540.86	**$903.24**	4.000
Install bathroom light/fan/heater, switch, finished ceiling/walls, average	EA	$381.36	$209.00	$590.36	**$985.90**	4.000
Install bathroom light/fan/heater, switch, finished ceiling/walls, premium	EA	$381.36	$269.50	$650.86	**$1,086.94**	4.000

Electrical

Bathroom Wall Heaters

> Within 10' of power source.
> No patching included.

Description	Unit	Direct Labor	Direct Materials	Direct Total	Selling Price	Man-hours
BATHROOM WALL HEATER, FORCED AIR HEAT						
Install wall heater, forced air, 1250W, open walls, economy	EA	$143.01	$192.50	$335.51	**$560.30**	1.500
Install wall heater, forced air, 1250W, open walls, average	EA	$143.01	$220.00	$363.01	**$606.23**	1.500
Install wall heater, forced air, 1250W, open walls, premium	EA	$143.01	$275.00	$418.01	**$698.08**	1.500
Install wall heater, forced air, 1250W, finished walls, economy	EA	$286.02	$192.50	$478.52	**$799.13**	3.000
Install wall heater, forced air, 1250W, finished walls, average	EA	$286.02	$220.00	$506.02	**$845.05**	3.000
Install wall heater, forced air, 1250W, finished walls, premium	EA	$286.02	$275.00	$561.02	**$936.90**	3.000
Install wall heater, forced air, 1500W, open walls, economy	EA	$143.01	$225.50	$368.51	**$615.41**	1.500
Install wall heater, forced air, 1500W, open walls, average	EA	$143.01	$253.00	$396.01	**$661.34**	1.500
Install wall heater, forced air, 1500W, open walls, premium	EA	$143.01	$308.00	$451.01	**$753.19**	1.500
Install wall heater, forced air, 1500W, finished walls, economy	EA	$286.02	$225.50	$511.52	**$854.24**	3.000
Install wall heater, forced air, 1500W, finished walls, average	EA	$286.02	$253.00	$539.02	**$900.16**	3.000
Install wall heater, forced air, 1500W, finished walls, premium	EA	$286.02	$308.00	$594.02	**$992.01**	3.000
BATHROOM WALL HEATER, RADIANT HEAT						
Install wall heater, radiant heat, 1250W, open walls, economy	EA	$143.01	$159.50	$302.51	**$505.19**	1.500
Install wall heater, radiant heat, 1250W, open walls, average	EA	$143.01	$187.00	$330.01	**$551.12**	1.500
Install wall heater, radiant heat, 1250W, open walls, premium	EA	$143.01	$247.50	$390.51	**$652.15**	1.500
Install wall heater, radiant heat, 1250W, finished walls, economy	EA	$286.02	$159.50	$445.52	**$744.02**	3.000
Install wall heater, radiant heat, 1250W, finished walls, average	EA	$286.02	$187.00	$473.02	**$789.94**	3.000
Install wall heater, radiant heat, 1250W, finished walls, premium	EA	$286.02	$247.50	$533.52	**$890.98**	3.000
Install wall heater, radiant heat, 1500W, open walls, economy	EA	$143.01	$192.50	$335.51	**$560.30**	1.500
Install wall heater, radiant heat, 1500W, open walls, average	EA	$143.01	$220.00	$363.01	**$606.23**	1.500
Install wall heater, radiant heat, 1500W, open walls, premium	EA	$143.01	$275.00	$418.01	**$698.08**	1.500
Install wall heater, radiant heat, 1500W, finished walls, economy	EA	$286.02	$192.50	$478.52	**$799.13**	3.000
Install wall heater, radiant heat, 1500W, finished walls, average	EA	$286.02	$220.00	$506.02	**$845.05**	3.000
Install wall heater, radiant heat, 1500W, finished walls, premium	EA	$286.02	$275.00	$561.02	**$936.90**	3.000

Electrical

Fans

> Within 10' of power source. No patching included.

Description	Unit	Direct Labor	Direct Materials	Direct Total	Selling Price	Man-hours
WHOLE HOUSE FAN						
Install whole house fan, 30" diameter	EA	$214.52	$528.00	$742.52	**$991.84**	2.250
Install whole house fan, 36" diameter	EA	$238.35	$583.00	$821.35	**$1,097.64**	2.500
Install whole house fan, 42" diameter	EA	$262.19	$660.00	$922.19	**$1,229.85**	2.750
Install whole house fan, 48" diameter	EA	$286.02	$792.00	$1,078.02	**$1,428.05**	3.000
CEILING FAN						
Install ceiling fan, existing wiring, economy	EA	$71.51	$192.50	$264.01	**$350.41**	0.750
Install ceiling fan, existing wiring, average	EA	$71.51	$286.00	$357.51	**$462.61**	0.750
Install ceiling fan, existing wiring, economy	EA	$71.51	$434.50	$506.01	**$640.81**	0.750
Install ceiling fan, new wiring, no switch, open ceiling & walls, economy	EA	$238.35	$220.00	$458.35	**$662.04**	2.500
Install ceiling fan, new wiring, no switch, open ceiling & walls, average	EA	$238.35	$313.50	$551.85	**$774.24**	2.500
Install ceiling fan, new wiring, no switch, open ceiling & walls, premium	EA	$238.35	$462.00	$700.35	**$952.44**	2.500
Install ceiling fan, new wiring, no switch, finished ceiling/walls, economy	EA	$381.36	$220.00	$601.36	**$900.87**	4.000
Install ceiling fan, new wiring, no switch, finished ceiling/walls, average	EA	$381.36	$313.50	$694.86	**$1,013.07**	4.000
Install ceiling fan, new wiring, no switch, finished ceiling/walls, premium	EA	$381.36	$462.00	$843.36	**$1,191.27**	4.000
Install ceiling fan, new wiring/switch, open ceiling and walls, economy	EA	$286.02	$236.50	$522.52	**$761.45**	3.000
Install ceiling fan, new wiring/switch, open ceiling and walls, average	EA	$286.02	$330.00	$616.02	**$873.65**	3.000
Install ceiling fan, new wiring/switch, open ceiling and walls, premium	EA	$286.02	$478.50	$764.52	**$1,051.85**	3.000
Install ceiling fan, new wiring/wall switch, finished ceiling/walls, economy	EA	$429.03	$236.50	$665.53	**$1,000.28**	4.500
Install ceiling fan, new wiring/wall switch, finished ceiling/walls, average	EA	$429.03	$330.00	$759.03	**$1,112.48**	4.500
Install ceiling fan, new wiring/wall switch, finished ceiling/walls, premium	EA	$429.03	$478.50	$907.53	**$1,290.68**	4.500
GABLE EXHAUST FAN						
Install gable fan, economy	EA	$190.68	$121.00	$311.68	**$463.64**	2.000
Install gable fan, average	EA	$190.68	$198.00	$388.68	**$556.04**	2.000
Install gable fan, premium	EA	$190.68	$275.00	$465.68	**$648.44**	2.000

Electrical

Electric Baseboard Heat

> Within 15' of power source.
> No patching included.

Description	Unit	Direct Labor	Direct Materials	Direct Total	Selling Price	Man-hours
ELECTRIC BASEBOARD HEAT, RADIANT						
Install electric baseboard, 1000W, 4' long, within 15' of power	EA	$190.68	$119.00	$309.68	**$461.24**	2.000
Install electric baseboard, 1500W, 6' long, within 15' of power	EA	$238.35	$163.00	$401.35	**$593.64**	2.500
Install electric baseboard, 2000W, 8' long, within 15' of power	EA	$286.02	$207.00	$493.02	**$726.05**	3.000
Install electric baseboard, 2500W, 10' long, within 15' of power	EA	$333.69	$251.00	$584.69	**$858.46**	3.500
ELECTRIC BASEBOARD HEAT, RECIRCULATING HOT WATER						
Install electric hot water baseboard, 750W, 4' long, within 15' of power	EA	$190.68	$182.00	$372.68	**$536.84**	2.000
Install electric hot water baseboard, 1000W, 5' long, within 15' of power	EA	$214.52	$209.00	$423.52	**$609.04**	2.250
Install electric hot water baseboard, 1380W, 6' long, within 15' of power	EA	$238.35	$237.00	$475.35	**$682.44**	2.500
Install electric hot water baseboard, 1500W, 7' long, within 15' of power	EA	$262.19	$270.00	$532.19	**$761.85**	2.750
Install electric hot water baseboard, 2000W, 8' long, within 15' of power	EA	$286.02	$292.00	$578.02	**$828.05**	3.000

Appliances

Appliance Rough-In, Open Walls and Open Ceiling Below

> Supply and gas rough-in, including cut-off valves. Electrical source within 15'.

Description	Unit	Direct Labor	Direct Materials	Direct Total	Selling Price	Man-hours
Disposer rough-in, includes electric & switch, open walls and ceiling	EA	$407.87	$43.62	$451.48	**$753.98**	4.000
Dishwasher rough-in, including electric, open walls and ceiling	EA	$407.87	$24.57	$432.44	**$722.18**	4.000
Trash compactor electric outlet, open walls and ceiling	EA	$95.34	$24.57	$119.91	**$200.26**	1.000
Refrigerator wall outlet, open walls and ceiling	EA	$95.34	$24.57	$119.91	**$200.26**	1.000
Oven rough-in, gas, including electric, open walls and ceiling	EA	$509.84	$49.87	$559.71	**$934.71**	5.000
Oven electric outlet, 30 amp, open walls and ceiling	EA	$166.85	$53.64	$220.48	**$368.20**	1.750
Cooktop rough-in, gas, including electric, open walls and ceiling	EA	$509.84	$49.87	$559.71	**$934.71**	5.000
Cooktop electric outlet, 30 amp, open walls and ceiling	EA	$166.85	$53.64	$220.48	**$368.20**	1.750
Range rough-in, gas, including electric, open walls and ceiling	EA	$509.84	$49.87	$559.71	**$934.71**	5.000
Range electric outlet, 50 amp, open walls and ceiling	EA	$166.85	$53.64	$220.48	**$368.20**	1.750
Hood & fan outlet, open walls and ceiling	EA	$95.34	$24.57	$119.91	**$200.26**	1.000
Dryer rough-in, gas, includes electric & vent, open walls and ceiling	EA	$509.84	$93.87	$603.71	**$1,008.19**	5.000
Dryer electric outlet, 40 amp, and vent, finished walls, open ceiling	EA	$166.85	$97.64	$264.48	**$441.68**	1.750
Gray box rough-in, open walls and ceiling	EA	$611.80	$102.56	$714.37	**$1,192.99**	6.000
Deduct for 2 fixtures roughed-in at same time	EA	-$152.95		-$152.95	**-$255.43**	-1.500
Deduct for 3 fixtures roughed-in at same time	EA	-$229.43		-$229.43	**-$383.14**	-2.250
Deduct for 4 fixtures roughed-in at same time	EA	-$280.41		-$280.41	**-$468.28**	-2.750

Appliances

Appliance Rough-In, Finished Walls and Open Ceiling Below

> Supply and gas rough-in, including cut-off valves. Electrical source within 15'. No patching included.

Description	Unit	Direct Labor	Direct Materials	Direct Total	Selling Price	Man-hours
Disposer rough-in, includes electric & switch, finished walls, open ceiling	EA	$509.84	$43.62	$553.45	**$924.26**	5.000
Dishwasher rough-in, including electric, finished walls, open ceiling	EA	$458.85	$24.57	$483.43	**$807.32**	4.500
Trash compactor electric outlet, finished walls, open ceiling	EA	$143.01	$24.57	$167.58	**$279.87**	1.500
Refrigerator wall outlet, finished walls, open ceiling	EA	$143.01	$24.57	$167.58	**$279.87**	1.500
Oven rough-in, gas, including electric, finished walls, open ceiling	EA	$560.82	$49.87	$610.69	**$1,019.86**	5.500
Oven electric outlet, 30 amp, finished walls, open ceiling	EA	$262.19	$53.64	$315.82	**$527.42**	2.750
Cooktop rough-in, gas, including electric, finished walls, open ceiling	EA	$560.82	$49.87	$610.69	**$1,019.86**	5.500
Cooktop electric outlet, 30 amp, finished walls, open ceiling	EA	$262.19	$53.64	$315.82	**$527.42**	2.750
Range rough-in, gas, including electric, finished walls, open ceiling	EA	$560.82	$49.87	$610.69	**$1,019.86**	5.500
Range electric outlet, 50 amp, finished walls, open ceiling	EA	$262.19	$53.64	$315.82	**$527.42**	2.750
Hood & fan outlet, finished walls, open ceiling	EA	$143.01	$24.57	$167.58	**$279.87**	1.500
Dryer rough-in, gas, includes electric & vent, finished walls, open ceiling	EA	$560.82	$93.87	$654.69	**$1,093.34**	5.500
Dryer electric outlet, 40 amp, and vent, finished walls, open ceiling	EA	$262.19	$97.64	$359.82	**$600.90**	2.750
Gray box rough-in, finished walls, open ceiling	EA	$713.77	$102.56	$816.33	**$1,363.28**	7.000
Deduct for 2 fixtures roughed-in at same time	EA	-$178.44		-$178.44	**-$298.00**	-1.750
Deduct for 3 fixtures roughed-in at same time	EA	-$254.92		-$254.92	**-$425.71**	-2.500
Deduct for 4 fixtures roughed-in at same time	EA	-$305.90		-$305.90	**-$510.85**	-3.000

Appliances

Appliance Rough-In, Finished Walls and Finished Ceiling Below

> Supply and gas rough-in, including cut-off valves. Electrical source within 15'. No patching included.

Description	Unit	Direct Labor	Direct Materials	Direct Total	Selling Price	Man-hours
Disposer rough-in, includes electric & switch, finished walls and ceiling	EA	$509.84	$43.62	$553.45	**$924.26**	5.000
Dishwasher rough-in, including electric, finished walls and ceiling	EA	$458.85	$24.57	$483.43	**$807.32**	4.500
Trash compactor electric outlet, finished walls and ceiling	EA	$190.68	$24.57	$215.25	**$359.47**	2.000
Refrigerator wall outlet, finished walls and ceiling	EA	$190.68	$24.57	$215.25	**$359.47**	2.000
Oven rough-in, gas, including electric, finished walls and ceiling	EA	$662.79	$49.87	$712.66	**$1,190.14**	6.500
Oven electric outlet, 30 amp, finished walls and ceiling	EA	$333.69	$53.64	$387.33	**$646.83**	3.500
Cooktop rough-in, gas, including electric, finished walls and ceiling	EA	$662.79	$49.87	$712.66	**$1,190.14**	6.500
Cooktop electric outlet, 30 amp, finished walls and ceiling	EA	$333.69	$53.64	$387.33	**$646.83**	3.500
Range rough-in, including electric, gas, finished walls and ceiling	EA	$662.79	$49.87	$712.66	**$1,190.14**	6.500
Range electric outlet, 50 amp, finished walls and ceiling	EA	$333.69	$53.64	$387.33	**$646.83**	3.500
Hood & fan outlet, finished walls and ceiling	EA	$190.68	$24.57	$215.25	**$359.47**	2.000
Dryer rough-in, gas, includes electric & vent, finished walls and ceiling	EA	$662.79	$93.87	$756.66	**$1,263.62**	6.500
Dryer electric outlet, 40 amp, and vent, finished walls and ceiling	EA	$333.69	$97.64	$431.33	**$720.31**	3.500
Gray box rough-in, finished walls and ceiling	EA	$815.74	$102.56	$918.30	**$1,533.56**	8.000
Deduct for 2 fixtures roughed-in at same time	EA	-$203.93		-$203.93	**-$340.57**	-2.000
Deduct for 3 fixtures roughed-in at same time	EA	-$305.90		-$305.90	**-$510.85**	-3.000
Deduct for 4 fixtures roughed-in at same time	EA	-$356.88		-$356.88	**-$596.00**	-3.500

26

Appliances

Remove Existing Appliance, Location Ready for New Appliance

Description	Unit	Direct Labor	Direct Materials	Direct Total	Selling Price	Man-hours
Disposer, remove	EA	$101.97		$101.97	**$170.28**	1.000
Dishwasher, remove	EA	$101.97		$101.97	**$170.28**	1.000
Trash compactor, remove	EA	$47.67		$47.67	**$79.61**	0.500
Refrigerator, remove	EA	$40.51		$40.51	**$67.65**	1.000
Oven, gas, remove	EA	$76.48		$76.48	**$127.71**	0.750
Oven, electric, remove	EA	$47.67		$47.67	**$79.61**	0.500
Cooktop, gas, remove	EA	$76.48		$76.48	**$127.71**	0.750
Cooktop, electric, remove	EA	$47.67		$47.67	**$79.61**	0.500
Range, gas, remove	EA	$76.48		$76.48	**$127.71**	0.750
Range, electric, remove	EA	$47.67		$47.67	**$79.61**	0.500
Range hood, remove	EA	$20.25		$20.25	**$33.82**	0.500
Dryer, gas, remove	EA	$76.48		$76.48	**$127.71**	0.750
Dryer, gas, remove, replace vent	EA	$152.95	$49.78	$202.73	**$338.55**	1.500
Dryer, electric, remove	EA	$40.51		$40.51	**$67.65**	1.000
Dryer, electric, remove, replace vent	EA	$81.02	$49.78	$130.79	**$218.42**	2.000
Washer, remove	EA	$60.76		$60.76	**$101.47**	1.500

Appliances

Install New Appliance in Prepared Location

> Install new appliance to cut-off valve or gray box, and existing electrical connection.

Description	Unit	Direct Labor	Direct Materials	Direct Total	Selling Price	Man-hours
Disposer, install	EA	$152.95		$152.95	**$255.43**	1.500
Dishwasher, install	EA	$152.95		$152.95	**$255.43**	1.500
Trash compactor, install	EA	$95.34		$95.34	**$159.22**	1.000
Refrigerator, install	EA	$40.51		$40.51	**$67.65**	1.000
Oven, gas, install	EA	$203.93		$203.93	**$340.57**	2.000
Oven, electric, install	EA	$95.34		$95.34	**$159.22**	1.000
Cooktop, gas, install	EA	$203.93		$203.93	**$340.57**	2.000
Cooktop, electric, install	EA	$95.34		$95.34	**$159.22**	1.000
Range, gas, install	EA	$203.93		$203.93	**$340.57**	2.000
Range, electric, install	EA	$95.34		$95.34	**$159.22**	1.000
Dryer, gas, install	EA	$203.93		$203.93	**$340.57**	2.000
Dryer, electric, install	EA	$60.76		$60.76	**$101.47**	1.500
Washer, install	EA	$81.02		$81.02	**$135.30**	2.000
Range hood, ducted	EA	$114.18		$114.18	**$190.68**	1.500
Range hood, ductless	EA	$76.12		$76.12	**$127.12**	1.000

26

Appliances

Refrigerators

> **Install in prepared location. No removal or rough-in included.**

Description	Unit	Direct Labor	Direct Materials	Direct Total	Selling Price	Man-hours
Refrigerator, 14 CF, economy	EA	$40.51	$620.00	$660.51	**$811.65**	1.000
Refrigerator, 14 CF, average	EA	$40.51	$636.00	$676.51	**$830.85**	1.000
Refrigerator, 14 CF, premium	EA	$40.51	$685.00	$725.51	**$889.65**	1.000
Refrigerator, 18 CF, economy	EA	$40.51	$674.00	$714.51	**$876.45**	1.000
Refrigerator, 18 CF, average	EA	$40.51	$779.00	$819.51	**$1,002.45**	1.000
Refrigerator, 18 CF, premium	EA	$40.51	$861.00	$901.51	**$1,100.85**	1.000
Refrigerator, 22 CF, economy	EA	$40.51	$919.00	$959.51	**$1,170.45**	1.000
Refrigerator, 22 CF, average	EA	$40.51	$1,004.00	$1,044.51	**$1,272.45**	1.000
Refrigerator, 22 CF, premium	EA	$40.51	$1,059.00	$1,099.51	**$1,338.45**	1.000
Refrigerator, 25 CF, economy	EA	$40.51	$1,151.00	$1,191.51	**$1,448.85**	1.000
Refrigerator, 25 CF, average	EA	$40.51	$1,318.00	$1,358.51	**$1,649.25**	1.000
Refrigerator, 25 CF, premium	EA	$40.51	$1,734.00	$1,774.51	**$2,148.45**	1.000
Built-in refrigerator, 36", economy	EA	$228.36	$2,418.00	$2,646.36	**$3,282.95**	3.000
Built-in refrigerator, 36", average	EA	$228.36	$4,436.00	$4,664.36	**$5,704.55**	3.000
Built-in refrigerator, 36", premium	EA	$228.36	$5,170.00	$5,398.36	**$6,585.35**	3.000
Built-in refrigerator, 42", economy	EA	$228.36	$4,212.00	$4,440.36	**$5,435.75**	3.000
Built-in refrigerator, 42", average	EA	$228.36	$5,420.00	$5,648.36	**$6,885.35**	3.000
Built-in refrigerator, 42", premium	EA	$228.36	$6,344.00	$6,572.36	**$7,994.15**	3.000
Built-in refrigerator, 48", economy	EA	$228.36	$4,888.00	$5,116.36	**$6,246.95**	3.000
Built-in refrigerator, 48", average	EA	$228.36	$5,963.00	$6,191.36	**$7,536.95**	3.000
Built-in refrigerator, 48", premium	EA	$228.36	$6,882.00	$7,110.36	**$8,639.75**	3.000

Appliances

Washers and Dryers

> Install in prepared location. No removal or rough-in included.

Description	Unit	Direct Labor	Direct Materials	Direct Total	Selling Price	Man-hours
CLOTHES WASHER						
Clothes washer, economy	EA	$81.02	$355.00	$436.02	**$561.30**	2.000
Clothes washer, average	EA	$81.02	$595.00	$676.02	**$849.30**	2.000
Clothes washer, premium	EA	$81.02	$1,099.00	$1,180.02	**$1,454.10**	2.000
CLOTHES DRYER						
Clothes dryer, electric, economy	EA	$60.76	$338.00	$398.76	**$507.07**	1.500
Clothes dryer, electric, average	EA	$60.76	$578.00	$638.76	**$795.07**	1.500
Clothes dryer, electric, premium	EA	$60.76	$1,052.00	$1,112.76	**$1,363.87**	1.500
Clothes dryer, gas, economy	EA	$203.93	$356.00	$559.93	**$767.77**	2.000
Clothes dryer, gas, average	EA	$203.93	$600.00	$803.93	**$1,060.57**	2.000
Clothes dryer, gas, premium	EA	$203.93	$1,078.00	$1,281.93	**$1,634.17**	2.000

Ranges

> Install in prepared location. No removal or rough-in included.

Description	Unit	Direct Labor	Direct Materials	Direct Total	Selling Price	Man-hours
Range, electric, economy	EA	$95.34	$578.00	$673.34	**$852.82**	1.000
Range, electric, average	EA	$95.34	$825.00	$920.34	**$1,149.22**	1.000
Range, electric, premium	EA	$95.34	$1,458.00	$1,553.34	**$1,908.82**	1.000
Range, gas, economy	EA	$203.93	$578.00	$781.93	**$1,034.17**	2.000
Range, gas, average	EA	$203.93	$825.00	$1,028.93	**$1,330.57**	2.000
Range, gas, premium	EA	$203.93	$1,458.00	$1,661.93	**$2,090.17**	2.000
Range, commercial, gas, 30"	EA	$407.87	$4,252.00	$4,659.87	**$5,783.54**	4.000
Range, commercial, gas, 36"	EA	$407.87	$4,792.00	$5,199.87	**$6,431.54**	4.000
Range, commercial, gas, 48"	EA	$407.87	$5,715.00	$6,122.87	**$7,539.14**	4.000

26

Appliances

Cooktops

> Install in prepared location.
> No removal or rough-in included.

Description	Unit	Direct Labor	Direct Materials	Direct Total	Selling Price	Man-hours
Cooktop, electric, economy	EA	$95.34	$422.00	$517.34	**$665.62**	1.000
Cooktop, electric, average	EA	$95.34	$538.00	$633.34	**$804.82**	1.000
Cooktop, electric, premium	EA	$95.34	$866.00	$961.34	**$1,198.42**	1.000
Cooktop, gas, economy	EA	$203.93	$422.00	$625.93	**$846.97**	2.000
Cooktop, gas, average	EA	$203.93	$538.00	$741.93	**$986.17**	2.000
Cooktop, gas, premium	EA	$203.93	$866.00	$1,069.93	**$1,379.77**	2.000

Ovens

> Install in prepared location.
> No removal or rough-in included.

Description	Unit	Direct Labor	Direct Materials	Direct Total	Selling Price	Man-hours
Wall oven, single, electric, economy	EA	$95.34	$419.00	$514.34	**$662.02**	1.000
Wall oven, single, electric, average	EA	$95.34	$572.00	$667.34	**$845.62**	1.000
Wall oven, single, electric, premium	EA	$95.34	$842.00	$937.34	**$1,169.62**	1.000
Wall oven, double, electric, economy	EA	$166.85	$572.00	$738.85	**$965.03**	1.750
Wall oven, double, electric, average	EA	$166.85	$906.00	$1,072.85	**$1,365.83**	1.750
Wall oven, double, electric, premium	EA	$166.85	$1,236.00	$1,402.85	**$1,761.83**	1.750
Wall oven, single, gas, economy	EA	$203.93	$419.00	$622.93	**$843.37**	2.000
Wall oven, single, gas, average	EA	$203.93	$572.00	$775.93	**$1,026.97**	2.000
Wall oven, single, gas, premium	EA	$203.93	$842.00	$1,045.93	**$1,350.97**	2.000
Wall oven, double, gas, economy	EA	$356.88	$572.00	$928.88	**$1,282.40**	3.500
Wall oven, double, gas, average	EA	$356.88	$906.00	$1,262.88	**$1,683.20**	3.500
Wall oven, double, gas, premium	EA	$356.88	$1,236.00	$1,592.88	**$2,079.20**	3.500

Trash Compactors

> Install in prepared location.
> No removal or rough-in included.

Description	Unit	Direct Labor	Direct Materials	Direct Total	Selling Price	Man-hours
Trash compactor, economy	EA	$95.34	$411.00	$506.34	**$652.42**	1.000
Trash compactor, average	EA	$95.34	$485.00	$580.34	**$741.22**	1.000
Trash compactor, premium	EA	$95.34	$639.00	$734.34	**$926.02**	1.000

Appliances

Range Hoods

> Install in prepared location. No removal or rough-in included.

Description	Unit	Direct Labor	Direct Materials	Direct Total	Selling Price	Man-hours
RANGE HOOD, DUCTED						
Range hood, ducted, 30", economy	EA	$114.18	$95.00	$209.18	**$304.68**	1.500
Range hood, ducted, 30", average	EA	$114.18	$134.00	$248.18	**$351.48**	1.500
Range hood, ducted, 30", premium	EA	$114.18	$188.00	$302.18	**$416.28**	1.500
Range hood, ducted, 36", economy	EA	$114.18	$105.00	$219.18	**$316.68**	1.500
Range hood, ducted, 36", average	EA	$114.18	$144.00	$258.18	**$363.48**	1.500
Range hood, ducted, 36", premium	EA	$114.18	$202.00	$316.18	**$433.08**	1.500
Range hood, ducted, 42", economy	EA	$114.18	$116.00	$230.18	**$329.88**	1.500
Range hood, ducted, 42", average	EA	$114.18	$158.00	$272.18	**$380.28**	1.500
Range hood, ducted, 42", premium	EA	$114.18	$219.00	$333.18	**$453.48**	1.500
RANGE HOOD, DUCTLESS						
Range hood, ductless, 30", economy	EA	$76.12	$106.00	$182.12	**$254.32**	1.000
Range hood, ductless, 30", average	EA	$76.12	$145.00	$221.12	**$301.12**	1.000
Range hood, ductless, 30", premium	EA	$76.12	$231.00	$307.12	**$404.32**	1.000
Range hood, ductless, 36", economy	EA	$76.12	$124.00	$200.12	**$275.92**	1.000
Range hood, ductless, 36", average	EA	$76.12	$158.00	$234.12	**$316.72**	1.000
Range hood, ductless, 36", premium	EA	$76.12	$254.00	$330.12	**$431.92**	1.000
Range hood, ductless, 42", economy	EA	$76.12	$132.00	$208.12	**$285.52**	1.000
Range hood, ductless, 42", average	EA	$76.12	$168.00	$244.12	**$328.72**	1.000
Range hood, ductless, 42", premium	EA	$76.12	$270.00	$346.12	**$451.12**	1.000

Appliances

Dishwashers

> Installation not included.
> No removal or rough-in included.

Description	Unit	Direct Labor	Direct Materials	Direct Total	Selling Price	Man-hours
Dishwasher, economy	EA		$348.00	$348.00	**$417.60**	1.500
Dishwasher, average	EA		$589.00	$589.00	**$706.80**	1.500
Dishwasher, premium	EA		$1,068.00	$1,068.00	**$1,281.60**	1.500

Disposers

> Installation not included.
> No removal or rough-in included.

Description	Unit	Direct Labor	Direct Materials	Direct Total	Selling Price	Man-hours
Disposer, 1/3 HP, economy	EA		$94.00	$94.00	**$112.80**	1.500
Disposer, 1/3 HP, average	EA		$122.00	$122.00	**$146.40**	1.500
Disposer, 1/3 HP, premium	EA		$171.00	$171.00	**$205.20**	1.500
Disposer, 1/2 HP, economy	EA		$142.00	$142.00	**$170.40**	1.500
Disposer, 1/2 HP, average	EA		$166.00	$166.00	**$199.20**	1.500
Disposer, 1/2 HP, premium	EA		$220.00	$220.00	**$264.00**	1.500
Disposer, 3/4 HP, economy	EA		$172.00	$172.00	**$206.40**	1.500
Disposer, 3/4 HP, average	EA		$243.00	$243.00	**$291.60**	1.500
Disposer, 3/4 HP, premium	EA		$392.00	$392.00	**$470.40**	1.500
Disposer, 1 HP, economy	EA		$302.00	$302.00	**$362.40**	1.500
Disposer, 1 HP, average	EA		$380.00	$380.00	**$456.00**	1.500
Disposer, 1 HP, premium	EA		$439.00	$439.00	**$526.80**	1.500

Insulation

Fiberglass Insulation, Unfaced

Description	Unit	Direct Labor	Direct Materials	Direct Total	Selling Price	Man-hours
FIBERGLASS INSULATION, UNFACED, R-11						
Install insulation, unfaced, in walls, R-11, 3-1/2" thick x 15" wide, 16"oc	SF	$0.65	$0.46	$1.11	**$1.86**	0.016
Install insulation, unfaced, in walls, R-11, 3-1/2" thick x 23" wide, 24"oc	SF	$0.45	$0.50	$0.94	**$1.57**	0.011
FIBERGLASS INSULATION, UNFACED, R-13						
Install insulation, unfaced, in walls, R-13, 3-1/2" thick x 15" wide, 16"oc	SF	$0.65	$0.54	$1.19	**$1.98**	0.016
Install insulation, unfaced, in walls, R-13, 3-1/2" thick x 23" wide, 24"oc	SF	$0.45	$0.58	$1.03	**$1.71**	0.011
FIBERGLASS INSULATION, UNFACED, R-19						
Install insulation, unfaced, laid flat, R-19, 6-1/4" thick x 15" wide, 16"oc	SF	$0.53	$0.74	$1.26	**$2.11**	0.013
Install insulation, unfaced, laid flat, R-19, 6-1/4" thick x 23" wide, 24"oc	SF	$0.36	$0.81	$1.18	**$1.97**	0.009
Install insulation, unfaced, rafters, R-19, 6-1/4" thick x 15" wide, 16"oc	SF	$0.81	$0.74	$1.55	**$2.59**	0.020
Install insulation, unfaced, rafters, R-19, 6-1/4" thick x 23" wide, 24"oc	SF	$0.53	$0.81	$1.34	**$2.24**	0.013
Install insulation, unfaced, in walls, R-19, 6-1/4" thick x 15" wide, 16"oc	SF	$0.65	$0.74	$1.39	**$2.31**	0.016
Install insulation, unfaced, in walls, R-19, 6-1/4" thick x 23" wide, 24"oc	SF	$0.45	$0.81	$1.26	**$2.10**	0.011
FIBERGLASS INSULATION, UNFACED, R-22						
Install insulation, unfaced, laid flat, R-22, 6-3/4" thick x 15" wide, 16"oc	SF	$0.53	$0.81	$1.34	**$2.24**	0.013
Install insulation, unfaced, laid flat, R-22, 6-3/4" thick x 23" wide, 24"oc	SF	$0.36	$0.86	$1.23	**$2.05**	0.009
Install insulation, unfaced, rafters, R-22, 6-3/4" thick x 15" wide, 16"oc	SF	$0.81	$0.81	$1.62	**$2.71**	0.020
Install insulation, unfaced, rafters, R-22, 6-3/4" thick x 23" wide, 24"oc	SF	$0.53	$0.86	$1.39	**$2.32**	0.013
Install insulation, unfaced, in walls, R-22, 6-3/4" thick x 15" wide, 16"oc	SF	$0.65	$0.81	$1.46	**$2.44**	0.016
Install insulation, unfaced, in walls, R-22, 6-3/4" thick x 23" wide, 24"oc	SF	$0.45	$0.86	$1.31	**$2.18**	0.011
FIBERGLASS INSULATION, UNFACED, R-30						
Install insulation, unfaced, laid flat, R-30, 9-1/2" thick x 16" wide, 16"oc	SF	$0.53	$1.28	$1.81	**$3.03**	0.013
Install insulation, unfaced, laid flat, R-30, 9-1/2" thick x 24" wide, 24"oc	SF	$0.36	$1.31	$1.67	**$2.80**	0.009
Install insulation, unfaced, rafters, R-30, 9-1/2" thick x 16" wide, 16"oc	SF	$0.81	$1.28	$2.10	**$3.50**	0.020
Install insulation, unfaced, rafters, R-30, 9-1/2" thick x 24" wide, 24"oc	SF	$0.53	$1.31	$1.84	**$3.07**	0.013
FIBERGLASS INSULATION, UNFACED, R-38						
Install insulation, unfaced, laid flat, R-38, 12" thick x 16" wide, 16"oc	SF	$0.53	$1.76	$2.28	**$3.81**	0.013
Install insulation, unfaced, laid flat, R-38, 12" thick x 24" wide, 24"oc	SF	$0.36	$1.78	$2.15	**$3.59**	0.009
Install insulation, unfaced, for rafters, R-38, 12" thick x 16" wide, 16"oc	SF	$0.81	$1.76	$2.57	**$4.29**	0.020
Install insulation, unfaced, for rafters, R-38, 12" thick x 24" wide, 24"oc	SF	$0.53	$1.78	$2.31	**$3.86**	0.013

Insulation

Fiberglass Insulation, Kraft Faced

Description	Unit	Direct Labor	Direct Materials	Direct Total	Selling Price	Man-hours
FIBERGLASS INSULATION, KRAFT FACED, R-11						
Install insulation, kraft faced, walls, R-11, 3-1/2" thick x 15" wide, 16"oc	SF	$0.65	$0.55	$1.20	**$2.00**	0.016
Install insulation, kraft faced, walls, R-11, 3-1/2" thick x 23" wide, 24"oc	SF	$0.45	$0.64	$1.09	**$1.82**	0.011
FIBERGLASS INSULATION, KRAFT FACED, R-13						
Install insulation, kraft faced, walls, R-13, 3-1/2" thick x 15" wide, 16"oc	SF	$0.65	$0.62	$1.27	**$2.12**	0.016
Install insulation, kraft faced, walls, R-13, 3-1/2" thick x 23" wide, 24"oc	SF	$0.45	$0.66	$1.11	**$1.85**	0.011
FIBERGLASS INSULATION, KRAFT FACED, R-19						
Install insulation, kraft faced, laid flat, R-19, 6-1/4" thick x 15" wide, 16"oc	SF	$0.53	$0.82	$1.35	**$2.25**	0.013
Install insulation, kraft faced, laid flat, R-19, 6-1/4" thick x 23" wide, 24"oc	SF	$0.36	$0.90	$1.26	**$2.10**	0.009
Install insulation, kraft faced,rafters, R-19, 6-1/4" thick x 15" wide, 16"oc	SF	$0.81	$0.82	$1.63	**$2.72**	0.020
Install insulation, kraft faced, rafters, R-19, 6-1/4" thick x 23" wide, 24"oc	SF	$0.53	$0.90	$1.42	**$2.37**	0.013
Install insulation, kraft faced, walls, R-19, 6-1/4" thick x 15" wide, 16"oc	SF	$0.65	$0.82	$1.47	**$2.45**	0.016
Install insulation, kraft faced, walls, R-19, 6-1/4" thick x 23" wide, 24"oc	SF	$0.45	$0.90	$1.34	**$2.24**	0.011
FIBERGLASS INSULATION, KRAFT FACED, R-22						
Install insulation, kraft faced, laid flat, R-22, 6-3/4" thick x 15" wide, 16"oc	SF	$0.53	$0.90	$1.42	**$2.37**	0.013
Install insulation, kraft faced, laid flat, R-22, 6-3/4" thick x 23" wide, 24"oc	SF	$0.36	$0.95	$1.31	**$2.19**	0.009
Install insulation, kraft faced, rafters, R-22, 6-3/4" thick x 15" wide, 16"oc	SF	$0.81	$0.90	$1.71	**$2.85**	0.020
Install insulation, kraft faced, rafters, R-22, 6-3/4" thick x 23" wide, 24"oc	SF	$0.53	$0.95	$1.47	**$2.46**	0.013
Install insulation, kraft faced, walls, R-22, 6-3/4" thick x 15" wide, 16"oc	SF	$0.65	$0.90	$1.54	**$2.58**	0.016
Install insulation, kraft faced, walls, R-22, 6-3/4" thick x 23" wide, 24"oc	SF	$0.45	$0.95	$1.39	**$2.32**	0.011
FIBERGLASS INSULATION, KRAFT FACED, R-30						
Install insulation, kraft faced, laid flat, R-30, 9-1/2" thick x 16" wide, 16"oc	SF	$0.53	$1.37	$1.89	**$3.16**	0.013
Install insulation, kraft faced, laid flat, R-30, 9-1/2" thick x 24" wide, 24"oc	SF	$0.36	$1.39	$1.76	**$2.93**	0.009
Install insulation, kraft faced, rafters, R-30, 9-1/2" thick x 16" wide, 16"oc	SF	$0.81	$1.37	$2.18	**$3.64**	0.020
Install insulation, kraft faced, rafters, R-30, 9-1/2" thick x 24" wide, 24"oc	SF	$0.53	$1.39	$1.92	**$3.21**	0.013
FIBERGLASS INSULATION, KRAFT FACED, R-38						
Install insulation, kraft faced, laid flat, R-38, 12" thick x 16" wide, 16"oc	SF	$0.53	$1.84	$2.37	**$3.95**	0.013
Install insulation, kraft faced, laid flat, R-38, 12" thick x 24" wide, 24"oc	SF	$0.36	$1.87	$2.23	**$3.72**	0.009
Install insulation, kraft faced, rafters, R-38, 12" thick x 16" wide, 16"oc	SF	$0.81	$1.84	$2.65	**$4.43**	0.020
Install insulation, kraft faced, rafters, R-38, 12" thick x 24" wide, 24"oc	SF	$0.53	$1.87	$2.39	**$3.99**	0.013

Insulation

Fiberglass Insulation, Foil Faced

Description	Unit	Direct Labor	Direct Materials	Direct Total	Selling Price	Man-hours
FIBERGLASS INSULATION, FOIL FACED, R-11						
Install insulation, foil faced, in walls, R-11, 3-1/2" thick x 15" wide, 16"oc	SF	$0.65	$0.59	$1.24	**$2.07**	0.016
Install insulation, foil faced, in walls, R-11, 3-1/2" thick x 23" wide, 24"oc	SF	$0.45	$0.62	$1.07	**$1.78**	0.011
FIBERGLASS INSULATION, FOIL FACED, R-13						
Install insulation, foil faced, in walls, R-13, 3-1/2" thick x 15" wide, 16"oc	SF	$0.65	$0.66	$1.31	**$2.19**	0.016
Install insulation, foil faced, in walls, R-13, 3-1/2" thick x 23" wide, 24"oc	SF	$0.45	$0.70	$1.15	**$1.92**	0.011
FIBERGLASS INSULATION, FOIL FACED, R-19						
Install insulation, foil faced, laid flat, R-19, 6-1/4" thick x 15" wide, 16"oc	SF	$0.53	$0.86	$1.39	**$2.32**	0.013
Install insulation, foil faced, laid flat, R-19, 6-1/4" thick x 23" wide, 24"oc	SF	$0.36	$0.94	$1.30	**$2.17**	0.009
Install insulation, foil faced, rafters, R-19, 6-1/4" thick x 15" wide, 16"oc	SF	$0.81	$0.86	$1.67	**$2.79**	0.020
Install insulation, foil faced, rafters, R-19, 6-1/4" thick x 23" wide, 24"oc	SF	$0.53	$0.94	$1.46	**$2.44**	0.013
Install insulation, foil faced, in walls, R-19, 6-1/4" thick x 15" wide, 16"oc	SF	$0.65	$0.86	$1.51	**$2.52**	0.016
Install insulation, foil faced, in walls, R-19, 6-1/4" thick x 23" wide, 24"oc	SF	$0.45	$0.94	$1.38	**$2.31**	0.011
FIBERGLASS INSULATION, FOIL FACED, R-22						
Install insulation, foil faced, laid flat, R-22, 6-3/4" thick x 15" wide, 16"oc	SF	$0.53	$0.94	$1.46	**$2.44**	0.013
Install insulation, foil faced, laid flat, R-22, 6-3/4" thick x 23" wide, 24"oc	SF	$0.36	$0.99	$1.35	**$2.26**	0.009
Install insulation, foil faced, rafters, R-22, 6-3/4" thick x 15" wide, 16"oc	SF	$0.81	$0.94	$1.75	**$2.92**	0.020
Install insulation, foil faced, rafters, R-22, 6-3/4" thick x 23" wide, 24"oc	SF	$0.53	$0.99	$1.51	**$2.53**	0.013
Install insulation, foil faced, in walls, R-22, 6-3/4" thick x 15" wide, 16"oc	SF	$0.65	$0.94	$1.58	**$2.65**	0.016
Install insulation, foil faced, in walls, R-22, 6-3/4" thick x 23" wide, 24"oc	SF	$0.45	$0.99	$1.43	**$2.39**	0.011
FIBERGLASS INSULATION, FOIL FACED, R-30						
Install insulation, foil faced, laid flat, R-30, 9-1/2" thick x 16" wide, 16"oc	SF	$0.53	$1.41	$1.94	**$3.23**	0.013
Install insulation, foil faced, laid flat, R-30, 9-1/2" thick x 24" wide, 24"oc	SF	$0.36	$1.43	$1.80	**$3.00**	0.009
Install insulation, foil faced, rafters, R-30, 9-1/2" thick x 16" wide, 16"oc	SF	$0.81	$1.41	$2.22	**$3.71**	0.020
Install insulation, foil faced, rafters, R-30, 9-1/2" thick x 24" wide, 24"oc	SF	$0.53	$1.43	$1.96	**$3.27**	0.013
FIBERGLASS INSULATION, FOIL FACED, R-38						
Install insulation, foil faced, laid flat, R-38, 12" thick x 16" wide, 16"oc	SF	$0.53	$1.88	$2.41	**$4.02**	0.013
Install insulation, foil faced, laid flat, R-38, 12" thick x 24" wide, 24"oc	SF	$0.36	$1.91	$2.27	**$3.79**	0.009
Install insulation, foil faced, for rafters, R-38, 12" thick x 16" wide, 16"oc	SF	$0.81	$1.88	$2.69	**$4.50**	0.020
Install insulation, foil faced, for rafters, R-38, 12" thick x 24" wide, 24"oc	SF	$0.53	$1.91	$2.43	**$4.06**	0.013

Insulation

Insulation Baffles

Description	Unit	Direct Labor	Direct Materials	Direct Total	Selling Price	Man-hours
Install baffle around light	EA	$12.68	$5.78	$18.45	**$30.82**	0.313
Install baffle around chimney	EA	$25.40	$14.58	$39.97	**$66.76**	0.627
Install baffle around fan	EA	$12.68	$5.78	$18.45	**$30.82**	0.313
Install baffle in rafter space	LF	$0.53	$0.53	$1.05	**$1.76**	0.013

Foam Sheathing

Description	Unit	Direct Labor	Direct Materials	Direct Total	Selling Price	Man-hours
Install foil faced foam sheathing, 1/2"	SF	$1.22	$0.30	$1.51	**$2.53**	0.016
Install foil faced foam sheathing, 5/8"	SF	$1.29	$0.34	$1.64	**$2.73**	0.017
Install foil faced foam sheathing, 3/4"	SF	$1.37	$0.40	$1.77	**$2.95**	0.018
Install foil faced foam sheathing, 1"	SF	$1.37	$0.45	$1.82	**$3.04**	0.018
Install foil faced foam sheathing, 2"	SF	$1.45	$0.79	$2.24	**$3.74**	0.019

Blown In Insulation

Description	Unit	Direct Labor	Direct Materials	Direct Total	Selling Price	Man-hours
Blow in insulation behind siding, R-13, 3-1/2" thick	SF	$2.44	$0.33	$2.77	**$4.62**	0.032
Blow in insulation behind siding, R-19, 5-1/2" thick	SF	$3.20	$0.54	$3.74	**$6.24**	0.042
Blow in insulation behind stucco, R-13, 3-1/2" thick	SF	$3.20	$0.33	$3.53	**$5.89**	0.042
Blow in insulation behind stucco, R-19, 5-1/2" thick	SF	$3.96	$0.54	$4.50	**$7.51**	0.052
Blow in insulation behind drywall, R-13, 3-1/2" thick	SF	$3.96	$0.33	$4.29	**$7.16**	0.052
Blow in insulation behind drywall, R-19, 5-1/2" thick	SF	$4.72	$0.54	$5.26	**$8.78**	0.062
Blow insulation between open joists, R-19, 6" thick	SF	$0.76	$0.48	$1.25	**$2.08**	0.010
Blow insulation between open joists, R-30, 10" thick	SF	$1.14	$0.80	$1.94	**$3.25**	0.015
Blow insulation between open joists, R-38, 12" thick	SF	$1.37	$0.97	$2.34	**$3.90**	0.018
Blow insulation between open joists, R-44, 14" thick	SF	$1.45	$1.13	$2.58	**$4.31**	0.019

Barriers and Sprays

Description	Unit	Direct Labor	Direct Materials	Direct Total	Selling Price	Man-hours
Vapor barrier, in crawlspace, 4 mil	SF	$0.16	$0.10	$0.26	**$0.44**	0.004
Vapor barrier, exterior wall, 6 mil	SF	$0.12	$0.11	$0.23	**$0.39**	0.003
Vapor barrier, ceiling, 6 mil	SF	$0.16	$0.11	$0.27	**$0.45**	0.004
Radiant barriers, foil heat shield	SF	$0.20	$0.26	$0.47	**$0.78**	0.005
Sprayed polystyrene, 1" thick, R-6	SF	$0.56	$0.72	$1.27	**$2.12**	0.010
Sprayed polystyrene, 2" thick, R-11	SF	$0.84	$1.47	$2.31	**$3.86**	0.015

Insulation

Roof Insulation

Description	Unit	Direct Labor	Direct Materials	Direct Total	Selling Price	Man-hours
Install roof insulation, fiberglass board, 3/4"	SF	$0.54	$0.44	$0.98	**$1.64**	0.007
Install roof insulation, fiberglass board, 1-1/8"	SF	$0.62	$0.55	$1.17	**$1.95**	0.008
Install roof insulation, fiberglass board, 1-1/2"	SF	$0.77	$0.81	$1.59	**$2.65**	0.010
Install roof insulation, perlite board, 1"	SF	$0.54	$0.55	$1.09	**$1.82**	0.007
Install roof insulation, perlite board, 1-1/2"	SF	$0.62	$0.77	$1.39	**$2.32**	0.008
Install roof insulation, perlite board, 2-1/2"	SF	$0.77	$1.21	$1.98	**$3.31**	0.010
Install roof insulation, perlite board, 4"	SF	$1.01	$1.94	$2.94	**$4.92**	0.013
Install roof insulation, polystyrene board, 1"	SF	$0.46	$0.50	$0.96	**$1.60**	0.006
Install roof insulation, polystyrene board, 1-1/2"	SF	$0.54	$0.61	$1.15	**$1.92**	0.007
Install roof insulation, polystyrene board, 2"	SF	$0.62	$0.77	$1.39	**$2.32**	0.008
Install roof insulation, urethane board, 3/4"	SF	$0.39	$0.53	$0.92	**$1.53**	0.005
Install roof insulation, urethane board, 1"	SF	$0.39	$0.66	$1.05	**$1.75**	0.005
Install roof insulation, urethane board, 1-1/2"	SF	$0.46	$0.94	$1.40	**$2.34**	0.006
Install roof insulation, urethane board, 2"	SF	$0.54	$1.27	$1.81	**$3.02**	0.007
Install roof insulation, composition board, 1-1/2"	SF	$0.62	$1.10	$1.72	**$2.87**	0.008
Install roof insulation, composition board, 2"	SF	$0.85	$2.15	$3.00	**$5.01**	0.011
Install roof insulation, composition board, 2-1/2"	SF	$1.01	$3.03	$4.03	**$6.73**	0.013

Wall Coverings

Drywall, Gypsum, Sheet Rock

Description	Unit	Direct Labor	Direct Materials	Direct Total	Selling Price	Man-hours
DRYWALL, STANDARD						
Install drywall, taped and finished, 3/8", over 300 SF	SF	$2.06	$0.38	$2.43	**$4.06**	0.027
Install drywall, taped and finished, 1/2", over 300 SF	SF	$2.13	$0.41	$2.54	**$4.24**	0.028
Install drywall, taped and finished, 5/8", over 300 SF	SF	$2.21	$0.46	$2.67	**$4.45**	0.029
Install drywall, hung only, 3/8", over 300 SF	SF	$0.76	$0.32	$1.09	**$1.81**	0.010
Install drywall, hung only, 1/2", over 300 SF	SF	$0.76	$0.35	$1.11	**$1.86**	0.010
Install drywall, hung only, 5/8", over 300 SF	SF	$0.84	$0.41	$1.24	**$2.08**	0.011
DRYWALL, STANDARD, SMALL AREA						
Install drywall, taped and finished, 3/8", 1/2" or 5/8", up to 32 SF	EA	$395.74	$20.28	$416.02	**$694.75**	5.199
Install drywall, taped and finished, 3/8", 1/2" or 5/8", up to 100 SF	EA	$476.20	$51.37	$527.57	**$881.05**	6.256
Install drywall, taped and finished, 3/8", 1/2" or 5/8", up to 200 SF	EA	$594.64	$100.05	$694.68	**$1,160.12**	7.812
Install drywall, taped and finished, 3/8", 1/2" or 5/8", up to 300 SF	EA	$713.08	$162.24	$875.31	**$1,461.78**	9.368
DRYWALL, MOISTURE RESISTANT						
Install drywall, taped and finished, 1/2" moisture resistant, over 300 SF	SF	$2.13	$0.51	$2.65	**$4.42**	0.028
Install drywall, hung only, 1/2" moisture resistant, over 300 SF	SF	$0.76	$0.51	$1.27	**$2.13**	0.010
DRYWALL, MOISTURE RESISTANT, SMALL AREA						
Install drywall, moisture resistant, finished, 1/2", up to 32 SF	EA	$395.74	$24.34	$420.08	**$701.53**	5.199
Install drywall, moisture resistant, finished, 1/2", up to 100 SF	EA	$476.20	$62.19	$538.39	**$899.11**	6.256
Install drywall, moisture resistant, finished, 1/2", up to 200 SF	EA	$594.64	$121.68	$716.31	**$1,196.25**	7.812
Install drywall, moisture resistant, finished, 1/2", up to 300 SF	EA	$713.08	$194.68	$907.76	**$1,515.96**	9.368
DRYWALL, FIRE RATED						
Install drywall, taped and finished, 1/2" fire rated, over 300 SF	SF	$2.13	$0.53	$2.66	**$4.44**	0.028
Install drywall, taped and finished, 5/8" fire rated, over 300 SF	SF	$2.21	$0.58	$2.79	**$4.66**	0.029
Install drywall, hung only, 1/2" fire rated, over 300 SF	SF	$0.76	$0.53	$1.29	**$2.15**	0.010
Install drywall, hung only, 5/8" fire rated, over 300 SF	SF	$0.84	$0.58	$1.42	**$2.37**	0.011
DRYWALL, FIRE RATED, SMALL AREA						
Install drywall, fire rated, finished, 1/2" or 5/8", up to 32 SF	EA	$395.74	$27.04	$422.78	**$706.04**	5.199
Install drywall, fire rated, finished, 1/2" or 5/8", up to 100 SF	EA	$476.20	$70.30	$546.50	**$912.65**	6.256
Install drywall, fire rated, finished, 1/2" or 5/8", up to 200 SF	EA	$594.64	$137.90	$732.54	**$1,223.34**	7.812
Install drywall, fire rated, finished, 1/2" or 5/8", up to 300 SF	EA	$713.08	$219.02	$932.10	**$1,556.60**	9.368
DRYWALL, BLUE BOARD						
Install drywall, hung only, 1/2" blue board, over 300 SF	SF	$0.76	$0.49	$1.25	**$2.08**	0.010

28

Wall Coverings

Plaster

Description	Unit	Direct Labor	Direct Materials	Direct Total	Selling Price	Man-hours
PLASTER ON EXISTING						
Apply 2 coats of plaster over existing gypsum lath	SF	$2.74	$0.62	$3.36	**$5.61**	0.036
Apply 3 coats of plaster over existing gypsum lath	SF	$3.81	$0.66	$4.47	**$7.46**	0.050
Apply 2 coats of plaster over existing masonry	SF	$2.82	$0.67	$3.49	**$5.83**	0.037
Apply 3 coats of plaster over existing masonry	SF	$3.81	$0.72	$4.52	**$7.55**	0.050
Apply 2 coats of plaster over existing metal lath	SF	$3.04	$0.78	$3.83	**$6.39**	0.040
Apply 3 coats of plaster over existing metal lath	SF	$3.96	$1.06	$5.02	**$8.38**	0.052
Apply 2 coats of plaster over existing wood lath	SF	$2.97	$0.66	$3.63	**$6.06**	0.039
Apply 3 coats of plaster over existing wood lath	SF	$3.96	$0.70	$4.66	**$7.78**	0.052
Apply skim-coat plaster over existing drywall	SF	$1.29	$0.17	$1.46	**$2.44**	0.017

Lath Installation

Description	Unit	Direct Labor	Direct Materials	Direct Total	Selling Price	Man-hours
Install 3/8" gypsum lath ready to receive plaster	SF	$1.29	$0.53	$1.83	**$3.05**	0.017
Install 1/2" gypsum lath ready to receive plaster	SF	$1.29	$0.58	$1.88	**$3.13**	0.017
Install metal lath ready to receive plaster	SF	$0.84	$0.47	$1.31	**$2.18**	0.011
Install wood lath ready to receive plaster	SF	$1.29	$1.00	$2.29	**$3.83**	0.017

Plaster and Drywall Repair

Description	Unit	Direct Labor	Direct Materials	Direct Total	Selling Price	Man-hours
Patch drywall hole, up to 8" diameter, 1 hole	EA	$418.65		$418.65	**$699.15**	5.500
Patch drywall hole, up to 8" diameter, up to 3 holes	EA	$532.83		$532.83	**$889.83**	7.000
Patch drywall hole, up to 8" diameter, up to 6 holes	EA	$704.10		$704.10	**$1,175.84**	9.250
Patch plaster hole, up to 8" diameter, 1 hole	EA	$532.83		$532.83	**$889.83**	7.000
Patch plaster hole, up to 8" diameter, up to 3 holes	EA	$647.01		$647.01	**$1,080.50**	8.500
Patch plaster hole, up to 8" diameter, up to 6 holes	EA	$818.27		$818.27	**$1,366.52**	10.750

Wall Coverings

Labor to Install Ceramic Wall Tile

> Does not include cost of ceramic tile. Includes installation of trim tiles.

Description	Unit	Direct Labor	Direct Materials	Direct Total	Selling Price	Man-hours
Install small (up to 1-12") back mount ceramic tile wall, in adhesive, grout and seal	SF	$6.98	$1.78	$8.76	**$14.62**	0.177
Install medium (up to 4-1/4") back mount ceramic tile wall, in adhesive, grout and seal	SF	$6.46	$1.78	$8.24	**$13.77**	0.164
Install small (up to 1-12") back mount ceramic tile wall, thin-set, grout and seal	SF	$8.83	$1.78	$10.61	**$17.72**	0.224
Install medium (up to 4-1/4") back mount ceramic tile wall, thin-set, grout and seal	SF	$7.96	$1.78	$9.74	**$16.27**	0.202
Install small (up to 1-12") back mount ceramic tile wall, mortar, grout and seal	SF	$12.61	$1.10	$13.71	**$22.90**	0.320
Install medium (up to 4-1/4") back mount ceramic tile wall, mortar, grout and seal	SF	$10.84	$1.10	$11.94	**$19.94**	0.275
Install 6 x 6 ceramic tile wall, in adhesive, grout and seal	SF	$8.08	$1.78	$9.86	**$16.47**	0.205
Install 9 x 9 ceramic tile wall, in adhesive, grout and seal	SF	$6.86	$1.78	$8.64	**$14.43**	0.174
Install 12 x 12 ceramic tile wall, in adhesive, grout and seal	SF	$6.03	$1.78	$7.81	**$13.04**	0.153
Install 6 x 6 ceramic tile wall, thin-set, grout and seal	SF	$11.00	$1.78	$12.78	**$21.34**	0.279
Install 9 x 9 ceramic tile wall, thin-set, grout and seal	SF	$9.38	$1.78	$11.16	**$18.64**	0.238
Install 12 x 12 ceramic tile wall, thin-set, grout and seal	SF	$7.02	$1.78	$8.80	**$14.69**	0.178
Install 6 x 6 ceramic tile wall, mortar, grout and seal	SF	$15.77	$1.10	$16.87	**$28.17**	0.400
Install 9 x 9 ceramic tile wall, mortar, grout and seal	SF	$13.40	$1.10	$14.50	**$24.22**	0.340
Install 12 x 12 ceramic tile wall, mortar, grout and seal	SF	$10.05	$1.10	$11.15	**$18.62**	0.255

Wall Coverings

Ceramic Wall Tile

> Cost of tile only. Add labor cost from 'Labor to Install Ceramic Wall Tile' section.

Description	Unit	Direct Labor	Direct Materials	Direct Total	Selling Price	Man-hours
CERAMIC TILE WALLS, MATERIALS ONLY (25% waste in costs)						
Back mount ceramic tile wall covering, small (up to 1-1/2"), at $3 SF	SF		$3.75	$3.75	**$6.26**	
Back mount ceramic tile wall covering, small (up to 1-1/2"), at $4 SF	SF		$5.00	$5.00	**$8.35**	
Back mount ceramic tile wall covering, small (up to 1-1/2"), at $5 SF	SF		$6.25	$6.25	**$10.44**	
Back mount ceramic tile wall covering, small (up to 1-1/2"), at $6 SF	SF		$7.50	$7.50	**$12.53**	
Back mount ceramic tile wall covering, small (up to 1-1/2"), at $8 SF	SF		$10.00	$10.00	**$16.70**	
Back mount ceramic tile wall covering, small (up to 1-1/2"), at $10 SF	SF		$12.50	$12.50	**$20.88**	
Back mount ceramic tile wall covering, medium (up to 4-1/4") at $3 SF	SF		$3.75	$3.75	**$6.26**	
Back mount ceramic tile wall covering, medium (up to 4-1/4") at $4 SF	SF		$5.00	$5.00	**$8.35**	
Back mount ceramic tile wall covering, medium (up to 4-1/4") at $5 SF	SF		$6.25	$6.25	**$10.44**	
Back mount ceramic tile wall covering, medium (up to 4-1/4") at $6 SF	SF		$7.50	$7.50	**$12.53**	
Back mount ceramic tile wall covering, medium (up to 4-1/4") at $8 SF	SF		$10.00	$10.00	**$16.70**	
Back mount ceramic tile wall covering, medium (up to 4-1/4") at $10 SF	SF		$12.50	$12.50	**$20.88**	
Ceramic tile wall covering, 4-1/4" to 12", at $2 SF	SF		$2.50	$2.50	**$4.18**	
Ceramic tile wall covering, 4-1/4" to 12", at $3 SF	SF		$3.75	$3.75	**$6.26**	
Ceramic tile wall covering, 4-1/4" to 12", at $4 SF	SF		$5.00	$5.00	**$8.35**	
Ceramic tile wall covering, 4-1/4" to 12", at $5 SF	SF		$6.25	$6.25	**$10.44**	
Ceramic tile wall covering, 4-1/4" to 12", at $6 SF	SF		$7.50	$7.50	**$12.53**	
Ceramic tile wall covering, 4-1/4" to 12", at $8 SF	SF		$10.00	$10.00	**$16.70**	
Ceramic tile wall covering, 4-1/4" to 12", at $10 SF	SF		$12.50	$12.50	**$20.88**	
Ceramic tile wall covering, 4-1/4" to 12", at $12 SF	SF		$15.00	$15.00	**$25.05**	

Wall Coverings

Prefinished Wall Paneling

> Average amount of trim included.

Description	Unit	Direct Labor	Direct Materials	Direct Total	Selling Price	Man-hours
PREFINISHED WALL PANELING (15% waste included in costs)						
Install prefinished paneling at $8.00 per 4' x 8' sheet	SF	$3.96	$0.46	$4.42	**$7.38**	0.052
Install prefinished paneling at $10.00 per 4' x 8' sheet	SF	$3.96	$0.59	$4.55	**$7.59**	0.052
Install prefinished paneling at $12.00 per 4' x 8' sheet	SF	$3.96	$0.70	$4.66	**$7.78**	0.052
Install prefinished paneling at $14.00 per 4' x 8' sheet	SF	$3.96	$0.76	$4.72	**$7.88**	0.052
Install prefinished paneling at $16.00 per 4' x 8' sheet	SF	$3.96	$0.86	$4.82	**$8.05**	0.052
Install prefinished paneling at $18.00 per 4' x 8' sheet	SF	$3.96	$0.97	$4.92	**$8.22**	0.052
Install prefinished paneling at $20.00 per 4' x 8' sheet	SF	$3.96	$1.01	$4.97	**$8.30**	0.052
Install prefinished paneling at $25.00 per 4' x 8' sheet	SF	$4.19	$1.26	$5.44	**$9.09**	0.055
Install prefinished paneling at $30.00 per 4' x 8' sheet	SF	$4.19	$1.51	$5.70	**$9.52**	0.055
Install prefinished paneling at $35.00 per 4' x 8' sheet	SF	$4.19	$2.02	$6.21	**$10.37**	0.055
Install prefinished paneling at $40.00 per 4' x 8' sheet	SF	$4.19	$2.30	$6.49	**$10.83**	0.055
Install prefinished paneling at $45.00 per 4' x 8' sheet	SF	$4.19	$2.59	$6.78	**$11.32**	0.055
Install prefinished paneling at $50.00 per 4' x 8' sheet	SF	$4.41	$2.15	$6.57	**$10.97**	0.058
Install prefinished paneling at $60.00 per 4' x 8' sheet	SF	$4.41	$2.59	$7.01	**$11.71**	0.058
Install prefinished paneling at $70.00 per 4' x 8' sheet	SF	$4.41	$3.02	$7.44	**$12.42**	0.058
Install prefinished paneling at $80.00 per 4' x 8' sheet	SF	$4.41	$3.45	$7.86	**$13.13**	0.058

Wall Coverings

Unfinished Wall Paneling

> Average amount of trim included.

Description	Unit	Direct Labor	Direct Materials	Direct Total	Selling Price	Man-hours
UNFINISHED WALL PANELING (15% waste included in costs)						
Install unfinished ash faced plywood paneling, 1/8", 4' x 8' sheet	SF	$3.96	$1.24	$5.20	**$8.68**	0.052
Install unfinished ash faced plywood paneling, 1/4", 4' x 8' sheet	SF	$4.34	$1.66	$6.00	**$10.02**	0.057
Install unfinished ash faced plywood paneling, 1/2", 4' x 8' sheet	SF	$4.72	$2.07	$6.79	**$11.35**	0.062
Install unfinished ash faced plywood paneling, 3/4", 4' x 8' sheet	SF	$5.02	$3.10	$8.13	**$13.57**	0.066
Install unfinished birch faced plywood paneling, 1/8", 4' x 8' sheet	SF	$3.96	$1.01	$4.97	**$8.30**	0.052
Install unfinished birch faced plywood paneling, 1/4", 4' x 8' sheet	SF	$4.34	$1.47	$5.81	**$9.70**	0.057
Install unfinished birch faced plywood paneling, 1/2", 4' x 8' sheet	SF	$4.72	$2.30	$7.02	**$11.73**	0.062
Install unfinished birch faced plywood paneling, 3/4", 4' x 8' sheet	SF	$5.02	$3.06	$8.08	**$13.50**	0.066
Install unfinished oak faced plywood paneling, 1/8", 4' x 8' sheet	SF	$3.96	$0.96	$4.92	**$8.21**	0.052
Install unfinished oak faced plywood paneling, 1/4", 4' x 8' sheet	SF	$4.34	$1.21	$5.55	**$9.27**	0.057
Install unfinished oak faced plywood paneling, 1/2", 4' x 8' sheet	SF	$4.72	$1.75	$6.47	**$10.80**	0.062
Install unfinished oak faced plywood paneling, 3/4", 4' x 8' sheet	SF	$5.02	$2.19	$7.21	**$12.05**	0.066
Install unfinished mahogany faced plywood paneling, 1/8", 4' x 8' sheet	SF	$3.96	$0.58	$4.54	**$7.58**	0.052
Install unfinished mahogany faced plywood paneling, 1/4", 4' x 8' sheet	SF	$4.34	$0.75	$5.09	**$8.51**	0.057
Install unfinished mahogany faced plywood paneling, 1/2", 4' x 8' sheet	SF	$4.72	$1.17	$5.89	**$9.83**	0.062
Install unfinished mahogany faced plywood paneling, 3/4", 4' x 8' sheet	SF	$5.02	$1.58	$6.61	**$11.03**	0.066
Install unfinished maple faced plywood paneling, 1/8", 4' x 8' sheet	SF	$3.96	$1.37	$5.33	**$8.90**	0.052
Install unfinished maple faced plywood paneling, 1/4", 4' x 8' sheet	SF	$4.34	$1.75	$6.09	**$10.17**	0.057
Install unfinished maple faced plywood paneling, 1/2", 4' x 8' sheet	SF	$4.72	$2.23	$6.95	**$11.61**	0.062
Install unfinished maple faced plywood paneling, 3/4", 4' x 8' sheet	SF	$5.02	$3.42	$8.44	**$14.10**	0.066
Install unfinished walnut faced plywood paneling, 1/8", 4' x 8' sheet	SF	$3.96	$1.37	$5.33	**$8.90**	0.052
Install unfinished walnut faced plywood paneling, 1/4", 4' x 8' sheet	SF	$4.34	$1.72	$6.05	**$10.11**	0.057
Install unfinished walnut faced plywood paneling, 1/2", 4' x 8' sheet	SF	$4.72	$2.25	$6.97	**$11.64**	0.062
Install unfinished walnut faced plywood paneling, 3/4", 4' x 8' sheet	SF	$5.02	$3.56	$8.59	**$14.34**	0.066

Wall Coverings

Unfinished Solid Wood Wall Paneling

> Average amount of trim included.

Description	Unit	Direct Labor	Direct Materials	Direct Total	Selling Price	Man-hours
UNFINISHED SOLID WOOD PANELING (15% waste included in costs)						
Install unfinished knotty pine 3/4" solid paneling	SF	$8.45	$2.90	$11.35	**$18.96**	0.111
Install unfinished cedar 3/4" solid paneling	SF	$8.45	$3.40	$11.85	**$19.79**	0.111
Install unfinished redwood 3/4" solid paneling	SF	$8.45	$5.71	$14.16	**$23.64**	0.111

Unfinished Hardboard Paneling

> No trim included.

Description	Unit	Direct Labor	Direct Materials	Direct Total	Selling Price	Man-hours
Install unfinished hardboard, surfaced 1 side, 1/8", 4' x 8' sheet	SF	$2.74	$0.25	$2.99	**$5.00**	0.036
Install unfinished hardboard, surfaced 1 side, 1/4", 4' x 8' sheet	SF	$2.97	$0.33	$3.30	**$5.51**	0.039
Install unfinished hardboard, surfaced 2 side, 1/8", 4' x 8' sheet	SF	$2.74	$0.42	$3.16	**$5.27**	0.036
Install unfinished hardboard, surfaced 2 side, 1/4", 4' x 8' sheet	SF	$2.97	$0.46	$3.43	**$5.73**	0.039

Cedar Closet Paneling

> No trim included.

Description	Unit	Direct Labor	Direct Materials	Direct Total	Selling Price	Man-hours
Install cedar chip panel closet lining, 1/4" thick	SF	$2.97	$1.12	$4.09	**$6.83**	0.039
Install cedar board closet lining, 1/4" thick x 3-3/4" wide	SF	$5.25	$2.48	$7.73	**$12.90**	0.069

28

Wall Coverings

Wallpaper Preparation

Description	Unit	Direct Labor	Direct Materials	Direct Total	Selling Price	Man-hours
Remove wallpaper with steam, single layer	SF	$0.45		$0.45	**$0.74**	0.008
Remove wallpaper with steam, several layers	SF	$0.72		$0.72	**$1.21**	0.013
Wash wall after paper removal, patch scrape marks	SF	$0.28		$0.28	**$0.47**	0.005

Paper Wallpaper

PAPER WALLPAPER, IN SMALL ROOM (15% waste included)

Description	Unit	Direct Labor	Direct Materials	Direct Total	Selling Price	Man-hours
Hang wallpaper, $10 per 28 SF roll, in bath or kitchen	SF	$1.45	$0.42	$1.87	**$3.12**	0.026
Hang wallpaper, $15 per 28 SF roll, in bath or kitchen	SF	$1.45	$0.63	$2.08	**$3.47**	0.026
Hang wallpaper, $20 per 28 SF roll, in bath or kitchen	SF	$1.50	$0.83	$2.33	**$3.90**	0.027
Hang wallpaper, $25 per 28 SF roll, in bath or kitchen	SF	$1.50	$1.04	$2.54	**$4.25**	0.027
Hang wallpaper, $30 per 28 SF roll, in bath or kitchen	SF	$1.61	$1.25	$2.86	**$4.78**	0.029
Hang wallpaper, $40 per 28 SF roll, in bath or kitchen	SF	$1.67	$1.65	$3.32	**$5.55**	0.030
Hang wallpaper, $50 per 28 SF roll, in bath or kitchen	SF	$1.78	$2.06	$3.84	**$6.42**	0.032

PAPER WALLPAPER, IN REGULAR ROOM (15% waste included)

Description	Unit	Direct Labor	Direct Materials	Direct Total	Selling Price	Man-hours
Hang wallpaper, $10 per 28 SF roll, in standard room	SF	$0.95	$0.42	$1.37	**$2.28**	0.017
Hang wallpaper, $15 per 28 SF roll, in standard room	SF	$0.95	$0.63	$1.58	**$2.63**	0.017
Hang wallpaper, $20 per 28 SF roll, in standard room	SF	$1.00	$0.83	$1.83	**$3.06**	0.018
Hang wallpaper, $25 per 28 SF roll, in standard room	SF	$1.00	$1.04	$2.04	**$3.41**	0.018
Hang wallpaper, $30 per 28 SF roll, in standard room	SF	$1.11	$1.25	$2.36	**$3.95**	0.020
Hang wallpaper, $40 per 28 SF roll, in standard room	SF	$1.11	$1.65	$2.76	**$4.62**	0.020
Hang wallpaper, $50 per 28 SF roll, in standard room	SF	$1.17	$2.06	$3.23	**$5.39**	0.021

PAPER WALLPAPER, BORDER (15% waste included)

Description	Unit	Direct Labor	Direct Materials	Direct Total	Selling Price	Man-hours
Hang coordinating border, 4" to 6" wide	LF	$0.67	$0.80	$1.47	**$2.45**	0.012

Wall Coverings

Vinyl Wallpaper

Description	Unit	Direct Labor	Direct Materials	Direct Total	Selling Price	Man-hours
VINYL WALLPAPER, IN SMALL ROOM (15% waste included)						
Hang vinyl wallpaper, $10 per 28 SF roll, in bath or kitchen	SF	$1.67	$0.42	$2.09	**$3.49**	0.030
Hang vinyl wallpaper, $15 per 28 SF roll, in bath or kitchen	SF	$1.67	$0.63	$2.30	**$3.84**	0.030
Hang vinyl wallpaper, $20 per 28 SF roll, in bath or kitchen	SF	$1.78	$0.83	$2.61	**$4.36**	0.032
Hang vinyl wallpaper, $25 per 28 SF roll, in bath or kitchen	SF	$1.78	$1.04	$2.82	**$4.71**	0.032
Hang vinyl wallpaper, $30 per 28 SF roll, in bath or kitchen	SF	$1.84	$1.25	$3.09	**$5.16**	0.033
Hang vinyl wallpaper, $40 per 28 SF roll, in bath or kitchen	SF	$2.00	$1.65	$3.65	**$6.10**	0.036
Hang vinyl wallpaper, $50 per 28 SF roll, in bath or kitchen	SF	$2.17	$2.06	$4.23	**$7.07**	0.039
VINYL WALLPAPER, IN REGULAR ROOM (15% waste included)						
Hang vinyl wallpaper, $10 per 28 SF roll, in standard room	SF	$1.17	$0.42	$1.59	**$2.65**	0.021
Hang vinyl wallpaper, $15 per 28 SF roll, in standard room	SF	$1.17	$0.63	$1.80	**$3.01**	0.021
Hang vinyl wallpaper, $20 per 28 SF roll, in standard room	SF	$1.28	$0.83	$2.11	**$3.53**	0.023
Hang vinyl wallpaper, $25 per 28 SF roll, in standard room	SF	$1.28	$1.04	$2.32	**$3.88**	0.023
Hang vinyl wallpaper, $30 per 28 SF roll, in standard room	SF	$1.34	$1.25	$2.59	**$4.32**	0.024
Hang vinyl wallpaper, $40 per 28 SF roll, in standard room	SF	$1.45	$1.65	$3.10	**$5.17**	0.026
Hang vinyl wallpaper, $50 per 28 SF roll, in standard room	SF	$1.50	$2.06	$3.56	**$5.95**	0.027
VINYL WALLPAPER, BORDER (15% waste included)						
Hang coordinating vinyl border, 4" to 6" wide	LF	$0.78	$1.00	$1.78	**$2.97**	0.014

Grasscloth Wallpaper

Description	Unit	Direct Labor	Direct Materials	Direct Total	Selling Price	Man-hours
GRASSCLOTH WALLPAPER, IN SMALL ROOM (15% waste included)						
Hang grass cloth, $0.50 SF, in bath or kitchen	SF	$2.62	$0.58	$3.20	**$5.34**	0.047
Hang grass cloth, $1.00 SF, in bath or kitchen	SF	$2.62	$1.15	$3.77	**$6.29**	0.047
Hang grass cloth, $1.50 SF, in bath or kitchen	SF	$2.62	$1.73	$4.35	**$7.26**	0.047
Hang grass cloth, $2.00 SF, in bath or kitchen	SF	$2.62	$2.30	$4.92	**$8.21**	0.047
GRASSCLOTH WALLPAPER, IN REGULAR ROOM (15% waste)						
Hang grass cloth, $0.50 SF, in standard room	SF	$2.00	$0.58	$2.58	**$4.32**	0.036
Hang grass cloth, $1.00 SF, in standard room	SF	$2.00	$1.15	$3.15	**$5.27**	0.036
Hang grass cloth, $1.50 SF, in standard room	SF	$2.00	$1.73	$3.73	**$6.24**	0.036
Hang grass cloth, $2.00 SF, in standard room	SF	$2.00	$2.30	$4.30	**$7.19**	0.036

Ceiling Coverings

Drywall, Gypsum, Sheet Rock Ceiling

Description	Unit	Direct Labor	Direct Materials	Direct Total	Selling Price	Man-hours
DRYWALL, STANDARD						
Install drywall ceiling, taped and finished, 3/8", over 300 SF	SF	$2.21	$0.38	$2.59	**$4.32**	0.029
Install drywall ceiling, taped and finished, 1/2", over 300 SF	SF	$2.28	$0.41	$2.69	**$4.49**	0.030
Install drywall ceiling, taped and finished, 5/8", over 300 SF	SF	$2.36	$0.46	$2.82	**$4.71**	0.031
Install drywall ceiling, hung only, 3/8", over 300 SF	SF	$0.84	$0.32	$1.16	**$1.94**	0.011
Install drywall ceiling, hung only, 1/2", over 300 SF	SF	$0.84	$0.35	$1.19	**$1.99**	0.011
Install drywall ceiling, hung only, 5/8", over 300 SF	SF	$0.91	$0.41	$1.32	**$2.20**	0.012
DRYWALL, STANDARD, SMALL AREA						
Install drywall ceiling, taped and finished, 3/8", 1/2" or 5/8", up to 32 SF	EA	$435.32	$20.28	$455.60	**$760.85**	5.719
Install drywall ceiling, taped and finished, 3/8", 1/2" or 5/8", up to 100 SF	EA	$523.85	$51.37	$575.22	**$960.62**	6.882
Install drywall ceiling, taped and finished, 3/8", 1/2" or 5/8", up to 200 SF	EA	$654.09	$100.05	$754.13	**$1,259.40**	8.593
Install drywall ceiling, taped and finished, 3/8", 1/2" or 5/8", up to 300 SF	EA	$784.40	$162.24	$946.64	**$1,580.88**	10.305
DRYWALL, MOISTURE RESISTANT						
Install drywall ceiling, finished, 1/2" moisture resistant, over 300 SF	SF	$2.28	$0.51	$2.80	**$4.67**	0.030
Install drywall ceiling, hung only, 1/2" moisture resistant, over 300 SF	SF	$0.84	$0.51	$1.35	**$2.26**	0.011
DRYWALL, MOISTURE RESISTANT, SMALL AREA						
Install drywall ceiling, moisture resistant, finished, 1/2", up to 32 SF	EA	$435.32	$24.34	$459.66	**$767.63**	5.719
Install drywall ceiling, moisture resistant, finished, 1/2", up to 100 SF	EA	$523.85	$62.19	$586.04	**$978.68**	6.882
Install drywall ceiling, moisture resistant, finished, 1/2", up to 200 SF	EA	$654.09	$121.68	$775.76	**$1,295.52**	8.593
Install drywall ceiling, moisture resistant, finished, 1/2", up to 300 SF	EA	$784.40	$194.68	$979.08	**$1,635.07**	10.305
DRYWALL, FIRE RATED						
Install drywall ceiling, taped and finished, 1/2" fire rated, over 300 SF	SF	$2.28	$0.53	$2.81	**$4.69**	0.030
Install drywall ceiling, taped and finished, 5/8" fire rated, over 300 SF	SF	$2.36	$0.58	$2.94	**$4.91**	0.031
Install drywall ceiling, hung only, 1/2" fire rated, over 300 SF	SF	$0.84	$0.53	$1.36	**$2.28**	0.011
Install drywall ceiling, hung only, 5/8" fire rated, over 300 SF	SF	$0.91	$0.58	$1.49	**$2.50**	0.012
DRYWALL, FIRE RATED, SMALL AREA						
Install drywall ceiling, fire rated, finished, 1/2" or 5/8", up to 32 SF	EA	$435.32	$27.04	$462.36	**$772.14**	5.719
Install drywall ceiling, fire rated, finished, 1/2" or 5/8", up to 100 SF	EA	$523.85	$70.30	$594.15	**$992.23**	6.882
Install drywall ceiling, fire rated, finished, 1/2" or 5/8", up to 200 SF	EA	$654.09	$137.90	$791.99	**$1,322.62**	8.593
Install drywall ceiling, fire rated, finished, 1/2" or 5/8", up to 300 SF	EA	$784.40	$219.02	$1,003.42	**$1,675.71**	10.305
DRYWALL, BLUE BOARD						
Install drywall ceiling, hung only, 1/2" blue board, over 300 SF	SF	$0.84	$0.49	$1.32	**$2.21**	0.011

29

Ceiling Coverings

Plaster Ceiling

Description	Unit	Direct Labor	Direct Materials	Direct Total	Selling Price	Man-hours
PLASTER ON EXISTING						
Apply 2 coats of plaster over existing gypsum lath on ceiling	SF	$0.16	$0.62	$0.78	**$1.31**	0.043
Apply 3 coats of plaster over existing gypsum lath on ceiling	SF	$4.57	$0.66	$5.23	**$8.73**	0.060
Apply 2 coats of plaster over existing masonry ceiling	SF	$3.35	$0.67	$4.02	**$6.72**	0.044
Apply 3 coats of plaster over existing masonry ceiling	SF	$4.57	$0.72	$5.28	**$8.82**	0.060
Apply 2 coats of plaster over existing metal lath on ceiling	SF	$3.65	$0.78	$4.43	**$7.41**	0.048
Apply 3 coats of plaster over existing metal lath on ceiling	SF	$4.80	$1.06	$5.85	**$9.78**	0.063
Apply 2 coats of plaster over existing wood lath on ceiling	SF	$3.58	$0.66	$4.24	**$7.08**	0.047
Apply 3 coats of plaster over existing wood lath on ceiling	SF	$4.80	$0.70	$5.50	**$9.18**	0.063
Apply skim-coat plaster over existing drywall on ceiling	SF	$1.60	$0.17	$1.76	**$2.95**	0.021

Lath Installation

Description	Unit	Direct Labor	Direct Materials	Direct Total	Selling Price	Man-hours
Install 3/8" gypsum lath on ceiling ready to receive plaster	SF	$1.52	$0.53	$2.05	**$3.43**	0.020
Install 1/2" gypsum lath on ceiling ready to receive plaster	SF	$1.52	$0.58	$2.10	**$3.51**	0.020
Install metal lath on ceiling ready to receive plaster	SF	$0.99	$0.47	$1.46	**$2.43**	0.013
Install wood lath on ceiling ready to receive plaster	SF	$1.45	$1.00	$2.45	**$4.08**	0.019

Plaster and Drywall Repair

Description	Unit	Direct Labor	Direct Materials	Direct Total	Selling Price	Man-hours
Patch drywall hole in ceiling, up to 8" diameter, 1 hole in ceiling	EA	$460.52		$460.52	**$769.06**	6.050
Patch drywall hole in ceiling, up to 8" diameter, up to 3 holes in ceiling	EA	$586.11		$586.11	**$978.81**	7.700
Patch drywall hole in ceiling, up to 8" diameter, up to 6 holes in ceiling	EA	$774.51		$774.51	**$1,293.42**	10.175
Patch plaster hole in ceiling, up to 8" diameter, 1 hole in ceiling	EA	$586.11		$586.11	**$978.81**	7.700
Patch plaster hole in ceiling, up to 8" diameter, up to 3 holes in ceiling	EA	$711.71		$711.71	**$1,188.55**	9.350
Patch plaster hole in ceiling, up to 8" diameter, up to 6 holes in ceiling	EA	$900.10		$900.10	**$1,503.17**	11.825

Ceiling Coverings

Ceiling Textures

Description	Unit	Direct Labor	Direct Materials	Direct Total	Selling Price	Man-hours
Paint drywall or plaster ceiling with brush, 1 coat, textured	SF	$0.72	$0.19	$0.92	**$1.53**	0.013
Paint drywall or plaster ceiling with roller, 1 coat, textured	SF	$0.61	$0.19	$0.81	**$1.34**	0.011
Spray acoustic ceiling, popcorn, thin layer	SF	$0.39	$0.15	$0.54	**$0.90**	0.007
Spray acoustic ceiling, popcorn, average layer	SF	$0.56	$0.21	$0.77	**$1.29**	0.010
Spray acoustic ceiling, popcorn, thick layer	SF	$0.67	$0.28	$0.95	**$1.58**	0.012

Ceiling Tiles

Description	Unit	Direct Labor	Direct Materials	Direct Total	Selling Price	Man-hours
FURRING STRIPS FOR ACOUSTIC TILE CEILING						
1" x 4" or 1" x 3", 12" oc, furring strips over wood for ceiling tile	SF	$1.07	$0.24	$1.31	**$2.18**	0.014
1" x 4" or 1" x 3", 12" oc, furring strips on drywall for ceiling tile	SF	$1.45	$0.24	$1.69	**$2.82**	0.019
1" x 4" or 1" x 3", 12" oc, furring strips on plaster for ceiling tile	SF	$167.77	$0.24	$168.01	**$280.57**	2.204
ACOUSTIC TILE CEILING						
Install ceiling tile, 12" x 12", at $ .50 SF	SF	$1.60	$0.55	$2.15	**$3.59**	0.021
Install ceiling tile, 12" x 12", at $ .60 SF	SF	$1.60	$0.66	$2.26	**$3.77**	0.021
Install ceiling tile, 12" x 12", at $ .70 SF	SF	$1.60	$0.77	$2.37	**$3.96**	0.021
Install ceiling tile, 12" x 12", at $ .80 SF	SF	$1.60	$0.88	$2.48	**$4.14**	0.021
Install ceiling tile, 12" x 12", at $ .90 SF	SF	$1.60	$0.99	$2.59	**$4.32**	0.021
Install ceiling tile, 12" x 12", at $1.00 SF	SF	$1.67	$1.10	$2.77	**$4.63**	0.022
Install ceiling tile, 12" x 12", at $1.25 SF	SF	$1.67	$1.38	$3.05	**$5.09**	0.022
Install ceiling tile, 12" x 12", at $1.50 SF	SF	$1.67	$1.65	$3.32	**$5.55**	0.022
Install ceiling tile, 12" x 12", at $2.00 SF	SF	$1.67	$2.20	$3.87	**$6.47**	0.022
Install ceiling tile, 12" x 12", at $2.25 SF	SF	$1.67	$2.48	$4.15	**$6.93**	0.022
Install ceiling tile, 12" x 12", at $2.50 SF	SF	$1.67	$2.75	$4.42	**$7.39**	0.022
Install ceiling tile, 12" x 12", at $2.75 SF	SF	$1.67	$3.03	$4.70	**$7.85**	0.022
Install ceiling tile, 12" x 12", at $3.00 SF	SF	$1.83	$3.30	$5.13	**$8.56**	0.024
Install ceiling tile, 12" x 12", at $3.50 SF	SF	$1.83	$3.85	$5.68	**$9.48**	0.024
Install ceiling tile, 12" x 12", at $4.00 SF	SF	$1.83	$4.40	$6.23	**$10.40**	0.024
Install ceiling tile, 12" x 12", at $4.50 SF	SF	$1.83	$4.95	$6.78	**$11.32**	0.024
Install ceiling tile, 12" x 12", at $5.00 SF	SF	$1.83	$5.50	$7.33	**$12.24**	0.024

Ceiling Coverings

Grid Ceilings, 24" x 24"

> Includes grid system. Does not include lighting.

Description	Unit	Direct Labor	Direct Materials	Direct Total	Selling Price	Man-hours
GRID CEILING, 24" x 24"						
Install 24" x 24" grid system, with panels at $ .40 SF ($1.60 per panel)	SF	$2.36	$1.08	$3.44	**$5.74**	0.031
Install 24" x 24" grid system, with panels at $ .50 SF ($2.00 per panel)	SF	$2.36	$1.18	$3.54	**$5.91**	0.031
Install 24" x 24" grid system, with panels at $ .60 SF ($2.40 per panel)	SF	$2.36	$1.28	$3.64	**$6.08**	0.031
Install 24" x 24" grid system, with panels at $ .70 SF ($2.80 per panel)	SF	$2.36	$1.46	$3.82	**$6.38**	0.031
Install 24" x 24" grid system, with panels at $ .80 SF ($3.20 per panel)	SF	$2.36	$1.57	$3.93	**$6.57**	0.031
Install 24" x 24" grid system, with panels at $ .90 SF ($3.60 per panel)	SF	$2.36	$1.68	$4.04	**$6.75**	0.031
Install 24" x 24" grid system, with panels at $1.00 SF ($4.00 per panel)	SF	$2.36	$1.79	$4.15	**$6.93**	0.031
Install 24" x 24" grid system, with panels at $1.10 SF ($4.40 per panel)	SF	$2.36	$1.90	$4.26	**$7.12**	0.031
Install 24" x 24" grid system, with panels at $1.20 SF ($4.80 per panel)	SF	$2.36	$2.01	$4.37	**$7.30**	0.031
Install 24" x 24" grid system, with panels at $1.30 SF ($5.20 per panel)	SF	$2.36	$2.12	$4.48	**$7.49**	0.031
Install 24" x 24" grid system, with panels at $1.40 SF ($5.60 per panel)	SF	$2.36	$2.23	$4.59	**$7.67**	0.031
Install 24" x 24" grid system, with panels at $1.50 SF ($6.00 per panel)	SF	$2.36	$2.34	$4.70	**$7.85**	0.031
Install 24" x 24" grid system, with panels at $1.60 SF ($6.40 per panel)	SF	$2.36	$2.45	$4.81	**$8.04**	0.031
Install 24" x 24" grid system, with panels at $1.70 SF ($6.80 per panel)	SF	$2.36	$2.56	$4.92	**$8.22**	0.031
Install 24" x 24" grid system, with panels at $1.80 SF ($7.20 per panel)	SF	$2.36	$2.67	$5.03	**$8.40**	0.031
Install 24" x 24" grid system, with panels at $1.90 SF ($7.60 per panel)	SF	$2.36	$2.78	$5.14	**$8.59**	0.031
Install 24" x 24" grid system, with panels at $2.00 SF ($8.00 per panel)	SF	$2.36	$2.89	$5.25	**$8.77**	0.031
Install 24" x 24" grid system, with panels at $2.10 SF ($8.40 per panel)	SF	$2.36	$3.00	$5.36	**$8.95**	0.031

Ceiling Coverings

Grid Ceilings, 24" x 48"

> Includes grid system. Does not include lighting.

Description	Unit	Direct Labor	Direct Materials	Direct Total	Selling Price	Man-hours
GRID CEILING, 24" x 48"						
Install 24" x 48" grid system, with panels at $ .40SF ($3.20 per panel)	SF	$2.21	$1.02	$3.23	**$5.39**	0.029
Install 24" x 48" grid system, with panels at $ .50 SF ($4.00 per panel)	SF	$2.21	$1.12	$3.33	**$5.56**	0.029
Install 24" x 48" grid system, with panels at $ .60 SF ($4.80 per panel)	SF	$2.21	$1.22	$3.43	**$5.72**	0.029
Install 24" x 48" grid system, with panels at $ .70 SF ($5.60 per panel)	SF	$2.21	$1.40	$3.60	**$6.02**	0.029
Install 24" x 48" grid system, with panels at $ .80 SF ($6.40 per panel)	SF	$2.21	$1.51	$3.71	**$6.20**	0.029
Install 24" x 48" grid system, with panels at $ .90 SF ($7.20 per panel)	SF	$2.21	$1.62	$3.82	**$6.39**	0.029
Install 24" x 48" grid system, with panels at $1.00 SF ($8.00 per panel)	SF	$2.21	$1.73	$3.93	**$6.57**	0.029
Install 24" x 48" grid system, with panels at $1.10 SF ($8.80 per panel)	SF	$2.21	$1.84	$4.04	**$6.75**	0.029
Install 24" x 48" grid system, with panels at $1.20 SF ($9.60 per panel)	SF	$2.21	$1.95	$4.15	**$6.94**	0.029
Install 24" x 48" grid system, with panels at $1.30 SF ($10.40 per panel)	SF	$2.21	$2.06	$4.26	**$7.12**	0.029
Install 24" x 48" grid system, with panels at $1.40 SF ($11.20 per panel)	SF	$2.21	$2.17	$4.37	**$7.31**	0.029
Install 24" x 48" grid system, with panels at $1.50 SF ($12.00 per panel)	SF	$2.21	$2.28	$4.48	**$7.49**	0.029
Install 24" x 48" grid system, with panels at $1.60 SF ($12.80 per panel)	SF	$2.21	$2.39	$4.59	**$7.67**	0.029
Install 24" x 48" grid system, with panels at $1.70 SF ($13.60 per panel)	SF	$2.21	$2.50	$4.70	**$7.86**	0.029
Install 24" x 48" grid system, with panels at $1.80 SF ($14.40 per panel)	SF	$2.21	$2.61	$4.81	**$8.04**	0.029
Install 24" x 48" grid system, with panels at $1.90 SF ($15.20 per panel)	SF	$2.21	$2.72	$4.92	**$8.22**	0.029
Install 24" x 48" grid system, with panels at $2.00 SF ($16.00 per panel)	SF	$2.21	$2.83	$5.03	**$8.41**	0.029
Install 24" x 48" grid system, with panels at $2.25 SF ($18.00 per panel)	SF	$2.21	$3.10	$5.31	**$8.87**	0.029
Install 24" x 48" grid system, with panels at $2.50 SF ($20.00 per panel)	SF	$2.21	$3.38	$5.58	**$9.33**	0.029
Install 24" x 48" grid system, with panels at $2.75 SF ($22.00 per panel)	SF	$2.21	$3.65	$5.86	**$9.79**	0.029
Install 24" x 48" grid system, with panels at $3.00 SF ($24.00 per panel)	SF	$2.21	$3.93	$6.13	**$10.24**	0.029

Interior Doors

Labor Costs to Install Interior Doors

> Labor costs do not include materials such as door slab, jamb, casings or other trim.

Description	Unit	Direct Labor	Direct Materials	Direct Total	Selling Price	Man-hours
LABOR TO INSTALL FIELD HUNG DOORS						
Install field hung interior door including jamb, casing 2 sides	EA	$228.36		$228.36	**$381.35**	3.000
Install double field hung interior door including jamb, casing 2 sides	Set	$342.53		$342.53	**$572.03**	4.500
Hang new door slab in existing jamb	EA	$114.18		$114.18	**$190.68**	1.500
LABOR TO INSTALL PRE-HUNG DOORS						
Install interior pre-hung door unit	EA	$114.18		$114.18	**$190.68**	1.500
Install double interior pre-hung door unit	Set	$152.24		$152.24	**$254.24**	2.000
LABOR TO INSTALL BI-FOLD DOORS						
Install 2 door bi-fold unit	Set	$190.30		$190.30	**$317.79**	2.500
Install 4 door bi-fold unit	Set	$266.41		$266.41	**$444.91**	3.500
LABOR TO INSTALL BYPASS OR SLIDING DOORS						
Install 2 door bypass or sliding unit	Set	$228.36		$228.36	**$381.35**	3.000
Install 3 door bypass or sliding unit	Set	$304.47		$304.47	**$508.47**	4.000
LABOR TO INSTALL POCKET DOORS						
Install pocket door in open wall including frame, casing 2 sides	EA	$380.59		$380.59	**$635.59**	5.000

Labor Costs to Remove Interior Doors

Description	Unit	Direct Labor	Direct Materials	Direct Total	Selling Price	Man-hours
LABOR TO REMOVE DOORS						
Remove single interior door, including jamb and casing	EA	$57.09		$57.09	**$95.34**	0.750
Remove double interior door, including jamb and casing	EA	$76.12		$76.12	**$127.12**	1.000
Remove 2 door bi-fold unit	Set	$57.09		$57.09	**$95.34**	0.750
Remove 4 door bi-fold unit	Set	$95.15		$95.15	**$158.90**	1.250
Remove 2 door bypass or sliding unit	Set	$57.09		$57.09	**$95.34**	0.750
Remove 3 door bypass or sliding unit	Set	$95.15		$95.15	**$158.90**	1.250
Remove door slab only	EA	$25.35		$25.35	**$42.33**	0.333

Interior Doors

Create Door Opening in Existing Wall

Description	Unit	Direct Labor	Direct Materials	Direct Total	Selling Price	Man-hours
CREATE DOOR OPENING IN DRYWALL WALL						
Create door opening up to 4' wide in interior drywall wall	EA	$304.47	$37.20	$341.67	**$570.60**	4.000
Create door opening up to 8' wide in interior drywall wall	EA	$418.65	$51.15	$469.80	**$784.57**	5.500
Create door opening up to 12' wide in interior drywall wall	EA	$532.83	$69.75	$602.58	**$1,006.31**	7.000
Create door opening up to 4' in drywall, case with pine stain grade	EA	$418.65	$105.15	$523.80	**$874.75**	5.500
Create door opening up to 8' in drywall, case with pine stain grade	EA	$551.86	$121.55	$673.41	**$1,124.59**	7.250
Create door opening up to 12' in drywall, case with pine stain grade	EA	$685.07	$141.06	$826.12	**$1,379.63**	9.000
Create door opening up to 4' in drywall wall, case with solid oak trim	EA	$456.71	$152.01	$608.72	**$1,016.56**	6.000
Create door opening up to 8' in drywall wall, case with solid oak trim	EA	$608.95	$175.80	$784.75	**$1,310.54**	8.000
Create door opening up to 12' in drywall wall, case with solid oak trim	EA	$761.18	$199.05	$960.24	**$1,603.60**	10.000
Create door opening up to 4' wide in drywall wall, finish with drywall	EA	$608.95	$62.78	$671.72	**$1,121.78**	8.000
Create door opening up to 8' wide in drywall wall, finish with drywall	EA	$742.16	$74.40	$816.56	**$1,363.65**	9.750
Create door opening up to 12' wide in drywall wall, finish with drywall	EA	$875.36	$93.00	$968.36	**$1,617.17**	11.500
CREATE DOOR OPENING IN PLASTER WALL						
Create door opening up to 4' wide in interior lath and plaster wall	EA	$380.59	$37.20	$417.79	**$697.71**	5.000
Create door opening up to 8' wide in interior lath and plaster wall	EA	$494.77	$51.15	$545.92	**$911.69**	6.500
Create door opening up to 12' wide in interior lath and plaster wall	EA	$608.95	$69.75	$678.70	**$1,133.43**	8.000
Create door opening to 4' in plaster wall, case with pine stain grade	EA	$494.77	$105.15	$599.92	**$1,001.86**	6.500
Create door opening to 8' in plaster wall, case with pine stain grade	EA	$627.98	$121.55	$749.53	**$1,251.71**	8.250
Create door opening to 12' in plaster wall, case with pine stain grade	EA	$799.24	$141.06	$940.30	**$1,570.30**	10.500
Create door opening up to 4' in plaster wall, case with solid oak trim	EA	$532.83	$152.01	$684.84	**$1,143.68**	7.000
Create door opening up to 8' in plaster wall, case with solid oak trim	EA	$666.04	$175.80	$841.84	**$1,405.88**	8.750
Create door opening up to 12' in plaster wall, case with solid oak trim	EA	$837.30	$199.05	$1,036.36	**$1,730.72**	11.000
Create door opening up to 4' wide in plaster wall, finish with drywall	EA	$723.13	$62.78	$785.90	**$1,312.45**	9.500
Create door opening up to 8' wide in plaster wall, finish with drywall	EA	$856.33	$74.40	$930.73	**$1,554.32**	11.250
Create door opening up to 12' wide in plaster wall, finish with drywall	EA	$989.54	$93.00	$1,082.54	**$1,807.84**	13.000

Interior Doors

Door Locks and Accessories

Description	Unit	Direct Labor	Direct Materials	Direct Total	Selling Price	Man-hours
Install interior passage set, premium quality	EA	$25.35	$84.00	$109.35	**$143.13**	0.333
Install interior passage set, average quality	EA	$25.35	$47.00	$72.35	**$98.73**	0.333
Install interior passage set, economy quality	EA	$25.35	$25.00	$50.35	**$72.33**	0.333
Install interior lock set, premium quality	EA	$25.35	$101.00	$126.35	**$163.53**	0.333
Install interior lock set, average quality	EA	$25.35	$62.00	$87.35	**$116.73**	0.333
Install interior lock set, economy quality	EA	$25.35	$32.00	$57.35	**$80.73**	0.333
Install interior dead bolt, premium quality	EA	$50.77	$90.00	$140.77	**$192.79**	0.667
Install interior dead bolt, average quality	EA	$50.77	$62.00	$112.77	**$159.19**	0.667
Install interior dead bolt, economy quality	EA	$50.77	$39.00	$89.77	**$131.59**	0.667
Install aluminum threshold	LF	$9.36	$4.61	$13.98	**$21.17**	0.123
Install oak threshold	LF	$9.36	$4.93	$14.29	**$21.55**	0.123
Install marble threshold	LF	$25.35	$7.28	$32.63	**$51.07**	0.333

Jamb and Casing for Field Hung Door

> Material Costs only. Labor is included in 'Labor to Install Field Hung Door' item.

Description	Unit	Direct Labor	Direct Materials	Direct Total	Selling Price	Man-hours
JAMB AND CASINGS FOR FIELD HUNG DOOR						
Paint grade pine jambs, casings 2 sides, up to 36"	EA		$77.93	$76.12	**$130.14**	
Stain grade pine jambs, casings 2 sides, up to 36"	EA		$87.54	$114.84	**$146.20**	
Solid oak jambs, casings 2 sides, up to 36"	EA		$109.95	$154.36	**$183.62**	
Paint grade pine jambs, casings 2 sides, 36" to 60"	EA		$85.74	$102.82	**$143.19**	
Stain grade pine jambs, casings 2 sides, 36" to 60"	EA		$99.19	$147.30	**$165.65**	
Solid oak jambs, casings 2 sides, 36" to 60"	EA		$122.83	$192.74	**$205.13**	
JAMB ONLY, NO CASINGS, FOR FIELD HUNG DOOR						
Paint grade pine jambs, no casings, up to 36"	EA		$42.85	$59.80	**$71.55**	
Stain grade pine jambs, no casings, up to 36"	EA		$60.04	$83.80	**$100.27**	
Solid oak jambs, no casings, up to 36"	EA		$64.69	$108.60	**$108.03**	
Paint grade pine jambs, no casings, 36" to 60"	EA		$51.59	$84.00	**$86.16**	
Stain grade pine jambs, no casings, 36" to 60"	EA		$68.55	$111.60	**$114.47**	
Solid oak jambs, no casings, 36" to 60"	EA		$72.19	$140.12	**$120.55**	

Interior Doors

Field Hung Panel Doors

> Material Costs only. Select labor item from 'Labor Costs to Install Doors' section.

Description	Unit	Direct Labor	Direct Materials	Direct Total	Selling Price	Man-hours
FIELD HUNG PANEL WOOD DOORS, FIR/PINE						
Interior fir/pine 6 panel door in existing jamb, 2-0 x 6-8	EA		$128.00	$128.00	**$153.60**	
Interior fir/pine 6 panel door in existing jamb, 2-4 x 6-8	EA		$133.00	$133.00	**$159.60**	
Interior fir/pine 6 panel door in existing jamb, 2-6 x 6-8	EA		$135.00	$135.00	**$162.00**	
Interior fir/pine 6 panel door in existing jamb, 2-8 x 6-8	EA		$138.00	$138.00	**$165.60**	
Interior fir/pine 6 panel door in existing jamb, 3-0 x 6-8	EA		$147.00	$147.00	**$176.40**	
FIELD HUNG PANEL WOOD DOORS, OAK						
Interior oak 6 panel door in existing jamb, 2-0 x 6-8	EA		$234.00	$234.00	**$280.80**	
Interior oak 6 panel door in existing jamb, 2-4 x 6-8	EA		$244.00	$244.00	**$292.80**	
Interior oak 6 panel door in existing jamb, 2-6 x 6-8	EA		$247.00	$247.00	**$296.40**	
Interior oak 6 panel door in existing jamb, 2-8 x 6-8	EA		$252.00	$252.00	**$302.40**	
Interior oak 6 panel door in existing jamb, 3-0 x 6-8	EA		$269.00	$269.00	**$322.80**	
FIELD HUNG PANEL WOOD DOORS, HARDBOARD						
Interior hardboard hollow core 6 panel door in existing jamb, 2-0 x 6-8	EA		$60.00	$60.00	**$72.00**	
Interior hardboard hollow core 6 panel door in existing jamb, 2-4 x 6-8	EA		$61.00	$61.00	**$73.20**	
Interior hardboard hollow core 6 panel door in existing jamb, 2-6 x 6-8	EA		$63.00	$63.00	**$75.60**	
Interior hardboard hollow core 6 panel door in existing jamb, 2-8 x 6-8	EA		$64.00	$64.00	**$76.80**	
Interior hardboard hollow core 6 panel door in existing jamb, 3-0 x 6-8	EA		$67.00	$67.00	**$80.40**	
Interior hardboard solid core 6 panel door in existing jamb, 2-0 x 6-8	EA		$96.00	$96.00	**$115.20**	
Interior hardboard solid core 6 panel door in existing jamb, 2-4 x 6-8	EA		$98.00	$98.00	**$117.60**	
Interior hardboard solid core 6 panel door in existing jamb, 2-6 x 6-8	EA		$101.00	$101.00	**$121.20**	
Interior hardboard solid core 6 panel door in existing jamb, 2-8 x 6-8	EA		$103.00	$103.00	**$123.60**	
Interior hardboard solid core 6 panel door in existing jamb, 3-0 x 6-8	EA		$108.00	$108.00	**$129.60**	

Interior Doors

Field Hung Louvered Wood Doors

> Material Costs only. Select labor item from 'Labor Costs to Install Doors' section.

Description	Unit	Direct Labor	Direct Materials	Direct Total	Selling Price	Man-hours
FIELD HUNG FULL LOUVERED WOOD DOORS, FIR/PINE						
Interior fir/pine full louvered door in existing jamb, 2-0 x 6-8	EA		$102.00	$102.00	**$122.40**	
Interior fir/pine full louvered door in existing jamb, 2-4 x 6-8	EA		$107.00	$107.00	**$128.40**	
Interior fir/pine full louvered door in existing jamb, 2-6 x 6-8	EA		$108.00	$108.00	**$129.60**	
Interior fir/pine full louvered door in existing jamb, 2-8 x 6-8	EA		$110.00	$110.00	**$132.00**	
Interior fir/pine full louvered door in existing jamb, 3-0 x 6-8	EA		$117.00	$117.00	**$140.40**	
FIELD HUNG HALF LOUVERED/HALF PANEL WOOD DOORS						
Interior fir/pine half louver/half panel door in existing jamb, 2-0 x 6-8	EA		$109.00	$109.00	**$130.80**	
Interior fir/pine half louver/half panel door in existing jamb, 2-4 x 6-8	EA		$113.00	$113.00	**$135.60**	
Interior fir/pine half louver/half panel door in existing jamb, 2-6 x 6-8	EA		$115.00	$115.00	**$138.00**	
Interior fir/pine half louver/half panel door in existing jamb, 2-8 x 6-8	EA		$117.00	$117.00	**$140.40**	
Interior fir/pine half louver/half panel door in existing jamb, 3-0 x 6-8	EA		$125.00	$125.00	**$150.00**	

Field Hung French Wood Doors

> Material Costs only. Select labor item from 'Labor Costs to Install Doors' section.

Description	Unit	Direct Labor	Direct Materials	Direct Total	Selling Price	Man-hours
FIELD HUNG FRENCH WOOD DOORS						
Interior french door in existing jamb, 5 lites, 2-0 x 6-8	EA		$127.00	$127.00	**$152.40**	
Interior french door in existing jamb, 5 lites, 2-4 x 6-8	EA		$136.00	$136.00	**$163.20**	
Interior french door in existing jamb, 5 lites, 2-6 x 6-8	EA		$142.00	$142.00	**$170.40**	
Interior french door in existing jamb, 5 lites, 2-8 x 6-8	EA		$148.00	$148.00	**$177.60**	
Interior french door in existing jamb, 5 lites, 3-0 x 6-8	EA		$155.00	$155.00	**$186.00**	
Interior french door in existing jamb, 2 rows of 5 lites, 2-0 x 6-8	EA		$167.00	$167.00	**$200.40**	
Interior french door in existing jamb, 2 rows of 5 lites, 2-4 x 6-8	EA		$176.00	$176.00	**$211.20**	
Interior french door in existing jamb, 2 rows of 5 lites, 2-6 x 6-8	EA		$184.00	$184.00	**$220.80**	
Interior french door in existing jamb, 2 rows of 5 lites, 2-8 x 6-8	EA		$192.00	$192.00	**$230.40**	
Interior french door in existing jamb, 2 rows of 5 lites, 3-0 x 6-8	EA		$200.00	$200.00	**$240.00**	
Interior french door in existing jamb, 3 rows of 5 lites, 2-6 x 6-8	EA		$224.00	$224.00	**$268.80**	
Interior french door in existing jamb, 3 rows of 5 lites, 2-8 x 6-8	EA		$234.00	$234.00	**$280.80**	
Interior french door in existing jamb, 3 rows of 5 lites, 3-0 x 6-8	EA		$251.00	$251.00	**$301.20**	

Interior Doors

Pre-Hung Flush Doors

> No removal of old door included.

Description	Unit	Direct Labor	Direct Materials	Direct Total	Selling Price	Man-hours
PRE-HUNG FLUSH WOOD DOORS, BIRCH HOLLOW CORE						
Pre-hung flush interior birch hollow core door unit, 2-0 x 6-8	EA	$114.18	$113.00	$227.18	**$326.28**	1.500
Pre-hung flush interior birch hollow core door unit, 2-4 x 6-8	EA	$114.18	$115.00	$229.18	**$328.68**	1.500
Pre-hung flush interior birch hollow core door unit, 2-6 x 6-8	EA	$114.18	$117.00	$231.18	**$331.08**	1.500
Pre-hung flush interior birch hollow core door unit, 2-8 x 6-8	EA	$114.18	$121.00	$235.18	**$335.88**	1.500
Pre-hung flush interior birch hollow core door unit, 3-0 x 6-8	EA	$114.18	$126.00	$240.18	**$341.88**	1.500
PRE-HUNG FLUSH WOOD DOORS, BIRCH SOLID CORE						
Pre-hung flush interior birch solid core door unit, 2-0 x 6-8	EA	$114.18	$138.00	$252.18	**$356.28**	1.500
Pre-hung flush interior birch solid core door unit, 2-4 x 6-8	EA	$114.18	$139.00	$253.18	**$357.48**	1.500
Pre-hung flush interior birch solid core door unit, 2-6 x 6-8	EA	$114.18	$142.00	$256.18	**$361.08**	1.500
Pre-hung flush interior birch solid core door unit, 2-8 x 6-8	EA	$114.18	$147.00	$261.18	**$367.08**	1.500
Pre-hung flush interior birch solid core door unit, 3-0 x 6-8	EA	$114.18	$153.00	$267.18	**$374.28**	1.500
PRE-HUNG FLUSH WOOD DOORS, OAK HOLLOW CORE						
Pre-hung flush interior oak hollow core door unit, 2-0 x 6-8	EA	$114.18	$153.00	$267.18	**$374.28**	1.500
Pre-hung flush interior oak hollow core door unit, 2-4 x 6-8	EA	$114.18	$161.00	$275.18	**$383.88**	1.500
Pre-hung flush interior oak hollow core door unit, 2-6 x 6-8	EA	$114.18	$163.00	$277.18	**$386.28**	1.500
Pre-hung flush interior oak hollow core door unit, 2-8 x 6-8	EA	$114.18	$168.00	$282.18	**$392.28**	1.500
Pre-hung flush interior oak hollow core door unit, 3-0 x 6-8	EA	$114.18	$174.00	$288.18	**$399.48**	1.500
PRE-HUNG FLUSH WOOD DOORS, WALNUT HOLLOW CORE						
Pre-hung flush interior walnut hollow core door unit, 2-0 x 6-8	EA	$114.18	$221.00	$335.18	**$455.88**	1.500
Pre-hung flush interior walnut hollow core door unit, 2-4 x 6-8	EA	$114.18	$225.00	$339.18	**$460.68**	1.500
Pre-hung flush interior walnut hollow core door unit, 2-6 x 6-8	EA	$114.18	$227.00	$341.18	**$463.08**	1.500
Pre-hung flush interior walnut hollow core door unit, 2-8 x 6-8	EA	$114.18	$230.00	$344.18	**$466.68**	1.500
Pre-hung flush interior walnut hollow core door unit, 3-0 x 6-8	EA	$114.18	$234.00	$348.18	**$471.48**	1.500
PRE-HUNG FLUSH WOOD DOORS, MAHOGANY HOLLOW CORE						
Pre-hung flush interior mahogany hollow core door unit, 2-0 x 6-8	EA	$114.18	$100.00	$214.18	**$310.68**	1.500
Pre-hung flush interior mahogany hollow core door unit, 2-4 x 6-8	EA	$114.18	$102.00	$216.18	**$313.08**	1.500
Pre-hung flush interior mahogany hollow core door unit, 2-6 x 6-8	EA	$114.18	$105.00	$219.18	**$316.68**	1.500
Pre-hung flush interior mahogany hollow core door unit, 2-8 x 6-8	EA	$114.18	$107.00	$221.18	**$319.08**	1.500
Pre-hung flush interior mahogany hollow core door unit, 3-0 x 6-8	EA	$114.18	$111.00	$225.18	**$323.88**	1.500
PRE-HUNG FLUSH DOORS, HARDBOARD HOLLOW CORE						
Pre-hung flush interior hardboard hollow core door unit, 2-0 x 6-8	EA	$114.18	$95.00	$209.18	**$304.68**	1.500
Pre-hung flush interior hardboard hollow core door unit, 2-4 x 6-8	EA	$114.18	$97.00	$211.18	**$307.08**	1.500
Pre-hung flush interior hardboard hollow core door unit, 2-6 x 6-8	EA	$114.18	$100.00	$214.18	**$310.68**	1.500
Pre-hung flush interior hardboard hollow core door unit, 2-8 x 6-8	EA	$114.18	$102.00	$216.18	**$313.08**	1.500
Pre-hung flush interior hardboard hollow core door unit, 3-0 x 6-8	EA	$114.18	$104.00	$218.18	**$315.48**	1.500

Interior Doors

Pre-Hung Panel Doors

> No removal of old door included.

Description	Unit	Direct Labor	Direct Materials	Direct Total	Selling Price	Man-hours
PRE-HUNG INTERIOR PANEL WOOD DOORS, FIR/PINE						
Interior pre-hung fir/pine 6 panel door unit, 2-0 x 6-8	EA	$114.18	$200.00	$314.18	**$430.68**	1.500
Interior pre-hung fir/pine 6 panel door unit, 2-4 x 6-8	EA	$114.18	$209.00	$323.18	**$441.48**	1.500
Interior pre-hung fir/pine 6 panel door unit, 2-6 x 6-8	EA	$114.18	$211.00	$325.18	**$443.88**	1.500
Interior pre-hung fir/pine 6 panel door unit, 2-8 x 6-8	EA	$114.18	$216.00	$330.18	**$449.88**	1.500
Interior pre-hung fir/pine 6 panel door unit, 3-0 x 6-8	EA	$114.18	$230.00	$344.18	**$466.68**	1.500
PRE-HUNG INTERIOR PANEL WOOD DOORS, OAK						
Interior pre-hung oak 6 panel door unit, 2-0 x 6-8	EA	$114.18	$300.00	$414.18	**$550.68**	1.500
Interior pre-hung oak 6 panel door unit, 2-4 x 6-8	EA	$114.18	$313.00	$427.18	**$566.28**	1.500
Interior pre-hung oak 6 panel door unit, 2-6 x 6-8	EA	$114.18	$317.00	$431.18	**$571.08**	1.500
Interior pre-hung oak 6 panel door unit, 2-8 x 6-8	EA	$114.18	$323.00	$437.18	**$578.28**	1.500
Interior pre-hung oak 6 panel door unit, 3-0 x 6-8	EA	$114.18	$345.00	$459.18	**$604.68**	1.500
PRE-HUNG INTERIOR PANEL DOORS, HARDBOARD						
Interior pre-hung hardboard hollow core door unit, 2-0 x 6-8	EA	$114.18	$111.00	$225.18	**$323.88**	1.500
Interior pre-hung hardboard hollow core door unit, 2-4 x 6-8	EA	$114.18	$113.00	$227.18	**$326.28**	1.500
Interior pre-hung hardboard hollow core door unit, 2-6 x 6-8	EA	$114.18	$117.00	$231.18	**$331.08**	1.500
Interior pre-hung hardboard hollow core door unit, 2-8 x 6-8	EA	$114.18	$120.00	$234.18	**$334.68**	1.500
Interior pre-hung hardboard hollow core door unit, 3-0 x 6-8	EA	$114.18	$125.00	$239.18	**$340.68**	1.500
Interior pre-hung hardboard solid core door unit, 2-0 x 6-8	EA	$114.18	$150.00	$264.18	**$370.68**	1.500
Interior pre-hung hardboard solid core door unit, 2-4 x 6-8	EA	$114.18	$153.00	$267.18	**$374.28**	1.500
Interior pre-hung hardboard solid core door unit, 2-6 x 6-8	EA	$114.18	$159.00	$273.18	**$381.48**	1.500
Interior pre-hung hardboard solid core door unit, 2-8 x 6-8	EA	$114.18	$161.00	$275.18	**$383.88**	1.500
Interior pre-hung hardboard solid core door unit, 3-0 x 6-8	EA	$114.18	$169.00	$283.18	**$393.48**	1.500

Interior Doors

Pre-Hung Louver Wood Doors

> No removal of old door included.

Description	Unit	Direct Labor	Direct Materials	Direct Total	Selling Price	Man-hours
PRE-HUNG INTERIOR FULL LOUVERED WOOD DOORS						
Interior pre-hung fir/pine full louvered door, 2-0 x 6-8	EA	$114.18	$146.00	$260.18	**$365.88**	1.500
Interior pre-hung fir/pine full louvered door, 2-4 x 6-8	EA	$114.18	$155.00	$269.18	**$376.68**	1.500
Interior pre-hung fir/pine full louvered door, 2-6 x 6-8	EA	$114.18	$158.00	$272.18	**$380.28**	1.500
Interior pre-hung fir/pine full louvered door, 2-8 x 6-8	EA	$114.18	$171.00	$285.18	**$395.88**	1.500
Interior pre-hung fir/pine full louvered door, 3-0 x 6-8	EA	$114.18	$185.00	$299.18	**$412.68**	1.500
PRE-HUNG INTERIOR HALF LOUVER/HALF PANEL WOOD DOORS						
Interior pre-hung fir/pine half louver/half panel door, 2-0 x 6-8	EA	$114.18	$153.00	$267.18	**$374.28**	1.500
Interior pre-hung fir/pine half louver/half panel door, 2-4 x 6-8	EA	$114.18	$163.00	$277.18	**$386.28**	1.500
Interior pre-hung fir/pine half louver/half panel door, 2-6 x 6-8	EA	$114.18	$165.00	$279.18	**$388.68**	1.500
Interior pre-hung fir/pine half louver/half panel door, 2-8 x 6-8	EA	$114.18	$179.00	$293.18	**$405.48**	1.500
Interior pre-hung fir/pine half louver/half panel door, 3-0 x 6-8	EA	$114.18	$193.00	$307.18	**$422.28**	1.500

Pre-Hung French Wood Doors

> No removal of old door included.

Description	Unit	Direct Labor	Direct Materials	Direct Total	Selling Price	Man-hours
PRE-HUNG FRENCH WOOD DOORS						
Interior pre-hung french door unit, 5 lites, 2-0 x 6-8	EA	$114.18	$197.00	$311.18	**$427.08**	1.500
Interior pre-hung french door unit, 5 lites, 2-4 x 6-8	EA	$114.18	$211.00	$325.18	**$443.88**	1.500
Interior pre-hung french door unit, 5 lites, 2-6 x 6-8	EA	$114.18	$220.00	$334.18	**$454.68**	1.500
Interior pre-hung french door unit, 5 lites, 2-8 x 6-8	EA	$114.18	$229.00	$343.18	**$465.48**	1.500
Interior pre-hung french door unit, 5 lites, 3-0 x 6-8	EA	$114.18	$240.00	$354.18	**$478.68**	1.500
Interior pre-hung french door unit, 2 rows of 5 lites, 2-0 x 6-8	EA	$114.18	$239.00	$353.18	**$477.48**	1.500
Interior pre-hung french door unit, 2 rows of 5 lites, 2-4 x 6-8	EA	$114.18	$252.00	$366.18	**$493.08**	1.500
Interior pre-hung french door unit, 2 rows of 5 lites, 2-6 x 6-8	EA	$114.18	$264.00	$378.18	**$507.48**	1.500
Interior pre-hung french door unit, 2 rows of 5 lites, 2-8 x 6-8	EA	$114.18	$274.00	$388.18	**$519.48**	1.500
Interior pre-hung french door unit, 2 rows of 5 lites, 3-0 x 6-8	EA	$114.18	$285.00	$399.18	**$532.68**	1.500
Interior pre-hung french door unit, 3 rows of 5 lites, 2-6 x 6-8	EA	$114.18	$298.00	$412.18	**$548.28**	1.500
Interior pre-hung french door unit, 3 rows of 5 lites, 2-8 x 6-8	EA	$114.18	$311.00	$425.18	**$563.88**	1.500
Interior pre-hung french door unit, 3 rows of 5 lites, 3-0 x 6-8	EA	$114.18	$334.00	$448.18	**$591.48**	1.500

Interior Doors

Bi-Fold Flush Doors

> No removal of old door included.

Description	Unit	Direct Labor	Direct Materials	Direct Total	Selling Price	Man-hours
INTERIOR BI-FOLD WOOD DOORS, FLUSH BIRCH						
Interior bi-fold flush birch hollow core, 2-6 x 6-8, 2 doors, hardware	Set	$190.30	$124.00	$314.30	**$466.59**	2.500
Interior bi-fold flush birch hollow core, 3-0 x 6-8, 2 doors, hardware	Set	$190.30	$138.00	$328.30	**$483.39**	2.500
Interior bi-fold flush birch hollow core, 4-0 x 6-8, 2 doors, hardware	Set	$190.30	$177.00	$367.30	**$530.19**	2.500
Interior bi-fold flush birch hollow core, 5-0 x 6-8, 4 doors, hardware	Set	$266.41	$207.00	$473.41	**$693.31**	3.500
Interior bi-fold flush birch hollow core, 6-0 x 6-8, 4 doors, hardware	Set	$266.41	$243.00	$509.41	**$736.51**	3.500
Interior bi-fold flush birch hollow core, 8-0 x 6-8, 4 doors, hardware	Set	$266.41	$318.00	$584.41	**$826.51**	3.500
Interior bi-fold flush birch hollow core, 4-0 x 8-0, 2 doors, hardware	Set	$190.30	$298.00	$488.30	**$675.39**	2.500
Interior bi-fold flush birch hollow core, 6-0 x 8-0, 4 doors, hardware	Set	$266.41	$377.00	$643.41	**$897.31**	3.500
Interior bi-fold flush birch hollow core, 8-0 x 8-0, 4 doors, hardware	Set	$266.41	$475.00	$741.41	**$1,014.91**	3.500
INTERIOR BI-FOLD WOOD DOORS, FLUSH OAK						
Interior bi-fold flush oak hollow core door, 2-6 x 6-8, 2 doors, hardware	Set	$190.30	$155.00	$345.30	**$503.79**	2.500
Interior bi-fold flush oak hollow core door, 3-0 x 6-8, 2 doors, hardware	Set	$190.30	$186.00	$376.30	**$540.99**	2.500
Interior bi-fold flush oak hollow core door, 4-0 x 6-8, 2 doors, hardware	Set	$190.30	$239.00	$429.30	**$604.59**	2.500
Interior bi-fold flush oak hollow core door, 5-0 x 6-8, 4 doors, hardware	Set	$266.41	$280.00	$546.41	**$780.91**	3.500
Interior bi-fold flush oak hollow core door, 6-0 x 6-8, 4 doors, hardware	Set	$266.41	$328.00	$594.41	**$838.51**	3.500
Interior bi-fold flush oak hollow core door, 8-0 x 6-8, 4 doors, hardware	Set	$266.41	$429.00	$695.41	**$959.71**	3.500
Interior bi-fold flush oak hollow core door, 4-0 x 8-0, 2 doors, hardware	Set	$190.30	$402.00	$592.30	**$800.19**	2.500
Interior bi-fold flush oak hollow core door, 6-0 x 8-0, 4 doors, hardware	Set	$266.41	$510.00	$776.41	**$1,056.91**	3.500
Interior bi-fold flush oak hollow core door, 8-0 x 8-0, 4 doors, hardware	Set	$266.41	$641.00	$907.41	**$1,214.11**	3.500
INTERIOR BI-FOLD DOORS, FLUSH MAHOGANY						
Interior bi-fold flush mahogany hollow, 2-6 x 6-8, 2 doors, hardware	Set	$190.30	$83.00	$273.30	**$417.39**	2.500
Interior bi-fold flush mahogany hollow, 3-0 x 6-8, 2 doors, hardware	Set	$190.30	$92.00	$282.30	**$428.19**	2.500
Interior bi-fold flush mahogany hollow, 4-0 x 6-8, 2 doors, hardware	Set	$190.30	$118.00	$308.30	**$459.39**	2.500
Interior bi-fold flush mahogany hollow, 5-0 x 6-8, 4 doors, hardware	Set	$266.41	$138.00	$404.41	**$610.51**	3.500
Interior bi-fold flush mahogany hollow, 6-0 x 6-8, 4 doors, hardware	Set	$266.41	$162.00	$428.41	**$639.31**	3.500
Interior bi-fold flush mahogany hollow, 8-0 x 6-8, 4 doors, hardware	Set	$266.41	$211.00	$477.41	**$698.11**	3.500
Interior bi-fold flush mahogany hollow, 4-0 x 8-0, 2 doors, hardware	Set	$190.30	$219.00	$409.30	**$580.59**	2.500
Interior bi-fold flush mahogany hollow, 6-0 x 8-0, 4 doors, hardware	Set	$266.41	$278.00	$544.41	**$778.51**	3.500
Interior bi-fold flush mahogany hollow, 8-0 x 8-0, 4 doors, hardware	Set	$266.41	$350.00	$616.41	**$864.91**	3.500
Bi-fold flush prefinished mahogany hollow, 2-0 x 6-8, 2 drs, hardware	Set	$190.30	$103.00	$293.30	**$441.39**	2.500
Bi-fold flush prefinished mahogany hollow, 4-0 x 6-8, 2 drs, hardware	Set	$190.30	$161.00	$351.30	**$510.99**	2.500
Bi-fold flush prefinished mahogany hollow, 6-0 x 6-8, 4 drs, hardware	Set	$266.41	$217.00	$483.41	**$705.31**	3.500

Interior Doors

Bi-Fold Flush Doors (cont.)

> No removal of old door included.

Description	Unit	Direct Labor	Direct Materials	Direct Total	Selling Price	Man-hours
INTERIOR BI-FOLD DOORS, FLUSH HARDBOARD						
Interior bi-fold flush hardboard hollow core, 2-6 x 6-8, 2 doors, hardware	Set	$190.30	$75.00	$265.30	**$407.79**	2.500
Interior bi-fold flush hardboard hollow core, 3-0 x 6-8, 2 doors, hardware	Set	$190.30	$83.00	$273.30	**$417.39**	2.500
Interior bi-fold flush hardboard hollow core, 4-0 x 6-8, 2 doors, hardware	Set	$190.30	$106.00	$296.30	**$444.99**	2.500
Interior bi-fold flush hardboard hollow core, 5-0 x 6-8, 4 doors, hardware	Set	$266.41	$124.00	$390.41	**$593.71**	3.500
Interior bi-fold flush hardboard hollow core, 6-0 x 6-8, 4 doors, hardware	Set	$266.41	$146.00	$412.41	**$620.11**	3.500
Interior bi-fold flush hardboard hollow core, 8-0 x 6-8, 4 doors, hardware	Set	$266.41	$191.00	$457.41	**$674.11**	3.500
Interior bi-fold flush hardboard hollow core, 4-0 x 8-0, 2 doors, hardware	Set	$190.30	$179.00	$369.30	**$532.59**	2.500
Interior bi-fold flush hardboard hollow core, 6-0 x 8-0, 4 doors, hardware	Set	$266.41	$226.00	$492.41	**$716.11**	3.500
Interior bi-fold flush hardboard hollow core, 8-0 x 8-0, 4 doors, hardware	Set	$266.41	$285.00	$551.41	**$786.91**	3.500

Bi-Fold Panel Doors

> No removal of old door included.

Description	Unit	Direct Labor	Direct Materials	Direct Total	Selling Price	Man-hours
INTERIOR BI-FOLD DOORS, PANEL FIR/PINE						
Interior bi-fold fir/pine 6 panel door, 2-6 x 6-8, 2 doors, hardware	Set	$190.30	$149.00	$339.30	**$496.59**	2.500
Interior bi-fold fir/pine 6 panel door, 3-0 x 6-8, 2 doors, hardware	Set	$190.30	$165.00	$355.30	**$515.79**	2.500
Interior bi-fold fir/pine 6 panel door, 4-0 x 6-8, 2 doors, hardware	Set	$190.30	$212.00	$402.30	**$572.19**	2.500
Interior bi-fold fir/pine 6 panel door, 5-0 x 6-8, 4 doors, hardware	Set	$266.41	$249.00	$515.41	**$743.71**	3.500
Interior bi-fold fir/pine 6 panel door, 6-0 x 6-8, 4 doors, hardware	Set	$266.41	$292.00	$558.41	**$795.31**	3.500
Interior bi-fold fir/pine 6 panel door, 8-0 x 6-8, 4 doors, hardware	Set	$266.41	$382.00	$648.41	**$903.31**	3.500
INTERIOR BI-FOLD DOORS, PANEL HARDBOARD						
Interior bi-fold hardboard 6 panel door, 2-6 x 6-8, 2 doors, hardware	Set	$190.30	$90.00	$280.30	**$425.79**	2.500
Interior bi-fold hardboard 6 panel door, 3-0 x 6-8, 2 doors, hardware	Set	$190.30	$99.00	$289.30	**$436.59**	2.500
Interior bi-fold hardboard 6 panel door, 4-0 x 6-8, 2 doors, hardware	Set	$190.30	$127.00	$317.30	**$470.19**	2.500
Interior bi-fold hardboard 6 panel door, 5-0 x 6-8, 4 doors, hardware	Set	$266.41	$149.00	$415.41	**$623.71**	3.500
Interior bi-fold hardboard 6 panel door, 6-0 x 6-8, 4 doors, hardware	Set	$266.41	$175.00	$441.41	**$654.91**	3.500
Interior bi-fold hardboard 6 panel door, 8-0 x 6-8, 4 doors, hardware	Set	$266.41	$229.00	$495.41	**$719.71**	3.500

Interior Doors

Bi-Fold Louvered Doors

> No removal of old door included.

Description	Unit	Direct Labor	Direct Materials	Direct Total	Selling Price	Man-hours
INTERIOR FULL LOUVERED DOORS, FIR/PINE						
Interior bi-fold fir/pine fully louvered door, 2-6 x 6-8, 2 doors, hardware	Set	$190.30	$127.00	$317.30	**$470.19**	2.500
Interior bi-fold fir/pine fully louvered door, 3-0 x 6-8, 2 doors, hardware	Set	$190.30	$141.00	$331.30	**$486.99**	2.500
Interior bi-fold fir/pine fully louvered door, 4-0 x 6-8, 2 doors, hardware	Set	$190.30	$180.00	$370.30	**$533.79**	2.500
Interior bi-fold fir/pine fully louvered door, 5-0 x 6-8, 4 doors, hardware	Set	$266.41	$211.00	$477.41	**$698.11**	3.500
Interior bi-fold fir/pine fully louvered door, 6-0 x 6-8, 4 doors, hardware	Set	$266.41	$248.00	$514.41	**$742.51**	3.500
Interior bi-fold fir/pine fully louvered door, 8-0 x 6-8, 4 doors, hardware	Set	$266.41	$324.00	$590.41	**$833.71**	3.500
INTERIOR HALF LOUVER/HALF PANEL DOORS						
Interior bi-fold fir/pine half louver/half panel, 2-6 x 6-8, 2 doors, hardware	Set	$190.30	$139.00	$329.30	**$484.59**	2.500
Interior bi-fold fir/pine half louver/half panel, 3-0 x 6-8, 2 doors, hardware	Set	$190.30	$155.00	$345.30	**$503.79**	2.500
Interior bi-fold fir/pine half louver/half panel, 4-0 x 6-8, 2 doors, hardware	Set	$190.30	$199.00	$389.30	**$556.59**	2.500
Interior bi-fold fir/pine half louver/half panel, 5-0 x 6-8, 4 doors, hardware	Set	$266.41	$232.00	$498.41	**$723.31**	3.500
Interior bi-fold fir/pine half louver/half panel, 6-0 x 6-8, 4 doors, hardware	Set	$266.41	$273.00	$539.41	**$772.51**	3.500
Interior bi-fold fir/pine half louver/half panel, 8-0 x 6-8, 4 doors, hardware	Set	$266.41	$357.00	$623.41	**$873.31**	3.500
INTERIOR HALF AND FULL LOUVERED DOORS, PREFINISHED						
Interior bi-fold prefinished fir/pine fully louvered, 2-0 x 6-8, 2 dr, hardware	Set	$190.30	$169.00	$359.30	**$520.59**	2.500
Interior bi-fold prefinished fir/pine fully louvered, 4-0 x 6-8, 2 dr, hardware	Set	$190.30	$330.00	$520.30	**$713.79**	2.500
Interior bi-fold prefinished fir/pine fully louvered, 6-0 x 6-8, 4 dr, hardware	Set	$266.41	$420.00	$686.41	**$948.91**	3.500
Bi-fold prefinished fir/pine half louver/half panel, 2-0 x 6-8, 2 dr, hardware	Set	$190.30	$179.00	$369.30	**$532.59**	2.500
Bi-fold prefinished fir/pine half louver/half panel, 4-0 x 6-8, 2 dr, hardware	Set	$190.30	$348.00	$538.30	**$735.39**	2.500
Bi-fold prefinished fir/pine half louver/half panel, 6-0 x 6-8, 4 dr, hardware	Set	$266.41	$420.00	$686.41	**$948.91**	3.500

Bi-Fold Mirrored Doors

> No removal of old door included.

Description	Unit	Direct Labor	Direct Materials	Direct Total	Selling Price	Man-hours
Interior bi-fold frameless mirrored door, 2-6 x 6-8, 2 doors, hardware	Set	$190.30	$174.00	$364.30	**$526.59**	2.500
Interior bi-fold frameless mirrored door, 3-0 x 6-8, 2 doors, hardware	Set	$190.30	$193.00	$383.30	**$549.39**	2.500
Interior bi-fold frameless mirrored door, 4-0 x 6-8, 2 doors, hardware	Set	$190.30	$248.00	$438.30	**$615.39**	2.500
Interior bi-fold frameless mirrored door, 5-0 x 6-8, 4 doors, hardware	Set	$266.41	$291.00	$557.41	**$794.11**	3.500
Interior bi-fold frameless mirrored door, 6-0 x 6-8, 4 doors, hardware	Set	$266.41	$341.00	$607.41	**$854.11**	3.500
Interior bi-fold frameless mirrored door, 8-0 x 6-8, 4 doors, hardware	Set	$266.41	$446.00	$712.41	**$980.11**	3.500

Interior Doors

Sliding Flush Doors

➤ No removal of old door included.

Description	Unit	Direct Labor	Direct Materials	Direct Total	Selling Price	Man-hours
INTERIOR SLIDING FLUSH DOORS, BIRCH						
Interior bypass/sliding flush birch hollow, 4-0 x 6-8, 2 drs, hardware	Set	$228.36	$162.00	$390.36	**$575.75**	3.000
Interior bypass/sliding flush birch hollow, 5-0 x 6-8, 2 drs, hardware	Set	$228.36	$212.00	$440.36	**$635.75**	3.000
Interior bypass/sliding flush birch hollow, 6-0 x 6-8, 2 drs, hardware	Set	$228.36	$251.00	$479.36	**$682.55**	3.000
Interior bypass/sliding flush birch hollow, 10-0 x 6-8, 3 drs, hardware	Set	$304.47	$381.00	$685.47	**$965.67**	4.000
Interior bypass/sliding flush birch hollow, 12-0 x 6-8, 3 drs, hardware	Set	$304.47	$459.00	$763.47	**$1,059.27**	4.000
Interior bypass/sliding flush birch hollow, 10-0 x 8-0, 3 drs, hardware	Set	$304.47	$594.00	$898.47	**$1,221.27**	4.000
Interior bypass/sliding flush birch hollow, 12-0 x 8-0, 3 drs, hardware	Set	$304.47	$706.00	$1,010.47	**$1,355.67**	4.000
INTERIOR SLIDING FLUSH DOORS, MAHOGANY						
Bypass/sliding flush mahogany hollow, 4-0 x 6-8, 2 doors, hardware	Set	$228.36	$122.00	$350.36	**$527.75**	3.000
Bypass/sliding flush mahogany hollow, 5-0 x 6-8, 2 doors, hardware	Set	$228.36	$159.00	$387.36	**$572.15**	3.000
Bypass/sliding flush mahogany hollow, 6-0 x 6-8, 2 doors, hardware	Set	$228.36	$188.00	$416.36	**$606.95**	3.000
Bypass/sliding flush mahogany hollow, 10-0 x 6-8, 3 drs, hardware	Set	$304.47	$286.00	$590.47	**$851.67**	4.000
Bypass/sliding flush mahogany hollow, 12-0 x 6-8, 3 drs, hardware	Set	$304.47	$344.00	$648.47	**$921.27**	4.000
Bypass/sliding flush mahogany hollow, 10-0 x 8-0, 3 drs, hardware	Set	$304.47	$445.00	$749.47	**$1,042.47**	4.000
Bypass/sliding flush mahogany hollow, 12-0 x 8-0, 3 drs, hardware	Set	$304.47	$529.00	$833.47	**$1,143.27**	4.000
INTERIOR SLIDING FLUSH DOORS, OAK						
Interior bypass/sliding flush oak hollow, 4-0 x 6-8, 2 drs, hardware	Set	$228.36	$195.00	$423.36	**$615.35**	3.000
Interior bypass/sliding flush oak hollow, 5-0 x 6-8, 2 drs, hardware	Set	$228.36	$254.00	$482.36	**$686.15**	3.000
Interior bypass/sliding flush oak hollow, 6-0 x 6-8, 2 drs, hardware	Set	$228.36	$301.00	$529.36	**$742.55**	3.000
Interior bypass/sliding flush oak hollow, 10-0 x 6-8, 3 drs, hardware	Set	$304.47	$457.00	$761.47	**$1,056.87**	4.000
Interior bypass/sliding flush oak hollow, 12-0 x 6-8, 3 drs, hardware	Set	$304.47	$551.00	$855.47	**$1,169.67**	4.000
Interior bypass/sliding flush oak hollow, 10-0 x 8-0, 3 drs, hardware	Set	$304.47	$712.00	$1,016.47	**$1,362.87**	4.000
Interior bypass/sliding flush oak hollow, 12-0 x 8-0, 3 drs, hardware	Set	$304.47	$847.00	$1,151.47	**$1,524.87**	4.000
INTERIOR SLIDING FLUSH DOORS, HARDBOARD						
Bypass/sliding flush hardboard hollow, 4-0 x 6-8, 2 drs, hardware	Set	$228.36	$106.00	$334.36	**$508.55**	3.000
Bypass/sliding flush hardboard hollow, 5-0 x 6-8, 2 drs, hardware	Set	$228.36	$138.00	$366.36	**$546.95**	3.000
Bypass/sliding flush hardboard hollow, 6-0 x 6-8, 2 drs, hardware	Set	$228.36	$163.00	$391.36	**$576.95**	3.000
Bypass/sliding flush hardboard hollow, 10-0 x 6-8, 3 drs, hardware	Set	$304.47	$248.00	$552.47	**$806.07**	4.000
Bypass/sliding flush hardboard hollow, 12-0 x 6-8, 3 drs, hardware	Set	$304.47	$298.00	$602.47	**$866.07**	4.000
Bypass/sliding flush hardboard hollow, 10-0 x 8-0, 3 drs, hardware	Set	$304.47	$386.00	$690.47	**$971.67**	4.000
Bypass/sliding flush hardboard hollow, 12-0 x 8-0, 3 drs, hardware	Set	$304.47	$459.00	$763.47	**$1,059.27**	4.000

Interior Doors

Sliding Panel Doors

> No removal of old door included.

Description	Unit	Direct Labor	Direct Materials	Direct Total	Selling Price	Man-hours
INTERIOR SLIDING PANEL DOORS, FIR/PINE						
Interior bypass/sliding fir/pine 6 panel door, 4-0 x 6-8, 2 doors, hardware	Set	$228.36	$214.00	$442.36	**$638.15**	3.000
Interior bypass/sliding fir/pine 6 panel door, 5-0 x 6-8, 2 doors, hardware	Set	$228.36	$279.00	$507.36	**$716.15**	3.000
Interior bypass/sliding fir/pine 6 panel door, 6-0 x 6-8, 2 doors, hardware	Set	$228.36	$331.00	$559.36	**$778.55**	3.000
Interior bypass/sliding fir/pine 6 panel door, 8-0 x 6-8, 3 doors, hardware	Set	$304.47	$503.00	$807.47	**$1,112.07**	4.000
Interior bypass/sliding fir/pine 6 panel door, 10-0 x 6-8, 3 doors, hardware	Set	$304.47	$606.00	$910.47	**$1,235.67**	4.000
INTERIOR SLIDING PANEL DOORS, HARDBOARD						
Bypass/sliding hardboard 6 panel door, 4-0 x 6-8, 2 doors, hardware	Set	$228.36	$117.00	$345.36	**$521.75**	3.000
Bypass/sliding hardboard 6 panel door, 5-0 x 6-8, 2 doors, hardware	Set	$228.36	$152.00	$380.36	**$563.75**	3.000
Bypass/sliding hardboard 6 panel door, 6-0 x 6-8, 2 doors, hardware	Set	$228.36	$181.00	$409.36	**$598.55**	3.000
Bypass/sliding hardboard 6 panel door, 8-0 x 6-8, 3 doors, hardware	Set	$304.47	$274.00	$578.47	**$837.27**	4.000
Bypass/sliding hardboard 6 panel door, 10-0 x 6-8, 3 doors, hardware	Set	$304.47	$331.00	$635.47	**$905.67**	4.000

Sliding Louvered Doors

> No removal of old door included.

Description	Unit	Direct Labor	Direct Materials	Direct Total	Selling Price	Man-hours
INTERIOR SLIDING LOUVERED DOORS, FIR/PINE						
Bypass/sliding fir/pine fully louvered door, 4-0 x 6-8, 2 doors, hardware	Set	$228.36	$171.00	$399.36	**$586.55**	3.000
Bypass/sliding fir/pine fully louvered door, 5-0 x 6-8, 2 doors, hardware	Set	$228.36	$222.00	$450.36	**$647.75**	3.000
Bypass/sliding fir/pine fully louvered door, 6-0 x 6-8, 2 doors, hardware	Set	$228.36	$263.00	$491.36	**$696.95**	3.000
Bypass/sliding fir/pine fully louvered door, 8-0 x 6-8, 3 doors, hardware	Set	$304.47	$400.00	$704.47	**$988.47**	4.000
Bypass/sliding fir/pine fully louvered door, 10-0 x 6-8, 3 doors, hardware	Set	$304.47	$482.00	$786.47	**$1,086.87**	4.000
INTERIOR SLIDING HALF LOUVER/HALF PANEL DOORS, FIR/PINE						
Bypass/sliding fir/pine half louver/half panel, 4-0 x 6-8, 2 drs, hardware	Set	$228.36	$182.00	$410.36	**$599.75**	3.000
Bypass/sliding fir/pine half louver/half panel, 5-0 x 6-8, 2 drs, hardware	Set	$228.36	$237.00	$465.36	**$665.75**	3.000
Bypass/sliding fir/pine half louver/half panel, 6-0 x 6-8, 2 drs, hardware	Set	$228.36	$281.00	$509.36	**$718.55**	3.000
Bypass/sliding fir/pine half louver/half panel, 8-0 x 6-8, 3 drs, hardware	Set	$304.47	$426.00	$730.47	**$1,019.67**	4.000
Bypass/sliding fir/pine half louver/half panel, 10-0 x 6-8, 3 drs, hardware	Set	$304.47	$514.00	$818.47	**$1,125.27**	4.000

Interior Doors

Sliding Mirrored Doors

> No removal of old door included.

Description	Unit	Direct Labor	Direct Materials	Direct Total	Selling Price	Man-hours
INTERIOR SLIDING MIRRORED DOORS, FRAMELESS						
Bypass/sliding frameless mirrored door, 4-0 x 6-8, 2 doors, hardware	Set	$228.36	$235.00	$463.36	**$663.35**	3.000
Bypass/sliding frameless mirrored door, 5-0 x 6-8, 2 doors, hardware	Set	$228.36	$269.00	$497.36	**$704.15**	3.000
Bypass/sliding frameless mirrored door, 6-0 x 6-8, 2 doors, hardware	Set	$228.36	$304.00	$532.36	**$746.15**	3.000
Bypass/sliding frameless mirrored door, 8-0 x 6-8, 3 doors, hardware	Set	$304.47	$368.00	$672.47	**$950.07**	4.000
Bypass/sliding frameless mirrored door, 10-0 x 6-8, 3 doors, hardware	Set	$304.47	$474.00	$778.47	**$1,077.27**	4.000
Bypass/sliding frameless mirrored door, 10-0 x 8-0, 3 doors, hardware	Set	$304.47	$560.00	$864.47	**$1,180.47**	4.000
Bypass/sliding frameless mirrored door, 12-0 x 8-0, 3 doors, hardware	Set	$304.47	$626.00	$930.47	**$1,259.67**	4.000
INTERIOR SLIDING MIRRORED DOORS, ALUMINUM FRAME						
Bypass/sliding aluminum mirrored door, 4-0 x 6-8, 2 dr, hardware	Set	$228.36	$176.00	$404.36	**$592.55**	3.000
Bypass/sliding aluminum mirrored door, 5-0 x 6-8, 2 dr, hardware	Set	$228.36	$202.00	$430.36	**$623.75**	3.000
Bypass/sliding aluminum mirrored door, 6-0 x 6-8, 2 dr, hardware	Set	$228.36	$228.00	$456.36	**$654.95**	3.000
Bypass/sliding aluminum mirrored door, 8-0 x 6-8, 3 dr, hardware	Set	$304.47	$276.00	$580.47	**$839.67**	4.000
Bypass/sliding aluminum mirrored door, 10-0 x 6-8, 3 dr, hardware	Set	$304.47	$355.00	$659.47	**$934.47**	4.000
Bypass/sliding aluminum mirrored door, 10-0 x 8-0, 3 dr, hardware	Set	$304.47	$420.00	$724.47	**$1,012.47**	4.000
Bypass/sliding aluminum mirrored door, 12-0 x 8-0, 3 dr, hardware	Set	$304.47	$470.00	$774.47	**$1,072.47**	4.000
INTERIOR SLIDING MIRRORED DOORS, OAK FRAME						
Bypass/sliding oak mirrored door, 4-0 x 6-8, 2 doors, hardware	Set	$228.36	$258.00	$486.36	**$690.95**	3.000
Bypass/sliding oak mirrored door, 5-0 x 6-8, 2 doors, hardware	Set	$228.36	$296.00	$524.36	**$736.55**	3.000
Bypass/sliding oak mirrored door, 6-0 x 6-8, 2 doors, hardware	Set	$228.36	$334.00	$562.36	**$782.15**	3.000
Bypass/sliding oak mirrored door, 8-0 x 6-8, 3 doors, hardware	Set	$304.47	$404.00	$708.47	**$993.27**	4.000
Bypass/sliding oak mirrored door, 10-0 x 6-8, 3 doors, hardware	Set	$304.47	$521.00	$825.47	**$1,133.67**	4.000
Bypass/sliding oak mirrored door, 10-0 x 8-0, 3 doors, hardware	Set	$304.47	$616.00	$920.47	**$1,247.67**	4.000
Bypass/sliding oak mirrored door, 12-0 x 8-0, 3 doors, hardware	Set	$304.47	$689.00	$993.47	**$1,335.27**	4.000

Interior Doors

Pocket Doors

> Installation in open wall.
> No removal of old door included.

Description	Unit	Direct Labor	Direct Materials	Direct Total	Selling Price	Man-hours
INTERIOR POCKET DOORS, FLUSH BIRCH						
Interior flush birch hollow core pocket door, 2-0 x 6-8, hardware included	EA	$380.59	$186.00	$566.59	**$858.79**	5.000
Interior flush birch hollow core pocket door, 2-4 x 6-8, hardware included	EA	$380.59	$187.00	$567.59	**$859.99**	5.000
Interior flush birch hollow core pocket door, 2-6 x 6-8, hardware included	EA	$380.59	$190.00	$570.59	**$863.59**	5.000
Interior flush birch hollow core pocket door, 2-8 x 6-8, hardware included	EA	$380.59	$194.00	$574.59	**$868.39**	5.000
Interior flush birch hollow core pocket door, 3-0 x 6-8, hardware included	EA	$380.59	$199.00	$579.59	**$874.39**	5.000
INTERIOR POCKET DOORS, FLUSH HARDBOARD						
Interior flush hardboard hollow core pocket door, 2-0 x 6-8, hardware	EA	$380.59	$133.00	$513.59	**$795.19**	5.000
Interior flush hardboard hollow core pocket door, 2-4 x 6-8, hardware	EA	$380.59	$134.00	$514.59	**$796.39**	5.000
Interior flush hardboard hollow core pocket door, 2-6 x 6-8, hardware	EA	$380.59	$136.00	$516.59	**$798.79**	5.000
Interior flush hardboard hollow core pocket door, 2-8 x 6-8, hardware	EA	$380.59	$137.00	$517.59	**$799.99**	5.000
Interior flush hardboard hollow core pocket door, 3-0 x 6-8, hardware	EA	$380.59	$140.00	$520.59	**$803.59**	5.000
INTERIOR POCKET DOORS, PANEL FIR/PINE						
Interior fir/pine 6 panel pocket door, 2-0 x 6-8, hardware included	EA	$380.59	$201.00	$581.59	**$876.79**	5.000
Interior fir/pine 6 panel pocket door, 2-4 x 6-8, hardware included	EA	$380.59	$206.00	$586.59	**$882.79**	5.000
Interior fir/pine 6 panel pocket door, 2-6 x 6-8, hardware included	EA	$380.59	$208.00	$588.59	**$885.19**	5.000
Interior fir/pine 6 panel pocket door, 2-8 x 6-8, hardware included	EA	$380.59	$210.00	$590.59	**$887.59**	5.000
Interior fir/pine 6 panel pocket door, 3-0 x 6-8, hardware included	EA	$380.59	$220.00	$600.59	**$899.59**	5.000
INTERIOR POCKET DOORS, PANEL OAK						
Interior oak 6 panel pocket door, 2-0 x 6-8, hardware included	EA	$380.59	$307.00	$687.59	**$1,003.99**	5.000
Interior oak 6 panel pocket door, 2-4 x 6-8, hardware included	EA	$380.59	$317.00	$697.59	**$1,015.99**	5.000
Interior oak 6 panel pocket door, 2-6 x 6-8, hardware included	EA	$380.59	$320.00	$700.59	**$1,019.59**	5.000
Interior oak 6 panel pocket door, 2-8 x 6-8, hardware included	EA	$380.59	$325.00	$705.59	**$1,025.59**	5.000
Interior oak 6 panel pocket door, 3-0 x 6-8, hardware included	EA	$380.59	$342.00	$722.59	**$1,045.99**	5.000

Interior Trim, Stairs and Accessories

Wood Casing, Pine

Description	Unit	Direct Labor	Direct Materials	Direct Total	Selling Price	Man-hours
UNFINISHED WOOD CASING, PINE						
Install pine casing, 1/2 x 1-5/8, plain	LF	$2.36	$0.90	$3.26	**$5.45**	0.031
Install pine casing, 1/2 x 1-5/8, decorative	LF	$2.36	$1.28	$3.64	**$6.07**	0.031
Install pine casing, 1/2 x 1-5/8, ornate	LF	$2.36	$1.62	$3.98	**$6.65**	0.031
Install pine casing, 5/8 x 1-5/8, plain	LF	$2.36	$1.00	$3.36	**$5.61**	0.031
Install pine casing, 5/8 x 1-5/8, decorative	LF	$2.36	$1.38	$3.74	**$6.24**	0.031
Install pine casing, 5/8 x 1-5/8, ornate	LF	$2.36	$1.72	$4.08	**$6.81**	0.031
Install pine casing, 11/16 x 2-1/4, plain	LF	$2.36	$1.24	$3.60	**$6.02**	0.031
Install pine casing, 11/16 x 2-1/4, decorative	LF	$2.36	$1.61	$3.96	**$6.62**	0.031
Install pine casing, 11/16 x 2-1/4, ornate	LF	$2.36	$2.10	$4.46	**$7.44**	0.031
Install pine casing, 5/8 x 2-1/2, plain	LF	$2.36	$1.41	$3.77	**$6.29**	0.031
Install pine casing, 5/8 x 2-1/2, decorative	LF	$2.36	$1.97	$4.33	**$7.22**	0.031
Install pine casing, 5/8 x 2-1/2, ornate	LF	$2.36	$2.54	$4.90	**$8.18**	0.031
Install pine casing, 11/16 x 2-1/2, plain	LF	$2.36	$1.67	$4.03	**$6.73**	0.031
Install pine casing, 11/16 x 2-1/2, decorative	LF	$2.36	$2.06	$4.42	**$7.39**	0.031
Install pine casing, 11/16 x 2-1/2, ornate	LF	$2.36	$2.93	$5.29	**$8.84**	0.031
Install pine casing, 11/16 x 2-7/8, plain	LF	$2.36	$1.79	$4.14	**$6.92**	0.031
Install pine casing, 11/16 x 2-7/8, decorative	LF	$2.36	$2.33	$4.69	**$7.82**	0.031
Install pine casing, 11/16 x 2-7/8, ornate	LF	$2.36	$3.26	$5.62	**$9.38**	0.031
Install pine casing, 1/2 x 3-1/4, plain	LF	$2.51	$1.79	$4.30	**$7.18**	0.033
Install pine casing, 1/2 x 3-1/4, decorative	LF	$2.51	$2.39	$4.90	**$8.19**	0.033
Install pine casing, 1/2 x 3-1/4, ornate	LF	$2.51	$3.34	$5.85	**$9.77**	0.033
Install pine casing, 11/16 x 3-1/4, plain	LF	$2.51	$2.11	$4.62	**$7.72**	0.033
Install pine casing, 11/16 x 3-1/4, decorative	LF	$2.51	$2.67	$5.18	**$8.65**	0.033
Install pine casing, 11/16 x 3-1/4, ornate	LF	$2.51	$3.90	$6.41	**$10.70**	0.033
Install pine casing, 1/2 x 3-1/2, plain	LF	$2.51	$1.93	$4.44	**$7.42**	0.033
Install pine casing, 1/2 x 3-1/2, decorative	LF	$2.51	$2.67	$5.18	**$8.65**	0.033
Install pine casing, 1/2 x 3-1/2, ornate	LF	$2.51	$2.05	$4.56	**$7.61**	0.033
Install pine casing, 11/16 x 3-1/2, plain	LF	$2.51	$2.28	$4.79	**$8.00**	0.033
Install pine casing, 11/16 x 3-1/2, decorative	LF	$2.51	$2.77	$5.28	**$8.82**	0.033
Install pine casing, 11/16 x 3-1/2, ornate	LF	$2.51	$4.13	$6.64	**$11.09**	0.033
Install pine casing, 11/16 x 4-1/4, plain	LF	$2.51	$2.60	$5.12	**$8.54**	0.033
Install pine casing, 11/16 x 4-1/4, decorative	LF	$2.51	$3.67	$6.18	**$10.32**	0.033
Install pine casing, 11/16 x 4-1/4, ornate	LF	$2.51	$5.00	$7.51	**$12.54**	0.033

Interior Trim, Stairs and Accessories

Wood Casing, Oak

Description	Unit	Direct Labor	Direct Materials	Direct Total	Selling Price	Man-hours
UNFINISHED WOOD CASING, OAK						
Install oak casing, 1/2 x 1-5/8, decorative	LF	$2.44	$1.48	$3.91	**$6.53**	0.032
Install oak casing, 1/2 x 1-5/8, ornate	LF	$2.44	$1.87	$4.31	**$7.20**	0.032
Install oak casing, 5/8 x 1-5/8, decorative	LF	$2.44	$1.59	$4.02	**$6.72**	0.032
Install oak casing, 5/8 x 1-5/8, ornate	LF	$2.44	$1.99	$4.42	**$7.39**	0.032
Install oak casing, 11/16 x 2-1/4, decorative	LF	$2.44	$1.85	$4.29	**$7.16**	0.032
Install oak casing, 11/16 x 2-1/4, ornate	LF	$2.44	$2.42	$4.86	**$8.11**	0.032
Install oak casing, 5/8 x 2-1/2, decorative	LF	$2.44	$2.27	$4.71	**$7.86**	0.032
Install oak casing, 5/8 x 2-1/2, ornate	LF	$2.44	$2.93	$5.37	**$8.96**	0.032
Install oak casing, 11/16 x 2-1/2, decorative	LF	$2.44	$2.38	$4.82	**$8.05**	0.032
Install oak casing, 11/16 x 2-1/2, ornate	LF	$2.44	$3.39	$5.82	**$9.72**	0.032
Install oak casing, 11/16 x 2-7/8, decorative	LF	$2.44	$2.69	$5.12	**$8.55**	0.032
Install oak casing, 11/16 x 2-7/8, ornate	LF	$2.44	$3.76	$6.20	**$10.35**	0.032
Install oak casing, 1/2 x 3-1/4, decorative	LF	$2.59	$2.76	$5.35	**$8.93**	0.034
Install oak casing, 1/2 x 3-1/4, ornate	LF	$2.59	$3.86	$6.45	**$10.77**	0.034
Install oak casing, 11/16 x 3-1/4, decorative	LF	$2.59	$3.08	$5.67	**$9.47**	0.034
Install oak casing, 11/16 x 3-1/4, ornate	LF	$2.59	$4.50	$7.09	**$11.84**	0.034
Install oak casing, 1/2 x 3-1/2, decorative	LF	$2.59	$3.08	$5.67	**$9.47**	0.034
Install oak casing, 1/2 x 3-1/2, ornate	LF	$2.59	$2.36	$4.95	**$8.27**	0.034
Install oak casing, 11/16 x 3-1/2, decorative	LF	$2.59	$3.20	$5.79	**$9.66**	0.034
Install oak casing, 11/16 x 3-1/2, ornate	LF	$2.59	$4.77	$7.36	**$12.28**	0.034
Install oak casing, 11/16 x 4-1/4, decorative	LF	$2.59	$4.24	$6.83	**$11.40**	0.034
Install oak casing, 11/16 x 4-1/4, ornate	LF	$2.59	$5.77	$8.36	**$13.96**	0.034

Wood Jamb and Casing

Description	Unit	Direct Labor	Direct Materials	Direct Total	Selling Price	Man-hours
Paint grade pine jambs, casings 2 sides, up to 36"	EA	$133.21	$77.93	$211.14	**$352.60**	1.750
Stain grade pine jambs, casings 2 sides, up to 36"	EA	$133.21	$87.54	$220.75	**$368.66**	1.750
Solid oak jambs, casings 2 sides, up to 36"	EA	$133.21	$109.95	$243.16	**$406.08**	1.750
Paint grade pine jambs, casings 2 sides, 36" to 60"	EA	$152.24	$85.74	$237.98	**$397.43**	2.000
Stain grade pine jambs, casings 2 sides, 36" to 60"	EA	$152.24	$99.19	$251.43	**$419.88**	2.000
Solid oak jambs, casings 2 sides, 36" to 60"	EA	$152.24	$122.83	$275.07	**$459.36**	2.000
Paint grade pine jambs, no casings, up to 36"	EA	$76.12	$42.85	$118.97	**$198.67**	1.000
Stain grade pine jambs, no casings, up to 36"	EA	$76.12	$60.04	$136.16	**$227.39**	1.000
Solid oak jambs, no casings, up to 36"	EA	$76.12	$64.69	$140.81	**$235.14**	1.000
Paint grade pine jambs, no casings, 36" to 60"	EA	$114.18	$51.59	$165.77	**$276.84**	1.500
Stain grade pine jambs, no casings, 36" to 60"	EA	$114.18	$68.55	$182.72	**$305.15**	1.500
Solid oak jambs, no casings, 36" to 60"	EA	$114.18	$72.19	$186.36	**$311.23**	1.500

Interior Trim, Stairs and Accessories

Wood Shoe Mould

Description	Unit	Direct Labor	Direct Materials	Direct Total	Selling Price	Man-hours
UNFINISHED WOOD SHOE MOULD						
Install base shoe mould, pine, 3/8 x 3/4	LF	$1.60	$0.90	$2.50	**$4.17**	0.021
Install base shoe mould, oak, 3/8 x 3/4	LF	$1.75	$1.08	$2.83	**$4.73**	0.023

Wood Base, Pine

Description	Unit	Direct Labor	Direct Materials	Direct Total	Selling Price	Man-hours
UNFINISHED WOOD BASE, PINE						
Install pine base, 7/16 x 2-1/2, plain	LF	$2.36	$1.56	$3.92	**$6.54**	0.031
Install pine base, 7/16 x 2-1/2, decorative	LF	$2.36	$2.11	$4.47	**$7.47**	0.031
Install pine base, 1/2 x 2-1/2, plain	LF	$2.36	$1.77	$4.13	**$6.89**	0.031
Install pine base, 1/2 x 2-1/2, decorative	LF	$2.36	$2.42	$4.78	**$7.99**	0.031
Install pine base, 7/16 x 3-1/4, plain	LF	$2.51	$1.72	$4.23	**$7.07**	0.033
Install pine base, 7/16 x 3-1/4, decorative	LF	$2.51	$2.23	$4.74	**$7.91**	0.033
Install pine base, 1/2 x 3-1/4, plain	LF	$2.51	$2.05	$4.56	**$7.61**	0.033
Install pine base, 1/2 x 3-1/4, decorative	LF	$2.51	$2.93	$5.44	**$9.09**	0.033
Install pine base, 7/16 x 3-1/2, plain	LF	$2.51	$1.80	$4.31	**$7.20**	0.033
Install pine base, 7/16 x 3-1/2, decorative	LF	$2.51	$2.42	$4.94	**$8.24**	0.033
Install pine base, 1/2 x 3-1/2, plain	LF	$2.51	$2.26	$4.77	**$7.97**	0.033
Install pine base, 1/2 x 3-1/2, decorative	LF	$2.51	$3.49	$6.00	**$10.02**	0.033
Install pine base, 1/2 x 4-1/4, plain	LF	$2.59	$2.77	$5.36	**$8.94**	0.034
Install pine base, 1/2 x 4-1/4, decorative	LF	$2.59	$4.24	$6.83	**$11.41**	0.034
Install pine base, 9/16 x 4-1/4, plain	LF	$2.59	$3.00	$5.59	**$9.33**	0.034
Install pine base, 9/16 x 4-1/4, decorative	LF	$2.59	$4.90	$7.49	**$12.50**	0.034
Install pine base, 1/2 x 4-1/2, plain	LF	$2.59	$2.77	$5.36	**$8.94**	0.034
Install pine base, 1/2 x 4-1/2, decorative	LF	$2.59	$4.67	$7.26	**$12.12**	0.034
Install pine base, 9/16 x 4-1/2, plain	LF	$2.59	$2.80	$5.39	**$9.00**	0.034
Install pine base, 9/16 x 4-1/2, decorative	LF	$2.59	$5.04	$7.63	**$12.75**	0.034
Install pine base, 9/16 x 5-1/4, plain	LF	$2.59	$3.29	$5.88	**$9.82**	0.034
Install pine base, 9/16 x 5-1/4, decorative	LF	$2.59	$5.88	$8.47	**$14.14**	0.034

Crown and Chair Moulding

Description	Unit	Direct Labor	Direct Materials	Direct Total	Selling Price	Man-hours
Install pine crown moulding, 2-1/4"	LF	$2.97	$2.93	$5.90	**$9.85**	0.039
Install pine crown moulding, 3-1/2"	LF	$3.20	$3.59	$6.78	**$11.33**	0.042
Install pine crown moulding, 4-1/4"	LF	$3.96	$4.41	$8.36	**$13.97**	0.052
Install pine crown moulding, 5-1/4"	LF	$4.41	$6.21	$10.62	**$17.74**	0.058
Install pine chair rail, 1-1/2"	LF	$3.96	$2.77	$6.73	**$11.23**	0.052
Install pine chair rail, 2-1/2"	LF	$4.41	$4.24	$8.66	**$14.46**	0.058

31

Interior Trim, Stairs and Accessories

Wood Base, Oak

Description	Unit	Direct Labor	Direct Materials	Direct Total	Selling Price	Man-hours
UNFINISHED WOOD BASE, OAK						
Install oak base, 7/16 x 2-1/2, plain	LF	$2.44	$1.80	$4.23	**$7.07**	0.032
Install oak base, 7/16 x 2-1/2, decorative	LF	$2.44	$2.44	$4.88	**$8.14**	0.032
Install oak base, 1/2 x 2-1/2, plain	LF	$2.44	$2.04	$4.48	**$7.48**	0.032
Install oak base, 1/2 x 2-1/2, decorative	LF	$2.44	$2.80	$5.24	**$8.74**	0.032
Install oak base, 7/16 x 3-1/4, plain	LF	$2.59	$1.99	$4.57	**$7.64**	0.034
Install oak base, 7/16 x 3-1/4, decorative	LF	$2.59	$2.57	$5.16	**$8.62**	0.034
Install oak base, 1/2 x 3-1/4, plain	LF	$2.59	$2.36	$4.95	**$8.27**	0.034
Install oak base, 1/2 x 3-1/4, decorative	LF	$2.59	$3.39	$5.97	**$9.98**	0.034
Install oak base, 7/16 x 3-1/2, plain	LF	$2.59	$2.08	$4.67	**$7.80**	0.034
Install oak base, 7/16 x 3-1/2, decorative	LF	$2.59	$2.80	$5.39	**$9.00**	0.034
Install oak base, 1/2 x 3-1/2, plain	LF	$2.59	$2.61	$5.20	**$8.68**	0.034
Install oak base, 1/2 x 3-1/2, decorative	LF	$2.59	$4.03	$6.62	**$11.05**	0.034
Install oak base, 1/2 x 4-1/4, plain	LF	$2.66	$3.20	$5.86	**$9.79**	0.035
Install oak base, 1/2 x 4-1/4, decorative	LF	$2.66	$4.90	$7.56	**$12.63**	0.035
Install oak base, 9/16 x 4-1/4, plain	LF	$2.66	$3.46	$6.13	**$10.23**	0.035
Install oak base, 9/16 x 4-1/4, decorative	LF	$2.66	$5.66	$8.32	**$13.90**	0.035
Install oak base, 1/2 x 4-1/2, plain	LF	$2.66	$3.20	$5.86	**$9.79**	0.035
Install oak base, 1/2 x 4-1/2, decorative	LF	$2.66	$5.39	$8.06	**$13.45**	0.035
Install oak base, 9/16 x 4-1/2, plain	LF	$2.66	$3.24	$5.90	**$9.85**	0.035
Install oak base, 9/16 x 4-1/2, decorative	LF	$2.66	$5.83	$8.49	**$14.18**	0.035
Install oak base, 9/16 x 5-1/4, plain	LF	$2.66	$3.80	$6.47	**$10.80**	0.035
Install oak base, 9/16 x 5-1/4, decorative	LF	$2.66	$6.79	$9.46	**$15.79**	0.035

Interior Wood Shutters

Description	Unit	Direct Labor	Direct Materials	Direct Total	Selling Price	Man-hours
Install operable interior shutters, pine, 27" wide x 20" tall	Set	$57.09	$85.00	$142.09	**$237.29**	0.750
Install operable interior shutters, pine, 27" wide x 24" tall	Set	$57.09	$96.00	$153.09	**$255.66**	0.750
Install operable interior shutters, pine, 27" wide x 28" tall	Set	$57.09	$106.00	$163.09	**$272.36**	0.750
Install operable interior shutters, pine, 31" wide x 20" tall	Set	$57.09	$93.00	$150.09	**$250.65**	0.750
Install operable interior shutters, pine, 31" wide x 24" tall	Set	$57.09	$104.00	$161.09	**$269.02**	0.750
Install operable interior shutters, pine, 31" wide x 28" tall	Set	$57.09	$117.00	$174.09	**$290.73**	0.750
Install operable interior shutters, pine, 35" wide x 20" tall	Set	$76.12	$101.00	$177.12	**$295.79**	1.000
Install operable interior shutters, pine, 35" wide x 24" tall	Set	$76.12	$117.00	$193.12	**$322.51**	1.000
Install operable interior shutters, pine, 35" wide x 28" tall	Set	$76.12	$130.00	$206.12	**$344.22**	1.000
Install operable interior shutters, pine, 39" wide x 20" tall	Set	$76.12	$109.00	$185.12	**$309.15**	1.000
Install operable interior shutters, pine, 39" wide x 24" tall	Set	$76.12	$125.00	$201.12	**$335.87**	1.000
Install operable interior shutters, pine, 39" wide x 28" tall	Set	$76.12	$141.00	$217.12	**$362.59**	1.000

Interior Trim, Stairs and Accessories

Fireplace Mantels and Surrounds

Description	Unit	Direct Labor	Direct Materials	Direct Total	Selling Price	Man-hours
MANTEL AND SURROUND						
Install mantel with surround, pine, 53" wide x 46" tall, economy	EA	$152.24	$233.00	$385.24	**$533.84**	2.000
Install mantel with surround, pine, 53" wide x 46" tall, average	EA	$304.47	$553.00	$857.47	**$1,172.07**	4.000
Install mantel with surround, pine, 53" wide x 46" tall, premium	EA	$380.59	$842.00	$1,222.59	**$1,645.99**	5.000
Install mantel with surround, pine, 59" wide x 46" tall, economy	EA	$152.24	$284.00	$436.24	**$595.04**	2.000
Install mantel with surround, pine, 59" wide x 46" tall, average	EA	$304.47	$648.00	$952.47	**$1,286.07**	4.000
Install mantel with surround, pine, 59" wide x 46" tall, premium	EA	$380.59	$999.00	$1,379.59	**$1,834.39**	5.000
Install mantel with surround, pine, 63" wide x 52" tall, economy	EA	$228.36	$350.00	$578.36	**$801.35**	3.000
Install mantel with surround, pine, 63" wide x 52" tall, average	EA	$380.59	$823.00	$1,203.59	**$1,623.19**	5.000
Install mantel with surround, pine, 63" wide x 52" tall, premium	EA	$456.71	$1,236.00	$1,692.71	**$2,245.91**	6.000
Install mantel with surround, pine, 70" wide x 52" tall, economy	EA	$228.36	$418.00	$646.36	**$882.95**	3.000
Install mantel with surround, pine, 70" wide x 52" tall, average	EA	$380.59	$905.00	$1,285.59	**$1,721.59**	5.000
Install mantel with surround, pine, 70" wide x 52" tall, premium	EA	$456.71	$1,357.00	$1,813.71	**$2,391.11**	6.000
MANTELS						
Install mantel, pine, economy	EA	$114.18	$105.00	$219.18	**$316.68**	1.500
Install mantel, pine, average	EA	$114.18	$209.00	$323.18	**$441.48**	1.500
Install mantel, pine, premium	EA	$114.18	$385.00	$499.18	**$652.68**	1.500
Install mantel, oak, economy	EA	$114.18	$171.00	$285.18	**$395.88**	1.500
Install mantel, oak, average	EA	$114.18	$391.00	$505.18	**$659.88**	1.500
Install mantel, oak, premium	EA	$114.18	$748.00	$862.18	**$1,088.28**	1.500

31

Interior Trim, Stairs and Accessories

Main Staircase

> Shop built by stair builder.

Description	Unit	Direct Labor	Direct Materials	Direct Total	Selling Price	Man-hours
MAIN STAIRCASE, CURVED, OPEN 1 SIDE						
Install curved oak stairway, balustrade, open one side, up to 9' high	EA	$1,522.37	$6,215.00	$7,737.37	**$10,000.36**	20.000
Install curved oak stairway, balustrade, open one side, 9' to 11' high	EA	$1,750.73	$7,128.00	$8,878.73	**$11,477.31**	23.000
MAIN STAIRCASE, CURVED, OPEN 2 SIDES						
Install curved oak stairway, balustrade, open two sides, up to 9' high	EA	$1,902.96	$10,791.00	$12,693.96	**$16,127.15**	25.000
Install curved oak stairway, balustrade, open two sides, 9' to 11' high	EA	$2,131.32	$12,265.00	$14,396.32	**$18,277.30**	28.000
MAIN STAIRCASE, STRAIGHT, OPEN 1 SIDE						
Install straight oak stairway, balustrade, open one side, up to 9' high	EA	$1,065.66	$2,272.00	$3,337.66	**$4,506.05**	14.000
Install straight oak stairway, balustrade, open one side, 9' to 11' high	EA	$1,217.90	$2,440.00	$3,657.90	**$4,961.89**	16.000
MAIN STAIRCASE, STRAIGHT, OPEN 2 SIDES						
Install straight oak stairway, balustrade, open two sides, up to 9' high	EA	$1,294.01	$2,480.00	$3,774.01	**$5,137.00**	17.000
Install straight oak stairway, balustrade, open two sides, 9' to 11' high	EA	$1,446.25	$2,666.40	$4,112.65	**$5,614.92**	19.000

Wood Stairs

Description	Unit	Direct Labor	Direct Materials	Direct Total	Selling Price	Man-hours
BOX STAIRS						
Install box stairs, oak treads, no handrails, 4' high x 3' wide	EA	$380.59	$415.00	$795.59	**$1,133.59**	5.000
Install box stairs, oak treads, no handrails, 8' high x 3' wide	EA	$532.83	$843.00	$1,375.83	**$1,901.43**	7.000
Install box stairs, pine treads, no handrails, 4' high x 3' wide	EA	$380.59	$260.00	$640.59	**$947.59**	5.000
Install box stairs, pine treads, no handrails, 8' high x 3' wide	EA	$532.83	$549.00	$1,081.83	**$1,548.63**	7.000
OPEN STAIRS						
Install open stairs, metal stringers, 3'-6" oak treads, 4' high	EA	$456.71	$817.00	$1,273.71	**$1,743.11**	6.000
Install open stairs, metal stringers, 3'-6" oak treads, 8' high	EA	$608.95	$1,538.00	$2,146.95	**$2,862.54**	8.000
RAILINGS AND BALUSTERS						
Install 3 piece wood railings and balusters, for stairs 4' high	EA	$152.24	$248.00	$400.24	**$551.84**	2.000
Install 3 piece wood railings and balusters, for stairs 8' high	EA	$247.39	$473.00	$720.39	**$980.73**	3.250

Interior Trim, Stairs and Accessories

Attic and Basement Steps

Description	Unit	Direct Labor	Direct Materials	Direct Total	Selling Price	Man-hours
BASEMENT STEPS						
Install fir/pine basement stairs, handrail, open risers, 3' wide x 8' high	EA	$608.95	$319.00	$927.95	**$1,399.74**	8.000
BASEMENT ENTRYWAY						
Replace existing basement entrance with new steel doors, up to 60" wide, 84" long, 26" tall	EA	$608.95	$692.00	$1,300.95	**$1,847.34**	8.000
Replace existing basement entrance with new steel doors and steel steps, up to 60" wide, 84" long, 26" tall	EA	$837.30	$1,095.00	$1,932.30	**$2,712.30**	11.000
ATTIC STEPS						
Install box stairs, pine treads, no handrails, 4' high x 3' wide	EA	$380.59	$260.00	$640.59	**$947.59**	5.000
Install box stairs, pine treads, no handrails, 8' high x 3' wide	EA	$532.83	$549.00	$1,081.83	**$1,548.63**	7.000
FOLDING ATTIC STEPS						
Open ceiling and install folding stairs, economy	EA	$380.59	$154.00	$534.59	**$820.39**	5.000
Open ceiling and install folding stairs, average	EA	$380.59	$285.00	$665.59	**$977.59**	5.000
Open ceiling and install folding stairs, premium	EA	$380.59	$427.00	$807.59	**$1,147.99**	5.000

Spiral Stairs

Description	Unit	Direct Labor	Direct Materials	Direct Total	Selling Price	Man-hours
Install oak spiral stairway with rail and balusters, 5' dia, up to 9' high	EA	$1,065.66	$4,180.00	$5,245.66	**$6,795.65**	14.000
Install oak spiral stairway with rail and balusters, 5' dia, 9' to 11' high	EA	$1,217.90	$4,472.00	$5,689.90	**$7,400.29**	16.000
Install oak spiral stairway with rail and balusters, 6' dia, up to 9' high	EA	$1,294.01	$5,018.00	$6,312.01	**$8,182.60**	17.000
Install oak spiral stairway with rail and balusters, 6' dia, 9' to 11' high	EA	$1,446.25	$5,368.00	$6,814.25	**$8,856.84**	19.000
Install aluminum spiral stairway with rail & balusters, 5' dia, up to 9' high	EA	$685.07	$1,681.00	$2,366.07	**$3,161.26**	9.000
Install aluminum spiral stairway with rail & balusters, 5' dia, 9' to 11' high	EA	$799.24	$1,868.00	$2,667.24	**$3,576.34**	10.500
Install aluminum spiral stairway with rail & balusters, 6' dia, up to 9' high	EA	$761.18	$2,138.00	$2,899.18	**$3,836.78**	10.000
Install aluminum spiral stairway with rail & balusters, 6' dia, 9' to 11' high	EA	$875.36	$2,376.00	$3,251.36	**$4,313.06**	11.500

31

Interior Trim, Stairs and Accessories

Concrete Steps and Slab

Description	Unit	Direct Labor	Direct Materials	Direct Total	Selling Price	Man-hours
SUSPENDED STEPS AND SLAB						
Suspended concrete slab for steps, up to 16 SF	EA	$341.09	$148.57	$489.65	**$817.72**	6.309
Suspended concrete slab for steps, 16 to 24 SF	EA	$454.78	$222.85	$677.63	**$1,131.64**	8.412
Suspended concrete slab for steps, 24 to 35 SF	EA	$636.71	$324.99	$961.69	**$1,606.03**	11.777
Suspended concrete slab for steps, over 35 SF	SF	$18.17	$9.29	$27.45	**$45.84**	0.336
Suspended step, 48" wide, per tread	EA	$159.16	$40.29	$199.45	**$333.09**	2.944
Suspended step, 60" wide, per tread	EA	$191.01	$50.36	$241.37	**$403.09**	3.533
Suspended step, 72" wide, per tread	EA	$219.66	$60.44	$280.10	**$467.76**	4.063
STEPS AND SLAB ON GRADE						
Concrete slab on grade for steps, up to 16 SF	EA	$306.97	$118.85	$425.83	**$711.13**	5.678
Concrete slab on grade for steps, 16 to 24 SF	EA	$409.32	$178.28	$587.59	**$981.28**	7.571
Concrete slab on grade for steps, 24 to 35 SF	EA	$573.02	$259.99	$833.01	**$1,391.13**	10.599
Concrete slab on grade for steps, over 35 SF	SF	$16.38	$7.43	$23.81	**$39.76**	0.303
Step on grade, 48" wide, per tread	EA	$143.27	$32.23	$175.50	**$293.09**	2.650
Step on grade, 60" wide, per tread	EA	$171.92	$40.29	$212.21	**$354.40**	3.180
Step on grade, 72" wide, per tread	EA	$197.71	$48.35	$246.06	**$410.92**	3.657

Exterior Wood Steps

Description	Unit	Direct Labor	Direct Materials	Direct Total	Selling Price	Man-hours
Install pressure treated step with open risers, 4' wide	EA	$38.06	$12.62	$50.68	**$84.64**	0.500
Install pressure treated step with treated risers, 4' wide	EA	$57.09	$16.45	$73.54	**$122.81**	0.750
Install cedar step with open riser, 4' wide	EA	$38.06	$9.03	$47.09	**$78.64**	0.500
Install cedar step with cedar riser, 4' wide	EA	$57.09	$11.89	$68.98	**$115.20**	0.750
Install redwood step with open riser, 4' wide	EA	$38.06	$13.05	$51.11	**$85.35**	0.500
Install redwood step with redwood riser, 4' wide	EA	$57.09	$17.00	$74.09	**$123.72**	0.750

Interior Trim, Stairs and Accessories

Wood Shelving

Description	Unit	Direct Labor	Direct Materials	Direct Total	Selling Price	Man-hours
Install open shelves on brackets and standards, pine, 10" deep	LF	$6.17	$3.58	$9.74	**$16.27**	0.081
Install open shelves on brackets and standards, pine, 12" deep	LF	$7.08	$4.68	$11.75	**$19.63**	0.093
Install open shelves on brackets and standards, oak, 10" deep	LF	$6.17	$8.20	$14.36	**$23.98**	0.081
Install open shelves on brackets and standards, oak, 12" deep	LF	$7.08	$10.40	$17.47	**$29.18**	0.093
Install open shelves on brackets and standards, birch plywood, 10" deep	LF	$7.23	$5.45	$12.68	**$21.17**	0.095
Install open shelves on brackets and standards, birch plywood, 12" deep	LF	$7.54	$6.55	$14.08	**$23.51**	0.099
Install open shelves on brackets and standards, MDF, 10" deep	LF	$7.23	$4.13	$11.36	**$18.96**	0.095
Install open shelves on brackets and standards, MDF, 12" deep	LF	$7.54	$4.95	$12.49	**$20.85**	0.099

Closet Organizer System

Description	Unit	Direct Labor	Direct Materials	Direct Total	Selling Price	Man-hours
CLOSET ORGANIZER SYSTEM, WIRE						
Install closet organizer, wire, economy	LF	$38.06	$28.68	$66.74	**$111.45**	0.500
Install closet organizer, wire, average	LF	$38.06	$40.48	$78.54	**$131.16**	0.500
Install closet organizer, wire, premium	LF	$38.06	$56.89	$94.95	**$158.57**	0.500
CLOSET ORGANIZER SYSTEM, MELAMINE BOARD						
Install closet organizer, melamine board, economy	LF	$57.09	$41.66	$98.75	**$164.91**	0.750
Install closet organizer, melamine board, average	LF	$57.09	$73.43	$130.51	**$217.96**	0.750
Install closet organizer, melamine board, premium	LF	$57.09	$97.34	$154.43	**$257.89**	0.750

Bathroom Accessories

Description	Unit	Direct Labor	Direct Materials	Direct Total	Selling Price	Man-hours
CUP AND TOOTHBRUSH HOLDER AND SOAP DISH						
Install cup and toothbrush holder or soap dish, chrome, economy	EA	$25.35	$7.70	$33.05	**$55.19**	0.333
Install cup and toothbrush holder or soap dish, chrome, average	EA	$25.35	$16.50	$41.85	**$69.89**	0.333
Install cup and toothbrush holder or soap dish, chrome, premium	EA	$25.35	$33.00	$58.35	**$97.44**	0.333
Install cup and toothbrush holder or soap dish, brass, economy	EA	$25.35	$13.20	$38.55	**$64.37**	0.333
Install cup and toothbrush holder or soap dish, brass, average	EA	$25.35	$27.50	$52.85	**$88.26**	0.333
Install cup and toothbrush holder or soap dish, brass, premium	EA	$25.35	$49.50	$74.85	**$125.00**	0.333
Install cup and toothbrush holder or soap dish, porcelain, economy	EA	$25.35	$11.00	$36.35	**$60.70**	0.333
Install cup and toothbrush holder or soap dish, porcelain, average	EA	$25.35	$22.00	$47.35	**$79.07**	0.333
Install cup and toothbrush holder or soap dish, porcelain, premium	EA	$25.35	$55.00	$80.35	**$134.18**	0.333
TOILET PAPER HOLDER						
Install toilet paper holder, recessed, chrome, economy	EA	$57.09	$16.50	$73.59	**$122.89**	0.750
Install toilet paper holder, recessed, chrome, average	EA	$57.09	$27.50	$84.59	**$141.26**	0.750
Install toilet paper holder, recessed, chrome, premium	EA	$57.09	$41.80	$98.89	**$165.14**	0.750
Install toilet paper holder, recessed, brass, economy	EA	$57.09	$24.20	$81.29	**$135.75**	0.750
Install toilet paper holder, recessed, brass, average	EA	$57.09	$33.00	$90.09	**$150.45**	0.750
Install toilet paper holder, recessed, brass, premium	EA	$57.09	$66.00	$123.09	**$205.56**	0.750
Install toilet paper holder, surface mount, chrome, economy	EA	$25.35	$7.70	$33.05	**$55.19**	0.333
Install toilet paper holder, surface mount, chrome, average	EA	$25.35	$16.50	$41.85	**$69.89**	0.333
Install toilet paper holder, surface mount, chrome, premium	EA	$25.35	$33.00	$58.35	**$97.44**	0.333
Install toilet paper holder, surface mount, brass, economy	EA	$25.35	$13.20	$38.55	**$64.37**	0.333
Install toilet paper holder, surface mount, brass, average	EA	$25.35	$27.50	$52.85	**$88.26**	0.333
Install toilet paper holder, surface mount, brass, premium	EA	$25.35	$49.50	$74.85	**$125.00**	0.333
SHOWER CURTAIN ROD						
Install shower curtain rod, chrome, 5' long	EA	$38.06	$22.00	$60.06	**$100.30**	0.500
Install shower curtain rod, chrome, 5-1/2' long	EA	$38.06	$26.40	$64.46	**$107.65**	0.500
Install shower curtain rod, stainless steel, 5' long	EA	$38.06	$35.20	$73.26	**$122.34**	0.500
Install shower curtain rod, stainless steel, 5-1/2' long	EA	$38.06	$41.80	$79.86	**$133.36**	0.500

Interior Trim, Stairs and Accessories

Bathroom Accessories (continued)

Description	Unit	Direct Labor	Direct Materials	Direct Total	Selling Price	Man-hours
TOWEL BAR						
Install towel bar, chrome, 15"	EA	$25.35	$27.50	$52.85	**$88.26**	0.333
Install towel bar, chrome, 18"	EA	$25.35	$33.00	$58.35	**$97.44**	0.333
Install towel bar, chrome, 24"	EA	$38.06	$36.30	$74.36	**$124.18**	0.500
Install towel bar, chrome, 30"	EA	$38.06	$44.00	$82.06	**$137.04**	0.500
Install towel bar, chrome, 36"	EA	$38.06	$50.60	$88.66	**$148.06**	0.500
Install towel ring, chrome	EA	$38.06	$24.20	$62.26	**$103.97**	0.500
Install towel bar, brass, 15"	EA	$25.35	$37.40	$62.75	**$104.79**	0.333
Install towel bar, brass, 18"	EA	$25.35	$42.90	$68.25	**$113.97**	0.333
Install towel bar, brass, 24"	EA	$38.06	$47.30	$85.36	**$142.55**	0.500
Install towel bar, brass, 30"	EA	$38.06	$56.10	$94.16	**$157.25**	0.500
Install towel bar, brass, 36"	EA	$38.06	$63.80	$101.86	**$170.10**	0.500
Install towel ring, brass	EA	$38.06	$34.10	$72.16	**$120.51**	0.500
GRAB BARS						
Install grab bar, chrome, straight, 16" long	EA	$38.06	$23.10	$61.16	**$102.14**	0.500
Install grab bar, chrome, straight, 24" long	EA	$38.06	$27.50	$65.56	**$109.48**	0.500
Install grab bar, chrome, straight, 32" long	EA	$38.06	$33.00	$71.06	**$118.67**	0.500
Install grab bar, chrome, straight, 36" long	EA	$38.06	$37.40	$75.46	**$126.02**	0.500
Install grab bar, chrome, angled, 16" by 36"	EA	$57.09	$66.00	$123.09	**$205.56**	0.750
Install grab bar, stainless steel, straight, 16" long	EA	$38.06	$34.10	$72.16	**$120.51**	0.500
Install grab bar, stainless steel, straight, 24" long	EA	$38.06	$40.70	$78.76	**$131.53**	0.500
Install grab bar, stainless steel, straight, 32" long	EA	$38.06	$48.40	$86.46	**$144.39**	0.500
Install grab bar, stainless steel, straight, 36" long	EA	$38.06	$55.00	$93.06	**$155.41**	0.500
Install grab bar, stainless steel, angled, 16" by 36"	EA	$57.09	$96.80	$153.89	**$256.99**	0.750

Cabinets and Countertops

Labor to Remove Kitchen Cabinets

Description	Unit	Direct Labor	Direct Materials	Direct Total	Selling Price	Man-hours
Remove kitchen cabinets, base or wall	LF	$12.64		$12.64	**$21.10**	0.166
Remove kitchen cabinets, base or wall units	EA	$38.06		$38.06	**$63.56**	0.500

Labor to Install Base Kitchen Cabinets

> Does not include the cost of cabinet.

Description	Unit	Direct Labor	Direct Materials	Direct Total	Selling Price	Man-hours
LABOR TO INSTALL BASE CABINETS						
Install base cabinets per lineal foot	LF	$25.35		$25.35	**$42.33**	0.333
Install medium sink/range base cabinets, 24 to 36 wide	EA	$76.12		$76.12	**$127.12**	1.000
Install wide sink/range base cabinets, 36 to 48 wide	EA	$95.15		$95.15	**$158.90**	1.250
Install narrow base cabinets, 12 to 24 wide	EA	$57.09		$57.09	**$95.34**	0.750
Install medium base cabinets, 24 to 36 wide	EA	$76.12		$76.12	**$127.12**	1.000
Install wide base cabinets, 36 to 48 wide	EA	$95.15		$95.15	**$158.90**	1.250
Install medium base corner cabinets, 27 to 36 wide	EA	$114.18		$114.18	**$190.68**	1.500
Install wide base corner cabinets, 36 to 48 wide	EA	$133.21		$133.21	**$222.46**	1.750
Install narrow island base cabinets, 24 wide	EA	$76.12		$76.12	**$127.12**	1.000
Install medium island base cabinets, 24 to 36 wide	EA	$95.15		$95.15	**$158.90**	1.250
Install wide island base cabinets, 36 to 48 wide	EA	$114.18		$114.18	**$190.68**	1.500

32

Cabinets and Countertops

Labor to Install Wall Kitchen Cabinets

> Does not include the cost of cabinet.

Description	Unit	Direct Labor	Direct Materials	Direct Total	Selling Price	Man-hours
LABOR TO INSTALL WALL CABINETS						
Wall cabinets per lineal foot	LF	$38.06		$38.06	**$63.56**	0.500
Install narrow 30" high wall cabinets, 12 to 24 wide	EA	$76.12		$76.12	**$127.12**	1.000
Install medium 30" high wall cabinets, 24 to 36 wide	EA	$95.15		$95.15	**$158.90**	1.250
Install wide 30" high wall cabinets, 36 to 48 wide	EA	$114.18		$114.18	**$190.68**	1.500
Install narrow 12" bridge cabinets, 30 to 42 wide	EA	$76.12		$76.12	**$127.12**	1.000
Install medium 15" bridge cabinets, 30 to 42 wide	EA	$85.63		$85.63	**$143.01**	1.125
Install medium 21" bridge cabinets, 30 to 42 wide	EA	$95.15		$95.15	**$158.90**	1.250
Install medium 24" bridge cabinets, 30 to 42 wide	EA	$114.18		$114.18	**$190.68**	1.500
Install narrow wall corner cabinets, 24 to 30 wide	EA	$114.18		$114.18	**$190.68**	1.500
Install medium wall corner cabinets, 30 to 36 wide	EA	$133.21		$133.21	**$222.46**	1.750
Install wide wall corner cabinets, 36 to 48 wide	EA	$152.24		$152.24	**$254.24**	2.000
Install medium hanging island wall cabinets, 30 wide	EA	$114.18		$114.18	**$190.68**	1.500
Install oven cabinet, full height	EA	$114.18		$114.18	**$190.68**	1.500
Install pantry, full height, 12 to 24 wide	EA	$114.18		$114.18	**$190.68**	1.500

Per Lineal Foot Cost of Kitchen Cabinets

Description	Unit	Direct Labor	Direct Materials	Direct Total	Selling Price	Man-hours
PER LINEAL FOOT COSTS OF KITCHEN CABINETS						
Economy grade base cabinets	LF	$25.35	$119.00	$144.35	**$185.13**	0.333
Average grade base cabinets	LF	$25.35	$160.00	$185.35	**$234.33**	0.333
Premium grade base cabinets	LF	$25.35	$199.00	$224.35	**$281.13**	0.333
Economy grade wall cabinets	LF	$38.06	$68.00	$106.06	**$145.16**	0.500
Average grade wall cabinets	LF	$38.06	$92.00	$130.06	**$173.96**	0.500
Premium grade wall cabinets	LF	$38.06	$114.00	$152.06	**$200.36**	0.500

Cabinets and Countertops

Base Kitchen Cabinet, PREMIUM

> Solid cherry drawer fronts and front frames. Solid cherry door frames, raised veneer panels.

Description	Unit	Direct Labor	Direct Materials	Direct Total	Selling Price	Man-hours
SINK BASE, PREMIUM						
Sink base, 24", 1 door	EA	$76.12	$281.00	$357.12	**$464.32**	1.000
Sink base, 27", 2 door	EA	$76.12	$354.00	$430.12	**$551.92**	1.000
Sink base, 30", 2 door	EA	$76.12	$362.00	$438.12	**$561.52**	1.000
Sink base, 33", 2 door	EA	$76.12	$373.00	$449.12	**$574.72**	1.000
Sink base, 36", 2 door	EA	$76.12	$398.00	$474.12	**$604.72**	1.000
Sink base, 39", 2 door	EA	$95.15	$424.00	$519.15	**$667.70**	1.250
Sink base, 42", 2 door	EA	$95.15	$451.00	$546.15	**$700.10**	1.250
Sink base, 48", 2 door	EA	$95.15	$508.00	$603.15	**$768.50**	1.250
BASE CABINET, 1 DOOR, PREMIUM						
Base cabinet, 9", 1 door	EA	$57.09	$192.00	$249.09	**$325.74**	0.750
BASE CABINET, 1 DRAWER, 1 DOOR, PREMIUM						
Base cabinet, 12", 1 drawer, 1 door	EA	$57.09	$241.00	$298.09	**$384.54**	0.750
Base cabinet, 15", 1 drawer, 1 door	EA	$57.09	$262.00	$319.09	**$409.74**	0.750
Base cabinet, 18", 1 drawer, 1 door	EA	$57.09	$281.00	$338.09	**$432.54**	0.750
Base cabinet, 21", 1 drawer, 1 door	EA	$57.09	$293.00	$350.09	**$446.94**	0.750
Base cabinet, 24", 1 drawer, 1 door	EA	$57.09	$319.00	$376.09	**$478.14**	0.750
BASE CABINET, 2 DRAWERS, 2 DOORS, PREMIUM						
Base cabinet, 27", 2 drawers, 2 doors	EA	$76.12	$414.00	$490.12	**$623.92**	1.000
Base cabinet, 30", 2 drawers, 2 doors	EA	$76.12	$431.00	$507.12	**$644.32**	1.000
Base cabinet, 33", 2 drawers, 2 doors	EA	$76.12	$451.00	$527.12	**$668.32**	1.000
Base cabinet, 36", 2 drawers, 2 doors	EA	$76.12	$470.00	$546.12	**$691.12**	1.000
Base cabinet, 39", 2 drawers, 2 doors	EA	$95.15	$506.00	$601.15	**$766.10**	1.250
Base cabinet, 42", 2 drawers, 2 doors	EA	$95.15	$535.00	$630.15	**$800.90**	1.250
Base cabinet, 48", 2 drawers, 2 doors	EA	$95.15	$581.00	$676.15	**$856.10**	1.250
BASE CABINET, 4 DRAWERS, PREMIUM						
Base cabinet, 12", 4 drawers	EA	$76.12	$302.00	$378.12	**$489.52**	1.000
Base cabinet, 15", 4 drawers	EA	$76.12	$323.00	$399.12	**$514.72**	1.000
Base cabinet, 18", 4 drawers	EA	$76.12	$353.00	$429.12	**$550.72**	1.000
Base cabinet, 21", 4 drawers	EA	$76.12	$370.00	$446.12	**$571.12**	1.000
Base cabinet, 24", 4 drawers	EA	$76.12	$401.00	$477.12	**$608.32**	1.000
Base cabinet, 30", 4 drawers	EA	$95.15	$455.00	$550.15	**$704.90**	1.250

Base Kitchen Cabinet, PREMIUM (continued)

> Solid cherry drawer fronts and front frames. Solid cherry door frames, raised veneer panels.

Description	Unit	Direct Labor	Direct Materials	Direct Total	Selling Price	Man-hours
BASE CABINET, 1 REGULAR , 2 DEEP DRAWERS, PREMIUM						
Base cabinet, 30", 1 regular, 2 deep drawers	EA	$95.15	$582.00	$677.15	**$857.30**	1.250
Base cabinet, 36", 1 regular, 2 deep drawers	EA	$95.15	$639.00	$734.15	**$925.70**	1.250
BASE ISLAND, 2 FACED, 1 DOOR EACH SIDE, PREMIUM						
Base, island, 2 faced, 24", 1 door each side	EA	$76.12	$721.00	$797.12	**$992.32**	1.000
BASE ISLAND, 2 FACED, 2 DOORS EACH SIDE, PREMIUM						
Base, island, 2 faced, 30", 2 doors each side	EA	$95.15	$812.00	$907.15	**$1,133.30**	1.250
Base, island, 2 faced, 36", 2 doors each side	EA	$95.15	$890.00	$985.15	**$1,226.90**	1.250
Base, island, 2 faced, 48", 2 doors each side	EA	$114.18	$1,093.00	$1,207.18	**$1,502.28**	1.500
BASE BLIND CORNER, 1 DRAWER, PREMIUM						
Base, blind corner, 27" 1 drawer, 1 door	EA	$114.18	$356.00	$470.18	**$617.88**	1.500
Base, blind corner, 30" 1 drawer, 1 door	EA	$114.18	$376.00	$490.18	**$641.88**	1.500
Base, blind corner, 36" 1 drawer, 1 door	EA	$114.18	$394.00	$508.18	**$663.48**	1.500
Base, blind corner, 42" 1 drawer, 1 door	EA	$133.21	$414.00	$547.21	**$719.26**	1.750
Base, blind corner, 48" 1 drawer, 1 door	EA	$133.21	$431.00	$564.21	**$739.66**	1.750
BASE LAZY SUSAN, PREMIUM						
Base, lazy susan, 36"	EA	$114.18	$641.00	$755.18	**$959.88**	1.500

Wall Kitchen Cabinet, PREMIUM

> Solid cherry drawer fronts and front frames. Solid cherry door frames, raised veneer panels.

Description	Unit	Direct Labor	Direct Materials	Direct Total	Selling Price	Man-hours
WALL CABINET, 1 DOOR, PREMIUM						
Wall cabinet, 12" x 30", 1 door	EA	$76.12	$180.00	$256.12	**$343.12**	1.000
Wall cabinet, 15" x 30", 1 door	EA	$76.12	$197.00	$273.12	**$363.52**	1.000
Wall cabinet, 18" x 30", 1 door	EA	$76.12	$215.00	$291.12	**$385.12**	1.000
Wall cabinet, 21" x 30", 1 door	EA	$76.12	$230.00	$306.12	**$403.12**	1.000
Wall cabinet, 24" x 30", 1 door	EA	$76.12	$256.00	$332.12	**$434.32**	1.000
Wall cabinet, 12" x 36", 1 door	EA	$76.12	$237.00	$313.12	**$411.52**	1.000
Wall cabinet, 15" x 36", 1 door	EA	$76.12	$254.00	$330.12	**$431.92**	1.000
Wall cabinet, 18" x 36", 1 door	EA	$76.12	$274.00	$350.12	**$455.92**	1.000
Wall cabinet, 21" x 36", 1 door	EA	$76.12	$302.00	$378.12	**$489.52**	1.000
Wall cabinet, 24" x 36", 1 door	EA	$76.12	$329.00	$405.12	**$521.92**	1.000
Wall cabinet, 12" x 42", 1 door	EA	$76.12	$278.00	$354.12	**$460.72**	1.000
Wall cabinet, 15" x 42", 1 door	EA	$76.12	$292.00	$368.12	**$477.52**	1.000
Wall cabinet, 15" x 42", 1 door	EA	$76.12	$316.00	$392.12	**$506.32**	1.000
Wall cabinet, 21" x 42", 1 door	EA	$76.12	$349.00	$425.12	**$545.92**	1.000
Wall cabinet, 24" x 42", 1 door	EA	$76.12	$376.00	$452.12	**$578.32**	1.000
Wall cabinet, 21" x 18", 1 door	EA	$76.12	$184.00	$260.12	**$347.92**	1.000
Wall cabinet, 24" x 18", 1 door	EA	$76.12	$195.00	$271.12	**$361.12**	1.000
Wall cabinet, 24" x 24", 1 door	EA	$76.12	$230.00	$306.12	**$403.12**	1.000
WALL CABINET, 2 DOOR, PREMIUM						
Wall cabinet, 27" x 24", 2 doors	EA	$95.15	$292.00	$387.15	**$509.30**	1.250
Wall cabinet, 30" x 24", 2 doors	EA	$95.15	$310.00	$405.15	**$530.90**	1.250
Wall cabinet, 33" x 24", 2 doors	EA	$95.15	$323.00	$418.15	**$546.50**	1.250
Wall cabinet, 36" x 24", 2 doors	EA	$95.15	$336.00	$431.15	**$562.10**	1.250
Wall cabinet, 39" x 24", 2 doors	EA	$114.18	$367.00	$481.18	**$631.08**	1.500
Wall cabinet, 42" x 24", 2 doors	EA	$114.18	$377.00	$491.18	**$643.08**	1.500
Wall cabinet, 48" x 24", 2 doors	EA	$114.18	$403.00	$517.18	**$674.28**	1.500
Wall cabinet, 30" x 27", 2 doors	EA	$95.15	$335.00	$430.15	**$560.90**	1.250

Wall Kitchen Cabinet, PREMIUM (continued)

> Solid cherry drawer fronts and front frames. Solid cherry door frames, raised veneer panels.

Description	Unit	Direct Labor	Direct Materials	Direct Total	Selling Price	Man-hours
WALL CABINET, 2 DOOR, PREMIUM (continued)						
Wall cabinet, 27" x 30", 2 doors	EA	$95.15	$316.00	$411.15	**$538.10**	1.250
Wall cabinet, 30" x 30", 2 doors	EA	$95.15	$338.00	$433.15	**$564.50**	1.250
Wall cabinet, 33" x 30", 2 doors	EA	$95.15	$362.00	$457.15	**$593.30**	1.250
Wall cabinet, 36" x 30", 2 doors	EA	$95.15	$374.00	$469.15	**$607.70**	1.250
Wall cabinet, 39" x 30", 2 doors	EA	$114.18	$395.00	$509.18	**$664.68**	1.500
Wall cabinet, 42" x 30", 2 doors	EA	$114.18	$418.00	$532.18	**$692.28**	1.500
Wall cabinet, 48" x 30", 2 doors	EA	$114.18	$460.00	$574.18	**$742.68**	1.500
Wall cabinet, 27" x 36", 2 doors	EA	$95.15	$401.00	$496.15	**$640.10**	1.250
Wall cabinet, 30" x 36", 2 doors	EA	$95.15	$421.00	$516.15	**$664.10**	1.250
Wall cabinet, 33" x 36", 2 doors	EA	$95.15	$446.00	$541.15	**$694.10**	1.250
Wall cabinet, 36" x 36", 2 doors	EA	$95.15	$458.00	$553.15	**$708.50**	1.250
Wall cabinet, 27" x 42", 2 doors	EA	$95.15	$456.00	$551.15	**$706.10**	1.250
Wall cabinet, 30" x 42", 2 doors	EA	$95.15	$475.00	$570.15	**$728.90**	1.250
Wall cabinet, 33" x 42", 2 doors	EA	$95.15	$498.00	$593.15	**$756.50**	1.250
Wall cabinet, 36" x 42", 2 doors	EA	$95.15	$514.00	$609.15	**$775.70**	1.250
WALL CABINET, 2 DOOR BRIDGE, PREMIUM						
Wall cabinet, 30" x 12", 2 door bridge	EA	$76.12	$198.00	$274.12	**$364.72**	1.000
Wall cabinet, 33" x 12", 2 door bridge	EA	$76.12	$211.00	$287.12	**$380.32**	1.000
Wall cabinet, 36" x 12", 2 door bridge	EA	$76.12	$221.00	$297.12	**$392.32**	1.000
Wall cabinet, 39" x 12", 2 door bridge	EA	$76.12	$230.00	$306.12	**$403.12**	1.000
Wall cabinet, 30" x 15", 2 door bridge	EA	$85.63	$214.00	$299.63	**$399.81**	1.125
Wall cabinet, 33" x 15", 2 door bridge	EA	$85.63	$225.00	$310.63	**$413.01**	1.125
Wall cabinet, 36" x 15", 2 door bridge	EA	$85.63	$236.00	$321.63	**$426.21**	1.125
Wall cabinet, 39" x 15", 2 door bridge	EA	$85.63	$265.00	$350.63	**$461.01**	1.125
Wall cabinet, 30" x 18", 2 door bridge	EA	$85.63	$232.00	$317.63	**$421.41**	1.125
Wall cabinet, 33" x 18", 2 door bridge	EA	$85.63	$259.00	$344.63	**$453.81**	1.125
Wall cabinet, 36" x 18", 2 door bridge	EA	$85.63	$274.00	$359.63	**$471.81**	1.125
Wall cabinet, 42" x 18", 2 door bridge	EA	$85.63	$304.00	$389.63	**$507.81**	1.125

Wall Kitchen Cabinet, PREMIUM (continued)

> Solid cherry drawer fronts and front frames. Solid cherry door frames, raised veneer panels.

Description	Unit	Direct Labor	Direct Materials	Direct Total	Selling Price	Man-hours
WALL CABINET, 2 DOOR BRIDGE, PREMIUM (continued)						
Wall cabinet, 30" x 21", 2 door bridge	EA	$95.15	$278.00	$373.15	**$492.50**	1.250
Wall cabinet, 33" x 21", 2 door bridge	EA	$95.15	$298.00	$393.15	**$516.50**	1.250
Wall cabinet, 36" x 21", 2 door bridge	EA	$95.15	$310.00	$405.15	**$530.90**	1.250
Wall cabinet, 36" x 24", 2 door bridge	EA	$114.18	$435.00	$549.18	**$712.68**	1.500
Wall cabinet, 39" x 24", 2 door bridge	EA	$114.18	$480.00	$594.18	**$766.68**	1.500
WALL BLIND CORNER, 1 DOOR, PREMIUM						
Wall, blind corner, 24" x 24", 1 door	EA	$114.18	$224.00	$338.18	**$459.48**	1.500
Wall, blind corner, 24" x 30", 1 door	EA	$114.18	$230.00	$344.18	**$466.68**	1.500
Wall, blind corner, 30" x 30", 1 door	EA	$114.18	$281.00	$395.18	**$527.88**	1.500
Wall, blind corner, 36" x 30", 1 door	EA	$114.18	$307.00	$421.18	**$559.08**	1.500
Wall, blind corner, 24" x 36", 1 door	EA	$133.21	$314.00	$447.21	**$599.26**	1.750
Wall, blind corner, 30" x 36", 1 door	EA	$133.21	$358.00	$491.21	**$652.06**	1.750
Wall, blind corner, 36" x 36", 1 door	EA	$133.21	$409.00	$542.21	**$713.26**	1.750
Wall, blind corner, 24" x 42", 1 door	EA	$152.24	$359.00	$511.24	**$685.04**	2.000
Wall, blind corner, 36" x 42", 1 door	EA	$152.24	$479.00	$631.24	**$829.04**	2.000
WALL BLIND CORNER, 2 DOOR, PREMIUM						
Wall, blind corner, 42" x 30", 2 doors	EA	$152.24	$388.00	$540.24	**$719.84**	2.000
Wall, blind corner, 48" x 30", 2 doors	EA	$152.24	$435.00	$587.24	**$776.24**	2.000
WALL DIAGONAL CORNER, PREMIUM						
Wall, diagonal corner, 24" x 24" x 30"	EA	$114.18	$304.00	$418.18	**$555.48**	1.500
Wall, diagonal corner, 24" x 24" x 36"	EA	$114.18	$401.00	$515.18	**$671.88**	1.500
Wall, diagonal corner, 24" x 24" x 42"	EA	$114.18	$465.00	$579.18	**$748.68**	1.500
Wall, diagonal corner, 27" x 27" x 30"	EA	$133.21	$332.00	$465.21	**$620.86**	1.750
Wall, diagonal corner, 27" x 27" x 36"	EA	$133.21	$432.00	$565.21	**$740.86**	1.750
Wall, diagonal corner, 27" x 27" x 42"	EA	$133.21	$502.00	$635.21	**$824.86**	1.750
WALL ISLAND, 2 FACED, 2 DOORS EACH SIDE, PREMIUM						
Wall, 2 faced, 30" x 30", 2 doors each side	EA	$114.18	$665.00	$779.18	**$988.68**	1.500

Cabinets and Countertops

Specialty Kitchen Cabinet, PREMIUM

> Solid cherry drawer fronts and front frames. Solid cherry door frames, raised veneer panels.

Description	Unit	Direct Labor	Direct Materials	Direct Total	Selling Price	Man-hours
PANTRY, 2 DOOR, OVER/UNDER, PREMIUM						
Pantry, 18" x 84" - 12" deep, 2 door, over/under	EA	$114.18	$599.00	$713.18	**$909.48**	1.500
Pantry, 18" x 90" - 12" deep, 2 door, over/under	EA	$114.18	$644.00	$758.18	**$963.48**	1.500
Pantry, 18" x 96" - 12" deep, 2 door, over/under	EA	$114.18	$668.00	$782.18	**$992.28**	1.500
Pantry, 18" x 84" - 24" deep, 2 door, over/under	EA	$114.18	$670.00	$784.18	**$994.68**	1.500
Pantry, 18" x 90" - 24" deep, 2 door, over/under	EA	$114.18	$699.00	$813.18	**$1,029.48**	1.500
Pantry, 18" x 96" - 24" deep, 2 door, over/under	EA	$114.18	$718.00	$832.18	**$1,052.28**	1.500
PANTRY, 4 DOOR, OVER/UNDER, PREMIUM						
Pantry, 24" x 84" - 12" deep, 4 door, over/under	EA	$114.18	$766.00	$880.18	**$1,109.88**	1.500
Pantry, 24" x 90" - 12" deep, 4 door, over/under	EA	$114.18	$763.00	$877.18	**$1,106.28**	1.500
Pantry, 24" x 96" - 12" deep, 4 door, over/under	EA	$114.18	$843.00	$957.18	**$1,202.28**	1.500
Pantry, 24" x 84" - 24" deep, 4 door, over/under	EA	$114.18	$825.00	$939.18	**$1,180.68**	1.500
Pantry, 24" x 90" - 24" deep, 4 door, over/under	EA	$114.18	$879.00	$993.18	**$1,245.48**	1.500
Pantry, 24" x 96" - 24" deep, 4 door, over/under	EA	$114.18	$906.00	$1,020.18	**$1,277.88**	1.500
OVEN CABINET, PREMIUM						
Oven cabinet, 30" x 84" - 24" deep	EA	$114.18	$974.00	$1,088.18	**$1,359.48**	1.500
Oven cabinet, 33" x 84" - 24" deep	EA	$114.18	$1,018.00	$1,132.18	**$1,412.28**	1.500
Oven cabinet, 30" x 90" - 24" deep	EA	$114.18	$1,086.00	$1,200.18	**$1,493.88**	1.500
Oven cabinet, 33" x 90" - 24" deep	EA	$114.18	$1,133.00	$1,247.18	**$1,550.28**	1.500
Oven cabinet, 30" x 96" - 24" deep	EA	$114.18	$1,158.00	$1,272.18	**$1,580.28**	1.500
Oven cabinet, 33" x 96" - 24" deep	EA	$114.18	$1,208.00	$1,322.18	**$1,640.28**	1.500

Cabinets and Countertops

Base Kitchen Cabinet, AVERAGE

> Solid oak drawer fronts and front frames. Solid oak door frames, raised veneer panels.

Description	Unit	Direct Labor	Direct Materials	Direct Total	Selling Price	Man-hours
SINK BASE, AVERAGE						
Sink base, 24", 1 door	EA	$76.12	$225.00	$301.12	**$397.12**	1.000
Sink base, 27", 2 door	EA	$76.12	$282.00	$358.12	**$465.52**	1.000
Sink base, 30", 2 door	EA	$76.12	$289.00	$365.12	**$473.92**	1.000
Sink base, 33", 2 door	EA	$76.12	$298.00	$374.12	**$484.72**	1.000
Sink base, 36", 2 door	EA	$76.12	$318.00	$394.12	**$508.72**	1.000
Sink base, 39", 2 door	EA	$95.15	$339.00	$434.15	**$565.70**	1.250
Sink base, 42", 2 door	EA	$95.15	$361.00	$456.15	**$592.10**	1.250
Sink base, 48", 2 door	EA	$95.15	$407.00	$502.15	**$647.30**	1.250
BASE CABINET, 1 DOOR, AVERAGE						
Base cabinet, 9", 1 door	EA	$57.09	$153.00	$210.09	**$278.94**	0.750
BASE CABINET, 1 DRAWER, 1 DOOR, AVERAGE						
Base cabinet, 12", 1 drawer, 1 door	EA	$57.09	$193.00	$250.09	**$326.94**	0.750
Base cabinet, 15", 1 drawer, 1 door	EA	$57.09	$210.00	$267.09	**$347.34**	0.750
Base cabinet, 18", 1 drawer, 1 door	EA	$57.09	$224.00	$281.09	**$364.14**	0.750
Base cabinet, 21", 1 drawer, 1 door	EA	$57.09	$234.00	$291.09	**$376.14**	0.750
Base cabinet, 24", 1 drawer, 1 door	EA	$57.09	$255.00	$312.09	**$401.34**	0.750
BASE CABINET, 2 DRAWERS, 2 DOORS, AVERAGE						
Base cabinet, 27", 2 drawers, 2 doors	EA	$76.12	$332.00	$408.12	**$525.52**	1.000
Base cabinet, 30", 2 drawers, 2 doors	EA	$76.12	$345.00	$421.12	**$541.12**	1.000
Base cabinet, 33", 2 drawers, 2 doors	EA	$76.12	$361.00	$437.12	**$560.32**	1.000
Base cabinet, 36", 2 drawers, 2 doors	EA	$76.12	$375.00	$451.12	**$577.12**	1.000
Base cabinet, 39", 2 drawers, 2 doors	EA	$76.12	$404.00	$480.12	**$611.92**	1.000
Base cabinet, 42", 2 drawers, 2 doors	EA	$76.12	$428.00	$504.12	**$640.72**	1.000
Base cabinet, 48", 2 drawers, 2 doors	EA	$76.12	$465.00	$541.12	**$685.12**	1.000
BASE CABINET, 4 DRAWERS, AVERAGE						
Base cabinet, 12", 4 drawers	EA	$76.12	$241.00	$317.12	**$416.32**	1.000
Base cabinet, 15", 4 drawers	EA	$76.12	$258.00	$334.12	**$436.72**	1.000
Base cabinet, 18", 4 drawers	EA	$76.12	$282.00	$358.12	**$465.52**	1.000
Base cabinet, 21", 4 drawers	EA	$76.12	$296.00	$372.12	**$482.32**	1.000
Base cabinet, 24", 4 drawers	EA	$76.12	$321.00	$397.12	**$512.32**	1.000
Base cabinet, 30", 4 drawers	EA	$95.15	$364.00	$459.15	**$595.70**	1.250

Cabinets and Countertops

Base Kitchen Cabinet, AVERAGE (continued)

> Solid oak drawer fronts and front frames. Solid oak door frames, raised veneer panels.

Description	Unit	Direct Labor	Direct Materials	Direct Total	Selling Price	Man-hours
BASE CABINET, 1 REGULAR , 2 DEEP DRAWERS, AVERAGE						
Base cabinet, 30", 1 regular, 2 deep drawers	EA	$95.15	$465.00	$560.15	**$716.90**	1.250
Base cabinet, 36", 1 regular, 2 deep drawers	EA	$95.15	$511.00	$606.15	**$772.10**	1.250
BASE ISLAND, 2 FACED, 1 DOOR EACH SIDE, AVERAGE						
Base, island, 2 faced, 24", 1 door each side	EA	$76.12	$577.00	$653.12	**$819.52**	1.000
BASE ISLAND, 2 FACED, 2 DOORS EACH SIDE, AVERAGE						
Base, island, 2 faced, 30", 2 doors each side	EA	$95.15	$650.00	$745.15	**$938.90**	1.250
Base, island, 2 faced, 36", 2 doors each side	EA	$95.15	$712.00	$807.15	**$1,013.30**	1.250
Base, island, 2 faced, 48", 2 doors each side	EA	$95.15	$874.00	$969.15	**$1,207.70**	1.250
BASE BLIND CORNER, 1 DRAWER, AVERAGE						
Base, blind corner, 27" 1 drawer, 1 door	EA	$114.18	$285.00	$399.18	**$532.68**	1.500
Base, blind corner, 30" 1 drawer, 1 door	EA	$114.18	$301.00	$415.18	**$551.88**	1.500
Base, blind corner, 36" 1 drawer, 1 door	EA	$114.18	$315.00	$429.18	**$568.68**	1.500
Base, blind corner, 42" 1 drawer, 1 door	EA	$133.21	$332.00	$465.21	**$620.86**	1.750
Base, blind corner, 48" 1 drawer, 1 door	EA	$133.21	$345.00	$478.21	**$636.46**	1.750
BASE LAZY SUSAN, AVERAGE						
Base, lazy susan, 36"	EA	$114.18	$513.00	$627.18	**$806.28**	1.500

Cabinets and Countertops

Wall Kitchen Cabinet, AVERAGE

> Solid oak drawer fronts and front frames. Solid oak door frames, raised veneer panels.

Description	Unit	Direct Labor	Direct Materials	Direct Total	Selling Price	Man-hours
WALL CABINET, 1 DOOR, AVERAGE						
Wall cabinet, 12" x 30", 1 door	EA	$76.12	$144.00	$220.12	**$299.92**	1.000
Wall cabinet, 15" x 30", 1 door	EA	$76.12	$157.00	$233.12	**$315.52**	1.000
Wall cabinet, 18" x 30", 1 door	EA	$76.12	$171.00	$247.12	**$332.32**	1.000
Wall cabinet, 21" x 30", 1 door	EA	$76.12	$184.00	$260.12	**$347.92**	1.000
Wall cabinet, 24" x 30", 1 door	EA	$76.12	$205.00	$281.12	**$373.12**	1.000
Wall cabinet, 12" x 36", 1 door	EA	$76.12	$190.00	$266.12	**$355.12**	1.000
Wall cabinet, 15" x 36", 1 door	EA	$76.12	$202.00	$278.12	**$369.52**	1.000
Wall cabinet, 18" x 36", 1 door	EA	$76.12	$219.00	$295.12	**$389.92**	1.000
Wall cabinet, 21" x 36", 1 door	EA	$76.12	$241.00	$317.12	**$416.32**	1.000
Wall cabinet, 24" x 36", 1 door	EA	$76.12	$263.00	$339.12	**$442.72**	1.000
Wall cabinet, 12" x 42", 1 door	EA	$76.12	$222.00	$298.12	**$393.52**	1.000
Wall cabinet, 15" x 42", 1 door	EA	$76.12	$234.00	$310.12	**$407.92**	1.000
Wall cabinet, 15" x 42", 1 door	EA	$76.12	$253.00	$329.12	**$430.72**	1.000
Wall cabinet, 21" x 42", 1 door	EA	$76.12	$279.00	$355.12	**$461.92**	1.000
Wall cabinet, 24" x 42", 1 door	EA	$76.12	$301.00	$377.12	**$488.32**	1.000
Wall cabinet, 21" x 18", 1 door	EA	$76.12	$147.00	$223.12	**$303.52**	1.000
Wall cabinet, 24" x 18", 1 door	EA	$76.12	$156.00	$232.12	**$314.32**	1.000
Wall cabinet, 24" x 24", 1 door	EA	$76.12	$184.00	$260.12	**$347.92**	1.000
WALL CABINET, 2 DOOR, AVERAGE						
Wall cabinet, 27" x 24", 2 doors	EA	$95.15	$234.00	$329.15	**$439.70**	1.250
Wall cabinet, 30" x 24", 2 doors	EA	$95.15	$247.00	$342.15	**$455.30**	1.250
Wall cabinet, 33" x 24", 2 doors	EA	$95.15	$258.00	$353.15	**$468.50**	1.250
Wall cabinet, 36" x 24", 2 doors	EA	$95.15	$268.00	$363.15	**$480.50**	1.250
Wall cabinet, 39" x 24", 2 doors	EA	$114.18	$294.00	$408.18	**$543.48**	1.500
Wall cabinet, 42" x 24", 2 doors	EA	$114.18	$301.00	$415.18	**$551.88**	1.500
Wall cabinet, 48" x 24", 2 doors	EA	$114.18	$323.00	$437.18	**$578.28**	1.500
Wall cabinet, 30" x 27", 2 doors	EA	$95.15	$268.00	$363.15	**$480.50**	1.250

Cabinets and Countertops

Wall Kitchen Cabinet, AVERAGE (continued) ➤ Solid oak drawer fronts and front frames. Solid oak door frames, raised veneer panels.

Description	Unit	Direct Labor	Direct Materials	Direct Total	Selling Price	Man-hours
WALL CABINET, 2 DOOR, AVERAGE (continued)						
Wall cabinet, 27" x 30", 2 doors	EA	$95.15	$253.00	$348.15	**$462.50**	1.250
Wall cabinet, 30" x 30", 2 doors	EA	$95.15	$270.00	$365.15	**$482.90**	1.250
Wall cabinet, 33" x 30", 2 doors	EA	$95.15	$289.00	$384.15	**$505.70**	1.250
Wall cabinet, 36" x 30", 2 doors	EA	$95.15	$298.00	$393.15	**$516.50**	1.250
Wall cabinet, 39" x 30", 2 doors	EA	$114.18	$315.00	$429.18	**$568.68**	1.500
Wall cabinet, 42" x 30", 2 doors	EA	$114.18	$334.00	$448.18	**$591.48**	1.500
Wall cabinet, 48" x 30", 2 doors	EA	$114.18	$368.00	$482.18	**$632.28**	1.500
Wall cabinet, 27" x 36", 2 doors	EA	$95.15	$321.00	$416.15	**$544.10**	1.250
Wall cabinet, 30" x 36", 2 doors	EA	$95.15	$336.00	$431.15	**$562.10**	1.250
Wall cabinet, 33" x 36", 2 doors	EA	$95.15	$357.00	$452.15	**$587.30**	1.250
Wall cabinet, 36" x 36", 2 doors	EA	$95.15	$366.00	$461.15	**$598.10**	1.250
Wall cabinet, 27" x 42", 2 doors	EA	$95.15	$364.00	$459.15	**$595.70**	1.250
Wall cabinet, 30" x 42", 2 doors	EA	$95.15	$380.00	$475.15	**$614.90**	1.250
Wall cabinet, 33" x 42", 2 doors	EA	$95.15	$399.00	$494.15	**$637.70**	1.250
Wall cabinet, 36" x 42", 2 doors	EA	$95.15	$411.00	$506.15	**$652.10**	1.250
WALL CABINET, 2 DOOR BRIDGE, AVERAGE						
Wall cabinet, 30" x 12", 2 door bridge	EA	$76.12	$159.00	$235.12	**$317.92**	1.000
Wall cabinet, 33" x 12", 2 door bridge	EA	$76.12	$168.00	$244.12	**$328.72**	1.000
Wall cabinet, 36" x 12", 2 door bridge	EA	$76.12	$176.00	$252.12	**$338.32**	1.000
Wall cabinet, 39" x 12", 2 door bridge	EA	$76.12	$184.00	$260.12	**$347.92**	1.000
Wall cabinet, 30" x 15", 2 door bridge	EA	$85.63	$171.00	$256.63	**$348.21**	1.125
Wall cabinet, 33" x 15", 2 door bridge	EA	$85.63	$180.00	$265.63	**$359.01**	1.125
Wall cabinet, 36" x 15", 2 door bridge	EA	$85.63	$188.00	$273.63	**$368.61**	1.125
Wall cabinet, 39" x 15", 2 door bridge	EA	$85.63	$211.00	$296.63	**$396.21**	1.125
Wall cabinet, 30" x 18", 2 door bridge	EA	$85.63	$185.00	$270.63	**$365.01**	1.125
Wall cabinet, 33" x 18", 2 door bridge	EA	$85.63	$207.00	$292.63	**$391.41**	1.125
Wall cabinet, 36" x 18", 2 door bridge	EA	$85.63	$219.00	$304.63	**$405.81**	1.125
Wall cabinet, 42" x 18", 2 door bridge	EA	$85.63	$243.00	$328.63	**$434.61**	1.125

Cabinets and Countertops

Wall Kitchen Cabinet, AVERAGE (continued)

> Solid oak drawer fronts and front frames. Solid oak door frames, raised veneer panels.

Description	Unit	Direct Labor	Direct Materials	Direct Total	Selling Price	Man-hours
WALL CABINET, 2 DOOR BRIDGE, AVERAGE (continued)						
Wall cabinet, 30" x 21", 2 door bridge	EA	$95.15	$222.00	$317.15	**$425.30**	1.250
Wall cabinet, 33" x 21", 2 door bridge	EA	$95.15	$238.00	$333.15	**$444.50**	1.250
Wall cabinet, 36" x 21", 2 door bridge	EA	$95.15	$247.00	$342.15	**$455.30**	1.250
Wall cabinet, 36" x 24", 2 door bridge	EA	$114.18	$348.00	$462.18	**$608.28**	1.500
Wall cabinet, 39" x 24", 2 door bridge	EA	$114.18	$383.00	$497.18	**$650.28**	1.500
WALL BLIND CORNER, 1 DOOR, AVERAGE						
Wall, blind corner, 24" x 24", 1 door	EA	$114.18	$178.00	$292.18	**$404.28**	1.500
Wall, blind corner, 24" x 30", 1 door	EA	$114.18	$184.00	$298.18	**$411.48**	1.500
Wall, blind corner, 30" x 30", 1 door	EA	$114.18	$224.00	$338.18	**$459.48**	1.500
Wall, blind corner, 36" x 30", 1 door	EA	$114.18	$246.00	$360.18	**$485.88**	1.500
Wall, blind corner, 24" x 36", 1 door	EA	$133.21	$251.00	$384.21	**$523.66**	1.750
Wall, blind corner, 30" x 36", 1 door	EA	$133.21	$286.00	$419.21	**$565.66**	1.750
Wall, blind corner, 36" x 36", 1 door	EA	$133.21	$327.00	$460.21	**$614.86**	1.750
Wall, blind corner, 24" x 42", 1 door	EA	$152.24	$287.00	$439.24	**$598.64**	2.000
Wall, blind corner, 36" x 42", 1 door	EA	$152.24	$383.00	$535.24	**$713.84**	2.000
WALL BLIND CORNER, 2 DOOR, AVERAGE						
Wall, blind corner, 42" x 30", 2 doors	EA	$152.24	$310.00	$462.24	**$626.24**	2.000
Wall, blind corner, 48" x 30", 2 doors	EA	$152.24	$348.00	$500.24	**$671.84**	2.000
WALL DIAGONAL CORNER, AVERAGE						
Wall, diagonal corner, 24" x 24" x 30"	EA	$114.18	$243.00	$357.18	**$482.28**	1.500
Wall, diagonal corner, 24" x 24" x 36"	EA	$114.18	$321.00	$435.18	**$575.88**	1.500
Wall, diagonal corner, 24" x 24" x 42"	EA	$114.18	$371.00	$485.18	**$635.88**	1.500
Wall, diagonal corner, 27" x 27" x 30"	EA	$133.21	$265.00	$398.21	**$540.46**	1.750
Wall, diagonal corner, 27" x 27" x 36"	EA	$133.21	$346.00	$479.21	**$637.66**	1.750
Wall, diagonal corner, 27" x 27" x 42"	EA	$133.21	$401.00	$534.21	**$703.66**	1.750
WALL ISLAND, 2 FACED, 2 DOORS EACH SIDE, AVERAGE						
Wall, 2 faced, 30" x 30", 2 doors each side	EA	$114.18	$532.00	$646.18	**$829.08**	1.500

Cabinets and Countertops

Specialty Kitchen Cabinet, AVERAGE

> Solid oak drawer fronts and front frames. Solid oak door frames, raised veneer panels.

Description	Unit	Direct Labor	Direct Materials	Direct Total	Selling Price	Man-hours
PANTRY, 2 DOOR, OVER/UNDER, AVERAGE						
Pantry, 18" x 84" - 12" deep, 2 door, over/under	EA	$114.18	$479.00	$593.18	**$765.48**	1.500
Pantry, 18" x 90" - 12" deep, 2 door, over/under	EA	$114.18	$514.00	$628.18	**$807.48**	1.500
Pantry, 18" x 96" - 12" deep, 2 door, over/under	EA	$114.18	$534.00	$648.18	**$831.48**	1.500
Pantry, 18" x 84" - 24" deep, 2 door, over/under	EA	$114.18	$536.00	$650.18	**$833.88**	1.500
Pantry, 18" x 90" - 24" deep, 2 door, over/under	EA	$114.18	$559.00	$673.18	**$861.48**	1.500
Pantry, 18" x 96" - 24" deep, 2 door, over/under	EA	$114.18	$574.00	$688.18	**$879.48**	1.500
PANTRY, 4 DOOR, OVER/UNDER, AVERAGE						
Pantry, 24" x 84" - 12" deep, 4 door, over/under	EA	$114.18	$613.00	$727.18	**$926.28**	1.500
Pantry, 24" x 90" - 12" deep, 4 door, over/under	EA	$114.18	$610.00	$724.18	**$922.68**	1.500
Pantry, 24" x 96" - 12" deep, 4 door, over/under	EA	$114.18	$674.00	$788.18	**$999.48**	1.500
Pantry, 24" x 84" - 24" deep, 4 door, over/under	EA	$114.18	$660.00	$774.18	**$982.68**	1.500
Pantry, 24" x 90" - 24" deep, 4 door, over/under	EA	$114.18	$702.00	$816.18	**$1,033.08**	1.500
Pantry, 24" x 96" - 24" deep, 4 door, over/under	EA	$114.18	$725.00	$839.18	**$1,060.68**	1.500
OVEN CABINET, AVERAGE						
Oven cabinet, 30" x 84" - 24" deep	EA	$114.18	$780.00	$894.18	**$1,126.68**	1.500
Oven cabinet, 33" x 84" - 24" deep	EA	$114.18	$814.00	$928.18	**$1,167.48**	1.500
Oven cabinet, 30" x 90" - 24" deep	EA	$114.18	$869.00	$983.18	**$1,233.48**	1.500
Oven cabinet, 33" x 90" - 24" deep	EA	$114.18	$906.00	$1,020.18	**$1,277.88**	1.500
Oven cabinet, 30" x 96" - 24" deep	EA	$114.18	$926.00	$1,040.18	**$1,301.88**	1.500
Oven cabinet, 33" x 96" - 24" deep	EA	$114.18	$966.00	$1,080.18	**$1,349.88**	1.500

Cabinets and Countertops

Base Kitchen Cabinet, ECONOMY

> Painted hardwood frames, thermofoil surface on drawers and doors.

Description	Unit	Direct Labor	Direct Materials	Direct Total	Selling Price	Man-hours
SINK BASE, ECONOMY						
Sink base, 24", 1 door	EA	$76.12	$186.00	$262.12	**$350.32**	1.000
Sink base, 27", 2 door	EA	$76.12	$233.00	$309.12	**$406.72**	1.000
Sink base, 30", 2 door	EA	$76.12	$239.00	$315.12	**$413.92**	1.000
Sink base, 33", 2 door	EA	$76.12	$246.00	$322.12	**$422.32**	1.000
Sink base, 36", 2 door	EA	$76.12	$262.00	$338.12	**$441.52**	1.000
Sink base, 39", 2 door	EA	$95.15	$279.00	$374.15	**$493.70**	1.250
Sink base, 42", 2 door	EA	$95.15	$298.00	$393.15	**$516.50**	1.250
Sink base, 48", 2 door	EA	$95.15	$336.00	$431.15	**$562.10**	1.250
BASE CABINET, 1 DOOR, ECONOMY						
Base cabinet, 9", 1 door	EA	$57.09	$126.00	$183.09	**$246.54**	0.750
BASE CABINET, 1 DRAWER, 1 DOOR, ECONOMY						
Base cabinet, 12", 1 drawer, 1 door	EA	$57.09	$159.00	$216.09	**$286.14**	0.750
Base cabinet, 15", 1 drawer, 1 door	EA	$57.09	$173.00	$230.09	**$302.94**	0.750
Base cabinet, 18", 1 drawer, 1 door	EA	$57.09	$185.00	$242.09	**$317.34**	0.750
Base cabinet, 21", 1 drawer, 1 door	EA	$57.09	$193.00	$250.09	**$326.94**	0.750
Base cabinet, 24", 1 drawer, 1 door	EA	$57.09	$211.00	$268.09	**$348.54**	0.750
BASE CABINET, 2 DRAWERS, 2 DOORS, ECONOMY						
Base cabinet, 27", 2 drawers, 2 doors	EA	$76.12	$228.00	$304.12	**$400.72**	1.000
Base cabinet, 30", 2 drawers, 2 doors	EA	$76.12	$237.00	$313.12	**$411.52**	1.000
Base cabinet, 33", 2 drawers, 2 doors	EA	$76.12	$248.00	$324.12	**$424.72**	1.000
Base cabinet, 36", 2 drawers, 2 doors	EA	$76.12	$258.00	$334.12	**$436.72**	1.000
Base cabinet, 39", 2 drawers, 2 doors	EA	$76.12	$278.00	$354.12	**$460.72**	1.000
Base cabinet, 42", 2 drawers, 2 doors	EA	$76.12	$294.00	$370.12	**$479.92**	1.000
Base cabinet, 48", 2 drawers, 2 doors	EA	$76.12	$320.00	$396.12	**$511.12**	1.000
BASE CABINET, 4 DRAWERS, ECONOMY						
Base cabinet, 12", 4 drawers	EA	$76.12	$166.00	$242.12	**$326.32**	1.000
Base cabinet, 15", 4 drawers	EA	$76.12	$177.00	$253.12	**$339.52**	1.000
Base cabinet, 18", 4 drawers	EA	$76.12	$194.00	$270.12	**$359.92**	1.000
Base cabinet, 21", 4 drawers	EA	$76.12	$203.00	$279.12	**$370.72**	1.000
Base cabinet, 24", 4 drawers	EA	$76.12	$221.00	$297.12	**$392.32**	1.000
Base cabinet, 30", 4 drawers	EA	$95.15	$250.00	$345.15	**$458.90**	1.250

Cabinets and Countertops

Base Kitchen Cabinet, ECONOMY (continued)

> Painted hardwood frames, thermofoil surface on drawers and doors.

Description	Unit	Direct Labor	Direct Materials	Direct Total	Selling Price	Man-hours
BASE CABINET, 1 REGULAR , 2 DEEP DRAWERS, ECONOMY						
Base cabinet, 30", 1 regular, 2 deep drawers	EA	$95.15	$320.00	$415.15	**$542.90**	1.250
Base cabinet, 36", 1 regular, 2 deep drawers	EA	$95.15	$351.00	$446.15	**$580.10**	1.250
BASE ISLAND, 2 FACED, 1 DOOR EACH SIDE, ECONOMY						
Base, island, 2 faced, 24", 1 door each side	EA	$76.12	$397.00	$473.12	**$603.52**	1.000
BASE ISLAND, 2 FACED, 2 DOORS EACH SIDE, ECONOMY						
Base, island, 2 faced, 30", 2 doors each side	EA	$95.15	$447.00	$542.15	**$695.30**	1.250
Base, island, 2 faced, 36", 2 doors each side	EA	$95.15	$490.00	$585.15	**$746.90**	1.250
Base, island, 2 faced, 48", 2 doors each side	EA	$95.15	$601.00	$696.15	**$880.10**	1.250
BASE BLIND CORNER, 1 DRAWER, ECONOMY						
Base, blind corner, 27" 1 drawer, 1 door	EA	$114.18	$196.00	$310.18	**$425.88**	1.500
Base, blind corner, 30" 1 drawer, 1 door	EA	$114.18	$207.00	$321.18	**$439.08**	1.500
Base, blind corner, 36" 1 drawer, 1 door	EA	$114.18	$217.00	$331.18	**$451.08**	1.500
Base, blind corner, 42" 1 drawer, 1 door	EA	$133.21	$228.00	$361.21	**$496.06**	1.750
Base, blind corner, 48" 1 drawer, 1 door	EA	$133.21	$237.00	$370.21	**$506.86**	1.750
BASE LAZY SUSAN, ECONOMY						
Base, lazy susan, 36"	EA	$114.18	$352.00	$466.18	**$613.08**	1.500

Cabinets and Countertops

Wall Kitchen Cabinet, ECONOMY

> Painted hardwood frames, thermofoil surface on drawers and doors.

Description	Unit	Direct Labor	Direct Materials	Direct Total	Selling Price	Man-hours
WALL CABINET, 1 DOOR, ECONOMY						
Wall cabinet, 12" x 30", 1 door	EA	$76.12	$99.00	$175.12	**$245.92**	1.000
Wall cabinet, 15" x 30", 1 door	EA	$76.12	$108.00	$184.12	**$256.72**	1.000
Wall cabinet, 18" x 30", 1 door	EA	$76.12	$118.00	$194.12	**$268.72**	1.000
Wall cabinet, 21" x 30", 1 door	EA	$76.12	$126.00	$202.12	**$278.32**	1.000
Wall cabinet, 24" x 30", 1 door	EA	$76.12	$141.00	$217.12	**$296.32**	1.000
Wall cabinet, 12" x 36", 1 door	EA	$76.12	$131.00	$207.12	**$284.32**	1.000
Wall cabinet, 15" x 36", 1 door	EA	$76.12	$139.00	$215.12	**$293.92**	1.000
Wall cabinet, 18" x 36", 1 door	EA	$76.12	$150.00	$226.12	**$307.12**	1.000
Wall cabinet, 21" x 36", 1 door	EA	$76.12	$166.00	$242.12	**$326.32**	1.000
Wall cabinet, 24" x 36", 1 door	EA	$76.12	$180.00	$256.12	**$343.12**	1.000
Wall cabinet, 12" x 42", 1 door	EA	$76.12	$153.00	$229.12	**$310.72**	1.000
Wall cabinet, 15" x 42", 1 door	EA	$76.12	$161.00	$237.12	**$320.32**	1.000
Wall cabinet, 15" x 42", 1 door	EA	$76.12	$174.00	$250.12	**$335.92**	1.000
Wall cabinet, 21" x 42", 1 door	EA	$76.12	$192.00	$268.12	**$357.52**	1.000
Wall cabinet, 24" x 42", 1 door	EA	$76.12	$207.00	$283.12	**$375.52**	1.000
Wall cabinet, 21" x 18", 1 door	EA	$76.12	$101.00	$177.12	**$248.32**	1.000
Wall cabinet, 24" x 18", 1 door	EA	$76.12	$107.00	$183.12	**$255.52**	1.000
Wall cabinet, 24" x 24", 1 door	EA	$76.12	$126.00	$202.12	**$278.32**	1.000
WALL CABINET, 2 DOOR, ECONOMY						
Wall cabinet, 27" x 24", 2 doors	EA	$95.15	$161.00	$256.15	**$352.10**	1.250
Wall cabinet, 30" x 24", 2 doors	EA	$95.15	$170.00	$265.15	**$362.90**	1.250
Wall cabinet, 33" x 24", 2 doors	EA	$95.15	$177.00	$272.15	**$371.30**	1.250
Wall cabinet, 36" x 24", 2 doors	EA	$95.15	$184.00	$279.15	**$379.70**	1.250
Wall cabinet, 39" x 24", 2 doors	EA	$114.18	$202.00	$316.18	**$433.08**	1.500
Wall cabinet, 42" x 24", 2 doors	EA	$114.18	$207.00	$321.18	**$439.08**	1.500
Wall cabinet, 48" x 24", 2 doors	EA	$114.18	$222.00	$336.18	**$457.08**	1.500
Wall cabinet, 30" x 27", 2 doors	EA	$95.15	$184.00	$279.15	**$379.70**	1.250

Wall Kitchen Cabinet, ECONOMY (continued)

> Painted hardwood frames, thermofoil surface on drawers and doors.

Description	Unit	Direct Labor	Direct Materials	Direct Total	Selling Price	Man-hours
WALL CABINET, 2 DOOR, ECONOMY (continued)						
Wall cabinet, 27" x 30", 2 doors	EA	$95.15	$174.00	$269.15	**$367.70**	1.250
Wall cabinet, 30" x 30", 2 doors	EA	$95.15	$185.00	$280.15	**$380.90**	1.250
Wall cabinet, 33" x 30", 2 doors	EA	$95.15	$199.00	$294.15	**$397.70**	1.250
Wall cabinet, 36" x 30", 2 doors	EA	$95.15	$205.00	$300.15	**$404.90**	1.250
Wall cabinet, 39" x 30", 2 doors	EA	$114.18	$217.00	$331.18	**$451.08**	1.500
Wall cabinet, 42" x 30", 2 doors	EA	$114.18	$230.00	$344.18	**$466.68**	1.500
Wall cabinet, 48" x 30", 2 doors	EA	$114.18	$253.00	$367.18	**$494.28**	1.500
Wall cabinet, 27" x 36", 2 doors	EA	$95.15	$221.00	$316.15	**$424.10**	1.250
Wall cabinet, 30" x 36", 2 doors	EA	$95.15	$231.00	$326.15	**$436.10**	1.250
Wall cabinet, 33" x 36", 2 doors	EA	$95.15	$245.00	$340.15	**$452.90**	1.250
Wall cabinet, 36" x 36", 2 doors	EA	$95.15	$251.00	$346.15	**$460.10**	1.250
Wall cabinet, 27" x 42", 2 doors	EA	$95.15	$250.00	$345.15	**$458.90**	1.250
Wall cabinet, 30" x 42", 2 doors	EA	$95.15	$261.00	$356.15	**$472.10**	1.250
Wall cabinet, 33" x 42", 2 doors	EA	$95.15	$274.00	$369.15	**$487.70**	1.250
Wall cabinet, 36" x 42", 2 doors	EA	$95.15	$283.00	$378.15	**$498.50**	1.250
WALL CABINET, 2 DOOR BRIDGE, ECONOMY						
Wall cabinet, 30" x 12", 2 door bridge	EA	$76.12	$109.00	$185.12	**$257.92**	1.000
Wall cabinet, 33" x 12", 2 door bridge	EA	$76.12	$116.00	$192.12	**$266.32**	1.000
Wall cabinet, 36" x 12", 2 door bridge	EA	$76.12	$121.00	$197.12	**$272.32**	1.000
Wall cabinet, 39" x 12", 2 door bridge	EA	$76.12	$126.00	$202.12	**$278.32**	1.000
Wall cabinet, 30" x 15", 2 door bridge	EA	$85.63	$118.00	$203.63	**$284.61**	1.125
Wall cabinet, 33" x 15", 2 door bridge	EA	$85.63	$124.00	$209.63	**$291.81**	1.125
Wall cabinet, 36" x 15", 2 door bridge	EA	$85.63	$129.00	$214.63	**$297.81**	1.125
Wall cabinet, 39" x 15", 2 door bridge	EA	$85.63	$145.00	$230.63	**$317.01**	1.125
Wall cabinet, 30" x 18", 2 door bridge	EA	$85.63	$128.00	$213.63	**$296.61**	1.125
Wall cabinet, 33" x 18", 2 door bridge	EA	$85.63	$142.00	$227.63	**$313.41**	1.125
Wall cabinet, 36" x 18", 2 door bridge	EA	$85.63	$150.00	$235.63	**$323.01**	1.125
Wall cabinet, 42" x 18", 2 door bridge	EA	$85.63	$167.00	$252.63	**$343.41**	1.125

Wall Kitchen Cabinet, ECONOMY (continued)

> Painted hardwood frames, thermofoil surface on drawers and doors.

Description	Unit	Direct Labor	Direct Materials	Direct Total	Selling Price	Man-hours
WALL CABINET, 2 DOOR BRIDGE, ECONOMY (continued)						
Wall cabinet, 30" x 21", 2 door bridge	EA	$95.15	$153.00	$248.15	**$342.50**	1.250
Wall cabinet, 33" x 21", 2 door bridge	EA	$95.15	$164.00	$259.15	**$355.70**	1.250
Wall cabinet, 36" x 21", 2 door bridge	EA	$95.15	$170.00	$265.15	**$362.90**	1.250
Wall cabinet, 36" x 24", 2 door bridge	EA	$114.18	$239.00	$353.18	**$477.48**	1.500
Wall cabinet, 39" x 24", 2 door bridge	EA	$114.18	$264.00	$378.18	**$507.48**	1.500
WALL BLIND CORNER, 1 DOOR, ECONOMY						
Wall, blind corner, 24" x 24", 1 door	EA	$114.18	$123.00	$237.18	**$338.28**	1.500
Wall, blind corner, 24" x 30", 1 door	EA	$114.18	$126.00	$240.18	**$341.88**	1.500
Wall, blind corner, 30" x 30", 1 door	EA	$114.18	$154.00	$268.18	**$375.48**	1.500
Wall, blind corner, 36" x 30", 1 door	EA	$114.18	$169.00	$283.18	**$393.48**	1.500
Wall, blind corner, 24" x 36", 1 door	EA	$133.21	$172.00	$305.21	**$428.86**	1.750
Wall, blind corner, 30" x 36", 1 door	EA	$133.21	$197.00	$330.21	**$458.86**	1.750
Wall, blind corner, 36" x 36", 1 door	EA	$133.21	$225.00	$358.21	**$492.46**	1.750
Wall, blind corner, 24" x 42", 1 door	EA	$152.24	$197.00	$349.24	**$490.64**	2.000
Wall, blind corner, 36" x 42", 1 door	EA	$152.24	$264.00	$416.24	**$571.04**	2.000
WALL BLIND CORNER, 2 DOOR, ECONOMY						
Wall, blind corner, 42" x 30", 2 doors	EA	$152.24	$213.00	$365.24	**$509.84**	2.000
Wall, blind corner, 48" x 30", 2 doors	EA	$152.24	$239.00	$391.24	**$541.04**	2.000
WALL DIAGONAL CORNER, ECONOMY						
Wall, diagonal corner, 24" x 24" x 30"	EA	$114.18	$167.00	$281.18	**$391.08**	1.500
Wall, diagonal corner, 24" x 24" x 36"	EA	$114.18	$221.00	$335.18	**$455.88**	1.500
Wall, diagonal corner, 24" x 24" x 42"	EA	$114.18	$255.00	$369.18	**$496.68**	1.500
Wall, diagonal corner, 27" x 27" x 30"	EA	$133.21	$182.00	$315.21	**$440.86**	1.750
Wall, diagonal corner, 27" x 27" x 36"	EA	$133.21	$238.00	$371.21	**$508.06**	1.750
Wall, diagonal corner, 27" x 27" x 42"	EA	$133.21	$276.00	$409.21	**$553.66**	1.750
WALL ISLAND, 2 FACED, 2 DOORS EACH SIDE, ECONOMY						
Wall, 2 faced, 30" x 30", 2 doors each side	EA	$114.18	$366.00	$480.18	**$629.88**	1.500

Cabinets and Countertops

Specialty Kitchen Cabinet, ECONOMY

> Painted hardwood frames, thermofoil surface on drawers and doors.

Description	Unit	Direct Labor	Direct Materials	Direct Total	Selling Price	Man-hours
PANTRY, 2 DOOR, OVER/UNDER, ECONOMY						
Pantry, 18" x 84" - 12" deep, 2 door, over/under	EA	$114.18	$330.00	$444.18	**$586.68**	1.500
Pantry, 18" x 90" - 12" deep, 2 door, over/under	EA	$114.18	$354.00	$468.18	**$615.48**	1.500
Pantry, 18" x 96" - 12" deep, 2 door, over/under	EA	$114.18	$367.00	$481.18	**$631.08**	1.500
Pantry, 18" x 84" - 24" deep, 2 door, over/under	EA	$114.18	$368.00	$482.18	**$632.28**	1.500
Pantry, 18" x 90" - 24" deep, 2 door, over/under	EA	$114.18	$384.00	$498.18	**$651.48**	1.500
Pantry, 18" x 96" - 24" deep, 2 door, over/under	EA	$114.18	$395.00	$509.18	**$664.68**	1.500
PANTRY, 4 DOOR, OVER/UNDER, ECONOMY						
Pantry, 24" x 84" - 12" deep, 4 door, over/under	EA	$114.18	$421.00	$535.18	**$695.88**	1.500
Pantry, 24" x 90" - 12" deep, 4 door, over/under	EA	$114.18	$419.00	$533.18	**$693.48**	1.500
Pantry, 24" x 96" - 12" deep, 4 door, over/under	EA	$114.18	$463.00	$577.18	**$746.28**	1.500
Pantry, 24" x 84" - 24" deep, 4 door, over/under	EA	$114.18	$454.00	$568.18	**$735.48**	1.500
Pantry, 24" x 90" - 24" deep, 4 door, over/under	EA	$114.18	$483.00	$597.18	**$770.28**	1.500
Pantry, 24" x 96" - 24" deep, 4 door, over/under	EA	$114.18	$498.00	$612.18	**$788.28**	1.500
OVEN CABINET, ECONOMY						
Oven cabinet, 30" x 84" - 24" deep	EA	$114.18	$536.00	$650.18	**$833.88**	1.500
Oven cabinet, 33" x 84" - 24" deep	EA	$114.18	$559.00	$673.18	**$861.48**	1.500
Oven cabinet, 30" x 90" - 24" deep	EA	$114.18	$598.00	$712.18	**$908.28**	1.500
Oven cabinet, 33" x 90" - 24" deep	EA	$114.18	$623.00	$737.18	**$938.28**	1.500
Oven cabinet, 30" x 96" - 24" deep	EA	$114.18	$637.00	$751.18	**$955.08**	1.500
Oven cabinet, 33" x 96" - 24" deep	EA	$114.18	$664.00	$778.18	**$987.48**	1.500

Cabinets and Countertops

Countertop Removal

> Does not include cost of countertop.

Description	Unit	Direct Labor	Direct Materials	Direct Total	Selling Price	Man-hours
Remove laminate countertop, no disconnect included	LF	$5.25		$5.25	**$8.77**	0.069
Remove solid surface countertop, no disconnect included	LF	$10.43		$10.43	**$17.42**	0.137
Remove stone countertop, no disconnect included	LF	$13.09		$13.09	**$21.86**	0.172
Remove tile countertop, no disconnect included	LF	$7.23		$7.23	**$12.08**	0.095

Laminate Countertops

Description	Unit	Direct Labor	Direct Materials	Direct Total	Selling Price	Man-hours
Install laminate countertop, post formed, 25" deep, 4" splash, economy	LF	$17.66	$27.50	$45.16	**$62.49**	0.232
Install laminate countertop, post formed, 25" deep, 4" splash, average	LF	$17.66	$34.10	$51.76	**$70.41**	0.232
Install laminate countertop, post formed, 25" deep, 4" splash, premium	LF	$17.66	$41.80	$59.46	**$79.65**	0.232
Install laminate countertop, double roll top, 25" deep, economy	LF	$15.22	$39.60	$54.82	**$72.94**	0.200
Install laminate countertop, double roll top, 25" deep, average	LF	$15.22	$44.00	$59.22	**$78.22**	0.200
Install laminate countertop, double roll top, 25" deep, premium	LF	$15.22	$52.80	$68.02	**$88.78**	0.200
Install laminate countertop, double roll top, 36" deep, economy	LF	$15.22	$48.40	$63.62	**$83.50**	0.200
Install laminate countertop, double roll top, 36" deep, average	LF	$15.22	$56.10	$71.32	**$92.74**	0.200
Install laminate countertop, double roll top, 36" deep, premium	LF	$15.22	$66.00	$81.22	**$104.62**	0.200
Install laminate countertop, post formed, square edge, 25" deep, 4" backsplash, economy	LF	$17.66	$35.20	$52.86	**$71.73**	0.232
Install laminate countertop, post formed, square edge, 25" deep, 4" backsplash, average	LF	$17.66	$41.80	$59.46	**$79.65**	0.232
Install laminate countertop, post formed, square edge, 25" deep, 4" backsplash, premium	LF	$17.66	$47.30	$64.96	**$86.25**	0.232

Solid Surface Countertops

Description	Unit	Direct Labor	Direct Materials	Direct Total	Selling Price	Man-hours
Install solid surface countertop, no backsplash, 25" deep, economy	LF	$29.61	$138.60	$168.21	**$215.77**	0.389
Install solid surface countertop, no backsplash, 25" deep, average	LF	$29.61	$162.80	$192.41	**$244.81**	0.389
Install solid surface countertop, no backsplash, 25" deep, premium	LF	$29.61	$189.20	$218.81	**$276.49**	0.389
Install solid surface backsplash, economy	LF	$9.90	$26.40	$36.30	**$48.21**	0.130
Install solid surface backsplash, average	LF	$9.90	$30.80	$40.70	**$53.49**	0.130
Install solid surface backsplash, premium	LF	$9.90	$36.30	$46.20	**$60.09**	0.130
Install solid surface countertop, integral backsplash, 25" deep, economy	LF	$29.61	$164.07	$193.68	**$246.33**	0.389
Install solid surface countertop, integral backsplash, 25" deep, average	LF	$29.61	$193.60	$223.21	**$281.77**	0.389
Install solid surface countertop, integral backsplash, 25" deep, premium	LF	$29.61	$225.50	$255.11	**$320.05**	0.389

Cabinets and Countertops

Granite and Marble Countertops

Description	Unit	Direct Labor	Direct Materials	Direct Total	Selling Price	Man-hours
Install granite countertop, average	SF	$39.51	$81.40	$120.91	**$163.65**	0.519
Install granite countertop, premium	SF	$39.51	$116.60	$156.11	**$205.89**	0.519
Install marble countertop, average	SF	$39.51	$74.80	$114.31	**$155.73**	0.519
Install marble countertop, premium	SF	$39.51	$108.90	$148.41	**$196.65**	0.519

Ceramic Countertops

Description	Unit	Direct Labor	Direct Materials	Direct Total	Selling Price	Man-hours
Ceramic tile countertop, at $2 SF material cost for tile	SF	$14.86	$5.78	$20.64	**$34.47**	0.377
Ceramic tile countertop, at $3 SF material cost for tile	SF	$14.86	$8.89	$23.75	**$39.66**	0.377
Ceramic tile countertop, at $4 SF material cost for tile	SF	$14.86	$11.54	$26.40	**$44.09**	0.377
Ceramic tile countertop, at $5 SF material cost for tile	SF	$14.86	$14.11	$28.97	**$48.38**	0.377
Ceramic tile countertop, at $6 SF material cost for tile	SF	$16.24	$17.54	$33.78	**$56.41**	0.412
Ceramic tile countertop, at $8 SF material cost for tile	SF	$16.24	$22.32	$38.56	**$64.40**	0.412
Ceramic tile countertop, at $10 SF material cost for tile	SF	$16.24	$27.54	$43.78	**$73.11**	0.412
Ceramic tile countertop, at $12 SF material cost for tile	SF	$16.24	$33.24	$49.48	**$82.63**	0.412

Cabinets and Countertops

Vanity

Description	Unit	Direct Labor	Direct Materials	Direct Total	Selling Price	Man-hours
Vanity, 20" x 16", 1 door, premium	EA	$57.09	$363.00	$420.09	**$530.94**	0.750
Vanity, 20" x 16", 1 door, average	EA	$57.09	$231.00	$288.09	**$372.54**	0.750
Vanity, 20" x 16", 1 door, economy	EA	$57.09	$143.00	$200.09	**$266.94**	0.750
Vanity, corner, 22" x 22", 1 door, premium	EA	$57.09	$396.00	$453.09	**$570.54**	0.750
Vanity, corner, 22" x 22", 1 door, average	EA	$57.09	$264.00	$321.09	**$412.14**	0.750
Vanity, corner, 22" x 22", 1 door, economy	EA	$57.09	$176.00	$233.09	**$306.54**	0.750
Vanity, 25" x 19", 1 door, premium	EA	$57.09	$418.00	$475.09	**$596.94**	0.750
Vanity, 25" x 19", 1 door, average	EA	$57.09	$286.00	$343.09	**$438.54**	0.750
Vanity, 25" x 19", 1 door, economy	EA	$57.09	$187.00	$244.09	**$319.74**	0.750
Vanity, 31" x 19", 2 door, premium	EA	$57.09	$462.00	$519.09	**$649.74**	0.750
Vanity, 31" x 19", 2 door, average	EA	$57.09	$308.00	$365.09	**$464.94**	0.750
Vanity, 31" x 19", 2 door, economy	EA	$57.09	$209.00	$266.09	**$346.14**	0.750
Vanity, 35" x 19", 2 door, premium	EA	$57.09	$495.00	$552.09	**$689.34**	0.750
Vanity, 35" x 19", 2 door, average	EA	$57.09	$352.00	$409.09	**$517.74**	0.750
Vanity, 35" x 19", 2 door, economy	EA	$57.09	$231.00	$288.09	**$372.54**	0.750
Vanity, 37" x 19", 2 door, 3 drawer, premium	EA	$57.09	$550.00	$607.09	**$755.34**	0.750
Vanity, 37" x 19", 2 door, 3 drawer, average	EA	$57.09	$440.00	$497.09	**$623.34**	0.750
Vanity, 37" x 19", 2 door, 3 drawer, economy	EA	$57.09	$286.00	$343.09	**$438.54**	0.750
Vanity, 49" x 19", 2 door, 3 drawer, premium	EA	$76.12	$638.00	$714.12	**$892.72**	1.000
Vanity, 49" x 19", 2 door, 3 drawer, average	EA	$76.12	$495.00	$571.12	**$721.12**	1.000
Vanity, 49" x 19", 2 door, 3 drawer, economy	EA	$76.12	$319.00	$395.12	**$509.92**	1.000
Vanity, 60" x 19", 2 door, 3 drawer, premium	EA	$76.12	$748.00	$824.12	**$1,024.72**	1.000
Vanity, 60" x 19", 2 door, 3 drawer, average	EA	$76.12	$583.00	$659.12	**$826.72**	1.000
Vanity, 60" x 19", 2 door, 3 drawer, economy	EA	$76.12	$363.00	$439.12	**$562.72**	1.000

Cabinets and Countertops

Vanity Top

Description	Unit	Direct Labor	Direct Materials	Direct Total	Selling Price	Man-hours
Cultured marble vanity top with integral sink, 25" x 19"	EA	$38.06	$110.00	$148.06	**$195.56**	0.500
Cultured marble vanity top with integral sink, 31" x 19"	EA	$38.06	$132.00	$170.06	**$221.96**	0.500
Cultured marble vanity top with integral sink, 35" x 19"	EA	$38.06	$154.00	$192.06	**$248.36**	0.500
Cultured marble vanity top with integral sink, 37" x 19"	EA	$38.06	$165.00	$203.06	**$261.56**	0.500
Laminate vanity top, 25" x 19"	EA	$38.06	$72.00	$110.06	**$149.96**	0.500
Laminate vanity top, 31" x 19"	EA	$38.06	$83.00	$121.06	**$163.16**	0.500
Laminate vanity top, 35" x 19"	EA	$38.06	$94.00	$132.06	**$176.36**	0.500
Laminate vanity top, 37" x 19"	EA	$38.06	$99.00	$137.06	**$182.36**	0.500
Laminate vanity top, 49" x 19"	EA	$57.09	$138.00	$195.09	**$260.94**	0.750
Laminate vanity top, 60" x 19"	EA	$57.09	$165.00	$222.09	**$293.34**	0.750
Granite vanity top, 25" x 19"	EA	$57.09	$264.00	$321.09	**$412.14**	0.750
Granite vanity top, 31" x 19"	EA	$57.09	$297.00	$354.09	**$451.74**	0.750
Granite vanity top, 35" x 19"	EA	$57.09	$330.00	$387.09	**$491.34**	0.750
Granite vanity top, 37" x 19"	EA	$57.09	$352.00	$409.09	**$517.74**	0.750
Granite vanity top, 49" x 19"	EA	$76.12	$396.00	$472.12	**$602.32**	1.000
Granite vanity top, 60" x 19"	EA	$76.12	$440.00	$516.12	**$655.12**	1.000
Solid surface vanity top, 25" x 19"	EA	$57.09	$303.00	$360.09	**$458.94**	0.750
Solid surface vanity top, 31" x 19"	EA	$57.09	$341.00	$398.09	**$504.54**	0.750
Solid surface vanity top, 35" x 19"	EA	$57.09	$380.00	$437.09	**$551.34**	0.750
Solid surface vanity top, 37" x 19"	EA	$57.09	$407.00	$464.09	**$583.74**	0.750
Solid surface vanity top, 49" x 19"	EA	$76.12	$457.00	$533.12	**$675.52**	1.000
Solid surface vanity top, 60" x 19"	EA	$76.12	$506.00	$582.12	**$734.32**	1.000

Cabinets and Countertops

Medicine Cabinets

Description	Unit	Direct Labor	Direct Materials	Direct Total	Selling Price	Man-hours
LABOR COSTS TO REMOVE MEDICINE CABINET						
Remove medicine cabinet, flush mount	EA	$19.03		$19.03	**$31.78**	0.250
Remove medicine cabinet, recessed	EA	$38.06		$38.06	**$63.56**	0.500
MEDICINE CABINETS, RECESSED						
Install white finish recessed medicine cabinets, 14 x 18	EA	$57.09	$66.00	$123.09	**$205.56**	0.750
Install white finish recessed medicine cabinets, 14 x 24	EA	$57.09	$77.00	$134.09	**$223.93**	0.750
Install stainless steel recessed medicine cabinets, 14 x 18	EA	$57.09	$83.00	$140.09	**$233.95**	0.750
Install stainless steel recessed medicine cabinets, 14 x 24	EA	$57.09	$94.00	$151.09	**$252.32**	0.750
Install polished brass recessed medicine cabinets, 14 x 18	EA	$57.09	$77.00	$134.09	**$223.93**	0.750
Install polished brass recessed medicine cabinets, 14 x 24	EA	$57.09	$88.00	$145.09	**$242.30**	0.750
Install frameless beveled mirror recessed medicine cabinets, 14 x 18	EA	$57.09	$94.00	$151.09	**$252.32**	0.750
Install frameless beveled mirror recessed medicine cabinets, 14 x 24	EA	$57.09	$105.00	$162.09	**$270.69**	0.750
Install natural oak recessed medicine cabinets, 14 x 18	EA	$57.09	$138.00	$195.09	**$325.80**	0.750
Install natural oak recessed medicine cabinets, 14 x 24	EA	$57.09	$160.00	$217.09	**$362.54**	0.750
MEDICINE CABINETS, SURFACE MOUNT						
Install swing door surface mount medicine cabinet 16 x 22	EA	$76.12	$61.00	$137.12	**$228.99**	1.000
Install swing door surface mount medicine cabinet 16 x 26	EA	$76.12	$77.00	$153.12	**$255.71**	1.000
Install sliding mirror, lighted stainless steel, surface mount medicine cabinet 24 x 16	EA	$76.12	$127.00	$203.12	**$339.21**	1.000
Install sliding mirror, lighted stainless steel, surface mount medicine cabinet 24 x 20	EA	$76.12	$154.00	$230.12	**$384.30**	1.000
Install sliding mirror, lighted stainless steel, surface mount medicine cabinet 28 x 20	EA	$95.15	$171.00	$266.15	**$444.47**	1.250
Install sliding mirror, lighted stainless steel, surface mount medicine cabinet 28 x 23	EA	$95.15	$193.00	$288.15	**$481.21**	1.250

Floor Covering

Labor To Install Flooring

> Labor costs do not include flooring material. Select flooring from 'Flooring' sections.

Description	Unit	Direct Labor	Direct Materials	Direct Total	Selling Price	Man-hours
LABOR TO INSTALL WOOD FLOORING						
Install unfinished solid wood strip flooring, up to 3" wide, no finishing	SF	$6.17		$6.17	**$10.30**	0.081
Install unfinished solid wood strip flooring, 3" to 5" wide, no finishing	SF	$4.57		$4.57	**$7.63**	0.060
Install unfinished solid wood strip flooring, 5" to 7" wide, no finishing	SF	$3.58		$3.58	**$5.97**	0.047
Install unfinished solid wood strip flooring, 7" to 10" wide, no finishing	SF	$3.12		$3.12	**$5.21**	0.041
Install prefinished solid wood strip flooring, up to 3" wide	SF	$6.93		$6.93	**$11.57**	0.091
Install prefinished solid wood strip flooring, 3" to 5" wide	SF	$5.33		$5.33	**$8.90**	0.070
Install prefinished solid wood strip flooring, 5" to 7" wide	SF	$4.34		$4.34	**$7.25**	0.057
Install prefinished solid wood strip flooring, 7" to 10" wide	SF	$3.81		$3.81	**$6.36**	0.050
Install unfinished wood flooring block (parquet), glued, no finishing	SF	$3.96		$3.96	**$6.61**	0.052
Install prefinished wood flooring block (parquet), glued	SF	$4.41		$4.41	**$7.37**	0.058
LABOR TO INSTALL LAMINATE AND ENGINEERED FLOORING						
Install laminate or engineered flooring, glued	SF	$3.12		$3.12	**$5.21**	0.041
Install laminate or engineered flooring, nailed	SF	$3.12		$3.12	**$5.21**	0.041
Install laminate or engineered flooring, float/interlock	SF	$2.36		$2.36	**$3.94**	0.031
LABOR TO INSTALL RESILIENT FLOORING						
Install resilient tile flooring on concrete floor	SF	$1.67		$1.67	**$2.80**	0.022
Install resilient tile flooring on wood floor	SF	$1.98		$1.98	**$3.31**	0.026
Install resilient sheet flooring on concrete floor	SY	$22.23		$22.23	**$37.12**	0.292
Install resilient sheet flooring on wood floor	SY	$25.35		$25.35	**$42.33**	0.333

Floor Covering

Labor To Install Flooring (continued)

> Labor costs do not include flooring material. Select flooring from 'Flooring' sections.

Description	Unit	Direct Labor	Direct Materials	Direct Total	Selling Price	Man-hours
LABOR TO INSTALL CERAMIC TILE FLOORING						
Install small (up to 1-12") back mount ceramic tile floor, in adhesive, grout and seal	SF	$6.07	$1.78	$7.85	**$13.11**	0.154
Install medium (up to 4-1/4") back mount ceramic tile floor, in adhesive, grout and seal	SF	$5.60	$1.78	$7.38	**$12.32**	0.142
Install small (up to 1-12") back mount ceramic tile floor, thin-set, grout and seal	SF	$7.65	$1.78	$9.43	**$15.74**	0.194
Install medium (up to 4-1/4") back mount ceramic tile floor, thin-set, grout and seal	SF	$6.94	$1.78	$8.72	**$14.56**	0.176
Install small (up to 1-12") back mount ceramic tile floor, mortar, grout and seal	SF	$11.00	$1.10	$12.10	**$20.20**	0.279
Install medium (up to 4-1/4") back mount ceramic tile floor, mortar, grout and seal	SF	$9.42	$1.10	$10.52	**$17.57**	0.239
Install 6 x 6 ceramic tile floor, in adhesive, grout and seal	SF	$7.02	$1.78	$8.80	**$14.69**	0.178
Install 9 x 9 ceramic tile floor, in adhesive, grout and seal	SF	$5.95	$1.78	$7.73	**$12.91**	0.151
Install 12 x 12 ceramic tile floor, in adhesive, grout and seal	SF	$5.24	$1.78	$7.02	**$11.73**	0.133
Install 6 x 6 ceramic tile floor, thin-set, grout and seal	SF	$9.58	$1.78	$11.36	**$18.97**	0.243
Install 9 x 9 ceramic tile floor, thin-set, grout and seal	SF	$8.16	$1.78	$9.94	**$16.60**	0.207
Install 12 x 12 ceramic tile floor, thin-set, grout and seal	SF	$6.11	$1.78	$7.89	**$13.18**	0.155
Install 6 x 6 ceramic tile floor, mortar, grout and seal	SF	$13.72	$1.10	$14.82	**$24.75**	0.348
Install 9 x 9 ceramic tile floor, mortar, grout and seal	SF	$11.67	$1.10	$12.77	**$21.32**	0.296
Install 12 x 12 ceramic tile floor, mortar, grout and seal	SF	$8.75	$1.10	$9.85	**$16.45**	0.222
LABOR TO INSTALL MARBLE, GRANITE AND STONE FLOORING						
Install 6 x 6 marble, granite, stone floor, thin-set, grout and seal	SF	$10.52	$1.78	$12.30	**$20.55**	0.267
Install 9 x 9 marble, granite, stone floor, thin-set, grout and seal	SF	$8.95	$1.78	$10.73	**$17.92**	0.227
Install 12 x 12 marble, granite, stone floor, thin-set, grout and seal	SF	$6.70	$1.78	$8.48	**$14.16**	0.170
Install 6 x 6 marble, granite, stone floor, mortar, grout and seal	SF	$15.10	$1.10	$16.20	**$27.05**	0.383
Install 9 x 9 marble, granite, stone floor, mortar, grout and seal	SF	$12.85	$1.10	$13.95	**$23.30**	0.326
Install 12 x 12 marble, granite, stone floor, thin-set, grout and seal	SF	$9.62	$1.10	$10.72	**$17.90**	0.244
LABOR TO INSTALL CARPET						
Install carpet and pad, includes tack strips, hot seams	SY	$15.53		$15.53	**$25.93**	0.204
Add for waterfall (box steps) stairways	Step	$9.90		$9.90	**$16.53**	0.130
Add for wrapped (open riser) stairways	Step	$19.71		$19.71	**$32.92**	0.259

Floor Covering

Labor To Remove Flooring

Description	Unit	Direct Labor	Direct Materials	Direct Total	Selling Price	Man-hours
LABOR TO REMOVE FLOORING, WOOD						
Remove solid wood strip flooring, nailed	SF	$1.22		$1.22	**$2.03**	0.030
Remove solid wood strip flooring, glued	SF	$1.66		$1.66	**$2.77**	0.041
Remove solid wood flooring block (parquet), glued	SF	$1.34		$1.34	**$2.23**	0.033
Remove molding or trim for wood flooring	LF	$0.41		$0.41	**$0.68**	0.010
LABOR TO REMOVE FLOORING, CERAMIC TILE						
Demolish ceramic tile floor, set in thin-set, over wood	SF	$2.31		$2.31	**$3.86**	0.057
Demolish ceramic tile floor, set in thin-set, over concrete	SF	$3.20		$3.20	**$5.34**	0.079
Demolish ceramic tile floor, set in mortar, over wood	SF	$3.04		$3.04	**$5.07**	0.075
Demolish ceramic tile floor, set in mortar, over concrete	SF	$3.61		$3.61	**$6.02**	0.089
LABOR TO REMOVE FLOORING, MARBLE, GRANITE, STONE						
Demolish marble, granite, stone floor, set in thin-set, over wood	SF	$2.63		$2.63	**$4.40**	0.065
Demolish marble, granite, stone floor, set in thin-set, over concrete	SF	$3.69		$3.69	**$6.16**	0.091
Demolish marble, granite, stone floor, set in mortar, over wood	SF	$3.48		$3.48	**$5.82**	0.086
Demolish marble, granite, stone floor, set in mortar, over concrete	SF	$4.17		$4.17	**$6.97**	0.103
LABOR TO REMOVE FLOORING, RESILIENT						
Remove resilient sheet flooring, adhesive set	SY	$6.56		$6.56	**$10.96**	0.162
Remove resilient tile flooring, adhesive set	SF	$0.81		$0.81	**$1.35**	0.020
Remove cove base molding	LF	$0.28		$0.28	**$0.47**	0.007
LABOR TO REMOVE FLOORING, CARPET						
Remove carpet, tack strips, padding	SY	$7.41		$7.41	**$12.38**	0.183
Remove adhesive set carpet	SY	$5.91		$5.91	**$9.88**	0.146
LABOR TO REMOVE FLOORING, FLOOR SHEATHING						
Demolish subfloor, 1" x 8" strips, laid straight	SF	$0.93		$0.93	**$1.56**	0.023
Demolish subfloor, 1" x 8" strips, laid diagonally	SF	$1.05		$1.05	**$1.76**	0.026
Demolish subfloor, 5/8" plywood sheathing, nailed only	SF	$0.65		$0.65	**$1.08**	0.016
Demolish subfloor, 5/8" plywood sheathing, nailed & glued	SF	$0.81		$0.81	**$1.35**	0.020
Demolish subfloor, 3/4" plywood sheathing, nailed only	SF	$0.69		$0.69	**$1.15**	0.017
Demolish subfloor, 3/4" plywood sheathing, nailed & glued	SF	$0.85		$0.85	**$1.42**	0.021
Demolish subfloor, 1-1/8" plywood sheathing, nailed only	SF	$0.93		$0.93	**$1.56**	0.023
Demolish subfloor, 1-1/8" plywood sheathing, nailed & glued	SF	$1.09		$1.09	**$1.83**	0.027
Demolish subfloor, 0.215" hardboard underlayment, nailed only	SF	$0.49		$0.49	**$0.81**	0.012
Demolish subfloor, 0.215" hardboard underlayment, nailed & glued	SF	$0.65		$0.65	**$1.08**	0.016

Floor Covering

Subfloor, Underlayment, Barriers

Description	Unit	Direct Labor	Direct Materials	Direct Total	Selling Price	Man-hours
SUBFLOOR, PLYWOOD						
Install plywood subfloor, 3/8"	SF	$1.22	$0.52	$1.74	**$2.90**	0.016
Install plywood subfloor, 1/2"	SF	$1.22	$0.58	$1.80	**$3.01**	0.016
Install plywood subfloor, 5/8"	SF	$1.29	$0.78	$2.07	**$3.46**	0.017
Install plywood subfloor, 3/4"	SF	$1.37	$0.98	$2.35	**$3.93**	0.018
Install plywood subfloor, 1-1/8"	SF	$1.37	$1.21	$2.58	**$4.30**	0.018
SUBFLOOR, ORIENTED STRAND BOARD (OSB)						
Install oriented strand board subfloor, 3/8"	SF	$1.22	$0.45	$1.67	**$2.79**	0.016
Install oriented strand board subfloor, 1/2"	SF	$1.22	$0.54	$1.76	**$2.93**	0.016
Install oriented strand board subfloor, 5/8"	SF	$1.29	$0.69	$1.98	**$3.31**	0.017
Install oriented strand board subfloor, 3/4"	SF	$1.37	$0.84	$2.21	**$3.69**	0.018
SUBFLOOR, TONGUE AND GROOVE PLYWOOD						
Install tongue and groove plywood subfloor, 5/8"	SF	$1.52	$0.95	$2.47	**$4.13**	0.020
Install tongue and groove plywood subfloor, 3/4"	SF	$1.60	$1.18	$2.77	**$4.63**	0.021
Install tongue and groove OSB subfloor, 5/8"	SF	$1.67	$0.80	$2.47	**$4.13**	0.022
Install tongue and groove OSB subfloor, 3/4"	SF	$1.75	$1.00	$2.75	**$4.60**	0.023
SUBFLOOR, STRIP						
Install strip subfloor, straight, 1" x 6" or 1" x 8"	SF	$2.06	$1.15	$3.20	**$5.35**	0.027
Install strip subfloor, diagonal, 1" x 6" or 1" x 8"	SF	$2.36	$1.45	$3.81	**$6.37**	0.031
UNDERLAYMENT						
Install cork underlayment, 1/8"	SF	$0.99	$0.61	$1.59	**$2.66**	0.013
Install cork underlayment, 1/4"	SF	$0.99	$1.33	$2.32	**$3.88**	0.013
Install cork underlayment, 1/2"	SF	$0.99	$2.84	$3.83	**$6.40**	0.013
Install hardboard underlayment, 0.215"	SF	$0.99	$0.54	$1.53	**$2.56**	0.013
Install underlayment, 15 lb asphalt felt	SF	$0.30	$0.08	$0.39	**$0.65**	0.004
VAPOR BARRIER						
Install vapor barrier, 8 mil poly	SF	$0.23	$0.10	$0.33	**$0.54**	0.003
CEMENT BOARD						
Install cement board/wonderboard/durock, 1/2"	SF	$3.73	$1.62	$5.35	**$8.94**	0.049

Floor Covering

Wood Floor Finishing

Description	Unit	Direct Labor	Direct Materials	Direct Total	Selling Price	Man-hours
WOOD FLOOR FINISHING						
Machine sand, fill and clear finish, new wood floor	SF	$1.67	$0.33	$2.00	**$3.34**	0.030
Machine sand, fill, stain and clear finish, new wood floor	SF	$2.28	$0.55	$2.83	**$4.73**	0.041
Machine sand, fill and clear finish, old/damaged wood floor	SF	$2.00	$0.33	$2.33	**$3.90**	0.036
Machine sand, fill, stain and clear finish, old/damaged wood floor	SF	$2.62	$0.55	$3.17	**$5.29**	0.047
Machine sand, fill and clear finish, new wood stairs	SF	$2.95	$0.44	$3.39	**$5.66**	0.053
Machine sand, fill, stain and clear finish, new wood stairs	SF	$4.01	$0.72	$4.72	**$7.89**	0.072
Machine sand, fill and clear finish, old/damaged wood stairs	SF	$3.56	$0.44	$4.00	**$6.69**	0.064
Machine sand, fill, stain and clear finish, old/damaged wood stairs	SF	$4.57	$0.72	$5.28	**$8.82**	0.082
Fill wood floor	SF	$0.33	$0.06	$0.39	**$0.65**	0.006
Machine sand wood floor, 3 passes	SF	$1.06	$0.11	$1.17	**$1.95**	0.019
Apply 2 coats of urethane to wood floor	SF	$0.67	$0.22	$0.89	**$1.48**	0.012
Apply 2 coats of lacquer to wood floor	SF	$1.00	$0.33	$1.33	**$2.23**	0.018
Apply 2 coats of stain/sealer to wood floors	SF	$0.67	$0.22	$0.89	**$1.48**	0.012

Floor Covering

Unfinished Wood Flooring, Red Oak

> Does not include old flooring removal or floor finishing.

Description	Unit	Direct Labor	Direct Materials	Direct Total	Selling Price	Man-hours
Red oak tongue & groove, clear, 3/4 x 2-1/4, unfinished, $6.30 SF	SF	$6.17	$7.25	$13.41	**$22.40**	0.081
Red oak tongue & groove, select, 3/4 x 2-1/4, unfinished, $5.20 SF	SF	$6.17	$5.98	$12.15	**$20.28**	0.081
Red oak tongue & groove, #1 common, 3/4 x 2-1/4, unfinished, $4.40 SF	SF	$6.17	$5.06	$11.23	**$18.75**	0.081
Red oak plank flooring, clear, 3/4 x 3, unfinished, $6.40 SF	SF	$6.17	$7.36	$13.53	**$22.59**	0.081
Red oak plank flooring, select, 3/4 x 3, unfinished, $6.00 SF	SF	$6.17	$6.90	$13.07	**$21.82**	0.081
Red oak plank flooring, #1 common, 3/4 x 3, unfinished, $4.90 SF	SF	$6.17	$5.64	$11.80	**$19.71**	0.081
Red oak plank flooring, clear, 3/4 x 4, unfinished, $6.40 SF	SF	$4.57	$7.36	$11.93	**$19.92**	0.060
Red oak plank flooring, select, 3/4 x 4, unfinished, $6.10 SF	SF	$4.57	$7.02	$11.58	**$19.34**	0.060
Red oak plank flooring, #1 common, 3/4 x 4, unfinished, $5.00 SF	SF	$4.57	$5.75	$10.32	**$17.23**	0.060
Red oak plank flooring, clear, 3/4 x 5, unfinished, $6.80 SF	SF	$4.57	$7.82	$12.39	**$20.69**	0.060
Red oak plank flooring, select, 3/4 x 5, unfinished, $6.40 SF	SF	$4.57	$7.36	$11.93	**$19.92**	0.060
Red oak plank flooring, #1 common, 3/4 x 5, unfinished, $6.00 SF	SF	$4.57	$6.90	$11.47	**$19.15**	0.060
Red oak plank flooring, clear, 3/4 x 6, unfinished, $7.20 SF	SF	$3.58	$8.28	$11.86	**$19.80**	0.047
Red oak plank flooring, select, 3/4 x 6, unfinished, $6.60 SF	SF	$3.58	$7.59	$11.17	**$18.65**	0.047
Red oak plank flooring, #1 common, 3/4 x 6, unfinished, $6.30 SF	SF	$3.58	$7.25	$10.82	**$18.07**	0.047

Unfinished Wood Flooring, White Oak

> Does not include old flooring removal or floor finishing.

Description	Unit	Direct Labor	Direct Materials	Direct Total	Selling Price	Man-hours
White oak tongue & groove, clear, 3/4 x 2-1/4, unfinished, $5.60 SF	SF	$6.17	$6.44	$12.61	**$21.05**	0.081
White oak tongue & groove, select, 3/4 x 2-1/4, unfinished, $4.80 SF	SF	$6.17	$5.52	$11.69	**$19.51**	0.081
White oak tongue/groove, #1 common, 3/4 x 2-1/4, unfinished, $4.20 SF	SF	$6.17	$4.83	$11.00	**$18.36**	0.081
White oak plank flooring, clear, 3/4 x 3, unfinished, $5.80 SF	SF	$6.17	$6.67	$12.84	**$21.44**	0.081
White oak plank flooring, select, 3/4 x 3, unfinished, $5.00 SF	SF	$6.17	$5.75	$11.92	**$19.90**	0.081
White oak plank flooring, #1 common, 3/4 x 3, unfinished, $4.60 SF	SF	$6.17	$5.29	$11.46	**$19.13**	0.081
White oak plank flooring, clear, 3/4 x 4, unfinished, $5.90 SF	SF	$4.57	$6.79	$11.35	**$18.96**	0.060
White oak plank flooring, select, 3/4 x 4, unfinished, $5.10 SF	SF	$4.57	$5.87	$10.43	**$17.42**	0.060
White oak plank flooring, #1 common, 3/4 x 4, unfinished, $4.80 SF	SF	$4.57	$5.52	$10.09	**$16.85**	0.060
White oak plank flooring, clear, 3/4 x 5, unfinished, $6.40 SF	SF	$4.57	$7.36	$11.93	**$19.92**	0.060
White oak plank flooring, select, 3/4 x 5, unfinished, $5.30 SF	SF	$4.57	$6.10	$10.66	**$17.81**	0.060
White oak plank flooring, #1 common, 3/4 x 5, unfinished, $4.80 SF	SF	$4.57	$5.52	$10.09	**$16.85**	0.060
White oak plank flooring, clear, 3/4 x 6, unfinished, $7.00 SF	SF	$3.58	$8.05	$11.63	**$19.42**	0.047
White oak plank flooring, select, 3/4 x 6, unfinished, $6.10 SF	SF	$3.58	$7.02	$10.59	**$17.69**	0.047
White oak plank flooring, #1 common, 3/4 x 6, unfinished, $5.50 SF	SF	$3.58	$6.33	$9.90	**$16.54**	0.047

Floor Covering

Unfinished Wood Flooring, Hard Maple

> Does not include old flooring removal or floor finishing.

Description	Unit	Direct Labor	Direct Materials	Direct Total	Selling Price	Man-hours
Hard maple tongue & groove, clear, 3/4 x 2-1/4, unfinished, $6.20 SF	SF	$6.17	$7.13	$13.30	**$22.20**	0.081
Hard maple tongue & groove, select, 3/4 x 2-1/4, unfinished, $5.50 SF	SF	$6.17	$6.33	$12.49	**$20.86**	0.081
Hard mapleT&G, #1 common, 3/4x 2-1/4, unfinished, $4.60SF	SF	$6.17	$5.29	$11.46	**$19.13**	0.081
Hard maple plank flooring, clear, 3/4 x 3, unfinished, $6.40 SF	SF	$6.17	$7.36	$13.53	**$22.59**	0.081
Hard maple plank flooring, select, 3/4 x 3, unfinished, $5.70 SF	SF	$6.17	$6.55	$12.72	**$21.24**	0.081
Hard maple plank flooring, #1 common, 3/4 x 3, unfinished, $4.80 SF	SF	$6.17	$5.52	$11.69	**$19.51**	0.081
Hard maple plank flooring, clear, 3/4 x 4, unfinished, $7.00 SF	SF	$4.57	$8.05	$12.62	**$21.07**	0.060
Hard maple plank flooring, select, 3/4 x 4, unfinished, $5.90 SF	SF	$4.57	$6.79	$11.35	**$18.96**	0.060
Hard maple plank flooring, #1 common, 3/4 x 4, unfinished, $5.10 SF	SF	$4.57	$5.87	$10.43	**$17.42**	0.060
Hard maple plank flooring, clear, 3/4 x 5, unfinished, $7.70 SF	SF	$4.57	$8.86	$13.42	**$22.41**	0.060
Hard maple plank flooring, select, 3/4 x 5, unfinished, $5.80 SF	SF	$4.57	$6.67	$11.24	**$18.77**	0.060
Hard maple plank flooring, #1 common, 3/4 x 5, unfinished, $5.20 SF	SF	$4.57	$5.98	$10.55	**$17.61**	0.060
Hard maple plank flooring, clear, 3/4 x 6, unfinished, $9.00 SF	SF	$3.58	$10.35	$13.93	**$23.26**	0.047
Hard maple plank flooring, select, 3/4 x 6, unfinished, $7.00 SF	SF	$3.58	$8.05	$11.63	**$19.42**	0.047
Hard maple plank flooring, #1 common, 3/4 x 6, unfinished, $5.80 SF	SF	$3.58	$6.67	$10.25	**$17.11**	0.047

Unfinished Wood Flooring, Hickory

> Does not include old flooring removal or floor finishing.

Description	Unit	Direct Labor	Direct Materials	Direct Total	Selling Price	Man-hours
Hickory tongue & groove, clear, 3/4 x 2-1/4, unfinished, $6.90 SF	SF	$6.17	$7.94	$14.10	**$23.55**	0.081
Hickory tongue & groove, select, 3/4 x 2-1/4, unfinished, $5.70 SF	SF	$6.17	$6.56	$12.72	**$21.24**	0.081
Hickory T&G, #1 common, 3/4 x 2-1/4, unfinished, $4.80 SF	SF	$6.17	$5.52	$11.69	**$19.52**	0.081
Hickory plank flooring, clear, 3/4 x 3, unfinished, $7.00 SF	SF	$6.17	$8.05	$14.22	**$23.74**	0.081
Hickory plank flooring, select, 3/4 x 3, unfinished, $6.60 SF	SF	$6.17	$7.59	$13.76	**$22.97**	0.081
Hickory plank flooring, #1 common, 3/4 x 3, unfinished, $5.40 SF	SF	$6.17	$6.21	$12.38	**$20.67**	0.081
Hickory plank flooring, clear, 3/4 x 4, unfinished, $7.00 SF	SF	$4.57	$8.05	$12.62	**$21.07**	0.060
Hickory plank flooring, select, 3/4 x 4, unfinished, $6.70 SF	SF	$4.57	$7.71	$12.27	**$20.50**	0.060
Hickory plank flooring, #1 common, 3/4 x 4, unfinished, $5.50 SF	SF	$4.57	$6.33	$10.89	**$18.19**	0.060
Hickory plank flooring, clear, 3/4 x 5, unfinished, $7.50 SF	SF	$4.57	$8.63	$13.19	**$22.03**	0.060
Hickory plank flooring, select, 3/4 x 5, unfinished, $7.00 SF	SF	$4.57	$8.05	$12.62	**$21.07**	0.060
Hickory plank flooring, #1 common, 3/4 x 5, unfinished, $6.60 SF	SF	$4.57	$7.59	$12.16	**$20.30**	0.060
Hickory plank flooring, clear, 3/4 x 6, unfinished, $7.90 SF	SF	$3.58	$9.08	$12.66	**$21.14**	0.047
Hickory plank flooring, select, 3/4 x 6, unfinished, $7.30 SF	SF	$3.58	$8.40	$11.97	**$19.99**	0.047
Hickory plank flooring, #1 common, 3/4 x 6, unfinished, $7.00 SF	SF	$3.58	$8.05	$11.63	**$19.42**	0.047

Floor Covering

Unfinished Wood Flooring, Cherry

> Does not include old flooring removal or floor finishing.

Description	Unit	Direct Labor	Direct Materials	Direct Total	Selling Price	Man-hours
Cherry tongue & groove flooring, clear, 3/4 x 2-1/4, unfinished, $7.40 SF	SF	$6.17	$8.51	$14.68	**$24.51**	0.081
Cherry tongue & groove flooring, select, 3/4 x 2-1/4, unfinished, $5.40 SF	SF	$6.17	$6.21	$12.38	**$20.67**	0.081
Cherry tongue & groove, #1 common, 3/4 x 2-1/4, unfinished, $4.70 SF	SF	$6.17	$5.41	$11.57	**$19.32**	0.081
Cherry plank flooring, clear, 3/4 x 3, unfinished, $8.00 SF	SF	$6.17	$9.20	$15.37	**$25.66**	0.081
Cherry plank flooring, select, 3/4 x 3, unfinished, $6.40 SF	SF	$6.17	$7.36	$13.53	**$22.59**	0.081
Cherry plank flooring, #1 common, 3/4 x 3, unfinished, $5.80 SF	SF	$6.17	$6.67	$12.84	**$21.44**	0.081
Cherry plank flooring, clear, 3/4 x 4, unfinished, $8.70 SF	SF	$4.57	$10.01	$14.57	**$24.34**	0.060
Cherry plank flooring, select, 3/4 x 4, unfinished, $7.30 SF	SF	$4.57	$8.40	$12.96	**$21.65**	0.060
Cherry plank flooring, #1 common, 3/4 x 4, unfinished, $6.00 SF	SF	$4.57	$6.90	$11.47	**$19.15**	0.060
Cherry plank flooring, clear, 3/4 x 5, unfinished, $9.50 SF	SF	$4.57	$10.93	$15.49	**$25.87**	0.060
Cherry plank flooring, select, 3/4 x 5, unfinished, $7.60 SF	SF	$4.57	$8.74	$13.31	**$22.22**	0.060
Cherry plank flooring, #1 common, 3/4 x 5, unfinished, $6.50 SF	SF	$4.57	$7.48	$12.04	**$20.11**	0.060
Cherry plank flooring, clear, 3/4 x 6, unfinished, $10.40 SF	SF	$3.58	$11.96	$15.54	**$25.95**	0.047
Cherry plank flooring, select, 3/4 x 6, unfinished, $8.60 SF	SF	$3.58	$9.89	$13.47	**$22.49**	0.047
Cherry plank flooring, #1 common, 3/4 x 6, unfinished, $6.90 SF	SF	$3.58	$7.94	$11.51	**$19.23**	0.047

Unfinished Wood Flooring, White Pine

> Does not include old flooring removal or floor finishing.

Description	Unit	Direct Labor	Direct Materials	Direct Total	Selling Price	Man-hours
White pine plank flooring, 3/4 x 4, unfinished, $2.70 SF	SF	$4.57	$3.11	$7.67	**$12.81**	0.060
White pine plank flooring, 3/4 x 6, unfinished, $3.00 SF	SF	$3.58	$3.45	$7.03	**$11.74**	0.047
White pine plank flooring, 3/4 x 8, unfinished, $3.00 SF	SF	$3.12	$3.45	$6.57	**$10.97**	0.041
White pine plank flooring, 3/4 x 10, unfinished, $3.20 SF	SF	$3.12	$3.68	$6.80	**$11.36**	0.041
White pine plank flooring, 3/4 x 12, unfinished, $3.60 SF	SF	$3.12	$4.14	$7.26	**$12.13**	0.041

Unfinished Wood Flooring, Yellow Pine

> Does not include old flooring removal or floor finishing.

Description	Unit	Direct Labor	Direct Materials	Direct Total	Selling Price	Man-hours
Yellow pine plank flooring, 3/4 x 4, unfinished, $2.90 SF	SF	$4.57	$3.34	$7.90	**$13.20**	0.060
Yellow pine plank flooring, 3/4 x 6, unfinished, $3.00 SF	SF	$3.58	$3.45	$7.03	**$11.74**	0.047
Yellow pine plank flooring, 3/4 x 8, unfinished, $3.00 SF	SF	$3.12	$3.45	$6.57	**$10.97**	0.041
Yellow pine plank flooring, 3/4 x 10, unfinished, $3.30 SF	SF	$3.12	$3.80	$6.92	**$11.55**	0.041
Yellow pine plank flooring, 3/4 x 12, unfinished, $3.70 SF	SF	$3.12	$4.26	$7.38	**$12.32**	0.041

Floor Covering

Unfinished Wood Flooring, Heart Pine

> Does not include old flooring removal or floor finishing.

Description	Unit	Direct Labor	Direct Materials	Direct Total	Selling Price	Man hours
Heart pine plank flooring, 3/4 x 4, unfinished, $4.80 SF	SF	$4.57	$5.52	$10.09	**$16.85**	0.060
Heart pine plank flooring, 3/4 x 6, unfinished, $5.30 SF	SF	$3.58	$6.10	$9.67	**$16.15**	0.047
Heart pine plank flooring, 3/4 x 8, unfinished, $5.60 SF	SF	$3.12	$6.44	$9.56	**$15.97**	0.041
Heart pine plank flooring, 3/4 x 10, unfinished, $6.10 SF	SF	$3.12	$7.02	$10.14	**$16.93**	0.041
Heart pine plank flooring, 3/4 x 12, unfinished, $6.90 SF	SF	$3.12	$7.94	$11.06	**$18.46**	0.041

Unfinished Wood Flooring, Bamboo

> Does not include old flooring removal or floor finishing.

Description	Unit	Direct Labor	Direct Materials	Direct Total	Selling Price	Man hours
Bamboo plank flooring, 1/2 x 3-5/8, unfinished, $4.70 SF	SF	$4.57	$5.41	$9.97	**$16.65**	0.060
Bamboo plank flooring, 9/16 x 3-5/8, unfinished, $5.10 SF	SF	$4.57	$5.87	$10.43	**$17.42**	0.060

Unfinished Wood Flooring, Parquet, Blocks

> Does not include old flooring removal or floor finishing.

Description	Unit	Direct Labor	Direct Materials	Direct Total	Selling Price	Man hours
Oak flooring blocks (parquet), 5/16 x12 x 12, unfinished, $4.50 SF	SF	$3.96	$5.18	$9.14	**$15.26**	0.052
Teak flooring blocks (parquet), 5/16 x 12 x 12, unfinished, $5.70 SF	SF	$3.96	$6.56	$10.51	**$17.56**	0.052

Wood Floor Trim

Description	Unit	Direct Labor	Direct Materials	Direct Total	Selling Price	Man hours
Base moulding, fir/pine, 2-1/4"	LF	$2.36	$1.97	$4.33	**$7.22**	0.031
Base moulding, fir/pine, 3-1/4"	LF	$2.51	$2.37	$4.89	**$8.16**	0.033
Base moulding, fir/pine, 4-1/4"	LF	$2.59	$3.77	$6.36	**$10.61**	0.034
Base moulding, fir/pine, 5-1/4"	LF	$2.59	$4.42	$7.01	**$11.71**	0.034
Base moulding, fir/pine, prefinished, 3-1/4"	LF	$2.74	$3.52	$6.26	**$10.46**	0.036
Base moulding, oak, 3-1/4"	LF	$2.59	$2.79	$5.38	**$8.98**	0.034
Base moulding, laminated bamboo, prefinished, 2"	LF	$2.97	$3.61	$6.57	**$10.98**	0.039
Base moulding, laminated bamboo, prefinished, 4"	LF	$3.20	$4.82	$8.01	**$13.38**	0.042
Shoe mould, oak, 1/2"x3/4"	LF	$1.75	$1.08	$2.83	**$4.73**	0.023
Shoe mould, fir/pine, 1/2"x3/4"	LF	$1.60	$0.90	$2.50	**$4.17**	0.021
Shoe mould, fir/pine, prefinished, 1/2"x3/4"	LF	$1.75	$1.15	$2.90	**$4.84**	0.023

Floor Covering

Prefinished Wood Flooring

> Does not include old flooring removal.

Description	Unit	Direct Labor	Direct Materials	Direct Total	Selling Price	Man-hours
PREFINISHED WOOD FLOORING, OAK						
Oak flooring, solid, prefinished, 3/4 x 2-1/4, $5.60 SF	SF	$6.93	$6.44	$13.37	**$22.33**	0.091
Oak flooring, solid, prefinished, 3/4 x 3-1/4, $7.00 SF	SF	$5.33	$8.05	$13.38	**$22.35**	0.070
Oak flooring, solid, prefinished, 3/4 x 4, $8.70 SF	SF	$5.33	$10.01	$15.33	**$25.61**	0.070
Oak flooring, solid, prefinished, 3/4 x 5, $9.20 SF	SF	$5.33	$10.58	$15.91	**$26.57**	0.070
PREFINISHED WOOD FLOORING, BIRCH						
Birch flooring, solid, prefinished, 3/4 x 2-1/4, $7.00 SF	SF	$6.93	$8.05	$14.98	**$25.02**	0.091
Birch flooring, solid, prefinished, 3/4 x 3-1/4, $8.40 SF	SF	$5.33	$9.66	$14.99	**$25.04**	0.070
PREFINISHED WOOD FLOORING, ASH						
Ash flooring, solid, prefinished, 3/4 x 2-1/4, $4.90 SF	SF	$6.93	$5.64	$12.56	**$20.98**	0.091
Ash flooring, solid, prefinished, 3/4 x 3-1/4, $6.30 SF	SF	$5.33	$7.25	$12.58	**$21.00**	0.070
PREFINISHED WOOD FLOORING, PARQUET, BLOCK						
Oak parquet, solid prefinished, acrylic impreg., 5/16x12x12, $7.70 SF	SF	$4.41	$8.86	$13.27	**$22.16**	0.058
Oak parquet, solid prefinished, urethane, 5/16x12x12, $4.40 SF	SF	$4.41	$5.06	$9.47	**$15.82**	0.058
Maple parquet, solid prefinished, acrylic impreg., 5/16x12x12, $8.30 SF	SF	$4.41	$9.55	$13.96	**$23.32**	0.058
Maple parquet, solid prefinished, urethane, 5/16x12x12, $5.30 SF	SF	$4.41	$6.10	$10.51	**$17.55**	0.058
Cherry parquet, solid prefinished, acrylic impreg., 5/16x12x12, $10.00 SF	SF	$4.41	$11.50	$15.91	**$26.58**	0.058
Cherry parquet, solid prefinished, urethane, 5/16x12x12, $7.50 SF	SF	$4.41	$8.63	$13.04	**$21.78**	0.058
Walnut parquet, solid prefinished, acrylic impreg., 5/16x12x12, $12.00 SF	SF	$4.41	$13.80	$18.21	**$30.42**	0.058
Walnut parquet, solid prefinished, urethane, 5/16x12x12, $9.50	SF	$4.41	$10.93	$15.34	**$25.62**	0.058

Floor Covering

Prefinished Engineered & Laminate Flooring

> Material Costs only. Select labor item from 'Labor Costs to Install Flooring' section.

Description	Unit	Direct Labor	Direct Materials	Direct Total	Selling Price	Man-hours
PREFINISHED ENGINEERED FLOORING						
Engineered flooring, prefinished, alum. oxide, 3/8 x 2-1/4, $5.00 SF	SF		$5.50	$5.50	**$9.19**	
Engineered flooring, prefinished, alum. oxide, 1/4 x 3, $4.70 SF	SF		$5.17	$5.17	**$8.63**	
Engineered flooring, prefinished, alum. oxide, 3/8 x 3, $6.60 SF	SF		$7.26	$7.26	**$12.12**	
Engineered flooring, prefinished, alum. oxide, 1/4 x 5, $4.70 SF	SF		$5.17	$5.17	**$8.63**	
Engineered flooring, prefinished, alum. oxide, 3/8 x 5, $6.60 SF	SF		$7.26	$7.26	**$12.12**	
Engineered floor, prefinished, alum. oxide, 8x48x3/8, $5.50 SF	SF		$6.05	$6.05	**$10.10**	
Engineered floor, prefinished, alum. oxide, 5x86-5/8x3/8, $6.00 SF	SF		$6.60	$6.60	**$11.02**	
Engineered floor, prefinished, alum. oxide, 5x86-5/8x1/2, $6.80 SF	SF		$7.55	$7.55	**$12.61**	
Engineered floor, prefinished, alum. oxide, 7-5/8x86-5/8x3/8, $4.70 SF	SF		$5.17	$5.17	**$8.63**	
Engineered floor, prefinished, alum. oxide, 7-5/8x86-5/8x1/2, $6.00 SF	SF		$6.60	$6.60	**$11.02**	
PREFINISHED LAMINATE FLOORING						
Laminate floor, prefinished, alum. oxide, 7-5/8x50-3/4x1/4, $2.40 SF	SF		$2.64	$2.64	**$4.41**	
Laminate floor, prefinished, alum. oxide, 7-5/8x47-1/4x5/16, $3.40 SF	SF		$3.74	$3.74	**$6.25**	
Laminate floor, prefinished, alum. oxide, 7-5/8x47-1/4x3/8, $4.30 SF	SF		$4.73	$4.73	**$7.90**	

Floor Covering

Resilient Flooring

> Material Costs only. Select labor item from 'Labor Costs to Install Flooring' section.

Description	Unit	Direct Labor	Direct Materials	Direct Total	Selling Price	Man-hours
RESILIENT FLOORING, TILE						
Asphalt tile flooring, 9 x 9 x 1/8 at $1.10 per tile	SF		$1.32	$1.32	**$2.20**	
Vinyl composition tile flooring, 9 x 9 x 1/16 at $0.90 per tile	SF		$1.08	$1.08	**$1.80**	
Vinyl composition tile flooring, 9 x 9 x 3/32 at $1.20 per tile	SF		$1.44	$1.44	**$2.40**	
Vinyl composition tile flooring, 9 x 9 x 1/8 at $1.90 per tile	SF		$2.28	$2.28	**$3.81**	
Vinyl composition tile flooring, 12 x 12 x 1/16, at $1.10 per tile	SF		$1.32	$1.32	**$2.20**	
Vinyl composition tile flooring, 12 x 12 x 3/32, at $1.50 per tile	SF		$1.80	$1.80	**$3.01**	
Vinyl composition tile flooring, 12 x 12 x 1/8, at $2.40 per tile	SF		$2.88	$2.88	**$4.81**	
Vinyl tile flooring, 9 x 9 x 1/16 at $1.30 per tile	SF		$1.56	$1.56	**$2.61**	
Vinyl tile flooring, 9 x 9 x 3/32 at $1.90 per tile	SF		$2.28	$2.28	**$3.81**	
Vinyl tile flooring, 9 x 9 x 1/8 at $3.40 per tile	SF		$4.08	$4.08	**$6.81**	
Vinyl tile flooring, 12 x 12 x 1/16, at $1.60 per tile	SF		$1.92	$1.92	**$3.21**	
Vinyl tile flooring, 12 x 12 x 3/32, at $2.20 per tile	SF		$2.64	$2.64	**$4.41**	
Vinyl tile flooring, 12 x 12 x 1/8, at $4.30 per tile	SF		$5.16	$5.16	**$8.62**	
RESILIENT FLOORING, SHEET GOODS						
Vinyl sheet flooring, .065" thick, 2 year, economy, at $12 SY	SY		$14.40	$14.40	**$24.05**	
Vinyl sheet flooring, .077" thick, 5 year, average, at $23 SY	SY		$27.60	$27.60	**$46.09**	
Vinyl sheet flooring, .090" thick, 10 year, premium, at $38 SY	SY		$45.60	$45.60	**$76.15**	
RESILIENT FLOORING, TRIM						
Vinyl base, 2-1/2"	LF	$2.21	$0.67	$2.87	**$4.80**	0.029
Vinyl base, 4"	LF	$2.44	$0.79	$3.22	**$5.38**	0.032
Vinyl base, 6"	LF	$2.74	$0.91	$3.65	**$6.09**	0.036

Floor Covering

Ceramic Tile Flooring

> Material Costs only. Select labor item from 'Labor Costs to Install Flooring' section.

Description	Unit	Direct Labor	Direct Materials	Direct Total	Selling Price	Man-hours
Back mount ceramic tile flooring, small (up to 1-1/2"), at $3 SF	SF		$3.75	$3.75	**$6.26**	
Back mount ceramic tile flooring, small (up to 1-1/2"), at $4 SF	SF		$5.00	$5.00	**$8.35**	
Back mount ceramic tile flooring, small (up to 1-1/2"), at $5 SF	SF		$6.25	$6.25	**$10.44**	
Back mount ceramic tile flooring, small (up to 1-1/2"), at $6 SF	SF		$7.50	$7.50	**$12.53**	
Back mount ceramic tile flooring, small (up to 1-1/2"), at $8 SF	SF		$10.00	$10.00	**$16.70**	
Back mount ceramic tile flooring, small (up to 1-1/2"), at $10 SF	SF		$12.50	$12.50	**$20.88**	
Back mount ceramic tile flooring, medium (up to 4-1/4") at $3 SF	SF		$3.75	$3.75	**$6.26**	
Back mount ceramic tile flooring, medium (up to 4-1/4") at $4 SF	SF		$5.00	$5.00	**$8.35**	
Back mount ceramic tile flooring, medium (up to 4-1/4") at $5 SF	SF		$6.25	$6.25	**$10.44**	
Back mount ceramic tile flooring, medium (up to 4-1/4") at $6 SF	SF		$7.50	$7.50	**$12.53**	
Back mount ceramic tile flooring, medium (up to 4-1/4") at $8 SF	SF		$10.00	$10.00	**$16.70**	
Back mount ceramic tile flooring, medium (up to 4-1/4") at $10 SF	SF		$12.50	$12.50	**$20.88**	
Ceramic tile flooring, 4-1/4" to 12", at $2 SF	SF		$2.50	$2.50	**$4.18**	
Ceramic tile flooring, 4-1/4" to 12", at $3 SF	SF		$3.75	$3.75	**$6.26**	
Ceramic tile flooring, 4-1/4" to 12", at $4 SF	SF		$5.00	$5.00	**$8.35**	
Ceramic tile flooring, 4-1/4" to 12", at $5 SF	SF		$6.25	$6.25	**$10.44**	
Ceramic tile flooring, 4-1/4" to 12", at $6 SF	SF		$7.50	$7.50	**$12.53**	
Ceramic tile flooring, 4-1/4" to 12", at $8 SF	SF		$10.00	$10.00	**$16.70**	
Ceramic tile flooring, 4-1/4" to 12", at $10 SF	SF		$12.50	$12.50	**$20.88**	
Ceramic tile flooring, 4-1/4" to 12", at $12 SF	SF		$15.00	$15.00	**$25.05**	

Floor Covering

Stone Flooring

> Material Costs only. Select labor item from 'Labor Costs to Install Flooring' section.

Description	Unit	Direct Labor	Direct Materials	Direct Total	Selling Price	Man-hours
TILE FLOORING, MARBLE						
Marble tile flooring, at $6.00 SF	SF		$7.50	$7.50	**$12.53**	
Marble tile flooring, at $8.00 SF	SF		$10.00	$10.00	**$16.70**	
Marble tile flooring, at $10.00 SF	SF		$12.50	$12.50	**$20.88**	
Marble tile flooring, at $12.00 SF	SF		$15.00	$15.00	**$25.05**	
Marble tile flooring, at $14.00 SF	SF		$17.50	$17.50	**$29.23**	
Marble tile flooring, at $16.00 SF	SF		$20.00	$20.00	**$33.40**	
TILE FLOORING, GRANITE						
Granite tile flooring, at $6.00 SF	SF		$7.50	$7.50	**$12.53**	
Granite tile flooring, at $8.00 SF	SF		$10.00	$10.00	**$16.70**	
Granite tile flooring, at $10.00 SF	SF		$12.50	$12.50	**$20.88**	
Granite tile flooring, at $12.00 SF	SF		$15.00	$15.00	**$25.05**	
Granite tile flooring, at $14.00 SF	SF		$17.50	$17.50	**$29.23**	
Granite tile flooring, at $16.00 SF	SF		$20.00	$20.00	**$33.40**	
TILE FLOORING, QUARRY						
Quarry tile flooring, at $2.00 SF	SF		$2.50	$2.50	**$4.18**	
Quarry tile flooring, at $3.00 SF	SF		$3.75	$3.75	**$6.26**	
Quarry tile flooring, at $4.00 SF	SF		$5.00	$5.00	**$8.35**	
Quarry tile flooring, at $5.00 SF	SF		$6.25	$6.25	**$10.44**	
Quarry tile flooring, at $6.00 SF	SF		$7.50	$7.50	**$12.53**	
Quarry tile flooring, at $7.00 SF	SF		$8.75	$8.75	**$14.61**	
TILE FLOORING, SLATE						
Slate tile flooring, at $4.00 SF	SF		$5.00	$5.00	**$8.35**	
Slate tile flooring, at $5.00 SF	SF		$6.25	$6.25	**$10.44**	
Slate tile flooring, at $6.00 SF	SF		$7.50	$7.50	**$12.53**	
Slate tile flooring, at $7.00 SF	SF		$8.75	$8.75	**$14.61**	
Slate tile flooring, at $8.00 SF	SF		$10.00	$10.00	**$16.70**	
Slate tile flooring, at $9.00 SF	SF		$11.25	$11.25	**$18.79**	

Floor Covering

Carpeting

> Material Costs only. Select labor item from 'Labor Costs to Install Flooring' section.

Description	Unit	Direct Labor	Direct Materials	Direct Total	Selling Price	Man-hours
CARPETING, INDOOR						
Interior carpeting with pad, at $10 SY	SY		$11.50	$11.50	**$13.80**	
Interior carpeting with pad, at $15 SY	SY		$17.25	$17.25	**$20.70**	
Interior carpeting with pad, at $20 SY	SY		$23.00	$23.00	**$27.60**	
Interior carpeting with pad, at $25 SY	SY		$28.75	$28.75	**$34.50**	
Interior carpeting with pad, at $30 SY	SY		$34.50	$34.50	**$41.40**	
Interior carpeting with pad, at $35 SY	SY		$40.25	$40.25	**$48.30**	
Interior carpeting with pad, at $40 SY	SY		$46.00	$46.00	**$55.20**	
Interior carpeting with pad, at $45 SY	SY		$51.75	$51.75	**$62.10**	
Interior carpeting with pad, at $50 SY	SY		$57.50	$57.50	**$69.00**	
Interior carpeting with pad, at $55 SY	SY		$63.25	$63.25	**$75.90**	
Interior carpeting with pad, at $60 SY	SY		$69.00	$69.00	**$82.80**	
CARPETING, INDOOR/OUTDOOR						
Indoor/outdoor carpeting, at $6 SY	SY		$6.90	$6.90	**$8.28**	
Indoor/outdoor carpeting, at $8 SY	SY		$9.20	$9.20	**$11.04**	
Indoor/outdoor carpeting, at $10 SY	SY		$11.50	$11.50	**$13.80**	
Indoor/outdoor carpeting, at $15 SY	SY		$17.25	$17.25	**$20.70**	
Indoor/outdoor carpeting, at $20 SY	SY		$23.00	$23.00	**$27.60**	
Indoor/outdoor carpeting, at $25 SY	SY		$28.75	$28.75	**$34.50**	

Exterior Painting

Exterior Painting Preparation

Description	Unit	Direct Labor	Direct Materials	Direct Total	Selling Price	Man-hours
SAND AND FILL						
Sand and fill wood siding, average	SF	$0.50		$0.50	**$0.84**	0.009
Sand & fill wood siding, extensive	SF	$0.61		$0.61	**$1.02**	0.011
Sand and fill exterior doors and windows	SF	$0.67		$0.67	**$1.12**	0.012
Sand and fill exterior wood trim, up to 5" wide, average	LF	$0.33		$0.33	**$0.56**	0.006
Sand and fill exterior wood trim, up to 5" wide, extensive	LF	$0.45		$0.45	**$0.74**	0.008
Sand and fill exterior wood trim, 5" to 10" wide, average	LF	$0.50		$0.50	**$0.84**	0.009
Sand and fill exterior wood trim, 5" to 10" wide, extensive	LF	$0.61		$0.61	**$1.02**	0.011
CONCRETE AND MASONRY PREPARATION						
Concrete or masonry surface preparation, average	SF	$0.45		$0.45	**$0.74**	0.008
Concrete or masonry surface preparation, extensive	SF	$0.50		$0.50	**$0.84**	0.009
METAL PREPARATION						
Metal surface preparation, average	SF	$0.33		$0.33	**$0.56**	0.006
Metal surface preparation, extensive	SF	$0.45		$0.45	**$0.74**	0.008
PAINT REMOVAL BY CHEMICAL						
Remove paint from wood siding with chemicals	SF	$2.00	$0.16	$2.17	**$3.62**	0.036
Remove paint from masonry with chemicals	SF	$2.17	$0.21	$2.39	**$3.98**	0.039
Remove paint from metal surface with chemicals	SF	$2.17	$0.21	$2.39	**$3.98**	0.039
Remove paint from exterior wood trim with chemicals	LF	$1.00	$0.11	$1.11	**$1.85**	0.018
Remove paint from wood roof with chemicals, to 5/12 slope	SF	$2.34	$0.21	$2.55	**$4.26**	0.042
Remove paint from wood roof with chemicals, over 5/12 slope	SF	$2.67	$0.21	$2.89	**$4.82**	0.048
Remove paint from metal roof with chemicals, to 5/12 slope	SF	$2.67	$0.32	$2.99	**$5.00**	0.048
Remove paint from metal roof with chemicals, over 5/12 slope	SF	$3.01	$0.32	$3.33	**$5.56**	0.054
PAINT REMOVAL BY BURNING OFF						
Burn paint from siding, average	SF	$2.51		$2.51	**$4.19**	0.045
Burn paint from siding, extensive	SF	$3.12		$3.12	**$5.21**	0.056
Burn paint from exterior trim	LF	$1.50		$1.50	**$2.51**	0.027
PAINT REMOVAL BY SANDBLASTING						
Remove paint from wood by sandblasting, average	SF	$3.40		$3.40	**$5.67**	0.061
Remove paint from wood by sandblasting, extensive	SF	$4.07		$4.07	**$6.79**	0.073
Remove paint from masonry by sandblasting, average	SF	$3.01		$3.01	**$5.02**	0.054
Remove paint from masonry by sandblasting, extensive	SF	$3.73		$3.73	**$6.23**	0.067
PRESSURE WASHING						
Pressure wash with TSP, light	SF	$0.28		$0.28	**$0.47**	0.005
Pressure wash with TSP, average	SF	$0.45		$0.45	**$0.74**	0.008
Pressure wash with TSP, extensive	SF	$0.72		$0.72	**$1.21**	0.013
Pressure wash gutters and trim with TSP	LF	$0.45		$0.45	**$0.74**	0.008

Exterior Painting

Paint Siding

Description	Unit	Direct Labor	Direct Materials	Direct Total	Selling Price	Man-hours
Paint wood siding with brush, 1 coat	SF	$0.56	$0.06	$0.62	**$1.04**	0.010
Paint wood siding with brush, 2 coats	SF	$0.95	$0.13	$1.08	**$1.80**	0.017
Paint wood siding with roller, 1 coat	SF	$0.45	$0.06	$0.51	**$0.85**	0.008
Paint wood siding with roller, 2 coats	SF	$0.67	$0.13	$0.80	**$1.33**	0.012
Paint wood siding with spray, 1 coat	SF	$0.28	$0.09	$0.36	**$0.61**	0.005
Paint wood siding with spray, 2 coats	SF	$0.45	$0.17	$0.62	**$1.03**	0.008
Paint aluminum siding with brush, 1 coat	SF	$0.39	$0.06	$0.45	**$0.76**	0.007
Paint aluminum siding with brush, 2 coats	SF	$0.56	$0.13	$0.69	**$1.14**	0.010
Paint aluminum siding with roller, 1 coat	SF	$0.33	$0.06	$0.40	**$0.67**	0.006
Paint aluminum siding with roller, 2 coats	SF	$0.50	$0.13	$0.63	**$1.05**	0.009
Paint aluminum siding with spray, 1 coat	SF	$0.28	$0.09	$0.36	**$0.61**	0.005
Paint aluminum siding with spray, 2 coats	SF	$0.45	$0.17	$0.62	**$1.03**	0.008
Additional charge for work above 1 story, per SF of work above 1 story	SF	$0.17		$0.17	**$0.28**	0.003

Stain Siding

Description	Unit	Direct Labor	Direct Materials	Direct Total	Selling Price	Man-hours
Stain wood siding with brush, 1 coat	SF	$0.45	$0.06	$0.51	**$0.85**	0.008
Stain wood siding with brush, 2 coats	SF	$0.84	$0.13	$0.96	**$1.61**	0.015
Stain wood siding with roller, 1 coat	SF	$0.45	$0.06	$0.51	**$0.85**	0.008
Stain wood siding with roller, 2 coats	SF	$0.61	$0.13	$0.74	**$1.24**	0.011
Stain wood siding with spray, 1 coat	SF	$0.28	$0.09	$0.36	**$0.61**	0.005
Stain wood siding with spray, 2 coats	SF	$0.45	$0.17	$0.62	**$1.03**	0.008
Additional charge for work above 1 story, per SF of work above 1 story	SF	$0.17		$0.17	**$0.28**	0.003

Exterior Painting

Paint Shingle Siding

Description	Unit	Direct Labor	Direct Materials	Direct Total	Selling Price	Man-hours
Paint wood shingle with brush, 1 coat	SF	$0.61	$0.09	$0.70	**$1.17**	0.011
Paint wood shingle with brush, 2 coats	SF	$1.00	$0.16	$1.16	**$1.94**	0.018
Paint wood shingle, with spray, 1 coat	SF	$0.33	$0.12	$0.45	**$0.75**	0.006
Paint wood shingle with spray, 2 coats	SF	$0.50	$0.16	$0.66	**$1.11**	0.009
Additional charge for work above 1 story, per SF of work above 1 story	SF	$0.17		$0.17	**$0.28**	0.003

Stain Shingle Siding

Description	Unit	Direct Labor	Direct Materials	Direct Total	Selling Price	Man-hours
Stain wood shingle, with brush, 1 coat	SF	$0.56	$0.06	$0.62	**$1.04**	0.010
Stain wood shingle, with brush, 2 coats	SF	$0.95	$0.12	$1.06	**$1.78**	0.017
Stain wood shingle, with spray, 1 coat	SF	$0.33	$0.09	$0.42	**$0.70**	0.006
Stain wood shingle, with spray, 2 coats	SF	$0.50	$0.16	$0.66	**$1.11**	0.009
Additional charge for work above 1 story, per SF of work above 1 story	SF	$0.17		$0.17	**$0.28**	0.003

Paint Masonry

Description	Unit	Direct Labor	Direct Materials	Direct Total	Selling Price	Man-hours
Paint smooth masonry with brush, 1 coat	SF	$0.56	$0.06	$0.62	**$1.04**	0.010
Paint smooth masonry with brush, 2 coats	SF	$0.95	$0.13	$1.08	**$1.80**	0.017
Paint smooth masonry with roller, 1 coat	SF	$0.45	$0.06	$0.51	**$0.85**	0.008
Paint smooth masonry with roller, 2 coats	SF	$0.67	$0.13	$0.80	**$1.33**	0.012
Paint smooth masonry with spray, 1 coat	SF	$0.28	$0.09	$0.36	**$0.61**	0.005
Paint smooth masonry with spray, 2 coats	SF	$0.45	$0.17	$0.62	**$1.03**	0.008
Paint porous masonry with brush, 1 coat	SF	$0.67	$0.13	$0.80	**$1.33**	0.012
Paint porous masonry with brush, 2 coats	SF	$1.11	$0.26	$1.37	**$2.29**	0.020
Paint porous masonry with roller, 1 coat	SF	$0.56	$0.13	$0.69	**$1.14**	0.010
Paint porous masonry with roller, 2 coats	SF	$1.00	$0.26	$1.26	**$2.10**	0.018
Paint porous masonry with spray, 1 coat	SF	$0.33	$0.17	$0.51	**$0.84**	0.006
Paint porous masonry with spray, 2 coats	SF	$0.61	$0.32	$0.93	**$1.56**	0.011
Additional charge for work above 1 story, per SF of work above 1 story	SF	$0.17		$0.17	**$0.28**	0.003

Exterior Painting

Paint Stucco

Description	Unit	Direct Labor	Direct Materials	Direct Total	Selling Price	Man-hours
Paint stucco with brush, 1 coat	SF	$0.56	$0.11	$0.66	**$1.11**	0.010
Paint stucco with brush, 2 coats	SF	$0.95	$0.17	$1.12	**$1.87**	0.017
Paint stucco with roller, 1 coat	SF	$0.45	$0.11	$0.55	**$0.92**	0.008
Paint stucco with roller, 2 coats	SF	$0.67	$0.17	$0.84	**$1.40**	0.012
Paint stucco with spray, 1 coat	SF	$0.28	$0.16	$0.44	**$0.73**	0.005
Paint stucco with spray, 2 coats	SF	$0.45	$0.26	$0.70	**$1.17**	0.008
Additional charge for work above 1 story, per SF of work above 1 story	SF	$0.17		$0.17	**$0.28**	0.003

Paint Concrete Floor

Description	Unit	Direct Labor	Direct Materials	Direct Total	Selling Price	Man-hours
Surface sealer, silicon	SF	$0.45	$0.16	$0.61	**$1.01**	0.008
Epoxy finish, 1 coat with brush over concrete floor	SF	$0.45	$0.32	$0.77	**$1.28**	0.008
Epoxy finish, 2 coats with brush over concrete floor	SF	$0.84	$0.56	$1.39	**$2.32**	0.015
Epoxy finish, 1 coat with roller over concrete floor	SF	$0.39	$0.32	$0.71	**$1.19**	0.007
Epoxy finish, 2 coats with roller over concrete floor	SF	$0.67	$0.56	$1.22	**$2.05**	0.012
Epoxy finish, 1 coat with spray over concrete floor	SF	$0.22	$0.37	$0.60	**$1.00**	0.004
Epoxy finish, 2 coats with spray over concrete floor	SF	$0.39	$0.62	$1.01	**$1.69**	0.007
Non-slip aluminum oxide finish on concrete	SF	$0.61	$0.30	$0.91	**$1.52**	0.011

Exterior Painting

Paint Trim

Description	Unit	Direct Labor	Direct Materials	Direct Total	Selling Price	Man-hours
Paint fascia and trim up to 6" wide with brush, 1 coat	LF	$0.67	$0.06	$0.73	**$1.22**	0.012
Paint fascia and trim up to 6" wide with brush, 2 coats	LF	$1.11	$0.11	$1.22	**$2.04**	0.020
Paint fascia and trim 6" to 10" wide with brush, 1 coat	LF	$0.95	$0.11	$1.05	**$1.76**	0.017
Paint fascia and trim 6" to 10" wide with brush, 2 coats	LF	$1.45	$0.18	$1.63	**$2.72**	0.026
Paint soffit with brush, 1 coat	SF	$0.67	$0.06	$0.73	**$1.22**	0.012
Paint soffit with brush, 2 coats	SF	$1.11	$0.11	$1.22	**$2.04**	0.020
Paint soffit with roller, 1 coat	SF	$0.56	$0.06	$0.62	**$1.04**	0.010
Paint soffit with roller, 2 coats	SF	$0.84	$0.11	$0.94	**$1.57**	0.015
Paint soffit with spray, 1 coat	SF	$0.28	$0.09	$0.36	**$0.61**	0.005
Paint soffit with spray, 2 coats	SF	$0.45	$0.16	$0.61	**$1.01**	0.008
Paint eaves, open rafters, brush, 1 coat	SF	$1.00	$0.11	$1.11	**$1.85**	0.018
Paint eaves, open rafters, brush, 2 coats	SF	$1.67	$0.16	$1.83	**$3.06**	0.030
Paint eaves, open rafters, spray, 1 coat	SF	$0.39	$0.15	$0.54	**$0.90**	0.007
Paint eaves, open rafters, spray, 2 coats	SF	$0.61	$0.24	$0.85	**$1.42**	0.011
Paint lattice with brush, 1 side, 1 coat	SF	$0.67	$0.04	$0.71	**$1.19**	0.012
Paint lattice with brush, 1 side, 2 coats	SF	$1.11	$0.06	$1.18	**$1.97**	0.020
Paint lattice with spray, 1 side, 1 coat	SF	$0.28	$0.09	$0.36	**$0.61**	0.005
Paint lattice with spray, 1 side, 2 coats	SF	$0.45	$0.16	$0.61	**$1.01**	0.008
Paint columns with brush, 1 coat	SF	$0.67	$0.06	$0.73	**$1.22**	0.012
Paint columns with brush, 2 coats	SF	$1.11	$0.11	$1.22	**$2.04**	0.020
Paint columns with spray, 1 coat	SF	$0.28	$0.09	$0.36	**$0.61**	0.005
Paint columns with spray, 2 coats	SF	$0.45	$0.16	$0.61	**$1.01**	0.008
Additional charge for work above 1 story, per SF of work above 1 story	SF	$0.17		$0.17	**$0.28**	0.003

Exterior Painting

Paint Deck and Porch

Description	Unit	Direct Labor	Direct Materials	Direct Total	Selling Price	Man-hours
Paint wood deck/porch floor with brush, 1 coat	SF	$0.50	$0.09	$0.59	**$0.98**	0.009
Paint wood deck/porch floor with brush, 2 coats	SF	$0.84	$0.13	$0.96	**$1.61**	0.015
Paint wood deck/porch floor with roller, 1 coat	SF	$0.39	$0.09	$0.48	**$0.79**	0.007
Paint wood deck/porch floor with roller, 2 coats	SF	$0.72	$0.13	$0.85	**$1.42**	0.013
Paint wood deck/porch floor with spray, 1 coat	SF	$0.28	$0.11	$0.39	**$0.64**	0.005
Paint wood deck/porch floor with spray, 2 coats	SF	$0.45	$0.17	$0.62	**$1.03**	0.008
Paint wood porch ceiling with brush, 1 coat	SF	$0.56	$0.09	$0.64	**$1.07**	0.010
Paint wood porch ceiling with brush, 2 coats	SF	$0.84	$0.13	$0.96	**$1.61**	0.015
Paint wood porch ceiling with roller, 1 coat	SF	$0.50	$0.09	$0.59	**$0.98**	0.009
Paint porch ceiling with roller, 2 coats	SF	$0.84	$0.13	$0.96	**$1.61**	0.015
Paint wood porch ceiling with spray, 1 coat	SF	$0.28	$0.11	$0.39	**$0.64**	0.005
Paint wood porch ceiling with spray, 2 coats	SF	$0.50	$0.17	$0.67	**$1.12**	0.009
Paint wood porch/deck railing with brush, 1 coat	SF	$1.28	$0.11	$1.39	**$2.32**	0.023
Paint porch/deck railing with brush, 2 coats	SF	$2.23	$0.17	$2.40	**$4.01**	0.040
Paint wood porch/deck railing with spray, 1 coat	SF	$0.45	$0.15	$0.60	**$0.99**	0.008
Paint wood porch/deck railing with spray, 2 coats	SF	$0.67	$0.24	$0.90	**$1.51**	0.012
Paint wood steps with brush, 1 coat	SF	$1.28	$0.11	$1.39	**$2.32**	0.023
Paint wood steps with brush, 2 coats	SF	$2.23	$0.17	$2.40	**$4.01**	0.040
Paint wood steps with spray, 1 coat	SF	$0.45	$0.15	$0.60	**$0.99**	0.008
Paint wood steps with spray, 2 coats	SF	$0.67	$0.24	$0.90	**$1.51**	0.012

Exterior Painting

Stain Deck and Porch

Description	Unit	Direct Labor	Direct Materials	Direct Total	Selling Price	Man-hours
Stain wood deck/porch floor with brush, 1 coat	SF	$0.45	$0.09	$0.53	**$0.89**	0.008
Stain wood deck/porch floor with brush, 2 coats	SF	$0.78	$0.13	$0.91	**$1.52**	0.014
Stain wood deck/porch floor with roller, 1 coat	SF	$0.39	$0.09	$0.48	**$0.79**	0.007
Stain wood deck/porch floor with roller, 2 coats	SF	$0.67	$0.13	$0.80	**$1.33**	0.012
Stain wood deck/porch floor with spray, 1 coat	SF	$0.28	$0.11	$0.39	**$0.64**	0.005
Stain wood deck/porch floor with spray, 2 coats	SF	$0.45	$0.17	$0.62	**$1.03**	0.008
Stain wood porch/deck railing with brush, 1 coat	SF	$1.17	$0.11	$1.28	**$2.13**	0.021
Stain wood porch/deck railing with brush, 2 coats	SF	$2.06	$0.17	$2.23	**$3.73**	0.037
Stain wood porch/deck railing with spray, 1 coat	SF	$0.45	$0.15	$0.60	**$0.99**	0.008
Stain wood porch/deck railing with spray, 2 coats	SF	$0.67	$0.24	$0.90	**$1.51**	0.012
Stain wood steps with brush, 1 coat	SF	$1.17	$0.11	$1.28	**$2.13**	0.021
Stain wood steps with brush, 2 coats	SF	$2.06	$0.17	$2.23	**$3.73**	0.037
Stain wood steps with spray, 1 coat	SF	$0.45	$0.15	$0.60	**$0.99**	0.008
Stain wood steps with spray, 2 coats	SF	$0.67	$0.24	$0.90	**$1.51**	0.012

Exterior Painting

Paint Windows

Description	Unit	Direct Labor	Direct Materials	Direct Total	Selling Price	Man-hours
Paint window screen, all sides, 1 coat	EA	$12.25	$0.64	$12.89	**$21.53**	0.220
Paint window screen, all sides, 2 coats	EA	$19.38	$1.18	$20.56	**$34.33**	0.348
Paint storm sash 1, all sides, coat	EA	$13.92	$0.64	$14.56	**$24.32**	0.250
Paint storm sash, all sides, 2 coats	EA	$21.94	$1.18	$23.12	**$38.61**	0.394
Paint window, frame, trim, up to 12 SF, up to 4 lites, 1 coat (per side)	EA	$20.22	$1.39	$21.61	**$36.08**	0.363
Paint window, frame, trim, up to 12 SF, up to 4 lites, 2 coats (per side)	EA	$37.09	$2.35	$39.44	**$65.87**	0.666
Paint window, frame, trim, 12 to 22 SF, up to 4 lites, 1 coat (per side)	EA	$33.75	$2.25	$35.99	**$60.11**	0.606
Paint window, frame, trim, 12 to 22 SF, up to 4 lites, 2 coats (per side)	EA	$60.70	$3.85	$64.55	**$107.80**	1.090
Paint window, frame, trim, 22 to 30 SF, up to 4 lites, 1 coat (per side)	EA	$43.83	$3.21	$47.04	**$78.55**	0.787
Paint window, frame, trim, 22 to 30 SF, up to 4 lites, 2 coats (per side)	EA	$74.18	$5.24	$79.42	**$132.63**	1.332
Paint window, frame, trim, up to 12 SF, over 4 lites, 1 coat (per side)	EA	$26.95	$1.61	$28.56	**$47.69**	0.484
Paint window, frame, trim, up to 12 SF, over 4 lites, 2 coats (per side)	EA	$47.22	$2.78	$50.01	**$83.51**	0.848
Paint window, frame, trim, 12 to 22 SF, over 4 lites, 1 coat (per side)	EA	$43.83	$2.68	$46.50	**$77.66**	0.787
Paint window, frame, trim, 12 to 22 SF, over 4 lites, 2 coats (per side)	EA	$74.18	$4.49	$78.67	**$131.38**	1.332
Paint window, frame, trim, 22 to 30 SF, over 4 lites, 1 coat (per side)	EA	$60.70	$3.75	$64.45	**$107.63**	1.090
Paint window, frame, trim, 22 to 30 SF, over 4 lites, 2 coats (per side)	EA	$97.79	$6.21	$104.00	**$173.67**	1.756
Paint window frame only, up to 12 SF, 1 coat (exterior only)	EA	$10.14	$0.80	$10.94	**$18.27**	0.182
Paint window frame only, up to 12 SF, 2 coats (exterior only)	EA	$16.87	$1.34	$18.21	**$30.41**	0.303
Paint window frame only, 12 to 22 SF, 1 coat (exterior only)	EA	$18.54	$1.34	$19.88	**$33.20**	0.333
Paint window frame only, 12 to 22 SF, 2 coats (exterior only)	EA	$28.68	$2.14	$30.82	**$51.47**	0.515
Paint window frame only, 22 to 30 SF, 1 coat (exterior only)	EA	$25.28	$1.87	$27.16	**$45.35**	0.454
Paint window frame only, 22 to 30 SF, 2 coats (exterior only)	EA	$40.49	$2.94	$43.43	**$72.53**	0.727
Additional charge for work above 1 story, per SF of work above 1 story	EA	$5.07		$5.07	**$8.46**	0.091

Exterior Painting

Stain Windows

Description	Unit	Direct Labor	Direct Materials	Direct Total	Selling Price	Man-hours
Stain window, frame, trim, up to 12 SF, up to 4 lites, 1 coat (per side)	EA	$20.22	$1.39	$21.61	**$36.08**	0.363
Stain window, frame, trim, up to 12 SF, up to 4 lites, 2 coats (per side)	EA	$37.09	$2.35	$39.44	**$65.87**	0.666
Stain window, frame, trim, up to 12 SF, up to 4 lites, 3 coats (per side)	EA	$53.96	$3.32	$57.28	**$95.66**	0.969
Stain window, frame, trim, 12 to 22 SF, up to 4 lites, 1 coat (per side)	EA	$33.75	$2.25	$35.99	**$60.11**	0.606
Stain window, frame, trim, 12 to 22 SF, up to 4 lites, 2 coats (per side)	EA	$60.70	$3.85	$64.55	**$107.80**	1.090
Stain window, frame, trim, 12 to 22 SF, up to 4 lites, 3 coats (per side)	EA	$87.66	$5.35	$93.01	**$155.32**	1.574
Stain window, frame, trim, 22 to 30 SF, up to 4 lites, 1 coat (per side)	EA	$43.83	$3.21	$47.04	**$78.55**	0.787
Stain window, frame, trim, 22 to 30 SF, up to 4 lites, 2 coats (per side)	EA	$74.18	$5.24	$79.42	**$132.63**	1.332
Stain window, frame, trim, 22 to 30 SF, up to 4 lites, 3 coats (per side)	EA	$104.53	$7.38	$111.91	**$186.89**	1.877
Stain window, frame, trim, up to 12 SF, over 4 lites, 1 coat (per side)	EA	$26.95	$1.61	$28.56	**$47.69**	0.484
Stain window, frame, trim, up to 12 SF, over 4 lites, 2 coats (per side)	EA	$47.22	$2.78	$50.01	**$83.51**	0.848
Stain window, frame, trim, up to 12 SF, over 4 lites, 3 coats (per side)	EA	$67.44	$3.96	$71.40	**$119.24**	1.211
Stain window, frame, trim, 12 to 22 SF, over 4 lites, 1 coat (per side)	EA	$43.83	$2.68	$46.50	**$77.66**	0.787
Stain window, frame, trim, 12 to 22 SF, over 4 lites, 2 coats (per side)	EA	$74.18	$4.49	$78.67	**$131.38**	1.332
Stain window, frame, trim, 12 to 22 SF, over 4 lites, 3 coats (per side)	EA	$104.53	$6.31	$110.84	**$185.11**	1.877
Stain window, frame, trim, 22 to 30 SF, over 4 lites, 1 coat (per side)	EA	$60.70	$3.75	$64.45	**$107.63**	1.090
Stain window, frame, trim, 22 to 30 SF, over 4 lites, 2 coats (per side)	EA	$97.79	$6.21	$104.00	**$173.67**	1.756
Stain window, frame, trim, 22 to 30 SF, over 4 lites, 3 coats (per side)	EA	$134.88	$8.67	$143.55	**$239.72**	2.422
Additional charge for work above 1 story, per SF of work above 1 story	EA	$6.74		$6.74	**$11.25**	0.121

Paint Shutters

Description	Unit	Direct Labor	Direct Materials	Direct Total	Selling Price	Man-hours
Paint louvered shutters with brush, 1 side, 1 coat	SF	$1.50	$0.11	$1.61	**$2.69**	0.027
Paint louvered shutters with brush, 1 side, 2 coats	SF	$2.51	$0.17	$2.68	**$4.47**	0.045
Paint louvered shutters with spray, 1 side, 1 coat	SF	$0.67	$0.15	$0.82	**$1.37**	0.012
Paint louvered shutters with spray, 1 side, 2 coats	SF	$1.17	$0.24	$1.40	**$2.35**	0.021
Paint paneled shutters with brush, 1 side, 1 coat	SF	$1.17	$0.11	$1.28	**$2.13**	0.021
Paint paneled shutters with brush, 1 side, 2 coats	SF	$2.00	$0.17	$2.18	**$3.63**	0.036
Paint paneled shutters with spray, 1 side, 1 coat	SF	$0.50	$0.15	$0.65	**$1.09**	0.009
Paint paneled shutters with spray, 1 side, 2 coats	SF	$0.84	$0.24	$1.07	**$1.79**	0.015
Additional charge for work above 1 story, per SF of work above 1 story	SF	$0.50		$0.50	**$0.84**	0.009

Exterior Painting

Paint Doors

> Includes door, jamb and trim.

Description	Unit	Direct Labor	Direct Materials	Direct Total	Selling Price	Man-hours
Paint exterior flush door with brush, 1 coat (per side)	EA	$16.87	$1.71	$18.59	**$31.04**	0.303
Paint exterior flush door with brush, 2 coats (per side)	EA	$29.13	$3.00	$32.12	**$53.64**	0.523
Paint exterior flush door with roller, 1 coat (per side)	EA	$12.64	$1.71	$14.35	**$23.97**	0.227
Paint exterior flush door with roller, 2 coats (per side)	EA	$21.50	$3.00	$24.49	**$40.90**	0.386
Paint exterior flush door with lite with brush, 1 coat (per side)	EA	$19.94	$1.71	$21.65	**$36.15**	0.358
Paint exterior flush door with lite with brush, 2 coats (per side)	EA	$33.75	$3.00	$36.74	**$61.36**	0.606
Paint exterior panel door with brush, 1 coat (per side)	EA	$25.34	$1.93	$27.26	**$45.53**	0.455
Paint exterior panel door with brush, 2 coats (per side)	EA	$42.94	$3.21	$46.15	**$77.06**	0.771
Paint exterior panel door with lite with brush, 1 coat (per side)	EA	$29.91	$1.93	$31.83	**$53.16**	0.537
Paint exterior panel door with lite with brush, 2 coats (per side)	EA	$49.12	$3.21	$52.33	**$87.39**	0.882
Paint exterior panel door with 1 sidelight with brush, 1 coat (per side)	EA	$50.62	$3.21	$53.83	**$89.90**	0.909
Paint exterior panel door with 1 sidelight with brush, 2 coats (per side)	EA	$85.93	$5.35	$91.28	**$152.44**	1.543
Paint exterior panel door with 2 sidelights with brush, 1 coat (per side)	EA	$75.96	$4.28	$80.24	**$134.00**	1.364
Paint exterior panel door with 2 sidelights with brush, 2 coats (per side)	EA	$128.87	$6.96	$135.82	**$226.82**	2.314
Paint exterior french door with brush, 5 lite, 1 coat (per side)	EA	$27.84	$1.28	$29.13	**$48.64**	0.500
Paint exterior french door, with brush, 5 lite, 2 coats (per side)	EA	$45.50	$2.14	$47.64	**$79.56**	0.817
Paint exterior french door with brush, 10 lite, 1 coat (per side)	EA	$42.99	$1.50	$44.49	**$74.30**	0.772
Paint exterior french door, with brush, 10 lite, 2 coats (per side)	EA	$75.85	$2.46	$78.31	**$130.78**	1.362
Paint exterior french door with brush, 15 lite, 1 coat (per side)	EA	$58.20	$1.71	$59.91	**$100.05**	1.045
Paint exterior french door, with brush, 15 lite, 2 coats (per side)	EA	$101.19	$2.78	$103.97	**$173.63**	1.817
Paint 2 panel patio door with brush, 1 coat (per side)	EA	$27.84	$2.14	$29.98	**$50.07**	0.500
Paint 2 panel patio door, with brush, 2 coats (per side)	EA	$47.22	$3.75	$50.97	**$85.12**	0.848
Paint 3 panel patio door, with brush, 1 coat (per side)	EA	$40.49	$3.21	$43.70	**$72.97**	0.727
Paint 3 panel patio door, with brush, 2 coats (per side)	EA	$70.84	$5.62	$76.45	**$127.68**	1.272
Paint 9x7 garage door, with brush, 1 coat (per side)	EA	$55.63	$6.74	$62.37	**$104.17**	0.999
Paint 9x7 garage door, with brush, 2 coats (per side)	EA	$97.79	$10.79	$109.30	**$181.32**	1.756
Paint 16x7 garage door, with brush, 1 coat (per side)	EA	$98.51	$11.98	$110.50	**$184.53**	1.769
Paint 16x7 garage door, with brush, 2 coats (per side)	EA	$168.63	$19.17	$187.80	**$313.63**	3.028
Paint 9x7 garage door, with spray, 1 coat (per side)	EA	$27.84	$7.42	$35.26	**$58.88**	0.500
Paint 9x7 garage door, with spray, 2 coats (per side)	EA	$50.57	$11.86	$62.43	**$104.26**	0.908
Paint 16x7 garage door, with spray, 1 coat (per side)	EA	$49.29	$13.18	$62.47	**$104.32**	0.885
Paint 16x7 garage door, with spray, 2 coats (per side)	EA	$94.39	$21.09	$115.49	**$192.86**	1.695

Exterior Painting

Stain Doors

> Includes door, jamb and trim.

Description	Unit	Direct Labor	Direct Materials	Direct Total	Selling Price	Man-hours
Stain exterior flush door with brush, 1 coat (per side)	EA	$27.84	$1.80	$29.64	**$49.50**	0.500
Stain exterior flush door with brush, 2 coats (per side)	EA	$47.22	$3.08	$50.31	**$84.01**	0.848
Stain exterior flush door with brush, 3 coats (per side)	EA	$67.44	$4.37	$71.81	**$119.92**	1.211
Stain exterior panel door with brush, 1 coat (per side)	EA	$37.14	$2.05	$39.20	**$65.46**	0.667
Stain exterior panel door with brush, 2 coats (per side)	EA	$60.70	$3.47	$64.17	**$107.16**	1.090
Stain exterior panel door with brush, 3 coats (per side)	EA	$84.31	$4.88	$89.19	**$148.95**	1.514
Stain exterior door with lite with brush, 1 coat (per side)	EA	$42.16	$2.05	$44.21	**$73.83**	0.757
Stain exterior door with lite with brush, 2 coats (per side)	EA	$70.84	$3.47	$74.30	**$124.09**	1.272
Stain exterior door with lite with brush, 3 coats (per side)	EA	$99.46	$4.88	$104.34	**$174.25**	1.786
Stain exterior french door with brush, 5 lite, 1 coat (per side)	EA	$55.63	$1.28	$56.92	**$95.05**	0.999
Stain exterior french door with brush, 5 lite, 2 coats (per side)	EA	$91.05	$2.18	$93.23	**$155.70**	1.635
Stain exterior french door with brush, 5 lite, 3 coats (per side)	EA	$126.47	$3.08	$129.55	**$216.35**	2.271
Stain exterior french door with brush, 10 lite, 1 coat (per side)	EA	$72.51	$1.73	$74.24	**$123.98**	1.302
Stain exterior french door with brush, 10 lite, 2 coats (per side)	EA	$107.93	$2.74	$110.67	**$184.82**	1.938
Stain exterior french door with brush, 10 lite, 3 coats (per side)	EA	$143.29	$3.76	$147.04	**$245.56**	2.573
Stain exterior french door with brush, 15 lite, 1 coat (per side)	EA	$89.38	$2.02	$91.40	**$152.64**	1.605
Stain exterior french door with brush, 15 lite, 2 coats (per side)	EA	$124.74	$4.04	$128.79	**$215.08**	2.240
Stain exterior french door with brush, 15 lite, 3 coats (per side)	EA	$160.16	$4.77	$164.93	**$275.43**	2.876
Stain 2 panel patio door with brush, 1 coat (per side)	EA	$42.16	$2.47	$44.63	**$74.53**	0.757
Stain 2 panel patio door with brush, 2 coats (per side)	EA	$70.84	$4.06	$74.90	**$125.08**	1.272
Stain 2 panel patio door with brush, 3 coats (per side)	EA	$99.46	$7.42	$106.88	**$178.48**	1.786
Stain 3 panel patio door with brush, 1 coat (per side)	EA	$62.37	$3.71	$66.08	**$110.35**	1.120
Stain 3 panel patio door with brush, 2 coats (per side)	EA	$106.20	$6.36	$112.56	**$187.97**	1.907
Stain 3 panel patio door with brush, 3 coats (per side)	EA	$146.69	$11.12	$157.81	**$263.54**	2.634

Exterior Painting

Paint Fence

Description	Unit	Direct Labor	Direct Materials	Direct Total	Selling Price	Man-hours
Paint board fence with brush, flat side only, 1 coat (one side)	SF	$0.50	$0.09	$0.59	**$0.98**	0.009
Paint board fence with brush, flat side only, 2 coats (one side)	SF	$0.84	$0.13	$0.96	**$1.61**	0.015
Paint board fence with spray, flat side only, 1 coat (one side)	SF	$0.28	$0.11	$0.39	**$0.64**	0.005
Paint board fence with spray, flat side only, 2 coats (one side)	SF	$0.45	$0.17	$0.62	**$1.03**	0.008
Paint board fence with brush, frame side only, 1 coat (one side)	SF	$1.00	$0.13	$1.13	**$1.89**	0.018
Paint board fence with brush, frame side only, 2 coats (one side)	SF	$1.67	$0.19	$1.86	**$3.11**	0.030
Paint board fence with spray, frame side only, 1 coat (one side)	SF	$0.45	$0.17	$0.62	**$1.03**	0.008
Paint board fence with spray, frame side only, 2 coats (one side)	SF	$0.84	$0.24	$1.07	**$1.79**	0.015
Paint picket fence both sides with brush, 1 coat (SF = 1 face)	SF	$1.67	$0.19	$1.86	**$3.11**	0.030
Paint picket fence both sides with brush, 2 coats (SF = 1 face)	SF	$2.84	$0.34	$3.18	**$5.31**	0.051
Paint picket fence both sides with spray, 1 coat (SF = 1 face)	SF	$0.56	$0.24	$0.79	**$1.32**	0.010
Paint picket fence both sides with spray, 2 coats (SF = 1 face)	SF	$0.89	$0.41	$1.30	**$2.17**	0.016
Paint chain link both sides with brush, 1 coat (SF = 1 face)	SF	$1.67	$0.13	$1.80	**$3.00**	0.030
Paint chain link both sides with brush, 2 coats (SF = 1 face)	SF	$2.84	$0.19	$3.03	**$5.06**	0.051
Paint chain link both sides with roller, 1 coat (SF = 1 face)	SF	$1.17	$0.13	$1.30	**$2.17**	0.021
Paint chain link both sides with roller, 2 coats (SF = 1 face)	SF	$2.00	$0.19	$2.20	**$3.67**	0.036
Paint chain link both sides with spray, 1 coat (SF = 1 face)	SF	$0.56	$0.15	$0.71	**$1.18**	0.010
Paint chain link both sides with spray, 2 coats (SF = 1 face)	SF	$0.89	$0.24	$1.13	**$1.88**	0.016

Paint Gutter and Downspout

Description	Unit	Direct Labor	Direct Materials	Direct Total	Selling Price	Man-hours
Paint metal gutter or downspout with brush, 1 coat	LF	$0.78	$0.06	$0.84	**$1.41**	0.014
Paint metal gutter or downspout with brush, 2 coats	LF	$1.28	$0.13	$1.41	**$2.35**	0.023
Paint metal gutter or downspout with spray, 1 coat	LF	$0.50	$0.11	$0.61	**$1.02**	0.009
Paint metal gutter or downspout with spray, 2 coats	LF	$0.84	$0.19	$1.03	**$1.72**	0.015
Additional charge for work above 1 story, per LF of work above 1 story	LF	$0.17		$0.17	**$0.28**	0.003

Exterior Painting

Paint and Stain Roof

Description	Unit	Direct Labor	Direct Materials	Direct Total	Selling Price	Man-hours
Aluminization with brush, 1 coat	SF	$1.17	$0.32	$1.49	**$2.49**	0.021
Aluminization with brush, 2 coats	SF	$2.34	$0.54	$2.87	**$4.80**	0.042
Paint metal roof with brush, 1 coat	SF	$0.56	$0.11	$0.66	**$1.11**	0.010
Paint metal roof with brush, 2 coats	SF	$1.00	$0.17	$1.17	**$1.96**	0.018
Paint roof shingles with brush, 1 coat	SF	$0.84	$0.15	$0.99	**$1.65**	0.015
Paint roof shingles with brush, 2 coats	SF	$1.34	$0.28	$1.61	**$2.70**	0.024
Paint roof shingles with spray, 1 coat	SF	$0.45	$0.17	$0.62	**$1.03**	0.008
Paint roof shingles with spray, 2 coats	SF	$0.84	$0.30	$1.13	**$1.90**	0.015
Stain roof shingles with brush, 1 coat	SF	$0.78	$0.13	$0.91	**$1.52**	0.014
Stain roof shingles with brush, 2 coats	SF	$1.23	$0.28	$1.50	**$2.51**	0.022
Stain roof shingles with spray, 1 coat	SF	$0.45	$0.15	$0.60	**$0.99**	0.008
Stain roof shingles with spray, 2 coats	SF	$0.84	$0.28	$1.11	**$1.86**	0.015

Waterproofing

Description	Unit	Direct Labor	Direct Materials	Direct Total	Selling Price	Man-hours
Apply waterproof paint, 2 coats	SF	$0.61	$0.18	$0.79	**$1.33**	0.011
Apply silicon paint with sprayer, 1 coat	SF	$0.28	$0.10	$0.37	**$0.63**	0.005
Apply parging, 1/2" thick, 2 coats	SF	$2.16	$0.43	$2.59	**$4.33**	0.040
Apply asphalt coating, 1 coat	SF	$0.65	$0.21	$0.86	**$1.44**	0.016
Apply asphalt coating, 2 coats	SF	$1.13	$0.37	$1.51	**$2.52**	0.028

Interior Painting and Wallpaper

Interior Painting Preparation

Description	Unit	Direct Labor	Direct Materials	Direct Total	Selling Price	Man-hours
SAND AND FILL						
Sand and fill walls	SF	$0.33		$0.33	**$0.56**	0.006
Sand and fill trim, up to 4" wide	LF	$0.28		$0.28	**$0.47**	0.005
Sand and fill trim, 4" to 8" wide	LF	$0.45		$0.45	**$0.74**	0.008
PAINT REMOVAL BY CHEMICAL						
Remove paint from walls with chemicals	SF	$1.67	$0.16	$1.83	**$3.06**	0.030
Remove paint from floor with chemicals	SF	$1.50	$0.16	$1.66	**$2.78**	0.027
Remove paint from trim with chemicals, up to 4" wide	LF	$0.84	$0.11	$0.94	**$1.57**	0.015
Remove paint from trim with chemicals, 4" to 8" wide	LF	$1.28	$0.16	$1.44	**$2.41**	0.023
Remove paint from door, up to 2-6 with chemicals, 1 side	EA	$83.53	$3.00	$86.53	**$144.51**	1.500
Remove paint from door, 2-6 to 3-0 with chemicals, 1side	EA	$111.38	$4.28	$115.66	**$193.15**	2.000
Remove paint from window, up to 16 SF with chemicals, 1 side	EA	$83.53	$3.00	$86.53	**$144.51**	1.500
Remove paint from window, 16 to 32 SF with chemicals, 1 side	EA	$111.38	$4.28	$115.66	**$193.15**	2.000
PAINT REMOVAL BY BURNING OFF						
Burn paint from walls	SF	$2.51		$2.51	**$4.19**	0.045
Burn paint from trim, up to 4" wide	LF	$1.50		$1.50	**$2.51**	0.027
Burn paint from trim, 4" to 8" wide	LF	$2.67		$2.67	**$4.46**	0.048
DE-GLOSS WALLS WITH CHEMICALS						
De-gloss walls with chemicals	SF	$0.50	$0.09	$0.59	**$0.98**	0.009
De-gloss trim with chemicals, up to 4" wide	LF	$0.28	$0.03	$0.31	**$0.52**	0.005
De-gloss trim with chemicals, 4" to 8" wide	LF	$0.33	$0.05	$0.39	**$0.65**	0.006
WASH SURFACE BEFORE PAINTING						
Wash walls with TSP	SF	$0.28		$0.28	**$0.47**	0.005
Wash door, jamb and casings with TSP, 1 side	EA	$5.90		$5.90	**$9.86**	0.106
Wash window and frame with TSP, 1 side	EA	$7.18		$7.18	**$12.00**	0.129
Wash moulding with TSP, up to 4" wide	LF	$0.22		$0.22	**$0.37**	0.004
Wash moulding with TSP, 4" to 8" wide	LF	$0.28		$0.28	**$0.47**	0.005
REMOVE WALLPAPER						
Remove wallpaper with steam, single layer	SF	$0.45		$0.45	**$0.74**	0.008
Remove wallpaper with steam, several layers	SF	$0.72		$0.72	**$1.21**	0.013
Wash wall after paper removal, patch scrape marks	SF	$0.28		$0.28	**$0.47**	0.005

Interior Painting and Wallpaper

Paint Doors

> Costs are per side of door.
> Includes door, jamb and casing, one side.

Description	Unit	Direct Labor	Direct Materials	Direct Total	Selling Price	Man-hours
Paint interior flush door with brush, 1 coat (per side)	EA	$13.92	$1.71	$15.63	**$26.11**	0.250
Paint interior flush door with brush, 2 coats (per side)	EA	$24.00	$3.00	$27.00	**$45.09**	0.431
Paint interior flush door with roller, 1 coat (per side)	EA	$10.41	$1.71	$12.13	**$20.25**	0.187
Paint interior flush door with roller, 2 coats (per side)	EA	$17.71	$3.00	$20.71	**$34.58**	0.318
Paint interior panel door with brush, 1 coat (per side)	EA	$20.88	$1.93	$22.81	**$38.09**	0.375
Paint interior panel door with brush, 2 coats (per side)	EA	$35.42	$3.21	$38.63	**$64.51**	0.636
Paint interior full louver door with brush, 1 coat (per side)	EA	$41.71	$2.57	$44.28	**$73.95**	0.749
Paint interior full louver door with brush, 2 coats (per side)	EA	$70.84	$4.28	$75.12	**$125.45**	1.272
Paint interior half louver door with brush, 1 coat (per side)	EA	$32.86	$2.35	$35.21	**$58.80**	0.590
Paint interior half louver door with brush, 2 coats (per side)	EA	$50.57	$4.07	$54.63	**$91.24**	0.908
Paint interior french door with brush, 5 lite, 1 coat (per side)	EA	$27.84	$1.28	$29.13	**$48.64**	0.500
Paint interior french door with brush, 5 lite, 2 coats (per side)	EA	$45.50	$2.14	$47.64	**$79.56**	0.817
Paint interior french door with brush, 10 lite, 1 coat (per side)	EA	$42.99	$1.50	$44.49	**$74.30**	0.772
Paint interior french door with brush, 10 lite, 2 coats (per side)	EA	$75.85	$2.46	$78.31	**$130.78**	1.362
Paint interior french door with brush, 15 lite, 1 coat (per side)	EA	$58.20	$1.71	$59.91	**$100.05**	1.045
Paint interior french door with brush, 15 lite, 2 coats (per side)	EA	$101.19	$2.78	$103.97	**$173.63**	1.817

Interior Painting and Wallpaper

Paint Doors, Bi-Fold

> Costs are per side of door. Includes door, jamb and casing, one side.

Description	Unit	Direct Labor	Direct Materials	Direct Total	Selling Price	Man-hours
Paint flush bi-fold door with brush, 1 coat, to 4' (per side)	EA	$16.43	$2.14	$18.57	**$31.01**	0.295
Paint flush bi-fold door with brush, 2 coats, to 4' (per side)	EA	$25.23	$3.42	$28.65	**$47.85**	0.453
Paint flush bi-fold door with brush, 1 coat, 4' to 6' (per side)	EA	$19.71	$2.57	$22.28	**$37.21**	0.354
Paint flush bi-fold door with brush, 2 coats, 4' to 6' (per side)	EA	$30.24	$4.11	$34.35	**$57.36**	0.543
Paint flush bi-fold door with brush, 1 coat, 6' to 8' (per side)	EA	$29.57	$3.85	$33.42	**$55.82**	0.531
Paint flush bi-fold door with brush, 2 coats, 6' to 8' (per side)	EA	$45.39	$6.16	$51.55	**$86.09**	0.815
Paint flush bi-fold door with roller, 1 coat, to 4' (per side)	EA	$13.42	$2.14	$15.56	**$25.99**	0.241
Paint flush bi-fold door with roller, 2 coats, to 4' (per side)	EA	$19.71	$3.42	$23.14	**$38.64**	0.354
Paint flush bi-fold door with roller, 1 coat, 4' to 6' (per side)	EA	$16.09	$2.57	$18.66	**$31.17**	0.289
Paint flush bi-fold door with roller, 2 coats, 4' to 6' (per side)	EA	$23.67	$4.11	$27.78	**$46.39**	0.425
Paint flush bi-fold door with roller, 1 coat, 6' to 8' (per side)	EA	$24.17	$3.85	$28.02	**$46.80**	0.434
Paint flush bi-fold door with roller, 2 coats, 6' to 8' (per side)	EA	$35.53	$6.16	$41.69	**$69.63**	0.638
Paint panel bi-fold door with brush, 1 coat, to 4' (per side)	EA	$24.67	$2.14	$26.81	**$44.77**	0.443
Paint panel bi-fold door with brush, 2 coats, to 4' (per side)	EA	$37.81	$3.42	$41.24	**$68.87**	0.679
Paint panel bi-fold door with brush, 1 coat, 4' to 6' (per side)	EA	$29.57	$2.57	$32.14	**$53.67**	0.531
Paint panel bi-fold door with brush, 2 coats, 4' to 6' (per side)	EA	$45.39	$4.11	$49.50	**$82.66**	0.815
Paint panel bi-fold door with brush, 1 coat, 6' to 8' (per side)	EA	$44.38	$3.85	$48.24	**$80.55**	0.797
Paint panel bi-fold door with brush, 2 coats, 6' to 8' (per side)	EA	$68.05	$6.16	$74.22	**$123.94**	1.222
Paint full louver bi-fold door with brush, 1 coat, to 4' (per side)	EA	$36.98	$2.78	$39.76	**$66.40**	0.664
Paint full louver bi-fold door with brush, 2 coats, to 4' (per side)	EA	$56.69	$4.45	$61.14	**$102.11**	1.018
Paint full louver bi-fold door with brush, 1 coat, 4' to 6' (per side)	EA	$44.38	$3.34	$47.72	**$79.70**	0.797
Paint full louver bi-fold door with brush, 2 coats, 4' to 6' (per side)	EA	$68.05	$5.34	$73.39	**$122.57**	1.222
Paint full louver bi-fold door with brush, 1 coat, 6' to 8' (per side)	EA	$66.60	$5.01	$71.61	**$119.59**	1.196
Paint full louver bi-fold door with brush, 2 coats, 6' to 8' (per side)	EA	$102.08	$8.01	$110.09	**$183.85**	1.833
Paint half louver bi-fold door with brush, 1 coat, to 4' (per side)	EA	$30.80	$2.46	$33.26	**$55.54**	0.553
Paint half louver bi-fold door with brush, 2 coats, to 4' (per side)	EA	$47.28	$3.94	$51.22	**$85.53**	0.849
Paint half louver bi-fold door with brush, 1 coat, 4' to 6' (per side)	EA	$36.98	$2.95	$39.93	**$66.68**	0.664
Paint half louver bi-fold door with brush, 2 coats, 4' to 6' (per side)	EA	$56.69	$4.73	$61.42	**$102.57**	1.018
Paint half louver bi-fold door with brush, 1 coat, 6' to 8' (per side)	EA	$55.47	$4.43	$59.90	**$100.03**	0.996
Paint half louver bi-fold door with brush, 2 coats, 6' to 8' (per side)	EA	$85.09	$7.09	$92.18	**$153.94**	1.528

Interior Painting and Wallpaper

Paint Doors, Sliding

> Costs are per side of door. Includes door, jamb and casing, one side.

Description	Unit	Direct Labor	Direct Materials	Direct Total	Selling Price	Man-hours
Paint flush sliding door with brush, 1 coat, to 5' (per side)	EA	$20.94	$2.85	$23.79	**$39.72**	0.376
Paint flush sliding door with brush, 2 coats, to 5' (per side)	EA	$32.13	$4.55	$36.69	**$61.27**	0.577
Paint flush sliding door with brush, 1 coat, 5' to 8' (per side)	EA	$25.17	$3.42	$28.59	**$47.74**	0.452
Paint flush sliding door with brush, 2 coats, 5' to 8' (per side)	EA	$38.59	$5.46	$44.06	**$73.58**	0.693
Paint flush sliding door with brush, 1 coat, 8' to 12' (per side)	EA	$37.70	$5.12	$42.82	**$71.52**	0.677
Paint flush sliding door with brush, 2 coats, 8' to 12' (per side)	EA	$57.86	$8.20	$66.06	**$110.32**	1.039
Paint flush sliding door with roller, 1 coat, to 5' (per side)	EA	$15.70	$2.85	$18.55	**$30.98**	0.282
Paint flush sliding door with roller, 2 coats, to 5' (per side)	EA	$24.11	$4.55	$28.67	**$47.87**	0.433
Paint flush sliding door with roller, 1 coat, 5' to 8' (per side)	EA	$18.88	$3.42	$22.29	**$37.23**	0.339
Paint flush sliding door with roller, 2 coats, 5' to 8' (per side)	EA	$28.90	$5.46	$34.37	**$57.39**	0.519
Paint flush sliding door with roller, 1 coat, 8' to 12' (per side)	EA	$28.29	$5.12	$33.41	**$55.80**	0.508
Paint flush sliding door with roller, 2 coats, 8' to 12' (per side)	EA	$43.38	$8.20	$51.58	**$86.14**	0.779
Paint panel sliding door with brush, 1 coat, to 5' (per side)	EA	$31.46	$2.85	$34.31	**$57.30**	0.565
Paint panel sliding door with brush, 2 coats, to 5' (per side)	EA	$48.23	$4.55	$52.78	**$88.14**	0.866
Paint panel sliding door with brush, 1 coat, 5' to 8' (per side)	EA	$37.70	$3.42	$41.12	**$68.67**	0.677
Paint panel sliding door with brush, 2 coats, 5' to 8' (per side)	EA	$57.86	$5.46	$63.33	**$105.75**	1.039
Paint panel sliding door with brush, 1 coat, 8' to 12' (per side)	EA	$56.58	$5.12	$61.70	**$103.05**	1.016
Paint panel sliding door with brush, 2 coats, 8' to 12' (per side)	EA	$86.76	$8.20	$94.96	**$158.59**	1.558
Paint full louver sliding door with brush, 1 coat, to 5' (per side)	EA	$47.17	$3.70	$50.87	**$84.95**	0.847
Paint full louver sliding door with brush, 2 coats, to 5' (per side)	EA	$72.28	$5.92	$78.20	**$130.60**	1.298
Paint full louver sliding door with brush, 1 coat, 5' to 8' (per side)	EA	$56.58	$4.44	$61.02	**$101.90**	1.016
Paint full louver sliding door with brush, 2 coats, 5' to 8' (per side)	EA	$86.76	$7.10	$93.87	**$156.76**	1.558
Paint full louver sliding door with brush, 1 coat, 8' to 12' (per side)	EA	$84.87	$6.66	$91.53	**$152.86**	1.524
Paint full louver sliding door with brush, 2 coats, 8' to 12' (per side)	EA	$130.15	$10.66	$140.80	**$235.14**	2.337
Paint half louver sliding door with brush, 1 coat, to 5' (per side)	EA	$39.32	$3.27	$42.59	**$71.13**	0.706
Paint half louver sliding door with brush, 2 coats, to 5' (per side)	EA	$60.26	$5.24	$65.49	**$109.37**	1.082
Paint half louver sliding door with brush, 1 coat, 5' to 8' (per side)	EA	$47.17	$3.93	$51.10	**$85.33**	0.847
Paint half louver sliding door with brush, 2 coats, 5' to 8' (per side)	EA	$72.28	$6.28	$78.57	**$131.21**	1.298
Paint half louver sliding door with brush, 1 coat, 8' to 12' (per side)	EA	$70.73	$5.89	$76.62	**$127.95**	1.270
Paint half louver sliding door with brush, 2 coats, 8' to 12' (per side)	EA	$108.48	$9.43	$117.91	**$196.91**	1.948

Interior Painting and Wallpaper

Stain Doors

> Costs are per side of door. Includes door, jamb and casing, one side.

Description	Unit	Direct Labor	Direct Materials	Direct Total	Selling Price	Man-hours
Stain interior flush door with brush, 1 coat (per side)	EA	$17.15	$1.88	$19.04	**$31.79**	0.308
Stain interior flush door with brush, 2 coats (per side)	EA	$29.63	$3.30	$32.92	**$54.98**	0.532
Stain interior flush door with brush, 3 coats (per side)	EA	$37.87	$4.71	$42.58	**$71.10**	0.680
Stain interior panel door with brush, 1 coat (per side)	EA	$25.73	$2.12	$27.85	**$46.50**	0.462
Stain interior panel door with brush, 2 coats (per side)	EA	$43.66	$3.53	$47.19	**$78.81**	0.784
Stain interior panel door with brush, 3 coats (per side)	EA	$55.02	$4.94	$59.96	**$100.14**	0.988
Stain interior full louver door with brush, 1 coat (per side)	EA	$51.46	$2.82	$54.28	**$90.65**	0.924
Stain interior full louver door with brush, 2 coats (per side)	EA	$87.32	$4.71	$92.03	**$153.69**	1.568
Stain interior full louver door with brush, 3 coats (per side)	EA	$112.55	$6.59	$119.14	**$198.96**	2.021
Stain interior half louver door with brush, 1 coat (per side)	EA	$40.54	$2.59	$43.13	**$72.03**	0.728
Stain interior half louver door with brush, 2 coats (per side)	EA	$62.37	$4.47	$66.84	**$111.63**	1.120
Stain interior half louver door with brush, 3 coats (per side)	EA	$78.47	$6.36	$84.82	**$141.65**	1.409

Stain Doors, Bi-Fold

> Costs are per side of door. Includes door, jamb and casing, one side.

Description	Unit	Direct Labor	Direct Materials	Direct Total	Selling Price	Man-hours
Stain interior flush bi-fold door with brush, 1 coat, to 4' (per side)	EA	$23.39	$2.35	$25.74	**$42.99**	0.420
Stain interior flush bi-fold door with brush, 2 coats, to 4' (per side)	EA	$35.86	$3.77	$39.63	**$66.18**	0.644
Stain interior flush bi-fold door with brush, 3 coats, to 4' (per side)	EA	$46.61	$5.18	$51.79	**$86.49**	0.837
Stain interior flush bi-fold door with brush, 1 coat, 4' to 6' (per side)	EA	$28.07	$2.82	$30.89	**$51.59**	0.504
Stain interior flush bi-fold door with brush, 2 coats, 4' to 6' (per side)	EA	$43.05	$4.52	$47.57	**$79.44**	0.773
Stain interior flush bi-fold door with brush, 3 coats, 4' to 6' (per side)	EA	$52.68	$7.13	$59.81	**$99.88**	0.946
Stain interior flush bi-fold door with brush, 1 coat, 6' to 8' (per side)	EA	$42.10	$4.24	$46.34	**$77.39**	0.756
Stain interior flush bi-fold door with brush, 2 coats, 6' to 8' (per side)	EA	$64.54	$6.78	$71.32	**$119.11**	1.159
Stain interior flush bi-fold door with brush, 3 coats, 6' to 8' (per side)	EA	$82.20	$9.33	$91.53	**$152.85**	1.476
Stain interior panel bi-fold door with brush, 1 coat, to 4' (per side)	EA	$35.08	$2.35	$37.44	**$62.52**	0.630
Stain interior panel bi-fold door with brush, 2 coats, to 4' (per side)	EA	$53.80	$3.77	$57.56	**$96.13**	0.966
Stain interior panel bi-fold door with brush, 3 coats, to 4' (per side)	EA	$67.05	$4.96	$72.01	**$120.26**	1.204
Stain interior panel bi-fold door with brush, 1 coat, 4' to 6' (per side)	EA	$42.10	$2.82	$44.93	**$75.03**	0.756
Stain interior panel bi-fold door with brush, 2 coats, 4' to 6' (per side)	EA	$64.54	$4.52	$69.06	**$115.34**	1.159
Stain interior panel bi-fold door with brush, 3 coats, 4' to 6' (per side)	EA	$82.20	$6.21	$88.40	**$147.63**	1.476

Interior Painting and Wallpaper

Stain Doors, Bi-Fold (continued)

> Costs are per side of door. Includes door, jamb and casing, one side.

Description	Unit	Direct Labor	Direct Materials	Direct Total	Selling Price	Man-hours
Stain interior panel bi-fold door with brush, 1 coat, 6' to 8' (per side)	EA	$63.15	$4.24	$67.39	**$112.54**	1.134
Stain interior panel bi-fold door with brush, 2 coats, 6' to 8' (per side)	EA	$96.84	$6.78	$103.62	**$173.05**	1.739
Stain interior panel bi-fold door with brush, 3 coats, 6' to 8' (per side)	EA	$122.13	$9.33	$131.46	**$219.53**	2.193
Stain full louver bi-fold door with brush, 1 coat, to 4' (per side)	EA	$52.63	$3.06	$55.69	**$93.00**	0.945
Stain full louver bi-fold door with brush, 2 coats, to 4' (per side)	EA	$80.69	$4.90	$85.59	**$142.94**	1.449
Stain full louver bi-fold door with brush, 3 coats, to 4' (per side)	EA	$100.96	$6.74	$107.71	**$179.87**	1.813
Stain full louver bi-fold door with brush, 1 coat, 4' to 6' (per side)	EA	$63.15	$3.67	$66.82	**$111.60**	1.134
Stain full louver bi-fold door with brush, 2 coats, 4' to 6' (per side)	EA	$96.84	$5.88	$102.72	**$171.54**	1.739
Stain full louver bi-fold door with brush, 3 coats, 4' to 6' (per side)	EA	$123.46	$8.08	$131.54	**$219.68**	2.217
Stain full louver bi-fold door with brush, 1 coat, 6' to 8' (per side)	EA	$94.73	$5.51	$100.24	**$167.39**	1.701
Stain full louver bi-fold door with brush, 2 coats, 6' to 8' (per side)	EA	$145.29	$8.81	$154.11	**$257.36**	2.609
Stain full louver bi-fold door with brush, 3 coats, 6' to 8' (per side)	EA	$183.72	$12.12	$195.84	**$327.06**	3.299
Stain half louver bi-fold door with brush, 1 coat, to 4' (per side)	EA	$43.88	$2.71	$46.59	**$77.81**	0.788
Stain half louver bi-fold door with brush, 2 coats, to 4' (per side)	EA	$67.27	$4.33	$71.60	**$119.58**	1.208
Stain half louver bi-fold door with brush, 3 coats, to 4' (per side)	EA	$84.09	$5.96	$90.05	**$150.39**	1.510
Stain half louver bi-fold door with brush, 1 coat, 4' to 6' (per side)	EA	$52.63	$3.25	$55.88	**$93.31**	0.945
Stain half louver bi-fold door with brush, 2 coats, 4' to 6' (per side)	EA	$80.69	$5.20	$85.89	**$143.44**	1.449
Stain half louver bi-fold door with brush, 3 coats, 4' to 6' (per side)	EA	$100.96	$7.15	$108.11	**$180.55**	1.813
Stain half louver bi-fold door with brush, 1 coat, 6' to 8' (per side)	EA	$78.97	$4.87	$83.84	**$140.01**	1.418
Stain half louver bi-fold door with brush, 2 coats, 6' to 8' (per side)	EA	$121.07	$7.80	$128.87	**$215.20**	2.174
Stain half louver bi-fold door with brush, 3 coats, 6' to 8' (per side)	EA	$151.36	$10.73	$162.10	**$270.70**	2.718

Stain Doors, Sliding

> Costs are per side of door. Includes door, jamb and casing, one side.

Description	Unit	Direct Labor	Direct Materials	Direct Total	Selling Price	Man-hours
Stain flush sliding door with brush, 1 coat, to 5' (per side)	EA	$26.34	$3.13	$29.47	**$49.22**	0.473
Stain flush sliding door with brush, 2 coats, to 5' (per side)	EA	$40.37	$5.01	$45.38	**$75.79**	0.725
Stain flush sliding door with brush, 3 coats, to 5' (per side)	EA	$51.85	$6.88	$58.73	**$98.07**	0.931
Stain flush sliding door with brush, 1 coat, 5' to 8' (per side)	EA	$31.58	$3.76	$35.33	**$59.01**	0.567
Stain flush sliding door with brush, 2 coats, 5' to 8' (per side)	EA	$48.45	$6.01	$54.46	**$90.95**	0.870
Stain flush sliding door with brush, 3 coats, 5' to 8' (per side)	EA	$61.59	$8.27	$69.86	**$116.67**	1.106

Interior Painting and Wallpaper

Stain Doors, Sliding (continued)

> Costs are per side of door.
> Includes door, jamb and casing, one side.

Description	Unit	Direct Labor	Direct Materials	Direct Total	Selling Price	Man-hours
Stain flush sliding door with brush, 1 coat, 8' to 12' (per side)	EA	$47.39	$5.64	$53.03	**$88.56**	0.851
Stain flush sliding door with brush, 2 coats, 8' to 12' (per side)	EA	$72.62	$9.02	$81.64	**$136.33**	1.304
Stain flush sliding door with brush, 3 coats, 8' to 12' (per side)	EA	$95.73	$12.40	$108.13	**$180.58**	1.719
Stain panel sliding door with brush, 1 coat, to 5' (per side)	EA	$52.63	$3.13	$55.76	**$93.11**	0.945
Stain panel sliding door with brush, 2 coats, to 5' (per side)	EA	$80.69	$5.01	$85.70	**$143.12**	1.449
Stain panel sliding door with brush, 3 coats, to 5' (per side)	EA	$100.96	$6.88	$107.85	**$180.10**	1.813
Stain panel sliding door with brush, 1 coat, 5' to 8' (per side)	EA	$63.15	$3.76	$66.91	**$111.74**	1.134
Stain panel sliding door with brush, 2 coats, 5' to 8' (per side)	EA	$96.84	$6.01	$102.86	**$171.77**	1.739
Stain panel sliding door with brush, 3 coats, 5' to 8' (per side)	EA	$125.69	$8.27	$133.96	**$223.72**	2.257
Stain panel sliding door with brush, 1 coat, 8' to 12' (per side)	EA	$94.73	$5.64	$100.36	**$167.61**	1.701
Stain panel sliding door with brush, 2 coats, 8' to 12' (per side)	EA	$145.29	$9.02	$154.31	**$257.70**	2.609
Stain panel sliding door with brush, 3 coats, 8' to 12' (per side)	EA	$185.22	$12.40	$197.62	**$330.03**	3.326
Stain full louver sliding door with brush, 1 coat, to 5' (per side)	EA	$78.97	$4.07	$83.04	**$138.67**	1.418
Stain full louver sliding door with brush, 2 coats, to 5' (per side)	EA	$121.07	$6.51	$127.58	**$213.06**	2.174
Stain full louver sliding door with brush, 3 coats, to 5' (per side)	EA	$157.55	$8.97	$166.51	**$278.07**	2.829
Stain full louver sliding door with brush, 1 coat, 5' to 8' (per side)	EA	$94.73	$4.88	$99.61	**$166.35**	1.701
Stain full louver sliding door with brush, 2 coats, 5' to 8' (per side)	EA	$145.29	$7.81	$153.11	**$255.69**	2.609
Stain full louver sliding door with brush, 3 coats, 5' to 8' (per side)	EA	$187.90	$10.74	$198.64	**$331.73**	3.374
Stain full louver sliding door with brush, 1 coat, 8' to 12' (per side)	EA	$142.12	$7.33	$149.45	**$249.57**	2.552
Stain full louver sliding door with brush, 2 coats, 8' to 12' (per side)	EA	$217.91	$11.72	$229.63	**$383.49**	3.913
Stain full louver sliding door with brush, 3 coats, 8' to 12' (per side)	EA	$273.88	$16.10	$289.98	**$484.27**	4.918
Stain half louver sliding door with brush, 1 coat, to 5' (per side)	EA	$65.77	$3.60	$69.37	**$115.85**	1.181
Stain half louver sliding door with brush, 2 coats, to 5' (per side)	EA	$100.91	$5.76	$106.67	**$178.14**	1.812
Stain half louver sliding door with brush, 3 coats, to 5' (per side)	EA	$125.69	$7.92	$133.61	**$223.13**	2.257
Stain half louver sliding door with brush, 1 coat, 5' to 8' (per side)	EA	$78.97	$4.32	$83.29	**$139.09**	1.418
Stain half louver sliding door with brush, 2 coats, 5' to 8' (per side)	EA	$121.07	$6.91	$127.98	**$213.73**	2.174
Stain half louver sliding door with brush, 3 coats, 5' to 8' (per side)	EA	$153.81	$9.50	$163.32	**$272.74**	2.762
Stain half louver sliding door with brush, 1 coat, 8' to 12' (per side)	EA	$118.45	$6.48	$124.93	**$208.64**	2.127
Stain half louver sliding door with brush, 2 coats, 8' to 12' (per side)	EA	$181.60	$10.37	$191.97	**$320.59**	3.261
Stain half louver sliding door with brush, 3 coats, 8' to 12' (per side)	EA	$232.50	$14.25	$246.76	**$412.08**	4.175

35

Interior Painting and Wallpaper

Paint Windows

> Includes window, frame and trim.

Description	Unit	Direct Labor	Direct Materials	Direct Total	Selling Price	Man-hours
Paint window, frame, trim, up to 12 SF, up to 4 lites, 1 coat (per side)	EA	$20.22	$1.39	$21.61	**$36.08**	0.363
Paint window, frame, trim, up to 12 SF, up to 4 lites, 2 coats (per side)	EA	$37.09	$2.35	$39.44	**$65.87**	0.666
Paint window, frame, trim, 12 to 22 SF, up to 4 lites, 1 coat (per side)	EA	$33.75	$2.25	$35.99	**$60.11**	0.606
Paint window, frame, trim, 12 to 22 SF, up to 4 lites, 2 coats (per side)	EA	$60.70	$3.85	$64.55	**$107.80**	1.090
Paint window, frame, trim, 22 to 30 SF, up to 4 lites, 1 coat (per side)	EA	$43.83	$3.21	$47.04	**$78.55**	0.787
Paint window, frame, trim, 22 to 30 SF, up to 4 lites, 2 coats (per side)	EA	$74.18	$5.24	$79.42	**$132.63**	1.332
Paint window, frame, trim, up to 12 SF, over 4 lites, 1 coat (per side)	EA	$26.95	$1.61	$28.56	**$47.69**	0.484
Paint window, frame, trim, up to 12 SF, over 4 lites, 2 coats (per side)	EA	$47.22	$2.78	$50.01	**$83.51**	0.848
Paint window, frame, trim, 12 to 22 SF, over 4 lites, 1 coat (per side)	EA	$43.83	$2.68	$46.50	**$77.66**	0.787
Paint window, frame, trim, 12 to 22 SF, over 4 lites, 2 coats (per side)	EA	$74.18	$4.49	$78.67	**$131.38**	1.332
Paint window, frame, trim, 22 to 30 SF, over 4 lites, 1 coat (per side)	EA	$60.70	$3.75	$64.45	**$107.63**	1.090
Paint window, frame, trim, 22 to 30 SF, over 4 lites, 2 coats (per side)	EA	$97.79	$6.21	$104.00	**$173.67**	1.756
Paint detachable light grilles, 1 coat	EA	$8.41	$0.75	$9.16	**$15.29**	0.151
Paint detachable light grilles, 2 coats	EA	$13.48	$1.28	$14.76	**$24.65**	0.242

Interior Painting and Wallpaper

Stain Windows

> Includes window, frame and trim.

Description	Unit	Direct Labor	Direct Materials	Direct Total	Selling Price	Man-hours
Stain window, frame, trim, up to 12 SF, up to 4 lites, 1 coat (per side)	EA	$20.22	$1.39	$21.61	**$36.08**	0.363
Stain window, frame, trim, up to 12 SF, up to 4 lites, 2 coats (per side)	EA	$37.09	$2.35	$39.44	**$65.87**	0.666
Stain window, frame, trim, up to 12 SF, up to 4 lites, 3 coats (per side)	EA	$53.96	$3.32	$57.28	**$95.66**	0.969
Stain window, frame, trim, 12 to 22 SF, up to 4 lites, 1 coat (per side)	EA	$33.75	$2.25	$35.99	**$60.11**	0.606
Stain window, frame, trim, 12 to 22 SF, up to 4 lites, 2 coats (per side)	EA	$60.70	$3.85	$64.55	**$107.80**	1.090
Stain window, frame, trim, 12 to 22 SF, up to 4 lites, 3 coats (per side)	EA	$87.66	$5.35	$93.01	**$155.32**	1.574
Stain window, frame, trim, 22 to 30 SF, up to 4 lites, 1 coat (per side)	EA	$43.83	$3.21	$47.04	**$78.55**	0.787
Stain window, frame, trim, 22 to 30 SF, up to 4 lites, 2 coats (per side)	EA	$74.18	$5.24	$79.42	**$132.63**	1.332
Stain window, frame, trim, 22 to 30 SF, up to 4 lites, 3 coats (per side)	EA	$104.53	$7.38	$111.91	**$186.89**	1.877
Stain window, frame, trim, up to 12 SF, over 4 lites, 1 coat (per side)	EA	$26.95	$1.61	$28.56	**$47.69**	0.484
Stain window, frame, trim, up to 12 SF, over 4 lites, 2 coats (per side)	EA	$47.22	$2.78	$50.01	**$83.51**	0.848
Stain window, frame, trim, up to 12 SF, over 4 lites, 3 coats (per side)	EA	$67.44	$3.96	$71.40	**$119.24**	1.211
Stain window, frame, trim, 12 to 22 SF, over 4 lites, 1 coat (per side)	EA	$43.83	$2.68	$46.50	**$77.66**	0.787
Stain window, frame, trim, 12 to 22 SF, over 4 lites, 2 coats (per side)	EA	$74.18	$4.49	$78.67	**$131.38**	1.332
Stain window, frame, trim, 12 to 22 SF, over 4 lites, 3 coats (per side)	EA	$104.53	$6.31	$110.84	**$185.11**	1.877
Stain window, frame, trim, 22 to 30 SF, over 4 lites, 1 coat (per side)	EA	$60.70	$3.75	$64.45	**$107.63**	1.090
Stain window, frame, trim, 22 to 30 SF, over 4 lites, 2 coats (per side)	EA	$97.79	$6.21	$104.00	**$173.67**	1.756
Stain window, frame, trim, 22 to 30 SF, over 4 lites, 3 coats (per side)	EA	$134.88	$8.67	$143.55	**$239.72**	2.422
Stain detachable light grilles, 1 coat	EA	$10.14	$0.86	$10.99	**$18.36**	0.182
Stain detachable light grilles, 2 coats	EA	$16.87	$1.50	$18.37	**$30.68**	0.303
Stain detachable light grilles, 3 coats	EA	$23.61	$2.14	$25.75	**$43.01**	0.424

35

Interior Painting and Wallpaper

Paint Walls

Description	Unit	Direct Labor	Direct Materials	Direct Total	Selling Price	Man-hours
Paint drywall or plaster wall with brush, 1 coat, smooth finish	SF	$0.45	$0.11	$0.55	**$0.92**	0.008
Paint drywall or plaster wall with brush, 2 coats, smooth finish	SF	$0.84	$0.17	$1.01	**$1.68**	0.015
Paint drywall or plaster wall with roller, 1 coat, smooth finish	SF	$0.39	$0.11	$0.50	**$0.83**	0.007
Paint drywall or plaster wall with roller, 2 coats, smooth finish	SF	$0.67	$0.17	$0.84	**$1.40**	0.012
Paint drywall or plaster wall with spray, 1 coat, smooth finish	SF	$0.22	$0.13	$0.35	**$0.59**	0.004
Paint drywall or plaster wall with spray, 2 coats, smooth finish	SF	$0.39	$0.21	$0.60	**$1.01**	0.007
Paint drywall or plaster wall with brush, 1 coat, sand finish	SF	$0.61	$0.15	$0.76	**$1.27**	0.011
Paint drywall or plaster wall with brush, 2 coats, sand finish	SF	$1.06	$0.24	$1.29	**$2.16**	0.019
Paint drywall or plaster wall with roller, 1 coat, sand finish	SF	$0.45	$0.15	$0.60	**$0.99**	0.008
Paint drywall or plaster wall with roller, 2 coats, sand finish	SF	$0.78	$0.24	$1.02	**$1.70**	0.014
Paint drywall or plaster wall with spray, 1 coat, sand finish	SF	$0.28	$0.19	$0.47	**$0.79**	0.005
Paint drywall or plaster wall with spray, 2 coats, sand finish	SF	$0.50	$0.32	$0.82	**$1.37**	0.009
Paint drywall or plaster wall with brush, 1 coat, textured	SF	$0.61	$0.19	$0.81	**$1.34**	0.011
Paint drywall or plaster wall with roller, 1 coat, textured	SF	$0.50	$0.19	$0.69	**$1.16**	0.009

Paint Ceiling

Description	Unit	Direct Labor	Direct Materials	Direct Total	Selling Price	Man-hours
Paint drywall or plaster ceiling with brush, 1 coat	SF	$0.56	$0.11	$0.66	**$1.11**	0.010
Paint drywall or plaster ceiling with brush, 2 coats	SF	$0.95	$0.17	$1.12	**$1.87**	0.017
Paint drywall or plaster ceiling with roller, 1 coat	SF	$0.45	$0.11	$0.55	**$0.92**	0.008
Paint drywall or plaster ceiling with roller, 2 coats	SF	$0.78	$0.17	$0.95	**$1.59**	0.014
Paint drywall or plaster ceiling with spray, 1 coat	SF	$0.28	$0.13	$0.41	**$0.68**	0.005
Paint drywall or plaster ceiling with spray, 2 coats	SF	$0.45	$0.21	$0.66	**$1.10**	0.008
Paint drywall or plaster ceiling with brush, 1 coat, textured	SF	$0.72	$0.19	$0.92	**$1.53**	0.013
Paint drywall or plaster ceiling with roller, 1 coat, textured	SF	$0.61	$0.19	$0.81	**$1.34**	0.011
Spray acoustic ceiling, popcorn, thin layer	SF	$0.39	$0.15	$0.54	**$0.90**	0.007
Spray acoustic ceiling, popcorn, average layer	SF	$0.56	$0.21	$0.77	**$1.29**	0.010
Spray acoustic ceiling, popcorn, thick layer	SF	$0.67	$0.28	$0.95	**$1.58**	0.012

Interior Painting and Wallpaper

Paint Trim

Description	Unit	Direct Labor	Direct Materials	Direct Total	Selling Price	Man-hours
Paint interior moulding, up to 4" wide, 1 coat	LF	$0.50	$0.04	$0.54	**$0.91**	0.009
Paint interior moulding, up to 4" wide, 2 coats	LF	$0.84	$0.07	$0.91	**$1.52**	0.015
Paint interior moulding, 4" to 8" wide, 1 coat	LF	$0.67	$0.07	$0.74	**$1.24**	0.012
Paint interior moulding, 4" to 8" wide, 2 coats	LF	$1.11	$0.11	$1.22	**$2.04**	0.020
Paint balusters and stain rail, 1 coat	LF	$8.63	$0.29	$8.92	**$14.90**	0.155
Paint balusters and stain rail, 2 coats	LF	$15.87	$0.54	$16.41	**$27.40**	0.285
Paint cased door opening, up to 3' wide, 1 coat (all sides)	EA	$18.54	$2.46	$21.01	**$35.08**	0.333
Paint cased door opening, up to 3' wide, 2 coats (all sides)	EA	$30.35	$4.07	$34.42	**$57.48**	0.545
Paint cased door opening, 3' to 6' wide, 1 coat (all sides)	EA	$23.61	$3.10	$26.72	**$44.61**	0.424
Paint cased door opening, 3' to 6' wide, 2 coats (all sides)	EA	$40.49	$4.60	$45.09	**$75.30**	0.727

Stain Trim

Description	Unit	Direct Labor	Direct Materials	Direct Total	Selling Price	Man-hours
Stain interior moulding, up to 4" wide, 1 coat	LF	$0.56	$0.06	$0.62	**$1.04**	0.010
Stain interior moulding, up to 4" wide, 2 coats	LF	$0.95	$0.11	$1.05	**$1.76**	0.017
Stain interior moulding, up to 4" wide, 3 coats	LF	$1.34	$0.15	$1.49	**$2.48**	0.024
Stain interior moulding, 4" to 8" wide, 1 coat		$0.72	$0.11	$0.83	**$1.39**	0.013
Stain interior moulding, 4"to 8" wide, 2 coats	LF	$1.06	$0.17	$1.23	**$2.05**	0.019
Stain interior moulding, 4"to 8" wide, 3 coats	LF	$1.39	$0.24	$1.63	**$2.72**	0.025
Stain balusters and rail, 1 coat	LF	$15.37	$0.37	$15.74	**$26.29**	0.276
Stain balusters and rail, 2 coats	LF	$27.68	$0.62	$28.30	**$47.26**	0.497
Stain cased door opening, up to 3' wide, 1 coat (all sides)	EA	$21.94	$2.78	$24.72	**$41.29**	0.394
Stain cased door opening, up to 3' wide, 2 coats (all sides)	EA	$35.42	$6.10	$41.52	**$69.33**	0.636
Stain cased door opening, up to 3' wide, 3 coats (all sides)	EA	$48.90	$7.06	$55.96	**$93.45**	0.878
Stain cased door opening, 3' to 6' wide, 1 coat (all sides)	EA	$28.68	$3.53	$32.21	**$53.79**	0.515
Stain cased door opening, 3' to 6' wide, 2 coats (all sides)	EA	$47.22	$6.42	$53.64	**$89.59**	0.848
Stain cased door opening, 3' to 6' wide, 3 coats (all sides)	EA	$65.77	$9.31	$75.08	**$125.38**	1.181

35

Interior Painting and Wallpaper

Paint Masonry

Description	Unit	Direct Labor	Direct Materials	Direct Total	Selling Price	Man-hours
Paint smooth masonry with brush, 1 coat	SF	$0.56	$0.06	$0.62	**$1.04**	0.010
Paint smooth masonry with brush, 2 coats	SF	$0.95	$0.13	$1.08	**$1.80**	0.017
Paint smooth masonry with roller, 1 coat	SF	$0.45	$0.06	$0.51	**$0.85**	0.008
Paint smooth masonry with roller, 2 coats	SF	$0.67	$0.13	$0.80	**$1.33**	0.012
Paint smooth masonry with spray, 1 coat	SF	$0.28	$0.09	$0.36	**$0.61**	0.005
Paint smooth masonry with spray, 2 coats	SF	$0.45	$0.17	$0.62	**$1.03**	0.008
Paint porous masonry with brush, 1 coat	SF	$0.67	$0.13	$0.80	**$1.33**	0.012
Paint porous masonry with brush, 2 coats	SF	$1.11	$0.26	$1.37	**$2.29**	0.020
Paint porous masonry with roller, 1 coat	SF	$0.56	$0.13	$0.69	**$1.14**	0.010
Paint porous masonry with roller, 2 coats	SF	$1.00	$0.26	$1.26	**$2.10**	0.018
Paint porous masonry with spray, 1 coat	SF	$0.33	$0.17	$0.51	**$0.84**	0.006
Paint porous masonry with spray, 2 coats	SF	$0.61	$0.32	$0.93	**$1.56**	0.011
Additional charge for scaffolding, per SF of work done using scaffold	SF	$0.17		$0.17	**$0.28**	0.003

Paper Wallpaper

Description	Unit	Direct Labor	Direct Materials	Direct Total	Selling Price	Man-hours
PAPER WALLPAPER, IN SMALL ROOM (15% waste included)						
Hang wallpaper, $10 per 28 SF roll, in bath or kitchen	SF	$1.45	$0.42	$1.87	**$3.12**	0.026
Hang wallpaper, $15 per 28 SF roll, in bath or kitchen	SF	$1.45	$0.63	$2.08	**$3.47**	0.026
Hang wallpaper, $20 per 28 SF roll, in bath or kitchen	SF	$1.50	$0.83	$2.33	**$3.90**	0.027
Hang wallpaper, $25 per 28 SF roll, in bath or kitchen	SF	$1.50	$1.04	$2.54	**$4.25**	0.027
Hang wallpaper, $30 per 28 SF roll, in bath or kitchen	SF	$1.61	$1.25	$2.86	**$4.78**	0.029
Hang wallpaper, $40 per 28 SF roll, in bath or kitchen	SF	$1.67	$1.65	$3.32	**$5.55**	0.030
Hang wallpaper, $50 per 28 SF roll, in bath or kitchen	SF	$1.78	$2.06	$3.84	**$6.42**	0.032
PAPER WALLPAPER, IN REGULAR ROOM (15% waste included)						
Hang wallpaper, $10 per 28 SF roll, in standard room	SF	$0.95	$0.42	$1.37	**$2.28**	0.017
Hang wallpaper, $15 per 28 SF roll, in standard room	SF	$0.95	$0.63	$1.58	**$2.63**	0.017
Hang wallpaper, $20 per 28 SF roll, in standard room	SF	$1.00	$0.83	$1.83	**$3.06**	0.018
Hang wallpaper, $25 per 28 SF roll, in standard room	SF	$1.00	$1.04	$2.04	**$3.41**	0.018
Hang wallpaper, $30 per 28 SF roll, in standard room	SF	$1.11	$1.25	$2.36	**$3.95**	0.020
Hang wallpaper, $40 per 28 SF roll, in standard room	SF	$1.11	$1.65	$2.76	**$4.62**	0.020
Hang wallpaper, $50 per 28 SF roll, in standard room	SF	$1.17	$2.06	$3.23	**$5.39**	0.021
PAPER WALLPAPER, BORDER (15% waste included)						
Hang coordinating border, 4" to 6" wide	LF	$0.67	$0.80	$1.47	**$2.45**	0.012

Interior Painting and Wallpaper

Vinyl Wallpaper

Description	Unit	Direct Labor	Direct Materials	Direct Total	Selling Price	Man-hours
VINYL WALLPAPER, IN SMALL ROOM (15% waste included)						
Hang vinyl wallpaper, $10 per 28 SF roll, in bath or kitchen	SF	$1.67	$0.42	$2.09	**$3.49**	0.030
Hang vinyl wallpaper, $15 per 28 SF roll, in bath or kitchen	SF	$1.67	$0.63	$2.30	**$3.84**	0.030
Hang vinyl wallpaper, $20 per 28 SF roll, in bath or kitchen	SF	$1.78	$0.83	$2.61	**$4.36**	0.032
Hang vinyl wallpaper, $25 per 28 SF roll, in bath or kitchen	SF	$1.78	$1.04	$2.82	**$4.71**	0.032
Hang vinyl wallpaper, $30 per 28 SF roll, in bath or kitchen	SF	$1.84	$1.25	$3.09	**$5.16**	0.033
Hang vinyl wallpaper, $40 per 28 SF roll, in bath or kitchen	SF	$2.00	$1.65	$3.65	**$6.10**	0.036
Hang vinyl wallpaper, $50 per 28 SF roll, in bath or kitchen	SF	$2.17	$2.06	$4.23	**$7.07**	0.039
VINYL WALLPAPER, IN REGULAR ROOM (15% waste included)						
Hang vinyl wallpaper, $10 per 28 SF roll, in standard room	SF	$1.17	$0.42	$1.59	**$2.65**	0.021
Hang vinyl wallpaper, $15 per 28 SF roll, in standard room	SF	$1.17	$0.63	$1.80	**$3.01**	0.021
Hang vinyl wallpaper, $20 per 28 SF roll, in standard room	SF	$1.28	$0.83	$2.11	**$3.53**	0.023
Hang vinyl wallpaper, $25 per 28 SF roll, in standard room	SF	$1.28	$1.04	$2.32	**$3.88**	0.023
Hang vinyl wallpaper, $30 per 28 SF roll, in standard room	SF	$1.34	$1.25	$2.59	**$4.32**	0.024
Hang vinyl wallpaper, $40 per 28 SF roll, in standard room	SF	$1.45	$1.65	$3.10	**$5.17**	0.026
Hang vinyl wallpaper, $50 per 28 SF roll, in standard room	SF	$1.50	$2.06	$3.56	**$5.95**	0.027
VINYL WALLPAPER, BORDER (15% waste included)						
Hang coordinating vinyl border, 4" to 6" wide	LF	$0.78	$1.00	$1.78	**$2.97**	0.014

Grasscloth Wallpaper

Description	Unit	Direct Labor	Direct Materials	Direct Total	Selling Price	Man-hours
GRASSCLOTH WALLPAPER, IN SMALL ROOM (15% waste included)						
Hang grass cloth, $0.50 SF, in bath or kitchen	SF	$2.62	$0.58	$3.20	**$5.34**	0.047
Hang grass cloth, $1.00 SF, in bath or kitchen	SF	$2.62	$1.15	$3.77	**$6.29**	0.047
Hang grass cloth, $1.50 SF, in bath or kitchen	SF	$2.62	$1.73	$4.35	**$7.26**	0.047
Hang grass cloth, $2.00 SF, in bath or kitchen	SF	$2.62	$2.30	$4.92	**$8.21**	0.047
GRASSCLOTH WALLPAPER, IN REGULAR ROOM (15% waste)						
Hang grass cloth, $0.50 SF, in standard room	SF	$2.00	$0.58	$2.58	**$4.32**	0.036
Hang grass cloth, $1.00 SF, in standard room	SF	$2.00	$1.15	$3.15	**$5.27**	0.036
Hang grass cloth, $1.50 SF, in standard room	SF	$2.00	$1.73	$3.73	**$6.24**	0.036
Hang grass cloth, $2.00 SF, in standard room	SF	$2.00	$2.30	$4.30	**$7.19**	0.036

Fencing and Landscaping

Picket Fence

> Intermediate posts in dry cement and sand mix. Gate and corner posts in wet cement.

Description	Unit	Direct Labor	Direct Materials	Direct Total	Selling Price	Man-hours
Install picket fence, pressure treated, 36" high	LF	$9.51	$6.72	$16.24	**$27.12**	0.125
Install picket gate, pressure treated, 42" wide, 36" high	EA	$114.18	$35.31	$149.48	**$249.64**	1.500
Install picket fence, pressure treated, 48" high	LF	$12.03	$9.33	$21.36	**$35.67**	0.158
Install picket gate, pressure treated, 42" wide, 48" high	EA	$114.18	$55.99	$170.16	**$284.17**	1.500
Install picket fence, cedar, 36" high	LF	$9.51	$5.75	$15.27	**$25.50**	0.125
Install picket gate, cedar, 42" wide, 36" high	EA	$114.18	$34.52	$148.70	**$248.33**	1.500
Install picket fence, cedar, 48" high	LF	$12.03	$7.98	$20.01	**$33.42**	0.158
Install picket gate, cedar, 42" wide, 48" high	EA	$114.18	$47.90	$162.08	**$270.67**	1.500
Install picket fence, redwood, 36" high	LF	$9.51	$7.67	$17.19	**$28.70**	0.125
Install picket gate, redwood, 42" wide, 36" high	EA	$114.18	$46.03	$160.21	**$267.55**	1.500
Install picket fence, redwood, 48" high	LF	$12.03	$10.65	$22.67	**$37.87**	0.158
Install picket gate, redwood, 42" wide, 48" high	EA	$114.18	$63.88	$178.06	**$297.36**	1.500

Solid Board Fence

> Intermediate posts in dry cement and sand mix. Gate and corner posts in wet cement.

Description	Unit	Direct Labor	Direct Materials	Direct Total	Selling Price	Man-hours
Install solid board fence, pressure treated, 1 x 6, 42" high	LF	$19.26	$8.22	$27.48	**$45.90**	0.253
Install solid board gate, pressure treated, 42" wide, 42" high	EA	$114.18	$49.34	$163.52	**$273.08**	1.500
Install solid board fence, pressure treated, 1 x 6, 72" high	LF	$20.70	$14.09	$34.79	**$58.11**	0.272
Install solid board fence, pressure treated, 1 x 8, 72" high	LF	$20.25	$14.46	$34.71	**$57.97**	0.266
Install solid board fence, pressure treated, 1 x 10, 72" high	LF	$19.71	$14.61	$34.32	**$57.32**	0.259
Install solid board gate, pressure treated, 42" wide, 72" high	EA	$152.24	$84.54	$236.77	**$395.41**	2.000
Install solid board fence, cedar, 1 x 6, 42" high	LF	$19.26	$7.04	$26.30	**$43.91**	0.253
Install solid board gate, cedar, 42" wide, 42" high	EA	$114.18	$42.23	$156.40	**$261.19**	1.500
Install solid board fence, cedar, 1 x 6, 72" high	LF	$20.70	$12.06	$32.76	**$54.71**	0.272
Install solid board fence, cedar, 1 x 8, 72" high	LF	$20.25	$12.38	$32.62	**$54.48**	0.266
Install solid board fence, cedar, 1 x 10, 72" high	LF	$19.71	$12.50	$32.21	**$53.80**	0.259
Install solid board gate, cedar, 42" wide, 72" high	EA	$152.24	$72.34	$224.58	**$375.05**	2.000
Install solid board fence, redwood, 1 x 6, 42" high	LF	$19.26	$9.38	$28.64	**$47.83**	0.253
Install solid board gate, redwood, 42" wide, 42" high	EA	$114.18	$56.30	$170.48	**$284.70**	1.500
Install solid board fence, redwood, 1 x 6, 72" high	LF	$20.70	$16.08	$36.78	**$61.42**	0.272
Install solid board fence, redwood, 1 x 8, 72" high	LF	$20.25	$16.50	$36.75	**$61.37**	0.266
Install solid board fence, redwood, 1 x 10, 72" high	LF	$19.71	$16.67	$36.38	**$60.76**	0.259
Install solid board gate, redwood, 42" wide, 72" high	EA	$152.24	$96.45	$248.69	**$415.31**	2.000

Fencing and Landscaping

Board on Board Fence

> Intermediate posts in dry cement and sand mix. Gate and corner posts in wet cement.

Description	Unit	Direct Labor	Direct Materials	Direct Total	Selling Price	Man-hours
Pressure treated board on board fence, 1 x 6, 42" high	LF	$19.26	$9.16	$28.41	**$47.45**	0.253
Pressure treated board on board gate, 42" wide, 42" high	EA	$114.18	$54.93	$169.11	**$282.41**	1.500
Pressure treated board on board fence, 1 x 6, 72" high	LF	$20.70	$14.88	$35.58	**$59.42**	0.272
Pressure treated board on board gate, 42" wide, 72" high	EA	$152.24	$89.26	$241.49	**$403.29**	2.000
Cedar board on board fence, 1 x 6, 42" high	LF	$19.26	$7.83	$27.09	**$45.24**	0.253
Cedar board on board gate, 42" wide, 42" high	EA	$114.18	$47.01	$161.18	**$269.18**	1.500
Cedar board on board fence, 1 x 6, 72" high	LF	$20.70	$12.73	$33.43	**$55.83**	0.272
Cedar board on board gate, 42" wide, 72" high	EA	$152.24	$76.38	$228.62	**$381.79**	2.000
Redwood board on board fence, 1 x 6, 42" high	LF	$19.26	$10.45	$29.70	**$49.60**	0.253
Redwood board on board gate, 42" wide, 42" high	EA	$114.18	$62.67	$176.85	**$295.34**	1.500
Redwood board on board fence, 1 x 6, 72" high	LF	$20.70	$16.97	$37.68	**$62.92**	0.272
Redwood board on board gate, 42" wide, 72" high	EA	$152.24	$101.84	$254.07	**$424.30**	2.000

Rail Fence

> Intermediate posts in dry cement and sand mix. Gate and corner posts in wet cement.

Description	Unit	Direct Labor	Direct Materials	Direct Total	Selling Price	Man-hours
Install cedar split rail fence, 2 rail, 36" high	LF	$8.91	$2.08	$10.98	**$18.34**	0.117
Install cedar split rail gate, 2 rail, 42" wide, 36" high	EA	$114.18	$24.32	$138.49	**$231.29**	1.500
Install cedar split rail fence, 2 rail, 42" high	LF	$9.59	$2.38	$11.97	**$19.99**	0.126
Install cedar split rail gate, 2 rail, 42" wide, 42" high	EA	$114.18	$26.50	$140.68	**$234.94**	1.500
Install cedar split rail fence, 3 rail, 48" high	LF	$10.35	$2.68	$13.45	**$21.76**	0.136
Install cedar split rail gate, 3 rail, 42" wide, 48" high	EA	$152.24	$28.69	$180.93	**$302.15**	2.000

Fencing and Landscaping

Chain Link Fence

> Fence and gate posts in cement.

Description	Unit	Direct Labor	Direct Materials	Direct Total	Selling Price	Man-hours
Install chain link fence, 11 gauge galvanized, 10'oc, 36" tall	LF	$10.66	$4.73	$15.39	**$25.70**	0.140
Install chain link fence, 11 gauge galvanized, 10'oc, 42" tall	LF	$11.11	$5.09	$16.21	**$27.06**	0.146
Install chain link fence, 11 gauge galvanized, 10'oc, 48" tall	LF	$11.72	$5.35	$17.07	**$28.50**	0.154
Install chain link fence, 11 gauge galvanized, 10'oc, 60" tall	LF	$13.02	$6.22	$19.23	**$32.12**	0.171
Install chain link fence, 11 gauge galvanized, 10'oc, 72" tall	LF	$14.69	$7.10	$21.79	**$36.38**	0.193
Install chain link gate, 11 gauge galvanized, 36" tall, 36" wide	EA	$76.12	$46.64	$122.76	**$205.01**	1.000
Install chain link gate, 11 gauge galvanized, 42" tall, 36" wide	EA	$76.12	$55.00	$131.12	**$218.97**	1.000
Install chain link gate, 11 gauge galvanized, 48" tall, 36" wide	EA	$76.12	$63.25	$139.37	**$232.75**	1.000
Install chain link gate, 11 gauge galvanized, 60" tall, 36" wide	EA	$114.18	$71.50	$185.68	**$310.08**	1.500
Install chain link gate, 11 gauge galvanized, 72" tall, 36" wide	EA	$114.18	$79.75	$193.93	**$323.86**	1.500
Install chain link fence, 9 gauge galvanized, 10'oc, 36" tall	LF	$10.66	$5.68	$16.33	**$27.28**	0.140
Install chain link fence, 9 gauge galvanized, 10'oc, 42" tall	LF	$11.11	$6.11	$17.22	**$28.77**	0.146
Install chain link fence, 9 gauge galvanized, 10'oc, 48" tall	LF	$11.72	$6.42	$18.14	**$30.29**	0.154
Install chain link fence, 9 gauge galvanized, 10'oc, 60" tall	LF	$13.02	$7.46	$20.47	**$34.19**	0.171
Install chain link fence, 9 gauge galvanized, 10'oc, 72" tall	LF	$14.69	$8.51	$23.20	**$38.75**	0.193
Install chain link gate, 9 gauge galvanized, 36" tall, 36" wide	EA	$114.18	$55.97	$170.15	**$284.14**	1.500
Install chain link gate, 9 gauge galvanized, 42" tall, 36" wide	EA	$114.18	$66.00	$180.18	**$300.90**	1.500
Install chain link gate, 9 gauge galvanized, 48" tall, 36" wide	EA	$114.18	$75.90	$190.08	**$317.43**	1.500
Install chain link gate, 9 gauge galvanized, 60" tall, 36" wide	EA	$152.24	$85.80	$238.04	**$397.52**	2.000
Install chain link gate, 9 gauge galvanized, 72" tall, 36" wide	EA	$152.24	$95.70	$247.94	**$414.05**	2.000

Fencing and Landscaping

Vinyl Fence

> Intermediate posts in dry cement and sand mix. Gate and corner posts in wet cement.

Description	Unit	Direct Labor	Direct Materials	Direct Total	Selling Price	Man-hours
Install vinyl fencing, 36" tall, economy	LF	$9.90	$17.60	$27.50	**$45.92**	0.130
Install vinyl fencing, 36" tall, average	LF	$9.90	$20.90	$30.80	**$51.43**	0.130
Install vinyl fencing, 36" tall, premium	LF	$9.90	$25.30	$35.20	**$58.78**	0.130
Install vinyl gate, 36" tall, 36" wide, economy	EA	$95.15	$48.13	$143.27	**$239.27**	1.250
Install vinyl gate, 36" tall, 36" wide, average	EA	$95.15	$56.38	$151.52	**$253.04**	1.250
Install vinyl gate, 36" tall, 36" wide, premium	EA	$95.15	$66.55	$161.70	**$270.04**	1.250
Install vinyl fencing, 48" tall, economy	LF	$10.50	$19.80	$30.30	**$50.61**	0.138
Install vinyl fencing, 48" tall, average	LF	$10.50	$24.20	$34.70	**$57.96**	0.138
Install vinyl fencing, 48" tall, premium	LF	$10.50	$29.70	$40.20	**$67.14**	0.138
Install vinyl gate, 48" tall, 36" wide, economy	EA	$114.18	$53.63	$167.80	**$280.23**	1.500
Install vinyl gate, 48" tall, 36" wide, average	EA	$114.18	$61.88	$176.05	**$294.01**	1.500
Install vinyl gate, 48" tall, 36" wide, premium	EA	$114.18	$66.83	$181.00	**$302.27**	1.500
Install vinyl fencing, 72" tall, economy	LF	$16.75	$27.50	$44.25	**$73.89**	0.220
Install vinyl fencing, 72" tall, average	LF	$16.75	$33.00	$49.75	**$83.08**	0.220
Install vinyl fencing, 72" tall, premium	LF	$16.75	$41.80	$58.55	**$97.77**	0.220
Install vinyl gate, 72" tall, 36" wide, economy	EA	$152.24	$69.58	$221.81	**$370.43**	2.000
Install vinyl gate, 72" tall, 36" wide, average	EA	$152.24	$81.95	$234.19	**$391.09**	2.000
Install vinyl gate, 72" tall, 36" wide, premium	EA	$152.24	$95.43	$247.66	**$413.60**	2.000

Ornamental Iron Fence

> Fence and gate posts in cement.

Description	Unit	Direct Labor	Direct Materials	Direct Total	Selling Price	Man-hours
Install ornamental iron fencing, 4' high, economy	LF	$20.10	$20.35	$40.45	**$67.54**	0.264
Install ornamental iron fencing, 4' high, average	LF	$20.10	$27.50	$47.60	**$79.48**	0.264
Install ornamental iron fencing, 4' high, premium	LF	$20.10	$40.15	$60.25	**$100.61**	0.264
Install ornamental iron gate, 4' high, 36" wide, economy	EA	$133.21	$91.58	$224.78	**$375.39**	1.750
Install ornamental iron gate, 4' high, 36" wide, average	EA	$133.21	$123.75	$256.96	**$429.12**	1.750
Install ornamental iron gate, 4' high, 36" wide, premium	EA	$133.21	$180.68	$313.88	**$524.18**	1.750
Install ornamental iron fencing, 6' high, economy	LF	$24.05	$30.53	$54.58	**$91.15**	0.316
Install ornamental iron fencing, 6' high, average	LF	$24.05	$41.25	$65.30	**$109.06**	0.316
Install ornamental iron fencing, 6' high, premium	LF	$24.05	$60.23	$84.28	**$140.74**	0.316
Install ornamental iron gate, 6' high, 36" wide, economy	EA	$171.27	$137.36	$308.63	**$515.41**	2.250
Install ornamental iron gate, 6' high, 36" wide, average	EA	$171.27	$185.63	$356.89	**$596.01**	2.250
Install ornamental iron gate, 6' high, 36" wide, premium	EA	$171.27	$271.01	$442.28	**$738.61**	2.250

Fencing and Landscaping

Brush, Tree and Stump Removal

Description	Unit	Direct Labor	Direct Materials	Direct Total	Selling Price	Man-hours
REMOVE TREE BY HAND						
Tree removal by hand, up to 7" diameter trunk	EA	$60.76		$60.76	**$101.47**	1.500
Tree removal by hand, 8" to 12" diameter trunk	EA	$101.27		$101.27	**$169.12**	2.500
Tree removal by hand, 13" to 18" diameter trunk	EA	$141.78		$141.78	**$236.77**	3.500
Tree removal by hand, 19" to 24" diameter trunk	EA	$222.80		$222.80	**$372.07**	5.500
Tree removal by hand, 25" to 30" diameter trunk	EA	$283.56		$283.56	**$473.55**	7.000
REMOVE STUMP BY HAND						
Stump removal by hand, up to 7" diameter trunk	EA	$88.84		$88.84	**$148.36**	2.193
Stump removal by hand, 8" to 12" diameter trunk	EA	$116.71		$116.71	**$194.90**	2.881
Stump removal by hand, 13" to 18" diameter trunk	EA	$144.37		$144.37	**$241.10**	3.564
Stump removal by hand, 19" to 24" diameter trunk	EA	$172.24		$172.24	**$287.65**	4.252
Stump removal by hand, 25" to 30" diameter trunk	EA	$183.50		$183.50	**$306.45**	4.530
REMOVE BRUSH BY MACHINE						
Clear brush by machine, light growth	SF	$0.12		$0.12	**$0.20**	0.003
Clear brush by machine, medium growth	SF	$0.16		$0.16	**$0.27**	0.004
Clear brush by machine, heavy growth	SF	$0.24		$0.24	**$0.41**	0.006

Backfill and Grading

Description	Unit	Direct Labor	Direct Materials	Direct Total	Selling Price	Man-hours
STRIP TOPSOIL BY MACHINE						
Strip topsoil by machine, 4" deep	SF	$0.22		$0.22	**$0.36**	0.003
Strip topsoil by machine, 6" deep	SF	$0.29		$0.29	**$0.49**	0.004
PLACE SOIL						
Backfill by hand from piles, no compaction, medium soil	CF	$1.42		$1.42	**$2.37**	0.035
Compaction by hand, 4"-6" deep layer, medium soil	SF	$0.36		$0.36	**$0.61**	0.009
Compaction by vibrating plate, 12" deep layer, medium soil	SF	$0.49		$0.49	**$0.81**	0.012
Place topsoil and grade by hand from piles, 4" deep	SF	$0.57		$0.57	**$0.95**	0.014
Place topsoil and grade by hand from piles, 6" deep	SF	$0.73		$0.73	**$1.22**	0.018
Spread topsoil by machine, 4"-6" deep	SF	$0.22		$0.22	**$0.36**	0.003
SEED AND SOD						
Place sod, roll and water	SF	$0.81	$0.50	$1.31	**$2.18**	0.020
Seed, rake, water by hand, tall fescue or equivalent	SF	$0.49	$0.09	$0.57	**$0.96**	0.012

Fencing and Landscaping

Patios and Walkways

Description	Unit	Direct Labor	Direct Materials	Direct Total	Selling Price	Man-hours
CONCRETE PAVERS						
Lay concrete pavers, 6" x 6", in sand on ground	SF	$4.94	$1.58	$6.52	**$10.89**	0.122
Lay concrete pavers, 6" x 6", in concrete bed on existing slab	SF	$9.93	$1.91	$11.84	**$19.78**	0.150
Lay concrete pavers, 6" x 12", in concrete bed on existing slab	SF	$8.74	$1.83	$10.57	**$17.65**	0.132
Lay concrete pavers, 12" x 12", in concrete bed on existing slab	SF	$7.55	$1.74	$9.29	**$15.52**	0.114
Lay concrete pavers, 12" x 18", in concrete bed on existing slab	SF	$6.16	$1.66	$7.82	**$13.06**	0.093
Lay round concrete stepping stones, 12" diameter	EA	$2.96	$3.16	$6.11	**$10.21**	0.073
Lay round concrete stepping stones, 18" diameter	EA	$3.97	$4.32	$8.29	**$13.84**	0.098
Lay round concrete stepping stones, 24" diameter	EA	$5.27	$6.48	$11.75	**$19.62**	0.130
BRICK PAVERS						
Lay standard paving brick, in sand on ground	SF	$5.27	$2.49	$7.76	**$12.96**	0.130
Lay standard paving brick, in concrete bed on existing slab	SF	$10.93	$2.91	$13.83	**$23.10**	0.165
Lay adobe brick paver, 6" x 12", in concrete bed on existing slab	SF	$8.74	$2.70	$11.44	**$19.11**	0.132
Lay adobe brick paver, 12" x 12", in concrete bed on existing slab	SF	$7.55	$2.41	$9.96	**$16.63**	0.114
SLATE AND FLAGSTONE PAVERS						
Lay flagstone, in sand on ground	SF	$9.56	$6.71	$16.27	**$27.17**	0.236
Lay flagstone, in concrete bed on existing slab	SF	$15.49	$7.26	$22.75	**$38.00**	0.234
Lay slate, in sand on ground	SF	$9.56	$8.36	$17.92	**$29.93**	0.236
Lay slate, in concrete bed on existing slab	SF	$15.49	$8.80	$24.29	**$40.57**	0.234

Retaining Wall

Description	Unit	Direct Labor	Direct Materials	Direct Total	Selling Price	Man-hours
Install retaining wall, 6"x8" pressure treated, 24" tall	LF	$27.48	$31.63	$59.10	**$98.70**	0.361
Install retaining wall, 6"x8" pressure treated, 36" tall	LF	$41.33	$47.44	$88.78	**$148.25**	0.543
Install retaining wall, 6"x8" pressure treated, 48" tall	LF	$54.96	$63.25	$118.21	**$197.41**	0.722
Install retaining wall, 6"x8" pressure treated, 60" tall	LF	$68.05	$79.07	$147.12	**$245.69**	0.894
Install retaining wall, 6"x8" pressure treated, 72" tall	LF	$82.36	$94.88	$177.24	**$295.98**	1.082
Drain pipe, 4" plastic, aggregate	LF	$5.94	$1.14	$7.08	**$11.83**	0.078

Project Finalization

General Cleaning

> All debris removed. Flooring cleaned. Windows and woodwork wiped clean.

Description	Unit	Direct Labor	Direct Materials	Direct Total	Selling Price	Man-hours
GENERAL CLEANING, ADDITION PROJECT						
Addition clean-up, up to 100 SF	EA	$512.45		$512.45	**$855.79**	13.000
Addition clean-up, 100 SF to 200 SF	EA	$581.44		$581.44	**$971.00**	14.750
Addition clean-up, 200 SF to 300 SF	EA	$650.42		$650.42	**$1,086.20**	16.500
Addition clean-up, 300 SF to 400 SF	EA	$719.40		$719.40	**$1,201.40**	18.250
Addition clean-up, over 400 SF	SF	$1.81		$1.81	**$3.03**	0.046
GENERAL CLEANING, 1ST FLOOR PROJECT						
Clean-up, 1st floor, up to 100 SF	EA	$206.95		$206.95	**$345.61**	5.250
Clean-up, 1st floor, 100 SF to 200 SF	EA	$256.23		$256.23	**$427.90**	6.500
Clean-up, 1st floor, 200 SF to 300 SF	EA	$305.50		$305.50	**$510.19**	7.750
Clean-up, 1st floor, 300 SF to 400 SF	EA	$354.77		$354.77	**$592.47**	9.000
Clean-up, 1st floor, over 400 SF	SF	$0.87		$0.87	**$1.45**	0.022
GENERAL CLEANING, UPPER LEVEL PROJECT						
Clean-up, above 1st floor, up to 100 SF	EA	$443.47		$443.47	**$740.59**	11.250
Clean-up, above 1st floor, 100 SF to 200 SF	EA	$492.74		$492.74	**$822.88**	12.500
Clean-up, above 1st floor, 200 SF to 300 SF	EA	$542.02		$542.02	**$905.17**	13.750
Clean-up, above 1st floor, 300 SF to 400 SF	EA	$591.29		$591.29	**$987.46**	15.000
Clean-up, above 1st floor, over 400 SF	SF	$1.50		$1.50	**$2.50**	0.038
GENERAL CLEANING, BASEMENT PROJECT						
Clean-up, basement, up to 100 SF	EA	$315.36		$315.36	**$526.64**	8.000
Clean-up, basement, 100 SF to 200 SF	EA	$364.63		$364.63	**$608.93**	9.250
Clean-up, basement, 200 SF to 300 SF	EA	$413.90		$413.90	**$691.22**	10.500
Clean-up, basement, 300 SF to 400 SF	EA	$473.03		$473.03	**$789.96**	12.000
Clean-up, basement, over 400 SF	SF	$1.18		$1.18	**$1.97**	0.030
GENERAL CLEANING, KITCHEN OR BATH PROJECT						
Kitchen or bathroom clean-up, up to 50 SF	EA	$157.68		$157.68	**$263.32**	4.000
Kitchen or bathroom clean-up, 50 SF to 100 SF	EA	$236.52		$236.52	**$394.98**	6.000
Kitchen or bathroom clean-up, 100 SF to 150 SF	EA	$315.36		$315.36	**$526.64**	8.000
Kitchen or bathroom clean-up, 150 SF to 200 SF	EA	$394.19		$394.19	**$658.30**	10.000
Kitchen or bathroom clean-up, over 200 SF	SF	$2.01		$2.01	**$3.36**	0.051
GENERAL CLEANING, DECK OR PORCH PROJECT						
Deck or porch clean-up, up to 100 SF	EA	$78.84		$78.84	**$131.66**	2.000
Deck or porch clean-up, 100 SF to 150 SF	EA	$108.40		$108.40	**$181.03**	2.750
Deck or porch clean-up, 150 SF to 200 SF	EA	$137.97		$137.97	**$230.41**	3.500
Deck or porch clean-up, 200 SF to 250 SF	EA	$167.53		$167.53	**$279.78**	4.250
Deck or porch clean-up, over 250 SF	SF	$0.71		$0.71	**$1.18**	0.018

CEILING continued on next page

DOORS continued on next page

PLYWOOD starts on next page

SINK continued on next page

WOOD continued on next page